# Teaching Disturbed and Disturbing Students

# Teaching Disturbed and Disturbing Students

## An Integrative Approach

### SECOND EDITION

Paul Zionts

pro·ed
8700 Shoal Creek Boulevard
Austin, Texas 78757-6897

**pro·ed**

©1996, 1985 by PRO-ED, Inc.
8700 Shoal Creek Boulevard
Austin, Texas 78757-6897

All rights reserved. No part of the material protected by this copyright notice may be reproduced or used in any form or by any means, electronic or mechanical, including photocopying, recording, or by any information storage and retrieval system, without the prior written permission of the copyright owner.

**Library of Congress Cataloging-in-Publication Data**

Zionts, Paul.
    Teaching disturbed and disturbing students : an integrative approach / Paul Zionts.—2nd ed.
      p.    cm.
    Includes bibliographical references and index.
    ISBN 0-89079-623-8
    1. Problem children—Education.   2. Classroom management.   3. Home and school.   4. Problem children—Discipline.   I. Title.
LB4801.Z56   1995
371.93—dc20
                                                             94-45437
                                                                 CIP

Production Manager: Alan Grimes
Production Coordinator: Karen Swain
Art Director: Lori Kopp
Reprints Buyer: Alicia Woods
Editor: Debra Berman
Editorial Assistant: Claudette Landry

Printed in the United States of America

1   2   3   4   5   6   7   8   9   10     00   99   98   97   96   95

*For my father and mother and my daughters, Polina and Emily,
and
to the memory of Gene Mulling who was
one of those students you can never let go.*

# Contents

| | |
|---|---|
| Preface | viii |
| **UNIT 1: Administrative Influences on Disturbance** | 2 |
| 1 Disturbance: Definitions, Influences, and Politics | 5 |
| 2 Factors that Influence the Teaching of Students with EBD | 35 |
| 3 Preassessment, Referral, Assessment, and Placement<br>*Christine Ormsbee, Richard L. Simpson, and Paul Zionts* | 71 |
| 4 Classroom Management: Instruction, Paraprofessionals, and Parents<br>*Paul Zionts and Patricia Daly* | 119 |
| 5 Classroom Management: Social Skills, Setting, and Behavior | 153 |
| Unit 1 References | 185 |
| **UNIT 2: Moral Development with Disturbed and Disturbing Students** | 208 |
| 6 Moral Development with Disturbed and Disturbing Students: Theory | 211 |
| 7 Moral Development: Application in the Classroom | 259 |
| Unit 2 References | 295 |
| **UNIT 3: Rational-Emotive Therapy in the Classroom** | 304 |
| 8 Rational-Emotive Therapy in the Classroom: Theory | 307 |
| 9 Rational-Emotive Therapy as an Intervention | 351 |
| 10 Rational-Emotive Therapy as a Mental Health Curriculum | 391 |
| Unit 3 References | 433 |
| Author Index | 439 |
| Subject Index | 451 |

# Preface

Lack of discipline is perceived by many American adults to be the greatest problem with which the public school teacher must deal. Blame for problem behaviors variously is placed on the student, teacher, administration, parents, peers, and/or community.

In growing numbers teachers attend workshops and inservices that offer classroom management techniques. Those teachers involved with mainstreaming disturbed and disturbing students most often cite their primary concern as being the effective behavioral handling of these students. The purpose of this book is to prepare educators who will be teaching students with emotional or behavioral problems.

Most college graduates who are trained to teach emotionally disturbed students can readily describe the theoretical rationale and name the major proponents of the biophysical, behavioral, ecological, psychodynamic, and counter-theoretical models of deviance. Few, however, are prepared to use these theories on a day-to-day basis. Many education students try to extract what they can from instruction, but they do not have the practical expertise to implement textbook knowledge. Definitional texts offer excellent perspectives on understanding children who are emotionally disturbed. Other books focus on a broad range of current intervention strategies. This book examines intervention through case studies, activities, and examples. The intention of this text is not only to interest educators, but to train them. The first unit attempts to provide techniques that will aid the teacher in dealing with the ecological influences on both disturbed and disturbing students and the administrative duties that are integral to teaching in the field of special education. The second and third units concentrate primarily on the teacher–student interactive process.

This textbook is organized in a developmental manner. Whereas much of Unit 1 is applicable to teachers of any grade, the intervention that is discussed is behavioral and ecological in nature. My contention is that behavioral interventions, when used as the teacher's sole approach, are extremely helpful in the lower elementary grades (K–4) but are less appropriate for older students. This contention is based on the notion that, although there are ecological influences that can promote disturbing behaviors, there are also internal or cognitive influences that become an increasingly pervasive factor as human beings age. Therefore, the intervention discussed in Unit 1, specifically in Chapter 4, differs philosophically and psychologically from the interventions presented in Units 2 and 3, which stress cognitive and cognitive-behavioral models, respectively. Unit 2 concentrates on the reasoning ability of students, which seems to be most appropriate as the primary intervention for Grades 4 through 12; Unit 3, which focusses on a classroom therapy, would be most appropriate for students who are reasoning beyond the lower moral developmental stages. I believe that all three units may be used together or they may stand on their own merits to supplement an existing program.

Unit 1 examines the teacher's role in administering a classroom of disturbed and disturbing youth. Administrative and educational definitions of disturbance illustrate the different perspectives that professionals, each charged with serving handicapped youth, have of the target population. The unit also suggests that an understanding of the referral, assessment, and placement processes is requisite to a successful teaching experience. It is hoped that these processes lead to specific and appropriate programming for the students. Academic, social-environmental, and behavioral considerations are presented to help the teacher provide a classroom that has a philosophy of preventing "ecological" disturbances. Finally, the theory and practice of communicating with parents is explored.

Unit 1 emphasizes those ecological and behavioral factors that can influence the education of disturbed and disturbing youth. The intervention presented is structured and, if implemented, could increase the chances of a successful teaching experience. The problem with using only the techniques in Unit 1 is that they ignore the fact that many students have internal difficulties, such as the inability to reason at higher levels. Aligned with these difficulties is the inability of some students to communicate effectively. Units 2 and 3 of this book attempt to introduce affective curricula that can better prepare students for life outside the special education setting. They are to be used in conjunction with the principles presented in Unit 1.

Unit 2 examines the impact of moral development and reasoning on the cognitions and behaviors of students. This unit suggests that, to prescribe successfully any classroom management technique or therapeutic intervention, the teacher should be aware of both behavioral and moral development. It may be necessary to ascertain whether the child's behavior is truly inappropriate for his or her stage of moral development, and more important to assess if the requested behavior is realistic to expect of the child. Theory and classroom examples are presented to assist the educator in correlating students' behaviors to the moral development models of Piaget and Kohlberg.

Unit 2 provides the teacher with the opportunity to integrate academics with the affective domain. Hardly any educator would argue that it is not within one's goals to teach students to increase their ability to reason. Through a structured process, the teacher attempts to teach the students to reason at a higher level, perceiving beyond their egocentric viewpoint and taking into consideration their peers and society. These are the maximal goals of Unit 2. The minimal goals include having a classroom in which discussion and communication are commonplace.

Although most disturbed and disturbing children respond positively to a well-planned classroom, some need specific therapeutic intervention. Unit 3 explores the implementation of rational-emotive therapy, a mental health curriculum. This program involves educational principles and techniques that combine cognitive, behavioral, and emotive components to teach students and teachers that they can effectively combat their own disturbed feelings. Rational-emotive therapy is included because of its efficient and practical use with individuals and small or large groups. Research suggests that this method is particularly successful and relatively easy to implement. In addition, many teachers have discovered that the techniques and ideas discussed in rational-emotive therapy are also applicable to their own professional and emotional growth. Unit 3 provides both the theory and the application of the educational component of rational-emotive therapy. Specific intervention and curricular exercises are included in this unit. I believe that the absence of such a thorough systematic approach has resulted in the failure of many teachers to adopt any therapeutic intervention.

No single technique is likely to work with all of the children in the classroom. Currently, if theory A is not working, then the educator tries theory B, and so forth, with the result that some disturbed and disturbing students encounter more theories of intervention during their public school career than some special educators receive in all of their undergraduate training. Realistically, one can be "eclectic" only if one can distinguish intelligently among theories and can understand why a particular intervention may be going awry. Through careful evaluation, a remedy may present itself. However, to evaluate any technique, one must know it well. Unless teachers thoroughly understand the intervention, they will not be able to diagnose and evaluate what is wrong. This text offers the educator the opportunity to be accountable for what he or she is attempting in the classroom.

This text is an attempt to provide the theory and application necessary for a successful classroom experience. The classroom vignettes, practical activities, and exercises are included to enhance and "test" the reader's understanding of the content. The text is not intended to be a composite of everything that works, but rather a systematic approach for preservice educators to begin their classroom experiences, or for an inservice educator to adapt to other educators' present expertise.

I would like to thank Barry Alford for again helping me with this edition by providing his reliable and insightful comments.

# UNIT 1

# Administrative Influences on Disturbance

The first unit of this text focuses on the administrative influences that must be considered when educating disturbed and disturbing students. The term *administrative* is used to connote the operations, and the dynamics of those operations, that currently exist in many schools. These influences have as direct an impact on the classroom as does any behavioral, emotive, or social intervention. An understanding of these processes, commonly treated as separate from the actual "working" with the students, is integral to a successful teaching and learning experience.

The influences that are discussed may be perceived as external, that is, as being part of the students' ecology. They may be as far reaching as the politics of school and community or as close to the students as the actual physical arrangement of the classroom. These influences can determine the mental health of the school and its teachers, as well as the students. I contend that, if students are affected by these factors, it would be those students who are, or who are potentially, disturbed or disturbing who would experience the greatest impact. Furthermore, these external influences differ from the psychological or internal problems commonly associated with this population, yet the behaviors exhibited by the students may be the same. Therefore, an understanding of these administrative influences will aid in the education of disturbed and disturbing youth.

Chapter 1 is an examination of the conditions that may both encourage and impede appropriate behaviors. This investigation begins with the frames of reference from which one perceives the target population. It is suggested that teachers, school administrators, social workers, and parents may each have different operational definitions of disturbance. The notion that many disturbing students are not disturbed, which perhaps accounts for these differences, is presented. Clearly, some people believe that some students should be included and some excluded from receiving help. The impact of social and political movements such as inclusion is also discussed.

Definitions of disturbance, including a practical version proposed by Wood (1979a), are provided and expanded upon throughout the unit. Wood's definition takes into account not only the students' personal problems, but also an environment that may be contributing to disturbance. However, no matter what definitions are used, schools do react in a remarkably similar manner to students who exhibit maladaptive behaviors. These reactions, both formal and informal, are examined in Chapter 1. Also, teacher reactions to disturbing students and these students' reactions to teachers are discussed to more fully account for the actual conditions currently present in the schools.

Chapters 2 and 3 explore some important processes that, if ignored, may confound the implementation of a special education program. Chapter 2 takes into account those aspects that are crucial to successfully teaching students with emotional and/or behavioral disorders. Teaching philosophies are presented and argued as necessary for teachers to possess before they enter the classroom. Teacher competencies (outcomes) are presented as a possible framework for educators to guide their professional careers. Finally, barriers that may impede successful teaching are discussed. Chapter 3 prepares the reader for the preassessment, referral, assessment, and placement procedures that are integral to special education. The chapter addresses the necessity of working with students before a formal referral is presented. Referral is an often-overlooked process that may in fact predetermine the educational status of disturbed and disturbing students. Examples of formats are presented to facilitate referral. The assessment section of Chapter 3 examines how assessment affects and is affected by the "disturber," the nature of the "problem behavior," the setting, and finally those who are the "disturbed." The natural follow-up to referral and assessment is how these processes are used in placement decisions. A mock multidisciplinary team meeting is presented in Chapter 3 to illustrate the dynamics of group decision making. Administrative factors that may expedite these team meetings are offered in hope of adequately meeting the goals of Public Law 94-142, the Education for All Handicapped Children Act.

No matter how carefully the educator considers external influences, referral, assessment, and placement, equal attention must be paid to the classroom. Chapters 4 and 5 investigate the utility element of any definition of disturbance: the programming of disturbed and disturbing students. A classroom management scheme is presented that can be implemented to ensure a sufficiently tranquil classroom for the teaching of academics. The physical arrangement of the classroom, schedules and routines, academic instructional considerations, and behavioral management are all specifically described and suggested to be essential to classroom management and, ultimately, programming. Finally, the theory and practice of encouraging parental and paraprofessional involvement is examined in Chapter 5.

Each chapter in Unit 1 is designed to help the educator better understand the responsibilities of educating disturbed and disturbing students. Indeed, although many of these responsibilities have a direct bearing on the success of the special education experience, they are carried out with little, if any, direct personal contact with the students themselves. However, the content of these chapters is as important in the education of these students as that of the chapters that detail curricula.

# 1

# Disturbance: Definitions, Influences, and Politics

Emotionally disturbed children have two major needs. First, there is a need for the removal of pathological, physiological, or environmental conditions contributing to their maladjustment or disturbance and a need for assistance in unlearning behavior that is destructive to self or society. Second, there is a need for assistance in developing their potential for social competence through the learning of social skills, including those related to academic achievement in school. (Wood, 1979b, p. 3)

Disruptive school behavior is on the increase and may be exacerbated by such societal factors as (a) an increasing divorce rate, (b) social conflict and dissension, (c) a declining respect for the autonomy of institutions, and (d) changing societal values. (Walker, 1982, p. 1)

The purpose of this chapter is to examine the factors that have a crucial impact on educating students described as emotionally and/or behaviorally disordered (EBD). Agreeing upon a definition of EBD, something seemingly obvious, has yet to be achieved, resulting in much confusion. Political forces influence not only who will be identified but how students are going to be serviced. Some students will not be serviced, even though they exhibit identical behaviors to those who will be, because the etiology of their behaviors is perceived differently. For example, an aggressive student may receive help if her problem is thought to be medical. Another may not receive help if his problem is thought to be caused by his social environment. This chapter examines not only students with EBD but also the impact of their teachers, schools, community, and society.

To understand the many dimensions of teaching students with EBD, one should be aware of the many factors with which both the teacher and these students are continually confronted. One of the fantasies that many high school and college-aged students have about teachers is that, when the time comes, the classroom door will be closed and they will work magic with their charges. It will not take long for this fantasy to be dispelled if their teaching assignment is in a special education classroom, especially in a classroom for students with EBD. That this disillusionment is predictable is a sure sign that some basic assumptions made about students with EBD are in error.

Teaching students with EBD can be extremely challenging and rewarding. It is crucial that teachers are aware of complexities of their students and their jobs. This awareness will allow teachers to have a complete repertoire to meet the challenges that most teachers will face: the politics of EBD, the politics of special education and regular education, and the politics of teaching.

# The Politics of EBD

Historically and currently, there have been two debates that have potential impact on teaching students with emotional and/or behavioral problems. These debates have focused on the federal definition and the particular label that should be attached to these students. Simply, there are problems with the current federal definition, as evidenced by the fact that states have widely varying prevalence rates (Quay, 1992). Other issues involve the effect politics has on various aspects within the field of EBD and the effect of institutional politics on teaching.

## The Federal Definition

The purpose of definitions is to provide guidelines for state departments of education, and ultimately local multidisciplinary teams, to identify and service students with EBD. The federal definition, adopted in its entirety by most states, has been the focus of much of the discussion. It states that serious emotional disturbance

> means a condition exhibiting one or more of the following characteristics over a long period of time and to a marked degree which adversely affects school performance:
> 
> (a) an inability to learn which cannot be explained by intellectual, sensory, or health factors;

(b) an inability to build or maintain satisfactory relationships with peers and teachers;

(c) inappropriate types of behavior or feelings under normal circumstances;

(d) a general pervasive mood of unhappiness or depression; or

(e) a tendency to develop physical symptoms or fears associated with personal or school problems.

Where a handicapped child is so disruptive in a regular classroom that the education of other students is significantly impaired, the needs of the handicapped child cannot be met in that environment. Therefore, regular placement would not be disruptive to his or her needs. (Federal Register, 1977)

This definition excludes students who are socially maladjusted unless it is determined that they are seriously emotionally disturbed.

On paper, the above descriptions may make sense. Yet, experience in attempting to operationalize the definition has led to frustration. Current definitions are inadequate with regard to providing practical guidelines for any educational or clinical situation. In fact, definitions may "place children in conceptual ball parks, but due to their vagueness, they may have little value for diagnostic, communicative and research purposes" (Hewett & Taylor, 1980, p. 37). In their examination of the ways in which the population labeled emotionally disturbed were identified in the research, Wood and Lakin (1979) found little detail about the specific behaviors or conditions of the groups studied. In other words, it has been almost impossible to generalize from the research because very little is known about the subjects studied. Clearly, almost two decades later, the fact that this discussion is still in the forefront indicates that the situation has not improved much.

From a practical standpoint for teachers, it seems imperative that any definition must contain educational implications. What is known about students when they are identified? Are their problems due to incompatible environments, or are they a result of internal problems? Is there a pattern to the behaviors? If so, what are the possible interventions?

Furthermore, what degree of severity in any of the federal descriptions should schools use to make a determination about a student? Professionals in the field of special education have been reluctant to use numbers. This has led others, such as lawyer Jane Slenkovitch, to attempt the task. Slenkovitch (1984) developed a very narrow legal interpretation of Public Law (P.L.) 94-142, the Education for All Handicapped Children Act (EHA). She noted that special educators, psychologists, and other education professionals do not make references to the law when they determine eligibility for services.

Slenkovitch (1984) argued that the only way a student may receive services is if "the student [is] so seriously emotionally disturbed that he cannot learn" (p. 274). With regard to length of time, she suggested that up to 2 years of exhibiting inappropriate feelings or behaviors may be an appropriate amount of time to wait before implementation of services. (However, what happens during this time?) In a somewhat confusing statement, Slenkovitch asserted, "the mere existence of a serious emotional disturbance, in and of itself, does not qualify the student as seriously emotionally disturbed under EHA" (p. 269).

Slenkovitch's (1984) argument best illustrates a legal interpretation of a federal definition that emanates from the medical conceptual model of emotional disturbance. In recent years, attempts to define this population have evolved because of the shift of popularity from the medical to the educational model. Rather than assigning the perception of emotional disturbance as an illness, the educational model encompasses such aspects as psychological problems, but also recognizes that difficulties in the classroom environment (or ecology) may contribute to the child's maladaptive behavior. Consequently, Skiba, Hugo, and Yell (1992) responded to Slenkovitch by asserting that "educational performance" should be defined by more than merely academic instruction. They believed that this is where Slenkovitch fell short. After an examination of case law, they found few cases that addressed the social maladjustment issue (see also Weinberg, 1992). This is probably due to the fact that students with EBD have few advocates. Coleman (1992) summarized the situation well by stating, "A common mistaken notion is that definitions have utility in identification of specific individuals to be served by programs" (p. 23).

## The Label for Students with EBD

Currently, the population discussed in the federal definition and in most of the literature is called "seriously emotionally disturbed" (SED). It is, in fact, the only population of students identified as disabled who are labeled with the qualifier "seriously." One commonly given reason for including "seriously" in the emotionally disturbed category has been to exclude those who are not *truly disabled,* but instead are socially maladjusted or conduct disordered. Ironically, Bower (1982), who has been given much of the credit for the development of the current definition, intended to include those who are socially maladjusted or conduct disordered. In fact, he originally labeled this population as emotionally handicapped (Bower, 1969). Since the advent of P.L. 94-142, an ongoing discussion has been whether students identified as socially maladjusted and/or conduct disordered should be serviced.

Conversely, the same scrutiny has not been applied to students identified as learning disabled, because it is believed that, regardless of the exactness of the classification process, these students are obviously in need of some type of services (Nelson, Rutherford, Center, & Walker, 1991). Furthermore, learning disabilities is a more "attractive" label to describe students who need help. This population of students, clearly the most overrepresented of special education categories, is not labeled with the term "seriously." Few people would argue with the notion that many students who are labeled learning disabled are not *truly disabled,* but instead have difficulties due to environmental factors (home, community, teachers, etc.).

Although teachers may find it appealing to help those with academic difficulties, they may be less willing to service those who are not "seriously" disturbed. In fact, by describing them as socially maladjusted or conduct disordered, professionals imply that the students are willfully acting disturbed or disturbing. "The term conduct disorders has been used to denote the problem of children who demonstrate a pattern of antisocial, rule breaking, or even aggressive behavior that not only impairs their own functioning but also is regarded as unmanageable by others" (Forness, Kavale, & Lopez, 1993, p. 101). Quay (1992) believed that "The option of ruling out conduct disorder [has] considerable downside risk. . . . It would eliminate the possibility of intensive special education services for the type of disorder that is most prevalent, has (with the exception of psychosis) the poorest prognosis and will eventually extract the greatest social cost" (p. 4).

The Council for Children with Behavioral Disorders (1990), in a position paper, perhaps summarized the definition problem best by reporting that "there is no widely accepted definition of social maladjustment, nor is there evidence that children who are socially maladjusted and those who are identified as emotionally disturbed represent two different populations" (p. 182). They further contended that "there are no assessment devices or techniques that are technically adequate for distinguishing social maladjustment from other conditions" (p. 183).

In reference to the above discussion on learning disabilities, the comparison again exists when noting that behaviors deemed socially maladjusted, conduct disordered, or disturbing certainly seem to be handicapping to both the students and their environment to at least the same degree as the behaviors of students who are not "seriously" learning disabled. Ironically, Bower (1982) and subsequent interpreters (Forness & Knitzer, 1992) have contended that the second criterion (b) of the existing definition argues for the inclusion of individuals identified as socially maladjusted or conduct disordered. The types of students who are identified or are at risk to be identified both as EBD and as socially maladjusted and conduct disordered are almost identical.

## The Exclusion Clause

Much discussion has occurred regarding the notion that individuals are not classified as EBD if they also have the characteristics of another disability. For example, teachers of students with learning disabilities often complain of the disturbing behaviors that their students exhibit, yet these students are not "dual identified" and consequently do not receive services for behavioral, social, or emotional problems.

To suggest that learning disabled students cannot be identified as EBD because their disability is a learning problem identified by a significant discrepancy between intelligence and performance, or that students with mental retardation cannot be identified as EBD because of their lower intelligence, is nonsensical. Not surprisingly, teachers of students with hearing impairments have identified significant numbers of their students as having emotional and behavioral problems that necessitate remediation, which is not possible because their primary label *excludes* them from such remediation (Zionts, Weddle, & Zebarah, 1981). It would seem appropriate, however, that if students need services, there should be mechanisms that would allow them to receive services.

## Students Who May Be Socially Maladjusted and/or Conduct Disordered

The general category of social maladjustment and conduct disorders (SM/CD) is multifaceted. Regardless of any specific characteristics that one could generate, research and literature have purported that these students could and/or should qualify for and benefit from special education services. However, little specific attention has been paid to nonschool factors that contribute to EBD. The following are brief discussions of the types of individuals who may be classified as having SM/CD.

***The Homeless.*** The plight of the homeless has received increased national attention. "Of the people in the United States with severe mental illnesses—estimated to be as many as 4 million—$\frac{1}{20}$ are homeless. . . . Of the estimated nearly 600,000 homeless people in the United States, $\frac{1}{3}$ of the single adults are believed to be mentally ill" (Task Force on Homelessness and Severe Mental Illness, 1992, p. 18). The problem of tracking and placing (probably unwanted) homeless children is monumental. Because of their circumstances, parental involvement is rare. Help is not likely to be found using other traditional avenues.

This problem is exacerbated by the fact that those homeless who are mentally ill rarely receive the help that they need. Tuma (1989) argued that the mental health care system has serious deficiencies, with major manpower deficiencies being a significant problem. He contended that the percentage of children receiving services today—approximately 15% to 19%—is about the same as at the turn of the century and that, of those, 70% to 80% do not receive appropriate services.

**The Culturally Diverse.** Students who are not members of the "majority culture" are among those who have had the greatest difficulty assimilating into the school system. Their differences in behaviors and/or values may result in their being referred for special education services. Cohen (1955) very early argued that school is a middle class institution and that those who are not members of the middle class are minimally at a disadvantage, and probably are punished for whatever differences exist. Research on how the culturally diverse are at a disadvantage with regard to most standardized tools has been well documented.

When examining dropout data, Blackorby, Edgar, and Kortering (1991) suggested that the data may be tainted because many students return. Perhaps "interruptions" is a more appropriate label. Regardless, they concluded that "it is plausible that the African American students and students labeled behavior disordered experience more disruptions than other groups because they have an incombatible fit in an essentially Anglocentric school system" (p. 111). It is not implausible to suggest that others with differences also do less well in school.

**The Poor.** With the advent of inclusion, many students with disabilities will receive quality services only if they come from economically advantaged homes. That is, they will probably need to have a support system that will strongly advocate for their rights. Those students who come from economically disadvantaged homes rarely receive the services that they need. Some students may not even have the luxury of housing. According to the Federal Task Force on Homelessness and Severe Mental Illness (1992), "Nearly 200,000 of our most vulnerable and disabled citizens are homeless and mentally ill, seemingly ignored by a society indifferent to their plight. Most lack permanent, safe, decent housing; a source of income or employment; treatment to provide relief from the disturbing symptoms of severe mental illnesses (and possibly substance abuse); basic health care; and any social support network" (p. 31). Takeuchi, Williams, and Adair (1991) found that the amount of time individuals spend in poverty seems to increase the likelihood of their exhibiting antisocial behaviors, both external (aggression) and internal (depression). Mattison, Morales, and Bauer (1992) noted, "The boys recommended for SED placement were specifically distinguished by poorer socioeconomic level, experience of major family stresses (broken home, a psychiatrically ill parent, and physical abuse), diagnosis of conduct or oppositional disorder as well as more than one DSM–III diagnosis at evaluation, clinician rating of poor function, and history of past treatment by a community mental health resource" (pp. 111–112).

**Substance Abusers.** In 1962 less than 4% of the school-aged population had tried drugs. In the 1980s that number increased to over 50% (Youcha & Seixas, 1989). Kress and Elias (1993) argued that special education populations, "particularly through preadolescence, are (or should be) prominent targets of primary and secondary efforts related to alcohol and other drug use. The very nature of their dysfunctions puts these students at high risk for substance abuse problems" (p. 37). This argument was substantiated by the research of Greenbaum, Prange, Friedman, and Silver (1991), who found that students with EBD used alcohol and marijuana with greater frequency than other populations. Accordingly, the learning and behavioral characteristics of this population seem to indicate that these students will be prime candidates for special education programming (Bauer, 1991; Bentley & Conley, 1992).

Morgan (1993) concluded through a review of the literature that "survey risk-factor data strongly suggest that students with behavioral disorders are at particularly high risk for substance use" (p. 172). Devlin and Elliot (1992) found that 51% of those with behavior disorders abused substances. They suggested that the use of substances may be due to the students' desires to be accepted by others (see also Milin, Halikas, Meller, & Morse, 1991).

Abusers of hard drugs are more likely than the general population to commit violent crimes (Simonds & Kashari, 1980). In fact, in one investigation (Fagan, Weis, & Cheng, 1990), 17% of those who committed violent offenses were found to have ingested significant amounts of drugs within a day of their offenses. Finally, a common misconception is that the population that abuses substances comprises urban dwellers. Novacek, Raskin, and Hogan (1991) found that there are many rural substance abusers as well.

**The Abused.** Child abuse cuts across all sectors of society. Types of abuse include sexual, emotional, physical, and neglect. Although types of abuse differ, the prevalence is equal for boys and girls (Gargiulo, 1990). The deleterious effects of abuse on self-concept (Oates, 1985) and social adjustment (Friedrich, Urquiza, & Beilke, 1984; Lamphear, 1985) obviously affect school success.

McGuire and Goldman (1991) argued that children with handicaps seem to be overrepresented among the abused. They contended that characteristics of the abused are similar to those of youth with EBD. They further hypothesized that "abusive messages from parents and other significant adults may be establishing the antecedents for behavior disorders" (p. 30). Normally, only one child in a family is a target for abuse, and if a child is handicapped, he or she becomes the one most at risk (Gargiulo, 1990). However it occurs, the victim of child abuse may never recover from it (Steele, 1986).

***Juvenile Delinquents.*** Clearly, the population of adolescents who engender the most concern because of the types of inappropriate behavior they display is juvenile delinquents. This group is the most frequently included in social maladjustment discussions. In an observational study of 884 police–citizen encounters, involving 1,798 citizens, Teplin (1984) found a higher incidence of arrests among the population with mental illness. It was suggested that these numbers may be due to the failure to adequately fund the mental health system.

Juvenile delinquents have been found to exhibit a wide array of conduct disorders, as well as other learning problems (Frick, et al., 1991). The exact relationship between poor achievement and juvenile delinquency is not understood (Tremblay, Perron, Lelanc, Schwartzman, & Ledingham, 1992). This relationship is most likely influenced by many of the factors that have been described in this section. Juvenile delinquency will be referred to in more depth throughout Unit 1.

## Choosing a Label

Even under the best conditions, identifying and classifying students as EBD can be difficult tasks. Parental and possibly administrative pressures exist to avoid the EBD label. In reaction to these pressures, students are often (mis)placed under the learning disabilities category with little subsequent EBD programming. More recently, many candidates for EBD programs have been referred to as having attention-deficit/hyperactivity disorder (ADHD) (an entire issue of *Exceptional Children,* 1993, was devoted to this subject).

Defining ADHD, however, although seemingly more accepted by parents (perhaps because of the absence of blame), is as difficult as defining EBD or learning disabilities. Goodman and Poillion (1992) conducted an extensive review of the literature and found 69 distinct characteristics of ADHD. Not one characteristic was listed by 80% of authors, and only 4 of 39 characteristics were similarly described by half of the authors. Furthermore, there was little agreement on etiology, although 48% of the articles agreed that genetics is a possible cause, but even those authors produced little empirical evidence to support their hypotheses.

Clearly, logical and emotional viewpoints influence who is selected to receive special education services. In fact, any discussion is incomplete without a review of the literature on the impact of "stigmatization" of the emotionally disturbed label. The discussion regarding a possible new definition

> **Window on Reality**
>
> Unquestionably, thousands of hours have been spent debating the differences between the supposed benefits of the labels emotional disturbance, emotional handicap, behavioral disorder, conduct disorder, social maladjustment, emotional/behavioral disorder, and so on. This is a clear example of the time and energy that has been wasted by professionals in special education. Has the debate resulted in any real changes with regard to the teaching and/or acceptance of these students? Does it matter to the students what they are labeled? Are informal labels already present (see Zionts & Simpson, 1988)? It is the informal labels, and not the educational process, that teachers and peers attach to students that probably cause the most "harm." Thus, changing the official or formal label may be merely an "academic" exercise.

has renewed concerns about the label for this population. Much attention has been devoted to the semantic label of serious emotional disturbance (SED). By changing the label, it has been argued, educators would know more about the student or at least reduce stigmatization.

Although research has not proven any significant differences among such terms as *emotional disturbance, behaviorally disordered, emotionally handicapped, acting out, and mentally ill,* when perceived in practical terms by teachers, the debate regarding the label continues. Coleman (1992) suggested that "the term behavior disordered is often seen as less stigmatizing, less severe, more socially acceptable, and more practical than the term emotionally disturbed. . . . Many educators seem to prefer behavior disordered because it seems more plausible to deal directly with disordered behavior than with disturbed emotions" (p. 22) (see also Huntze, 1985; Walker & Bullis, 1991). Coleman further argued that the label behavior disordered suggests "less impaired" and that the label emotionally disturbed may connote "more impaired."

## The Label Emotionally/Behaviorally Disordered

Center (1990) believed that the reason why the current definition is narrow is because of its psychodynamic influence. He called for a broadened definition to include rather than exclude students who may need help. The Council for Children with Behavioral Disorders (1989), in consultation with a mental health alliance, proposed the following new label and definition for this population:

Behavioral or Emotional Disorder (BED) refers to a condition in which behavioral or emotional responses of an individual in school are so different from his/her generally accepted, age-appropriate, ethnic or cultural norms as to result in significant impairment in his/her self care, social relationships, school progress, classroom demeanor, work adjustment, or related functioning.

The condition may include, but is not necessarily limited to, clinical entities such as schizophrenia, depression, anxiety disorders, attention-deficit hyperactivity disorders, autism, or other sustained disturbances of conduct or adjustment.

The condition is not a transient, expected response to stressors in the individual's environment nor misbehavior that can generally be corrected by routine environmental intervention, e.g., feedback to the individual, advice to his/her parents or family, guidance to his/her teacher, supervision by his/her employer, and the like.

The condition is also not mental retardation, learning disability, speech or language handicap, physical or sensory impairment, or juvenile delinquency, although it may exist concurrently with these conditions; nor is it merely conflict between the individual and a political/governmental entity.

It is also assumed that the condition will be diagnosed on the basis of multiple sources of data about the individual's behavioral or emotional functioning. If the condition is solely a behavior disorder, it must further be exhibited in at least two different settings with the individual's environment, i.e., home and classroom, classroom and playground, or other combinations, at least one of which must be in school.

The above label has been since modified from BED to EBD. Forness et al. (1993) clarified the benefits of the EBD definition:

(a) EBD is more than a transient expected response to stressors and persists or would be expected to persist even with prereferral interventions

(b) Eligibility must be based on multiple measures and across settings

(c) EBD can coexist with other disabilities

(d) EBD may include but is not limited to schizophrenic, affective or anxiety disorders, or other disturbances of conduct or adjustment. (p. 106)

Kauffman (1991) appreciated the ambiguity of the "new" definition. EBD is still a new field; Kauffman (1993) compared its development with adolescence, as it has yet to mature to adulthood. He somewhat pessimistically predicted that it would be 10 years before this definition was adopted by everyone.

## Disburbed or Disturbing?

Implicit in the debate regarding characteristics and labels is the practical issue of how educators teach students with EBD. Regardless of the definition used, apparently two types of students will be placed in the classroom: disturbed and disturbing.

Truly disturbed students, as reflected in the current federal definition, are relatively easy to identify. In other words, most observers (evaluators, diagnosticians) would agree regarding the identification of these students. Their problems may be the result of neurological or psychological imbalances, and their behavior is consistent regardless of the environment. Disturbed students may exhibit their disabilities in two ways: internally or externally. Examples of internalizing are extreme worries, fears, and somatic complaints, whereas examples of externalizing are aggression, overactivity, temper tantrums, and delinquency (Coleman, 1992).

Although depression and extreme withdrawal are characterized as disturbed behaviors, students with these problems are often not referred for services. Perhaps these behaviors are misinterpreted as shy or quiet. However, it is not unusual to find many patients of adolescent psychiatric wards having these severe problems. Interestingly, they were never referred for special education services, probably because they were not disrupting the classroom routine. The concept of disturbed suggests that a disability exists, and remediation, if possible, will be through specific individual or group interventions.

If a student's problems are caused by environmental (community, home, school, classroom) factors, the student may be disturbing; however, observers (evaluators, diagnosticians) might disagree about a particular student's problem. Disturbing behaviors are those that interfere with learning and teaching. Not surprisingly, Safran, Safran, and Barcikowski (1985) contended that severe inner disturbingness is more tolerable than severe external disturbingness. Consequently, a change in the environment or in teaching the students how to cope with the environment may result in the students' being "cured." This model, rather than focusing solely on the

---

### Window on Reality

A common misconception of some professionals and laypeople is that it is "healthy" for an individual to openly display feelings and emotions—for example, screaming and crying are considered "better" than repression or withdrawal. Either of these displays of feelings and behavior, however, is extremely serious, and neither is better or easier to treat than the other.

> ### Exercise
>
> Discuss the different types of environmental expectations and reactions that will create the 6-hour disturbing student. How do authority figures respond to noncompliance? How does that effect the consequential student behaviors?

child, reacts also to the systems with which the students must interact. It is also based on the belief that appropriate educational programs can be developed for disturbing students without making inferential judgments about their "essence" (i.e., "Bob is disturbed").

It is crucial to understand that a student may be both disturbing and disturbed. However, the theory underlying the concept of disturbing also suggests that most disturbing students are not disturbed. Like some students with mild mental retardation, who are considered "6-hour retarded students," some students may be disturbing only at school and not at home or in the community, and thus be considered "6-hour disturbing students."

Attention should be paid to the responses of teachers and other significant people (parents, school administrators) to students' behaviors. The perception of disturbingness in a classroom is often a function of each teacher's flexibility or tolerance. Teachers have not approached the concept of discipline in a well-defined manner. The general agreement is that few discipline problems will occur if the classroom is exciting, challenging, and interesting (Ausubel, 1961). Some teachers find this goal to be very difficult to achieve when confronted with students who are from different social classes or who are handicapped, especially in the face of heavy class sizes. Teachers must be prepared to examine their own contributions to the identification of students as disturbing.

For practical purposes, it might be worthwhile to conceptualize disturbed and disturbing as a continuum (see Table 1.1). Disturbed students may externalize and/or internalize their emotions and behaviors. Disurbing students will externalize their behaviors *and they are not disturbed*. The following continuum of behavioral examples, developed by Bower (1959), the author of the original EBD definition, may be a useful reference point from which to begin when developing criteria for definitions:

Stage 1: Children who experience and demonstrate the normal problems of everyday living, growing, exploration and reality testing.

Stage 2: Children who develop a greater number and degree of symptoms of emotional problems as a result of a crisis or traumatic experience.

**TABLE 1.1**
**The Disturbing–Disturbed Continuum**

|  | **Disturbing** | **Disturbed** |
| --- | --- | --- |
| **Identification** | Varies with evaluator | Is obvious to most evaluators |
| **Etiology** | May be a result of environment | May be a result of psychological or biophysical factors |
| **Behaviors** | Are flux, may change with environment | Are not necessarily dependent upon environment |
| **Intervention** | Is by ecological manipulation | Is by individual or group therapy |

Stage 3: Children in whom symptoms persist to some extent beyond normal expectation but who can manage an adequate school adjustment.

Stage 4: Children with fixed and recurring symptoms of emotional disturbance, who can, with help, maintain some positive relationships in a school setting.

Stage 5: Children with fixed and recurring symptoms of emotional difficulties, who are best educated in a residential school setting or temporarily in a home setting. (p. 10)

Stage 1 students are those who, like most people, exhibit disturbing behaviors at some time in their lives. Teachers and other caregivers should be careful not to overreact to an isolated event. All of these students probably belong in the general classroom setting. Whereas Bower's (1959) continuum is somewhat psychodynamic in nature, allowance is made for students who exhibit problem behaviors that result from the environment. Students in Stage 2 might do best in the general classroom with support services, those in Stage 3 might need a part-time special class, and those in Stage 4 probably need a self-contained special class. It should be reiterated that placements may not dictate specific services. In reality, the placement decisions depend on the available resources. Communities that are small or lack resources rarely have the full range of services that may be available to special education students in more populated and/or affluent areas.

An important feature of Bower's (1959) continuum is that the concept of normalcy is addressed in Stage 1. What are the "normal" behaviors that one can expect from children based on sex, social status, race, and religion? Are all overactive preschool children EBD? Clearly not. Most of these children obviously develop into at least somewhat normal adults. When should educators attempt interventions? Compounding the problem of defining normalcy is that educators possess different perspectives regarding the nature of culturally different students. For example, students of some cultures lower their eyes when being reprimanded as a sign of respect. A teacher may misinterpret their actions as "guilt" because they "won't look me in the eye." Countless such examples occur daily.

## The Underserved

It was originally estimated that 2% of the general population would be identified as EBD, and that estimation was deemed conservative (Kauffman, 1993). Most states, however, are hard put to identify 1%. Many professionals believe that students with EBD have been grossly underidentified (Center & Obringer, 1987; Forness, 1991; Kauffman, 1993). Forness and Knitzer (1992) blamed the existing terminology as the cause of this underrepresentation. The dropout rate of students with EBD is over 40%, and less than half are in general education settings (U.S. Department of Education, 1990). Finally, the academic progress of this population is the lowest of groups identified with mild handicaps (Cullinan, Epstein, & Sarbonie, 1992; U.S. Department of Education, 1990).

Any incidence data will reflect the problems that are inherent to any definition that is not widely accepted by everyone. Vague definitions result in different decisions not only on who is "disturbed," but on how many are disturbing. As mentioned above, the evaluators are key factors in determining incidence (Wood & Zabel, 1978). Although administrators have identified low numbers of students with EBD (U.S. Department of Education, 1990), teachers report numbers that may be tenfold those officially identified (Glavin, 1972; Kelly, Bullock, & Dykes, 1977). Consequently, teachers contend that clinical labels are not helpful when one is faced with this type of disability. Some administrators do discourage teacher referrals because of the resources required to service the students (Christenson, Ysseldyke, & Algozzine, 1982). Ignoring the financial costs, many administrators have difficulty finding qualified personnel to staff EBD classrooms. It has been estimated that 50% more EBD teachers are needed than those with endorsements in either learning disabilities or mental retardation (U.S. Department of Education, 1988).

The numbers of students actually disturbed are probably somewhere between administrators' and teachers' estimates. However, if a teacher believes that a student is disturbing or disturbed, some type of assistance should be forthcoming (as one might expect if a student had a significant learning problem). Perhaps another 7% to 10% of the general education population are in need of service (Coleman, 1992). Brandenburg, Friedman, and Silver (1990) found consistency in their review of the research regarding the prevalence of children with significant psychiatric problems:

The prevalence over each of the previous 10 years ranged between 14% and 20%.

Coffey (1988) expressed the need for special education services in prisons. Prison inmates "exhibit 20 times the illiteracy rate of the population at large and 8 times the unemployment rate" (p. 98). Rutherford, Nelson, and Wolford (1985) estimated the number of juvenile delinquents with EBD to be around 28%, with 81% of those receiving special education. Interestingly, only 28% of their teachers are special education certified. This country's rate of incarceration is among the highest in the world and seems to be growing. Lewis, Swartz, and Ianacone (1988) argued that services for the adjudicated are being neglected. There is a need for procedures and for transfer of information. Juvenile delinquents are lost in the system, and they have basically lost their right to a "free and appropriate education."

Bauer (1993) expressed concern about those 400,000 children and youth residing in foster care situations, 25% of whom are disabled. These individuals are shifted from home to home and often from school to school. Research has indicated that many of these students exhibit internalizing and externalizing behaviors, such as the failure to make friends, poor connections, and substance abuse.

Possible reasons for underidentification include the fact that many parents of students with EBD are not an integral part of the education process, and the shortage of EBD teachers may prompt multidisciplinary teams to provide different labels to this population (Forness et al., 1993). Regardless, it is evident that much time and effort have been devoted to bringing these important issues to those (who should be) concerned.

Perhaps a workable solution, albeit simplistic, was provided by Quay (1992) who suggested determining answers to two questions: (a) Does the student have EBD? and (b) Does it interfere with regular class learning? Implementing this suggestion is not simplistic, but might best be done by referring to Wood's (1979) six elements that should be included in any definition:

1. The "disturbed" element: What or who is perceived to be the focus of the problem?

2. The "problem behavior" element: How is the problem described?

3. The "setting" element: In what setting does the problem behavior occur?

4. The "disturbed" element: Who regards the behavior as a problem?

5. The "operationalizing" element: Through what operations and by whom is the definition used to differentiate disturbers from non-disturbers. Does it assess the needs of the disturbers?

6. The "utility" element: Does the definition when operationalized provide the basis for planning activities that will benefit those labeled such as needs assessment, individual assessment, program evaluation, etc. (pp. 7–8)

Although Wood's elements are not a definition per se, they do provide the implications for understanding and working with the students and/or their environment. By now, it should be evident to the reader that there are no simple answers to these issues.

## The Politics of Special Education and General Education

The field of special education is young. It has been a mere two decades since the passing of P.L. 94-142, the Education for All Handicapped Children Act. Academic and social movements have made significant impacts upon the interpretation and application of this very important law. Mainstreaming, the Regular Education Initiative (REI), and inclusion movements have attempted to destigmatize and more effectively integrate students with disabilities or handicaps into the regular education setting. It is important to understand that mainstreaming, REI, and inclusion are all social movements, predicated on the idea that schools "should" reflect society and society "should" insist upon full integration of all individuals to the fullest extent possible. Although there is little controversy in the philosophy of creating a society in which all people are treated (and instructed) equally, these movements have met much opposition.

It would be faulty to assume that all parents and professionals have the same perceptions of successful inclusion. For example, some people believe that special education should be abolished, forcing regular education to embrace, or at least tolerate, those who are different. Others believe that the process should be slow, guaranteeing students the benefits of both social and academic inclusion. Still others are very reluctant to place students with disabilities in any kind of threatening environment, assuming an extremely protective attitude.

### Inclusion in the Regular Education Setting

Reynolds, Wang, and Walberg (1992) argued that students in special education get less general instruction and less reading instruction than if they were in regular education settings. Proponents of reform believe that

## Window on Reality

An 18-year-old young woman stands in front of her classmates, explaining why she is qualified to become Student Council class treasurer. She is poised, self-assured and vibrant. She can be your daughter, or the daughter of your friends. But she is Suzy, my very special daughter, who traveled a long, long way before arriving at that exciting day when she was elected class treasurer.

Suzy is handicapped. Over the course of many years, we have experienced the educational opportunities available in both the public school system and private sector. I have to make it quite clear that I am not opposed to inclusion in the event that a child can be included both academically and socially in his or her school. Having said that, however, it is clear to me that we are deluding ourselves into believing that all handicapped children can be successfully placed into regular classrooms, even with the necessary modifications and sensitivity training.

Early on, we knew that Suzy was handicapped. Schools, however, were not mandated to provide a free appropriate [public] education until the special needs child was school-age. I instinctively knew that I could not spend the next five years waiting for the schools to assume their obligation.

As an infant, I took her to a rehabilitation center which began intensive therapy and taught me how to work with her at home. When she was about 3, I learned about ECLC, a school for learning disabled children, which included a program for handicapped preschoolers. After visiting the class, I enrolled Suzy and assumed all tuition costs for the program, since the school board was not obligated at that time to assist us.

Suzy remained at ECLC for several years. When she turned school-age, special services offered us the opportunity to enroll Suzy in the public school program. I declined, since the program at ECLC seemed to be "the perfect fit." Why tempt fate? It was not until Suzy's ninth birthday that I considered bringing her back to the public school.

I was approached by the district's director of special services, who agreed that Suzy's progress at ECLC was very encouraging. He also agreed that the program in our town must be modeled after the one at ECLC. Additional staff would be hired, including an aide to shadow Suzy in the lunch room and on the playground.

The transition to our public school could only be successful if the professionals at ECLC were willing to act as consultants and counsel the district as to the kinds of materials, staff ratio and modifications needed in the classroom. Even an interview with the individual who was to become Suzy's teacher was arranged. Not a stone was left unturned. With tremendous trepidation, but with total support and encouragement from all our private professionals, including the ECLC staff, I agreed to return Suzy to the district's self-contained class for a trial period.

Suzy's teacher was wonderful. The district maintained all its promises and everyone devoted much time and effort to making the placement work. I became totally absorbed in the town committee named Parents of Children with Special Needs.

Suzy remained in the elementary school for several years. Socialization became the most pressing issue. We started an after-school recreational program that met once a week. Suzy's best friends became her teachers, therapists, family members, and other significant adults.

Suzy continued to make slow progress academically, but socially she was very lonely and isolated. I cannot emphasize enough how painful this

*(continues)*

**Window on Reality** (Continued)

problem was, and how it was to last for years. She continually verbalized her desire for friendships with her own peers.

I suppose the turning point in Suzy's life came in middle school. As a result of an outstanding effort to accommodate Suzy and the commitment on the part of the professionals, she continued in public school. Suzy began to express her loneliness in very subtle ways. Camp became the highlight of Suzy's life. It was a seven-week utopia in which she was in her world surrounded by other children just like herself.

In any event, Suzy's spirits were flagging. She was mainstreamed in home room and special classes such as art and music. There truly was an all-out effort to compensate for the rejection and isolation Suzy was feeling. When Suzy was at the middle school for a few years and approaching her 13th birthday, a very astute psychologist on our team approached me with some serious problems she believed Suzy was facing. "Stop putting Band-Aids on," she scolded. "You can't change the world. You cannot eliminate the rejection. The reality is kids at this age are brutal, and Suzy is a target. She is prey. Spend a day in her shadows and watch her." And so I did.

In the classroom, she socialized primarily with the teachers. However, once she left the confines of the classroom, she walked alone. The knot in my stomach tightened as the day continued. I stood behind a tree at recess and watched Suzy standing alone. Regardless of all the programs and safety nets that were implemented, Suzy's disabilities prevented her from participating in a world that, at best, tolerated her, but much more often rejected her and denied her access.

As I became aware of Suzy's pain and desperation, I knew a change in placement was imminent and necessary. I decided to let Suzy visit ECLC. Suzy agreed with great excitement. Her initial reaction was the first clue that she desperately wanted to escape her current placement. After spending a day at ECLC, Suzy requested that she be allowed to transfer there. She explained that she had already made a friend and there was so much that she could do at the school. As she chatted on, it became very clear that my Suzy had found her world at ECLC—a place where she could be herself.

After a few weeks, Suzy joined the cheerleaders club and invited me to come watch her. As I entered the gym, and observed these darling girls, about 10 of them, in their adorable uniforms, a glaring question began to haunt me. Would these girls have had an opportunity to be cheerleaders in a public school?

The year progressed and Suzy joined the Key Club, Drama Club and a teen social club. The culminating activity for the year was a prom sponsored by ECLC. When the evening arrived. . . Suzy was the focal point instead of the observer. Now, of course, one might question why this scenario could not become reality at our local high school. The answer to this question was at the ECLC prom itself.

As I watched all these "special" youngsters, the same hounding question consumed me. "Where could these kids be free to be themselves at an event which would be devoid of judgmental attitudes?" They were laughing, supporting one another, encouraging the shy individuals to participate, and totally understanding each other's strengths and weaknesses.

As the months passed . . . the events and opportunities which bolstered Suzy's self-esteem, confidence and self-worth were endless. There were certainly too many to discuss in one evening. One special event, however, occurred a few months ago and typified all that I have tried to describe. Suzy was nominated to run for Student Council class treasurer.

*(continues)*

> **Window on Reality** (Continued)
>
> The day before the election Suzy [spoke] to the student body. I'm thrilled to say she won the election. However, envision this young lady with a significant speech and language disability, involved learning problems, and an eye condition which makes it difficult for her to focus, standing up and addressing her audience.
>
> She entered ECLC feeling insecure, dejected and self-conscious, and now she was proclaiming that she was a competent and capable individual worthy of such an important position. I ask you—I would like to ask all the supporters of inclusive education for children like my Suzy—would this have happened at our local high school? Yes, she and children like herself might attend these events, but only as spectators watching everyone else receive the kudos. No more is Suzy isolated. She is part of a world which not only accepts her, but enjoys and appreciates the wonderful, rare human being who only requests a little piece of this life—the right to be herself.
>
> I must again emphasize that I am not opposed to inclusion.... However to make a blanket statement that includes all handicapped children . . . will only cause our movement to regress, and children like my Suzy to be destroyed. Do not allow yourselves to be convinced that schools like ECLC are unrealistic because eventually our children will have to face the world. Our children will always need support and protection. By preserving their self-esteem, we only help them to have the strength to accept and address their challenges in the future.
>
> Let us work together to make certain that no child be forced into a setting that, at best, is unrealistic, but even worse, destructive, leading to isolation, loneliness or perhaps total withdrawal. (Reprinted with permission from "A Parent's Struggle: When Inclusion Becomes Exclusion" by J. Fischer, 1993, *Counterpoint, 14*(2), p. 13. Copyright 1993 by LRP Publications, Horsham, PA. All rights reserved.)

evidence is unclear that special education works (Carlberg & Kavale, 1980). Lipsky and Gartner (1991) contended that "The current system of special education needs to be changed for a basic reason: It does not work. That is, it fails to serve well the students. Although particular practices are faulty, the cause is not in practice but in basic conception" (p. 43). Furthermore, Safran and Safran (1987) suggested that special educators are not any more tolerant of inappropriate behaviors than are regular educators. Consequently, according to Stainbeck and Stainbeck (1984), if there are no differences in these important areas, then regular education can and should make the modifications to include all people. They proposed that it may be time for schools to recognize that all students have individual needs and that the suggestion that one type is regular and one type is special is false and discriminating. They further stressed that special education is both academically and fiscally inefficient. It is more expensive to operate the current dual system. A more cynical belief was espoused by Reynolds (1990), who suggested in an article about students with mild handicaps (rather than specifically EBD) that special education advocacy groups are simply trying to hold on to their turf.

## Arguments Against Inclusion of Students with EBD

Although it certainly is desirable for both regular and special educators to share the responsibilities of educating learners with handicaps, many educators have expressed a pessimistic view regarding the impacts of such previous reforms in the classroom (Algozzine, Ysseldyke, Kauffman, & Landrum, 1991). Algozzine et al. (1991) expressed concern that, "depending on how the issues are framed, the reform movement may leave students with behavior problems particularly vulnerable to neglect" (p. 10).

Walker and Bullis (1991) argued against mainstreaming for the sake of mainstreaming: "Nor do we believe that mere placement in the regular classroom is in any way equivalent nor synonymous with best practice when implemented in the absence of other critical considerations such as the design and delivery of an appropriate educational program" (p. 75). In addition, they contended that "the hope that the student will progress academically and benefit socially from mere placement in a regular classroom setting will likely not be realized; in fact, the opposite set of outcomes (lack of teacher acceptance, rejection by nonhandicapped peers, and academic failure with concomitant decrements in self esteem) are far more likely" (p. 76) (see also Gresham, 1982). Walker and Bullis further argued that claims about the purported failure of special education are false. In fact, they suggested that it is the regular education settings in public schools that have failed the populations with EBD. They questioned any evidence that would suggest that public school personnel have demonstrated major attitude changes that would call for an inclusive atmosphere (see also Pappanikou, 1979).

In refuting the notion that the regular education setting is more healthy for EBD students, research and literature have been highly suggestive that nonhandicapped peers reject students with EBD (Konopasek, 1990; Larrivee & Horne, 1991; Roberts & Zubrick, 1993; Sarbonie, 1987). In fact, Larrivee and Horne (1991) also found that nonhandicapped students in low-reading groups were less accepted by their peers. Often, this information is confused with research that has found more peer acceptance of students with learning disabilities (LD) (Walker & Bullis, 1991). There is a wide gap between the ways peers accept students with LD and those with EBD (Sarbonie, Kauffman, Ellis, Marshall, & Elksnin, 1987–1988).

Furthermore, some research suggests that teachers do not like disturbing students in their classrooms (Gable & Laycock, 1991; Landrum, 1992; Lewin, Nelson, & Tollefson, 1983). Teachers see inclusion as more work, are unsure of their own abilities to teach this population, and are unsure of the possible benefits (Carter, 1991; Gersten, Walker, & Darch, 1988; Landrum, 1992). It is not surprising that teachers feel this way, as research has suggested that colleges and universities are not delivering or requiring the classes that will allow preteachers to integrate students with handicaps. How can teachers have good attitudes about teaching these students, if they do not know how to help them (Kearney & Durand, 1992)?

The sanctity of the regular education setting was also called into question by Gable, Hendrickson, and Rutherford (1991), who concluded through their literature review that "not all students with behavior disorders are best served in regular classroom situations" (p. 27). They also identified factors that should be situationally considered:

1. Knowledge of demands of LRE [least restrictive environment]
2. Climate for collaboration
3. Level of administrative support
4. Complexity of required programming
5. Intrusiveness of required programming
6. Duration of required programming
7. Acceptability of programming demands
8. Possible side effects of programming
9. Teacher motivation
10. Student motivation (p. 28)

Each of these factors is addressed fully in Unit 1 of this book.

As mentioned above, one criticism of the professionals arguing for separation is that they are being protective not only of students with EBD, but also of their own jobs. Braaten, Kauffman, Braaten, Polsgrove, and Nelson (1988) refuted this claim by suggesting that "BD students placed in regular classes present particular problems because their characteristics demand additional instructional resources, including specially trained staff to manage extremely disruptive and dangerous behavior. Other students' rights to a safe and supportive learning environment are neither minor nor moot when the assumption that nobody should be segregated forces the integration of BD students" (p. 23). To implement wholesale inclusion implies that the behaviors of students with EBD are simply a function of being labeled as such and, when integrated with others, they will no longer be EBD; that teaching students with EBD is identical to teaching regular education students; and that regular education teachers now possess the necessary skills and attitudes to teach students with EBD (Braaten, Kauffman, et al., 1988).

There is little sympathy for individuals with EBD when they are exhibiting their handicaps. Furthermore, no national parent support groups exist to advocate for the rights of these children. Thus, one concern is that total inclusion will result in children and youth with EBD being suspended, expelled, pushed, or elbowed out of school. Diamond (1993) cautioned that "If we regard inclusion as a religious principle, if we disregard the differences among the students we consider disabled, if we continue to insist that the least restrictive environment is some absolute standard rather than a continuum of variability that has truth only for each individual in question, we will lose some of the most valuable and creative and lovable citizens in our community" (p. 6).

Needless to say, there is not a simple answer to this complex problem. Is it true, as Lipsky and Gartner (1991) contended, that P.L. 94-142 was right for its time and has now assured access for all? More important, are those teachers "in the trenches" also excited about this movement? The Executive Committee of the Council for Children with Behavioral Disorders (1989) stated that these movements are the agenda of "certain government officials and highly vocal minority of special educators and school administrators" (p. 203). Certainly the past does not suggest success with a single system of education. Has education (and society) progressed to the point that only one is sufficient now? Or, is the situation simply that students with EBD are among the least mainstreamable (Braaten, Kauffman, et al., 1988)? Special education law does not mandate these movements. It does, however, require that students must be placed in the least restrictive environment.

## Least Restrictive Environment

The phrase *least restrictive environment* (LRE) has different meanings to different people. It seems that the original conception of LRE was developed with the spirit of providing an environment that is as close as possible to what is considered "normal." The term *normal* also engenders different connotations for different people. With the advent of "inclusive education," it is appropriate that the concept of LRE is revisited.

The least restrictive environment is the environment in which an individual's disability is not handicapping to him or her. Therefore, if the behavioral, social, affective, pedagogical, and learning characteristics in an environment prevent learning from occurring, then the student is not in the least restrictive environment. Consequently, if a student is able to read (behave?) on a third-grade level and the seatwork in a particular class calls for sixth-grade reading (behaviors/social skills), then he or she is handicapped because of a disability, *and thus is in a restrictive environment*. Note, however, that this definition does not account for the "choice" of the student not to participate. For example, if a student can read and decides not to read, he or she then is not handicapped (given that the student is "normal" in all other areas).

***A Functional LRE Definition.*** If LRE is to be a functional concept, someone should develop written guidelines that detail what percentage of the time an individual can, in fact, be handicapped in the LRE. Is 5%, or 10%, or 50% acceptable? Certainly, some individuals with handicaps can be handicapped in a classroom with few consequences to others. However, students with EBD cannot be handicapped to the same extent, because when they cannot meet, *because of their disability*, the learning and behavioral expectations of a particular setting, they will normally intrude on the rights of others, creating a restrictive environment for the nonhandicapped. In other words, when students with EBD are not learning, their disability will be more visible and certainly more disturbing.

***Where Do Educators Go from Here?*** The inclusion of LRE in the special education laws made sense in the 1970s. They make sense now. Even Slenkovitch (1984) argued that P.L. 94-142 is not a social law; it is an education law. All schools need to implement LRE so that hundreds of disabled students do not lose a free and appropriate education under the guise of inclusion. When inclusive education innovations allow a classroom to become the LRE, then and only then is it an example of true "inclusion."

---

### Window on Reality

The reader of this book will surely confront professionals and parents who are firmly placed in either camp. Hopefully, the reader will be cognizant of the different arguments and of their ramifications to the students. Regardless, the effects of how a particular student is "included" must be examined. For example, such variables as teacher–student interactions and the effect of students on the general classroom ecology is integral to any success. In Chapter 4, specific guidelines are introduced to implement possible reintegration.

---

# Politics of Teaching

Teachers confront numerous political influences each day on the job. The availability of adequate services for their students and the reactions of administrators and fellow teachers to disturbing behaviors by students who are EBD will have significant impact on the success of any program. Teachers need to be aware of these realities so they can learn to work with or change these influences.

## Institutional Reactions to Students with EBD

If, as has been suggested, the school is a microcosm of society, the turmoil evidenced in schools during recent years should not be surprising. Criminal behaviors by high school as well as elementary students are no longer unusual. Predictions for the future do not seem much better. Reynolds (1990) contended that schools and society need to prepare for "(a) a higher percentage from economically poor families; (b) a higher percentage from minority families; (c) increasing proportions living with one or neither natural parent; and (d) increasing proportions surviving low birth weight or congenital anomalies" (Reynolds, 1990, p. 64).

Schools and teachers cannot continue to ignore this information. The trials and tribulations that many children experience daily do not go away at the classroom door. The irony of any discussion regarding inclusion is that the school must be ready to accommodate those who are different and be willing to remediate those who are significantly deviant. Nevertheless, "the majority of students exhibiting undesirable behavior in school settings generally receive no services, inadequate services under auspices of regular education programs, or special education services applied piecemeal or too late to be beneficial" (Nelson, Rutherford, et al., 1991, p. 411). Perhaps schools and teachers are too narrow with regard to their expectations and demands. This is clearly evident with regard to their reactions to students with disturbing behaviors.

Schools seem to have two equally pertinent reactions to deviance: formal and informal. Formal reactions are those that are actively followed as school policy. Sometimes, "actively following policy" may involve purposely doing nothing about a situation. Informal reactions are subtle behaviors exhibited by some administrators, teachers, and students that represent discrimination of the "good" student from the "bad" student.

## Administrators' Reactions to Students with EBD

One of the most difficult tasks regular educators must face is that of understanding that the behaviors exhibited by students with EBD are as "normal" for them as not having sight is "normal" for students who are visually impaired. However, the behaviors of students with EBD often prevent teachers from teaching and students from learning. More important, they also break the codes of the school. Thus, the management of these students can become a monumental task.

Walker (1979) identified three common responses that schools have to disturbances: blame the student's behaviors on parents, teachers, or community; medicate the student; or remove the student from the regular education setting. Despite the legal decisions described later in this section,

> **Window on Reality**
>
> Although state laws limit the number of days students may be suspended (10 days per year in many states), students with EBD are still being suspended in a routine manner from many schools. After 10 days, some schools convene a multidisciplinary team meeting and devise a "new" Individualized Education Program (IEP) to increase the suspension by another 10 days. Most of these school districts are not being sued by anyone.
>
> Few people stand up for the types of behaviors that these students exhibit. Many of the behaviors exhibited by students with EBD are simply too deviant for the school to manage. Pressures, both economic and social, are preventing these students from being placed in more appropriate settings (i.e., restrictive), and suspension is perceived as the only reasonable alternative. Nevertheless, these students are being denied their civil rights.

suspension from school is still commonplace. Students with EBD are more likely to be expelled than are students who are either learning disabled or mentally retarded (Rose, 1988).

Students are suspended for tardiness, absenteeism, "vulgar" language, and even the possession of tobacco. A suspension may also be used as a means of having a student transfer out of the school district ("Transfer and we won't expel you"). A 3-day suspension may last for much longer when the stipulation is added that the student must return with a parent.

Hindman's (1986) review of court decisions led her to write, "The pendulum has clearly swung from the schools having virtually unquestioned authority regarding disciplinary action to their facing costly lawsuits for infringing upon the rights of certain classes of students. Courts, in their attempt to protect federally guaranteed rights, have placed school officials in increasingly compromising positions" (p. 287). Her predictions were accurate.

The U.S. Supreme Court has ruled that students could no longer be expelled from school if their behaviors evolved from their handicap. Leone (1984) suggested that there should be a special clause in school discipline codes for determining if students who violate the code are handicapped, and to decide if the act is a result of their disability. Bartlett (1989) commented that "student vandalism, assault, insubordination, masturbation, smoking, sexual misconduct, and sale of drugs can no longer be dealt with swiftly and freely when the perpetrator is handicapped" (p. 357). Students cannot be denied services because of the disability. This lack of action would deny these students their civil rights.

Directly related to suspension is purposely creating a hostile environment that encourages nonattendance ("Jose, one false move and you're out!"). Another formal school reaction is for teachers and administrators to spend less time identifying and tracking down disturbing nonattendees. When students leave a school district (an increasingly common occurrence), follow-up to determine if they are attending another school is rare. Another reaction to potential disturbers is the refusal to admit students to school without the appropriate paperwork or to postpone their admission until the beginning of the following term. The Task Force on Children Out of School (1971) identified the following administrative responses to nonattendees:

1. *Denial:* I deny that children are being excluded from school or that such things are happening to them. Prove it.
2. *Exception:* The examples you have given me are exceptions. Prove that they are widespread.
3. *Demurrer:* I admit the facts, but feel that you have not presented a problem which is that important.
4. *Confession and Avoidance:* I admit the fact and feel very concerned. But, there are overriding considerations which free me from responsibility for acting to solve the problems.
5. *Improper Jurisdiction:* I understand the problem, but feel it is not the school's responsibility. It is the task of the family and other institutions.
6. *Prematurity of Request:* We knew all along that these things were happening, and have made plans to correct the situation. Our efforts must be given a chance.
7. *Generalized Guilt:* What you say is true, but other school systems have similar problems. We are not worse than they are.
8. *Improper Forum:* The problem is really in the hands of the state and federal government. There is little that we can do.
9. *Recrimination:* I admit that children are out of school, but it is their own fault. It wouldn't happen if their parents really cared.
10. *Further Study:* The problem has been referred to the proper official for future study. We hope to develop a plan sometime in the future. (p. 67)

The existence of these reactions more than 20 years later is probably quite prevalent. There is debate on whose responsibility it is not to educate, but to care for children and youth with EBD. It would be simplistic to suggest that administrators are the demons and must shoulder that responsibility. Prior to being referred to administrators, these students most often have interacted with teachers.

## Teachers' Reactions to Students with EBD

A reasonable assumption is that "bad" behaviors usually evoke bad reactions. Coleman and Gilliam (1983) believed that "a student with behavior problems may encounter negative teacher expectations for his/her behavior problems and academic achievement, which, under given conditions, could translate into a self-fulfilling prophecy of failure" (p. 122). A research investigation determined that, even when their problem behaviors had improved, students with EBD were still treated in a negative manner by their student teachers (Lewin et al., 1983).

Teachers often blame the students, their parents, the community, and the above-mentioned school administrators for problems in their classrooms. Although such factors may be present, it could be a case of avoiding the essential issue if teachers are not considered in the equation. Clearly, teachers' attitudes will have a significant impact on their students' subsequent behaviors (Safran et al., 1985).

Furthermore, it is not surprising that the higher efficacy teachers are assigned to teach the more difficult classes, and the lower efficacy teachers are assigned to the easier classes (Dembo & Gibson, 1985). Consequently, students who need the "best" teachers may not be receiving them.

Teachers have traditionally been considered as highly reliable predictors and identifiers of disturbed and disturbing students. Walker and Bullis (1991) wrote that research is needed on teacher–peer interactions and their effect on the classroom ecology. This research would focus on external behaviors that are teacher related (e.g., acting out, teacher defiance, noncompliance) and peer related (e.g., some acceptance, some rejection, negative aggressive social behavior), as well as internal behavior patterns that are teacher related (e.g., problems with self, low achievement, nonassertive behavior patterns) and peer related (e.g., neglected or rejected peer status, social isolation, withdrawal).

The purpose of this text is not to place blame on teachers or administrators. The competencies needed to effectively teach disturbed and disturbing students in both regular education and special education settings are expanding. Kearney and Durand's (1992) research suggested that colleges and universities are not delivering or requiring the classes that will allow preteachers to integrate students with handicaps. This leads to the more important question: How can teachers have good attitudes about students with handicaps if they do not know how to deal with them? Chapter 2 examines the effective school and teaching factors that will enhance the possibilities for the success of both students and teachers.

## Summary and Conclusions

Teaching disturbed and disturbing students is not an easy job. One would think that arriving at a definition for this population would be a necessary first step before undertaking this task. After reviewing this chapter, however, the reader may be struck with the notion that almost any disturbing student could be included or excluded from services. The reader might very well be correct in this assumption. It should be reiterated that, simply because some students are "disturbing," it does not necessarily follow that their problems are transitory. Unless they are dealt with on a systematic basis, many disturbing behaviors will not fade away. Teachers should understand that many disturbing behaviors may be the result of school or teacher behaviors, and that these may be the "easiest" to remediate. It is the disturbing students, not the disturbed students, with whom teachers have the greatest opportunity to achieve success. Most likely, the disturbed child will benefit only from intensive individual therapy; subtle environmental changes may not greatly enhance this child's chances for success.

Although some educators may believe that the answer to educating these students lies in placement, others focus on programming. Or maybe, as argued by Audette and Algozzine (1992), "special educators have spent too much time addressing the wrong questions. The penchant for seeking the right definition for the right type of students is obvious. The results are less than impressive. . . . Time spent seeking definitions, tests, or criteria is not time spent improving the processes of teaching and learning" (p. 17). More probably, there needs to be a compromise of the two with the reality that, if there is to be federal funding for special education, some type of identification procedure will have to be in place. Ideally, it will have an educational purpose.

# 2

# Factors That Influence the Teaching of Students with EBD

Educating students with EBD is probably among the most demanding jobs in the teaching profession. It is a multifaceted job. An EBD teacher educates, collaborates, counsels, consults, and manages. The job is challenging under the best of circumstances, and under the worst of circumstances it can be extremely burdensome. If, as suggested in Chapter 1, this category of students is grossly underrepresented, then it would make sense that only those who exhibit the most severe behaviors currently find their way into special education classrooms. If teachers are going to teach, then it makes sense that they should do so under the "best of circumstances."

The challenge of teaching students with EBD is multiplied when they are integrated, as much as possible, into general education settings (or for that matter into the general mainstream of society). Traditionally, the model of integration has been a special education "expert" model. "Efforts have been made to sensitize general education to special education programs and the accomplishments of special education; to gain acceptance and access for atypical children into general education classrooms and programs" (Goodman, 1985, p. 102). The expert model certainly must be revisited if integration is going to be collaborative and, ultimately, successful.

This chapter presents the qualities of schools that can enable effective teaching. Additionally, the ever-broadening specific tasks and behaviors that teachers must understand and demonstrate are outlined and ultimately serve as a framework for the remainder of this book. The chapter provides the educator with realistic methods to use in the context of their environment. The word "realistic" is used because teaching should not be a 24-hour-a-day job. Those teachers who make teaching their sole preoccupation are the ones who most frequently "burn out," and their students burn out along with them. Consequently, the discussion is confined to procedures and techniques that can be accomplished during a somewhat regular 40-hour-a-week schedule.

This chapter also will examine the challenges of teaching students with EBD and discuss factors that promote or inhibit effective school climates and school teachers. Regardless of the impact of students' backgrounds, the way schools and teachers approach education can have a significant impact on student learning. These factors lead to the evolving role of the special educator. No longer is the model of the isolated special education classroom commonplace. Consequently, teachers of students with EBD will be faced with the decision of creating an environment that focuses on remediation or accommodation. Further, "simple behavior management" will not be accepted as the primary role of the job description. Teachers will need to consider and learn new techniques of delivering instruction, working with administrators, and consulting and collaborating with their peers. All of these behaviors will be taken within newer contexts, for example, the implementation of a successful transition from school to work.

# Factors that Contribute to Inviting and Effective Schools

The importance and educational implications of establishing a positive school climate have received attention in educational research and literature (Bickel, 1983; Edmonds, 1979, 1981; Mackenzie, 1983; Purkey & Smith, 1982). Although having a significant effect on a school's climate is probably beyond the capacity of any one teacher, it seems necessary that teachers understand the climate of their own particular schools. With the renewed focus on inclusion, the concept of effective schools has even greater weight. The dual notion of education (separation of general and special education) will certainly be subject to reform, and to suggest that general education can learn from special education, and not vice versa, is folly indeed. The research and literature surveyed in this chapter are, for the most part, general education findings. They impact and indeed may be the most powerful predictors of both teacher and student success.

It would be simplistic to suggest that all teachers or all schools possess all or none of the characteristics necessary to guarantee good teaching (Johnson, 1987). Clearly, many general education teachers are well prepared to accept students with mild handicaps and others are not. Many general education teachers have positive attitudes toward individuals with disabilities and others do not. It does not require a stretch of the imagination to replace "general education teachers" in the previous two sentences with "special education teachers." What certainly will complicate matters for any type of educators, however, is if those individuals with mild handicaps exhibit them in a disturbing manner.

The type of school and its leadership may strongly influence any changes. "In effective schools, the principal (or other appropriate administrative personnel) provides leadership by demonstrating commitment to goals, coupled with flexibility in pursuing them. There is also an emphasis on outcomes over procedures, the presence of high levels of informal interaction and the use of problem-solving and evaluation techniques to monitor performance objectives. There are clear and consistent school policies in effective schools; and policies emphasize shared responsibilities; the policies emphasize shared responsibility for the overall school climate" (Bickel & Bickel, 1986, p. 490).

### Window on Reality

Many well-intentioned classroom management programs fall short of success when the school's (i.e., administrator's) reactions to disturbances differ markedly from those of the teacher who developed the classroom management design. For example, some principals may be more concerned with the level of noise coming from a room than the amount of learning that is occurring. Or, if a student with severe EBD is placed inappropriately in a setting, misguided administrators may expect the "certified special education teacher" to cure the disability.

As mentioned, it is unrealistic to expect that the variables inherent to a positive school environment can be measured as either all good or all bad. The following are essential components of school climate that require a continual process of assessment (and practice):

1. Ambiance of the environment (Is it clean and inviting?)
2. Workable class sizes
3. Positive leadership from the principal
4. Adequate resources
5. Collaboration and cooperation among the faculty
6. School philosophy (Are there high expectations for all, tutoring programs, etc.?)

7. Reinforcers (Is there recognition to faculty, staff, and students?)

Christenson, Ysseldyke, and Thurlow (1989) complemented this list with (8) the importance of establishing parent–teacher contact and (9) the presence of appropriate building maintenance. All of these components pervade the aspects of educational outcomes that are demonstrated in curriculum, instruction, evaluation, and community and parent support.

## Disinviting and Ineffective Schools

In 1940 the top seven disciplinary problems cited by teachers were talking out of turn, chewing gum, making noise, running in the halls, cutting in line, dress code violations, and littering. In 1990 teachers face the effects of drug abuse, alcohol abuse, pregnancy, suicide, rape, robbery, and assault (Toch, Gest, & Guttman, 1993). Even though problems have changed with the times, it is safe to assume that the problems of 1940 still exist and are probably troubling to many teachers. Although most of the above-stated problems of 1990 are most appropriately dealt with by law enforcement officials, they also make their way into the classroom. The quality of these 1990 problems is different from those of 1940. Consequently, it is a concern when educators treat the "crimes" of the 1940s as if they were crimes of the 1990s. For example, some schools suspend students for the same or longer periods of time for disturbing the classroom or skipping school than for committing assault.

Most schools informally react to disturbing and disturbed behaviors in a highly consistent manner. Rarely are disturbing and certainly disturbed students welcome to participate in school events. They do not belong to clubs, do not attend school functions, and are not asked to participate in athletics. There are also de facto obstacles that preclude many students from participation. For instance, many activities (e.g., sports, drama) require money for equipment, and activities scheduled for after school exclude students who have to work. Large impersonal schools also contribute to disturbing behaviors. Barker and Hall (1964) found that the smaller the school, the greater the percentage of participation by the students, suggesting that the students felt more a "part" of the school. The uninvited in the larger schools are alienated and do not have any particular bonding to the school. It would be shortsighted, however, to interpret Barker and Hall's findings as generalizable to *all* schools. Grabe (1981) essentially agreed with Barker and Hall, but also found that many students, especially the boys, who went to small schools felt alienated and were more likely to feel the pressure to succeed.

It would be easy simply to blame the size of school or society or some other factor for the learning and behavioral problems currently being experienced. However, the nature of education in the schools and ultimately those who staff the schools also should shoulder some of the responsibility. Ysseldyke, Algozzine, and Thurlow (1992) listed three controversial reasons for some of the school's problems. The first is that "schools are doing an inadequate, perhaps deplorable job of educating students and indeed . . . the schools are not designed to teach" (p. 202). This is based on the notion that the students from lower socioeconomic status groups do not do well in school and that schools today are ill prepared to care for these populations. The second reason is that "schools are designed to teach, . . . teachers are prepared to do an adequate job of teaching, but . . . many students simply have too many defects, deficiencies, or disabilities to profit from instruction" (p. 203). Finally, "school failure (is due) to a combination of internal constraints, external pressures, and unattainable objectives" (p. 203).

There are no simple solutions to any of these problems. For example, high teacher expectations are often cited to be an enviable school attribute. However, these high expectations can also be disinviting to those who cannot reach them. It would take skilled teachers to have the intuition with regard to how students may perceive their intentions. Regular education teachers do have high expectations. They expect adaptive behaviors and consequently are less tolerant of inappropriate responses (Walker & Rankin, 1983).

In summary, disinviting school reactions to disturbing and disturbed children involve either overt or subtle exclusion. If students do not possess the social skills, and perhaps the economic stability, necessary to actively participate in school functions, then they are rarely invited to those functions. Those who have the necessary attributes are welcome as the social leaders of the school or as members of an "in" crowd.

## Inviting and Disinviting Teachers

Although the nature of schools and family and community factors may engender disturbing behaviors from certain students, they are certainly not the sole contributors to the students' problems in the classroom. When examining the factors that may be precipitating disturbing behaviors, the teacher is often ignored. Research identifying teacher behaviors that may contribute to certain student reactions is rare.

Purkey and Novak (1984), in their excellent book *Inviting School Success*, discussed four types of teachers and ways they may promote or discourage problem behaviors. When reading these descriptions, readers will probably be able to attach these descriptions to teachers they may have experienced.

***Intentionally Disinviting Teachers.*** Intentionally disinviting teachers are characterized by being not only prejudiced, but also discriminatory toward certain students, holding such attitudes as "survival of the fittest" or "sink or swim" and making consequential stereotypical remarks about these students. Intentionally disinviting teachers also exhibit low levels of tolerance. They get frustrated or angry quite rapidly. Many of their comments and behaviors are exhibited during these times. For example, these teachers may implement corporal punishment as part (or all!) of their classroom management system because "these students don't know how to behave."

Surely, most readers will disavow any chances of becoming a teacher such as this. Most will think, "I love students; that's why I got into teaching!" Intentionally disinviting teachers probably went into teaching for the same reasons, yet something probably happened to change these feelings. Intentionally disinviting teachers are rarely found in large numbers, but even one in a school certainly will make his or her presence felt.

***Unintentionally Disinviting Teachers.*** Unintentionally disinviting teachers are much more common in the schools and are potentially a much greater problem than intentionally disinviting teachers. Many of these teachers are "well meaning and high minded" but simply are not teaching effectively. They may, in fact, be overly protective of students who do not do well. They may praise incorrect or barely passable work. When this happens, students very quickly realize that they have to submit little effort to be acceptable. The curriculum of these teachers is often characterized by "busywork," complete with reams of copy machine paper. "Teacher behavior perceived by students as sexist, racist, patronizing, or thoughtless is likely to be interpreted as disinviting despite the teacher's good intention" (Purkey & Novak, 1984, p. 18). Interactions with students are perceived by these teachers as being only positive.

Some disinviting comments from either the intentionally or unintentionally disinviting teachers include:

> Don't be so stupid.
>
> Why do you bother coming to school?
>
> That is dead wrong.
>
> I know you're not that stupid.
>
> They don't want to learn.
>
> He can't be disturbed. (Purkey & Novak, 1984, p. 132)

Some disinviting behaviors from either the intentionally or unintentionally disinviting teachers include:

> Using sarcasm
>
> Hitting someone
>
> Breaking a promise

Shaking your finger at someone

Showing a lack of concern (Purkey & Novak, 1984, p. 133)

It should not be a surprise if students' reactions to these behaviors include an unwillingness to take risks or even to participate in class activities. It is important to understand that many teachers who are considered *effective* for many students, may be unintentionally disinviting for others. Because of their intense focus on academics, these teachers may have a consequent low tolerance for disturbing behaviors (perhaps especially for students with EBD).

***Unintentionally Inviting Teachers.*** These teachers are commonly referred to as "natural born"—they simply behave in a manner that makes students feel part of the educational process. What comes naturally to these teachers are often attributes professed to be successful classroom factors in the literature and in teacher training institutions. However, these attributes are probably less a reflection of their professional training than of the makeup of their personalities, or perhaps the way they were nurtured. No matter how dramatically depressing certain school environments are, unintentionally inviting teachers may be found. Despite the "students' background" and "lack of administrative support," these individuals get the job done.

Problems may occur with these teachers, however, when they are asked to explain their behaviors in "theoretical terms" or, more seriously, when something goes wrong and they have to remediate. Teaching "from the top of one's head" may lead to inconsistency and confusion from even the best of these teachers.

***Intentionally Inviting Teachers.*** Most teachers attempt to be intentionally inviting. Utilizing carefully designed curriculum and instruction, contacting parents, and learning the special needs of their students are all goals of these teachers. One student once remarked about a particular high school teacher, "I especially like this teacher; he took the time to know my name and I was hardly ever there!" Students from kindergarten through doctoral studies need to feel important, and teachers who can meet this need are often the most successful ones. In most instances, intentionally inviting teachers are characterized by the constant desire to learn by attending graduate classes, inservice training, and professional conferences.

Some inviting comments from either intentionally or unintentionally inviting teachers include:

Good morning!

I enjoy having you here.

I've been thinking about you.

Of course I have time.

I think you can do it. (Purkey & Novak, 1984, p. 132)

Some inviting behaviors from either intentionally or unintentionally inviting teachers include:

Shaking hands

Smiling

Learning names quickly

Noticing new clothes

Congratulating someone

Giving a thumbs-up sign (Purkey & Novak, 1984, p. 133)

The primary focus of these teachers is instruction. Their goals are clear and well defined. They are responsive to the individual academic and social needs of their students.

Teachers frequently find reasons why their classrooms seem to be in a constant state of chaos, or why each year two or three students are consistently being suspended. Parents, the community, and lack of administrative support often rank high on the blame list. Although these factors may be present, it may be avoiding the essential issue not to determine into which category of invitedness the teacher fits. It may be the behaviors of intentionally or unintentionally disinviting teachers that engender problematic student responses. The focus of Chapter 4 (and this book) is to give some more specific behaviors for those teachers who desire to become intentionally inviting.

The purpose of the following exercise is to help the reader differentiate among the four types of teaching behavior. This ability would seem to be a prerequisite to the reader's self-evaluation process.

---

### Exercise

Using Purkey and Novak's (1984) four types of teachers, identify the teachers in the following vignettes:

1. These teachers are constantly sending home monthly newsletters and have weekly individual talks with each student. They

*(continues)*

> **Exercise** (Continued)
>
> are not afraid (although they may experience anxiety) to try new techniques. They provide other teachers with information that they have received from inservices and other sources.
>
> 2. These teachers are liked by everyone. Students enjoy being in their classes. They don't complain about students or administrators. They are always smiling.
>
> 3. These teachers are proud of the fine academic achievement and standardized test scores of their students. They demand hard work and love students who "really care" about school. They do not spend much time with slower students because they feel that they can make "little difference."
>
> 4. These teachers are very organized! They are always making copies at the copy machine. They have already ordered movies for every week of the school year. Their lessons plans are finished weeks in advance. They are always busy correcting workbook sheets. They believe that the classroom should be reflective of success, success, success. That is why they use workbooks.

Hopefully, under the best of circumstances, inviting teachers will be matched with inviting schools, and the students will become the beneficiaries. For this to happen, however, teachers must be able to carefully define who they are, what they do, and what they want to achieve for their students.

## The Role of the Special Educator: Remediation or Accommodation?

The implications of the information presented thus far can be overwhelming. There are conflicting messages for teachers both in the schools and in the university classroom. Is the major role of teachers to remediate their students or is it to make the necessary accommodations so that the student will remain "EBD" and learn within a "normal" setting? Philosophically, it would be hard to argue with the accommodation viewpoint. In practice, however, the normal setting must desire to accommodate, must have the tools to accommodate, and must work hard to accommodate. Otherwise, the student with EBD suffers.

## A Definition of Remediation

Even within the accommodation argument, the role of the teacher remains unclear. Remediation is a process that purports to result in a cure; that is, it results in those previously labeled people as being no longer identifiable as emotionally or behaviorally disordered. In other words, a person is remediated, or cured, when he or she possesses behaviors, emotions, and/or feelings that fall within a "normal range of functioning." A person is not remediated if he or she is still identified by others as having a disorder (Becker, 1963). Hallahan and Kauffman (1988) argued convincingly that, although most normal people experience behavior disorders, few are identified as behaviorally disordered or in need of remediation. Accordingly, the concept of "cure" is relative.

"Emotional/behavioral disorder remediation" relates to a process that is called for by society, that is, by a school, a workplace, the community, or the family. People with mild maladaptive behaviors or feelings who initiate self-help actions, such as those who seek counseling because they feel they are beginning to lose control, are not identifiable as concerns by society and therefore do not fall within the definition of somebody needing EBD remediation.

## The Philosophies of Remediation and Accommodation

Remediation drastically differs from accommodation in philosophy. One extreme view of accommodation is as a "holding" situation, one in which the individual with EBD is held in abeyance. At the other extreme, it is a concept of a society creating the necessary structural changes, attitudinal as well as physical, to allow individuals with EBD to retain their "EBD-ness" and not encounter undue discrimination.

There is irony in the argument that, if education would have been successful in remediation, the problems of today (homelessness, suicide, juvenile delinquency, etc.) would not exist. Education is not the panacea for society's ills. Teachers in the 1990s and the 2000s need to understand those pressures that students face on a daily basis. Furthermore, the societal influences on child development are unlike those that have existed at any previous point in history. For example, Epstein, Kauffman, and Cullinan (1985) suggested that "it is distinctly unlikely that the majority of teachers who rate children today are as keenly aware of childhood depression as they are of childhood aggression and disruption" (p. 133). Bettes and Walker (1986) argued that depression can lead to suicidal ideations or behavior. Furthermore, those depressed individuals who are unidentified as having EBD may ultimately commit aggressive acts.

Because many students with EBD are not identified in public schools, it is absurd to argue that schools have not succeeded in "curing" them all. To carry this argument to its conclusion, one can recall the countless case histories of seemingly "normal" people who have committed atrocities: mass murders in a McDonalds' restaurant in San Diego and in a schoolyard in Stockton, California, an attempt on former President Reagan's life, suicides, suicide pacts among friends, and so on. Invariably, former classmates, teachers, and family members are interviewed to arrive at a clearer understanding of the assailant's motives. Usually, they describe the assailant as a quiet, shy, "keeps-to-himself" kind of person. Identification efforts in this area have been almost nonexistent, rendering remediation attempts impossible.

Remediation is an appropriate goal. It should be the main goal. It is a system of guided change that is designed to achieve a better fit between students with EBD and the world in which they live. The philosophy of remediation is clear: "You have the opportunity to learn to fit, to be not discriminated against because of your present feelings and behaviors, to learn that 'EBD' or 'emotionally disturbed' or 'crazy' does not accurately describe your essence. It describes a condition that you are experiencing, a condition that most people have experienced one time or another in their lives. It is a condition that, with much hard work, may be reduced to the point that you may fit in with others without being identified as being different."

Where does society look for the goal of remediation to be attempted? To the schools, and ultimately to the teachers who are charged with the responsibility to change behavior. Good, and one must emphasize the word good, teachers of students with EBD view themselves as change agents, and not merely jail keepers, baby-sitters, or other types of accommodations. Effective school literature, while describing some features of accommodation such as class size, focuses on instructional and behavioral remediation (Edmonds, 1979, 1981). Rarely do alternative schools omit as a central goal the need to remediate (Duke & Perry, 1981).

The goal of education of students with EBD is to help the students help themselves. That change may happen through such success-documented interventions as behavior modification, social skills training, cognitive-behavior therapy, or psychodynamic counseling interventions. Ecological interventions also may be appropriate when they teach individuals or remediate them to such a degree that their new behaviors or feelings can be generalized to the environment to which they return. Otherwise, any so-called environmental interventions are simply accommodations that render students unmainstreamable (segregated). The following statements should help clarify the difference between accommodations and remediations.

- Classrooms that are designed to teach students with EBD only academic skills ignore the supposed reason for these students' entrance to special education. They serve as *accommodations*. Classrooms that teach behavioral, emotional, and social skills, in addition to academics, allow students with EBD to work on those problems that placed them into special education. These classrooms are *remediations*.

- Special education classrooms that are ditto-sheet and workbook-driven are *accommodations*. Special education classrooms that are interactive-learning driven are *remediations*.
- Time-out is an *accommodation*. Teaching how to prevent those behaviors from occurring and to learn new behaviors or feelings to replace the inappropriate ones is *remediation*.
- Vocational schools, art classes, and music and dance schools are *accommodations* when students are placed in them, and ultimately fail in them, because they cannot behave well enough in the general classroom. Vocational schools, art classes, and music and dance schools are *remediations* when individuals are taught behaviors to allow them to "fit."
- Most reform schools are *accommodations*. Reform schools that teach new social skills, feelings, or behaviors that are congruent with those expected by the outside world are *remediations*.
- General education classrooms are *accommodations* for students who are ill prepared to behaviorally or emotionally adapt to the expectations of those environments (Gresham, 1981). Consequently, homebound instruction, suspension, and expulsion (despite the decision rendered in *Honig v. Doe*, 1988) become further *accommodations*.

Remediation is not a passive process. It is not a magical formula that a teacher "does" to a child. It involves active participation of the individual with EBD and the environment. It is extremely difficult to change a harmful feeling or behavior if one wants to do so; it is near impossible to do so if one is resistant. The goals of remediation are self-control and self-management.

Although emotional and/or behavioral disorder may be a "lifelong disability," individuals can learn to live with their disabilities. Certainly, emotional and/or behavioral disorders can occur at any time during a person's life (see Thomas & Chess, 1976, who suggest, for example, that the period of adolescence embodies a totally new set of demands that, combined with one's previous experiences, can impact emotional and/or behavioral disorders). Some evidence indicates that there are early indications of future problems. For example, in a 31-year longitudinal study, highly aggressive children who did not receive remediation remained aggressive over time (Lerner, Hertzog, Hooker, Hassibi, & Thomas, 1988). In fact, Cowen, Pederson, Babigan, Izzo, and Trost's (1973) 11- to 13-year follow-up study supported Lerner et al. (1988), and also found significantly fewer appearances at a community-wide psychiatric center for those subjects who actively participated in a preventative school-based mental health program (see also Thomas & Chess, 1984).

Research on remediation techniques has suggested much success for many individuals with behavioral disorders. To cite only a few examples, research has demonstrated successes with children who:

- Have excessive fears (Graziano, DeGiovanni, & Garcia, 1979, who reviewed behavioral approaches)
- Have impulsiveness, hyperactivity, or poor self-control (Meichenbaum & Goodman, 1971, who used cognitive-behavioral modification)
- Are withdrawn (Strain & Fox, 1981, who used peers as change agents; O'Connor, 1972, who used filmed models)
- Experience severe depression (Butler, Miezitis, Friedman, & Cole, 1980, using a form of psychotherapy, behavior modification, and self-control therapy; Frame, Matson, Sonis, Failkov, & Kazdin, 1982, using behavior modification)
- Have aggressive behaviors (Bailey, Wolf, & Phillips, 1970; Phillips, 1968, who used behavior modification; Patterson, Reid, Jones, & Conger, 1975, who used a social learning model)
- Are adolescents at high risk for behavior disorders (Arbuthnot & Gordon, 1986, with a moral development curriculum)
- Have anxiety (Miller & Kassinove, 1978; Warren, Deffenbacher, & Brading, 1976, who employed cognitive-behavior techniques)
- Have low self-concept (Cangelosi, Gressard & Mines, 1980, who used rational-emotive therapy)
- Are juvenile delinquents with major school problems (Bailey et al., 1970; Leschied, Coolman, & Williams, 1984; Meichenbaum, Bowers, & Ross, 1968, all employing behavior modification)

Granted, the field of EBD is young as a research discipline. The field can be likened to an infant of the larger field of special education (or at least, as Kauffman, 1991, contended, an "adolescent"). There is little question that the original focus of special education was to identify handicapped students for services. Today, access to special education, while still a concern, is no longer the only focus. Today, focus should be upon quality. And quality is remediation. Quality is programming. Quality is specially designed instruction, not specially designed accommodation. Perhaps, it is access back to the general education environment and society that requires remediation to take place.

The fact remains that a very large population of people who are disturbed are being left uncared for, figuratively and literally, in society. It is time that educators help these individuals to help themselves. It is left open to conjecture regarding the number of students who can be prevented from becoming identified as EBD if interventions are used as a preventative.

The goal of special education should be remediation instead of accommodation. Remediation can work. Every person who has worked with a student who has EBD and observed significant changes in feelings and behaviors knows this fact. Every person who can recount success stories after success stories of those students who had been given little chance of achieving that success knows this fact. Even if anecdotal experiences and classroom research had been less promising than they have been, the field must not give up searching for an intervention that might succeed.

Only two decades have passed since P.L. 94-142, the Education for All Handicapped Children Act, became legislation. Academic and social movements have made significant impacts upon the interpretation and application of this very important law. Teachers must take an active role in the education of students with emotional and behavioral disorders to help them become participants in society. The responsibility must be collaborative and include the students, their parents or guardians; their teachers, and their community.

# Job Description of Teachers of Students with EBD

University professionals and public administrators constantly attempt to define the desired competencies that all teachers should possess to effectively teach students. These competencies are listed in various ways and eventually find their way into college and university programs and state education department endorsement programs. Morsink, Fardig, Algozzine, and Algozzine (1987) reviewed the literature comparing the competencies of general and special educators and found, for the most part, that the competencies were similar. The differences that did exist revolved around the special educators using "teacher-directed instruction" (direct instruction, mastery learning, precision teaching), "active academic responding or controlled practice," contingent reinforcement, and adaptive instruction to meet the individual needs of students. Furthermore, they found that teachers of students with EBD (they used the label EH, or emotionally handicapped) were:

1. Implementing individual behavior management plans with rules and positive/negative consequences to modify deviant behaviors and increase appropriate behaviors. . . .

2. Implementing programs that enable EH students to assess and manage their own behavior, rather than relying on external controls.

3. Teaching specific social skills to EH students, such as taking turns, asking mainstream teachers for assistance, and developing interpersonal relationships.

4. Assist EH students, one-to-one or in small groups, in dealing with personal problems and in coping with daily occurrences which may interfere with classroom learning; use active listening, stress management, or affective curricula. ( pp. 115–116)

What "should be" in the job descriptions of special educators often differs from "what is" in the actual job duties. Fink and Janssen (1993) asked experienced teachers to rank the importance of the various components of educating students with EBD. The teachers who responded to the survey listed behavior management and social skills development as the most important areas of their jobs, with assessment, knowledge of the disability region, and technology as the least important. The authors also found that "two objectives received ratings of definitely relevant by all participants: (a) establish realistic, appropriate instructional goals and (b) know the legal basis for the educational placement of EBD students" (p. 14). Attempts to list the competencies (which are sometimes discussed and measured in terms of "student outcomes") have been made by the Center for Quality Special Education (1990), which developed a series of outcomes for each disability area (e.g., Emotional Impairment), and by the Institute for Adolescents with Behavioral Disorders (1994), which developed a detailed list of competencies that is an extension of those recommended by the Council for Exceptional Children (1992). The institute divided the competencies into knowledge and skill levels of areas such as the characteristics of learners, assessment and diagnosis, instructional content and practice, managing the learning environment, managing student behavior, transitions, monitoring and evaluation, cultural and linguistic diversity, communication and collaboration, families, community resources, legal and administrative structure, and professional and ethical practice (see Table 2.1). Although the competencies listed in Table 2.1 are extensive, they are not exhaustive. The list is included in this book because it serves as an excellent self-evaluation for the reader.

In an attempt to determine what teachers actually do each week, Gable, Hendrickson, Young, and Shooki-Yetka (1992) surveyed teachers of students with EBD. These teachers reported that they worked 56 hours per week, 41.6% of which had to do with instruction and teaching. They did not feel prepared in consultation and administrative skills, areas that are rarely learned in the undergraduate experience. Consequently, the areas of delivering instruction and dealing with administration (and support people) need to be more fully explored for teachers.

## Delivering Instruction

In 1992 less than half of students with EBD were educated in the general education classroom for at least part of the time (U.S. Department of Education, 1990, 1992). Although arguments have been made to combine students with EBD, learning disabilities, and mental retardation in the classroom, competencies required for teaching students with EBD differ significantly from those required for teaching students who are learning disabled and mentally retarded (Carri, 1985; see also Graves, Landers, Lokerson,

## TABLE 2.1
## EBD Teacher Competencies

Mark proficiency "X"   1 = none or little   2 = somewhat   3 = moderate   4 = strong   5 = mastery

### Characteristics of Learners

#### Knowledge of:

| | 1 | 2 | 3 | 4 | 5 |
|---|---|---|---|---|---|
| Physical and psychological needs of normal child/adolescent | ☐ | ☐ | ☐ | ☐ | ☐ |
| Factors affecting contemporary youth culture | ☐ | ☐ | ☐ | ☐ | ☐ |
| Difficulties defining normal/abnormal behavior | ☐ | ☐ | ☐ | ☐ | ☐ |
| History and theoretical perspectives re: | | | | | |
|     child and adolescent development | ☐ | ☐ | ☐ | ☐ | ☐ |
|     the nature of EBD | ☐ | ☐ | ☐ | ☐ | ☐ |
|     the nature of aggression | ☐ | ☐ | ☐ | ☐ | ☐ |
|     the nature of delinquency | ☐ | ☐ | ☐ | ☐ | ☐ |
| EBD classification systems and trends | ☐ | ☐ | ☐ | ☐ | ☐ |
| Factors related to the development of EBD | ☐ | ☐ | ☐ | ☐ | ☐ |
| Definitions of emotional and behavioral disorders | ☐ | ☐ | ☐ | ☐ | ☐ |
| Characteristics of students with EBD | ☐ | ☐ | ☐ | ☐ | ☐ |
|     of students with multiple diagnoses | ☐ | ☐ | ☐ | ☐ | ☐ |
|     of abused/neglected students | ☐ | ☐ | ☐ | ☐ | ☐ |
|     of students abusing or addicted to drugs | ☐ | ☐ | ☐ | ☐ | ☐ |
|     of students who are depressed/suicidal | ☐ | ☐ | ☐ | ☐ | ☐ |
|     of students with conduct disorders | ☐ | ☐ | ☐ | ☐ | ☐ |
|     of students with attention-deficit/hyperactivity disorder | ☐ | ☐ | ☐ | ☐ | ☐ |
| Prevalence/incidence rates of EBD | ☐ | ☐ | ☐ | ☐ | ☐ |

#### Skill in:

| | 1 | 2 | 3 | 4 | 5 |
|---|---|---|---|---|---|
| Describing factors influencing youth development | ☐ | ☐ | ☐ | ☐ | ☐ |
| Comparing and contrasting elements of various definitions | ☐ | ☐ | ☐ | ☐ | ☐ |
| Comparing and contrasting theoretical perspectives | ☐ | ☐ | ☐ | ☐ | ☐ |
| Comparing and contrasting medical, psychological, behavioral, and educational classification systems | ☐ | ☐ | ☐ | ☐ | ☐ |
| Articulation of current accepted definition | ☐ | ☐ | ☐ | ☐ | ☐ |
| Formulating a personal definition of EBD | ☐ | ☐ | ☐ | ☐ | ☐ |

*(continues)*

**TABLE 2.1** (*Continued*)

**Assessment and Diagnosis of EBD**

*Knowledge of:*

| | 1 | 2 | 3 | 4 | 5 |
|---|---|---|---|---|---|
| Basic terminology used in assessment | ☐ | ☐ | ☐ | ☐ | ☐ |
| Role of teacher and others in assessment/diagnosis | ☐ | ☐ | ☐ | ☐ | ☐ |
| Procedures required by law and regulations | ☐ | ☐ | ☐ | ☐ | ☐ |
| Instruments and procedures linked with theoretical perspectives | ☐ | ☐ | ☐ | ☐ | ☐ |
| Ethical concerns related to assessment | ☐ | ☐ | ☐ | ☐ | ☐ |
| Appropriate use and limitations of each instrument | ☐ | ☐ | ☐ | ☐ | ☐ |
| Appropriate application and interpretation of scores | ☐ | ☐ | ☐ | ☐ | ☐ |
| Instruments for use in screening and prereferral | ☐ | ☐ | ☐ | ☐ | ☐ |
| Techniques for the evaluation/placement process | ☐ | ☐ | ☐ | ☐ | ☐ |
| Appropriate instruments for assessing academic skills | ☐ | ☐ | ☐ | ☐ | ☐ |
| Influence of development and diversity on assessment | ☐ | ☐ | ☐ | ☐ | ☐ |
| Learning styles | ☐ | ☐ | ☐ | ☐ | ☐ |
| Methods for monitoring process | ☐ | ☐ | ☐ | ☐ | ☐ |

*Skill in:*

| | 1 | 2 | 3 | 4 | 5 |
|---|---|---|---|---|---|
| Collaborating with parents and other professionals | ☐ | ☐ | ☐ | ☐ | ☐ |
| Development and maintenance of records | ☐ | ☐ | ☐ | ☐ | ☐ |
| Administration of various types of assessment: | | | | | |
|     norm referenced | ☐ | ☐ | ☐ | ☐ | ☐ |
|     curriculum-based | ☐ | ☐ | ☐ | ☐ | ☐ |
|     work samples/portfolio | ☐ | ☐ | ☐ | ☐ | ☐ |
|     observations | ☐ | ☐ | ☐ | ☐ | ☐ |
|     informal and individualized data | ☐ | ☐ | ☐ | ☐ | ☐ |
| Interpretation of results and reporting | ☐ | ☐ | ☐ | ☐ | ☐ |
| Utilizing assessment data from other professionals | ☐ | ☐ | ☐ | ☐ | ☐ |
| Development of individualized plan | ☐ | ☐ | ☐ | ☐ | ☐ |
| Evaluation of intervention plan and modifications | ☐ | ☐ | ☐ | ☐ | ☐ |

**Instructional Content and Practice**

*Knowledge of:*

| | 1 | 2 | 3 | 4 | 5 |
|---|---|---|---|---|---|
| Research-based best practices for effective teaching | ☐ | ☐ | ☐ | ☐ | ☐ |

(*continues*)

**TABLE 2.1**  (Continued)

| | 1 | 2 | 3 | 4 | 5 |
|---|---|---|---|---|---|
| Basic instructional approaches for content areas | ☐ | ☐ | ☐ | ☐ | ☐ |
|     Deciding what to teach | ☐ | ☐ | ☐ | ☐ | ☐ |
|     Deciding how to teach | ☐ | ☐ | ☐ | ☐ | ☐ |
|     Preparing for instruction | ☐ | ☐ | ☐ | ☐ | ☐ |
| Standard curriculum for various grade levels | ☐ | ☐ | ☐ | ☐ | ☐ |
| Methods for techniques for teaching basic skill areas | ☐ | ☐ | ☐ | ☐ | ☐ |
|     reading, language arts, and math | ☐ | ☐ | ☐ | ☐ | ☐ |
|     life, career, and vocational skills | ☐ | ☐ | ☐ | ☐ | ☐ |
|     social skills | ☐ | ☐ | ☐ | ☐ | ☐ |
| Demands of various learning environments | | | | | |
|     individual and group | ☐ | ☐ | ☐ | ☐ | ☐ |
|     special and general class | ☐ | ☐ | ☐ | ☐ | ☐ |
| Techniques for modifying instructional materials and methods | ☐ | ☐ | ☐ | ☐ | ☐ |
| Strategies for combining semi-independent and independent practice | ☐ | ☐ | ☐ | ☐ | ☐ |
| Errorless training techniques | ☐ | ☐ | ☐ | ☐ | ☐ |
| Task analysis | ☐ | ☐ | ☐ | ☐ | ☐ |
| Applications of technology | | | | | |
|     operation of various types of equipment | ☐ | ☐ | ☐ | ☐ | ☐ |
|     selecting appropriate materials | ☐ | ☐ | ☐ | ☐ | ☐ |

**Skill in:**

| | 1 | 2 | 3 | 4 | 5 |
|---|---|---|---|---|---|
| Interpreting and using assessment data for instructional planning | ☐ | ☐ | ☐ | ☐ | ☐ |
| Identifying prerequisite skills for a given curriculum | ☐ | ☐ | ☐ | ☐ | ☐ |
| Selecting and writing goals and objectives for individuals and groups | ☐ | ☐ | ☐ | ☐ | ☐ |
| Developing instructional units | ☐ | ☐ | ☐ | ☐ | ☐ |
| Preparing appropriate lesson plans | ☐ | ☐ | ☐ | ☐ | ☐ |
| Selecting and using materials that respond to cultural, linguistic, gender, and developmental differences | ☐ | ☐ | ☐ | ☐ | ☐ |
| Selecting and adapting instructional strategies to characteristics of students | ☐ | ☐ | ☐ | ☐ | ☐ |

(continues)

**TABLE 2.1** (*Continued*)

|  | 1 | 2 | 3 | 4 | 5 |
|---|---|---|---|---|---|
| to learning styles of students | ☐ | ☐ | ☐ | ☐ | ☐ |
| to skill levels of students | ☐ | ☐ | ☐ | ☐ | ☐ |
| Modifying instructional materials to meet student needs | ☐ | ☐ | ☐ | ☐ | ☐ |
| Planning procedures and activities and working with | | | | | |
| large groups | ☐ | ☐ | ☐ | ☐ | ☐ |
| small groups | ☐ | ☐ | ☐ | ☐ | ☐ |
| individuals | ☐ | ☐ | ☐ | ☐ | ☐ |
| Using various instructional strategies (e.g., modeling, rehearsal, inquiry, prompting, cueing, corrective feedback, consequation) in isolation and in combination | ☐ | ☐ | ☐ | ☐ | ☐ |
| Proper use of instructional time | ☐ | ☐ | ☐ | ☐ | ☐ |
| Using questions at various cognitive levels | ☐ | ☐ | ☐ | ☐ | ☐ |
| Teaching learning strategies | ☐ | ☐ | ☐ | ☐ | ☐ |
| Using audiovisual equipment and material in instruction | ☐ | ☐ | ☐ | ☐ | ☐ |
| Using computers in instruction | | | | | |
| operation of hardware | ☐ | ☐ | ☐ | ☐ | ☐ |
| selection and use of software | ☐ | ☐ | ☐ | ☐ | ☐ |
| computer retrieval/communication systems | ☐ | ☐ | ☐ | ☐ | ☐ |
| data management systems | ☐ | ☐ | ☐ | ☐ | ☐ |
| Using motivational rapport | ☐ | ☐ | ☐ | ☐ | ☐ |
| Reinforcing academic achievement | ☐ | ☐ | ☐ | ☐ | ☐ |
| Using strategies to maintain and generalize skills | ☐ | ☐ | ☐ | ☐ | ☐ |
| Evaluating student progress | ☐ | ☐ | ☐ | ☐ | ☐ |
| Conducting self-evaluation of instruction | ☐ | ☐ | ☐ | ☐ | ☐ |

**Managing the Learning Environment**

*Knowledge of:*

|  | 1 | 2 | 3 | 4 | 5 |
|---|---|---|---|---|---|
| Effects of environmental variables on learning and behavior | ☐ | ☐ | ☐ | ☐ | ☐ |
| Strategies to create safe, supportive environment | ☐ | ☐ | ☐ | ☐ | ☐ |
| Room organization and structure of routines to facilitate learning | ☐ | ☐ | ☐ | ☐ | ☐ |
| Strategies to facilitate functional integration with others | ☐ | ☐ | ☐ | ☐ | ☐ |
| Directing activities of paraprofessionals, volunteers, others | ☐ | ☐ | ☐ | ☐ | ☐ |

(*continues*)

**TABLE 2.1** (Continued)

| Skill in: | 1 | 2 | 3 | 4 | 5 |
|---|---|---|---|---|---|
| Establishing and maintaining environment that is safe | ☐ | ☐ | ☐ | ☐ | ☐ |
|     stimulating and flexible | ☐ | ☐ | ☐ | ☐ | ☐ |
|     tension free | ☐ | ☐ | ☐ | ☐ | ☐ |
|     functional | ☐ | ☐ | ☐ | ☐ | ☐ |
| Establishing time for academic and social routines | ☐ | ☐ | ☐ | ☐ | ☐ |
| Preparing and organizing materials for daily lesson plans | ☐ | ☐ | ☐ | ☐ | ☐ |
| Design that encourages participation in a variety of activities | ☐ | ☐ | ☐ | ☐ | ☐ |
| Planning scope and sequence of activities | ☐ | ☐ | ☐ | ☐ | ☐ |
| Directing the activities of others | | | | | |
|     paraprofessional or aide | ☐ | ☐ | ☐ | ☐ | ☐ |
|     volunteer | ☐ | ☐ | ☐ | ☐ | ☐ |
|     peer tutor | ☐ | ☐ | ☐ | ☐ | ☐ |
| Coordinating activities with other staff | ☐ | ☐ | ☐ | ☐ | ☐ |

**Managing Student Behavior**

| Knowledge in: | 1 | 2 | 3 | 4 | 5 |
|---|---|---|---|---|---|
| Techniques related to theoretical perspectives | | | | | |
|     psychodynamic-psychoeducational | ☐ | ☐ | ☐ | ☐ | ☐ |
|     behavioral-applied behavior analysis | ☐ | ☐ | ☐ | ☐ | ☐ |
|     ecological | ☐ | ☐ | ☐ | ☐ | ☐ |
|     biophysical | ☐ | ☐ | ☐ | ☐ | ☐ |
| Laws, policies, and ethics related to behavior management | ☐ | ☐ | ☐ | ☐ | ☐ |
| Strategies for observing and recording behavior | ☐ | ☐ | ☐ | ☐ | ☐ |
| Environmental influences on behavior | ☐ | ☐ | ☐ | ☐ | ☐ |
| Age-appropriate social skills | ☐ | ☐ | ☐ | ☐ | ☐ |
| Community and cultural norms and behavioral expectations | ☐ | ☐ | ☐ | ☐ | ☐ |
| Commercial materials for social development and instruction | | | | | |
|     social skills training | ☐ | ☐ | ☐ | ☐ | ☐ |
|     conflict resolution | ☐ | ☐ | ☐ | ☐ | ☐ |
|     self-esteem building | ☐ | ☐ | ☐ | ☐ | ☐ |
|     stress management | ☐ | ☐ | ☐ | ☐ | ☐ |

(continues)

**TABLE 2.1** (Continued)

| | 1 | 2 | 3 | 4 | 5 |
|---|---|---|---|---|---|
| Components of affective education | ☐ | ☐ | ☐ | ☐ | ☐ |
| Components of a continuum of services/intervention model | ☐ | ☐ | ☐ | ☐ | ☐ |
| Components of an individualized education plan | ☐ | ☐ | ☐ | ☐ | ☐ |
| Strategies that reduce verbal and physical aggression | ☐ | ☐ | ☐ | ☐ | ☐ |
| Strategies that increase or decrease other behaviors | ☐ | ☐ | ☐ | ☐ | ☐ |
| Strategies for crisis prevention and intervention | ☐ | ☐ | ☐ | ☐ | ☐ |
| Effects of medication and illicit drugs on behavior | ☐ | ☐ | ☐ | ☐ | ☐ |
| Teacher behaviors that influence student behaviors | ☐ | ☐ | ☐ | ☐ | ☐ |
| Selecting individual and/or group strategies | ☐ | ☐ | ☐ | ☐ | ☐ |
| Techniques often cited in the literature, e.g. | | | | | |
|     assertive discipline | ☐ | ☐ | ☐ | ☐ | ☐ |
|     teacher effectiveness training | ☐ | ☐ | ☐ | ☐ | ☐ |
|     positive peer culture | ☐ | ☐ | ☐ | ☐ | ☐ |
|     reality therapy | ☐ | ☐ | ☐ | ☐ | ☐ |
|     rational-emotive therapy | ☐ | ☐ | ☐ | ☐ | ☐ |
|     life space interview | ☐ | ☐ | ☐ | ☐ | ☐ |
| Strategies for maintaining and generalizing behaviors | ☐ | ☐ | ☐ | ☐ | ☐ |
| Strategies for providing student feedback | ☐ | ☐ | ☐ | ☐ | ☐ |

**Skill in:**

| | 1 | 2 | 3 | 4 | 5 |
|---|---|---|---|---|---|
| Systematic observation of social-behavioral patterns | ☐ | ☐ | ☐ | ☐ | ☐ |
| Identifying behavior patterns from recorded data | ☐ | ☐ | ☐ | ☐ | ☐ |
| Identifying environmental influences on behavior | ☐ | ☐ | ☐ | ☐ | ☐ |
| Developing functional and realistic norms for the classroom | ☐ | ☐ | ☐ | ☐ | ☐ |
| Establishing and maintaining a structured classroom | ☐ | ☐ | ☐ | ☐ | ☐ |
| Developing positive classroom rules | ☐ | ☐ | ☐ | ☐ | ☐ |
| Arranging the environment to promote prosocial behavior | ☐ | ☐ | ☐ | ☐ | ☐ |
| Scheduling time and activities to promote social interaction | ☐ | ☐ | ☐ | ☐ | ☐ |
| Selecting age-appropriate target behaviors and activities | ☐ | ☐ | ☐ | ☐ | ☐ |
| Identifying appropriate reinforcers for individuals and groups | ☐ | ☐ | ☐ | ☐ | ☐ |

*(continues)*

**TABLE 2.1**  (*Continued*)

| | | | | | |
|---|---|---|---|---|---|
| Applying behavioral strategies to increase behaviors | | | | | |
|     contracts | ☐ | ☐ | ☐ | ☐ | ☐ |
|     point system/token economy | ☐ | ☐ | ☐ | ☐ | ☐ |
|     level system | ☐ | ☐ | ☐ | ☐ | ☐ |
| Applying behavioral strategies to decrease behaviors | | | | | |
|     differential reinforcement | ☐ | ☐ | ☐ | ☐ | ☐ |
|     loss of privileges | ☐ | ☐ | ☐ | ☐ | ☐ |
|     time out | ☐ | ☐ | ☐ | ☐ | ☐ |
|     dismissal or suspension | ☐ | ☐ | ☐ | ☐ | ☐ |
| Using basic counseling techniques in individual or group problem-solving sessions | ☐ | ☐ | ☐ | ☐ | ☐ |
| Teaching social skills important to school success | ☐ | ☐ | ☐ | ☐ | ☐ |
| Teaching critical thinking, problem-solving, and decision-making skills | ☐ | ☐ | ☐ | ☐ | ☐ |
| Demonstrating, teaching, and directing role-play of appropriate social skills | ☐ | ☐ | ☐ | ☐ | ☐ |
| Performing crisis intervention and counseling | | | | | |
|     diffusion of verbal aggression | ☐ | ☐ | ☐ | ☐ | ☐ |
|     active listening | ☐ | ☐ | ☐ | ☐ | ☐ |
|     reflection | ☐ | ☐ | ☐ | ☐ | ☐ |
|     restatement | ☐ | ☐ | ☐ | ☐ | ☐ |
|     questioning | ☐ | ☐ | ☐ | ☐ | ☐ |
|     problem-solving | ☐ | ☐ | ☐ | ☐ | ☐ |
|     safe physical holding | ☐ | ☐ | ☐ | ☐ | ☐ |
|     referral | ☐ | ☐ | ☐ | ☐ | ☐ |
|     first aid and cardiopulmonary resuscitation | ☐ | ☐ | ☐ | ☐ | ☐ |
| Using nonverbal methods of influencing behavior | ☐ | ☐ | ☐ | ☐ | ☐ |
| Selecting appropriate management strategies in various situations as related to verbal interventions | ☐ | ☐ | ☐ | ☐ | ☐ |
| Implementing a hierarchy of interventions along a continuum of least to most intrusive | ☐ | ☐ | ☐ | ☐ | ☐ |
| Use of paraprofessional or volunteers | ☐ | ☐ | ☐ | ☐ | ☐ |

(*continues*)

**TABLE 2.1** (Continued)

Generalization and maintenance of acquired social skills
- school–home–community plans
- special class–general class plans

## Transitions

**Knowledge of:**  1  2  3  4  5

- Carl Perkins Act
- Principles and components of career education
- Principles and components of vocational education
- Role and provisions of vocational rehabilitation agencies
- Need for career/vocational education for students with EBD
- Service learning

***Skill in:***  1  2  3  4  5

- Administering vocational aptitude and interest instruments
- Planning and teaching career information
- Teaching daily living skills
  - home and family management
  - consumer responsibility
  - using community resources
  - use of leisure time
  - civic responsibility
- Teaching skills for locating, securing, and maintaining a job
- Selecting and evaluating community-based instruction sites
- Using coaching techniques in applied settings
- Providing opportunities for guidance from various sources

## Monitoring and Evaluation

**Knowledge of:**  1  2  3  4  5

- Essential elements, methods of record keeping
- Appropriate measures of specific target behaviors
- Recording and reporting procedures for target behaviors

*(continues)*

**TABLE 2.1** (Continued)

| Skill in: | 1 | 2 | 3 | 4 | 5 |
|---|---|---|---|---|---|
| Using a variety of recording procedures | ☐ | ☐ | ☐ | ☐ | ☐ |
|     event recording | ☐ | ☐ | ☐ | ☐ | ☐ |
|     duration recording | ☐ | ☐ | ☐ | ☐ | ☐ |
|     interval recording | ☐ | ☐ | ☐ | ☐ | ☐ |
|     permanent products | ☐ | ☐ | ☐ | ☐ | ☐ |
| Pinpointing students' entering behaviors | ☐ | ☐ | ☐ | ☐ | ☐ |
| Providing visual display-charting target behaviors | ☐ | ☐ | ☐ | ☐ | ☐ |
| Evaluating effectiveness of instruction or intervention | ☐ | ☐ | ☐ | ☐ | ☐ |
| Constructing criterion-referenced tests | ☐ | ☐ | ☐ | ☐ | ☐ |
| Teaching self-monitoring, self-evaluation | ☐ | ☐ | ☐ | ☐ | ☐ |
| Determining readiness for integration or reintegration | ☐ | ☐ | ☐ | ☐ | ☐ |
| Reporting progress to parents and other professionals | ☐ | ☐ | ☐ | ☐ | ☐ |

**Cultural and Linguistic Diversity**

| Knowledge of: | 1 | 2 | 3 | 4 | 5 |
|---|---|---|---|---|---|
| Variations in beliefs, traditions, and cultural values | ☐ | ☐ | ☐ | ☐ | ☐ |
| Major theories regarding relationships of diversity to EBD | | | | | |
|     Sociocultural influences on behavior | ☐ | ☐ | ☐ | ☐ | ☐ |
| Effects of cultural and linguistic diversity on assessment | ☐ | ☐ | ☐ | ☐ | ☐ |
| Personal culture and beliefs and influence on perceptions | ☐ | ☐ | ☐ | ☐ | ☐ |

| Skill in: | 1 | 2 | 3 | 4 | 5 |
|---|---|---|---|---|---|
| Supporting ethnic or cultural differences in students | ☐ | ☐ | ☐ | ☐ | ☐ |
| Creating supportive climate that values diversity | ☐ | ☐ | ☐ | ☐ | ☐ |
| Working with students, parents, and professionals of diverse cultural and/or ethnic backgrounds | | | | | |
|     adapting teaching style and techniques to learning styles | ☐ | ☐ | ☐ | ☐ | ☐ |
|     adapting interaction style to fit local customs | ☐ | ☐ | ☐ | ☐ | ☐ |

**Communication and Collaboration**

| Knowledge of: | 1 | 2 | 3 | 4 | 5 |
|---|---|---|---|---|---|
| Importance and benefits of communication and collaboration | ☐ | ☐ | ☐ | ☐ | ☐ |

(continues)

**TABLE 2.1** (*Continued*)

| | 1 | 2 | 3 | 4 | 5 |
|---|---|---|---|---|---|
| Typical concerns of parents and others about EBD students | ☐ | ☐ | ☐ | ☐ | ☐ |
| Ethical practices for confidential communication | ☐ | ☐ | ☐ | ☐ | ☐ |
| Distinctions between consultation and collaboration | ☐ | ☐ | ☐ | ☐ | ☐ |
| Roles of various school professionals involved | ☐ | ☐ | ☐ | ☐ | ☐ |
| Role of the special education teacher on the team | ☐ | ☐ | ☐ | ☐ | ☐ |
| Roles of various local, state/province, or national agencies | ☐ | ☐ | ☐ | ☐ | ☐ |

***Skill in:***

| | 1 | 2 | 3 | 4 | 5 |
|---|---|---|---|---|---|
| Establishing and maintaining open communication with parents, teachers, administrators, and other staff | ☐ | ☐ | ☐ | ☐ | ☐ |
| Accurately collecting and contributing information | ☐ | ☐ | ☐ | ☐ | ☐ |
| Explaining characteristics and needs of students with EBD | ☐ | ☐ | ☐ | ☐ | ☐ |
| Use of collaborative strategies with school personnel | ☐ | ☐ | ☐ | ☐ | ☐ |
| Consulting with various involved professionals | ☐ | ☐ | ☐ | ☐ | ☐ |

**Families**

***Knowledge of:***

| | 1 | 2 | 3 | 4 | 5 |
|---|---|---|---|---|---|
| Major functions and evolving role of families | ☐ | ☐ | ☐ | ☐ | ☐ |
| Special needs of families of students with EBD | ☐ | ☐ | ☐ | ☐ | ☐ |
|     impact on parents and siblings | ☐ | ☐ | ☐ | ☐ | ☐ |
|     for services | ☐ | ☐ | ☐ | ☐ | ☐ |
|     for advocacy | ☐ | ☐ | ☐ | ☐ | ☐ |
|     nontraditional families | ☐ | ☐ | ☐ | ☐ | ☐ |
| Parental rights and responsibilities | | | | | |
|     confidentiality of data | ☐ | ☐ | ☐ | ☐ | ☐ |
|     participation in decisions | ☐ | ☐ | ☐ | ☐ | ☐ |
|     access to information | ☐ | ☐ | ☐ | ☐ | ☐ |

***Skill in:***

| | 1 | 2 | 3 | 4 | 5 |
|---|---|---|---|---|---|
| Developing and maintaining open lines of communication | ☐ | ☐ | ☐ | ☐ | ☐ |
| Planning and conducting parent conferences | ☐ | ☐ | ☐ | ☐ | ☐ |
| Planning and implementing daily/weekly report system to communicate with parents regarding student progress | ☐ | ☐ | ☐ | ☐ | ☐ |

(*continues*)

**TABLE 2.1** (Continued)

| | 1 | 2 | 3 | 4 | 5 |
|---|---|---|---|---|---|
| Developing, implementing, and evaluating home–school intervention program | ☐ | ☐ | ☐ | ☐ | ☐ |
| Planning and conducting parent training sessions related to student's educational program | ☐ | ☐ | ☐ | ☐ | ☐ |

**Community Resources**

*Knowledge of:*

| | 1 | 2 | 3 | 4 | 5 |
|---|---|---|---|---|---|
| Social, medical, mental health, and legal resources available in the community | ☐ | ☐ | ☐ | ☐ | ☐ |
| Roles and responsibilities of community resources | ☐ | ☐ | ☐ | ☐ | ☐ |
| Procedures for referral to community resources | ☐ | ☐ | ☐ | ☐ | ☐ |

*Skill in:*

| | 1 | 2 | 3 | 4 | 5 |
|---|---|---|---|---|---|
| Identifying appropriate agencies for provision of related services | ☐ | ☐ | ☐ | ☐ | ☐ |
| Making appropriate contacts and referrals | ☐ | ☐ | ☐ | ☐ | ☐ |
| Maintaining collaborative communication | ☐ | ☐ | ☐ | ☐ | ☐ |

**Legal and Administrative Structure**

*Knowledge of:*

| | 1 | 2 | 3 | 4 | 5 |
|---|---|---|---|---|---|
| Major provisions of public laws (e.g., 94-142, 99-457) | ☐ | ☐ | ☐ | ☐ | ☐ |
| Case law related to education/treatment of students with EBD | ☐ | ☐ | ☐ | ☐ | ☐ |
| Federal and state provisions and regulations related to EBD | ☐ | ☐ | ☐ | ☐ | ☐ |
| Local district policies and procedures | ☐ | ☐ | ☐ | ☐ | ☐ |
| Continuum of services for exceptional students | ☐ | ☐ | ☐ | ☐ | ☐ |
| Teacher's role in various service delivery models | ☐ | ☐ | ☐ | ☐ | ☐ |

*Skill in:*

| | 1 | 2 | 3 | 4 | 5 |
|---|---|---|---|---|---|
| Conducting instruction and professional activities according to requirements of law, regulations, and local procedures | ☐ | ☐ | ☐ | ☐ | ☐ |
| Adapting instructional techniques, procedures for collaboration and consultation, and other skills to match requirements of the educational setting | ☐ | ☐ | ☐ | ☐ | ☐ |

*(continues)*

**TABLE 2.1** (Continued)
**Professional and Ethical Practice**

| Knowledge of: | 1 | 2 | 3 | 4 | 5 |
|---|---|---|---|---|---|
| Code of Ethics and Professional Standards of the Council for Exceptional Children | ☐ | ☐ | ☐ | ☐ | ☐ |
| Legal and ethical issues related to the school and classroom | ☐ | ☐ | ☐ | ☐ | ☐ |
| Current national and international trends related to EBD | ☐ | ☐ | ☐ | ☐ | ☐ |
| Program models and evaluation procedures | ☐ | ☐ | ☐ | ☐ | ☐ |
| Current research results and implications of in the field of EBD | ☐ | ☐ | ☐ | ☐ | ☐ |
| Major professional organizations and their purpose | ☐ | ☐ | ☐ | ☐ | ☐ |

| Skill in: | 1 | 2 | 3 | 4 | 5 |
|---|---|---|---|---|---|
| Showing commitment to the highest educational quality | ☐ | ☐ | ☐ | ☐ | ☐ |
| Conducting professional activities in a legal and ethical manner | ☐ | ☐ | ☐ | ☐ | ☐ |
| Modeling appropriate social-emotional, intellectual, and achievement skills for students and colleagues | ☐ | ☐ | ☐ | ☐ | ☐ |
| Showing fairness, sensitivity, empathy, persistence, and other crucial human values in work with students and colleagues | ☐ | ☐ | ☐ | ☐ | ☐ |
| Describing and evaluating program components | ☐ | ☐ | ☐ | ☐ | ☐ |
| Reading and evaluating current research literature | ☐ | ☐ | ☐ | ☐ | ☐ |
| Translating research results into effective teaching skills | ☐ | ☐ | ☐ | ☐ | ☐ |
| Adopting teaching practices that produce positive results | ☐ | ☐ | ☐ | ☐ | ☐ |
| Proficiency in oral and written communication | ☐ | ☐ | ☐ | ☐ | ☐ |
| Continuing skill growth through professional involvement | ☐ | ☐ | ☐ | ☐ | ☐ |

From *EBD Teacher Competencies* by The Institute for Adolescents with Behavioral Disorders, 1993, Arden Hills, MN: Author. Reprinted with permission.

Luchow, & Horvath, 1993). According to Graves et al. (1993), teachers believed that it is difficult to argue that students with learning disabilities and mental retardation can be taught in the same ways as students with EBD because "little [is] known regarding optimal strategies for teaching basic skills and less is known about teaching content area information to such students" (p. 189).

Traditionally, and perhaps because of the nature of the disability, very few students with EBD are in general education classrooms (Steinberg &

> **Window on Reality**
>
> One should not assume that being a special education teacher is more difficult than being a general education teacher. As Rauth (1981) suggested, general education teachers need to be "mentally alert and responsive to 20 to 30 minds at one time for 3, 4, or 5 consecutive hours a day" (p. 28). The amount of work faced by general educators precludes them from having the time to think about such special concerns as learning styles, identifying possible victims of abuse, and so on.

Knitzer, 1992). Interestingly, it may not be only the behavior of these students that is impeding successful integration. "The emphasis on higher achievement scores brought on by the effective schools movement may dampen the enthusiasm of service providers for implementing a full-time mainstreaming model" (Semmel, Abernathy, Butera, & Lesar, 1991, p. 19).

Research has revealed that students with EBD score lower on standardized achievement tests, and that they have more problems with math than reading (Epstein, Kinder, & Bursuck, 1989). Students with EBD also do not achieve as well as general education students with regard to knowledge in those subject areas that seem contingent upon success in general settings, such as social studies, science, and writing (Mastropieri, Jenkins, & Scruggs, 1985), although they were not as far behind in word recognition and calculation (Foley, Epstein, & Cullinan, 1991). Clearly, more attention needs to be paid to content areas (see also Kauffman, Cullinan, & Epstein, 1987).

Lower scores on achievement tests and the current focus on skill rather than content teaching go hand-in-hand. Ruhl and Berlinghoff's (1992) review of the research found little focus on the teaching of academics to students with EBD. More startling is the revelation that students referred to special education were getting less reading instruction than those in general education (Allington & McGill-Franzen, 1989).

Fad and Ryser (1993) suggested that academics may not be the key to success, yet most resource rooms and self-contained settings focus almost entirely in this area. Oddly, in one study, the most important behavior identified by both general and special educators was "work turned in on time" (Bursuck, Kinder, & Epstein, 1989). Teaching social skills and management of emotions and behaviors should also be part of the curriculum (Jones, 1992). Students with EBD need to understand and learn to express their feelings in an appropriate manner.

The daily behavioral demands of teaching students with EBD are of interest. McManus and Kauffman (1991) found that 9.6% of resource room teachers and 25% of self-contained teachers surveyed expected to deal with disruptive behavior more than 22 times per day. Also, 7.5% of resource room teachers and 19.7% of self-contained teachers were verbally threatened on a daily basis. Each day 1.9% of resource room teachers and 8.5% of self-contained teachers were physically threatened. During the year resource room teachers reported 2.91 average physical attacks, compared with 4.35 attacks by the teachers in self-contained settings. When teachers have these kinds of difficulties with students, it is no surprise that teacher burnout may result (Zabel, Boomer, & King, 1984). Consequently, it should be little surprise that there is confusion about what a curriculum for EBD students should be (Grosenick, 1989).

---

### Window on Reality

The challenges described in the previous text may seem minimal compared with those encountered by teachers during the next two decades. Children often referred to as belonging to "emerging populations" are now entering the public schools. "No one knows how many crack babies there are; however, a national total of one to two percent of all live births or 40,000 to 80,000 seems like a realistic figure" (Besharov, 1990, p. 22). The March of Dimes estimated that by the year 2000 these numbers may rise to 4 million (Rist, 1990). It has been the rare diagnostician who would blame parents for the cause of their child's EBD. Yet, today many mothers can be blamed, because they give birth to children addicted to drugs and/or alcohol. The challenge of teaching these students needs to be met by both general and special educators.

---

## Dealing with Administration and Stress

Although completing administrative tasks and interacting with administrators are necessary competencies for successful special education teachers, these important variables rarely surface in special education texts. Inadequate administrative support and poor communication have been cited as major causes of stress (Lawrenson & McKinnon, 1982), and teachers of EBD have been found to be among the least satisfied with working conditions (Abelson, 1986). For example, the majority of the resource room teachers in Maine reported that they received little or no supervision, and when they did get supervision, it did not deal with their specific teaching (Breton & Donaldson, 1991).

Many teachers, in both general and special education, feel stress. Stress was reported as a problem by 78% of teachers as early as 1967 (National Education Association, 1967). More recently, Frank and McKenzie (1993) conducted a 5-year examination of burnout and concluded that emotional exhaustion was a slow but steady phenomenon. Teachers of students with EBD scored higher on four of the six "stress" subtests. The following variables were reported to increase or maintain stress by 410 teachers in a study conducted by Wheeler, Reilly, and Donahue (1984):

Administration (37%)

Student behavior (26%)

Pressure (20%)

Paperwork (18%)

Incompetence (12%)

Parents (12%)

Although administrative variables were identified as the most stressful, the teachers "were unwilling to confront the administration, and when they did they were met with postponement, indifference, and/or promises that were seldom kept" (p. 92). This is in congruence with the research by Zabel and Zabel (1982), who found that when supervisors offered support, teachers experienced lower levels of burnout.

The results of Pulliss (1992) review suggest that schools in the 21st century will experience a major shortage of teachers for students with EBD (see also Billingsley & Cross, 1992). Pullis listed the following factors as contributors to teacher stress and the eventual fleeing from the teaching profession:

inadequate discipline policy of school

attitudes and behavior of administrators

evaluation of administrators/supervisors

attitudes and behavior of other teachers/professionals

too much work to do

poor career opportunities

low status of the teaching profession

lack of recognition of good teaching

loud, noisy pupils

dealing with parents (p. 194)

Dedrick and Raschke (1988) surveyed teachers of EBD, who listed the following stressors:

1. student unmet needs
2. uncooperative students

3. unhelpful administrators
4. nonsupportive parents
5. paperwork
6. lack of support from specialized services
7. lack of preparation time
8. general class teachers' attitudes
9. insufficient resources
10. lengthy meetings
11. larger teacher/pupil ratio
12. isolation from colleagues (p. 180)

When perusing these lists, one might conclude that role conflict and/or ambiguity are major contributors of stress (Crane & Iwanicki, 1986). Perhaps this is due to the expectations that individuals bring to their jobs. Interestingly, Crane and Iwanicki (1986) also found that older and more experienced teachers reported having less stress, suggesting that these teachers successfully altered their expectations.

One way to combat stress is to focus on the positive aspects of the job. Dedrick and Raschke (1988) listed the areas of jobs that teachers liked:

1. student progress (56%)
2. students (44%)
3. curricular challenge (37%)
4. freedom to implement (25%)
5. colleagues (18%) (p. 183)

They also listed aspects of the school environment, that teachers would choose to change:

1. more administrative support (46%)
2. more parent involvement (30%)
3. less paperwork (24%)
4. increases in planning time (16%)
5. more cooperation from general teachers (12%) (p. 183)

Fimian (1986) supported the previously cited research by contending that the "receipt of peer or supervisory support could act as a key moderator of teacher stress. Evidently, teachers are more apt to receive aid and support from peers in times of stress than they are to receive it from supervisors . . . Support plays a major role in moderating both the perceived strength and frequency of teacher stress. Those not receiving supervisory support received more stress" (p. 441). Accordingly, the teachers surveyed would have little argument with the notion that "differences in leadership styles do make a difference in the overall achievement of children and the well-being and enthusiasm of teachers" (Goodman, 1985, p. 104).

Directly related to administrative support is the need to obtain adequate resources (Schmid, et al., 1990). Perhaps the definition of stress is "teaching," as Mueller (1993) has suggested in a personal essay. If so, then if the special education field is to retain teachers of quality, the above-stated factors will have to be addressed during both preservice and inservice in a unified manner. Although it would be unrealistic to suggest that the readers of this text will be allowed the opportunity to change school "systems," educators can enact specific actions to seek possible relief from many of the classroom stressors that they may encounter (see Chapters 4, 10, and 11).

## Consultation and Collaboration

One of the more difficult and frustrating roles of the special education teacher is that of consultation. These consultative behavior often focus on talking to general classroom teachers regarding the progress of their students. Ideally, these responsibilities would include helping teachers integrate students with EBD and serving as liaisons to support people and community agencies. If students with EBD are to be successful in any environment, then the opportunities for consultation and collaboration must exist.

Chapter 1 indicates that education is currently undergoing another push toward full integration. This movement has not been embraced by all teachers. One reason for this hesitancy may be that general and special education teachers are not dissatisfied with the current special education delivery system and feel strongly that it should be protected. In fact, less than one third of teachers in one study believed that the consultation services needed for full inclusion would be successful (Semmel et al., 1991). Furthermore, some evidence indicates that, when consultation opportunities are offered, teachers may not utilize them (Myles & Simpson, 1992). Nevertheless, the hue and cry for appropriate placements and support for students in these placements have not subsided (Leone, 1989).

The *continuum of services* is a concept that has expanded rather than narrowed with the movements of regular education initiative and inclusion. For example, Knitzer (1993) called for a link between school and mental health services because of her belief that mental health services are often ignored (see also Knitzer, Steinberg, & Fleisch, 1990). Even within the school setting, it is clear that counseling, an important related service, and one that is included in special education law, is not being delivered in EBD classes. Ironically, receiving a special education label virtually guarantees that these students will not receive counseling services (Hutton & Kinnison, 1991). Ironically, perhaps up to 50% of students placed in psychiatric hospitals are there only because their local school districts did not have placements on the more "restrictive" end of the continuum (Behar, 1990). Psychiatric hospitals are often one of the few options available to students with EBD. "Possibly more so than any other special education category, related services, effective interagency models, and family-focused programs for children and youth with EBD are in short supply" (Epstein et al., 1993, p. 127). Forness (1992) contended that a major factor for having a more restrictive federal or state definition for the population of students with EBD is the lack of available services.

Although professionals such as Gable and Laycock (1991) have argued for a full continuum of services for students with EBD in schools, others have less hope for these students after graduation. For example, Edgar (1987) concluded that "there are not (and never will be) adequate community-based programs to serve all of the special education students who leave school" (p. 560). There has been a call for multidisciplinary support systems in research, as well as "real support" (Edgar, 1991; Peacock Hill Working Group, 1991). Needless to say, the need for collaboration and consultation has never been greater.

## Transition

Professionals who work with students who have special needs need to be aware of the importance of making transitions between the different types of school experiences within the public school system. Changes from preschool to elementary to middle or junior high school to high school often occur without preparation, yet the learning and affective attitudes of these institutions are quite different (Kelly et al., 1977; Spivack, Swift, & Prewitt, 1971; Stone, Wilson, & Spence, 1969). For example, the amount of physical and emotional contact between teacher and student diminishes progressively as one moves to each of these settings, perhaps with the end result being a "last name" or a "number" in a high school. Another transition that must be considered is the move from the small intimate environment of the special education classroom to the general setting (see Chapter 4).

Schools need to consider transition attitudes to enable students to find success as they move from setting to setting. It is important to emphasize that this discussion involves the natural shocks that "normal" students experience, which may create stressful periods for some students. For example, the event of entering school for the first time and the onset of adolescence can certainly be difficult times for even the most stable individual. Bower (1964) suggested that the crisis of school entrance may be lessened by the active involvement of parents and the astute observation of teachers. In dealing with the onset of adolescence, Bower offered two approaches: (a) Have junior high school students work with younger students to observe and comment upon their behaviors, and (b) use games to build stress immunity through values exploration and role playing.

If students with EBD are going to be successful in life, they must be helped not only in the classroom but also in the world of work. Clearly, additional services and coordination are needed (Mattison, Morales, & Bauer, 1992). Consequently, the continuum of services is being broadened to include community resources, postsecondary education, and the world of work. The track record for helping students with EBD has not been very good. Research indicates, for instance, that students with EBD are not likely to use community services (Frank, Sitlington, Cooper, & Cool, 1990; Hasazi, Gordon, & Roe, 1985; Neel, Meadows, Levine, & Edgar, 1988; Sitlington, Frank, & Carson, 1993). In fact, many graduates continue to live at home after graduation (Mithaug, Horiuchi, & Fanning, 1985; Neel et al., 1988; Sitlington et al., 1993).

It is not surprising that students with EBD who graduate from high school are much less likely to enroll in postsecondary school programming. However, variables such as education of parents, socioeconomic status, and the student's placement in the graduating high school class are powerful indicators of success (Neel et al., 1988; Sitlington et al., 1993).

Youth with disabilities have higher degrees of unemployment and underemployment. The need for transition programs is evident (Edgar, 1988, 1990; Rusch & Phelps, 1987). Research confirms that the population with EBD not only meets with little success immediately after leaving high school, but fares less well than other groups as the individuals grow older (Chadsey-Rusch, Rusch, & O'Reilly, 1991; Sitlington et al., 1993). Ultimately, it seems that individuals with EBD fail on jobs because they lack appropriate social and problem solving skills (Sabatino, Allen, Paulson, & Sedlak, 1984). Incredibly, vocational goals were found on only 6% of the Individualized Education Programs for students with EBD in one investigation (Nickles, Cronis, Justan, & Smith, 1992). More important is the content of these goals. The skills and behaviors that are necessary for success in the workplace must be considered before arriving at particular goals. These may differ significantly from many of the behaviors that are currently being attended to in the classroom (see Chapter 4 for these goals and the teaching of these goals).

## Summary and Conclusions

This chapter explored some of the variables that have a significant impact on teaching children with emotional and/or behavioral problems. Many of these variables are beyond the influence of the classroom teacher. For example, the environments of the school, community, and family all play important roles in the progress of students and, although it may be beyond the purview of a teacher to change these environments, the teacher needs to understand their effects.

Each teacher of students with EBD should conduct a self-assessment before attempting interventions. Knowing his or her type of teaching personality can certainly engender teaching implications. Levels of inviting behavior, which range from intentionally disinviting to intentionally inviting, may correlate directly with the teacher's expectations of what attributes students should possess. It is likely that handling a disturbing student may in fact require changes in the teacher's behavior. On the pages of a textbook, these changes seem relatively simple, especially with the cooperation of a positive support system (peers, administration, mate). However, most changes probably will be difficult to institute. The teacher, parent, or administrator who may be influencing disturbing behaviors may not be "receptive" to suggestions. Furthermore, administrators, peers, or mates may not offer full support, both practical and emotional, in a teacher's endeavors for the student. This certainly may be a formidable problem for *any* educator, let alone the novice. Inherent to the success of any teaching position are openness to change and possession of the diplomacy to implement change.

It is crucial that, before teachers enter their classrooms, they should have an understanding of what they are trying to accomplish within their structure: remediation or accommodation. Knowing their "philosophy" should lead to the types of teacher competencies that they should possess, and/or have the resources to learn, as they pursue their professions. Teachers also need general competencies in areas that encompass such diverse and yet overlapping elements as delivering instruction, dealing with administration, dealing with stress, consultation and collaboration, and intraschool and interschool transition. Even the experienced teacher might feel overwhelmed by the enormity of teaching students with EBD. However, once the teacher understands these competencies and the philosophic underpinnings of the classroom, specific assessment and identification procedures (as explained in the next chapter) should follow.

# 3

# Preassessment, Referral, Assessment, and Placement

*Christine Ormsbee, Richard L. Simpson, and Paul Zionts*

According to Knitzer, Steinberg, and Fleisch (1990), approximately .96% of school-aged children and youth were identified by school professionals as having emotional and/or behavioral disorders (EBD) during the 1986–1987 school year. The U.S. Department of Education (1991, 1992) reported similar data. However, estimates are that the number of students with EBD far exceeds the number of children and youth being identified. Moreover, national estimates are that 5% to 10% of school-aged children and youth have emotional and behavioral difficulties, confirming that underidentification continues to be a significant concern (Coleman, 1992; Kazdin, 1989; Pelavin Associates, 1990; Wagner & Shavers, 1989). Knitzer et al. (1990) also reported that over 80% of students identified as EBD attended regular public schools; these data are supported by the Fourteenth Annual Report to Congress on the Implementation of The Individuals with Disabilities Education Act (U.S. Department of Education, 1992). Furthermore, there are strong indications that support services for students with EBD are lacking. In this regard, Paul and Epanchin (1991) and Simpson (1990) reported limited parent and family mental health involvement; Zionts and Simpson (1988) observed minimal continuity or congruence among educational, legal, and mental health programs; and Knitzer et al. (1990) noted that the majority of districts surveyed revealed that they did not provide counseling services. Finally, there are strong indications that preassessment and other problem-solving programs for students experiencing EBD are lacking (Carter & Sugai, 1989), and that mainstreaming support programs for students with EBD are in significant need of improvement (Grosenick, George, & George, 1987; Myles & Simpson, 1992).

Professionals also have reported that EBD identification may depend on various factors external to a child's behavior and needs, including local tolerance levels, resource availability, or the student's race, class, or socioeconomic status (Ysseldyke, Algozzine, & Thurlow, 1992). Knitzer and colleagues (1990), for example, noted that students are often identified because they are 'mad, bad, sad, and can't add," and because their teachers are unable to tolerate them, rather than because of diagnoses based on valid clinical assessments. These and other variables (e.g., the exceptionally high school dropout rate for students with EBD) translate into an obvious need for professionals to become more effective in (a) implementing effective preassessment and problem-solving programs, (b) making accurate referrals of students experiencing emotional and behavioral problems, (c) conducting accurate and utilitarian assessment of students purported to have EBD, and (d) utilizing these processes in well-designed multidisciplinary team meetings.

# Implementing Effective Preassessment and Problem-Solving Programs

Since the passage of P.L. 94-142, professionals have sought ways to provide support and expertise to teachers with students with EBD. A particularly resilient model for early intervention and teacher support has been the preassessment or prereferral team. Mandated in over half of the states, preassessment teams work as collaborative problem-solving units with general classroom teachers to provide early consultation services before a student is referred for comprehensive multidisciplinary special education evaluation. This procedure has helped reduce special education evaluations by helping teachers make modifications in the classroom, thereby eliminating the need to label a student and remove him or her from the general education environment. This section presents issues of early intervention, a description of preassessment procedures, and suggestions for establishing a preassessment team.

### Early Classroom Interventions

General classroom teachers are typically the first educational professionals to identify a student with EBD. This determination often occurs when a student consistently demonstrates inappropriate behaviors or substandard achievement to the extent that the student's progress is not commensurate with that of same-age peers. At this point, the general classroom teacher implements informal interventions designed to remediate the areas of difficulty.

Often some form of professional collaboration occurs regarding a student experiencing difficulty. During lunch, while supervising recess, passing in the halls, or standing in an office, general educators, and sometimes special educators, engage in informal collaboration. A conversation might begin with the statement, "I have this student who . . . . Have you ever worked with anyone with this problem?" During these informal exchanges, educators share past experiences regarding effective modifications for specific academic and behavioral problems. This informal consultation probably accounts for the majority of collaboration that occurs among educators.

***Categories of Interventions.*** Most teachers begin applying some basic remediation techniques that can be categorized into three areas: (a) curricular, (b) environmental, and (c) management. Table 3.1 provides examples of curricular, environmental, and management modifications that may be suggested in informal collaborative situations. It is meant to provide some examples but is not exhaustive.

*Curricular modifications* target the academic tasks required in the classroom. The classroom teacher analyzes and modifies the learning objectives, materials, and teaching methods to ensure a better academic match between the teacher's instructional objectives and the student's demonstrated academic or social behaviors. Taping lessons or texts, using parallel instructional materials, or giving a test in segments are examples of curricular modifications that teachers may use to provide support to a student experiencing academic difficulties.

*Environmental modifications* focus on analyzing and adapting the classroom ecology to accommodate the learner. For example, the general educator may provide preferential seating, establish time expectations for assignment completion, or move instructional supplies to reduce distractions to help a student experience success in the classroom.

*Management modifications* are designed to provide behavioral support to a student. These adaptations offer reinforcements and environmental–behavioral support for students. Providing daily or weekly progress reports, using nonverbal signals to monitor behavior, or using tangible reinforcers are only a few examples of early interventions that may be implemented for students experiencing behavioral difficulties.

***Documentation of Interventions.*** Teachers should keep formal records of any interventions or modifications that have been implemented for a student experiencing learning and/or behavioral difficulties. These records

## TABLE 3.1
### Chart of Curricular, Environmental, and Management Modification Examples

| Curricular Modifications | Environmental Modifications | Management Modifications |
|---|---|---|
| • Tape lessons or instructions for student | • Change the student's seat assignment | • Establish home–school communication system |
| • Simplify vocabulary of test items, practice sheets | • Assign preferential seating | • Post rules and consequences for behavior |
| • Provide tests in segments | • Post class routine | • Put student on daily or weekly progress report |
| • Provide visual or memory aids such as number lines, formulas, pictures, and charts | • Move location of classroom supplies to minimize distractions | • Keep graphs, charts, or calendars of student progress |
| • Highlight main ideas and supporting details in text | • Assign student study partner | • Establish contingency contract |
| • Provide study outlines and guides | • Provide one-on-one tutoring | • Ignore inappropriate behavior |
| • Reduce quantity of material to be read | • Use small group instruction | • Give verbal or nonverbal signals to monitor behavior (winks, hand signals, ect.) |
| • Have student keep an assignment notebook | • Provide a monitoring buddy | • Move closer to student to monitor behavior |
| • Provide a sample or practice test | • Establish time expectations for assignment completion | • Establish list of reinforcers for student |
| • Provide opportunities for extra drill | • Provide verbal cues to indicate beginning and ending instructional time | • Offer social reinforcers for student |
| • Use special supplementary material | • Provide visual, tactile, or auditory prompts to indicate appropriate behavior | • Offer tangible reinforcers (points, tokens, stickers) |
| • Provide text written at student's reading level | | • Establish home–school communication system |
| • Provide self-checking materials | | • Provide immediate reinforcement for correct responses |
| • Provide immediate correction of errors | | • Implement a token or point system |
| • Teach learning strategies | | • Implement self-recording of behavior |
| • Ask student to repeat directions | | |

should contain information about the (a) type of interventions implemented, (b) duration of implementation, and (c) results of interventions. There are many ways to collect and present this data. A form such as that presented in Figure 3.1 provides a structure for keeping data in a manageable and readable form. Whatever form an educator uses, it is imperative that any modifications made are carefully documented to record the teacher's efforts to accommodate the student and assist educators in decisions about student progress. Moreover, detailed documentation provides a clearer picture of student problems if adequate progress is not observed.

## The Preassessment Process

Multidisciplinary teams (MDTs) were originally conceptualized and mandated by P.L. 94-142 as a procedural safeguard for identification and placement of students in special education (Pryzwansky & Rzepski, 1983). The function of these teams was to assist general educators in their efforts to support students in the least restrictive settings. The team decision-making requirement was based on the premise that group decision making was superior to individual decision making (Abelson & Woodman, 1983).

Since the early 1980s the role of teams in schools has expanded. Today MDTs may also function as a problem-solving unit to assist teachers in maintaining students in general classrooms (Pryzwansky & Rzepski, 1983). Specifically, school team roles have taken two general forms: teacher assistance teams and preassessment teams. The teacher assistance team (TAT) model engages within-building personnel in collaborative and problem-solving processes. The TAT can be used to clarify classroom problems, develop interventions, set instructional or management goals, modify curriculum, generate strategies for whole classes, and/or prepare for parent conferences (Chalfant & Van Dusen Pysh, 1989). Since TATs were established, investigations of team effectiveness have reported success in intervening in classroom difficulties (Gilmer, 1985; Talley, 1988). High levels of teacher and team satisfaction with the process also have been reported (Chalfant & Van Dusen Pysh, 1985).

The primary function of a preassessment team is to reduce the number of inappropriate referrals while delineating interventions that allow students to experience success in the general classroom (Graden, Casey, & Christenson, 1985). According to Abelson and Woodman (1983), "a team is two or more interdependent individuals who work and communicate directly in a coordinated manner in order to reach an agreed upon goal(s)" (p. 126). Preassessment procedures also have been defined by delineating the purpose of the preassessment process: "The purpose of Preassessment is to provide support and assistance to regular classroom teachers so that they may deal effectively with students who exhibit learning or behavior

```
┌─────────────────────────────────────────────────────────┐
│                 Intervention Data Summary                │
├─────────────────────────────────────────────────────────┤
│  Student name: _____  │
│  Grade: _____  │
│  Age: _____  │
│  Reason(s) for modifications:                            │
│                                                          │
│                                                          │
│                                                          │
│                                                          │
│                                                          │
│                                                          │
│  Other relevant information:                             │
│                                                          │
└─────────────────────────────────────────────────────────┘
```

**FIGURE 3.1.** Intervention data summary.

difficulties for which their usual approaches have proven unsuccessful" (Kansas State Department of Education, 1987, p. II-1). Preassessment team procedures that provide assistance to teachers prior to special education referral have been adopted by many states (Carter & Sugai, 1989).

Pugach and Johnson (1989) identified the five common purposes of a preassessment team: (a) acknowledging the limitations of identification and diagnostic procedures mandated by P.L. 94-142, (b) redistributing the resources of special educators toward integration with general educators in a problem-solving focus, (c) providing a forum for problem-solving systems that do not otherwise exist in education, (d) supporting classroom teachers' ability to problem solve and offer strategies for students exhibiting classroom difficulties, and (e) resolving educational difficulties exhibited by students at the site of their occurrence—the general classroom.

According to Chalfant, Pysh, and Moutrie (1979), general educators encounter particular difficulties when attempting to serve students with behavior and learning problems in the general classroom. These concerns included:

1. Many general classroom teachers lack the training and the confidence to manage the behavior of or individualize instruction for these students.
2. General educators typically have limited resources to provide assistance.
3. General classroom teachers' day-to-day classroom problems are often compounded when students with identified disabilities are mainstreamed. (pp. 85–86)

Chalfant et al. suggested that these problems have resulted in teachers referring as many as 20% of their students for comprehensive, multidisciplinary special education evaluation. In response to these problems, preassessment teams were developed as an alternative model for early intervention.

## Suggestions for Preassessment Procedures

Preassessment teams function as day-to-day problem-solving units for teachers within a building, not as substitutes for traditional multidisciplinary teams that conduct comprehensive special education evaluations. The major benefits of this procedure are that more students with disabilities can be maintained in the least restrictive environment, general classroom instruction may improve, and less time may be spent on unnecessary assessment activities (Harrington & Gibson, 1986). Moreover, students who do not qualify for special education services, but demonstrate low achievement or underachievement, can also benefit from preassessment procedures. These students, who are increasing in numbers and represent a growing concern among teachers and administrators (Cooley, McVey, & Barrett-Jones, 1988), account for 20% of the general school population (Will, 1986). For these students, the preassessment process can be used as a monitoring device to determine whether students brought before the preassessment team can perform better in the general education classroom if individualized changes are made in curriculum and/or teaching techniques.

Preassessment procedures should be established in a school building specifically to meet the needs of the teachers assigned to that school. Because different schools and students present unique problems, a generic preassessment model may not provide the support needed by the teaching staff. Hence, a preassessment model, if it is to be utilized and effective, should be viewed as positive and helpful by the building teachers.

One of the first things that can be done to establish an effective preassessment team is to survey the building teachers to determine whom they believe should be on the team. That is, teachers should be offered the opportunity to select colleagues who will serve as regular team members for the school year. If the team comprises educators who are viewed as leaders and are trusted by the staff, teams will probably be accessed more often. Researchers have attempted to determine who typically is on preassessment teams and found that the building principal, the students' teachers, and the special education teacher are most often found on early intervention teams (Chalfant & Van Dusen Pysh, 1989; Cooley et al., 1988; Ormsbee, Myles, & Simpson, 1993; Poland, Thurlow, Ysseldyke, & Mirkin, 1982). Thus, although it seems that a common core of education professionals is represented on preassessment teams, it is critical that building teachers select team participants who meet their needs.

Building teachers should not only select who is on the team, but also identify the role and functions of the preassessment team. In particular, educators should consider exactly what kind of support they want from the team. Should the team serve as a collaborative resource that guides the classroom teacher in designing interventions, or should the team design specific interventions for the classroom teacher? Should the preassessment team help collect intervention data through observation of the student or teacher? These are critical questions that merit discussion, because often educators do not agree on exactly what teams should do. Many general and special educators prefer that preassessment teams (a) clarify student referral problems, (b) design general curriculum interventions, (c) review student records, (d) conduct direct observations, and (e) analyze student products (Ormsbee et al., 1993).

Once selected, the team members should identify the team's operating procedures. Specifically, a meeting schedule, meeting procedures, and appropriate referral procedures should be developed by team members and shared with the building teachers. The team may choose to meet weekly, monthly, or on an as-needed basis. Whatever meeting time is established for the preassessment team, it is imperative that the schedule is designed to provide ongoing support for teachers and students.

Procedures also should be generated for the preassessment team meetings. In particular, arrangements should be made for a team member to keep minutes of the meeting. These minutes can be especially crucial when reviewing previous interventions suggested or designed by the team to determine student progress. In addition, a referral form should be used (see Figure 3.2) to guide a teacher through a process of identifying the nature of the problem objectively and to provide information on the types and durations of interventions already implemented.

After a referral form has been filed with the preassessment team, the referring teacher attends a team meeting to discuss his or her concerns and to engage in a structured problem-solving session. During the team meeting, the referring teacher should be viewed as a team member participating in

---

**Preassessment Referral Form**

Student name: _____

Grade: _____

Age: _____

Reason(s) for referral to preassessment team:
_____
_____
_____

Intervention(s) implemented by classroom teacher and results:
_____
_____
_____
_____
_____
_____

Other relevant information:
_____
_____
_____

Referring teacher: _____

---

**FIGURE 3.2.** Preassessment referral form.

brainstorming, developing interventions, and documenting methods. Team members may generate intervention suggestions, request additional information, schedule observations, or assign the referring teacher a task. In addition, the team should decide the duration of intervention implementation, ensuring that adequate time is allotted for a student to experience the full effect of the modification. Generally, a 6- to 8-week implementation period gives students enough time to respond to well-designed interventions. These decisions should be based on the individual needs of the student and the referring teacher.

In addition, the team should develop follow-up procedures for team- or teacher-designed interventions or to review additional information. How does the preassessment team know that their work with a student is successful? What kind of information should be collected to ensure that an intervention is effective and that the student is now experiencing success? The team should generate a variety of validation methods to be flexible in dealing with the varying needs of students. For example, student observations, student work products, report cards, or teacher reports may be used to determine success or failure of specially designed interventions. Furthermore, the team should develop a method for dealing with students who have not progressed after possible classroom modifications have been exhausted.

## Referral for Assessment

If attempts to provide curricular, environmental, or management adaptations are unsuccessful, the preassessment team may wish to refer the student for a comprehensive multidisciplinary special education evaluation. Referral for testing should occur only if the team has exhausted the options available for accommodating the student in the general classroom. This is critical according to early research documenting relatively high referral, identification, and placement rates (Algozzine, Christenson, & Ysseldyke, 1982). A recent study surveyed elementary teachers to determine the frequency and percentage of students in their classrooms who were referred to a building preassessment team, referred for special education assessment, and identified as eligible for special education classification during the 1991–1992 school year. Teachers reported that a mean number of 3.95 ($SD$ = 5.84) students were brought before the preassessment team during a 1-year period, representing approximately 11% of respondents' class populations. More than half of the students brought before the preassessment teams were eventually referred for a full, comprehensive multidisciplinary special education evaluation ($M$ = 2.36, $SD$ = 3.23, range = 0–20). Of those students who were evaluated, approximately half were identified as being eligible for special education classification and subsequently placed in a special education program ($M$ = 1.34, $SD$ = 2.07, range = 0–10) (Ormsbee et al., 1993).

For referral procedures to yield helpful information about a student, the process must be systematic. According to Larsen and Poplin (1980), a systematic referral process allows educators to do the following:

1. Distinguish between those students likely to meet the criteria for inclusion in a handicapped condition and those effectively managed through other, already existing non–special education programs.
2. Plan the best assessment strategies to be utilized during the evaluation phase.
3. Contact parents for the purpose of informing them that their child is exhibiting difficulties in the educational environment and may undergo an educational or medical evaluation.
4. Begin a general screening procedure to yield data regarding potential problem areas in the student's environment that may be causing or maintaining the educational disability.
5. Conduct an initial screening meeting on the referral that includes appropriate professionals and parents to determine whether formal evaluation is desirable and/or needed. (p. 49)

Hence, clear, methodical referral procedures have the potential to bring together interested parties to investigate the nature of the problems exhibited by the student and to generate the best possible educational situation.

## Formal and Informal Assessment Guidelines

Once the decision has been made to assess a student, and parental permission has been obtained, the MDT should outline an assessment plan. Professionals on the team should discuss specifically the types of information needed and who will be responsible for obtaining that information. Assessment information may be collected using formal or informal methods.

Using both formal and informal methods will help overcome shortcomings of evaluations. In fact, the benefits of special education assessment have been widely questioned (Hammill, 1987; Ysseldyke et al., 1992), particularly as related to classroom application and instructional utility. Wallace and Larsen (1978) observed that students experiencing school problems "are administered various educational assessment techniques for two major purposes: (a) to identify and sometimes label for administrative purposes those children experiencing learning problems who will probably require special educational help, and (b) to gather additional information that might be helpful in establishing instructional objectives and remedial strategies for those children identified as handicapped learners" (p. 5). Primary evaluation emphasis is, without argument, placed on identification and labeling; however, the information used to qualify youngsters for special education or other programs may have limited educational planning value (Shapiro & Lintz, 1986). Hence, professionals must be able to use informal assessment methods in conjunction with other formal assessment procedures to understand adequately students and their families and to implement effectively programs to address their needs.

*Formal Assessment.* Formal assessment procedures are typically perceived as standardized pencil-and-paper group test format or individual scales administered by psychologists or highly trained teachers, diagnosticians, or psychometricians. These procedures are administered under highly structured and standardized conditions; students are evaluated using standardized methods; and students' responses are interpreted in accordance with precise statistical norms. Formal evaluation results that are norm referenced are designed to compare individual student performance with that of peers or a norm group, and those that are criterion referenced are designed to evaluate individual performance relative to a set of objectives or skills. Thus, formal evaluations result in data about a student's academic or behavioral standing relative to other students or curricula. Unfortunately, formal evaluation information rarely is specific enough to provide programming guidance, and thus is typically used primarily for eligibility decisions.

*Informal Assessment.* Information and data ensuing from informal evaluations, on the other hand, are not primarily structured around the notion that children being evaluated should be compared with their same-age peers relative to particular strengths, weaknesses, or levels of performance, or in reference to set objectives and skills. Rather, informal assessment procedures are designed to yield information about specific students' educational strengths and weaknesses in particular settings and, in the case of academic assessment, with particular materials.

**Interviews.** Interviews may be conducted with students' teachers, program administrators, and other professionals; parents or legal custodians; and students themselves. According to Hammill (1987), interview results "can be used to study attitudes, perceptions, and feelings about the causes, nature, and consequences of a particular problem area; settings and situations in which problems occur; and countless other nuances associated with a suspected difficulty" (p. 21). Interview purposes and areas of discussion will vary with the nature and circumstances of a problem, available information, and assessment hypotheses; however, interviews are universally designed to generate information from individuals involved with a problem such that a clearer understanding of its participants, factors, and possible solutions may be gained.

The parent interview typically focuses on information related to a student's attitude toward school, friends, family, and leisure time activities. In this instance, special attention is given to atypical behavior patterns and interactions (or lack of interactions) with peers and adults. Although parents may frequently dismiss the significance of observed problems or changes as only a function of childhood or adolescence, the overall importance of this information, especially when paired with other observations, may be great. Parent and family interviews also focus on evaluating the goals and expectations of parents and family members. Discrepancies between the expectations of the parents and those of the student and the teacher are given special note.

Among the most significant areas of interest in parent interviews is the student's school history as perceived by parents and family members. Specifically, discussions involving school history are designed to reveal patterns of behavioral excess and deficits, academic success and failure, and previous professional procedures undertaken to diagnose or remediate home or school problems. Because diagnosticians may have school records, the information generated through the interview may be compared with school documents. Examples of teacher and parent interview formats are shown in Figures 3.3 and 3.4, respectively (Simpson & Regan, 1988).

**Record Review.** In the course of students' educational careers, schools gather numerous reports, records, and other types of information. A record review may provide diagnosticians and teachers opportunities for understanding and instructional planning insight. In particular, records and data may assist professionals in understanding students' (a) cognitive abilities; (b) physical, sensory, and medical history; (c) home and community background; (d) personality, behavioral, and social strengths and weaknesses; (e) academic skills, deficits, performance characteristics, and intervention program history; (f) speech and language factors; (g) prevocational and vocational skills; and (h) other important data and information. Effective use of student records is one of the most important and basic elements of informal assessment. Although this source of information requires organizational time and pattern analysis, its importance to assessment of students is clear.

**Direct Observation.** Direct observations of students are particularly important in gaining an understanding of behavior and social skills and deficits. Observations make no assumptions about the meaning of a student's response to contrived situations or stimuli. Rather, direct observations are made in situations and under circumstances directly associated with a student's problems. Thus, for example, a student who reportedly hits other children on the playground during recess would be observed for hitting during recess. Similarly, a student who displays limited attention to task during independent seat-work activities would be directly observed during periods when expectations for independent working exist.

Direct observations may be highly structured or simply designed to aid in forming an impression of a child and his or her educational environment. Thus, direct observation options range from making anecdotal

## Teacher Interview Form

Interviewer: _____ Date: _____
Informant: _____
Student: _____ Sex: M  F  Race: _____
Date of birth: _____ Grade: _____
Home address/phone: _____
Teacher statement of student problem: _____
_____

### EDUCATIONAL SETTING
1. No. of students in class: boys:_____ girls:_____
2. No. of full-time teachers: _____ aides:_____
3. Description of class (regular vs. special, traditional vs. open concept): _____
4. Description of teaching style (structured vs. unstructured): _____
5. Description of class seating arrangement(s) (including rows, clusters, isolation booths): _____
6. Special seating for student (including proximity to board or teacher; isolation; other): _____
7. Important physical features of the class: _____
8. Additional information: _____

### PARENT COMMUNICATION
1. No. of parent conferences this year: _____ attending parent(s):_____
2. Special parent communication systems in operation (including a description of type of frequency): _____
   parent role/follow through in communication systems: _____
3. Other specialists/agencies involved: _____
4. Description of teacher relationship with parents (including parent attitude toward school/cooperation): _____
5. Additional information: _____

### HEALTH/PHYSICAL CONSIDERATIONS
1. Current medications: _____
2. Allergies: _____
3. Seizures or convulsions: _____
4. Vision: _____
5. Hearing: _____
6. Speech problems: _____
7. Motor skills: fine: _____ gross: _____
8. Other health/physical problems: _____

*(continues)*

**FIGURE 3.3.** Teacher interview form.

9. Classroom or teaching modifications as a result of health/physical considerations (including special PE, motor programming, limited recess, modified behavior programs): _____
10. Additional information: _____

## ACADEMIC FUNCTIONING

1. Academic strengths: _____
   weaknesses: _____
2. Academic likes: _____
   dislikes: _____
3. Test data:
   IQ _____ Source(s) _____
   Reading _____ Source(s) _____
   Math _____ Source(s) _____
   Spelling _____ Source(s) _____
   Language arts _____ Source(s) _____
   Speech _____ Source(s) _____
   Other _____ Source(s) _____
4. Performance levels:
   Reading _____
   Math _____
   Spelling _____
   Language arts _____
   Speech _____
   Other _____
5. Spec. ed. services received: _____
6. Rate of learning (including progress on academic goals): _____
7. Impression(s) of school attitude: _____
8. Additional information: _____

## PERSONAL AND SOCIAL ADJUSTMENT

1. Behavior Checklist: _____
2. Management techniques: _____
3. Reinforcers/likes (identify spontaneous vs. elicited) _____
4. Punishers/dislikes (identify spontaneous vs. elicited) _____
5. Leisure-time activities: _____
6. Other special problems or situations (including reactions to lunch, field trips, specials, substitutes): _____
7. Additional information: _____

## IMPRESSIONS

(Include a statement of teacher and student needs and goals, responses or comments from other school personnel concerning the student, overall teacher impressionss of the student, special parent considerations or areas to probe.)

From *Management of Autistic Behavior* by R. L. Simpson and M. R. Regan, 1988, Austin, TX: PRO-ED. Copyright 1988 by PRO-ED, Inc. Reprinted with permission.

**FIGURE 3.3** (*Continued*)

## Parent Interview Form

Interviewer: _____ Date: _____ Informant: _____
Student: _____ Sex: M   F   Race: _____
Date of birth: _____ Grade: _____
Home address/phone: _____
Parent statement of student problem: _____

### FAMILY CONSTELLATION
(Including all household members)

| Name | Relationship | Age | Education | Employment & phone | Addresss (if different from above) |
|------|--------------|-----|-----------|--------------------|-----------------------------------|
|      |              |     |           |                    |                                   |
|      |              |     |           |                    |                                   |
|      |              |     |           |                    |                                   |
|      |              |     |           |                    |                                   |
|      |              |     |           |                    |                                   |
|      |              |     |           |                    |                                   |
|      |              |     |           |                    |                                   |
|      |              |     |           |                    |                                   |

Indicate with a star the person(s) in the family whom the child likes to be around or to engage in an activity.

### FAMILY BACKGROUND

1. Marital status: M   D   S
2. Are extended family members in the area?   No   Yes
3. Emergency contact: _____
   Phone: _____
4. Source(s) of child care/respite: _____
5. Family activities: _____
6. Additional information (including relationship among family members, home climate, significant events): _____

### DEVELOPMENTAL AND MEDICAL INFORMATION

1. Description of pregnancy and delivery (including term of pregnancy, birth complications):
   _____

2. Developmental milestones (approximate times): Sat up _____ Walked _____
   First words _____ Toilet trained _____
   Other information (including regressions): _____

*(continues)*

**FIGURE 3.4.** Parent interview form.

3. Relevant family medical history: _____
4. History of medications: _____
5. Current medications: _____
6. Allergies: _____
7. Seizures or convulsions: _____
8. Vision: _____
9. Hearing: _____
10. Speech problems: _____
11. Current health (including physicals strengths and limitations; physical complaints);

12. Physician: _____ Phone: _____
13. Date of last physical: _____
14. Other specialists/agencies involved (request release of information): __

15. Additional information: _____

## SCHOOL HISTORY

1. Schools attended: _____

2. Special services received in the past (including special education classes, speech therapy, motor programming, and counseling): _____

3. Academic strengths: _____ weaknesses: _____
4. Academic likes: _____ dislikes: _____
5. Approximate reading level: _____ math level: _____
6. School attitude: _____
7. Successful management techniques applied in the past: _____

8. Additional information (including a description of past school experiences): _____

## PERSONAL AND SOCIAL ADJUSTMENT

1. Description of sociability (including initiations and responses toward strangers and familiar people): _____

2. Description of independent functioning: (indicate alone or with help)
   Asking for needed help: _____ Grooming: _____
   Dressing: _____ Self-identification: _____

*(continues)*

**FIGURE 3.4** *(Continued)*

> Running errands: _____ Toileting: _____
> Feeding: _____ Others: _____
> 3. Mode(s) of communication: _____
> 4. Self-direction (including use of leisure time, initiation of activity, passivity, appropriate response to danger): _____
>
> 5. Ability to follow directions: _____
> 6. Reactions to changes in routine: _____
> 7. Eye contact: _____
> 8. Self-stimulatory behavior including spinning objects, overactivity, inappropriate laughter, facial distortions, inappropriate verbalization: _____
>
> 9. Unusual preoccupations (including fixations on fictional characters, objects): _____
>
> 10. Antisocial behavior (including temper tantrums, self-destructive behaviors, disruptive or resistive behavior, physical violence, attempts to run away): _____
>
> 11. Other odd mannerisms: _____
> 12. Leisure-time activities: _____
> 13. Methods of discipline used at home with child:
>     a. Effective: _____
>     b. Ineffective: _____
> 14. Effective reinforcers: _____
>
> 15. Additional information: _____
>
> ### IMPRESSIONS
> (Include a statement of parent and student needs and goals, receptiveness to district programs, receptiveness to behavior treatments, and observations of parent-child interactions.)
>
> From *Management of Autistic Behavior* by R. L. Simpson and M. R. Regan, 1988, Austin, TX: PRO-ED. Copyright 1988 by PRO-ED, Inc. Reprinted with permission.

**FIGURE 3.4** *(Continued)*

records or mental notes of students' performance on particular tasks to formalized analyses of specified target responses. In either case direct observation of students' behavior and performance is a crucial and basic part of informal assessment. An example of one structured observation method (Simpson & Regan, 1988) is highlighted in Figure 3.5.

## Adaptation of the Nelson Modified Deviant Classroom Observation Scale

### Observation Procedures

Observation is conducted in a task situation for which the rules are clearly defined (e.g., during individual academic seatwork). Data are not to be taken during group situations where rules tend to be unclear. The observer sits closely enough to the student under study to be able to hear what he or she is saying and to see what he or she is doing without being obtrusive. The observer does not interact with the student or the class. The observer observes each student (one at a time) for 20 seconds and then records for 10 seconds the symbol(s) describing the student's behavior on the Nelson Scale recording sheet (see accompanying form). Behaviors occurring during the 10-second recording period are not recorded. Thus there are two observations per minute. Observation sessions last for 16 minutes daily.

### Behavior Definitions

*Being on Task (S):* This behavior is defined as having eyes applied to the task material or to the teacher for a period of no less than 15 out of 20 seconds of observation. Exceptions to this include instances when the child is clearly seen working on task even though his or her eyes are off his or her work, for example, counting on fingers or working out loud. Deviant behaviors may be recorded while the student is on task; the converse is not possible.

*Being Out of Seat (X):* This behavior is operationally defined as occurring when the normal seating surface of neither buttock is applied to the child's seat or when the child moves his or her desk or chair so as to alter its ultimate stationary position (thus swinging a seat on its axis or tilting a chair on its legs are excluded). When a child is performing a permitted out-of-seat activity such as sharpening a pencil (after receiving permission from the teacher), he or she is not marked as being out of seat except: (a) when deviant behaviors occur during the permitted act such as taking side trips, looking at things on the teacher's desk, or stopping to talk; or (b) when the permitted activity is prolonged beyond a reasonable period of time or altered in some significant way.

*Physical Contact or Disturbing Others Directly (P):* This behavior is operationally defined as initiating any physical contact or reciprocating another person's action independent of the intent of the child (aggression or affection). This category inlcudes making physical contact with another person by means of an object such as a book held in a hand or an object thrown, or disturbing another person or child by making contact not with the other's body but with objects about him or her such as work or desk (e.g., grabbing objects or work, knocking objects off another's desk, destroying property, pushing the desk).

*(continues)*

**FIGURE 3.5.** Adaptation of the Nelson Modified Deviant Classroom Observation Scale.

*Making Audible Noises (N):* This behavior is operationally defined as making any nonvocal, nonrespiratory noise that is clearly audible and that is not an integral part of a nondeviant activity. Examples include tapping, pencil twirling, tapping feet, rattling or tearing papers, throwing a book on a desk, and slamming a desk closed.

*Making a 90-Degree Turn, Seated (X):* This behavior is operationally defined as turning the head and/or body more than 90 degrees (using the desk as a reference point). The exception is when the student wishes to attract the teacher's attention and turns in an obvious gesture for teacher help.

*Vocalizing (V):* This behavior is operationally defined as vocalizing or making other respiratory noises such as whistling which are not task related and which are not physiological (normal coughing or sneezing). Examples include answering the teacher without first raising a hand, talking to others without permission, making strange, unintelligible sounds, muttering, and swearing. Direct responses to a teacher's questions are not scored except when the content of what is said is clearly deviant, such as stating refusal to do work, putting off obeying instructions, and swearing. Working out loud is not included.

*Behaving in Other Deviant Ways (Ø):* This category encompasses behaviors that do not fit easily into any of the categories previously listed and that are situational rather than absolutely deviant. An example is engaging in a task other than that which is assigned, such as reading instead of doing arithmetic, drawing instead of reading. Behaviors such as playing with clothes, playing with self, chewing gum, and playing with a pencil are not considereds deviant. Also included in this category are sterotyped and autistic-like behaviors.

*Making Positive Teacher-Initiated Contact (T):* This behavior is operationally defined as occurring when any person interacts positively with the student. Any positive contact between the teacher and the student, which is initiated by the adult, is scored here. This includes direct contacts such as talking to the child and less obvious ones such as gesturing, smiling at the child, and giving materials to the child.

*Making Positive Child-Initiated Contact (t):* This behavior iss operationally defined as occurring when the child interacts positively with other students or adults in the classroom. This includes hand raising, gesturing, giving or taking materials from others, playing with others, etc.

*Making Negative Teacher-Initiated Contact (T̄):* This behavior is operationally defined as occurring when any adult interacts negatively with the child. Any negative contact between the teacher and the student, which is initiated by the adult, is scored here. This includes obvious contacts such as yelling at or shaking the child and less obvious ones such as frowning and gesturing.

*(continues)*

**FIGURE 3.5** *(Continued)*

*Isolating the Child (I):* This behavior is operationally defined as occurring when the teacher/aide effectively interrupts inappropriate behavior(s). This includes removal to another room or having the child place his or her head on the desk.

## ADDITIONAL BEHAVIOR DEFINITIONS

Definitions of other behaviors that may be observed during assessment of autistic children include the following:

*Daydreaming (D):* This behavior is operationally defined as occurring when a child is off task for more than 5 seconds, staring into space rather than being involved in some active endeavor.

*Behaving Aggressively (A):* This behavior is operationally defined as presenting physical threats to or attacking another person in the room through such behaviors as hitting, pushing, or slapping.

*Throwing (Th):* This behavior is operationally defined as moving the arm purposely to propel an object in any direction. This does not include pushing objects off a desk or dropping objects.

*Stimulating the Self (SS):* This behavior is operationally defined as performing any repetitious, distracting, and self-inflicted act that is not related to the activity in which the child is engaged, such as whirling, hand tapping, face slapping, and biting hands and arms. Any series of movements within a 5-second period should be considered as one instance of self-stimulatory behavior.

*Ruminating (R):* This behavior is operationally defined as moving food from stomach to mouth voluntarily. Included is an in-and-out jerky movement of the stomach to begin the behavior and puffing of the cheeks and chewing motions signifying the presence of food in the mouth. Only the definite presence of food in the mouth is necessary for rumination to be counted.

*Thumbsucking (TS):* This behavior is operationally defined as the insertion of the thumb in the mouth.

## BEHAVIOR INTERPRETATION

The Observation Scale below allows for preliminary investigations of significant operant behavior of autistic-like pupils. Further, graphing of these responses over time provides an objective longitudinal analysis of students' classroom behavior. Such comparisons yield invaluable data for validating individual student progress and overall program efficacy.

Even though the procedure is designed for preliminary behavioral evaluataions, its general format allows an analysis of ideosyncratic student behavior. That is, as noted in the "Additional Behavior Definitions" section, the procedure can be modified to assess specific responses of individual students.

*(continues)*

**FIGURE 3.5** *(Continued)*

**OBSERVATION SCALE***

Subject: _____ Observer: _____
Date: _____ School: _____
Teacher: _____ Time: _____

| S | X | P | N | X̸ | V | Ø | T | t | 7̸ | I | S | X | P | N | X̸ | V | Ø | T | t | 7̸ | I |
|---|---|---|---|---|---|---|---|---|---|---|---|---|---|---|---|---|---|---|---|---|---|
|   |   |   |   |   |   |   |   |   |   |   |   |   |   |   |   |   |   |   |   |   |   |

**Key**
S – On task
X – Out of seat
P – Physical contact or disturbing others
N – Audible noise
X̸ – 90-degree turn, seated

V – Vocalization
Ø – Other deviant behavior: _____
T – Positive teacher-initiated contact
t – Positive child-initiated contact
7̸ – Negative teacher-initiated contact
I – Isolation

**Totals**
S____ ; X____ ; P____ ; N____ ; X̸____ ; V____ ; Ø____ ; T____ ; t____ ; 7̸____ ; I____

*Adapted with permission from the *Nelson Modified Deviant Classroom Observational Scale.*

**FIGURE 3.5** (Continued)

**Product Analysis.** Useful informal assessment information about a student can also be derived from analysis of student work products. These products allow educators and diagnosticians first-hand access to student performance, and thus direct information about the student's academic and social problems. Samples appropriate for review include homework assignments, examination papers, worksheets, handwriting papers, and videotapes and audiotapes of academic, social, vocational, and speech–language performances. When combined with other sources of formal and informal assessment information, these products can be extremely beneficial in developing and refining diagnostic questions and hypotheses.

Inspection and analysis of student products and work samples may also lead to understanding of and hypotheses about student–teacher relationships and areas of conflict. For example, papers revealing teachers' critical or supportive comments may be correlated with student–teacher classroom interactions. Similarly, analysis of a highly creative English composition paper judged to be of failing quality may reveal poor spelling and grammar to be the problem, thereby providing insight into the values and expectations of the grader and possible areas for intervention and/or remediation.

**Trial Teaching.** Perhaps no area of informal assessment provides more potential for valuable information than clinical or diagnostic teaching. Trial teaching can be invaluable in specifying students' educational strengths and weaknesses; identifying instructional techniques and strategies; and formulating and testing assessment hypotheses. With this type of informal assessment, children and youth are systematically presented with instructional stimuli and response requests, thereby providing teachers and evaluation personnel opportunities for investigating students' problem-solving and work strategies, performance factors, motivational and behavioral patterns, and other data. Information and data ensuing from these analyses are used to formulate hypotheses regarding the nature of students' problems and possible strategies for their solution; to establish performance baselines against which progress resulting from interventions can be judged; and to monitor progress over time. Thus, clinical or diagnostic teaching can result in highly functional and utilitarian assessment data and information.

**Uses for Informal Assessment Information.** Informal assessment can be used in several ways to assess and plan for students experiencing emotional and behavioral problems. These include (a) differential diagnosis and placement, (b) instructional planning and decision making, and (c) progress monitoring. Informal assessment information can and should be used, along with formal testing results and clinical judgments, to make EBD diagnostic and placement decisions. For instance, information and data gathered from trial teaching and direct observation can be used to investigate to what extent a student who may have an EBD displays "an inability to build or maintain satisfactory interpersonal relationships with peers and teachers" (Individuals with Disabilities Education Act, 1990). Similarly, informal methods can be used to determine to what extent a student thought to have a learning disability exhibits a significant discrepancy between expected and actual achievement and evidences an uneven pattern of academic growth and development. Although informal assessment methods are not designed exclusively to be used in making EBD diagnostic and placement decisions, information and data from use of these procedures are useful in making these decisions.

Informal assessment methods are also particularly effective in the area of instructional planning and decision making. That is, informal assessment methods can be used to answer basic, relevant questions:

1. What general areas of strength and weakness does a student display?
2. What are a student's specific strengths and weaknesses within each area identified as a problem?
3. In what sequence should skills within a problem area be addressed?
4. To which instructional procedures is a student most apt to be responsive?
5. What are the conditions (e.g., antecedent factors, environmental conditions) under which a student is most and least likely to be effective?
6. What historical factors and patterns exist to explain a student's behaviors and educational strengths and weaknesses?

The items identified above constitute the matters with which most teachers must contend, including those teachers who serve students with EBD in general education settings. That is, teachers and other direct instruction persons must (a) determine what a student can and cannot do; (b) identify, within major curricular categories and domains, the student's specific instructional and social needs; (c) specify instructional and behavioral priorities and sequencing strategies; and (d) isolate and evaluate management and teaching techniques and strategies appropriate for the student. Accordingly, informal assessment procedures provide the most functional and utilitarian means of planning for the unique needs of children and youth experiencing academic and school difficulty.

Another purpose of informal assessment is to monitor progress of students and, specifically, to assess the success or failure of intervention procedures and curricular modifications. While not an element of initial assessment, such efforts provide teachers and other educators data on which they may base important decisions, including whether to continue to modify a particular strategy or supplant it with an alternate approach, and whether to recommend a more or less restrictive classroom placement.

Informal assessment monitoring methods also allow teachers an opportunity to make progress reports to parents and other teachers in ways that are meaningful, understandable, and pertinent to individual student programs and expectations. One general education teacher, who was involved in mainstreaming a child with a behavior disorder, observed that she had little interest in knowing how her student compared with other third-grade students in terms of reading abilities. She noted, however, that she was extremely impressed when the student's resource room teacher showed her a progress chart that linked use of specific instructional techniques and procedures with reading recognition and comprehension gains.

Finally, informal assessment procedures can be used to evaluate student progress in meeting Individualized Education Program (IEP) short-term objectives. IEPs are designed to reflect the unique goals and objectives of an individual student. Informal evaluation methods are often required to assess the degree to which they are achieved. In this regard, one informal assessment instrument designed to analyze problem behavior and setting elements as they apply to differential diagnosis and placement, instructional planning and decision making, and progress monitoring (Zionts & Wood, 1983) is shown in Figure 3.6.

## Assessment

When adults have concerns about the emotions and behaviors of children and youth, five basic elements should be considered in evaluations: (a) cognitive–intellectual abilities; (b) academic and other educationally related abilities; (c) physical, motor, and sensory strengths and weaknesses; (d) emotional, social, behavioral, and/or personality strengths and weaknesses; and (e) home and community environmental information.

### Cognitive Ability

For a number of reasons, cognitive–intellectual ability measures are commonly employed in evaluations of children and youth undergoing assessments. Primarily, these measures provide important information about a student's potential for academic achievement and overall prognosis (Coleman, 1992; Robbins, 1966, 1972). Moreover, a discrepancy between student intellectual ability and academic achievement remains among the most significant diagnostic indicators for an emotional or behavioral disturbance. Thus, in that the goal of comprehensive, multidisciplinary special education evaluation is both accurate diagnosis and a suitable intervention plan, cognitive ability should be considered. Because the accurate measurement of intelligence requires specialized training, this component of the evaluation is usually conducted by school psychologists and other similarly trained professionals.

Much of the information and data generated within the cognitive–intellectual domain comes from standardized intellectual measures. Results of these evaluations have produced rather consistent results: children and youth with EBD tend to earn lower intelligence test scores than their nondisabled peers (Coleman, 1992). In addition, the more severe the emotional disturbance, the lower the IQ score, with many individuals diagnosed with psychotic conditions functioning at a retarded level (DeMyer et al., 1974).

A variety of intellectual–cognitive measures are designed for either group or individual administration. However, relative to assessing students with EBD, psychologists and other diagnosticians prefer individual scales. The most widely used measures are the Wechsler scales, which cover ages 2 to

## The Pupil Assessment Summary

**The Disturber Element:** Who or what is perceived to be the focus of the problems?

1. List pertinent demographic and historic events:

   Name:
   Age:
   Sex:
   Parent or Guardian:
   Previous Educational Placement:
   Significant Historic Events:

2. Is the child's intellectual functioning a problem?
   Does the child have an unusual variation among subtests?
   List the intelligence test documentation here:

3. What personality characteristics does the child exhibit?
   List brief personality test summaries (projective tests, peer evaluations, self-ratings, and teacher ratings):

4. Does the child have perceptual-motor or other specific psychoeducational strengths or weaknesses? List them:

5. How is the student functioning academically? List evidence:

6. What patterns of behavior does the child exhibit? (Describe intensity, frequency, and duration if available).

   Rating scale or checklist information:

   Observational information:

**The Problem Behavior Element:** What specific behaviors does the child exhibit (or not exhibit) that create a problem?

List the student's behavioral characteristics (you may use information from Disturber Element no. 6) and have rater/observer define them as they relate to student.

**The Setting Element:** In what setting(s) does the problem behavior occur? (There may be multiple settings if student is disturbed rather than disturbing.)

1. List the specific educational settings (math, English, social studies, special education, gym)
2. List the nonacademic school settings (playground, recess, lunchroom, bus)

*(continues)*

**FIGURE 3.6.** The Pupil Assessment Summary.

> 3. List the social settings (home, community, agency clubs)
> 4. How does student's behavior compare to that of other students in that setting?
>
> **The Disturbed Element:** Who regards the behavior as a problem?
>
> 1. Diagnostician
> 2. Previous teacher(s)
> 3. Present teacher(s)
> 4. Parent(s)
> 5. Peer(s)
> 6. Others
>
> From *The Pupil Assessment Summary* by P. Zionts and P. Wood, 1983, Mt. Pleasant, MI: RETCO. Reprinted with permission.

**FIGURE 3.6** (*Continued*)

adulthood. These measures (*Wechsler Preschool and Primary Scale of Intelligence–Revised* [Wechsler, 1989] for young children; the *Wechsler Intelligence Scale for Children–Third Edition* [Wechsler, 1991] for children and youth aged 6 to 16; and the *Wechsler Adult Intelligence Scale–Revised* [Wechsler, 1981] for youth over age 16) provide an overall IQ along with Verbal and Performance IQ scores and, perhaps most importantly, opportunities for diagnosticians to make clinical observations. Knowledge of student intellectual functioning allows diagnostic teams to assess differences between students' academic performance and potential achievement. More specifically, professionals can evaluate subscales to assess various strengths and weaknesses, thus allowing diagnosticians to compare various types of verbal and nonverbal performance.

## Academic and Educational Ability

Evaluations of student academic achievement are important in making diagnostic judgments about children and youth with emotional and behavioral problems. Currently, the federal definition of serious emotional disturbance identifies academic problems as a salient consideration. Moreover, even when compared with expected academic achievement based on cognitive functioning, students identified with EBD almost always demonstrate academic deficits (Forness, Bennett, & Tose, 1983). Finally, and perhaps most important, accurate information regarding academic achievement is needed to plan effective individualized programs for students. Accordingly, a variety of formal and informal procedures are routinely used as a part of academic evaluation efforts.

Formal assessment of student academic achievement is accomplished using a variety of instruments and procedures, almost all of which focus on assessing performance in the areas of reading, mathematics, and language arts. Like cognitive measures, these tests are designed for group or individual administration. Group achievement test results are typically considered as a part of the referral and screening process; individualized achievement tests are used during formal academic achievement evaluations.

Although most achievement tests are not particularly good at pinpointing specific learner deficits and suggesting remediation strategies, they are nonetheless an important part of evaluations of children and youth with suspected EBD. They permit comparisons with a norm group of same-age peers, and they allow assessment teams to compare student academic performance with their cognitive–intellectual capacity. When formal and informal procedures are used together, they provide diagnostic teams a global picture of the student's functioning.

Among the most commonly used of the academic achievement tests is the *Woodcock–Johnson Psycho-Educational Battery–Revised* (Woodcock, 1991). This instrument, designed for a wide range of ages, is actually a comprehensive test battery designed to assess cognitive ability, scholastic aptitude, interests, independent functioning, and academic achievement. However, the academic achievement component of the test is the most widely used, and is often used independently, of the other components of the battery. In particular, the academic achievement element of the battery allows diagnosticians to evaluate students' performance in five basic academic areas: reading, mathematics, written language, general knowledge, and skills.

## Health and Physical Abilities

Information and data related to student physical status and functioning, including sensory strengths and weaknesses, health, motor abilities, neurological deficits, and disease factors, are also a significant component of evaluations of students considered to have emotional and behavioral problems. In recognition of the importance of this domain, the revised third edition of the *Diagnostic and Statistical Manual of Mental Disorders (DSM-III-R)* (American Psychiatric Association, 1987) lists physical disorders and conditions as an important element of its multiaxial diagnostic system. Educators have also long known that sensory, medical, and other physical variables may contribute to or be associated with problems of behavior and emotional stability. Although medical professionals are obviously the primary diagnosticians relative to specific health problems, this information is very important in educational assessments of children and youth with emotional and behavioral problems. Moreover, educators are in a unique position to recognize and screen factors and conditions contributing to student behavior and emotional excesses and deficits.

Professionals agree that emotional and behavioral problems can be associated with or exacerbated by a variety of physical factors such as malnutrition, health problems, alcohol or drug use, and sensory deficits. Accordingly, consideration of physical variables is a necessary and basic element of comprehensive and multidisciplinary special education evaluations of students with purported EBD. Evaluation within this domain often relies on informal methods; however, formal, standardized methods also exist for assessing students' physical functioning.

Relative to diagnostic attention to the physical domain, professionals are encouraged to be particularly sensitive to the following: (a) frequent school absence; (b) signs of chronic fatigue and physical illness; (c) inability to focus attention; (d) poor muscle control; (e) signs of visual problems (e.g., excessive blinking, reddening of eyes); (f) signs of auditory problems (e.g., frequent colds or sinus infection, requests to repeat directions, turning one ear toward a speaker); (g) frequent signs of extreme excitability, anxiety, or other strong emotion; (h) signs of depression or chronic sadness; (i) frequent strong mood swings; (j) frequent headaches, stomachaches, or other physical complaints; and (k) signs of drug and alcohol use. The above list is not comprehensive; however, it does point to the wide variety of symptoms that should be considered during evaluations. Moreover, sensitivity to the above, along with similar behavior patterns, allows educators to employ appropriate formal and informal evaluation methods to assess particular motor, sensory, medical, and other physical problems. Finally, such awareness facilitates educators making timely and appropriate referrals for further assessment to professionals with expertise in areas corresponding to students' problems.

The consideration of most physical factors relies largely on informal procedures such as observations, interviews, and record reviews. The exceptions to this rule are in the area of perceptual motor functioning, auditory discrimination, and speech–language performance assessment, where there are well-established formal measures. It is also important to remember that information and data within the physical domain is often most valuable when integrated with other findings; that is, specific analysis of factors within the physical domain often result from observations and findings from other components of evaluations, such as was the case with one student who alerted diagnostic staff to a possible hearing loss by frequently asking that clinical interview questions be repeated.

## Behavioral and Emotional Functioning

Children and youth with alleged emotional and behavioral problems are primarily a concern to adults because of their behavior and affect. Hence, it is understandable that professionals who evaluate these children would place utmost importance on the behavioral and emotional domain.

Although a variety of assessment methods are used, most are categorized as tests, interview methods, observations, and rating scales. These formal and informal methods often serve to generate information and data that will ultimately determine students' diagnoses. Accordingly, information within this domain is typically considered to be of primary importance to diagnosticians, program planners, and family members.

Formal evaluation techniques used to assess a student's behavioral and emotional functioning include projective tests and rating scales. Although the utility of projective tests has been severely challenged (Salvia & Ysseldyke, 1988), their use continues. Because of such use in school and clinical settings, two well-known projective procedures are discussed. One of the oldest and best known projective measures is Rorschach's (1942) Test. The Rorschach test, like other projective instruments, consists of ambiguous stimuli which the individual under evaluation interprets according to his or her own personality and emotional needs. The test consists of 10 inkblots; the person being examined is instructed to indicate what the blots look like, what they might be, or what they make the individual think of. These spontaneous free-association responses are followed by examiner inquiries regarding the location of each response and the properties of the stimuli that evoke each.

In spite of its traditional acceptance and continued usage, the utility of the Rorschach technique, especially with regard to school-related problems, is seriously questioned. As noted by O'Leary (1972), "the Rorschach appears to qualify as an instrument for research, but it has not met requirements which demonstrate its utility in the decision-making process of diagnosis or treatment" (p. 23).

Another relatively popular projective technique is *The Thematic Apperception Test* (TAT) (Murray, 1943). Originally developed as a test to study fantasy, the TAT consists of 31 drawings and photographs, such as a child staring reflectively at a violin. Certain stimulus items are designed for specific age and gender groups. Individuals being administered the test are asked to make up a story about each stimulus card. Subjects are specifically instructed to indicate what is happening, what led up to it, how the individuals involved feel, and how the story will turn out.

Because of the TAT's time requirements for administration, scoring, and interpretation and relatively poor reliability and validity, it, like the Rorschach, is a questionable technique. In addition, the relevant information that the TAT yields is usually available through simpler and less expensive means.

Rating scales are perhaps the most widely used means of assessing children's and youth's behavior and emotional status, and are often the source of information given the most weight in diagnostic evaluations. Rating scales involve teachers, parents, and other persons who are familiar with children and youth, who rate the extent to which a student demonstrates certain behavioral excesses and deficits. Thus, rating scales involve use of checklists that allow diagnosticians to compare children and youth with a standardized norm group on behavioral patterns believed to represent signs of emotional and behavioral disorders.

Literally dozens of behavior rating checklists exist from which diagnostic teams may choose. One popular and effective rating scale is the *Behavior Rating Profile–Second Edition* (BRP–2) (Brown & Hammill, 1990). This instrument is noteworthy because it allows the gathering and comparison of information from four independent sources: the teacher, the parent/family, peers, and the student. The teacher rating scale of the BRP–2 is shown in Figure 3.7.

## Home and Community

Analysis of environmental factors relevant to understanding children and youth undergoing evaluations for EBD rely primarily on informal methods such as interviews and observations. One of the most effective ways of learning more about a student's out-of-school environments is to interview parents and family members. Interviews allow parents (and other family members) opportunities to discuss the perceptions of the child's behavior, including behavioral patterns about which they and school personnel may have concerns.

Evaluation of students' non-school environments is also a basic element of a comprehensive and multidisciplinary assessment. Consideration of this factor recognizes the significant and unique effect that parents, families, and other environmental influences have on children and youth. In this regard Opler (1965) suggested that considering the family along with the individual under evaluation "leads to a more accurate diagnosis, a better chance for successful treatment, less pressure for repeated clinical visits, and faster progress toward sound solutions" (p. 235). In addition, because P.L. 94-142 clearly specifies that parents must be given the opportunity to be involved in their child's education, it is only logical that the diagnostic process include parents. This strategy not only will serve to facilitate compliance in the subsequent Individuals with Disabilities Education Act (IDEA), but also will aid in gaining a more comprehensive understanding of the student under study. Moreover, because educators frequently assume that a child's or youth's behavior problems are a function of environmental factors that are responsive to environmental changes, it is necessary that information relative to this area be made available.

Finally, information about aspects of a child's sociocultural environment should be collected. This information may be obtained most readily through school records or other sources. Specific sociological information that evaluation teams often find important include the composition of the family and its

### INSTRUCTIONS

This behavior rating form contains a list of descriptive words and phrases. Some of these items will describe the referred student quite well. Some will not. What we wish to know is this: Which of these behaviors are you concerned about at this particular time and to what extent do you see them as problems?

Take for example item #1, "Is sent to the principal for discipline." If the child frequently is sent to the principal's office, the rater might check the "Very Much Like" space. If the child is sent to the principal's office on an infrequent but regular basis, the rater might check the "Somewhat Like" space. If the child has been sent to the principal's office on rare occasions, a check in the "Not Much Like" space might be appropriate. If the child never has been disciplined by the principal, the "Not At All Like" space would be indicated. These ratings should reflect your perceptions of the child's behavior. Please do not confer with other teachers in completing this form.

| The student . . . . . | Very Much Like the Student | Like the Student | Not Much Like the Student | Not At All Like the Student |
|---|---|---|---|---|
| 1. Is sent to the principal for discipline............ | ☐ | ☐ | ☐ | ☐ |
| 2. Is verbally aggressive to teachers or peers...... | ☐ | ☐ | ☐ | ☐ |
| 3. Is disrespectful of others' property rights........ | ☐ | ☐ | ☐ | ☐ |
| 4. Tattles on classmates............... | ☐ | ☐ | ☐ | ☐ |
| 5. Is lazy................. | ☐ | ☐ | ☐ | ☐ |
| 6. Lacks motivation and interest.... | ☐ | ☐ | ☐ | ☐ |
| 7. Disrupts the classroom............. | ☐ | ☐ | ☐ | ☐ |
| 8. Argues with teachers and classmates........... | ☐ | ☐ | ☐ | ☐ |
| 9. Doesn't follow directions......... | ☐ | ☐ | ☐ | ☐ |
| 10. Steals................. | ☐ | ☐ | ☐ | ☐ |
| 11. Has poor personal hygiene habits................. | ☐ | ☐ | ☐ | ☐ |
| 12. Is passive and withdrawing...... | ☐ | ☐ | ☐ | ☐ |
| 13. Says that other children don't like him/her........... | ☐ | ☐ | ☐ | ☐ |
| 14. Can't seem to concentrate in class................. | ☐ | ☐ | ☐ | ☐ |
| 15. Pouts, whines, snivels............... | ☐ | ☐ | ☐ | ☐ |

**FIGURE 3.7.** Selected items from the Teacher Rating Scale of the *Behavior Rating Profile–Second Edition*. From *Behavior Rating Profile–Second Edition* by L. Brown and D. D. Hammill, 1990, Austin, TX: PRO-ED. Copyright 1990 by PRO-ED, Inc. Reproduced with permission.

cultural and ethnic makeup; the occupations of the parents; the physical and mental health of the family; languages other than English spoken by the parents or others in the family; child-rearing practices of the parents; agencies that may be involved with the child or family; and supervision provided the child. Cultural and language factors, in addition to providing environmental information, are also useful in selecting appropriate evaluation procedures. Consideration of the community and neighborhood characteristics may also be a useful source of diagnostic information. For instance, knowing that children or adolescents must contend daily with neighborhood gang violence or similar problems may shed light on their school behavior.

## Implementing Effective Multidisciplinary Teams

Wood (1979) suggested that, for a definition of emotional disturbance to be adequate, the operationalizing element, which is a placement process enabling decision making about the nature of the behavioral disturbance, must be in place. To determine if the operationalizing element is satisfied, the following question should be addressed: "Through what operations and by whom is the definition used to differentiate disturbers from nondisturbers or to assess the needs of disturbers? (Note: At this point, many traditional definitions move rapidly from descriptions of behavior to inference of disturbance.)" (Wood, 1979, p. 8). Normally the above question is answered at the multidisciplinary team meeting (MTM). After a careful examination of the information compiled in the referral and assessment process, the team usually makes a decision about the possible diagnostic labeling of the student. When the student is considered for special education services, two new, separate processes begin: (a) placement of the student in the "least restrictive environment" and (b) educational programming for the student in the emotional, behavioral, social, and academic domains. With these two processes, a controversy occurs: Should the student first be placed in a type of classroom, such as the self-contained classroom or resource room, and the specific program subsequently be prescribed, or vice versa? It would seem that this question should be addressed if special educators are to fully understand their roles in the programming and placement process.

It would seem ideal that educators first determine the needs of the student, and then locate a classroom and teacher in an attempt to meet those needs. This scenario is not unusual when the student's problems are essentially academic. However, when the student is disturbed or disturbing, programming and placement may very well be the same process because of the theoretical and/or philosophical biases of the teacher. Some students with EBD may have socialization problems, some may simply not have learned appropriate behaviors, some may have deep-rooted psychological problems, and still others may have emotional problems primarily of a biophysical nature. Because of fiscal constraints, it is highly unlikely in most school districts that there will be a choice of classrooms devoted to the prescriptive programming needed to meet these varying student problems. In such cases, placement decisions do not necessarily imply specific behavioral and emotional remediation.

It may be unrealistic to suggest that school districts provide individual classrooms to meet the needs of each group of students who have similar problems. It should also be evident that educators who subscribe to one particular educational orientation cannot and should not expect to be meeting the emotional and behavioral needs of each student in their classrooms. Herein lies the most crucial step, and issue, in the special education process: the placement and programming of students with the goal of remediating problems so that the students may progress to the classroom environment that is most beneficial to them.

The purpose of this section is to examine how placement procedures are implemented. The intent is not to suggest that there is only one appropriate process, but rather that there are guidelines that should be included in any procedure. By further examining Wood's (1979) operationalizing element, two placement facets are examined: (a) the dynamics of the multidisciplinary team meeting (the interaction among MTM members, the perceived influence of participants, and the goals of MTMs) and (b) administrative factors that could lead to a consistency among MTMs. The aspects of the role of handicapped students in the placement continuum, planning for their school day as well as for their future, are among the key issues in this area. An exercise is provided to enable the reader to become more familiar with the placement process.

## Multidisciplinary Team Meetings

A sometimes unspoken responsibility of special educators is their role in the MTM process. Much research and thought have been devoted to both this role and the process itself. Rucker and Vautour (1981, p. 5) suggested that previous teams of MTMs "seemed based more on folklore than on any hard research data" (see also Ysseldyke et al., 1992). Hopefully, the model of operation of the MTMs has changed since the advent of P.L. 94-142 in order to more accurately prescribe the placement and programming of students. Many investigations have recently been conducted on MTMs, primarily because of their mandated role in special education decision making.

Research and literature have highlighted some specific needs of both special and general educators (Fenton, Yoshida, Maxwell, & Kaufman, 1979; Goldstein, Arkell, Ashcroft, Hurley, & Lilly, 1975; Yoshida, Fenton,

Maxwell, & Kaufman, 1978). Ironically, general educators are rarely active participants in the development of IEPs for students they teach. They are not required to attend the MTM, even though they referred the students and will probably be required to teach them (see Pugach, 1982).

Ironically, much of the research on IEPs has focused on the process of the forms and how they are followed and not the process itself. For example, Smith and Simpson (1989) found that IEPs are not completed as required and that they rarely serve as instructional guides. The actual instructional goals have been criticized as being too specific, perhaps reflecting only a behavioral perspective (Ballard, 1987; Goodman & Bond, 1993). Most revealing is the research by Fielder and Knight (1986), who found a poor relationship between the assessment presented at MTMs and the instruction. They suggested that this may be due to "two possibilities: (a) little of the information transmitted is actually understood, or (b) the information is understood but, for unknown reasons, is not acted upon" (p. 26). Improvement in IEPs may occur if teams can begin "positing alternative objectives, using portfolios and videotapes to document behavior, employing personal judgments to supplement or replace measured gain, and substituting methods of instruction for instructional objectives" (Goodman & Bond, 1993, p. 418).

More information and practice in MTMs (both actual and mock) are needed so that educators may fully understand their roles and make greater contributions to the MTM process. Rucker's studies (Crowell & Rucker, 1977; Vautour & Rucker, 1977) indicated the need for a knowledge base not only about the child, but also about the alternative placement options. This point should be emphasized. Teachers often feel that their responsibilities begin and end with their students in the classrooms, yet the politics of such activities as the MTM and working with peers, administrators, and parents cannot be ignored because these are extremely important factors that do affect students in the classrooms. Research and literature have often touted the value of parent and student participation, yet little has been published that explains how to facilitate such participation (Van Ruesen & Bos, 1994). Gilliam and Coleman (1981) found that parents and principals were initially ranked as being highly influential in team meetings; however, after the actual meetings, their influence dwindled. Those team members who presented data were considered the most influential. Information from MTMs can help teachers transcend the information provider–gatherer role that they may now play. Another benefit of training would be to increase teachers' frequency of contact with MTMs, so that their knowledge about the process will increase.

The following exercise is intended to provide the reader with experience in making placement decisions, so as to gain a more thorough understanding of the MTM process. To achieve the latter goal, the reader is encouraged to use this exercise as a group activity, progressing through the following steps:

1. Complete the exercise individually.
2. Divide into small groups and arrive at consensus on student placement, simulating a MTM.
3. Compare group placements.
4. Compare individual scores with group scores to determine "influence."

---

## Exercise

Following are brief descriptions of children actually referred for special education services. For each student, choose what you think would be the best educational setting at this time from among the seven possibilities in the continuum given below. (You would actually need more information before placing most of these students, but please make your best judgments based on the information provided.) Assume that all types of placement programs are available and competently staffed, and that placements within the continuum are flexible and it is possible for a student to be moved up or down the scale after treatment.

### POSSIBLE PLACEMENTS

1. *Out*—Student placed in a residential school, hospital program, treatment center, or similar facility.
2. *Full-time special class*—Student assigned to a self-contained special class on a full-time basis.
3. *Part-time special class*—Student enrolled in a special class for the majority of each day, but enters regular classroom for certain subjects.
4. *Resource room*—Regular classroom with resource room services (special education teacher providing supplemental instruction) provided on a continuing basis in which the student can participate for as much as 2 hours each day.
5. *Consultation + direct services*—Regular classroom with specialists available in the school to consult with teacher and provide short-term direct services to student.
6. *Consultation*—Regular classroom with specialists available to consult with teacher (or parent) whenever needed.
7. *Regular classroom*—With no basic change in teaching procedures.

*(continues)*

**Exercise** (Continued)

## DESCRIPTION OF STUDENTS

1. Myron is a sixth grader who often becomes aggressive in class. His relationships with other children are usually quarrelsome, and he is prone to get into trouble when left alone.

2. Ed repeated kindergarten because of his immaturity and is now having trouble doing his first-grade work. If he is in a group activity, he constantly teases the smaller children. He has to be watched at all times or he will destroy their work in a sadistic manner.

3. Christopher is a very articulate second grader with many interests. He works very slowly, particularly in reading. He is weak in phonetic analysis, can't seem to retain reading skills, and any academic growth on his part depends on a great deal of drill.

4. Leroy beat another first grader so severely that minor surgery was required. He has bitten a number of his classmates and has to be supervised constantly.

5. Fred is a 10-year-old fourth grader who was retained in first grade. His motivation for classroom work is very low, but improves markedly in a one-to-one relationship. He has difficulty with reading, spelling, and arithmetic concepts. His oral performance indicates that he is far more able than his written work would indicate.

6. Annalou is new to her present fifth-grade class. She seems anxious while she is in school, but is much calmer as soon as she leaves the school grounds. Her school work is slightly below average, but she is quite responsive if encouraged.

7. Ray, age 12, is a two-time repeater with above average potential; he has great difficulty remembering material presented in a visual manner and, in spite of a great deal of remedial reading instruction, remains a nonreader.

8. Bob is a third grader who wants friends, but his classmates continually make him a scapegoat. Although he is apparently bright, he is very forgetful and seems unaware of what is expected by his teacher.

9. Virginia is an 8-year-old who does little work in school. She is capable of verbal and physical attacks on anyone when angry. She doesn't seem to care about any school relationships and neither threats nor praise are effective in dealing with her.

*(continues)*

> **Exercise** (Continued)
> 
> 10. Tom, age 8, doesn't seem to acquire new skills as quickly as most students; he needs to have instructions repeated several times. He has difficulty working individually and needs a great deal of encouragement and supervision.
> 
> Reprinted by permission from *Rucker–Gable Educational Programming Scale* by C. N. Rucker and R. K. Gable, 1973, Storrs, CT: Rucker–Gable Associates. This exercise is a modification of one developed by Jerry Chaffin of the University of Kansas.

If this exercise was conducted with groups and MTMs were simulated, each group should consider the following questions:

1. Did the members assign roles to each other?
2. Did the members of the group introduce themselves, and were name cards with names (and roles) completed to enhance familiarity?
3. Were rules created?
4. Was the most aggressive person also the most influential?
5. Was the most knowledgeable person also the most influential?
6. What were the differences of results among groups? How do you account for these differences?

Because this exercise simulates a MTM, the first question has important implications. Although Gilliam and Coleman's (1981) research indicates that the most influential individual is also the most knowledgeable, a power structure based on roles nevertheless exists in some MTMs. Does the psychologist report his or her data first, or does the referring teacher or parent? Is all of the information discussed in practical, educational terms? Roles and labels can either clarify or cloud the purposes of the MTM, so their use in a simulation may be revealing.

Question 2 is closely related to the first question. What means were taken to make all individuals feel comfortable? Although name cards are a familiar device to at least remember names (and titles), in many cases they are not used. Did group members remember the names of other participants? Question 3 asks about the ground rules for the MTM. What were the goals of the MTM? Were any procedures followed? Questions 4, 5, and 6 all relate to the literature cited above. How actively involved was each group member in the process? More important, what prompted individuals to take a greater or lesser role?

In an investigation of the functions of a MTM, five groups of graduate students (4 to 5 in each group), each of whom was teaching in special education classrooms in Michigan, completed this exercise. Their results are presented in Table 3.2; the numbers given are their placements of each student according to the list of possible placements in the exercise. Experts' placements of the students, compiled by Rucker and Gable (1973), are presented in Table 3.3. Upon examination of the data, discrepancies with regard to the most appropriate placement for each student can be observed. Although the discrepancy may be minimal with some students, there seems to be a wide variance with others. The expert scores were obviously averaged, so that in reality within that population there was also a variance with the scores.

The implications of this investigation are that, given a student's particular social or academic profile, there is not and probably cannot be unanimous agreement upon placements. When the same student is examined by various groups, his or her actual placement may vary anywhere from a self-contained setting to a regular classroom with supportive help. Each team completes its duties with as much dedication to its task as any other group, yet differences exist. If placements are not "carved in stone," this discrepancy is not a major problem. Special education law states that, if placements are not appropriate, the student should be transferred to a more suitable placement. However, this fluidity of movement between placements is not common.

Those completing this placement exercise did so with the instruction that each placement was competently staffed. The effects of placement decisions when actual teachers' personalities are involved can only be left

**TABLE 3.2**
**Graduate Students' Results on Placement Activity**

| Students to Be Placed | Group | | | | |
|---|---|---|---|---|---|
| | 1 | 2 | 3 | 4 | 5 |
| Myron | 5 | 4 | 5 | 6 | 5 |
| Ed | 2 | 2 | 3 | 3 | 3 |
| Christopher | 4 | 4 | 4 | 4 | 4 |
| Leroy | 2 | 2 | 1 | 3 | 2 |
| Fred | 3 | 3 | 4 | 3 | 4 |
| Annalou | 7 | 6 | 6 | 6 | 6 |
| Ray | 3 | 3 | 3 | 2 | 3 |
| Bob | 5 | 5 | 6 | 6 | 5 |
| Virginia | 2 | 2 | 5 | 2 | 2 |
| Tom | 4 | 4 | 4 | 3 | 4 |

**TABLE 3.3**
**Experts' Results on Placement Activity (N = 35)**

| Students To Be Placed | Experts' Placements |
|---|---|
| Myron | 5.3 |
| Ed | 4.3 |
| Christopher | 4.6 |
| Leroy | 2.7 |
| Fred | 4.0 |
| Annalou | 6.4 |
| Ray | 3.5 |
| Bob | 5.7 |
| Virginia | 3.2 |
| Tom | 5.0 |

Data from Rucker and Gable (1973).

to conjecture. These "imperfect" decisions may help understand those teachers who believe that IEPs are not useful (Dudley-Marling, 1985).

Furthermore, this exercise, like regular MTMs, assumes that participants understand the breadth of each placement option. The resource room concept, for example, has been hailed as the least restrictive environment for many mildly handicapped youth (Glavin, Quay, Annesley, & Werry, 1971; Hammill & Wiederholt, 1972; Wiederholt, Hammill, & Brown, 1978), yet Bullock (1980) suggested that the resource room does not address "the quality nor the generalizability of such services" (p. 5). In reality, there are no prototypical placement options. Different people have different perceptions of each particular setting. Add to these problems the philosophies of mainstreaming, the Regular Education Initiative, and inclusion, and one could only speculate the diversity of personal and political agendas that multidisciplinary team members will bring to the planning table.

To summarize, placement may be influenced by the composition of the multidisciplinary team, as well as other factors such as the meeting time, the number of meetings conducted that day, the readily available services (Gerber, 1981), and the perceived competence of the teachers who are directly responsible for these services. An example of extraneous influences on placement is Goldbaum and Rucker's (1977) finding that team members were likely to place students in more restrictive (segregated) settings if they received norm-referenced rather than criterion-referenced assessment data, although each case study essentially described the same child.

The reader should be cautioned against assuming that the MTM process, because of its unpredictability, is imperfect and should be eliminated. The fact that there are differences among teams is problematic and should not simply be accepted if they are due mostly to the personalities involved (Knoff, 1983). Instead, the MTM can be a carefully designed evaluation and prescription process relating to both the student's needs and the available resources. However, it seems that a uniform procedure is needed to more consistently meet these goals. The following section examines the factors that could facilitate such a procedure.

## Administrative Factors of the MTM

Administrative factors are those that explicitly use the criteria for special placement both to place students in special education and to provide the means to allow them to exit the special education placement. Although they are not the only factors that team members may choose, the point of the previous section and this section is that some agreed-upon guidelines should be determined before teams meet. Educators are encouraged to list these factors and others that they deem to be crucial to the MTM on index cards for reference during the meetings. Educators often rely purely on memory, and after the meeting remember what "should have been covered." Many of the factors discussed in this section have been developed from Cawley (1977; personal communication, 1980).

***Define the Student's Least Restrictive Environment.*** The fact that the learner attends (and learns) all day suggests that when students are in the public schools they must be in the least restrictive environment, which is defined as the most appropriate environment for the student. For example, a self-contained classroom may be the least restrictive environment for students with severe emotional disturbances; the mainstreamed classroom certainly is not the most beneficial to them. The least restrictive environment dictum is often cited as a major emphasis of P.L. 94-142, but in actual practice its function is somewhat questionable (Meyen & Lehr, 1980). Consider the case of Joe, who is reading, especially in the comprehension area, well below grade level. Suppose that reading is Joe's only problem. His skills in both the academic and the social–emotional areas are acceptable to both the team and Joe's parents. Basing their decision on Joe's reading deficiency, the team places Joe in a special education resource room. Realizing that attempting to remediate a 3-year deficit is not an easy task, the team members argue about how much help is actually needed.

The team is divided into two camps. Group 1 suggests that Joe's schedule remain similar to its present format. Their changes include taking him out of his English class all week and out of his gym/art/music period 2 days a week to put him in the resource room for special reading help. Group 2 argues that, although Joe is achieving acceptable levels in his other classes, he must be performing "magic" because his reading level indicates he cannot do most of the reading assigned in any content area. They argue that Joe should be placed in a special education class during reading, science, social studies, and English classes.

Group 1 becomes outraged, contending that the other group's idea of placement is not in the spirit of P.L. 94-142 and the least restrictive environment statement. Group 2 retorts that any placement in which students cannot function because of their handicap is indeed "restrictive" and, furthermore, that literature and classroom experience suggest that handicapped students need as much if not more instruction time than nonhandicapped students, and yet Group 1 wants to place Joe in situations in which reading is commonplace, rendering him incapacitated during those times.

Group 2 has determined that the least restrictive environment is defined in such a way that in no case will the child be exposed to failure-producing situations, arguing that, if Joe is required to read in any class, he will be rendered helpless. Their arguments are in contrast to the literature, which asserts that the least restrictive environment is the general education classroom (inclusion) and that it is preferable for students to be placed in this setting (Dunn, 1968; Lilly, 1970). Group 2 instead contends that the least restrictive environment is one that is the most effective in meeting the needs of the child.

The assumption that the regular classroom is both socially and emotionally beneficial to acting-out students was debated in Chapter 1 and also has been questioned by Gresham (1982). In an extensive review of the research, Gresham concluded, "Clearly, the intent of the least restrictive environment is to prevent wholesale exclusion of exceptional children from the mainstream of the regular school environment. Part of the present difficulty may have come about when many state and local education authorities interpreted these requirements to mean that most, if not all, handicapped children should be mainstreamed" (p. 430). This is not what the law states, and Gresham found that students who do not have acceptable social skills are in fact isolated from their regular education peers and teachers. In other words to be placed in a regular "mainstreamed" classroom does not mean that one will necessarily benefit from it. Strain and Shores (1983) criticized Gresham for having misinterpreted some of the research he cited, yet they did agree with his major assumptions.

Nevertheless, to take Joe out of classrooms in which he could handle most of the work, except for the reading, seems unfair to him, because he does have many skills similar to those of his peers. This problem, although not difficult to understand, certainly has many ramifications that are integral to the issue of inclusion. Pappanikou (1979) asserted that, for mainstreaming to work, "the system must be ready to accept handicapping conditions as part of and not apart from the ability, performance, and/or emotional distribution" (p. 52). The system will have to cooperate if Joe is to remain in his general education classrooms.

For Joe to be in an environment in which he can be exposed to meaningful learning all day (Group 1) and be in a classroom in which he can benefit from the interaction of which he is capable (Group 2), the following may be proposed:

1. Determine what the system (in each class on his schedule) requires with regard to his deficiency (reading). If a class is 80% reading with 10 minutes of interaction, then it is probably too restrictive for Joe. If the class is at least 50% interaction, alternatives may be attempted.

2. Determine if the teacher (system) can arrange interactions with Joe in weekly time blocks that are regularly scheduled. These would include all of the activities (movies, tapes, etc.) in which Joe can participate.

3. Schedule Joe to be in the regular classroom during the times in which there is interaction and in the special classroom for reading (if possible in the content area) during other times.

To implement this plan, the cooperation needed from the regular educators is actually minimal. Besides rescheduling their reading times, they are not required to do many of the tasks commonly assigned to them as a result of the MTMs, such as taping lessons, holding individual sessions with each special education student, and/or giving oral tests. Finally, if the above steps are enacted, students like Joe can attend and learn all day in school. In other words, the *potential* for him to learn is now available.

**Determine Individualized Versus Generalized Treatment.** The concept of the learner as one of many students refers to the often-cited remark by teachers in the regular education setting that carefully planning curricula for, say, 27 students is certainly a difficult duty, yet they are requested to plan additional curricula for each of their special education students. Furthermore, they argue that, if students are not ready for the regular classroom, the amount of teacher time required for them is quite high (see Thompson, White, & Morgan, 1982).

If a team decides that students are to be placed in the regular classroom, the decision should be because the students are ready for it. Unfortunately, students who are moved from special education settings often are ill prepared to handle the regular classroom. These students may very well have been excellent students in the special settings, but the demands and environmental expectations of the two settings may differ radically. For example, in the special class requests for help may be automatically met, whereas in the regular class students have to "wait their turn." Also, the student's educational program in the special education setting might be highly individualized, whereas the curriculum in the regular setting is devised to meet the needs of the entire class. Consideration of what actually is required of students in the general education setting should be part of the special education program for all students needing special services.

An unfortunate consequence of inclusion is the influx of students with special programming needs into cooperative, receptive classrooms, creating an imbalance in those classes. Cooperation by regular educators with special education services personnel will certainly diminish if students still in need of special services are placed in their classrooms. This type of remedy does not seem to be the intent of P.L. 94-142.

One method of fostering cooperation among school personnel is to provide techniques for the regular classroom teacher that benefit not only the special education students, but also the other members of the class. The classroom management program presented in Chapter 4 is designed for both populations. Other techniques that can be explored include how to implement peer tutoring, time management techniques, specific remedial techniques, and uses of the overhead projector and other audiovisual aids. Certainly this list is not exhaustive. In many cases, teachers can readily identify areas in which they would like to improve. Again, because the learner is

## Window on Reality

An example of the type of problem that can result from the differences between placement and program can occur in any environment. Suppose that the classroom management system of a special education teacher reflects a behavior modification orientation. Not all students react favorably to any one intervention, yet this classroom teacher, Mr. Marinelli, has been particularly successful in implementing this approach. In fact, most of his students previously had extreme difficulty in their regular classroom and were not progressing in an adequate manner.

Sally, a particularly intelligent and economically wealthy student, has been diagnosed as disturbed and is placed in Mr. Marinelli's classroom. The psychologist suggests that Sally is extremely averse to any structure, but can be quite productive when allowed to explore on her own volition. Also, the use of rewards in the classroom is somewhat meaningless to Sally because she can buy whatever she chooses, and the use of punishments (e.g., timeout) does not seem to affect her. Should Mr. Marinelli follow the team's suggestions on the IEP and allow the other students to observe the inconsistency with which he treats Sally? What would Sally's presence do to the classroom management system and to the rights of the other students?

one of many students, teachers must remember that, although students may have similar emotional labels, their needs are probably different.

Sally's situation is not unique with regard to placements for students with EBD. In many cases, placements and programming are equivalent, and considerations, even with IEP recommendations, of the effect of Sally's placement on other students and their IEPs should be determined. Even in special education settings, the learner is one of many students.

***Establish Differing Educational Practices at Each Level of Education.*** Educational practices differ at the preschool, elementary, middle, and secondary levels with regard to both the academic and the affective practices of the schools. These institutional requirements of the school should be considered as integral to the assessment process. The teams should address these differences when students are about to progress through the school system (i.e., move from one level to the next).

Two major practices dramatically change from preschool to secondary school: the influence of significant others and the nature of education. When children are young, they are highly influenced by the adults in their lives. Upon arrival at school, they become teacher oriented and behave in such a manner as to either please or avoid the disapproval of their teachers. When students reach the later grades of elementary school, they begin to be more influenced by their peers and behave in a manner designed to gain peer approval. These developmental influences on a child are in direct contrast to the nature of education during those periods. Preschools and elementary schools tend to be more child oriented, concentrating on both the affective and cognitive domains, whereas middle and secondary schools tend to be more subject or context oriented and less tolerant of deviant affective behavior.

The dilemma is obvious. When students approach adolescence, a potentially turbulent time even for the "normal" teenager, the emphasis of the schools switches to an impersonal institutional approach. The lack of person-oriented curricula in high schools has been well documented (McDowell & Brown, 1978; Nelson & Kauffman, 1977). It would seem to be the multidisciplinary team's responsibility to determine if the needs of the student with EBD call for such programming.

***Set Long-Term Goals in Education.*** The learner's education ranges from preschool through secondary schooling, and awareness of the total span of time a student spends in school leads to recognition of the need for setting long-term goals for the student during the MTM. Long-term goals are generally interpreted by the team as a period of 1 or 2 years, during which time a particular skill is to be obtained. Consideration of this administrative factor suggests that this time frame is insufficient, and that the concept of "long term" needs to be expanded. For example, discussion and planning for the student's middle school program may begin as early as third grade. Similarly, career exploration should be the topic of programming as early as sixth grade.

An example of this issue once occurred in a MTM. The student, a 16-year-old girl diagnosed as mildly retarded, had been living at home since birth. She had progressed to the point where she could help her mother with many household chores. When a team member discussed the option of placing the girl in a group home, the mother was shocked. She resisted any change in her daughter's program. Nobody had ever spoken to her about the possible options that would be open, and it seemed that for years she had been talking herself into the "reality" that her daughter would be living with her all of her life.

Long-term goals are necessary to any student's educational programming, and these goals can be flexible. Regular education students have these goals already instituted for them as part of the ongoing system. It seems obvious that special education students should also receive this planning.

***Provide Specially Designed Instruction.*** An important tenet of P.L. 94-142 defines special education as specially designed instruction. The major stress in education since P.L. 94-142 was first enacted by Congress has been to provide access to programs for handicapped children and youth. Phrases such as "free and appropriate public education" and "least restrictive environment" have been used as slogans to ensure the right to education for students with special needs. Needless to say, access is a concept that is integral to the implementation of P.L. 94-142. However, it would seem that it is now time for the concept of specially designed instruction, also stated in P.L. 94-142, to be stressed. For example, Reiher's (1992) research detected a weak "diagnostic–instructional link" between the IEP and the classroom.

Special education classrooms were not intended to be miniature regular education classrooms, yet, upon visiting many such classrooms, one would be hard put to identify anything "special," adding valuable fuel to the total inclusion argument. MTMs should lead to multidisciplinary programming (see Gallivan-Fenlon, 1994). The team's work is not complete when an IEP is devised that specifically delineates what services the student will receive in special education that are not available in regular education, especially in the case of disturbed and disturbing youth. If remediation cannot be planned for these students, educators are in effect excluding the students from regular education without any specific special education exit criteria except, perhaps, that "the student will behave in a more socialized fashion." For an IEP and a team to have any meaning, specific programming based on the child's deficiencies should be planned. Even for students with EBD, instructional goals on IEPs are twice as likely to be academic as social/affective/behavioral (Reiher, 1992). Perhaps Reiher (1992) said it best when he concluded, "When one considers the amount of time, the number of highly trained personnel, and the large sums of money that are expended in this process, these data demonstrating a lack of congruence become a sad commentary" (p. 176). The obvious desired outcome is behavioral change, and the means to achieve it could be an intervention chosen from the myriad that are currently available, or from one of the three types (behavioral management, moral development, rational-emotive therapy) examined in this text.

## Summary and Conclusions

A variety of issues confront school personnel who attempt to effectively serve children and youth with emotional and behavioral disorders (McIntyre, 1993; Rizzo & Zabel, 1988; Simpson, Myles, Walker, Ormsbee, & Downing, 1991). Progress in dealing with each of the issues discussed in this chapter (and many others as well) is directly associated with educators improving their skills and knowledge in engaging in utilitarian preassessment activities, making appropriate referrals for service, and conducting accurate and timely student evaluations. Moreover, the success in these activities and ultimately in multidisciplinary team meetings is a basic step to adequately meeting the needs of students with EBD and other students who experience problems of behavior and affect.

This chapter examined the special educator's role in the placement process. An effort was made to explain to the reader the sometimes subtle differences between placement (where the student is located) and programming (the education plan for the student). Also discussed were the multidisciplinary team meeting (MTM) and five guidelines that can serve as goals for the placement of students. Research was reviewed to highlight the efficiency of group decisions over individual decisions, the perceived influence of the MTM members, and the goals of the MTM, in order to more fully understand the dynamics of this very important procedure. A mock placement exercise was presented to illustrate a MTM and the problems that may be inherent in it.

Five administrative factors or considerations were discussed that were developed by Cawley (1977) and modified to provide consistency among MTMs and to facilitate the actual MTM process in meeting the goals of P.L. 94-142. These factors were (a) that the learner attends (and learns) all day, which suggests that academic, behavioral, and emotional programming must be appropriate in each placement option, consistent with the least restrictive environment concept; (b) that the learner is one of many students, which suggests that the other students, and perhaps the entire milieu of the classroom, should be taken into consideration before placement is made; (c) that educational practices differ at the preschool, elementary, middle, and secondary levels, which implies that the affective and cognitive requirements of the institutions themselves and how they may influence placement must be examined; (d) that the learner's education is preschool through secondary, so that schooling must be considered a long-term developmental process rather than one that consists of a series of 1-year behavioral objectives; and (e) that an important tenet of P.L. 94-142 defines special education as specifically designed instruction, which implies that the purpose of special education is more than access to classes—it includes prescriptive, appropriate remediation.

# 4

# Classroom Management: Instruction, Paraprofessionals, and Parents

*Paul Zionts and Patricia Daly*

Classroom management has many dimensions. Unfortunately, most seminars and inservices focus only on rules and consequences. Teachers flock to these sessions looking for the miracle solution to their classroom woes. There are no miracle cures. Although these topics are important, to suggest that they encompass the totality of how a classroom is managed is shortsighted. To be effective in the classroom requires time and hard work. This chapter examines the components of teaching that have an enormous impact on the behaviors of students with emotional and behavioral problems: instruction, working with paraprofessionals, and communicating with parents.

## Instruction

Whether disturbing behaviors lead to academic underachievement or vice versa is unclear (Kauffman, 1981). Much of the confusion may be due to the methodology of the research that has been conducted in this area. In many investigations, students who exhibited disturbing behaviors in the classroom were observed and rated, and generalizations about those behaviors were developed for instructional purposes. However, specific observations of the classroom's instructional methodologies and how they relate to disturbing behaviors have been rare. In a study by Thompson, White, and Morgan (1982), 12 third-grade teachers were observed; not surprisingly, most of their classroom day was spent interacting with disturbing children. Thus, much of their time was devoted to procedural and behavioral activities rather than to academic instruction. Another aspect to consider is that many plans for students with emotional and behavioral disorders (EBD) focus on eliminating inappropriate behaviors rather than teaching new desired behaviors (Neel & Cessna, 1993b).

One of the most important factors of any classroom management schema is that of instruction. According to the Chesapeake Institute (1994), students with serious emotional disturbance have lower grades than any other groups of students with disabilities. They more frequently fail courses and minimum competency examinations than do other students with disabilities; they also are retained at grade level more often at the end of the school year. The obvious dilemma with regard to instruction is the question of whether the students' primary disability of emotional and behavioral problems is getting in the way of learning or whether secondary learning problems are also in evidence. Whatever the social reasons for full inclusion, evidence seems to be mounting that students whose academic needs are unmet will fall further behind in the general education setting (Parmar, Cawley, & Miller, 1994). For example, Kinder and Bursuck's (1993) review found an absence of students with EBD in history classes. Consequently, it is not unbelievable that students with EBD lack even the most basic history knowledge.

In fact, little research has been done on what works well with students who have EBD in the general education environment (Ruhl & Berlinghoff, 1992). For a general education placement to be appropriate, teachers need to learn how to continually challenge these students and still understand that they will not learn at the pace of others. The concept of specially designed instruction, integral to P.L. 94-142, must be reinvestigated and perhaps redefined in the 21st century. Will students with disabilities have their instructional needs met in the general education content setting?

Another dilemma is the focus of the curriculum. Students with EBD need to understand their disability and the world (home, school, community, and society) around them. One of the most frequent problems in teaching students with EBD is keeping them on task. If teachers can help students stay on task as much as possible, it would follow that it would be more difficult for them to be off task. The research and literature is adamant in its claims that teachers and their teaching methods do make a difference (Berliner, 1988; Brophy & Good, 1986; Christenson, Ysseldyke,

& Thurlow, 1989). Lower achieving students who are on task less time actually have less teacher time than others in the classroom (Greenwood, Arreaga-Mayer, & Carta, 1994). If students with disabilities are to be successful in the general education setting, they probably need to be able to listen to lectures, take notes, take written assignments, read from textbooks, and take tests (Putnam, 1992).

Other philosophical decisions also must be made. A familiar dictum is that special education students need structure. Almost all management plans call for very structured environments because students do respond well to them. Howard-Rose and Rose (1994) found that students who were in special education settings (as opposed to those in general education classrooms) were encouraged to self-monitor, self-evaluate, and be more accountable for their class work. Although these are admirable goals, they may come into conflict with the world outside of the special education classroom. Because the real world is not structured, if students with EBD are going to learn to succeed, then they have to learn in an unstructured environment.

This section on instruction is based on the literature on students who have learning problems because similar research has not been reported for students with EBD. This tact does not suggest that students with various disabilities are identical (see Scruggs & Mastropieri, 1986) or that their teaching needs are the same (Kauffman & Wong, 1991). Nevertheless, students with EBD, mental retardation, and learning disabilities are currently being taught in similar manners (Ysseldyke, Christenson, Thurlow, & Bakewell, 1989). This finding, however, does not suggest that these students are necessarily getting their needs met. One would not expect that students within any disability category, much less across disability categories, have the same strengths and weaknesses. Therefore, readers should be cautioned about any information they read or hear that is based on research but is generalized inappropriately. Although Cawley and Parmar (1992) were referring to arithmetic, their comments were appropriate to all instruction: "Should we continue with our present practices that attempt to teach traditional arithmetic in fairly routine ways and change the cognitive status of the children so they may respond more effectively? or Should we consider changing the format of arithmetic to bring forth a renaissance in teacher behavior, curriculum and instructional organization and cognitive processing on the part of the child?" (p. 6). This chapter is an attempt to undertake the latter challenge.

Because students have different levels of competence within a classroom, teachers must employ different methodologies to meet their students' specific needs. The choices educators must make are apparent. Teachers may group the students whenever possible to afford more relevant instructional time. Alternatively, they may provide the students with less instructional time and, in turn, expect them to do meaningful work, be challenged, and not disturb others when they are having difficulty or are bored with busywork.

While planning more instructional time, the issue of *quality* teaching should not be ignored. One approach to careful planning is to take into account the learner's own purposes and goals of education. Jones and Jones (1981, pp. 41–50) listed 10 academic needs of students that should be considered in planning:

1. *The need to understand the teacher's goal.* Part of the student's IEP [Individualized Education Program] can be sharing the long- and short-term goals of the learning experience. This process may also help to keep the teacher on task.

2. *The need to be actively involved in the learning process.* Students tend to learn more from experiences than they do from lectures or reading.

3. *The need to relate subject matter to their own lives.* It is suggested that teachers inventory their students to determine their actual interests. For example, a common misconception is that students enjoy reading about the things they like to do (e.g., basketball or driving a car), but research has been scarce in support of this contention.

4. *The need to follow their own interests.* It is clear that much of the curriculum taught in school is inappropriate to many students, handicapped or not. This discrepancy revolves around what educators feel students *need* to learn and what students aged 16 to 18 *want* to learn. A compromise should be attempted between these two concerns.

5. *The need to experience success.* Life has its frustrations, and total avoidance of them will ill prepare students to cope with the many problems they will encounter. Lessons should be properly planned at a level that is both challenging and attainable. If the work is too difficult and failure becomes a minor pattern, the assignments should be modified.

6. *The need to receive realistic and immediate feedback.* Much of the research suggests that learning can be facilitated when students know in which areas they are doing well, because this is motivating. Furthermore, remediation can be attempted, especially in developmental tasks, before the failure is compounded.

7. *The need for the appropriate amount of structure.* Disturbed and disturbing students seem, at least initially, to need more guidance than other students. Too little structure can create anxiety, and too much may be stifling to the students.

8. *The need for time to integrate learning.* Piaget (1963) provided evidence that assimilation and accommodation are needed for a student to truly learn new information. Heaping activity after activity upon the students may confuse them and give them little time to fully understand the concepts.

9. *The need to have positive contact with peers.* Special attention should be paid to the setting in which this contact is established. When students are supposed to be attending to schoolwork, peer contact is not desired. Specific times for interaction should be determined, perhaps during science or sports or through group discussion.
10. *The need for instruction matched to students' cognitive development and learning styles.* This factor is as important as prescribing relevant content for students. Even those students not diagnosed as learning disabled have strengths and weaknesses with regard to their most appropriate learning style.

Instructional procedures, as well as the time scheduled for instruction, seem to have an effect on the prevalence of disturbing behaviors (Reith, Polsgrove, & Semmel, 1981; Reith, Polsgrove, Semmel, & Cohen, 1980). It has been found that the more instructional time allotted, the greater the amount of learning that occurs, leading to less time for disturbing behavior to be exhibited. The investigators recommended that the affective and academic components of the curriculum be combined to enhance the students' learning experiences. (Units 2 and 3 of this text attempt to illustrate how this combination may be accomplished.)

Learning the concept of instruction as integral to classroom management is difficult for teachers because they often can recite the important theories and principles, yet when they are in the "trenches" they find it difficult to use them (Algozzine & Ysseldyke, 1992). Although the research on instruction has been almost exclusively on students with learning disabilities and mental retardation, indications are that students with behavioral disorders also respond well to good teaching (Scruggs & Marsing, 1987).

Instruction is a multifaceted concept. Algozzine and Ysseldyke (1992), for example, divided the components of instruction into (a) planning, which is deciding what and how to teach as well as how to communicate realistic expectations; (b) managing, which is preparing, using time, and establishing a positive environment; (c) delivering, which is presenting instruction, teaching thinking skills, motivation, feedback, practice, and modifying instruction; and (d) evaluation, which is checking for understanding, engaged time, and progress, and using data to make decisions.

## Teaching Skills and Content

Teaching students to read and compute has encompassed the traditional special education job description. If the movements of mainstreaming, Regular Education Initiative, and inclusion have taught the field anything, it is that the traditional special education job description needs to be reformed. Regardless of age or grade level, students need to learn about the world around them. Reading and computation skills taught in isolation do little to prepare students for the real world, especially if taught in the general education classroom. Parmar and Cawley's (1993) review of the research suggested that special education students do less well than general education students in content areas than in skill areas. Science, for instance, is not generally taught in the special education setting. Students with mild disabilities do much better when instruction is taught with a context (Scruggs, Mastropieri, & Sullivan, 1994). Students need to know how to apply these skills to content, to information.

## Recall and Reasoning

Learning specific skills is important. Methods such as direct instruction, precision teaching, and mastery learning have demonstrated success with helping students recall and practice instruction. These methods are excellent for students who need to learn specific steps of a process (see Gajria & Salvia, 1992). However, and perhaps due to the success of this process, the importance of integrating skills with other processes has been ignored. For example, Dowis and Schloss (1992) found that students did less well when rules and skills were taught separately from the writing process. Also, many students with handicaps who are integrated in the general education setting have comparable computation skills, yet they are far behind with regard to their understanding of basic skills (Parmar, Cawley, & Miller, 1994).

Cawley and Parmar (1992) presented the issue well when they remarked that in current arithmetic instruction, teachers commonly teach students "a routine and [give] a large number of problems to apply that routine to in a relatively short period of time" (p. 7). They further stated that "The most striking aspect of the concern with computation is not so much that, day after day and year after year, children with handicaps can be observed using ditto sheets in rote- and drill-focused modes. What is most striking about these practices is that they reinforce, if not develop, a kind of passive and rote response behavior" (Parmar & Cawley, 1991, p. 23). This type of learning allows very little actual decision making, yet educators implore students throughout their school careers to apply decision making that they are not expected to apply in their classroom activities.

Woodward (1994) contended that methods such as direct instruction stilts learning. Learning is more than words with definitions. It is thinking, probing, and reasoning. Students can generate their own explanations for phenomena and seem to do as well when called on to recall instruction (Scruggs et al., 1994).

## Learning Strategies

The idea that educators need to meet the instructional needs of students is "easier said than done." Although they focused primarily on students with learning disabilities, Deshler and Shumaker (1986) developed strategies designed to enhance their education. These strategies included matching instruction with curriculum demands, using a structured teaching methodology, deliberately promoting generalization, applying critical teaching behaviors, using scope and sequence in teaching, ensuring that teaching decisions are governed by outcome goals, maximizing student involvement, and maintaining a realistic point of view (e.g., understanding that no "single" intervention can serve as a panacea).

Many resources exist to help educators teach. For example, *Intervention in the School and Clinic, Teaching Exceptional Children,* and *Remedial and Special Education* are excellent journals that have many practical teaching ideas, such as using graphic organizers to help students learn content (Ellis, 1994), using a newspaper to teach students how to work collaboratively (Hetfield, 1994), or using the following steps to make a study guide (Lovitt & Horton, 1994):

1. Analyze the material to be read for both subject matter and level of difficulty.

2. Select the content to be emphasized during the lesson.

3. Decide on the processes that students must use in acquiring that content (e.g., comprehending the material with respect to literal, interpretive, or applied responses).

4. Consider students' abilities to read, write, listen, and organize in relation to the content and processes to be emphasized. Vary the structure of study guides with respect to question type, format, and method of implementation to increase chances that the effects of treatment will generalize.

5. Make the study guides as aesthetically pleasing as possible (e.g., avoid overcrowding the print). (p. 107)

## Behaviors That Enable Instruction

One theme that runs rampant throughout the literature is that little is known about what makes general educators effective with special education students (Brady, Swank, Taylor, & Freiberg, 1992) or, for that matter, whether they are more effective than special educators. Larivee (1985) suggested that effective teaching includes behaviors such as using little time for student transitions, asking questions that students will be able to answer, and presenting learning tasks for which students will have a high success rate. Research that enables instruction and increases time on task includes the following:

- Sufficient time allocated for academics (Christenson et al., 1989)
- A choice of tasks (Munk & Repp, 1994)
- A variety of tasks during the classroom period (Munk & Repp, 1994)
- Clearly presented lessons with specific instructional procedures (Christenson et al., 1989)
- Rapidly paced instruction (Greenwood et al., 1994; Munk & Repp, 1994)
- Reviewing instruction using adaptations of such games as Bingo, War, and Scrabble (Wesson, Wilson, & Mandlebaum, 1988)
- Active monitoring of student progress and understanding (Christenson et al., 1989)
- Feedback to the students (Greenwood et al., 1994)

Using mnemonics has recently been found effective with students with disabilities in the teaching of science and social studies content (Mastropieri, Scruggs, Whittaker, & Bakken, 1994; Scruggs & Mastropieri, 1992). The investigators found that both teachers and students enjoyed developing mnemonics.

## Teaching in the Content Areas

The emphasis of teaching subject matter content in general education has been increasing, even in the elementary grades. Teachers believe that there are pressures to cover content and cover it quickly (Vaughn & Schumm, 1994). One of the most important decisions that teachers may have to make is what information needs to be taught.

***Effectively Teaching Content.*** Christenson et al. (1989) identified four elements needed to ensure instructional clarity. The first element is reminiscent of direct instruction, mastery learning, and precision teaching, in that the teacher will *demonstrate* the concept, *prompt* the student through guided instruction and error correction procedures, and *practice* (practice, practice). More specifically, direct instruction has the following features:

1. Goals for students' learning are made clear;
2. Progress through tasks is carefully organized and sequenced;

3. The teacher clearly explains and illustrates what students are to learn;

4. The teacher frequently asks direct questions to monitor students' progress and checks their understanding;

5. Students are given ample opportunity to practice with prompts and feedback to insure success and to correct errors;

6. Students work with a skill until it is overlearned and automatic;

7. The teacher reviews regularly and holds students accountable for work. (Doyle, 1985, p. 61)

The second element of instructional clarity is "a well-organized, step-by-step instructional presentation that articulates *what* skill is to be learned, *why* the skill is important, *when* the skill is useful, and *how* to apply the skill" (Christenson et al., 1989, p. 24). The third element is that teachers need to check for student understanding (see later section on Cawley's, 1979, process regulator). Finally, it is imperative to use sound learning principles. For example, behaviors that enable teachers to gain student attention and use reinforcement techniques are examples of instructional practices that can facilitate teaching.

Special education teachers will frequently be called upon to help general educators adapt material for students with disabilities. Nolet and Tindal (1993) suggested that content area teachers identify the content, complete with attributes and examples, that they view as critical, and then special educators can help with the delivery of this information. Chalmers (1991) presented the following ideas that may be recommended for the general education teacher who has students with learning problems:

1. Preteach vocabulary and preview major concepts.
2. State a purpose for reading.
3. Provide for repetition of instruction.
4. Provide clear directions and examples.
5. Make time adjustment.
6. Provide feedback.
7. Have students keep an assignment notebook.
8. Provide an alternative assignment.
9. Read orally.
10. Allow manipulatives.
11. Highlight textbooks. (pp. 41–42)

A quick review of these hints should serve as a useful reminder that all are appropriate for most students in any classroom setting. Good special education is good general education, and vice versa.

***Some Problems with Current Modes of Instruction.*** Textbooks are the primary mode of instruction in the general education environment, and the assignments and tests are not exactly "friendly" for those with learning problems (Kantor, Anderson, & Armbruster, 1983; Kinder & Bursuck, 1993; Lovitt & Horton, 1994; Parmar, DeLuca, & Janczak, 1994; Putnam, 1992; Woodward, 1994). The following is a common general classroom experience: "instruction . . . is delivered by teacher lectures and demonstrations. Students are passive rather than active learners, working independently rather than in groups. . . . Textbooks militate against the full participation of students with disabilities because many of these students have reading difficulties. . . . The paper and pencil format of the textbook denies students with disabilities access to the content and processes of science, and it denies them opportunities to demonstrate knowledge and process competencies in evaluation. . . . In effect, thinking as an act of pondering, reflection, and the analysis of options and outcomes is infrequent" (Cawley, 1994, p. 69).

Textbooks rarely provide teachers with specific teaching ideas to meet the needs of students with disabilities, and many teachers use publisher-provided tests for all students (Putnam, 1992; Schumm, Vaughn, Haager, & Klinger, 1994). Lovitt and Horton (1994) provided the following ideas to adapt the traditional instruction that is associated with textbooks:

1. Modify only textbook chapters or passages within chapters that have proven difficult for students or that clearly lack organization.

2. Collaborate with other teachers who use the same text by dividing the modification load and sharing materials.

3. Use curriculum-based assessments prior to instruction to determine which students can interact with the text at an independent level and which students will need materials modifications.

4. Computerize the materials adaptation process by using commercial software, thereby developing a continuous store of materials.

5. Encourage general and special education teachers to co-teach certain subjects and to modify the materials cooperatively.

6. Urge teachers, through textbook adoption committees, to demand that textbook publishers offer study guides, graphic organizers, vocabulary exercises, computer programs, or other adaptations of material in addition to basic textbooks and supplementary materials. (p. 107)

## Thematic Units

The focus on differences rather than similarities has clouded the teaching of students with disabilities. It seems that, in educators' attempts to individualize, curriculum has been weakened so that all students can learn. The consequence of this action may be the lessening of student interest. Educators have forgotten that good instruction may very well result, and probably should result, in different student outcomes. Furthermore, the efficacy research on teaching students "one-to-one" as a primary mode of instruction *is not convincing.* In fact, group instruction is usually more effective because it provides more contact with the teacher, as well as collaborative and observational learning (Polloway, Cronin, & Patton, 1986), although "grouping" students without careful monitoring can have negative effects (Bickel & Bickel, 1986). If it is important to deliver information, then the opportunity to learn must be present.

Most instructional units are traditionally presented as content oriented. Cawley (1994) suggested that an additional layer of principles should also be included. These principles (e.g., justice) can help teachers explain the content. It is also evident that the curriculum of many students with disabilities should differ in certain ways from the traditional curriculum. A life-skills or functional curriculum approach can fit within the theme format. Functional (or any other) curriculum should include considerations of *assessment,* or what the students need or want to learn; *design,* or how this information will be used in their lives; and *teaching,* or how instruction will be used (Weaver, Landers, & Adams, 1991). Clark (1994) suggested that the following should be considered when developing a functional curriculum:

- Is the instructional content of the student's current educational placement appropriate for meeting the student's personal-social, daily living, and occupational adjustment needs? That is,

- Does the content focus on necessary knowledge and skills to function as independently as possible in the home, school, or community?

- Does the content provide a scope and sequence for meeting future needs?

- Do the student's parents think the content is important for both current and future needs?

- Does the student think the content is important for current and future needs?

- Is the content appropriate for the student's chronological age and current intellectual, academic, or behavioral performance level(s)?

- What are the consequences to the student of not learning the concepts and skills inherent in the current educational placement? (p. 37)

Educators working with students with learning problems should also consider teaching strategies that will help deliver the content and principles. Although there are many learning strategy presentations, one relatively easy program to implement is that designed by Cawley (1979), which can be described as the process regulator.

## Cawley's Process Regulator

The following examination of learning styles is only one of many currently being developed. Its inclusion in this chapter, along with its mathematical application, serves only as an example of exemplary work in progress. Cawley (1979, 1985) proposed the use of a process regulator, a 16-interaction instructional model to facilitate the teaching of content. According to Cawley, learning styles incorporate both input (how the student receives the information) and output (how the student communicates the information). These interactions may be grouped under five categories:

1. *Manipulate* (M). This consists of the manipulation of the learning environment through movements, expressions, or actions. Either teacher input or student output can be manipulated.

2. *Display* (D). Pictures of three-dimensional objects are shown to the student. Numerals, letters of the alphabet, and other symbols cannot be presented. Presenting occurs only through teacher input.

3. *Identify* (I) (output only). Students are to point to or mark the appropriate answer, that is, one option of two or more choices.

4. *Say* (S). The verbalization of content that can be either teacher input or student output.

5. *Write* (W). Letters, numerals, and other symbols that convey messages on paper. (Note the differences between "Display" and "Write.")

---

### Window on Reality

A common misconception of learning styles is demonstrated by teachers who try to teach to the "visual," "kinesthetic," or "auditory" learner. Although many students may learn best visually, they may not communicate their information best through the visual mode. In fact, they may communicate best through one of the other three outputs. A good teacher may inaccurately assume that auditory learners should take oral tests when a multiple choice test may serve them best. Remember, according to Cawley's (1979, 1985) model, there are 16 possible interactions to use.

As shown in Figure 4.1, teacher–student interactions can be recorded on a grid to help a teacher understand what interaction types he or she encourages in the classroom. Most teacher–student interactions that occur in classrooms are S/S, S/W, W/W, and perhaps W/I. Inviting teachers can increase the types of interactions used in each lesson and, by doing so, may more effectively meet the needs of all students (see Harding, Gust, Goldhawk, & Bierman, 1993). When some students in the classroom are learning primarily from particular interactions, other students can benefit at the same time because those interactions may reinforce the content for them.

To more fully demonstrate the concept of the process regulator (16 interactions), Table 4.1 shows how the same information may be taught using each type of interaction. Exposing students to the same content in 16 different ways enhances the possibility that they will assimilate that information.

Although Table 4.1 provides a simple example, almost any piece of information can be taught 9, 12, or even 16 ways. Repeating information via

|  | INPUT | INSTRUCTOR | | |
|---|---|---|---|---|
| OUTPUT | MANIPULATE | DISPLAY | SAY | WRITE |
| MANIPULATE | | | | |
| IDENTIFY | | | | |
| SAY | | | | |
| WRITE | | | | |

**FIGURE 4.1.** Grid for recording teacher–student interaction categories.

**TABLE 4.1**
**Using Cawley's Process Regulator Model to Teach Addition of Single-Digit Numbers**

| Interaction | Instructor | Learner |
|---|---|---|
| M/M | Takes two objects from box. | Takes two objects from box. |
| M/I | Takes two objects from box. | Chooses the numeral 2 when given the options 1, 2, and 3. |
| M/S | Takes two objects from box. | Says "2." |
| M/W | Takes two objects from box. | Writes "2." |
| D/M | Shows picture with 2 objects. | Takes two objects from box. |
| D/I | Shows picture with 2 objects. | Chooses the numeral 2 when given the options 1, 2, and 3. |
| D/S | Shows picture with 2 objects. | Says "2." |
| D/W | Shows picture with 2 objects. | Writes "2." |
| S/M | Says "Take 2 objects from box." | Takes two objects from box. |
| S/I | Says "Choose the the number 2." | Points to number 2 when given the options 1, 2, and 3. |
| S/S | Says "What is 1 + 1?" | Says "2." |
| S/W | Says "Write the sum of 1 + 1." | Writes "2." |
| W/M | Writes on paper, "Bring the teacher 2 objects." | Takes two objects from box. |
| W/I | Writes on paper, "1 + 1 = 1, 2, or 3." | Writes "2." |
| W/S | Writes on paper, "1 + 1 = ___." | Says "2." |
| W/W | Writes on paper, "1 + 1 = ___." | Writes "2." |

*Note:* M = manipulate; I = identify; S = say; W = write; D = display.
From Cawley, J. F. (1980). *Mathematics and the handicapped: Emphasis on diagnostics training packet.* Presentation at Central Michigan University, Mt. Pleasant, Michigan, April 1980. Adapted with permission.

varied types of intereactions will merely serve as review for some students, whereas the process may be the only way that other students can understand the information presented. The reader should be cautioned not to assume that M/M, because it is the most "concrete," is the first interaction to use with each student. For some students, this interaction may be the most difficult.

# An Instructional Design for Teaching Students with Different Abilities

One method of increasing instructional time entails adopting a slightly different conceptualization of individualized instruction. As mentioned above, individualized instruction is often interpreted as one-to-one teaching; however, with this interpretation, if there are 10 students in a classroom at the same time, the average time allotted to each child would be 6 minutes per hour. If one student receives more teacher instructional time, obviously the others receive less. For students to obtain more instructional time, groupings of those with similar strengths and weaknesses *in each content area* should be attempted. Ideally, concepts can then be taught to the entire class, meeting each individual's needs in a general way. An hour of instruction could then be organized in the following manner:

| | |
|---|---|
| 9:00–9:10 | Introduce concept to entire class. |
| 9:10–9:25 | Work with "slower" group to reinforce instruction, review concepts, and go over examples. |
| 9:25–9:30 | Check the work of the "faster" group and start the "slower" group on seat work. |
| 9:30–9:40 | Work with the middle group on any problems they may be having. If work is progressing, expand on some points. |
| 9:40–9:45 | Check the work of the "slower" group. |
| 9:45–9:55 | Work with the "faster" group. Their initial assignment should be completed by now and teacher and/or students can lead a more divergent discussion. |

Note that this design requires organizational skills, time, and planning by the teacher. The increased teacher contact time (25 to 30 minutes per hour) is surely more beneficial to students than the traditional contact time (6 minutes per hour).

# Peer Tutoring

Many teachers expect students to know how to behave in the classroom. However, research suggests that some students "possess neither the basic academic skills to succeed in content area courses nor the requisite work-related habits to compensate for their academic skill deficits" (Maheady,

Sacca, & Harper, 1988, p. 52). One approach to teach these students is have their fellow students work with them.

Peer tutoring increases the opportunities for students to respond. It has been used for a variety of purposes, including oral reading, math facts, comprehension questions, and word lists (Delquadri, Greenwood, Whorton, Carta, & Hall, 1986). Hopefully, higher level activities can also be attempted, perhaps in a collaborative learning activity.

Peer tutoring has worked well with helping students in academics (Hogan & Prater, 1993; Maheady et al., 1988). Tutoring can also help students in the affective domain. A reverse-role tutoring program increased the tutees' perceptions of students with EBD (Shisler, Osguthorpe, & Eiserman, 1987). The authors recommended that instruction on similarities should be presented to general education students. Fowler (1986) suggested that teaching acceptable classroom behavior, assigning management roles, and teacher supervision and feedback should assure that occasions for learning can occur. Peer tutoring may benefit both the tutor and the tutee.

Morgan and Jensen (1988) offered the following guidelines for implementation of a peer tutoring system:

1. A period of approximately 30 minutes per day is required. Each student receives 10 minutes of tutoring and tutors for 10 minutes, and 5 to 10 minutes are spent counting points and posting results.

2. Tutor–tutee pairs for the week are randomly selected each Monday. The pair sit next to or across from each other. They begin a 10-minute session with one as tutor and the other as tutee when the teacher sounds a signal to begin. . . . At the end of the 10 minutes the roles are reversed.

3. During tutoring sessions, the teacher circulates among the students and awards bonus points for correct tutoring behavior. The teacher also divides the class into two teams. . . .

4. At the end of the second 10-minute session, each student counts the number of points earned as both tutor and tutee and calls out the grand total when the teacher calls his or her name. . . .

5. At the end of each week . . . the teacher may conduct a more intensive assessment of each student's progress on the skills from that week. (p. 312)

Cooperative learning groups allow the slower students to learn the skills that they need to complete activities. They allow the students to take responsibility for their own learning. Students who have been taught cooperative skills increase time on task, learn to care about other members of the group, and produce quality work. The group's composition, the length of the particular task, and the task difficulty must be considered for this process to work well (McKenzie, 1991). Cooperative learning is appropriate to use with special and general education students. Johnson and Johnson (1986) called this type of learning positive interdependence. They suggested that cooperative learning works best when groups consist of two to six students and when the teacher explains the task, sets up a goal, structures individual accountability, structures intergroup cooperation (with reinforcers), explains criteria for success, and specifies the desired behavior. Monitoring the activity must occur. Students can monitor themselves and each other, although teacher interventions may be necessary if inappropriate behaviors occur. Evaluation is twofold: on the group process and on the learning that took place.

## Self-Monitoring

One of the more attractive approaches described in the literature is self-monitoring because it entails less involvement by teachers. Major components of a self-monitoring program should include defining the behavior; teaching the behavior; teaching the student to self-monitor, practice, and choose a reinforcer; fading the intervention by increasing the time that the student may receive points; increasing the amount of work required prior to winning an award; changing the reinforcer from tangible to social; and evaluating its effectiveness (Burke, 1992; DiGangi & Maag. 1992). See the next chapter for a discussion of reinforcers and for how to use self-monitoring when dealing with inappropriate behaviors.

## Motivation

Regardless of the approach that teachers choose to implement, they must present the information in a manner that will invite and motivate their students. Motivation is influenced by knowledge of results, interest, relevance of activity, and success that is in line with effort (Cohen & deBettencourt, 1991). It should be modeled by the teacher. Curwin (1994) believed that teachers who truly love to teach can demonstrate motivation. He provided the following excellent advice:

- Remember why you wanted to be a teacher. Keep those reasons in mind every day you teach.

- Understand what you love to teach and what you don't. Teach more of what you love. Find ways to energize yourself for teaching what you don't love by using techniques and methods you enjoy or by teaching it in a way that the kids enjoy.

- Do at least one activity you love once a day, or once a period for secondary teachers. The special activities might only take five minutes of class time. On your way to school, focus on how much you are looking forward to teaching this activity.

- Ignore cynical teachers or administrators. Do not let them diminish your love of teaching.
- Strive to be a great teacher every day. Take pride in your profession and your ability to do it well. . . .
- Don't be afraid to show off. Let yourself go and be a ham every now and then for your students.
- Let your students know why you love teaching and why you love what you teach. Do this with energy and commitment, not preaching.
- Do the unexpected; surprise your students and surprise yourself. Make your classroom an event. Look forward to being there and do things that get your students to think, "I wonder what will happen next?" rather than "I wonder if I can make it through another class?" (p. 29)

Fuhler (1991) added that teachers should strive for relevance, give positive and negative feedback, allow students to make some choices, set high but manageable expectations, push students' boundaries, encourage activity and interaction, and encourage students to explore the world outside their classroom environment.

Certainly, many of the above suggestions are easier said than done. To implement them requires commitment, hard work, and constant self-evaluation. For example, with regard to self-evaluation, teachers will need to provide evidence that students are actively involved in planning: Are students setting personal and classroom goals for instruction? Do they do it collaboratively (in dyads or small groups), or is the teacher constantly presiding with a hidden curriculum? Are students asking questions in class?

---

### Window on Reality

Even though articles and books such as this plead for teachers to provide interesting content and literature, the reality is that no matter what teachers attempt, some students may complain of boredom.

There may be a variety of reasons for this boredom, including things the teacher is or is not doing, or other factors may be involved, such as these students' families may not hold education in high esteem, or perhaps the students simply do not care to learn.

Although doing so may be risky, educators should seek continuing evaluations by students, trusted peers, and supervisors. The teacher requesting evaluations should be explicit about what the evaluators are to observe and on what to provide feedback.

# Working with Paraprofessionals

Most teachers would be pleased when informed that a paraprofessional is being assigned to their special education classrooms. However, one of the tasks that few new teachers are prepared to do is to work with, supervise, and/or evaluate paraprofessionals (Boomer, 1980). Working in concert with another individual is not an easy task and has often been compared with marriage: "Just like marriages, effective collaboration as team members in a classroom or center involves many skills and efforts and is not likely to occur by accident or without deliberation" (Blalock, 1991). The only addition to the analogy of marriage is that it is probably more likely an "arranged" marriage, meaning that the two adults are often placed in the same environment by others with little regard to compatibility. Furthermore, research has suggested that paraprofessionals do not work independently (creating the need for more teacher planning) and do not necessarily make the special educator's job easier (Boomer, 1994). In fact, paraprofessionals may make or break the management of the classroom.

First-year teachers may find themselves involved in hiring or interviewing a paraprofessional despite having little competence in this important and far-reaching task (see Boomer, 1980, for some excellent interview questions). Also, these professionals most likely have had little training on how to work and communicate with each other. Although literature is available on "how to work with paraprofessionals," little efficacy research has been done on this information (Jones & Bender, 1993). The available literature has focused on the quality of relationships between the teachers and the paraprofessionals.

Communication will enhance any working relationship. "Effective teamwork, of whatever kind, requires well defined, but different, levels of responsibility" (Boomer, 1982). Blalock (1991) suggested listing specific duties that may take place on a daily or weekly basis. Starting and finishing times should be established, as well as appropriate in-classroom behaviors (e.g., in classroom to work, not to read paper, etc.). The teacher may have to teach the paraprofessional how to perform tasks. Paraprofessionals can help by working in the general education setting or allowing the special education teacher to do so. They also can help with communications to students' homes. Duties in other environments (e.g., bus, playground, cafeteria) should be outlined. Boomer (1981) suggested that on-the-spot communication is also necessary because of the frequent student and schedule changes. As for anyone else in the classroom, it is crucial that the teacher provide to the paraprofessional both positive and negative feedback that is specific and constructive.

Although the teacher will certainly be the primary person responsible for the classroom, the paraprofessional can make valuable contributions with regard to perceptions of student progress or any other ideas that may facilitate the classroom environment. Boomer (1982) suggested that paraprofessionals can also "help the teacher develop a more complete and accurate picture of the child" (p. 195). Furthermore, they can learn to teach the students new skills, such as direct instruction, behavior recording, and assessing (Jones & Bender, 1993). They can also assist in the many emergency procedures that may be part of the school or the classroom (see Chapter 5).

An important issue in teaching students with disabilities is that of confidentiality. Paraprofessionals need to understand that they cannot talk about the identities of the children who are in the classroom. This may be particularly difficult if they live in the same town as the school.

---

### Window on Reality

June, a first-year teacher, is taking a job where she is inheriting not only a classroom of 10 students with severe EBD, but also a paraprofessional with 10 years of experience in that particular room. This assertive, in fact aggressive, paraprofessional had a very close relationship with the previous teacher and is intent on keeping the classroom the same.

Unfortunately for June, this classroom also demonstrates much of what she has learned to be inappropriate (total reliance on skill sheets, free time, little self-responsibility). The paraprofessional is very upset with June's ideas and has told all who would listen about their differences.

What would you do if you were June? What kinds of open communication would best fit this situation?

---

Certainly, June has a worry in addition to her 10 students. Perhaps the best idea is to persevere and avoid Blalock's (1991) problems that might occur in a dysfunctional teacher–paraprofessional relationship: "(a) absence of job descriptions, (b) arbitrary and often inequitable assignment of general school duties, (c) excessive and unreasonable use of paraprofessionals as substitutes in special and regular education, (d) scarcity of time for joint planning, and (e) an occasional perspective (emanating from the principal) that paraprofessionals are not valued or important" (pp. 201–202). The consequences of these problems may be minor, or they may sabotage the entire classroom. To paraphrase Boomer (1981), instead of asking, "Now, what do I do with this person?" the question should be, "How can he or she best help me reach the goals of the classroom?"

## Working with Parents of Students with EBD

Teachers should develop and maintain working relationships with parents and families of students with EBD for several reasons. These include the need to develop in parents (a) an awareness of what the term *public educa-*

*tion* implies, (b) the understanding that the child develops and learns in an ecosystem and not in the isolation of either home or school, and (c) the fact that informing parents of and involving them in educational plans is mandated by law. It may also be fruitful to explore some of the reasons why some parents choose not to be involved. The nature of this involvement and the types of services offered by schools for families have changed radically in concert with the move to reduce residential placement and increase home-based treatment approaches for these students.

Four basic reasons exist for establishing links between teachers and families, as discussed in the following paragraphs.

1. *Legal mandates.* P.L. 94-142 and subsequently the Individuals with Disabilities Education Act (1990) mandate parental involvement in all stages of the process of identification of and educational intervention for students with EBD. To say that parents must be involved in these processes is not the same as saying they are skilled enough or knowledgeable enough to participate effectively. A large responsibility in any parent-teacher relationship is knowledge sharing. This is a two-way arrangement: Teachers must help parents to learn whatever they need to know in order to advocate for their child, whereas parents must share information about their child that is useful to teachers in program planning for the child.

A mistake that educators often make is thinking that, because parent involvement is mandated legislatively, involvement will necessarily occur. Many parents of disturbed or disturbing children wonder as to the extent of their involvement under the well-intentioned law that mandates such participation. Part of the problem of schools' not making the most complete use of parental involvement is the nature of the law itself. Although there are penalties for noncompliance with the law, it is difficult to ascertain exactly what constitutes noncompliance. Some school officials view their role regarding parents as simply one of disseminating information to them. In the loosest interpretation of the law, this will probably suffice as compliance. However, if one views the goal of team programming as that of truly helping children with EBD and their families, this dissemination in and of itself is woefully inadequate.

2. *Nature of EBD.* The complex nature of EBD, combined with the current view of the student as an integral part of a family system, leads naturally to the notion that the student cannot be treated in an isolated manner. Frequently, the families of students with EBD experience problems that reduce their potential to function as supportive environments. These problems may be financial, employment, social, housing, educational, and so on. Most teachers readily admit that the 5-hour school day, no matter how well organized or intensive, cannot counteract a seriously deficient home and family environment where the student spends at least three times as much time. Although it is unreasonable to expect teachers to radically change the home environments of their students, teachers can arrange, or at least provide information about, many services for families.

To determine what assistance is needed, teachers and families must have well-established communications.

3. *Potential for treatment extension.* Skilled teachers of students with EBD arrange complex behavior management programs for their classrooms. They manage behavior, teach behavior, and teach content. Teaching new behavior repertoires is time-consuming and requires expertise. Extending those repertoires to multiple environments and ultimately untaught situations is an important goal. This becomes more possible when other supporters of new repertoires, especially parents, become active. Behavioral interactions taught and practiced in school classrooms can be extended to appropriate home situations if parents know when and how to prompt and support them. This can be accomplished by parent training and workshop opportunities made possible by strong parent–teacher relationships.

4. *Parents want what is best for their child.* Parents, for the most part, believe they are doing what is best for their child. Most parents want school to accomplish certain goals to benefit their child. This is not to say that teachers and parents always agree on those goals or the means to accomplish them. When teachers believe that, at heart, most parents want their children to do well (however "well" is defined), they will acknowledge the need to work with those parents at least on those areas on which they agree.

Given these reasons, most teachers will be motivated to establish good parent–teacher relationships. It is most often in the hands of teachers to make initial contacts in this regard. What can be rather frustrating for enthusiastic teachers is lack of parent response to invitations to discuss progress or problems. Teachers need to be aware of some reasons for refusals by parents to participate in typical school contacts and not interpret those necessarily as lack of interest or poor parenting.

---

### Window on Reality

Typical good residential treatment programs for children and youth with EBD include family therapy or counseling as a requirement for residency of the child. Although the child receives extensive and intensive treatment while the family undergoes separate counseling, the nature of family interactions is changed in essential ways when the child with EBD is not living in the home. When the child returns to the family after such a program, it is frequently difficult to prevent the recurrence of old ineffective patterns of interaction between family and child. In other words, removing the child and treating the child and family separately has been found to be insufficient in many cases, because new family interaction patterns need to be taught to the family as a whole.

## Obstacles to Inviting Parent Participation

Major changes in family structures have occurred during the past 25 years. The full range of family arrangements is likely to be met by teachers in many school districts. Not everyone's life revolves around the standard school day. Families of students with EBD may have work schedule problems, lack of travel resources, and child-care needs that cannot be met in order for parents to attend school meetings. School personnel are becoming more sensitive to these considerations by arranging evening and off-campus communications. It may not be as easy for parents of a child with EBD to arrange for child care; however, some schools now organize student activities during teacher–parent meetings so the student can accompany parents. It may be necessary to use telephone communications for some families, but others may have no telephone service. Teachers need to use all their creativity to organize times and places of mutual convenience for family–school meetings. The bottom line is that some parents do not turn up because they cannot.

Many parents do not attend school meetings or functions because they do not have good memories of school themselves. For complex reasons they have lost faith in education. They feel ignorant whenever they try to communicate with teachers and they quickly stop trying. Some of these parents are angry at schools for how they were treated when they were students. Others may be angry because teachers have implied poor parenting skills on their part when discussing a child's behavioral or academic problems. They may feel this way particularly when they have a child with EBD if they are contacted by the school and local authorities only when there is a problem. They may feel let down by schools and teachers. Some parents feel teachers have no idea of what their lives are like and that teachers belong to different classes or races and simply would not understand.

Another reason for the inability of many schools and teachers to institute parent involvement programs is that such programs have emanated from the school to fulfill *its* needs rather than being a joint venture. McAfee and Vergason (1979) suggested that most school-oriented involvement programs have failed to consider that:

1. Parents are the single most important influence on the development of children.

2. People (parents) who are disenfranchised will not actively seek to support the organization (educational system); in fact, they generally will work against it in some way.

3. When the goals and values of two groups are incongruent, an active process must work between them to ensure that both groups will influence a final agreement if those groups have any desire to

produce a joint product (in this case parents and educators producing educated children).
4. Mutual agreements have some means of enforcement.
5. Merely teaching parents about education does not ensure their support.
6. Neither parents nor educators can be held solely *responsible* for the educational achievement of children.
7. Parental responsibility cannot be dictated, but it can be developed if American education is to be improved. (pp. 3–4)

These contentions listed by McAfee and Vergason are very real concerns and may be only the tip of the iceberg, because they fail to take into consideration the problems of involving parents who have children in high school.

Some parents do not attend meetings because, when they did at first, they did not feel welcome. Some teachers resist making teacher–parent relationships. They feel parents should let them do their job and interfere as little as possible in the process. These teachers certainly are not in the majority, but they do exist. Parents have the power to intimidate teachers and some do. Teachers have varied talents in their personal interaction skills. Some interact better with students than with parents. Some teachers feel poorly prepared to establish relationships with parents whose lives are very different from their own.

Clarizio and McCoy (1983) remarked about the possible disadvantages of actively involving parents. Choosing the "appropriate" approach is largely guesswork because research has not supported the value of any one program over another. The authors suggested that many training models are inefficient, in that they do not account for parental differences. Finally, the age-old issue that some parents simply will or do not want to become involved for a variety of reasons adds to the frustration of educators, especially after the parents initially indicate their willingness to participate in concert with the teacher. Alexander, Kroth, Simpson, and Poppelreiter (1982) noted a possible reason for this: "Another problem (with eliciting parental involvement) is that taking the child to therapy sessions, working with the child at home, and attending workshops and meetings take a large amount of time and energy, so that the parents have little time for themselves or other members of the family. The price of cooperation with the school may be paid at home" (p. 306). A major disadvantage of involving parents that is cited by teachers is that, despite the possible benefits, initiating contact with parents after working with students all day is both time-consuming and energy draining. Coupled with grading papers and lesson planning, it is little wonder that teachers question when their own private time begins (Jones & Jones, 1981). Teacher preparation programs carry a heavy burden to prepare new teachers and retain established teachers so they can begin and carry out the delicate process of making solid, workable parent contacts and then maintain them.

## Typical Parent–Teacher Contact Opportunities

The literature on communicating with parents suggests that a variety of negative feelings and behaviors occur when parents are told their child is handicapped. Although teachers need to know how to respond when parents react adversely, they also should realize that the need to tell parents does not happen every day.

Some parents of disturbed children may not be surprised that their child has been acting out in school, especially if the child also has behavior problems at home. Others may *seem* initially shocked because they believe that is the way they are supposed to act. Neither of these behaviors seems to have much bearing on whether the parents are going to be motivated and/or cooperative in efforts to institute a program for the child. Some parents *are* genuinely surprised that their child is having difficulties in the school, and their initial reactions may be quite harsh. Walker (1979) suggested that only half of the students who are behavior problems at school are also behavior problems at home. "Teachers should expect some degree of discomfort and defensiveness on the part of the parents whose children are experiencing problems at school. It is extremely important not to personalize parents' critical remarks" (Jones, 1980, p. 270). If both parties become upset, little progress will be made.

Marion (1981) discussed variables that may affect parental reaction. Frequently, the parents want to know if a genetic factor is involved in the problem; this usually is not the case in children labeled as emotionally disturbed. The social acceptability of the handicap is another important variable to consider—the label of "learning disability" is certainly more acceptable than "emotional disturbance" or "mental retardation." This is further substantiated by the lack of any national support group for parents of children who are emotionally disturbed, although groups exist for parents of children who have autism (Autism Society of America), mental retardation (Association of Retarded Citizens), and learning disabilities (Association of Children with Learning Disabilities).

Occasionally when parents are told that their child is emotionally disturbed or otherwise handicapped, they may go "doctor shopping" for an opinion that differs. Mercer (1981) reminded educators that there is a difference between doctor shopping and attempting to validate a label that has been placed upon the child. Should the parents frequent many doctors, one may infer that their intention is the former rather than the latter. Inherent in doctor shopping is the concept of denial. "Parents of children who do not experience emotional disorders until after they enter school (regular disturbance) are often more susceptible to denial. The child they see at home may be different from the child seen by the classroom teacher. The behaviors exhibited at home may be different from the behaviors that caused the teachers to be concerned" (Mercer, 1981, p. 275).

The educator is cautioned not to smugly think or assert to peers that "these parents are lying . . . covering up for their kids" or that "they don't even 'know' Joe." The parents may be telling the truth. Behaviors required in school (more abstract) are different from those required at home (more concrete).

---

### Window on Reality

Teachers should not stereotype parents. A forceful reminder of this occurred when one of the authors (Zionts) participated in a multidisciplinary team meeting in which he was told that Joe's grandmother was an alcoholic. Each time the counselor or psychologist had called her, she slurred her words and was incoherent. When Joe entered the special education class, a home visit was made and it was discovered that Joe's grandmother's face was half-paralyzed as a result of a stroke, causing her to slur her words.

---

Another parental reaction may be blaming someone else for the child's problem. Incriminated parties may include the classroom teacher, the school in general, or the student's peers. It is important when dealing with such parents to actively listen to what they are saying in hopes of defusing their emotions. This may be accomplished by presenting a calm professional manner and placing emphasis on the specific data (see Chapter 2) used to arrive at the label.

Parents may demonstrate or feel guilt, sorrow, grief or mourning, rejection, or withdrawal when told that their child is disturbed. It is extremely important that these feelings be expressed and explored; if not, secondary disturbances may surface (Fallen & McGovern, 1978). An example of this is when parents argue that their child is purposely *not trying* to behave or to read (Samuels, 1981). Kroth (1975) suggested that, following parental reaction, one should attempt to determine who "owns the problem." This owner may be determined to be the disturber (the child), the disturbed (peers, teachers, parents), or the situation (the interaction between these two). The question is whether the problem is with the child's behavior; overreaction to the child's behavior on the part of peers, teachers, and parents (perhaps exacerbating the situation); or the incompatibility of the two sides to the degree that disturbing behavior by the child results?

Regardless, it is crucial that teachers and parents get together. Occasions that provide opportunities or require parents and teachers to meet include the following:

- Referral for assessment
- Assessment process
- Scheduled conferences
- Special events (positive)
- Special events (negative)
- Parent-initiated contacts

The most formal of these are the first two. Parental approval is required prior to individualized assessment for identification or placement in special education. For EBD assessment, it is likely that parents will be interviewed. Parental input at this stage is vital. The experience parents have with the school during this process may be important for the potential of making a good teacher–parent relationship later. Scheduled conferences are also fairly formal as they usually have tight time constraints and meeting times to suit the majority.

A key opportunity to meet parents is the positive special event, which can be classwide, gradewide, or schoolwide. Some form of performance, presentation, or accomplishment is celebrated. It is usually attended by the students themselves and by as many family members as possible. When an event is for the class only, more time flexibility is possible. When gradewide or schoolwide, the focus is less likely to be on the special education aspect of the students. At this type of event, an additional advantage is the opportunity for parents to meet other parents.

### Window on Reality

In a residential treatment program divided into four units of 11 youngsters, each unit organized an Open House for families. The students cooked and froze food for several weeks prior to the event and participated in much of the organization. Volunteer workers assisted on the night of the Open House. Families were shown around the facility by their child "host," and special emphasis was placed on specific accomplishments in social and academic behavior. Charts of behavioral improvement were highlighted. Staff took opportunities to informally chat with family members.

Organizing such a special event is a risk. One important consideration is to establish some contingency plan for the student whose family promised to come but fails to arrive.

Many teachers are familiar with the necessity of contacting parents in the event of an emergency. When the student breaks a major school rule, runs away, smashes a window, assaults a faculty member, or injures a peer, the parent contact may provide the opportunity to discuss a problem that may otherwise not be faced.

Parent-initiated contacts, the final item in the previous list, are both cherished and dreaded by teachers. It is a good idea for the teacher to think through a plan of action for when an angry or frustrated parent turns up at the door during class time. Such a plan may include arranging a more appropriate time or scheduling a meeting, arranging for another member of the school staff to stay with the parent until the teacher has time to meet, or arranging an emergency supervisor for the class while the teacher meets briefly with the parent. Although it is important that parents feel welcome in the classroom, it is equally important that teachers set the boundaries for parents working in or visiting the classroom.

## Current Conceptualization of the Teacher–Parent Relationship

In line with the previous discussion of the current focus on working with the family instead of only the child with EBD, Friesen and Wahlers (1993) discussed the notion of "family support." Given the reduced emphasis on residential placement, more families are being asked to deal with their children with EBD in the home. Residential placements are becoming less popular for two reasons: (a) Residential treatment is extremely expensive (Simpson & Carter, 1993) and (b) there is an increasing recognition of the interactive nature of emotional and behavioral problems within the family structure. Family support is defined by the Federation of Families for Children's Mental Health (1992) as "a constellation of formal and informal services and tangible goods that are defined and determined by families. It is 'whatever it takes' for a family to care for and live with a child or adolescent who has an emotional, behavioral, or mental disorder. It also includes supports needed to assist families to maintain close involvement with their children who are in out-of-the home placements and to help families when their children are ready to return home" (p. 1).

Within this framework, a teacher's responsibilities change from communicator of information and builder of parent–teacher relationships to a much broader one. The problems encountered in the classroom are viewed within the larger family structure. Families of children with EBD have many needs beyond those of the child of focus, and many service agencies in a given community may need to become involved. Typically such social service agencies become involved but do not communicate with each other.

Families may be receiving assistance with finances, housing, transportation, and so forth, but no coordination of services exists. What is being proposed is central coordination of all the services a family needs. Consequently, the actual needs of a given family and how those needs will be met will be decided in large part with the active involvement of the family. P.L. 99-457, The Education of the Handicapped Act Amendments, passed in 1986, mandated the creation of the Individualized Family Service Plan, in which the specific needs of the family with a child who is handicapped are documented and a treatment plan developed that includes attention to these needs.

Epstein, Cullinan, Quinn, and Cumblad (1994) stressed the concept of "multidisciplinary networks of services" (p. 52) for families of youth with EBD to keep them in the home. Such plans are in essence family based, community centered, and comprehensive in nature. Interagency collaboration among all agencies contributing to the needs of a particular family is required. The provision of categorical services by individual agencies is no longer acceptable or desirable.

## Keeping Parents Informed: Reporting Pupil Progress

The teacher's responsibilities to parents do not end with pupil placement or with the development of the Individualized Education Program. Parents have the right to be kept abreast of their child's progress. Furthermore, if communication is truly a two-way undertaking aimed at providing maximum benefit to the child with EBD, parents and teachers must be cognizant of the progress being made within both settings—school and home. This will allow for coordination of and consistency in planning.

The mention of reporting pupil progress generally conjures up images of report cards and letter grades in the minds of most persons involved in education. Although this is the most universal form of reporting progress, it is not the only or necessarily the best method. In fact, a standardized report card may be inconsistent with the notion of an *Individualized* Education Program (IEP). This is not to suggest that report cards should be abandoned; rather, they should be viewed as only one component of a system for reporting pupil progress. Other components of such a system might include feedback on assignments, notes home, telephone calls, conversations at school functions, and parent–teacher conferences.

Probably the best method of reporting pupil progress is through properly structured parent–teacher conferences. Such meetings allow for exchanging information about the student and clearing up misconceptions about the student's program. Parents may ask questions about areas that might otherwise be unclear or misunderstood. The key to conducting meaningful conferences is planning. The following are some general considerations to bear in mind when setting up conferences:

1. Allow enough time to adequately discuss each student.
2. Be aware that some parents may have conflicts with the allotted times; they should be allowed to make appointments at other times.
3. Develop some structure or format for keeping the conference on-task and flowing.
4. Communicate in clearly understandable language, avoiding educational jargon.
5. Make the setting comfortable, but businesslike.
6. Allow for questions during the course of the conference, not only at the end.
7. Make provisions for parents who may have to bring young children.
8. Make provisions for parents who arrive early and have to wait for their appointment.
9. Be on time.
10. Have folders available containing representative samples of the student's schoolwork (parents who arrive early may examine these while waiting).
11. Be flexible, but make every attempt to follow the schedule.
12. If problem areas are identified, inform parents how they may help in resolving the problems.

These guidelines are only one facet of the planning process. Planning is also important in structuring the individual conferences. There are two basic questions to be addressed before meeting with the parents: "What information do I wish to impart?" and "What information do I wish to obtain?" Once these questions have been addressed, a specific format for conferencing can be developed. Table 4.2 provides an outline of the types of information that should be exchanged in a parent–teacher conference. Note that the items listed in the table are not all-inclusive; they are provided only as examples. Readers are encouraged to develop outlines of their own in conjunction with the table.

Families have complex needs and rarely in the categorical system of service provision is attention paid to the overall plan of assistance. When a vehicle for arranging this interagency collaboration and coordination of services does not formally exist in a community, schools may be the focal point for developing this. Schools may help by establishing a framework for such services to exist. These services include specific contact people within the school, designated information centers, and a concerted effort to involve teachers, students, and parents in an understanding of roles in the IEP process as well as a better understanding of diversity (e.g., disabilities and cultural differences).

**TABLE 4.2**
**Information Flow in Parent–Teacher Conference**

| Information to Impart | Information to Obtain |
|---|---|
| 1. Progress under the four areas of<br>    a. social development<br>    b. physical development<br>    c. emotional development<br>    d. intellectual development | 1. Parental expectations under the four areas of<br>    a. social development<br>    b. physical development<br>    c. emotional development<br>    d. intellectual development |
| 2. Attitude toward school | 2. Attitude toward school in the home |
| 3. Perceived potentials | 3. Parent's perception of child's potential |
| 4. Attendance | 4. Student's outside interest |
| 5. Teacher expectations | 5. How much freedom or restriction parent allows or imposes |
| 6. Grading system | 6. Influences in the home that may interfere with progress |
| 7. Student's learning style | 7. Behavior in the home |
| 8. Ways to improve | |
| 9. Behavior at school | |

Simpson and Carter (1993) elaborated on the types of services to be provided in a comprehensive family support plan, and their work is used extensively in the following section. The authors recommended that schools provide services to families in five areas: "community programs and services; informational services; advocacy and resource use; home and community parent and family training programs; and parent/family support, counseling, and consultation" (p. 22). Each is discussed below.

***Community Programs and Services.*** Parents and families of children with EBD often have complex needs, typically considered beyond the purview of schools, such as health, legal, housing, recreating, employment, and financial. It is suggested that either satellite offices from relevant agencies be put in schools or a referral system be set up so more than a name, address, and phone number is provided by teachers to families.

***Informational Services.*** A two-way system of informational services needs to be established between families and service providers. Families need access to jargon-free information available on programs and interventions, and all consultative and support services. Families need to supply information to service providers on developmental history, family goals and expectations, school history, and so forth.

***Advocacy and Resource Use.*** Although parents have considerable legal power in the process of getting services for their children, many need to be informed on how to use that power effectively. Parents need training on their rights and responsibilities and on how best to advocate for their child's needs with professionals.

***Home and Community Parent and Family Training Programs.*** Because the problems of children with EBD extend beyond the classroom to the community and home, if treatment programs are to follow these children, a vital method of doing so is to train parents in intervention techniques. This extends treatment from the classroom to the other environments the child inhabits. There is much evidence that such training can be effective—with adequate supervision—and the whole process improves home–school communications.

***Parent/Family Support, Counseling, and Consultation.*** After children and youth with EBD have been in highly structured residential programs where parent counseling was provided, and then they begin to attend public school, parents and families may continue to need general or specific (problem-related) counseling services. The school's role is not to be the direct provider of such services, but to procure these services for parents.

Parents' styles of interaction with their children may also change within the same family. Parents may be good with children and tough with adolescents (Jones, 1980). When children reach adolescence, it is not uncommon for the parents to be experiencing turmoil themselves. Jones (1980) and Lillie (1981) suggested that many of these parents are in their early 40s and may be going through career or marriage changes. The literature and research have only recently begun to examine the needs of this parent population. Therefore, before parental involvement is considered, the educators should examine the needs of the parents. Also, teachers need to understand some of the additional dynamics that may be occurring in the home:

1. Mothers and fathers are striving for self-fulfillment and self-esteem which seem to them to be more obtainable outside the home than inside the home.
2. The role identity of a father and a mother is unclear and vague.

3. Professional careers of mother and father, particularly in the early years of marriage, may cause high family stress.
4. What today's generation of parents learned about being a parent from their parents is difficult to apply in today's world. (Lillie, 1981, p. 92)

For another perspective of the needs of parents who have children with handicaps, Turnbull and Turnbull (1985) compiled a book written by parents titled *Parents Speak Out: Then and Now.* It tells succinctly of the struggles, both positive and negative, that these parents experienced while raising their children.

Simpson and Carter (1993) discussed the relationship between the extent to which families can participate in the educational process of their child and the specific characteristics of the families' capabilities and problems. Families can participate more or less depending on such variables as their interests, the severity of the child's problems, the impact of the child's problems on the family members, work availability and hours, and availability of respite care.

Also, if services are to be provided that meet the expressed needs of the family in a team format, the burden of training rests on all members of the team—the school, the family, and the service agencies. Simpson and Carter (1994) stressed the need for all team members to learn how to work with all other members. Communication and collaborative skills are important, as well as organization and flexibility.

To involve parents in the education of their child, the teacher must establish and maintain open lines of communication between home and school. True communication is often elusive, particularly when the communication is between an expert and a lay person. The teacher's language is often laced with jargon that is foreign to parents; instead of impressing their intended audience, teachers often confuse and alienate parents. Effective communication is not served by using language that is understood only by a select few.

In this society a basic fallacy exists regarding communication, which might be best illustrated with an example. Following a parent–teacher conference of which 30 minutes had been spent discussing the child's progress, potential, and problems, the teacher concluded with the statement, "Thank you, Mrs. Jones, it's been nice talking to you." People spend a great deal of time talking "to" one another, and teachers are probably more guilty of it than any other group, with the possible exceptions of politicians and lawyers. Talking "to" is not communication. If a person desires to be talked "to," he or she can turn on the radio. The fallacy is that people think communication is occurring when, in fact, it is not. Communication is not something that happens *to* an individual; it is something in which one participates or engages. According to Anderson (1972), communication is a symbolic interaction between and among people. The key term in the definition is *interaction*.

Another fallacy surrounding communication is that all participants *must* talk. The problem is that if communication is to occur someone has to listen. This may seem contradictory to the previous paragraph about interaction, but it is crucial that communication occur in an atmosphere where the participants feel they may interact. Ideally, there will be give and take, and all participants will contribute; however, everyone will not participate by talking a great deal. Hopefully, all will participate by actively listening to all other parties involved.

In summary, communication involves sending, receiving, and perceiving information. This is reasonably straightforward and seemingly simple; however, effective communication is complex. For it to occur there must be careful structuring by the facilitator, in this case the teacher. Consideration of the parents' philosophical and moral orientation is certainly integral to this structure.

## Summary and Conclusions

The concept of classroom management has to expand beyond the commonly accepted definition. Developing a rule system and expecting it to be the major factor in minimizing inappropriate behaviors is shortsighted. This chapter examined three critical factors that can enable the management of a classroom: instruction, working with paraprofessionals, and communicating with parents.

Teaching content to students with EBD has been amazingly absent in the literature and probably in the classroom. Keeping students actively engaged in learning is one way to ensure that they will remain on task and, more important, that they will learn information that will be useful to them.

One way to facilitate learning and teaching in the classroom is to develop a plan for working with paraprofessionals. Many classrooms of students with EBD have paraprofessionals. The techniques presented in this chapter are designed to help teachers and paraprofessionals work together so that students can learn.

To meet the needs of a child with EBD, teachers must establish good communication with the family. The complexity of EBD problems extends outside the classroom to the community and home. It is important that teachers understand where the parents are, what their strengths are, and what they can contribute to the educational process of their child at any given stage. Seeing the child with EBD as an element of an interactive family system requires the coordination of services to meet the complex needs of that family system. Schools may need to be the central coordinating agent for these services.

# 5

# Classroom Management: Social Skills, Setting, and Behavior

Thus far, this text has been expanding upon the six elements in Wood's (1979) definition of emotional disturbance in order to treat these elements as a framework for delivering a special education program for disturbed and disturbing students. Wood suggested that a programming element should be present in a good definition of emotional disturbance. The remainder of this chapter examines the implications of this sixth element: "Does the definition when operationalized provide the basis for planning activities that will benefit those labeled, such as needs assessment, individual assessment, program evaluation, etc.?" (p. 8).

Before any intervention can be effectively implemented, careful planning regarding aspects of classroom management should be considered, because an effective management program may be the only remediation a student with emotional and/or behavioral disorder (EBD) requires. A particular classroom management system may include or exclude certain students from a particular setting. For example, a student diagnosed as needing a structured behavioral environment may need to be excluded from an environment that frequently utilizes free-play therapy.

Although I developed the classroom management program discussed in this chapter, I culled many of its concepts from both classroom peers and the literature. The program is ecological and behavioral in nature and is intended to provide the educator with a structured classroom environment in which both teacher and student expectations are fixed. This program is intended to complement the two types of intervention that complete this text.

The most careful adherence to the principles and techniques discussed thus far may be rendered useless unless appropriate programming for the student is developed. Unfortunately, the workings of the referral, assessment, and placement processes are sometimes perceived as entities separate from programming; thus, when the student is placed in a special education classroom, a new process may begin that in fact duplicates much of the work already accomplished by the multidisciplinary team meeting (MTM).

It is difficult to suggest that a special education teacher can faithfully follow each Individualized Education Program (IEP) completed by the various multidisciplinary teams and still realistically expect to operate a structured, orderly classroom. The behaviors of the child may be attributed to a variety of etiologies, depending upon the philosophical orientations of team members, and therefore a variety of emotional and behavioral interventions may be prescribed. One has only to peruse many of the current textbooks in the field of educating disturbed and disturbing students to begin to grasp the number of options currently available.

Even the most intentionally inviting teacher (see Chapter 2) may have difficulties with classroom management. Kauffman and Wong (1991) suggested that "more effective teachers of students with behavioral disorders might be those who (a) can readily bring a student's behavior into line with their standards and tolerance, (b) are less demanding and more tolerant of the kinds of behavior that most teachers find unacceptable, or (c) will readily modify their standards and tolerance to accommodate the needs of any exceptional student" (p. 228).

The philosophy of a classroom should be to *prevent* maladaptive behaviors from occurring, rather than to simply react to them. I believe that a structured management system is integral to a successful teaching experience with disturbing students. This chapter briefly examines the social skills needed for students to behave in a school setting. A classroom design is offered that consists of the physical arrangement of the classroom, classroom schedules and routines, and behavioral management. The central purpose of this chapter is to provide the natural extension of the previously examined skills and procedures: referral, assessment, and placement. Its stress is on the classroom ecosystem that naturally includes a combination of the psychoeducational model with the observation of adaptive and maladaptive behaviors. The chapter has application for students who are in grades K through 12; however, these are not the *only* interventions that are appropriate for students. The cognitive and cognitive-behavioral approaches discussed in Units 2 and 3 are alternative models that may be integrated with this chapter or treated as separate entities. Programming allows the teacher to utilize the previous three chapters in a practical manner.

This chapter is divided into two sections: (a) characteristics of the classroom, which includes the teaching of social skills, the classroom structure, the physical arrangement of the classroom, and classroom schedules and routines, (b) behavioral management, which includes pre-rule setting, considering rules, presenting rules, developing consequences, administering positive consequences, administering negative consequences, level systems and token economies, and crisis intervention.

## Teaching Social Skills

Social skills training has been evident in many classes for students with EBD since the early 1980s. Perhaps the seminal article by Gresham (1982), who argued that students with behavioral disorders need more than simply to be placed among "normal" acting peers, provided the legitimacy needed to include social skills in the curriculum. Meadows, Neel, Parker, and Timo (1991) contended that social skills are related to "all aspects of students' lives: educational, social and employment" (p. 200). Reviews of the research demonstrate that the largest differences between students with mild handicaps and those with no handicaps were evident in the area of classroom survival skills. Furthermore, "children who exhibit social skills deficits experience both short- and long-term negative consequences, and these negative consequences appear to be precursors of more severe problems in adolescence and adulthood" (Gresham, Elliott, & Black, 1987, p. 78). Likewise, Schloss, Schloss, Wood, and Kiehl (1986) concluded from their review of the research that "social skill deficiencies may be the most critical deterrent to adult adjustment for behaviorally disordered youth" (p. 1).

Interestingly, various authors and speakers provide different definitions of social skills. Some describe social skills as getting along with others in social situations. Others define the term as classroom behaviors that students need to exhibit in order to become a member of the classroom. Still others may combine the two definitions to form a third definition. Strayhorn, Strain, and Walker (1993) listed the following skills as those that "promote harmonious relationships":

- noticing positive examples of behavior in another person
- giving immediate enthusiastic approval or thanks for positive behaviors in another person
- providing real-life and fictional models of kind acts
- taking pleasure in trying to make the other person feel good
- noticing the verbal and nonverbal indicators of another person's feelings

- listening empathically to the other person
- having conversations that are fun for both people
- playing well with another person
- modeling enthusiasm when participating in joint activities
- withholding unnecessary commands and directives
- giving clear directives when they are necessary
- making correct decisions about how much to expect and ask of another person
- giving fluent explanations of how to do tasks
- enforcing directives in a kind yet firm way
- ignoring trivial negative behaviors
- remaining calm and rational when the other does undesirable things
- deciding which negative behaviors to punish or reprimand
- using only humane punishment or reprimands
- not accepting invitations for a hostile argument with the other person
- listing options and choosing among them rationally when joint decisions are to be made (p. 16)

This list may be helpful to the reader as a resource when designing IEP goals for students. When students with behavioral disorders were asked to describe critical social skills, they disagreed with the perceptions of general and special education teachers. These students did not feel that "being of assistance to the teacher," "avoiding confrontations and problems with adults," and "disagreeing with adults in an acceptable way" were important skills for them to learn (Meadows et al., 1991).

In determining the specific skills that should be targeted for remediation, the teacher needs first to consider two questions: Are the skills valued by the students (or their teachers)? Are the skills going to contribute to students' success in the classroom setting? To ensure success, skills that are "easier to learn" should be attempted first. McConnell (1987) suggested that teachers should "select behaviors that will be maintained after the intervention is terminated; . . . that will generalize across settings or other behaviors; [and] . . . that will covary with specific social behaviors of peers" (pp. 254–255).

For social skills training to be successful, it should be conducted in a group setting. Having students model the appropriate behaviors has been an effective technique with teaching these skills (Carter & Sugai, 1988; Gresham, 1981; Knapcyzk, 1992). Even videotaped modeling was effec-

> **Window on Reality**
>
> After examining Strayhorn et al.'s list of social skills, the reader should list the skills that seem crucial for students with EBD. Are they the same skills as those that would be listed by general educators? Are they the skills that are expected to be demonstrated by general education students?
>
> When students are referred for special education services because of their emotions or behaviors, do the teachers consider the set of skills necessary for the students to function in the real world, or are they concerned with appropriate classroom behaviors? Perhaps, the reality is that the behaviors that general education teachers want to see altered are those that are disturbing and consequently in the way of their teaching or the learning of others.

tive as a training technique with juvenile delinquents (Thelen, Fry, Dollinger, & Paul, 1976).

Regardless of the specific program, the teaching of social skills seems to follow similar procedures. First, the skill is presented. It is defined, taught, and/or modeled. Next, the students role-play the appropriate behavior. Feedback and reinforcement (discussed later) are given to the students, and homework and generalization follow. Individual contracts may be developed to ensure that the new behavior is continued. Clearly, the most difficult aspect of social skills training is that of generalization. Sasso, Melloy, and Kavale (1990) used a structured learning approach with three students. They found that "training which uses modeling, role-playing, behavioral rehearsal, reinforcement, and self-recording can be effective in teaching skills which maintain over time and generalize to untreated settings" (p. 18). However, generalization did not occur readily. The same environmental cues are usually not available in general education settings.

Current research and literature have taken polar approaches to the problem of generalizing behaviors to different settings. Students are either taught specific social skills or taught to cognitively interpret and solve problems. A review by Coleman, Wheeler, and Webber (1993) identified the following components of most problem-solving training:

- Identify/define the problem.
- Generate alternate solutions.
- Anticipate consequences.
- Make a decision and evaluate it. (p. 26)

Their review of the literature also yielded strong support of this approach when students role-played or provided verbal responses to dilemmas.

Camp and Bash's (1981) *Think Aloud* program requires the student to ask, What is my problem? How can I solve it? Am I using the best plan? and How did I do? They provide graphics to make the process more inviting to the students. The goal of these programs is to teach students to think about their problems. If this process can be achieved, then perhaps the students will generalize the strategy to other problem-solving opportunities.

## Classroom Structure

The issue of degree of structure in the classroom transcends instruction: Unmanageable behavior can destroy the most carefully designed floor plan and the most careful adherence to routines, schedules, and instructional practices. Conversely, if these structural considerations are well maintained, behavior management may not be a problem. It has often been claimed that exciting educational programs, using as many interactions as possible, rarely produce children with behavior problems. This may be true for many of the students labeled disturbing.

To suggest that *all* disturbing behaviors are the result of teacher interactions is faulty reasoning. Students, either disturbed or disturbing, do not leave their home, community, or peer situations outside the door when they enter the classroom. Many students who are disturbing and/or disturbed may be so as a result of never having learned appropriate school and social behaviors. The remainder of this chapter presents (a) an educational–behavioral system designed to identify and remediate maladaptive classroom behaviors and (b) a behavioral management rules system for the everyday operation of the class.

### Classroom Characteristics

Few teachers have the luxury of time to adequately prepare a classroom management program. The characteristics of their room may change often during the year. Nevertheless, knowing and planning for all variables possible will allow teachers to do their best so that they may prevent inappropriate behaviors from occurring. For example, the information in this chapter may have to be modified depending upon the number of students expected in each class and the numbers teachers might expect to reach during any given year.

Specific information regarding students' ages, grade ranges, and types of disabilities is crucial in order to adequately plan. Approaches and both affective and academic content will differ if students have mental retardation, learning disabilities, and/or EBD. Will adults such as paraprofessionals, student teachers, or volunteers be assisting in the classroom? The dynamics of their presence must be considered.

## Physical Arrangement of the Classroom

An often-ignored dimension of preventing behavior problems is the physical arrangement of the classroom (Rich, 1982). The structure of the room should be planned in a manner to meet the educator's instruction-related goals. If these goals include allowing the student the space to work uninterrupted, as well as the ability to "take a break" from seat work while not necessarily being distracted by peers or distracting them, a careful floor plan should be devised. Figure 5.1 shows a floor plan that could be used for either elementary or secondary school students. It is uncluttered and there is ample space between desks. The desks are in rows to avoid the interaction that may occur in round table settings. The purpose of the learning table in the back of the room is twofold: to provide for small group and individual interaction and to allow the teacher to observe any inappropriate student interaction.

On each desk is a portable "office," similar to a carrel. Depending on the fiscal condition of the educator's school district, these may be either purchased or constructed by the teachers *and the students* (if it can be made by the teacher, it certainly can be made by the students!). Sturdy cartons like those found in bookstores or cafeterias can be cut and spray-painted white. A student schedule and a clock with moveable hands are placed on the inside of the office (secondary students may have a calendar instead of a clock). Otherwise, the students may decorate these offices as they see fit. The teacher might tell the class that the rule of thumb with regard to "good taste" is for each student to ask, "Would the principal or my parents mind seeing that?"

If each student has a permanent desk, the office can be attached to it. If not, when not in use, the office can be placed to one side of the room, and the teacher can attach to it both work that needs to be corrected and work that has been checked by the teacher. The students can remove the offices from their desks or move to the sides of their desks for discussions and class participation. When students are seated in their offices, any attempt to disturb peers would be easily observable because the student would have to move a chair or stand up. The benefits of having offices include allowing the students to "own" part of the classroom; something in the room is their property.

Other students are not allowed in a student's office without permission. Furthermore, the office gives the students quiet space in which to work. If students choose not to work at their desks, they may move to alternate private offices (see offices 3–8 on the floor plan in Figure 5.1; utilization of private offices 1 and 2 on this floor plan is discussed in the later section titled "Behavioral Management Rules System"). Occasionally, teachers of secondary students suggest that this office concept would be rejected by their students as infantile. One alternative could be to use traditional desks

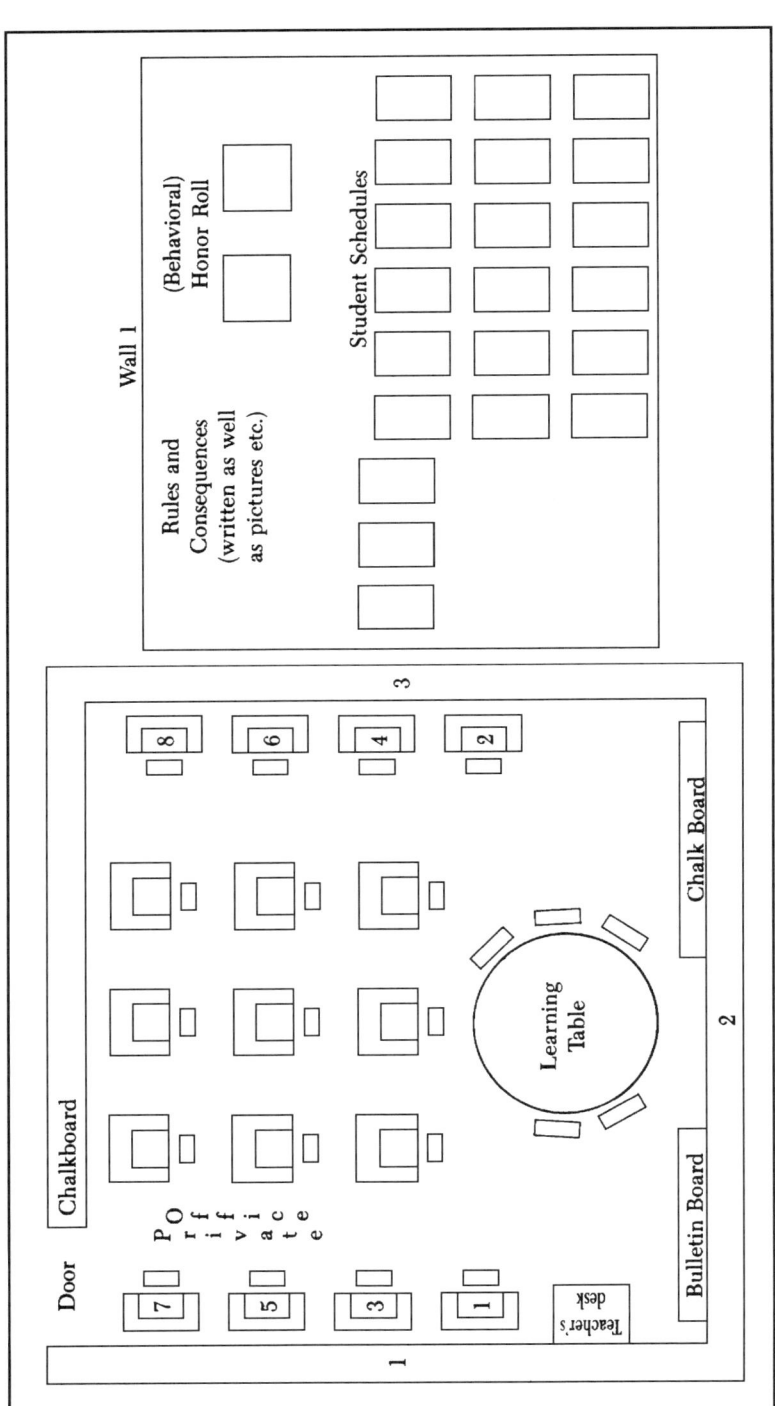

**FIGURE 5.1.** Sample school floor plan for disturbed and disturbing students.

*(continues)*

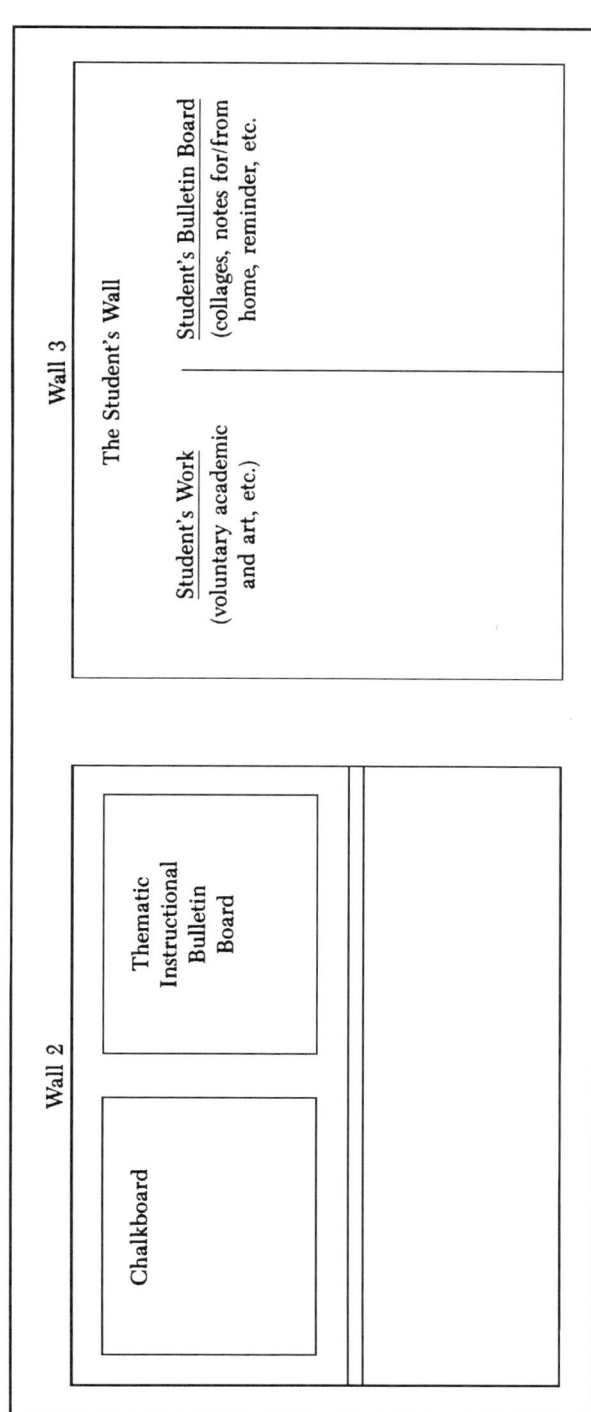

FIGURE 5.1. (Continued)

> **Window on Reality**
>
> The concept of ownership in the classroom cannot be overemphasized, especially in the elementary self-contained setting. If the classroom is not equipped with desks in which the students can store personal effects, an effort should be made to provide some personal space for them. Large empty ice-cream cylinders would suit this purpose; these can be obtained from many restaurants. Other possibilities include placing lockers or even hooks in the room with the students' names on them.

in the middle of the room and offer the offices on the sides of the room as an option. If the students gravitate toward these offices, the teachers' concerns may be alleviated and use of individual offices instituted.

A slightly different floor plan would be appropriate for classrooms with students who are severely disturbing (to each other and to themselves) (see Figure 5.2). The philosophy of this floor plan is clearly more restrictive. The teacher has direct eye contact with each student and is still able to conduct small group instruction. The information on the walls would be identical to that in the floor plan in Figure 5.1.

In summary, the physical arrangement of the classroom can set the tone for the school year. The floor plans and ideas provided are intended to be starting points for new teachers and perhaps alternatives for teachers who are currently experiencing problems. However, the design of a classroom alone will not eliminate all problems that may occur.

## Classroom Schedules and Routines

Another structural component of classroom management involves schedules and routines. It is important that teachers (a) schedule particular events and/or subject matter and (b) make certain that students understand the social routines expected of them.

*Scheduling* pertains to fixed course content and/or activities that the teacher announces daily, weekly, monthly, and even yearly. If the classroom is self-contained with little in-and-out traffic, scheduling is easier to implement because a master schedule can be devised for the entire group. If students are in a teacher's class for only a period or two, individual schedules are necessary for both the student and the teacher.

Gallagher (1979) suggested using blank schedule sheets because they are useful for completing progress records to determine if the schedule is being met. She added, "Regardless of the format, each student receives a daily schedule of activities and, thus, expectations and order of activities

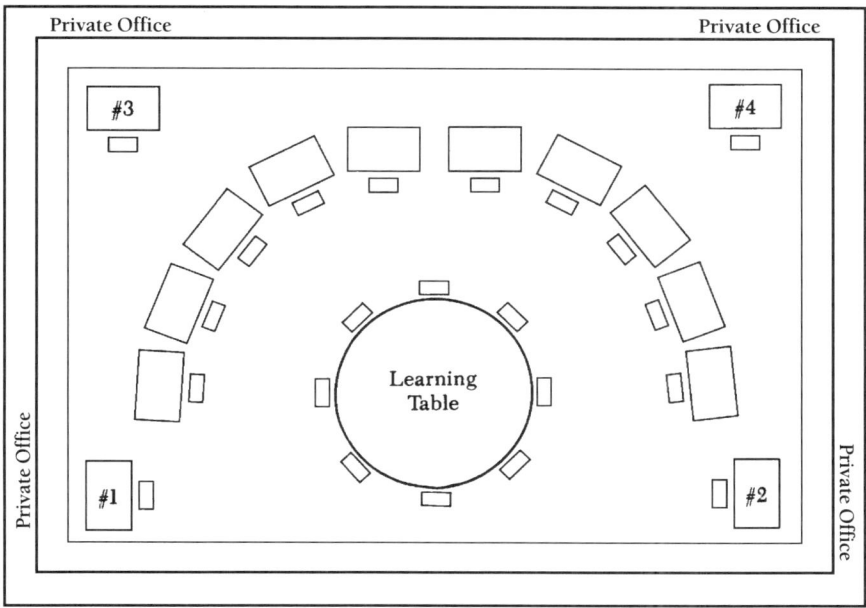

**FIGURE 5.2.** Alternative floor plan for severely disturbing students. Wall layouts are identical to those in Figure 5.1.

are known in advance. Students may not always like the work that is to be completed, but they know what is planned and what the options are. There is little room for argument since the schedule is a 'black and white' arrangement" (p. 244). If the particular assignment is too easy or difficult, adjustments should be made; however, the specific subject area should not be altered.

Scheduling benefits the students in many ways. Besides the comfort of "knowing what's coming," it guarantees that the subject area will be discussed in class. Unfortunately, some teachers tend to avoid certain teaching subjects (e.g., mathematics, science) because of their own lack of skills, perhaps justifying this by saying that "reading is more important." When a subject is ignored, students are shortchanged because they must compete in the content as well as in the skill areas.

Another benefit for both student and teacher is the knowledge that "something was covered that day." Because of the individualized nature in some special education classrooms, students can be on page 12 in a lesson, miss 2 weeks of school, and be scheduled to work on page 13 upon their return. The message to the students is clear: "You didn't miss anything." Hopefully, this is not the message educators want to convey. Students can be assigned homework for the work not completed on the daily schedule.

Another preventative measure requires some teacher planning. Disturbing behaviors frequently occur when students are frustrated with their work and require help from the teacher. Although the teacher may be actively engaged in working with another student, he or she cannot ask the student needing help to sit quietly for a few moments. If this request could be met by these students on a regular basis, they probably would not be in a classroom for the emotionally disturbed. Instead of taking the chance to tempt these students, the teacher could develop a folder for each student with review work in it. By handing this folder to the student who is waiting for the teacher, the teacher can encourage the student to participate in class until help is available.

Once schedules have been determined, the teacher can introduce the *routines* that will be required of the students. Routines are integral to a well-structured preventative classroom. They "are clearly established ways of operating, that define what the classroom expectations are and how they are to be met" (Epanchin, 1982, p. 328). The students' lack of understanding the concepts and practice of routines can frequently promote disturbing behaviors. Many of the skills that social skills curricula concentrate upon actually relate to the various aspects of routines with which disturbing children have trouble.

Teaching such routines as lining up to leave the room; corridor, playground, cafeteria, and auditorium behavior; asking for bathroom passes; sharpening pencils; waiting for help from the teacher; moving within the classroom setting; and leaving and entering the classroom, can alleviate problems for both the teacher and the students. Teachers too often assume that students *should* know these behaviors and may punish those who do not. For example, before Kevin began kindergarten, like many preschoolers, the only "procedures" he encountered were those at home. He was taught that when his parents requested something, he must obey *immediately* or suffer the consequences. On Kevin's first day of school, the teacher told the class to "line up for the playground," and Kevin rushed to the door. The teacher, who was not operating under the same routine, shouted, "Kevin! You immediately march yourself back to your desk and when everyone is lined up, then, and only then, you can join the rest of the group." Kevin was punished for following the only routine he knew.

As discussed in the chapters on moral development in Unit 2, simply explaining routines to students will not necessarily guarantee that the routines will be followed. Role-playing, observing videotapes, participating in discussion groups, and using behavioral techniques may all be effective in teaching the students the concepts of routine. Affleck, Lowenbraun, and Archer (1980) developed several sample explanations of some daily routines that teachers may use to ensure that all students are aware of the school's and teacher's routines. For example, for entering the classroom following lunch or recess, the teacher might say, "When the bell rings, you should line up outside of the door. When everyone is quiet, we will go into the classroom. You should hang up your coat and quickly take your seat."

Sometimes schedules and routines are disrupted by special events, such as class trips, parties, and even school assemblies. These events can be exciting to the students; in fact, they may sometimes be too exciting. Problems that may occur as a result of this excitement may be attributed to teacher interaction. For example, when a party or special assembly is to be held, a teacher may try to use it as a reward or punishment and hold it over the students' heads. This may be appropriate if the teacher actually intends to withhold the event, but if it is simply a threat, student anxiety or hostility, and at least teacher inconsistency, will be the product. Another teacher behavior that occasionally accompanies special events is the tendency not to schedule work for the students because the classroom periods are shortened (this may also occur at the end of the grading period or school year). This lack of planning may directly increase the frequency of disturbing behaviors.

## Behavioral Management Rules System

The remainder of this chapter presents methods designed to help teachers manage their classrooms. Although these sections may be interpreted by some readers as the nuts and bolts of teaching, I would warn that all of the text previous to this point has been designed to minimize the importance of these sections. That is, if one is prepared to teach, can teach, and does teach, then the maladaptive behaviors present in a setting may be few.

### Pre–Rule Setting

Most presentations of management systems discuss the development and importance of rules and consequences. The structured rule program presented in this chapter can be even more effective for teachers who understand the "warning" process. Even the most experienced teachers are often reluctant to give that "first warning." One of the most common errors that teachers exhibit is ignoring students' inappropriate behaviors when those same behaviors may be strongly reinforced by peers or by the students' not doing the assigned tasks. Ignoring can work if it is part of the *ignore–attend–praise* technique (Jackson, Jackson, & Monroe, 1983). The teacher is to ignore the student's inappropriate behavior, specifically praise another student who is on task, and praise the first student when/if that student returns to task. For example, Bob is playing with his shoes during silent reading time. The teacher ignores Bob's behavior and praises Frank by saying, "Nice going, Frank! You are doing a good job during silent reading!"

> **Window on Reality**
>
> When using programs such as *Getting Along with Others* (Jackson et al., 1983), older and more intelligent students may learn the administration of techniques. They may parrot "Good job! Now I'm reading." The teacher should try not to let their behavior interfere with the fact that they are learning the program. The teacher may tell the students that he or she uses ignore–attend–praise before giving them warnings. It is all right to let students know the system.

If Bob returns to silent reading, the teacher praises him by saying, "Nice going, Bob! You are doing well at reading silently."

Another management technique described by Jackson et al. (1983) is *direct prompt*. If students are off task, the teacher should tell them in a quiet, calm, and firm voice exactly what he or she would like them to do. The teacher should then praise the students for exhibiting the appropriate behaviors.

Another nonintrusive way for the teacher to let students know that he or she is aware that they are not on task is to give them a variety of cues. For example, walking near the students or having them sit near the teacher or paraprofessional can be very effective. This procedure is called proximity control. Hand signals, coughs, and asking students simple, related questions may also bring them back to task. Rich, Beck, and Coleman (1982) supported the use of rule reminders, which act as preventative measures that can be implemented before problems occur. They suggested that reminders are effective "when emotions are high or events in minor violation of the classroom rules . . . statements such as *Remember, you must remain in your seat* or the rule is *'keep your hands to yourself'* should be made as reminders before violations occur" (p. 152). Rearranging the setting so that disruptive students can sit closer to appropriately behaving models or to the teacher can also prevent maladaptive behaviors.

## Considering Rules

Students' misbehaviors are often a "shared responsibility." The research of Gunter, Jack, Shores, Carrell, and Flowers (1993) suggested that students with EBD exhibited behaviors that were related to those of their teachers. When the teachers changed their conduct, the students reduced their maladaptive behaviors. Walker and Buckley (1973) found that students who exhibit deviant behaviors receive more teacher attention than those who display appropriate student behaviors. To remedy this situation, a behavioral management system should be instituted that increases attention to appropriate behaviors and minimizes the time involved in dealing with maladaptive behaviors. Most such systems contain similar components: rules and consequences, both positive and negative, that are clear and easy to implement. This text addresses these factors, as well as how to operate the management program with the support of the school and parents.

The purpose of rules is to let the students know what behaviors are expected of them and what behaviors are inappropriate in the classroom. Literature conflicts with regard to who should create the rules: the teacher, the students, or both. Although there are many theories as to which approach to developing rules is more effective, studies to support any one method are scarce.

One means of generating rules is through the democratic process. The rationale behind this group process is that "when people help make rules they are more likely to see them as reasonable and they are more likely to follow them" (Charles, 1981, p. 141). First, the students and the teacher brainstorm rules that they feel are important to the smooth operation of the classroom. Next, they rank the rules, with perhaps only the top six rules being instituted. A problem with this approach is that there may be rules that the students generate that the teacher would feel uncomfortable implementing. If the teacher is not flexible enough to utilize these rules, then new ones may eventually surface. Most students, especially those who are older, will quickly perceive the "hidden agenda" of the teacher and realize that the earlier democratic process was only a teacher's ploy.

Another approach to developing rules is to have teachers decide which rules would allow them to manage the classroom in a fluid and fair manner. After the rules are developed, the teacher should present them on a piece of paper to the students for discussion and have the students agree to them by signing the bottom of the paper. Distribute the rules to other teachers, parents, counselors, and administrators.

The literature is almost universal in agreement upon the need to set few rules (Affleck et al., 1980; Epanchin, 1982; Lovitt, 1978; Rich et al., 1982). Walker (1979) suggested that one rule of thumb could be that the students should be able to remember each rule, and that the rules should apply to everyone. Implicit in Walker's suggestion is the idea that rules need to be taught to students as well as explained. Lecturing students about appropriate and inappropriate behaviors does not guarantee that they will understand what is expected of them. The work of Piaget (1948) indicates that many elementary students may be too young developmentally to fully understand the concept of rules.

Regardless of how they are chosen, the rules should be stated in positive behavioral terms. Ginott (1971) suggested that the more succinctly rules are written, the easier they are to understand. Walker (1979, pp. 81–82) listed examples illustrating differences between good and poor rules:

|     Good Rules                              |     Poor Rules              |
|---------------------------------------------|-----------------------------|
| 1. Raise your hand before asking a question. | 1. Be considerate of others. |
| 2. Listen carefully to teacher directions.   | 2. Behave in class.          |
| 3. Pay attention to the assignment and complete your work. | 3. Do what you are told. |
| 4. Do not talk to others during work time.   | 4. Don't disturb others.     |
| 5. Take your turn in group activities.       | 5. Work hard.                |

Good rules are specific and are observable. Poor rules may be open to question and are vague. Good rules need to be presented in a clear and understandable manner.

## Presenting Rules

When presenting the rules, teachers should try to explain them using specific examples. If the rule is to listen carefully to teacher directions, all facets of the rule can be explored; listening checks to determine if the students understand the concept can be most helpful. Viewing videotapes of students behaving and misbehaving so that the students can correctly identify the appropriate behaviors is another excellent technique. Teachers can use former students, present students, or even neighborhood children to act in the videotape.

Frequent reviews and simulations of proper behaviors are effective techniques to reinforce the rules. Quizzes may be another means to determine if the students are aware of the classroom expectations. In this way the teacher can determine if (a) any rules are unclear, (b) there are any rules that the students think the teacher may have forgotten (this allows the teacher the right to accept or reject suggestions), and (c) there are any rules that students think are unfair. If no problems are discovered, the teacher then makes it clear that these are the rules that will be followed in the classroom.

Rules should be presented on the first day of school and implemented immediately. Occasionally, teachers are told to begin the school year with a very firm hand and loosen up as the school year progresses. This can be extremely unfair to disturbed and disturbing students, because many of them will be unable to determine when it is a "firm" day or when it is a "loose" day. Recently, I consulted in an intermediate school where the teacher was in the process of displaying a new set of rules. She exclaimed,

"Okay, here are the new rules. And this time I mean it!" The teacher's problem was probably not with the content of the rules, but rather with her inconsistency in following them.

When maladaptive behaviors do occur, the following sequence of consequences may be applied (adapted from Affleck et al., 1980). The numbers indicate each incident.

1. *Warning*—This could be either written on the chalkboard or verbal (as little as two or three words can suffice). If it is verbal, the teacher should keep a reminder pad. The teacher should be aware that students may react to the warning in different ways. Some students, especially older ones, may hate the thought of their name going on the board and may react more negatively to this than they did in their initial behavior.

2. *Removal to office for 10 minutes*—On the floor plan referred to earlier in this chapter, there were two "offices" (1 and 2) that were empty. Students committing a second offense are to immediately go to these offices with their work. They may listen to class discussion, but they may not participate. The purpose of this intervention is to physically cue the students that they are misbehaving and yet still allow them to succeed in their schoolwork.

3. *Warning.*

4. *Removal to the office for 10 minutes.*

5. *Warning.*

6. *Ten minutes in office and 10 minutes before or after school*—Before school is an excellent time for detention for three reasons:
   (a) School buses usually arrive early (and they leave early);
   (b) teachers usually are in their classrooms early so that the detention is not a punishment for them; and (c) before school is a very active social period for many students, whether it be in the playground or in the halls. After school, few people are around.

7. *Warning.*

8. *Removal to timeout room for 5 minutes and phone call to parents.* (The concept of timeout is discussed later.)

9. *Warning.*

10. *Removal of student to principal's (or designee's) office for a new series of interventions.*

The specific interventions taken by the principal depend on his or her cooperation and philosophy. Some school administrators are not likely to actively engage in disciplinary actions, whereas others may react too harshly. Teachers need to work with the administrators and determine interventions with which both feel comfortable. These interventions may actually require *no* interaction from the administrator. Because some administrators believe that teachers who send students to the office cannot control their classrooms, teachers should sit down with their school administrators and explain their management program and share the above intervention schedule. Then it would be evident that sending the student to the principal's office is a last resort.

Student cooperation relates directly to the manner in which the consequences are delivered. Accepting negative feedback is not an easy behavior to learn, even for the most "normal" individuals. Most people sometimes cringe when given "constructive, helpful criticism" by loved ones, parents, or supervisors. Many students with EBD are constantly corrected for their behaviors. Teachers can teach students through role-playing and behavioral demonstration that a warning is simply that, no more, no less. The teacher can communicate to the students concern about their behavior and desire for them to remain in the setting. It is counterproductive when teachers attach blame or guilt or lecture students when they misbehave. If this occurs the student may react to the teacher's behavior rather than to the intervention. Furthermore, healthy teacher–student relations may become impaired.

An examination of this program should reveal two important elements: The program is designed to keep the student in the classroom for as long as possible, and the environmental expectations are clear. Copies of rules and consequences should be given to students and administrators, as well as to guidance counselors and parents. Meetings should be scheduled to explain the program to those concerned. Some teachers may question the use of so many interventions, yet successful application of this program will eliminate much of the classroom discussion (lectures and warnings) that is prevalent when disturbing behaviors occur. In most cases, the amount of teacher time used when a student misbehaves five times is equivalent to less than a minute.

This type of intervention plan is appropriate for most problem behaviors that occur in the classroom. However, different management may be needed for other, more serious misbehaviors, such as physically striking a peer or adult, destroying school property, or use of drugs or alcohol. Also, this plan is inappropriate in cases of some milder misbehaviors such as tardiness or not doing homework, because these infractions are typically exhibited only once a day or period. For example, one can only be tardy once during the day; consequently, a warning carries little weight. Therefore, a second facet of the management system should be implemented. Specific consequences similar to the following could be utilized:

- Immediate removal to the principal's office for any *serious* misbehaviors, such as physical space intrusion or possession of contraband.

- Immediate removal to the principal's office for a student who refuses to cooperate with the interventions in the management program.
- For each minute that the student is tardy to class, 2 minutes in before-school detention.

The second consequence is particularly crucial. Teachers should not try to cajole or coerce the student into cooperation. If the student does not cooperate within 30 seconds, he or she should be removed from the setting. Each teacher should also have a plan to remove students who refuse to cooperate. This plan may involve the assistance of a paraprofessional, a colleague in the next room, or the school administrator. Also, this plan should be developed *before* such occurrences and explained to the students as the consequences of not complying. To continually threaten removal will only increase the problem.

Curwin and Mendler (1988) in *Discipline with Dignity,* suggested nine ways to administer consequences, which can serve as an effective review of this important topic:

1. Always implement a consequence: Be consistent.
2. Simply state the rule and consequence.
3. Be as physically close as possible when you implement a consequence: Use the power of proximity.
4. Make direct eye contact when you deliver a consequence (this is dependent upon ethnicity and culture).
5. Use a soft voice.
6. Catch a student being good.
7. Don't embarrass the student in front of his peers.
8. Be firm and anger free when giving your consequence.
9. Do not accept excuses, bargaining, or whining. (pp. 95–99)

## Developing Consequences

Hewett and Taylor (1980) suggested that rules have both positive and negative consequences. Inherent in a successful behavioral program should be "rewards" for those who exhibit appropriate behavior and "punishments" for those who exhibit inappropriate behaviors.

***Positive Consequences.*** The management system described above needs to have a positive reinforcement component. One way teachers can implement this component is to offer a variety of reinforcers that the students can earn. To create an inviting environment, I encourage the use of a modified response cost system. Response cost is the loss of reinforcers, such as television privileges, following inappropriate behaviors.

One useful technique is for the teacher to create a series of strong reinforcers and announce to the students that they are all going to receive these awards. The teacher might announce, for example, "Friday we are going to have a pizza party for lunch. You are all invited." They should be told, however, that individuals will not be allowed to have pizza if they receive a designated number of warnings for the remainder of the week. This is a reversal of the traditional special education practice of earning points to receive rewards. The teacher can develop group and individual contests.

Hewett and Forness (1977) identified six types of positive consequences: (a) acquisition of knowledge and skill, (b) knowledge of results, (c) social approval, (d) multisensory stimulation and activity, (e) task completion, and (f) tangible rewards. Stephens (1978), perhaps realistically, excluded the items of Hewett and Forness that pertain to acquisition of knowledge, knowledge of results, and task completion. These list differences may be due to the authors' different perspectives of who benefits from management programs. Is the same student who finds learning to be a positive consequence the one who will necessarily be disturbing to the class?

Acquiring meaningful rewards, especially for students in the upper grades, requires teachers to be resourceful. If teachers are not in a financially wealthy school district, they may have to provide their own rewards. Some rewards—movies, filmstrips, and school privileges such as erasing the chalkboards or running errands—are relatively easy to deliver in the school. Other rewards that are surprisingly available to creative and somewhat assertive teachers include free haircuts at barber or hair-dressing schools, free admission to regularly scheduled matinees or free bowling in exchange for cleanup, free meals at many fast-food franchises (usually on a yearly basis; arrangements must be made far in advance), and free admission to dress rehearsals of plays.

Such rewards may be more meaningful to some students than rewards that are normally awarded in school. Teachers should explore all possible options and not be disappointed if they are rejected by a retailer or two. Many others are willing to cooperate in aiding "exceptional children," and some have established programs to do so. Summers are an excellent time for teachers to arrange year-round rewards. Teachers report that gathering rewards during the first year may be a somewhat slow process, but, with the appropriate class thank-you notes and diligence, school-year reward calendars can usually be filled. One oft-neglected reward is that of personal teacher time. I actually offered chopping wood and staying at my home overnight as a choice for reward, and the interested student list (and chopped wood) was endless!

Giving praise may be difficult for some teachers. Initially, the teacher might use a common phrase, such as "Good job" or "Nice going," to let the student know that he or she acted in an appropriate manner. Then, the teacher can describe the behavior in observable terms to let the student (and others) know exactly what he or she did well: "Good job! You have been in class every day this week!" When administering praise, teachers should avoid comparisons to previous inappropriate behaviors or to other students, such as "Good job! Your clothes are much neater today than they were yesterday!" and "Good job! You are doing as well as every one else now."

For praise to be effective, it must be true. Students are aware of fake praise and will either consider the teachers to be disinviting or lose their own motivation to work hard ("Why bother if everything is a good job?").

**Negative Consequences.** When students break the rules, teachers should administer consequences immediately and without emotion. Generally, two types of negative consequences can be applied: specific consequences that correspond to the specific behavior and graduated degrees of consequences that correspond to the frequency of the behaviors. The first category may be beneficial because it allows the student to understand that some misbehaviors are unmistakably more serious than others. However, behaviors that some teachers consider crucial to learning may be ignored by other teachers (see Chapter 1). Consequently, this category may be somewhat troublesome to administer because it may be difficult for the students to remember each specific rule and its penalty. Another common problem associated with the first category is the tendency to overpunish for the first offense of a serious maladaptive behavior. When a student misbehaves more than once, what would then be the punishment? One still more severe? Finally, some students misbehave so that they *can* be punished; therefore, the consequence may be rewarding to the student, no matter how aversive it is considered by the teacher.

Braaten, Simpson, Rosell, and Reilly (1988) contended that, if intrusive punishments are going to be used, the following guidelines must be considered and shared with all involved: "(1) information on the use and abuse of punishment procedures; (2) staff training requirements; (3) approved punishment procedures; (4) record maintenance and retention procedures; (5) complain and appeal procedures; (6) punishment issues and cautions; and (7) procedures for periodic review" (p. 80).

**Timeout.** A brief timeout, the eighth intervention in the behavior program described previously, can be therapeutic for the student. Note that "going to the office" is not considered timeout. Timeout remains controversial because of "erroneous definitions, the incorrect labeling of extended periods of seclusion as timeout, ineffective use of unknowledgeable persons, the occurrence of paradoxical effects, the potential for abuse and legal and ethical concerns" (Harris, 1985).

Smith (1981) contended that timeout is "(1) an escape from a stressful environment, (2) a safe place for venting cathartic anger, (3) a consistent signal to the child that he/she is upset . . . and finally, (4) reduced environmental stimuli" (p. 248). For the purpose of this management program, timeout can be considered a mild punishment, and one that is used after seven other interventions.

The timeout room or area should be isolated from peers, fairly spacious, well lighted, ventilated, and safe. Ideally, a one-way mirror and intercom system should be installed to monitor the student's behavior if necessary. If a separate room is not available, partitions can be placed in some area within a room. There should also be a written log near the timeout area with the names of the students who occupied it, as well as their lengths of stay.

Timeout is a concept that "although indisputably effective . . . is potentially a highly aversive procedure if used improperly" (Gast & Nelson, 1977, p. 461). For example, there is little therapeutic value in placing the student in timeout for long periods of time—except, perhaps, to the teacher. Teachers are encouraged to limit timeouts to 5 minutes. Gast and Nelson (1977) concurred, suggesting that "one to five minutes generally is sufficient. It is doubtful that timeout periods exceeding 15 minutes serve the purpose for which they were intended (i.e., temporary withholding of positive reinforcement)" (p. 463). Another issue that is integral to timeout is that, if "timein" is not reinforcing and a positive place to be, timeout may actually be rewarding. Walker (1979) suggested, therefore, that the timeout area should be dull and uninteresting. On the other hand, Gallagher (1979) contended that a multipurpose timeout area can be a viable alternative that may not only separate the students from others, but also increase their learning time.

Teachers can have students practice taking timeouts by asking the students to sit in the office for 5 minutes when they have not been misbehaving. The teacher then asks them if it was difficult to take the timeout and discusses the teacher's intentions for administering timeouts.

It should be stated that prosocial behaviors will not occur simply because of timeout. Any new behaviors must be learned by the student (Rutherford & Neel, 1978). The reader is urged to consult Rutherford and Nelson (1982) for an excellent review on the efficacy of timeout as an intervention.

***Suspension and Expulsion.*** The most intrusive negative consequences that schools administer are suspension and expulsion. In general, students with EBD who exhibit significantly intense or frequent inappropriate behaviors may be suspended for up to 10 days (Katsiyannis & Prillaman, 1989). If students are to be suspended for more than 10 days (usually

> **Window on Reality**
>
> The availability of more restrictive environments for students has decreased in many areas because of the movements of inclusion and some harsh economic realities (insurance limitations, less federal support, lower property millages). Some schools schedule IEP meetings after 10 days of suspension to make slight changes in suspended students' programs. However, a "change of placement" may not be possible in some schools. In fact, many school districts are placing students with EBD on half days because the schools can no longer handle the students' disruptive behaviors. Although sending students home during the afternoons is clearly exclusionary, schools are making use of this alternative. Time will only tell if this practice will be allowed to continue.

cumulative), then their behaviors and handicaps must be reassessed. If their behaviors are a result of their handicaps, then a change of program or placement is in order.

In a position statement, the Michigan State Board of Education (1989) proposed a series of guidelines to enable schools to enact a long-term suspension or expulsion of students with handicaps. At the multidisciplinary team meeting, the student's misbehavior must be identified. The following questions were developed to assist in determining whether the misbehavior is a manifestation of the student's handicap:

1. Was the student told of the school's policy regulating the inappropriate behavior?
2. Is it reasonable to believe the student understood the school's regulations given the student's handicapping condition?
3. Given the handicapping condition and given the student understood, is it reasonable to believe the student could control his or her behavior in the context in which it occurred?
4. Is it reasonable to believe that the programs and services, the method of delivery, or the environment in which they were delivered did not precipitate the inappropriate behavior? (pp. 4–5)

Clearly, numbers 3 and 4 are the most crucial to any decision-making policy. The team also must remember that students cannot be excluded from an educational program because of their handicap.

## Administering Positive Consequences

With experience, most teachers will be able to predict powerful positive reinforcers for their students. Depending upon the intervention, reinforcers should be both classwide and individualized. Certain considerations must be contemplated by the teacher, such as how reinforcers will be delivered (how frequently? how long?); how reinforcers will be evaluated (did they work?); and whether reinforcers should be individualized or for all students (Downing, Moran, Myles, & Ormsbee, 1991).

## Administering Negative Consequences

One of the most difficult tasks that teachers must undertake is administering consequences. Although the constant reminder of being *consistent* is everpresent, rarely have techniques been described as to how to be consistent. Possible reasons for teacher inconsistency may include the following:

- *Revenge*—I don't like what you did this time and I am going to punish you.

- *Fear of retribution*—I am concerned that there will be negative consequences if I administer the punishment. Will it get worse? Will you be mad at me?

- *Concern for flow of lesson*—If I punish you, I will have to interrupt my lesson.

Although each of these reasons may have merit, each can be disputed because of its possible consequences. Revenge is not the reason to negatively reinforce certain behaviors and not others. Fear will be communicated to students, who may take advantage of it and continue their inappropriate behavior. Finally, if students exhibit inappropriate behavior and the teacher chooses not to act, not only may the behavior continue to interrupt the lesson, but also peers may reinforce the behavior.

One way for the teacher to communicate that he or she is in control and is simply administering consequences is to calmly cite the warning or infraction. The teacher should remain quiet if the student wants to argue the point. The teacher may tell the class that any student can discuss infractions 1 hour after they take timeout.

## Level Systems and Token Economies

Many classrooms for special education students utilize a level system and/or a token economy, sometimes used interchangeably. Smith and Farrell (1993) wrote that "level systems commonly incorporate positive reinforcement and shaping, combine token economies with hierarchies of behavioral expectations or levels, and often include social skills and self-management curricula" (p. 252). Each level is developmentally based on a series of behaviors. Normally, students receive points or other tokens as they demonstrate these desirable behaviors with consistency. Each level is usually correlated to a series of responsibilities and privileges leading toward increasing independence. Mastropieri, Jenne, and Scruggs (1988) implemented a successful level system with high school students exhibiting problem behaviors by giving the higher level students the responsibility of self-monitoring their behavior in general education settings. Bauer, Shea, and Keppler (1986) presented the following 11-step process that would enable a classroom-level system:

1. Determine the usual entry level behaviors of the student population with whom the system is applied.
2. Determine the terminal behavioral expectations for the students.
3. List at least two but not more than four sets of behavioral expectations which seem to be appropriate steps between those described in Steps 1 and 2.
4. Write the sets of graduated expectations on separate sheets of paper. Label them "Level 1" through "Level 4."
5. Consider using a disciplinary or ground level.
6. Consider using a transition level which would include part time placement in the special program and part time in regular education.
7. Determine the privileges appropriate for students beginning the program (i.e., Level 1).
8. Determine the privileges appropriate for students preparing to terminate the program (i.e., at the highest level).
9. For each level developed in Step 3, list appropriate privileges evenly distributed among the levels.
10. Finally consider:
    - How frequently and in what way will a student's status be reviewed?
    - Will a minimum stay be required at each level?
    - Who will review the student's status?
    - What level of appropriate behavior will be required to remain at the level?
    - What self-monitoring and teacher-monitoring procedures will be needed?
11. Determine the communication system to be used among special education and regular education staff, parents, and students. (pp. 33–34)

These guidelines are intended to help students learn appropriate behaviors within both special and general education settings.

Token economies may or may not be associated with a level system. Sometimes, they may be merely a structure in which to provide positive reinforcers. Within a level system, token economies provide a means of measurement to categorize the position of the students. Burke (1992) presented the following guidelines for implementing a token economy program:

1. The program should emphasize behaviors that are considered positive . . . .
2. Initially, students should be rewarded for the positive behaviors throughout the day.
3. The amount of the reinforcement should be in direct proportion to the amount of good behavior shown during the time period . . . and in relation to the back-up reinforcers that are being used . . . .
4. Students must be taught that tokens are valued. This can be done by allowing students frequent opportunities to exchange them during the initial phase.
5. Students must be taught to save tokens and to wait increasingly longer periods of time to exchange them for a back-up reinforcer.
6. A token economy program may need to be individualized for students with special needs.
7. If a response–cost component is added, the teacher should implement it for well-defined behaviors and ensure that the students have many opportunities to earn tokens.
8. The teacher should have a plan to fade the program. (p. 100)

Administering a token or level system can be cumbersome because it requires that teachers carefully record behaviors, either positive or negative. Frequency counts may be taken with a wrist or golf counter, index cards, beads-in-a-pocket, or a calculator that will print the data (Koorland, Monda, & Vail, 1988). A stopwatch, video camera, or tape recorder can determine the duration of behaviors.

As mentioned in the previous chapter, students also can be taught to monitor their own behavior. The advantage is less teacher involvement. Carr and Punzo (1993) had three adolescents with EBD learn self-monitoring procedures and found that, "according to the teacher's anecdotal records, students eagerly recorded daily scores on weekly subject area charts and seemed aware of their improvement" (p. 248). Self-management is best learned when it includes self-instruction, self-monitoring, and self-evaluation and/or self-reinforcement (DiGangi & Maag, 1992). In a review of the research, Nelson, Smith, Young, and Dodd (1991) examined the efficacy of self-management with students who have EBD. They found that this approach can be successful in helping students learn both social and academic behaviors, although they questioned the ability of students to generalize their new behaviors.

## Crisis Intervention

As mentioned earlier, the philosophy of any good management program should be to prevent inappropriate problems. Clearly, the message of this chapter and unit has been for teachers to carefully plan for as many potential problems as possible to allow students to learn as much as possible. When working with students who have EBD, the possibilities of a crisis exist, regardless of the quality of the program (Gilliam, 1993).

Simply defined, a crisis exists when there is a real or potential danger to self or others. Consequently, safety for all must be the first point of order. For a crisis management program to work well, trust between teacher and students must exist. This trust is developed by fair and open teachers who teach to the best of their abilities and who have followed their rule systems fairly and without rancor.

Teachers need to plan for crises to occur. It is helpful to know the students and their tendencies. Are they crisis prone? What were the characteristics of the setting before crises occurred? How quickly do the students normally calm down? Have there been actual aggressive acts? Does the presence of an audience or of an authority figure affect their behaviors? Finally, are cultural differences (the teacher's or students') involved in the crisis? Beyond the obvious discrimination of those who are different, other more subtle forms of potential crisis ignition or maintenance may occur. For example, some cultures teach the avoidance of eye contact when being reprimanded, whereas others demand it. The implications of these different expectations should be quite obvious.

Greenstone and Leviton (1993) outlined six steps for effective crisis intervention. Step 1 is to *act immediately to stop emotional bleeding*. This is necessary to relieve anxiety, and to ensure that students do not harm themselves or others. Step 2 is to *take control*. Taking control can be accomplished by avoiding a power situation and entering the situation with caution. The teacher should use eyes and voice rather than the threat of physical force. The purpose of crisis intervention is to reduce the magnitude of the situation. The teacher needs to appear stable and supportive. Greenstone and Leviton directed teachers to "be clear in your introductory statements. The opening questions, directions, and other information you give the victim will often assist in gaining and in maintaining control" (p. 11). Teachers should not communicate that they can fix a problem. Teachers must be creative in taking control. One helpful technique is to remove the students in crisis. If that is impossible, the teacher should remove the audience. The teacher can also try redirecting the activities. Also, if more than one student is involved, the teacher can try to break the students' eye contact.

Step 3 is to *assess the situation*. What is causing the crisis? Are there multiple problems? If there are multiple problems, the teacher needs to determine which one to address first. Some students communicate crises through nonverbal means (e.g., body language). To help students understand and verbalize their crises, the teacher can ask short, specific, and direct questions such as "What is wrong?" or "How do you feel?" The teacher must allow plenty of time for the students to answer the questions. The teacher should demonstrate empathy and support, and remind the students that almost all crises are temporary and this one, too, shall pass.

Step 4 is to *decide how to handle the situation after assessing it*. Greenstone and Leviton (1993) suggested that "Heightened stress closes down options and generally produces 'tunnel vision' in the victim. When effective intervention occurs the victim becomes more receptive to exploring options, thinking creatively and solving problems" (p. 15). The teacher needs to work collaboratively with the students to identify solutions. The teacher should communicate that successful solutions may be available. If more than one student is involved, the teacher should try to have them arrive at an agreement. However, if the crisis has subsided, the teacher might choose to save the student agreement process for a later time.

Step 5 of crisis intervention is to *refer as needed and to follow up if possible or as agreed*. Because the students' crises may very well be non–school based, school counselors, psychologists, social workers, and administrators may prove helpful to the students. The teacher can develop a list of community crisis centers, hotlines, and other resources, and always have it available for students. The teacher should try to include reliable contact people on this list, which requires regular updates).

Step 6—*follow up with victims to ensure that they made contact with the referral agency (or person)*—is critical. If the purpose of classroom management is prevention, then it would seem necessary to help the student achieve the ammunition necessary to combat future problems. Furthermore, this will communicate to students that the teacher does care about them and their progress.

These six steps should enable the teacher to defuse most crises. If the teacher is involved in a setting where crises are frequent, specific techniques need to be learned by both teacher and students. Wood and Long's (1991) *Life Space Intervention: Talking With Children and Youth in Crisis* is an excellent resource that summarizes an approach designed to break the "conflict cycle" (see Figure 5.3).

When students are in or near crisis, opportunities for them to avert the crisis must be constantly present. Teachers *may* help by letting the stu-

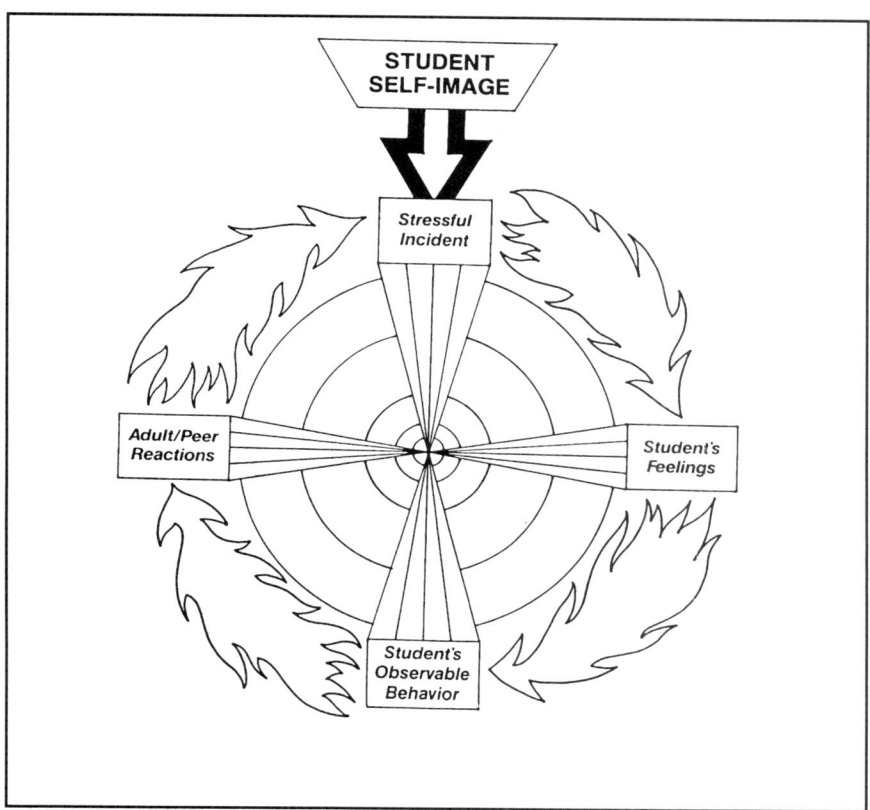

**FIGURE 5.3.** The student's conflict cycle.

dents keep their dignity, avoiding power struggles, remaining calm, and attempting redirection (Gilliam, 1993). Teacher behaviors that may allow students to keep their dignity include speaking to them at their eye level with as much eye contact as possible, giving them instructions on what to do rather than what not to do, using their names, and softly speaking to them. Also, teachers should keep quiet when students "talk back" and not argue with them even if it means letting them have the last word.

A common error that teachers make during crisis situations is to ask students rhetorical questions such as "Why did you do that?" (Would one expect or accept the answer "Because you're boring"?) Most often, the teacher means that the students "shouldn't have done that." Also, if there are no real choices for the student, the teacher must not give them any. For example, instead of saying "Do you want to leave now?" the teacher should say "Please leave the room now." Saying "please" softens any directive and avoids the perception of unnecessary power. Teachers should never make threats. Students should know what is going to happen as a result of their behavior, and teachers should calmly and consistently implement the consequences. If teachers lose control, they are sending an unclear message to their students.

Other possible alternatives for avoiding crises include giving the students an "out" by redirecting their activity. Teachers should ask them to do something else when a crisis is about to occur. Teachers can ask students to signal when they are feeling stress by, for instance, tapping a pencil to request an alternative setting.

Crisis plans need to be explained, taught, and practiced. Teachers must stay out of striking range (at least two good "kicks" away) and present themselves at an angle (to avoid a full frontal attack). At the point of intervention, the teacher should tell the student why he or she should stop the behavior with as little action and few words as possible (Gilliam, 1993). If students promise to "be good," apologize, or cry, the teacher should be gentle and reassuring but firm about following through with the consequences.

Physical management, which normally involves manual restraint, may be needed when teaching very aggressive students. The school trains the teachers to administer these procedures. Schloss and Smith (1987) suggested that the following considerations are important when using physical management in the public schools:

1. Maladaptive behaviors to be modified or replaced are identified in objective terms and there is written documentation of the preintervention behavior strength.

2. Goals of the intervention plan emphasize the development of adaptive responses that are consistent with the principles of normalization.

3. There are observable and measurable objectives, stated in behavioral terms, for meeting each goal.

4. The method of implementation is clearly and specifically stated . . . and is consistent with current literature and research.

5. The professionals using manual restraint procedures are thoroughly trained in the appropriate use of such techniques. . . .

6. Educational strategies (e.g., behavior rehearsal, modeling, and shaping) are used to develop alternative prosocial responses not presently found in the learner's repertoire. . . .

7. Reinforcement procedures are implemented to increase the likelihood that alternative prosocial responses will be used. . . .

8. Aversive procedures are used only after systematic trials have demonstrated the ineffectiveness of less restrictive methods. . . .

9. Potential benefits and consequences of the procedures are discussed with the student prior to implementation of the program. . . .

10. The procedures reflect the evaluation and decisions of the multidisciplinary team including parents or guardians and are incorporated into the youth's Individualized Education Program.

11. The behavior management program includes provisions for review with the intent of utilizing increasingly less restrictive procedures. (p. 210)

The teacher and administration should develop a plan for crises that includes emergency procedures, which should be used when necessary. Ignoring the possibility of crises will only create havoc when they occur.

## Summary and Conclusions

The application of a classroom management program has many advantages. In general, these programs have been shown to be effective in aiding students who react positively to the structure provided. Although it does require time and effort to successfully implement, a management program is probably more efficient than many procedures (or lack of procedures) that teachers currently use (Jones & Jones, 1981). Most problems in implementing a management system are the result not of the system but of the people who operate it.

This chapter presented a classroom management system that was intended to be a follow-up to Chapter 4. The teaching of social skills and rules is important to prevent problems from occurring. Carefully arranging classroom space can help maximize instructional time and minimize misbehaviors. Scheduling and teaching routines to students are additional preventive aspects of classroom management.

The disadvantages of using *only* a behavioral management program include teachers' tendencies to ignore their own behaviors that may be contributing to the students' disturbing behaviors. Because this type of program concentrates only on observable, external behaviors, it ignores problems of a psychological, internal nature. Units 2 and 3 of this text explore how educators can implement a behavioral management program while taking into consideration the psychological dimension of human behavior.

# Unit 1 References

Abelson, A. G. (1986). A factor analytic study of job dissatisfaction among special educators. *Education and Psychological Measurement, 46,* 37–43.

Abelson, M. A., & Woodman, R. W. (1983). Review of research on team effectiveness: Implications for teams in schools. *School Psychology Review, 12*(2), 125–136.

Affleck, J. Q., Lowenbraun, S., & Archer, A. (1980). *Teaching the mildly handicapped in the regular classroom* (2nd ed.). Columbus, OH: Merrill.

Alexander, R. N., Kroth, R. L., Simpson, R. L., & Poppelreiter, T. (1982). The parent role in special education. In R. L. McDowell, G. W. Adamson, & F. H. Wood (Eds.), *Teaching emotionally disturbed children.* Boston: Little, Brown.

Algozzine, B., Christenson, S., & Ysseldyke, J. E. (1982). Probabilities associated with the referral to placement process. *Teacher Education and Special Education, 5,* 19–23.

Algozzine, B., & Ysseldyke, J. E. (1992). *Strategies and tactics for effective instruction.* Longmont, CO: Sopris West.

Algozzine, B., Ysseldyke, J. E., Kauffman, J. M., & Landrum, T. J. (1991). Implications of school reform in the 1990s for teachers of students with behavior problems. *Preventing School Failure, 35,* 6–10.

Allington, R. L., & McGill-Franzen, A. (1989). School response to reading failure: Instruction for Chapter I and special education students in grades two, four, and eight. *The Elementary School Journal, 89,* 529–542.

American Psychiatric Association. (1987). *Diagnostic and statistical manual of mental disorders* (3rd ed., rev.). Washington, DC: Author.

Anderson, K. E. (1972). *Introduction to communication theory and practice.* Menlo Park, CA: Cummings.

Arbuthnot, J., & Gordon, D. A. (1986). Behavioral and cognitive effects of a moral reasoning development intervention for high-risk behavior-disordered adolescents. *Journal of Counseling and Clinical Psychology, 54,* 208–216.

Audette, B., & Algozzine, B. (1992). Free and appropriate education for all students: Total quality and the transformation of American public education. *Remedial and Special Education, 13*(6), 8–18.

Ausubel, D. P. (1961). A new look at classroom discipline. *Phi Delta Kappan, 43,* 25–30.

Bailey, J. S., Wolf, M., & Phillips, E. L. (1970). Home based reinforcement and the modification of pre-delinquents' classroom behavior. *Journal of Applied Behavioral Analysis, 3,* 223–233.

Ballard, R. D. (1987). The limitation of behavioral approaches to teaching: Some implications for special education. *Exceptional Child, 34,* 197–212.

Barker, R., & Hall, E. (1964). Participation in interschool events and extraschool activities. In R. Barker & P. Gump (Eds.), *Big school, small school: High school size and student behavior.* Stanford, CA: Stanford University Press.

Bartlett, L. (1989). Disciplining handicapped students: Legal issues in light of Honig v. Doe. *Exceptional Children, 55,* 357–366.

Bauer, A. M. (1991). Drug and alcohol exposed children: Implications for special education for students identified as behaviorally disordered. *Behavioral Disorders, 12,* 72–79.

Bauer, A. M. (1993). Children and youth in foster care. *Intervention, 28,* 134–142.

Bauer, A. M., Shea, T. M., & Keppler, R. (1986). Level systems: A framework for the individualization of behavior management. *Behavioral Disorders, 12,* 28–35.

Becker, H. S. (1963). *The outsiders: Studies in the sociology of deviance.* New York: Free Press of Glencoe.

Behar, L. (1990). Financing mental health services for children and adolescents. *Bulletin of the Menninger Clinic, 54,* 127–139.

Bentley, J. L., & Conley, M. W. (1992). Making connections between substance abuse and literacy difficulties. *Journal of Reading, 35,* 386–389.

Berliner, D. C. (1988). The half-full glass: A review of the research on teaching. In E. L. Meyen, G. A. Vergason, & R. J. Whelan (Eds.), *Effective instructional strategies for exceptional children* (pp. 7–31). Denver: Love.

Besharov, D. J. (1990). Crack children in foster care: Re-examining the balance between children's rights and parent's rights. *Children Today, 19*(4), 21–25, 35.

Bettes, B. A., & Walker, E. (1986). Symptoms associated with suicidal behavior in childhood and adolescence. *Journal of Abnormal Child Psychology, 14,* 591–604.

Bickel, W. E. (1983). Effective schools: Knowledge, dissemination, inquiry. *Education Researcher, 4,* 3–5.

Bickel, W. E., & Bickel, D. D. (1986). Effective schools, classrooms and instruction: Implications for special education. *Exceptional Children, 52,* 489–500.

Billingsley, B. S., & Cross, L. H. (1992). Predictors of commitment, job satisfaction, and intent to stay in teaching: A comparison of general and special educators. *Journal of Special Education, 25,* 453–471.

Blackorby, J., Edgar, E., & Kortering, L. J. (1991). A third of our youth? A look at the problem of high school dropout among students with mild handicaps. *Journal of Special Education, 25,* 102–113.

Blalock, G. (1991). Paraprofessionals: Critical team members in our special education programs. *Intervention in School and Clinic, 26,* 200–214.

Boomer, L. W. (1980). Special education paraprofessionals: A guide for teachers. *Teaching Exceptional Children, 12,* 146–149.

Boomer, L. W. (1981). Meeting common goals through effective teacher–paraprofessional communication. *Teaching Exceptional Children, 13,* 51–53.

Boomer, L. W. (1982). The paraprofessional: A valued resource for special children and their teachers. *Teaching Exceptional Children, 14,* 194–197.

Boomer, L. W. (1994). The utilization of paraprofessionals in programs for students with autism. *Focus on Autistic Behavior, 9*(2), 1–8.

Bower, E. M. (1959). The emotionally handicapped and the school. *Exceptional Children, 26,* 6–11.

Bower, E. M. (1964). The modification, mediation and utilization of stress during the school years. *American Journal of Orthopsychiatry, 34,* 667–674.
Bower, E. M. (1969). *Early identification of emotionally handicapped children in school* (2nd ed.). Springfield, IL: Charles C. Thomas.
Bower, E. M. (1982). Defining emotional disturbance: Public policy and research. *Psychology in the Schools, 19,* 55–60.
Braaten, S., Kauffman, J. M., Braaten, B., Polsgrove, L., & Nelson, C. M. (1988). The Regular Education Initiative: Patent medicine for behavior disorders. *Exceptional Children, 55,* 21–27.
Braaten, S., Simpson, R., Rosell, J., & Reilly, T. (1988). Using punishment with exceptional children: A dilemma for educators. *Teaching Exceptional Children, 20*(2), 79–81.
Brady, M. P., Swank, P. R., Taylor, R. D., & Freiberg, J. (1992). Teacher interactions in mainstream social studies and science classes. *Exceptional Children, 58,* 530–540.
Brandenburg, N. A., Friedman, R. M., & Silver, S. E. (1990). The epidemiology of childhood psychiatric disorders: Recent prevalence findings and methodologic issues. *Journal of the American Academy of Child and Adolescent Psychiatry, 29,* 76–83.
Breton, W. A., & Donaldson, Jr., G. A. (1991). Too little, too late? The supervision of Maine resource room teachers. *Journal of Special Education, 25,* 114–125.
Brophy, J. E., & Good, T. L. (1986). Teacher behavior and student achievement. In M. C. Wittrock (Ed.), *Handbook on research on achievement* (3rd ed., pp. 328–375). New York: Macmillan.
Brown, L. L., & Hammill, D. D. (1990). *Behavior Rating Profile–Second Edition.* Austin, TX: PRO-ED.
Bullock, L. M. (1980). A glimpse of the past and a look at the future. In R. B. Rutherford, Jr., A. G. Prieto, & J. E. McGlothen (Eds.), *Monograph in behavior disorders: Severe behavior disorders of children and youth.* Reston, VA: Council for Children with Behavioral Disorders.
Burke, J. C. (1992). *Decreasing classroom behavior problems.* San Diego: Singular.
Bursuck, B., Kinder, D., & Epstein, M. H. (1989). Teacher ratings of school survival skills and setting demands in junior high school settings. In S. L. Braaten, R. B. Rutherford, Jr., T. F. Reilly, & S. A. DiGangi (Eds.), *Programming for adolescents with behavior disorders* (Vol. 4, pp. 1–9). Reston, VA: Council for Children with Behavioral Disorders.
Butler, L., Miezitis, S., Friedman, R., & Cole, E. (1980). The effect of two school-based intervention programs on depressive symptoms in preadolescents. *American Educational Research Journal, 17,* 111–119.
Camp, B. W., & Bash, M. A. S. (1981). *Think aloud.* Champaign, IL: Research Press.
Cangelosi, A., Gressard, C. F., & Mines, R. A. (1980). The effects of a rational thinking group on self-concepts in adolescents. *The School Counselor, 27,* 357–361.
Carlberg, C., & Kavale, K. (1980). The efficacy of special class versus regular class placement for exceptional children: A metaanalysis. *Journal of Special Education, 14,* 295–309.
Carr, S. C., & Punzo, R. P. (1993). The effects of self-monitoring of academic accuracy and productivity on the performance of students with behavior disorders. *Behavioral Disorders, 18,* 241–250.

Carri, L. (1985). Inservice teachers' assessed needs in behavioral disorders, mental retardation, and learning disabilities: Are they similar? *Exceptional Children, 51*, 411–416.

Carter, J. F. (1991). REI: What regular educators are saying. In R. B. Rutherford, Jr., S. A. DiGangi, & S. R. Mathur (Eds.), *Severe behavior disorders of children and youth* (Vol. 14, pp. 11–17). Reston, VA: Council for Children with Behavioral Disorders.

Carter, J., & Sugai, G. (1988). Teaching social skills. *Teaching Exceptional Children, 20*(3), 68–71.

Carter, J., & Sugai, G. (1989). Questionnaire on prereferrals to state departments of education. *Exceptional Children, 55*, 298–302.

Cawley, J. F. (1977). Curriculum: One perspective for special education. In R. D. Kneedler & S. Tarver (Eds.), *Changing perspectives in special education*. Columbus, OH: Merrill.

Cawley, J. F. (1979). *Meeting the learning and behavioral needs of handicapped children via subject related IEPs*. Portland, ME: Psycho-Educational Associates.

Cawley, J. F. (1980, April). *Mathematics and the handicapped: Emphasis on diagnostics training packet*. Presentation at Central Michigan University, Mt. Pleasant, MI.

Cawley, J. F. (1985). *Secondary school mathematics*. Austin, TX: PRO-ED.

Cawley, J. F. (1994). Science for students with disabilities. *Remedial and Special Education, 15*, 67–71.

Cawley, J. F., & Parmar, R. S. (1992). Arithmetic programming for students with disabilities: An alternative. *Remedial and Special Education, 13*(3), 6–18.

Center, D. B. (1990). Social maladjustment: An interpretation. *Behavioral Disorders, 15*, 141–148.

Center, D., & Obringer, J. (1987). A search for variables affecting underidentification of behaviorally disordered students. *Behavioral Disorders, 12*, 169–175.

Center for Quality Special Education. (1990). *Special education program outcomes guide: Emotional impairment*. East Lansing, MI: Author.

Chadsey-Rusch, J., Rusch, F. R., & O'Reilly, M. F. (1991). Transition from school to integrated communities. *Remedial and Special Education, 12*(6), 22–33.

Chalfant, J. C., Pysh, M. V., & Moutrie, R. (1979). Teacher assistance teams: A model for within-building problem solving. *Learning Disability Quarterly, 2*, 85–94.

Chalfant, J. C., & Van Dusen Pysh, M. V. (1985). *Teacher assistance team report. State of Maryland*. Baltimore: State of Maryland.

Chalfant, J. C., & Van Dusen Pysh, M. V. (1989). Teacher assistance teams: Five descriptive studies on 96 teams. *Remedial and Special Education, 10*(6), 49–58.

Chalmers, L. (1991). Classroom modifications for the mainstreamed student with mild handicaps. *Intervention in School and Clinic, 27*, 40–42, 51.

Charles, C. M. (1981). *Building classroom discipline*. New York: Longman.

Chesapeake Institute. (1994). *National agenda for achieving better results for children and youth with serious emotional disturbance*. Washington, DC: Author.

Christenson, S., Ysseldyke, J. E., & Algozzine, B. (1982). Institutional and external pressures influencing referral decisions. *Psychology in the Schools, 19*, 341–345.

Christenson, S. L., Ysseldyke, J. E., & Thurlow, M. L. (1989). Critical instructional factors for students with mild handicaps: An integrative review. *Remedial and Special Education, 10*(5), 21–31.

Clarizio, H. F., & McCoy, G. F. (1983). *Behavior disorders in children* (3rd ed.). New York: Crowell.
Clark, G. M. (1994). Is a functional curriculum approach compatible with an inclusive education model? *Teaching Exceptional Children, 26*(2), 36–39.
Coffey, O. D. (1988). Handicapped youth and young adults in prison: Forgotten clients in search of assistance. In R. B. Rutherford, Jr., & J. W. Maag (Eds.), *Monograph in behavioral disorders: Severe behavior disorders of children and youth* (Vol. 11, pp. 97–105). Reston, VA: Council for Children with Behavioral Disorders.
Cohen, A. K. (1955). *Delinquent boys.* New York: Free Press.
Cohen, S. B., & deBettencourt, L. V. (1991). Dropout: Intervening with the reluctant learner. *Intervention in School and Clinic, 26,* 262–271.
Coleman, M. C. (1992). *Behavior disorders* (2nd ed.). Boston: Allyn & Bacon.
Coleman, M. C., & Gilliam, J. E. (1983). Disturbing behaviors in the classroom: A survey of teacher attitudes. *Journal of Special Education, 17,* 121–129.
Coleman, M. C., Wheeler, L., & Webber, J. (1993). Research on interpersonal problem-solving training: A review. *Remedial and Special Edcuation, 14*(2), 25–37.
Cooley, S. A., McVey, D. L., & Barrett-Jones, K. (1988). *Evaluation of identification and preassessment procedures in Kansas.* Topeka: Special Education Administration Section, Kansas State Department of Education.
Council for Children with Behavioral Disorders. (1989). *A proposed definition and terminology to replace "serious emotional disturbance" in Education of Handicapped Act.* Reston, VA: Author.
Council for Children with Behavioral Disorders. (1990). Position paper on the provision of service to children with conduct disorders. *Behavioral Disorders, 15,* 180–189.
Council for Exceptional Children. (1992). *Common core of knowledge and skills essential for all beginning special education teachers.* Reston, VA: Council for Exceptional Children.
Cowen, E. L., Pederson, A., Babigan, D., Izzo, L. D., & Trost, M. A. (1973). Long term follow-up of early detected vulnerable children. *Journal of Consulting and Clinical Psychology, 41,* 438–446.
Crane, S. J., & Iwanicki, E. F. (1986). Perceived role conflict, role ambiguity, and burnout among special education teachers. *Remedial and Special Education, 7*(2), 24–31.
Crowell, A. R., Jr., & Rucker, C. N. (1977). Influence of regular education involvement on child study teams. In J. A. C. Vautour & C. N. Rucker (Eds.), *Child study team training program book of readings.* Austin, TX: Special Education Associates.
Cullinan, D., Epstein, M. H., & Sarbonie, E. J. (1992). Selected characteristics of a national sample of seriously emotionally disturbed adolescents. *Behavioral Disorders, 17,* 273–280.
Curwin, R. (1994). Helping students rediscover hope. *Journal of Emotional and Behavioral Problems, 3,* 27–30.
Curwin, R. L., & Mendler, A. N. (1988). *Discipline with dignity.* Alexandria, VA: Association for Supervision and Curriculum Development.
Dedrick, C. V. L., & Raschke, D. B. (1988). Stress and the special educator. In R. B. Rutherford, Jr., & J. W. Maag (Eds.), *Monograph in behavioral disorders:*

*Severe behavior disorders of children and youth* (Vol. 11, pp. 177–187). Reston, VA: Council for Children with Behavioral Disorders.

Delquadri, J., Greenwood, C. R., Whorton, D., Carta, J. J., & Hall, R. V. (1986). Classwide peer tutoring. *Exceptional Children, 52,* 535–542.

Dembo, M. H., & Gibson, S. (1985). Teachers' sense of efficacy: An important factor in school improvement. *Elementary School Journal, 86,* 173–184.

DeMyer, M., Barton, S., Alpern, G., Kimberlin, C., Allen, J., Yang, E., & Steele, R. (1974). The measured intelligence of autistic children. *Journal of Autism and Childhood Schizophrenia, 4,* 42–60.

Deshler, D. D., & Shumaker, J. B. (1986). Learning strategies: An instructional alternative for low-achieving students. *Exceptional Children, 52,* 583–590.

Devlin, S. D., & Elliot, R. N. (1992). Drug use patterns of adolescents with behavioral disorders. *Behavioral Disorders, 17,* 264–272.

Diamond, S. C. (1993). Special education and the great God, inclusion. *Beyond Behavior, 4,* 3–6.

DiGangi, S. A., & Maag, J. W. (1992). A component analysis of self-management training with behaviorally disordered youth. *Behavioral Disorders, 17,* 281–290.

Dowis, C. L., & Schloss, P. (1992). The impact of mini-lessons on writing skills. *Remedial and Special Education, 13*(5), 34–42.

Downing, J. A., Moran, M. R., Myles, B. S., & Ormsbee, C. K. (1991). Using reinforcement in the classroom. *Intervention in School and Clinic, 27,* 85–90.

Doyle, W. (1985). Effective secondary practices. In R. M. J. Kyle (Ed.), *Reaching for excellence* (pp. 55–70). Washington, DC: National Institute of Education.

Dudley-Marling, C. (1985). Perceptions of the usefulness of the IEP by teachers of learning disabilities and emotionally disturbed children. *Psychology in the School, 51,* 411–416.

Duke, D. L., & Perry, C. (1981). Can alternative schools succeed where Benjamin Spock, Spiro Agnew, and B. F. Skinner have failed? *Adolescence, 13,* 376–392.

Dunn, L. M. (1968). Special education for the mildly retarded—Is it justified? *Exceptional Children, 35,* 5–22.

Edgar, E. (1987). Secondary programs in special education: Are many of them justifiable? *Exceptional Children, 53,* 555–561.

Edgar, E. (1988). Employment as an outcome for mildly handicapped students: Current status and future directions. *Focus on Exceptional Children, 21*(1), 1–8.

Edgar, E. (1990). Is it time to change our view of the world? *Beyond Behavior, 1,* 9–13.

Edgar, E. (1991). System support and transition to adulthood for adolescents with serious disordered behaviors: Orchestrating successful transitions. In S. L. Braaten & E. Wild (Eds.), *Programming for adolescents with behavior disorders* (Vol. 5, pp. 1–19). Reston, VA: Council for Children with Behavioral Disorders.

Edmonds, R. R. (1979). Some schools work and more can. *Social Policy, 9,* 28–32.

Edmonds, R. R. (1981). Making public schools effective. *Social Policy, 12,* 56–60.

Ellis, E. S. (1994). Integrating writing strategy instruction with content-area instruction: Part II. Writing processes. *Interventions in School and Clinic 29,* 219–228.

Epanchin, B. C. (1982). Behavior management. In J. C. Paul & B. C. Epanchin (Eds.), *Emotional disturbance in children.* Columbus, OH: Merrill.

Epstein, M. H., Cullinan, D., Quinn, K. P., & Cumblad, C. (1994). Characteristics of children with emotional and behavioral disorders in community-based programs designed to prevent placement in residential facilities. *Journal of Emotional and Behavioral Disorders, 2*(1), 51–57.

Epstein, M. H., Kauffman, J. M., & Cullinan, D. (1985). Patterns of maladjustment among the behaviorally disordered: II. Boys aged 6–11, boys aged 12–18, girls aged 6–11, and girls aged 12–18. *Behavioral Disorders, 10,* 125–135.

Epstein, M. H., Kinder, D., & Bursuck, B. (1989). The academic status of adolescents with behavioral disorders. *Behavioral Disorders, 14,* 157–165.

Epstein, M. H., Nelson, C. M., Polsgrove, L., Coutinho, M., Cumblad, C., & Quinn, K. (1993). A comprehensive community-based approach to serving students with emotional and behavioral disorders. *Journal of Emotional and Behavioral Disorders, 1,* 127–133.

*Exceptional Children.* (1993). Issues in the education of children with attention deficit disorder [Special issue]. *Exceptional Children, 60,* 97–192.

Fad, K. S., & Ryser, G. R. (1993). Social/behavioral variables related to success in general education. *Remedial and Special Education, 14,* 25–35.

Fagan, J., Weis, J. G., & Cheng, Y. (1990). Delinquency and substance abuse among inner-city students. *Journal of Drug Issues, 20,* 352–399.

Fallen, N. H., & McGovern, J. E. (1978). *Young children with special needs.* Columbus, OH: Merrill.

Federal Register. (August 23, 1977). *Education of handicapped children. Regulations implementing Education of All Handicapped Children Act of 1975.*

Federal Task Force on Homelessness and Severe Mental Illness. (1992). *Outcasts on Main Street.* Rockville, MD: National Institute of Mental Health.

Federation of Families for Children's Mental Health. (1992). *Family support statement.* Alexandria, VA: Author.

Fenton, K. S., Yoshida, R. K., Maxwell, J. P., & Kaufman, M. S. (1979). Recognition of team goals: An essential step toward rational decision making. *Exceptional Children, 45,* 638–644.

Fielder, J. F., & Knight, R. R. (1986). Congruence between assessed needs and IEP goals of identified behaviorally disordered students. *Behavioral Disorders, 12,* 22–27.

Fimian, M. J. (1986). Social support and occupational stress in special education. *Exceptional Children, 52,* 426–442.

Fink, A. H., & Janssen, K. N. (1993). Competencies for teaching students with emotional-behavioral disabilites. *Preventing School Failure, 37*(2), 11–15.

Fischer, J. (1993). A parent's struggle: When inclusion becomes exclusion. *Counterpoint, 14*(2), 13.

Foley, R. M., Epstein, M. H., & Cullinan, D. (1991). Achievement, locus of control, and study orientation of adolescents with and without behavior disorders. In S. L. Braaten & E. Wild (Eds.), *Programming for adolescents with behavior disorders* (Vol. 5, pp. 35–45). Reston, VA: Council for Children with Behavioral Disorders.

Forness, S. R. (1991). Resolving the definitional and diagnostic issue of serious emotional disturbance in the schools. In S. Braaten & G. Wrobel (Eds.),

*Perspectives on the diagnosis and treatment of students with emotional/behavioral disorders* (pp. 1–15). Minneapolis: Minnesota Educators of the Emotionally Disturbed–Minnesota Council for Children with Behavioral Disorders.

Forness, S. R. (1992). Broadening the cultural-organizational perspective in exclusion of youth with social maladjustment: First invited reaction to the Maag and Howell paper. *Remedial and Special Education, 13,* 55–59.

Forness, S., Bennett, M. A., & Tose, B. A. (1983). Academic benefits in emotionally disturbed children revisited. *Journal of the American Academy of Child Psychiatry, 22,* 140–144.

Forness, S. R., Kavale, K. A., & Lopez, M. (1993). Conduct disorders in school: Special education eligibility and comorbidity. *Journal of Emotional and Behavioral Disorders, 1,* 101–108.

Forness, S. R., & Knitzer, J. (1992). A new proposed definition and terminology to replace "serious emotional disturbance" in the Individuals with Disabilities Education Act. *School Psychology Review, 21,* 12–20.

Fowler, S. A. (1986). Peer-monitoring and self-monitoring: Alternatives to traditional teacher management. *Exceptional Children, 52,* 573–581.

Frame, C., Matson, J. L., Sonis, W. A., Failkov, M. J., & Kazdin, A. E. (1982). Behavioral treatment of depression in a prepubertal child. *Journal of Behavioral Therapy and Experimental Psychiatry, 13,* 239–243.

Frank, A. R., & McKenzie, R. (1993). The development of burnout among special educators. *Teacher Education and Special Education, 16,* 161–170.

Frank, A. R., Sitlington, P. L., Cooper, L., & Cool, V. (1990). Adult adjustment of individuals enrolled in Iowa mental disabilities programs. *Education and Training in Mental Retardation, 25,* 62–75.

Frick, P., Kamphaus, R., Lahey, B., Lober, R., Christ, M., Hart, E., & Tannenbaum, L. (1991). Academic underachievement and the disruptive behavior disorders. *Journal of Consulting and Clinical Psychology, 59,* 289–294.

Friedrich, W. N., Urquiza, A. J., & Beilke, R. L. (1984). Behavior problems in sexually abused young children. *Journal of Pediatric Psychiatry, 11,* 47–57.

Friesen, B. J., & Wahlers, D. (1993). Respect and real help: Family support and children's mental health. *Journal of Emotional and Behavioral Problems, 2*(4), 12–15.

Fuhler, C. J. (1991). Searching for the right key: Unlocking the doors to motivation. *Intervention in the School and Clinic, 26,* 216–220.

Gable, R. A., Hendrickson, J. M., & Rutherford, R. B., Jr. (1991). Strategies for integrating students with behavioral disorders into general education. In R. B. Rutherford, Jr., S. A. DiGangi, & S. R. Mathur (Eds.), *Monograph in behavioral disorders: Severe behavior disorders of children and youth* (Vol. 14, pp. 18–32). Reston, VA: Council for Children with Behavioral Disorders.

Gable, R. A., Hendrickson, J. M., Young, C. C., & Shooki-Yetka, M. (1992). Preservice preparation and classroom practices of teachers of students with emotional/behavioral disorders. *Behavioral Disorders, 17,* 126–134.

Gable, R. A., & Laycock, V. K. (1991). Regular classroom integration of adolescents with emotional/behavioral disorders in perspective. In S. L. Braaten & E. Wild (Eds.), *Programming for adolescents with behavior disorders* (Vol. 5, pp. 1–19). Reston, VA: Council for Children with Behavioral Disorders.

Gajria, M., & Salvia, J. (1992). The effects of summarization instruction on text comprehension of students with learning disabilities. *Exceptional Children, 58,* 508–516.

Gallagher, P. A. (1979). *Teaching students with behavior disorders.* Denver: Love.
Gallivan-Fenlon, A. (1994). Integrated transdisciplinary teams. *Teaching Exceptional Children, 26* (3), 16–20.
Gargiulo, R. M. (1990). Child abuse and neglect: An overview. In R. L.Goldman & R. M. Gargiulo (Eds.), *Children at risk.* Austin, TX: PRO-ED.
Gast, D. L., & Nelson, D. M. (1977). Time out in the classroom: Implications for special education. *Exceptional Children, 43,* 461–464.
Gerber, M. M. (1981). Economic considerations of "appropriate" education for exceptional children. *Exceptional Education Quarterly, 2,* 49–57.
Gersten, R., Walker, H., & Darch, C. (1988). Relationship between teachers' effectiveness and their tolerance of handicapped students. *Exceptional Children, 54,* 433–438.
Gilliam, J. E. (1993). Crisis management for students with emotional/behavioral problems. *Intervention in School and Clinic, 28,* 224–230.
Gilliam, J. E., & Coleman, M. C. (1981). Who influences IEP decisions? *Exceptional Children, 47,* 642–644.
Gilmer, J. F. (1985). *Factors related to the success and failure of teacher assistance teams in elementary school.* Unpublished doctoral dissertation, University of Arizona, Tucson.
Ginott, H. (1971). *Teacher and child.* New York: Macmillan.
Glavin, J. P. (1972). Persistence of behavior disorders in children. *Exceptional Children, 38,* 367–376.
Glavin, J., Quay, H. C., Annesley, F. R., & Werry, J. S. (1971). An experimental resource room for behavior problem children. *Exceptional Children, 38,* 131–137.
Goldbaum, J. L., & Rucker, C. N. (1977). Assessment data and the child study team. In J. A. C. Vautour & C. N. Rucker (Eds.), *Child study team training book of readings.* Austin, TX: Special Education Associates.
Goldstein, H., Arkell, C., Ashcroft, C. C., Hurley, O. L., & Lilly, M. S. (1975). Schools. In N. Hobbs (Ed.), *Issues in the classifications of children* (Vol. 2). San Francisco: Jossey-Bass.
Goodman, G., & Poillion, M. J. (1992). ADD: Acronym for any dysfunction or difficulty. *Journal of Special Education, 26,* 37–56.
Goodman, J. F., & Bond, L. (1993). The Individualized Education Program: A retrospective critique. *Journal of Special Education, 26,* 408–422.
Goodman, L. (1985). The effective schools movement and special education. *Teaching Exceptional Children, 17,* 102–105.
Grabe, M. (1981). School size and the importance of school activities. *Adolescence, 16,* 21–31.
Graden, J., Casey, A., & Christenson, S. (1985). Implementing a pre-referral intervention system: The model. *Exceptional Children, 5,* 377–384.
Graves, A., Landers, M. F., Lokerson, J., Luchow, J., & Horvath, M. (1993). The development of a competency list for teachers of students with learning disabilities. *Learning Disabilities Research & Practice, 8*(3), 188–199.
Graziano, A., DeGiovanni, I., & Garcia, K. (1979). Behavioral treatments of children's fears: A review. *Psychological Bulletin, 86,* 804–830.
Greenbaum, P. E., Prange, M. E., Friedman, R. M., & Silver, S. E. (1991). Substance abuse prevalence and comorbidity with other psychiatric disorders among adolescents with severe emotional disturbances. *Journal of the American Academy of Child and Adolescent Psychiatry, 30,* 773–775.

Greenstone, J. L., & Leviton, S. C. (1993). *Elements of crisis intervention.* Pacific Grove, CA: Brooks Cole.

Greenwood, C. R., Arreaga-Mayer, C., & Carta, J. J. (1994). Identification and translation of effective teacher-developed instructional procedures for general practice. *Remedial and Special Education, 15,* 140–151.

Gresham, F. M. (1981). Social skills training with handicapped children: A review. *Review of Educational Research, 51,* 139–176.

Gresham, F. M. (1982). Misguided mainstreaming: The case for social skills training with handicapped children. *Exceptional Children, 48,* 422–433.

Gresham, F. M., Elliott, S. N., & Black, F. L. (1987). Teacher-rated social skills of mainstreamed mildly handicapped and nonhandicapped children. *School Psychology Review, 16,* 78–88.

Grosenick, J. K. (1989). School service for behaviorally disordered students: A national perspective. In R. B. Rutherford, Jr., & S. A. DiGangi (Eds.), *Monograph in behavioral disorders: Severe behavior disorders of children and youth* (Vol. 12, pp. 11–20). Reston, VA: Council for Children with Behavioral Disorders.

Grosenick, J. K., George, M. P., & George, N. L. (1987). A profile of school program for the behaviorally disordered: Twenty years after Morse, Cutler and Fink. *Behavioral Disorders, 12,* 159–168.

Gunter, P. L., Jack, S. L., Shores, R. E., Carrell, D. E., & Flowers, J. (1993). Lag sequential analysis as a tool for functional analysis of student disruptive behavior in classrooms. *Journal of Emotional and Behavioral Disorders, 1,* 138–148, 198.

Hallahan, D. P., & Kauffman, J. M. (1988). *Exceptional children: Introduction to special education* (4th ed.). Englewood Cliffs, NJ: Prentice-Hall.

Hammill, D. D. (Ed.). (1987). *Assessing the abilities and instructional needs of students: A practical guide for educators, psychologists, speech pathologists, and diagnosticians.* Austin: PRO-ED.

Hammill, D. D., & Wiederholt, J. L. (1972). *The resource room: Rationale and implementation.* Philadelphia: Journal of Special Education Press.

Harding, D. C., Gust, A. M., Goldhawk, S. L., & Bierman, M. M. (1993). The effects of the interactive unit on the computation skills of students with learning disabilities and students with mild cognitive impairments. *Learning Disabilities, 4,* 53–65.

Harrington, R. G., & Gibson, E. (1986). Preassessment procedures for learning disabled students: Are they effective? *Journal of Learning Disabilities, 19,* 538–541.

Harris, K. R. (1985). Definitional, parametric, and procedural considerations in timeout interventions and research. *Exceptional Children, 51,* 279–288.

Hasazi, S., Gordon, L., & Roe, C. (1985). Factors associated with the employment status of handicapped youth exiting high school from 1879–1983. *Exceptional Children, 51,* 455–469.

Hetfield, P. (1994). Using a student newspaper to motivate students with behavior disorders. *Teaching Exceptional Children, 26*(2), 6–9.

Hewett, F. M., & Forness, S. R. (1977). *Education of exceptional learners* (2nd ed.). Boston: Allyn & Bacon.

Hewett, F. M., & Taylor, F. D. (1980). *The emotionally disturbed child in the classroom: The orchestration of success* (2nd ed.). Boston: Allyn & Bacon.

Hindman, S. E. (1986). The law, the courts, and the education of behaviorally disordered students. *Behavioral Disorders, 11,* 280–289.

Hogan, S., & Prater, M. A. (1993). The effects of peer tutoring and self-management training on on-task, academic, and disruptive behaviors. *Behavioral Disorders, 18,* 118–128.

Honig v. Doe (1988), 56 S.Ct.27.

Howard-Rose, D., & Rose, C. (1994). Student's adaptation to task environments in resource room and regular class settings. *Journal of Special Education, 28,* 3–26.

Huntze, S. (1985). A position paper of the Council for Children with Behavioral Disorders. *Behavioral Disorders, 10,* 167–174.

Hutton, J. B., & Kinnison, L. (1991). Counseling as a related service: Are emotionally disturbed students being left out? In S. L. Braaten & E. Wild (Eds.), *Programming for adolescents with behavior disorders* (Vol. 5, pp. 91–99). Reston, VA: Council for Children with Behavioral Disorders.

Individuals with Disabilities Education Act. (1990). *To assure the free public education of all handicapped children: Twelfth annual report to Congress on the implementation of the Education of the Handicapped Act.* Washington, DC: U.S. Government Printing Office.

Institute for Adolescents with Behavioral Disorders. (1994). *EBD teacher competencies.* Arden Hills, MN: Author.

Jackson, N. E., Jackson, D. A., & Monroe, C. (1983). *Getting along with others.* Champaign, IL: Research Press.

Johnson, A. B. (1987). Attitudes toward mainstreaming: Implications for inservice training and teaching the handicapped. *Education, 107,* 229–233.

Johnson, D. W., & Johnson, R. T. (1986). Mainstreaming and cooperative learning strategies. *Exceptional Children, 52,* 553–561.

Jones, K. H., & Bender, W. N. (1993). Utilization of paraprofessionals in special education: A review of the literature. *Remedial and Special Education, 14*(1), 7–14.

Jones, V. F. (1980). *Adolescents with behavioral problems: Strategies for teaching counseling and parent involvement.* Boston: Allyn & Bacon.

Jones, V. F. (1992). Integrating behavioral and insight-oriented treatment in school based programs for seriously emotionally disturbed students. *Behavioral Disorders, 17,* 225–236.

Jones, V. F., & Jones, L. S. (1981). *Responsible classroom discipline.* Boston: Allyn & Bacon.

Kansas State Department of Education. (1987). *Kansas guidelines for identifying children and youth with specific learning disabilities.* Topeka, KS: Special Education Commission.

Kantor, R. N., Anderson, T. H., & Armbruster, B. B. (1983). How inconsiderate are children's textbooks? *Journal of Curriculum Studies, 15,* 6–72.

Katsiyannis, A., & Prillaman, D. (1989). Suspension and expulsion of handicapped students: National trends and the case of Virginia. *Behavioral Disorders, 15,* 35–40.

Kauffman, J. M. (1981). *Characteristics of children's behavior disorders* (2nd ed.). Columbus, OH: Merrill.

Kauffman, J. M. (1991). Purposeful ambiguity: Its value in defining emotional or behavioral disorders. In R. B. Rutherford, Jr., S. A. DiGangi, & S. R. Mathur

(Eds.), *Monograph in behavior disorders: Severe behavior disorders of children and youth* (Vol. 14, pp. 1–7). Reston, VA: Council for Children with Behavioral Disorders.

Kauffman, J. M. (1993). *Characteristics of emotional and behavioral disorders of children and youth* (5th ed.). New York: Merrill.

Kauffman, J., Cullinan, D., & Epstein, M. (1987). Characteristics of students placed in special programs for the seriously emotionally disturbed. *Behavioral Disorders, 12,* 175–184.

Kauffman, J. M., & Wong, K. L. H. (1991). Effective teachers of students with behavioral disorders: Are generic teaching skills enough? *Behavioral Disorders, 16,* 225–237.

Kazdin, A. (1989). Developmental psychopathology: Current research, issues and directions. *American Psychologist, 44,* 180–187.

Kearney, C. A., & Durand, V. M. (1992). How prepared are our teachers for mainstreamed classroom settings? A survey of postsecondary schools of education in New York State. *Exceptional Children, 59,* 6–11.

Kelly, T. J., Bullock, L. M., & Dykes, M. K. (1977). Behavioral disorders: Teacher's perceptions. *Exceptional Children, 43,* 316–318.

Kinder, D., & Bursuck, W. (1993). History strategy instruction: Problem–solution–effect analysis, timeline, and vocabulary instruction. *Exceptional Children, 59,* 324–335.

Knapcyzk, D. R. (1992). Effects of developing alternative responses on aggressive behavior of adolescents. *Behavioral Disorders, 17,* 247–263.

Knitzer, J. (1993). Children's mental health policy: Challenging the future. *Journal of Emotional and Behavioral Disorders, 1,* 8–16.

Knitzer, J., Steinberg, Z., & Fleisch, B. (1990). *At the schoolhouse door: An examination of programs and policies for children with behavioral and emotional problems.* New York: Bank Street College of Education.

Knoff, H. M. (1983). Investigating disproportionate influence and status in multidisciplinary child study teams. *Exceptional Children, 49,* 367–370.

Konopasek, D. E. (1990). Priests on my shoulder. In R. B. Rutherford, Jr., & S. A. DiGangi (Eds.), *Monograph in behavioral disorders: Severe behavior disorders of children and youth* (Vol. 13, pp. 11–17). Reston, VA: Council for Children with Behavioral Disorders.

Koorland, M. A., Monda, L. E., & Vail, C. O. (1988). Recording behavior with ease. *Teaching Exceptional Children, 21*(1), 59–61.

Kress, J. S., & Elias, M. J. (1993). Substance abuse prevention in special education populations: Review and recommendations. *Journal of Special Education, 27,* 35–51.

Kroth, R. L. (1975). *Communicating with parents of exceptional children.* Denver: Love.

Lamphear, V. S. (1985). The impact of maltreatment on children's psychosocial adjustment: A review of the literature. *Child Abuse and Neglect, 9,* 251–263.

Landrum, T. J. (1992). Teachers as victims: An interactional analysis of the teacher's role in educating atypical learners. *Behavioral Disorders, 17,* 135–144.

Larivee, B. (1985). *Effective teaching for successful mainstreaming.* New York: Longman.

Larrivee, B., & Horne, M. D. (1991). Social status: A comparison of mainstreamed students with peers of different ability levels. *Journal of Special Education, 25,* 90–101.

Larsen, S. C., & Poplin, M. C. (1980). *Methods for educating the handicapped: An individualized education program approach.* Boston: Allyn & Bacon.

Lawrenson, G. M., & McKinnon, A. F. (1982). A survey of classroom teachers of the emotionally disturbed: Attrition and burnout factors. *Behavioral Disorders, 8,* 41–49.

Leone, P. E. (1984). Reconciling educational rights of handicapped pupils with the school disciplinary code. In R. B. Rutherford, Jr., & C. M. Nelson (Eds.), *Monograph in behavioral disorders: Severe behavior disorders of children and youth* (Vol. 4). Reston, VA: Council for Children with Behavioral Disorders.

Leone, P. E. (1989). Beyond fixing bad behavior and bad boys: Multiple perspectives on education and treatment of troubled and troubling youth. In R. B. Rutherford, Jr., & S. A. DiGangi (Eds.), *Monograph in behavioral disorders: Severe behavior disorders of children and youth* (Vol. 12). Reston, VA: Council for Children with Behavioral Disorders.

Lerner, J. V., Hertzog, C., Hooker, K. A., Hassibi, M., & Thomas, A. (1988). A longitudinal study of negative emotional states and adjustment from early childhood through adolescence. *Child Development, 59,* 356–366.

Leschied, A. W., Coolman, M., & Williams, S. (1984). Addressing the needs of school failures in a delinquent population. *Behavioral Disorders, 10,* 40–46.

Lewin, P., Nelson, R. E., & Tollefson, N. (1983). Teacher attitudes toward disruptive students. *Elementary School Guidance and Counseling, 17,* 188–193.

Lewis, K. A., Swartz, G. M., & Ianacone, R. N. (1988). Service coordination between correctional and public school systems for handicapped juvenile offenders. *Exceptional Children, 55,* 66–70.

Lillie, D. (1981). Educational psychological strategies for working with parents. In J. L. Paul (Ed.), *Understanding and working with parents of children with special needs.* New York: Holt, Rinehart & Winston.

Lilly, M. S. (1970). Special education: A teapot in the tempest. *Exceptional Children, 37,* 43–49.

Lipsky, D. K., & Gartner, A. (1991). Restructuring for quality. In J. W. Lloyd, N. N. Singh, & A. C. Repp (Eds.), *The Regular Education Initiative: Alternative perspectives on concepts, issues, and models* (pp. 43–56). Sycamore, IL: Sycamore.

Lovitt, T. C. (1978). *Managing inappropriate behaviors in the classroom.* Reston, VA: Council for Exceptional Children.

Lovitt, T. C., & Horton, S. V. (1994). Strategies for adapting science textbooks for youth with learning disabilities. *Remedial and Special Education, 15,* 105–116.

Mackenzie, D. E. (1983). Research for school improvement: An appraisal of some recent trends. *Educational Researcher, 4,* 5–13.

Maheady, L., Sacca, M., & Harper, G. (1988). Classwide peer tutoring with mildly handicapped high school students. *Exceptional Children, 55,* 52–59.

Marion, R. L. (1981). *Educators, parents, and exceptional children.* Rockville, MD: Aspen Systems.

Mastropieri, M. A., Jenkins, V., & Scruggs, T. E. (1985). Academic and intellectual characteristics of behaviorally disordered children and youth. In R. B. Rutherford (Ed.), *Monograph in behavioral disorders: Severe behavior disorders of children and youth* (Vol. 8, pp. 86–104). Reston, VA: Council for Children with Behavioral Disorders.

Mastropieri, M. A., Jenne, T., & Scruggs, T. E. (1988). A level system for managing problem behaviors in a high school resource program. *Behavioral Disorders, 13,* 202–208.

Mastropieri, M. A., Scruggs, T. E., Whittaker, M. E. S., & Bakken, J. P. (1994). Applications of mnemonic strategies with students with mild mental disabilities. *Remedial and Special Education, 15*(1), 34–43.

Mattison, R. E., Morales, J., & Bauer, M. A. (1992). Distinguishing characteristics of elementary schoolboys recommended for SED placement. *Behavioral Disorders, 17,* 107–114.

McAfee, J. K., & Vergason, G. A. (1979). Parent involvement in the process of special education: Establishing the new partnership. *Focus on Exceptional Children, 11*(2), 1–15.

McConnell, S. R. (1987). Entrapment effects and the generalization and maintenance of social skills training for elementary school students with behavioral disorders. *Behavioral Disorders, 12,* 252–263.

McDowell, R. L., & Brown, G. B. (1978). The emotionally disturbed adolescent: Development of program alternatives in secondary education. *Focus on Exceptional Children, 10*(4), 1–15.

McGuire, M. D., & Goldman, R. L. (1991). Targets for abuse: Children and youth with behavioral disorders. In S. L. Braaten & E. Wild (Eds.), *Programming for adolescents with behavior disorders* (Vol. 5, pp. 21–33). Reston, VA: Council for Children with Behavioral Disorders.

McIntyre, T. (1993). Reflections on the new definition for emotional or behavioral disorders: Who still falls through the cracks and why. *Behavioral Disorders, 18,* 148–160.

McKenzie, R. G. (1991). Developing study skills through cooperative learning activities. *Intervention in School and Clinic, 26,* 227–229.

McManus, M. E., & Kauffman, J. M. (1991). Working conditions of teachers of students with behavioral disorders: A national survey. *Behavioral Disorders, 16,* 247–259.

Meadows, N., Neel, R. S., Parker, G., & Timo, K. (1991). A validation of social skills for students with behavioral disorders. *Behavioral Disorders, 16,* 200–210.

Meichenbaum, D. H., Bowers, K. S., & Ross, R. R. (1968). Modification of classroom behavior of institutionalized female adolescent offenders. *Behavior Research and Therapy, 6,* 343–353.

Meichenbaum, D., & Goodman, J. (1971). Training impulsive children to talk to themselves: A means of developing self-control. *Journal of Abnormal Psychology, 77,* 115–126.

Mercer, C. D. (1981). Parent involvement. In R. E. Algozzine, R. Schmid, & C. D. Mercer (Eds.), *Childhood behavior disorders*. Rockville, MD: Aspen Systems.

Meyen, E. L., & Lehr, D. H. (1980). Least restrictive environments: Instructional implications. *Focus on Exceptional Children, 12*(7), 1–8.

Michigan State Board of Education. (1989). *Position statement: Suspension and expulsion of handicapped students.* Lansing, MI: Author.

Milin, R., Halikas, J., Meller, J., & Morse, C. (1991). Psychopathology among substance abusing juvenile offenders. *Journal of the American Academy of Child and Adolescent Psychiatry, 30,* 569–573.

Miller, N., & Kassinove, H. (1978). Effects of lecture, rehearsal, written homework, and IQ on the efficacy of a rational emotive school mental health program. *Journal of Community Psychology, 6,* 366–373.
Mithaug, D. E., Horiuchi, C. N., & Fanning, P. N. (1985). A report on the Colorado statewide follow-up survey of special education students. *Exceptional Children, 51,* 397–404.
Morgan, D. P. (1993). Substance abuse prevention and students with behavioral disorders: Guidelines for school professionals. *Journal of Emotional and Behavioral Disorders, 1,* 170–178.
Morgan, D., & Jensen, W. (1988). *Teaching behaviorally disordered students.* Columbus, OH: Merrill.
Morsink, C. V., Fardig, D. B., Algozzine, K., & Algozzine, B. (1987). Competencies for teachers of students with high incidence handicaps. *B.C. Journal of Special Education, 11,* 109–122.
Mueller, F. (1993). Teaching and stress: A personal view. *Beyond Behavior, 5*(1), 3.
Munk, D. D., & Repp, A. C. (1994). The relationship between instructional variables and problem behavior: A review. *Exceptional Children, 60,* 390–401.
Murray, H. (1943). *Thematic Apperception Test Manual.* Cambridge, MA: Harvard University Press.
Myles, B. S., & Simpson, R. L. (1992). General educators' mainstreaming preferences that facilitate acceptance of students with behavioral disorders and learning disabilities. *Behavioral Disorders, 17,* 305–315.
National Education Association. (1967). Teacher's problems. *Research Bulletin, 45,* 116–117.
Neel, R. S., & Cessna, K. K. (1993b). Instructional themes: A pragmatic response to complexity. In K. K. Cessna (Ed.), *Instructionally differentiated programming* (pp. 41–50). Denver: Colorado Department of Education.
Neel, R. S., Meadows, N., Levine, P., & Edgar, E. (1988). What happens after special education: A statewide follow-up of secondary students who have behavioral disorders. *Behavioral Disorders, 13,* 209–216.
Nelson, C. M., & Kauffman, J. M. (1977). Educational programming for secondary school age delinquent and maladjusted pupils. *Behavioral Disorders, 2,* 102–113.
Nelson, C. M., Rutherford, R. B., Jr., Center, D. B., & Walker, H. M. (1991). Do public schools have an obligation to serve troubled and troubling youth? *Exceptional Children, 57,* 406–415.
Nelson, R. N., Smith, D. J., Young, R. K., & Dodd, J. M. (1991). A review of self-management outcome research conducted with students who exhibit behavioral disorders. *Behavioral Disorders, 16,* 169–179.
Nickles, J. L., Cronis, T. G., Justan, J. E., III, & Smith, G. J. (1992). Individualized Education Programs: A comparison of students with BD, LD, and MMR. *Intervention, 28,* 41–44.
Nolet, V., & Tindal, G. (1993). Special education in content area classes: Development of a model and practical procedures. *Remedial and Special Education, 14*(1), 36–48.
Novacek, J., Raskin, J., & Hogan, R. (1991). Why do adolescents use drugs? Age, sex, and user differences. *Journal of Youth and Adolescence, 20,* 475–492.
O'Connor, R. D. (1972). The relative efficacy of modeling, shaping and combined procedures. *Journal of Abnormal Psychology, 72,* 327–334.

O'Leary, K. D. (1972). The assessment of psychopathology in children. In H. C. Quay & J. S. Werry (Eds.), *Psychopathological disorders of childhood* (pp. 16–38). New York: Wiley.

Opler, M. K. (1965). Cultural determinants of mental disorders. In B. B. Wolman (Ed.), *Handbook of clinical psychology* (pp. 228–244). New York: McGraw-Hill.

Pappanikou, A. J. (1979). Mainstreaming. *Teacher Education and Special Education, 2,* 51–55.

Parmar, R. S., & Cawley, J. F. (1991). Challenging the routines and passivity that characterize arithmetic instruction for children with mild handicaps. *Remedial and Special Education, 12*(5), 23–32, 43.

Parmar, R. S., & Cawley, J. F. (1993). Analysis of science textbook recommendations provided for students with disabilities. *Exceptional Children, 59,* 518–531.

Parmar, R. S., Cawley, J. F., & Miller, J. H. (1994). Differences in mathematics performance between students with learning disabilities and students with mental retardation. *Exceptional Children, 60,* 549–563.

Parmar, R. S., DeLuca, C. B., & Janczak, T. M. (1994). Investigations into the relationship between science and language abilities of students with mild disabilities. *Remedial and Special Education, 15,* 117–126.

Patterson, G. R., Reid, J. B., Jones, R. R., & Conger, R. E. (1975). *A social learning approach to family interaction* (Vol. 1). Eugene, OR: Castalia.

Paul, J. L., & Epanchin, B. C. (1991). *Educating emotionally disturbed children and youth.* New York: Merrill.

Peacock Hill Working Group. (1991). Problems and promises in special education and related services for children and youth with emotional or behavioral disorders. *Behavioral Disorders, 16,* 299–313.

Pelavin Associates. (1990). *Identification of children with behavioral or emotional disorders: A report prepared under contract to U.S. Department of Education.* Washington, DC: Author.

Phillips, E. L. (1968). Achievement Place: Token reinforcement procedures in a home-style rehabilitation setting for "pre-delinquent" boys. *Journal of Applied Behavior Analysis, 1,* 214–223.

Piaget, J. (1963). *The child's conception of the world.* Paterson, NJ: Littlefield, Adams.

Piaget, J. (1948). *The moral judgment of the child* [Trans. by M. Gabain]. Glencoe, IL: Free Press.

Poland, S. F., Thurlow, M. L., Ysseldyke, J. E., & Mirkin, P. K. (1982). Current psychoeducational assessment and decision-making practices as reported by directors of special education. *Journal of School Psychology, 20,* 171–179.

Polloway, E. A., Cronin, M. E., & Patton, J. R. (1986). The efficacy of group versus one-to-one instruction. *Remedial and Special Education, 7*(1), 22–30.

Pryzwansky, W., & Rzepski, B. (1983). School-based teams: An untapped resource for consultation and technical assistance. *School Psychology Review, 12*(2), 174–178.

Pugach, M. C. (1982). Regular classroom teacher involvement in the development and utilization of IEPs. *Exceptional Children, 48,* 371–374.

Pugach, M. C., & Johnson, L. J. (1989). Prereferral interventions: Progress, problems and challenges. *Exceptional Children, 56,* 217–226.

Pullis, M. (1992). An analysis of the occupational stress of teachers of the behaviorally disordered: Sources, effects, and strategies for coping. *Behavioral Disorders, 17,* 191–201.
Purkey, S. C., & Smith, M. S. (1982). Too soon to cheer? Synthesis of research on effective schools. *Educational Leadership, 40,* 64–69.
Purkey, W. W., & Novak, J. M. (1984). *Inviting school success* (2nd ed.). Belmont, CA: Wadsworth.
Putnam, M. L. (1992). Testing practices of mainstream secondary classroom teachers. *Remedial and Special Education, 13*(5), 11–21.
Quay, H. C. (1992). Defining behavior disorder and determining eligibility for special education services: Interrelated but separate processes. In R. B. Rutherford, Jr., & S. R. Mathur (Eds.), *Monograph in behavior disorders: Severe behavior disorders of children and youth* (Vol. 15, pp. 1–4). Reston, VA: Council for Children with Behavioral Disorders.
Rauth, M. (1981). What can be expected of the regular education teacher? Ideals and realities. *Exceptional Education Quarterly, 2*(7), 27–36.
Reiher, T. C. (1992). Identified deficits and their congruence to the IEP for behaviorally disordered students. *Behavioral Disorders, 17,* 167–177.
Reith, H. J., Polsgrove, L., & Semmel, M. I. (1981). Instructional variables that make a difference: Attention to task and beyond. *Exceptional Education Quarterly, 2,* 61–71.
Reith, H. J., Polsgrove, L., Semmel, M., & Cohen, R. (1980). An experimental analysis of the effects of increased instructional time on the academic achievement of a "behaviorally disordered" high school pupil. In R. B. Rutherford, A. G. Prieto, & J. E. McGlothlin (Eds.), *Monograph in behavior disorders: Severe behavior disorders of children and youth* (pp. 134–141). Reston, VA: Council for Children with Behavioral Disorders.
Reynolds, M. C. (1990). Noncategorical special education. In M. C. Wang, M. C. Reynolds, & H. J. Walberg (Eds.), *Special education: Research and practice: Synthesis of findings* (pp. 57–80). Oxford, England: Pergamon.
Reynolds, M. C., Wang, M. C., & Walberg, H. J. (1992). The knowledge bases for special and general education. *Remedial and Special Education, 13*(5), 33–43.
Rich, H. L. (1982). *Disturbed students.* Baltimore: University Park Press.
Rich, H. L., Beck, M. A., & Coleman, T. W. (1982). Behavioral management: The psychoeducational model. In R. L McDowell, G. W. Adamson, & F. H. Wood (Eds.), *Teaching emotionally disturbed children.* Boston: Little, Brown.
Rist, M. C. (1990). The shadow children. *American School Board Journal, 117,* 18–24.
Rizzo, J. V., & Zabel, R. H. (1988). *Educating children and adolescents with behavioral disorders: An integrative approach.* Boston: Allyn & Bacon.
Roberts, C., & Zubrick, S. (1993). Factors influencing the social status of children with mild academic disabilities in regular classrooms. *Exceptional Children, 59,* 192–202.
Robbins, L. N. (1966). *Deviant children grow up.* Baltimore: Williams and Wilkins.
Robbins, L. N. (1972). Follow-up studies of behavior disorders in children. In H. C. Quay & J. S. Werry (Eds.), *Psychopathological disorders in childhood* (pp. 414–450). New York: Wiley.
Rorschach, H. (1942). *Psychodiagnostics.* Berne, Switzerland: Verlag Hans Huber.

Rose, T. L. (1988). Current disciplinary practices with handicapped students: Suspensions and expulsions. *Exceptional Children, 55,* 230–239.
Rucker, C. N., & Gable, R. K. (1973). *Rucker–Gamble Educational Programming Scale.* Storrs, CT: Rucker–Gable Associates.
Rucker, C. N., & Vautour, J. A. C. (1981). The child study team training programming: Research and development. *Teacher Education and Special Education, 4,* 5–12.
Ruhl, K. L., & Berlinghoff, D. H. (1992). Research on improving behaviorally disordered students' academic performance: A review of the literature. *Behavioral Disorders, 17,* 178–190.
Rusch, F. R., & Phelps, L. A. (1987). Secondary special education and transition from school to work: A national priority. *Exceptional Children, 53,* 487–492.
Rutherford, R. B., Jr., & Neel, R. S. (1978). The role of punishment with behaviorally disordered children. In R. B. Rutherford, Jr., & A. G. Prieto (Eds.), *Monograph in behavioral disorders: Severe behavioral disorders of children and youth* (pp. 69–76). Reston, VA: Council for Children with Behavioral Disorders.
Rutherford, R. B., & Nelson, C. M. (1982). Analysis of the response contingent timeout literature with behaviorally disordered students in classroom settings. In R. B. Rutherford, (Ed.), *Monograph in behavioral disorders: Severe behavior disorders of children and youth* (Vol. 5). Reston, VA: Council for Children with Behavioral Disorders.
Rutherford, R. B., Nelson, C. M., & Wolford, B. (1985). Special education in the most restrictive environment: Corrections/special education. *Journal of Special Education, 19,* 59–71.
Sabatino, D. A., Allen, D., Paulson, D., & Sedlak, R. (1984). Integrating vocational education: Techniques. *Techniques: A Journal for Remedial Education and Counseling, 1,* 53–64.
Safran, J. S., & Safran, S. P. (1987). Teachers' judgments of problem behaviors. *Exceptional Children, 54,* 240–244.
Safran, S. P., Safran, J. S., & Barcikowski, R. S. (1985). Differences in teacher tolerance: An illusory phenomena? *Behavioral Disorders, 11,* 11–16.
Salvia, J., & Ysseldyke, J. E. (1988). *Assessment in special and remedial education.* Boston: Houghton Mifflin.
Samuels, S. (1981). *Disturbed exceptional children.* New York: Human Sciences Press.
Sarbonie, E. J. (1987). Bi-directional social status of behaviorally disordered and non-handicapped elementary school pupils. *Behavioral Disorders, 13,* 45–57.
Sarbonie, E. J., Kauffman, J. M., Ellis, E. S., Marshall, K. J., & Elksnin, L. K. (1987–1988). Bi-directional and cross-categorical social status of learning disabled, behaviorally disordered, and nonhandicapped adolescents. *Journal of Special Education, 21,* 39–56.
Sasso, G. M., Melloy, K. J., & Kavale, K. A. (1990). Generalization, maintenance, and behavioral covariation associated with social skills training through structured learning. *Behavioral Disorders, 16,* 9–22.
Schloss, P. J., Schloss, C. N., Wood, C. E., & Kiehl, W. S. (1986). A critical review of social skills research in behaviorally disordered students. *Behavioral Disorders, 12,* 1–14.

Schloss, P. J., & Smith, M. A. (1987). Guidelines for ethical use of manual restraint in public school settings for behaviorally disordered students. *Behavioral Disorders, 12,* 207–213.

Schmid, K. D., Schatz, C. J., Walter, M. B., Shidla, M. C., Leone, P. E., & Trickett, E. J. (1990). Providing help: Characteristics and correlates of stress, burnout, and accomplishment across three groups of teachers. In R. B. Rutherford, Jr., & S. A. DiGangi (Eds.), *Monograph in behavioral disorders: Severe behavior disorders of children and youth* (Vol. 13, pp. 115–122). Reston, VA: Council for Children with Behavioral Disorders.

Schumm, J. S., Vaughn, S., Haager, D., & Klinger, J. K. (1994). Literacy instruction for mainstreamed students: What suggestions are provided in basal reading series? *Remedial and Special Education, 15*(1), 14–20.

Scruggs, T. E., & Marsing, L. (1987). Teaching test-taking skills to behaviorally disordered students. *Behavioral Disorders, 13,* 240–244.

Scruggs, T. E., & Mastropieri, M. A. (1986). Academic characteristics of behaviorally disordered and learning disabled students. *Behavioral Disorders, 11,* 184–190.

Scruggs, T. E., & Mastropieri, M. A. (1992). Classroom applications of mnemonic instruction: Acquisition, maintenance, and generalization. *Exceptional Children, 58,* 219–229.

Scruggs, T. E., Mastropieri, M. A., & Sullivan, G. S. (1994). Promoting relational thinking: Elaborative interrogation for students with mild disabilities. *Exceptional Children, 60,* 450–457.

Semmel, M. I., Abernathy, T. V., Butera, G., & Lesar, S. (1991). Teacher perceptions of the Regular Education Initiative. *Exceptional Children, 58,* 9–23.

Shapiro, E. S., & Lintz, F. E. (1986). Behavioral assessment of academic skills. In T. R. Kratochwill (Ed.), *Advances in school psychology* (Vol. 5, pp. 87–139). Hillsdale, NJ: Erlbaum.

Shisler, L., Osguthorpe, R. T., & Eiserman, W. D. (1987). The effects of reverse-role tutoring on the social acceptance of students with behavioral disorders. *Behavioral Disorders, 13,* 35–44.

Simonds, J. F., & Kashari, J. (1980). Specific drug use and violence in delinquent boys. *American Journal of Drug and Alcohol Abuse, 7,* 305–322.

Simpson, R. L. (1990). *Conferencing parents of exceptional children.* Austin, TX: PRO-ED.

Simpson, R. L., & Carter, W. J., Jr. (1993). Comprehensive, inexpensive, and convenient services for parents and families of students with behavior disorders: If only Sam Walton had been an educator. *Preventing School Failure, 37*(2), 21–25.

Simpson, R. L., Myles, B. S., Walker, B. L., Ormsbee, C. K., & Downing, J. A. (1991). *Programming for aggressive and violent students.* Reston, VA: Council for Exceptional Children.

Simpson, R. L., Ormsbee, C. K., & Miles, B. S. (in press). General and special educators' perceptions of preassessment-related activities and team members. *Exceptionality.*

Simpson, R. L., & Regan, M. R. (1988). *Management of autistic behavior.* Austin, TX: PRO-ED.

Sitlington, P. L., Frank, A. R., & Carson, R. (1993). Adult adjustment among high school graduates with mild disabilities. *Exceptional Children, 59,* 221–233.

Skiba, R., Hugo, K. E., & Yell, M. (1992). Legal issues in exclusion: Academics and behavior in SED eligibility. In R. B. Rutherford, Jr., & S. R. Mathur (Eds.), *Monograph in behavior disorders: Severe behavior disorders of children and youth* (Vol. 15, pp. 5–17). Reston, VA: Council for Children with Behavioral Disorders.

Slenkovitch, J. E. (1984). *Understanding special education law* (Vol. 1). Cupertino, CA: Kinghorn.

Smith, D. E. P. (1981). Is isolation room time-out a punisher? *Behavioral Disorders, 6,* 247–256.

Smith, S. W., & Farrel, D. T. (1993). Level system use in special education: Classroom intervention with prima facie appeal. *Behavioral Disorders, 18,* 251–264.

Smith, S. W., & Simpson, R. L. (1989). An analysis of Individualized Education Programs (IEPs) for students with behavioral disorders. *Behavioral Disorders, 14,* 107–116.

Spivack, G., Swift, M., & Prewitt, J. (1971). Syndromes of disturbed classroom behavior: A behavioral diagnostic system for elementary schools. *The Journal of Special Education, 5,* 269–292.

Stainbeck, W., & Stainbeck, S. (1984). A rationale for the merger of special and regular education. *Exceptional Children, 51,* 102–111.

Steele, B. F. (1986). Notes on the lasting effects of early child abuse throughout the life cycle. *Child Abuse and Neglect, 10,* 283–291.

Steinberg, Z., & Knitzer, J. (1992). Classrooms for emotionally and behaviorally disturbed students: Facing the challenge. *Behavioral Disorders, 17,* 145–156.

Stephens, T. M. (1978). *Social skills in the classroom.* Columbus, OH: Merrill.

Stone, F., Wilson, B., & Spence, M. (1969). A survey of elementary school children's behavior problems. *American Journal of Orthopsychiatry, 39,* 289–290.

Strain, P. S., & Fox, J. J. (1981). Peers as behavior change agents for withdrawing classmates. In B. B. Leahy & A. E. Kazdin (Eds.), *Advances in clinical child psychology* (Vol. 4). New York: Plenum Press.

Strayhorn, J. M., Jr., Strain, P. S., & Walker, H. M. (1993). The case of interaction skills training in the context of tutoring as a preventative mental health intervention in schools. *Behavioral Disorders, 19,* 11–26.

Takeuchi, D., Williams, D., & Adair, R. (1991). Economic stress in the family and children's emotional and behavioral problems. *Journal of Marriage and Family, 53,* 1031–1041.

Talley, R. (1988). *End of year school psychological services report: School year 1987–88.* Jefferson, KY: Jefferson County Public Schools.

Task Force on Children Out of School. (1971). *The way we go to school: The exclusion of children in Boston.* Boston: Beacon Press.

Task Force on Homelessness and Severe Mental Illness. (1992). *Outcasts on Main Street.* Rockville, MD: National Institute of Mental Health.

Teplin, L. A. (1984). Criminalizing mental disorder: The comparative arrest rate of the mentally ill. *American Psychologist, 39,* 794–803.

Thelen, M., Fry, R., Dollinger, S. J., & Paul, S. (1976). Use of videotaped models to improve the interpersonal adjustment of delinquents. *Journal of Consulting and Clinical Psychology, 44,* 492–493.

Thomas, A., & Chess, S. (1976). Evolution of behavior disorders into adolescence. *American Journal of Psychiatry, 133,* 539–542.

Thomas, A., & Chess, S. (1984). Genesis of evolution of behavioral disorders: From infancy to early adult life. *American Journal of Psychiatry, 141,* 1–9.

Thompson, R. H., White, K. R., & Morgan, D. P. (1982). Teacher–student interactions patterns in classrooms with mainstreamed mildly handicapped students. *American Education Research Journal, 19,* 220–237.

Toch, T., Gest, T., & Guttman, M. (1993, November 8). Violence in the schools. *United States News and World Report, 111*(18), 30–37.

Tremblay, R. E., Perron, B. M., Lelanc, M., Schwartzman, A. E., & Ledingham, J. E. (1992). Early disruptive behavior, poor school achievement, delinquent behavior and delinquent personality: Longitudinal analysis. *Journal of Consulting and Consulting Psychology, 60,* 64–72.

Tuma, J. M. (1989). Mental health services for children: The state of the art. *American Psychologist, 44,* 188–199.

Turnbull, A. P., & Turnbull, H. R. (1985). *Parents speak out: Then and now.* Columbus, OH: Merrill.

U.S. Department of Education. (1988). *Tenth annual report to Congress on the implementation of the Education of the Handicapped Act.* Washington, DC: U.S. Department of Education, Office of Special Education.

U.S. Department of Education. (1990). To assure the free public education of all handicapped children: Twelfth annual report to Congress on the implementation of the Education of the Handicapped Act. Washington, DC: U.S. Government Printing Office.

U.S. Department of Education. (1991). *Thirteenth annual report to Congress on the implementation of the Individuals with Disabilities Education Act.* Washington, DC: Author.

U.S. Department of Education. (1992). *Fourteenth annual report to Congress on the implementation of the Individuals with Disabilities Education Act.* Washington, DC: Author.

Van Reusen, A. K., & Bos, C. S. (1994). Facilitating student participation in Individualized Education Programs through motivation strategy instruction. *Exceptional Children, 60,* 466–475.

Vaughn, S., & Schumm, J. S. (1994). Middle school teachers' planning for students with learning disabilities. *Remedial and Special Education, 15,* 152–161.

Vautour, J. A. C., & Rucker, C. N. (1977). The efficacy of child study teams. In J. A. C. Vautour & C. N. Rucker (Eds.), *Child study team training program book of readings.* Austin, TX: Special Education Associates.

Wagner, M., & Shavers, D. M. (1989, March). *Educational Progress and Achievement of Secondary Special Education Students: Findings from the National Longitudinal Study.* Paper presented at the Annual Meeting of the American Educational Research Association, San Francisco.

Walker, H. M. (1979). *The acting out child: Coping with classroom disruption.* Boston: Allyn & Bacon.

Walker, H. M., & Buckley, N. K. (1973). Teacher attention to appropriate and inappropriate classroom: An individual case study. *Focus on Exceptional Children, 5*(3), 5–11.

Walker, H. M., & Bullis, M. (1991). Behavior disorders and the social context of regular class integration: A conceptual dilemma? In J. W. Lloyd, N. N. Singh,

& A. C. Repp (Eds.), *The Regular Education Initiative: Alternative perspectives on concepts, issues, and models* (pp. 75–93). Sycamore, IL: Sycamore.

Walker, H. M., & Rankin, R. (1983). Assessing the behavior expectations and demands of less restrictive settings. *School Psychology Review, 12,* 274–284.

Wallace, G., & Larsen, S. (1978). *Educational assessment of learning problems: Testing for teaching.* Boston: Allyn & Bacon.

Warren, R., Deffenbacher, J. L., & Brading, P. (1976). Rational-emotive therapy and the reduction of test anxiety in elementary school students. *Rational Living, 11*(2), 26–29.

Weaver, R., Landers, M. F., & Adams, S. (1991). Making curriculum functional: Special education and beyond. *Intervention in School and Clinic, 26,* 284–287.

Wechsler, D. (1981). *Wechsler Adult Intelligence Scale–Revised.* San Antonio: Psychological Corporation.

Wechsler, D. (1989). *Wechsler Preschool and Primary Scale of Intelligence–Revised.* San Antonio: Psychological Corporation.

Wechsler, D. (1991). *Wechsler Intelligence Scale for Children–Third Edition.* San Antonio: Psychological Corporation.

Weinberg, L. A. (1992). The relevance of choice in distinguishing seriously emotionally disturbed from socially maladjusted students. *Behavioral Disorders, 17,* 99–106.

Wesson, C., Wilson, R., & Mandlebaum, L. H. (1988). Learning games for active student responding. *Teaching Exceptional Children, 20*(2), 12–14.

Wheeler, L. J., Reilly, T. F., & Donahue, C. (1984). Teacher's perception of stress and coping skills. In R. B. Rutherford, Jr., & C. M. Nelson (Eds.), *Monograph in behavioral disorders: Severe behavior disorders of children and youth* (Vol. 4). Reston, VA: Council for Children with Behavioral Disorders.

Wiederholt, J. L., Hammill, D. D., & Brown, V. (1978). *The resource teacher: A guide to effective practices.* Boston: Allyn & Bacon.

Will, M. (1986). Educating students with learning problems: A shared responsibility. *Exceptional Children, 52,* 411–416.

Wood, F. H. (1979a). Defining disturbing and disturbed behavior. In F. H. Wood & K. C. Lakin (Eds.), *Disturbing, disordered, or disturbed? Perspectives on the definition of problem behavior in educational settings.* Minneapolis: Department of Psychoeducational Studies, University of Minnesota.

Wood, F. H. (1979b). Issues in training teachers for the seriously emotionally disturbed. In R. B. Rutherford, Jr., & A. G. Prieto (Eds.), *Monograph in behavioral disorders: Severe behavioral disorders in children and youth.* Reston, VA: Council for Children with Behavioral Disorders.

Wood, F. H., & Lakin, K. C. (1979). Defining emotionally disturbed/behaviorally disordered populations for research purposes. In F. H. Wood & K. C. Lakin (Eds.), *Disturbing, disordered, or disturbed? Perspectives on the definition of problem behavior in educational settings.* Minneapolis, MN: Department of Psychoeducational Studies, University of Minnesota.

Wood, F. H., & Zabel, R. H. (1978). Making sense of reports of the incidence of behavior disorders/emotional disturbance in school-aged populations. *Psychology in the Schools, 15,* 45–51.

Wood, M., & Long, N. (1991). *Life Space Intervention: Talking with children and youth in crisis.* Austin: PRO-ED.

Woodcock, R. (1991). *Woodcock–Johnson Psycho-Educational Battery–Revised.* Hingham, MA: Teaching Resources Corp.

Woodward, J. (1994). The role of models in secondary science instruction. *Remedial and Special Education, 15,* 94–104.

Youcha, G., & Seixas, J. S. (1989). *Drugs, alcohol and your children.* New York: Crown.

Yoshida, R. K., Fenton, F. S., Maxwell, J. P., & Kaufman, M. J. (1978). Group decision making in the planning team process: Myth and reality. *Journal of School Psychology, 16,* 237–244.

Ysseldyke, J. E., Algozzine, B., & Thurlow, M. L. (1992). *Critical issues in special education* (2nd ed.). Boston: Houghton Mifflin.

Ysseldyke, J. E., Christenson, S. L., Thurlow, M. L., & Bakewell, D. (1989). Are different kinds of instructional tasks used by different categories of students in different settings? *School Psychology Review, 18,* 98–111.

Zabel, R. H., Boomer, L. W., & King, T. R. (1984). A model of stress and burnout among teachers of behaviorally disordered students. *Behavioral Disorders, 10,* 215–221.

Zabel, R. H., & Zabel, M. K. (1982). Factors in burnout among teachers of exceptional children. *Exceptional Children, 49,* 261–263.

Zionts, P., & Simpson, R. L. (1988). *Understanding children and youth with emotional and behavioral problems.* Austin, TX: PRO-ED.

Zionts, P., Weddle, C., & Zebarah, J. (1981). A study of the emotional problems in the hearing impaired public school population. *Journal of Childhood Communication Disorders, 5,* 136–144.

Zionts, P., & Wood, P. (1983). *The Pupil Assessment Summary.* Mt. Pleasant, MI: RETCO.

# UNIT 2

## Moral Development with Disturbed and Disturbing Students

The students' problems discussed in Unit 1 generally are those of an observable nature. Unit 2 looks at problems that may be due to the students' inability to reason (i.e., problems that are not readily observable). Chapters 6 and 7 explore the belief that a lack of appropriate values and ethics may be engendering behaviors not conducive to the classroom. Polls have suggested that developing students' moral and ethical character has not received enough attention in school curricula. In fact, current educational practice is to control inappropriate behavior and to treat it as a separate entity from moral and ethical behavior.

Except for some short-term research projects, little evidence suggests that cohesive and understandable affective curricula are being implemented in schools today. The literature on the mainstreaming of students who are emotionally disturbed suggests that either the students or the system is failing (Pappanikou & Paul, 1977). Unquestionably, those teachers who consistently employ a behavioral program have had positive results. More often than not, however, special education students have been unable to generalize their "learned" behaviors to the regular classroom. Successful affective education encompasses more than teaching the ability to respond correctly in certain environments.

Special education teachers claim that their students do very well in their classrooms and express perplexity about the students' failures in the general education environment; some even blame their colleagues for the students' problems. Model students from special education classes probably are good students in that setting, where the environmental demands are clear and authority is consistent. However, the real world is far from clear and consistent, and what results for these students outside that classroom may be confusion and failure.

Integral to the philosophy of simply putting students in special education is that the removal from the regular education setting, or placement of the student in a smaller class, will in itself be "the cure." However, the special education placement (especially the resource room) may be inadequate because systematic affective educational programming may not be taking place; the teacher's emphasis may be only on academics. Complicating matters further is the expectation that, when a specific program intervention is suggested, the teacher possesses the skills necessary to implement it. The fact is that, with the exception of behavior modification, Hewett's engineered classroom (Hewett & Taylor, 1980), and rational-emotive therapy, few approaches to dealing with students who are emotionally disturbed provide the structure (i.e., the systematic "how-to" design) that invites classroom use.

The affective program presented in Chapters 6 and 7 suggests one approach—moral development—for teaching disturbed and disturbing students how to think about various conflicts. Furthermore, the program may be considered a natural extension of the behavioral approach presented in Unit 1. Unit 2 presents the theory and methods necessary to enable the student to understand situations and choose among the behavioral alternatives available. This curriculum attempts to teach students in a systematic manner the means to identify and perhaps choose appropriate responses, rather than simply responding to a situation. Students may not always behave properly, but integral to the approach described in the following chapters is the notion that they will indeed "know better."

# 6

# Moral Development with Disturbed and Disturbing Students: Theory

How do we explain the fact that children resist temptations, act against their own immediate self-interest, or obey laws even when no parents, police, or authority figures are around? How do we explain the fact that children come to make judgments concerning the "oughts" of behavior—to distinguish between good and bad, right and wrong, just and unjust? How do we account for the emergence of moral feelings, especially the feeling of guilt that accompanies violation of one's own moral judgments? (Cowan, 1978, p. 172)

Factors other than environmental influences may influence behaviors.

Value systems, ethical behavior, and moral attitudes have been identified as essential to the definition of citizenship, including school citizenship. Moral development and the ability to reason and make decisions have been ignored in both the diagnosis and the treatment of disturbed and disturbing students. Morse (1977) contended that some students who are labeled disturbed may instead be "value deviant." Inherent in the examination of values is the fact that, to attain or possess values in a discerning manner, one must be able to choose among the alternatives available. Currently, various kinds of affective programs are used in schools; they range from allowing the individual "free choice" to a rather dogmatic inculcation of values. These are discussed in this chapter.

After a brief examination of these educational programs, the chapter presents Piaget's work on moral judgment and its relevance to teaching disturbed and disturbing students. How children perceive and apply rules, as well as their perceptions of specific actions of others, is discussed. Specific exercises to enhance students' developmental growth are provided throughout the chapter.

# Indoctrinative Education, Values Clarification, and Moral Development

The indoctrination of appropriate values, values clarification, and moral development are examples of curricula that concentrate on value systems, ethical behaviors, and moral attitudes. These three types of affective programming may be placed on a continuum ranging from rigid to flexible:

| **Rigid** | **Flexible** |
|---|---|
| Indoctrinative----------------Moral Development--------------------Values | |
| Education | Clarification |

Each has a uniquely different philosophy and different implications for the education for disturbed and disturbing youth.

How does a teacher decide which curriculum to implement? Proponents of affective curricula often claim that their programs are destined to cure all students' ills. Before deciding upon any approach, one should study its philosophical and psychological implications. The philosophy of any approach must be congruent with the teacher's philosophy. Would an intentionally disinviting teacher feel comfortable with the openness of a values clarification program, or an unintentionally disinviting teacher with a moral development curriculum?

## Indoctrinative Education

Indoctrinative education is the most rigid of the three approaches because it does not allow self-exploration of morality and the practice of decision-making skills. It presents values of society—in this case, the school—as sacred, and the student must conform or be alienated. Scharf (1978) found that most indoctrinative approaches share the following features:

1. They define morality in terms of moral rules, values, and virtues of a particular society at a particular point in history . . . these values tend to be presented in terms of rules . . . rather than generalizable moral principles.

2. Indoctrinative educators assume that moral values can be taught through inculcation, modeling repetition and reinforcement.

3. Most indoctrinative educators assume that society's values will remain more or less constant; that values taught to a child today will have validity in the years to come; that the norms of respect and honor, lawfulness and pride in one's country should have the moral validity in the year A.D. 2000 that they do today. (p. 23)

Indoctrinative education views the child as a "miniature adult": The means of growth is supplied by the adult in the form of providing information that the child is lacking. Implicit in this information is the notion of conformity. Indoctrinative education claims that the norms and mores of one particular society or culture *should* be universal. In society at large, problems arise when an American confronts a Russian, Chinese, or English person with his or her "universal" American values. Cohen (1955) noted the obvious parallels in U.S. schools, which, as middle class institutions, routinely punish those who are different—that is, the minority cultures of U.S. society. Indoctrinative education is rigid, allowing little if any questioning of the "system."

The implications of indoctrinative education for teaching disturbed and disturbing students are clear. These students, especially those referred to as disturbing, commonly fall victim to teachers who *expect their pupils to behave.* Unfortunately, many disturbing students have never learned the behaviors that are expected of them in school, yet these same students often know how to behave at home. Differential behaviors, which are usually observed as being negative by teachers, are often the result of this situation.

Although developing an indoctrinative environment can make the lives of teachers and parents easier, other consequences may occur. For example, students who are forced to follow any particular doctrine may ultimately rebel because of their perceived powerlessness, or they may fall prey to inappropriate indoctrinative "leaders," such as gang leaders, strong maladaptive peers, and so on.

## Values Clarification

Values clarification is on the opposite end of the moral educational continuum from indoctrinative education. Values clarification is open ended, and students are encouraged to express their opinions about various ideas, *each of which has as much value as any other.* There is no one correct value, as one might expect with indoctrinative education. Values clarification allows the individual to choose values that may be contrary to the norms and mores of the majority society.

Most values clarification programs share the following features:

1. Values are, to a large extent, a matter of personal opinion. No person can tell another person what is right for him or her. While values in

order to be considered as such meet specific criteria, there exists the assumption that a particular value is neither right nor wrong.
2. Learning . . . is largely a matter of increasing awareness of the self. Values clarification sees the child as developing his or her own values apart from social others rather than accepting society's values.
3. There is the implicit assumption that the moral norms of society have largely broken down, and further, that the moral pluralism of today's society forces individuals to define their own value commitments. (Scharf, 1978, p. 27)

Raths, Harmin, and Simon (1966) suggested that values must be chosen freely from alternatives after careful consideration of the consequence of each alternative. The individual should be happy with the choice made and willing to affirm the choice publicly. Next, the individual should do something with the choice, repeatedly, in some pattern during life.

Ironically, many teachers hope that their students will freely choose beliefs and behaviors that are consistent with societal norms. Often, even teachers who claim to favor values clarification use as models the "good" students who choose values consistent with societal norms—the same students who would be chosen by a teacher who is indoctrinative—in hopes of influencing those students who poorly choose their values (e.g., those who choose values that are potentially disruptive to the system). Although such modeling may be effective, the teacher may be falsely assuming that students possess the ability to understand underlying values. Furthermore, other students may choose to model maladaptive behaviors.

### Window on Reality

A teacher asked Frank, a middle school student who is a member of a gang, for his opinion about a story that involves a male–female relationship issue. He commented that if he were the boy in the story, he would smack the girl "until she was sorry."

The teacher was left speechless. She wondered how she could ignore such an inappropriate value.

Problems such as that posed by Frank can frustrate teachers who implement a values clarification program. Kohlberg (1975) suggested that, although values clarification has the above-stated limitations, it can be a very important first step in moral development. It offers a vehicle to encourage the child to arrive at his or her own conclusions about issues, rather than deciding to choose what an authority says is the correct way to think and act. Hersh, Paolitto, and Reimer (1979) suggested that the problem of values clarification is that it does not help students cope with value conflicts. In many situations, an arbitrary authority may be determining value choices for the students. Disturbing students are only too aware that schools do not operate as an all-accepting society, and that their values do not necessarily have equal weight with those of their teachers.

## Moral Development

Moral development can be found in the middle of the continuum of education models. The philosophical and practical weaknesses of indoctrinative education and values clarification are clear when one attempts to apply these models as they exist. Moral development is the progressive development of moral judgment as a cognitive process that allows the person to reflect on values and order them in a logical hierarchy. Development refers to "a progressive change towards some more complex level, a change usually of an irreversible nature" (Downey & Kelley, 1978, p. 63). Moral development differs from the two previously discussed models in two major areas:

1. It suggests that the teacher should be philosophically guided by universal ethical principles rather than by either societal values or the student's personal values.

2. It suggests that a child's moral learning takes place through the changing of his or her ideas of right and wrong in a series of moral stages, rather than through the internalization of societal behavior norms or by an increased awareness of his or her own inner values. (Scharf, 1978, p. 27)

Both students and teachers are confronted daily with a multitude of moral issues, such as self-preservation, respect of property, authority, sexual relationships, and civil rights. The resolution of these issues can help students understand and develop positions on the norms and mores that regulate society.

### Window on Reality

Fred is a smaller than average student who exhibits behaviors that annoy many of his peers. He is often persecuted for his attention-getting demonstrations. Rarely does a week pass when the teacher does not notice Jim teasing Fred because of a perceived shortcoming or handicap.

Normally, the teacher attempts to explain that "Fred can't help having his handicap" or that "You shouldn't hit Fred just because he is different." These efforts rarely result in any change of behavior by Fred or his peers.

A teacher applying moral development would try to help Jim, as well as others, take the perspective of Fred, or initiate a discussion about being fair to others. Will Jim stop teasing Fred simply because his teacher says he should not do such things in school? Maybe. Will he stop after a discussion of the concept of fairness? The fact that some students may have the ability to take the perspective of Fred and disclose how they would feel if they were teased, and others may not, is a very important aspect of moral development. The development of such abilities is what parents and teachers seem to consider a social priority in schools (Gallup, 1981). Moral development theory attempts to teach students to consider the perspectives and needs of others, be they teachers, peers, or parents.

Moral education is analogous to civic education, rather than having religious connotations. In fact, Kohlberg's stages of moral judgment clearly resemble political levels. His higher stages reflect concern for convention, authority, and political institutions. Moral development stresses "arousal of genuine moral conflict, uncertainty and disagreement about genuinely problematic situations" (Blatt & Kohlberg, 1975, p. 130). More important, moral development attempts to allow students to make decisions and solve problems (Rest, 1974). It has been suggested that moral judgment is a necessary but not sufficient condition for moral action (Fenton, 1976). In other words, to act morally one must be able to at least think morally, but if one thinks morally one may not necessarily act morally. This latter point was of concern to Kauffman (1981) in his characteristics textbook. Although he suggested that more research is needed, Kauffman hypothesized that "it may be the case that once moral judgment or moral behavior has gone awry, special techniques will be required to rectify the problem" (p. 272).

Considerable moral education research has been done with disturbing and disturbed populations. For example, Campagna and Hunter (1975) compared 21 individuals with significant social adjustment problems with 23 "normal" working class individuals who were matched on age, IQ, and socioeconomic status. The former individuals were significantly less mature in their moral reasoning than were the latter. Similar results have been found with students with emotional disturbance (Chandler, Greenspan, & Barenboim, 1974) and juvenile delinquent populations (Fodor, 1972; Hains & Miller, 1980). Denno (1979) noted the need to implement moral development rehabilitation in conjunction with other techniques when working with delinquent youth. The strong relationship between discipline and moral development has also been noted by George (1980), Lickona (1980), and Zionts and Weddle (1983). Research that focused primarily on Kohlberg's model is presented later in this chapter.

The research cited suggests a relationship between moral judgment and action. Implicit in this notion is that those individuals operating at lower stages of moral judgment or reasoning do not have the ability to fully interpret situations and conflicts as they occur. The presence of such ability does not necessarily guarantee that those people operating at higher stages will behave more appropriately; rather, it suggests that they will understand the consequences of their own long-term goals, the possible options of behavior, and the perspectives of others.

The purpose of introducing a moral development curriculum into the special education classroom is to enhance the reasoning ability of students who have EBD. This will allow this population to examine situations from both their own perspective and the perspective of others. To implement moral development exercises and techniques in an efficient manner, and to be able to remediate difficulties as they occur, teachers need to examine the theory of moral development. Otherwise, educators may use exercises that simply seem interesting. If roadblocks do occur, the educator may be tempted to discard the curriculum rather than to diagnose where and why the problems exist.

Jean Piaget provided much of the early research that suggested that moral judgment is a cognitive process. He contended that a student's moral judgment progresses through a series of interactions with the environment. How students perceive (cognitively) those interactions is integral to their advancement through the stages. Piaget's work laid the foundation for Lawrence Kohlberg and his associates, who have developed applicable classroom curricula.

## Piagetian Theory of Moral Judgment

Although Piaget is known primarily for his work in the cognitive domain, he made a noted departure in the late 1920s with his research on moral development. His goal as stated in *The Moral Judgment of the Child* (1948) was to stimulate further thought and research on moral judgment. He perceived that development is "clearly related to—is actually a product of— the human mind's tendency to systemize its processes into coherent systems and adapt those systems to changing environmental stimuli" (Hersh et al., 1979, pp. 23–24). Piaget (1948) defined morality as "a system of rules" and said that "the essence of all morality is to be sought for in the respect which the individual acquires for these rules" (p. 1).

Piaget was interested in two phenomena that are integral to understanding rules: *practice*—the ways children of different ages apply rules— and *consciousness*—the perceptions that children of different ages have of how rules are formed, where they originate, and whether they can be changed. What the actual rules entail (their content) was of little interest to Piaget. He believed that children do not attain growth, affective or cognitive, without interaction with their environment. This interaction, combined with the ability to reflect upon events, enables the developmental process. Piaget "always insisted that the cognitive and the moral are inseparably correlative aspects of a unified human development, that there is a parallelism in their respective structures and in their evolution" (Lewis, 1979, p. 174).

Piaget's concept of *decalage* suggests horizontal growth (the generalization of learning) across both cognitive and affective domains. Research has supported the notion of horizontal decalage in moral judgment, because cognitive maturity has been determined to be one of the prerequisites for moral growth. For example, if individuals have IQ scores in the 130 range, many teachers would consider them "gifted." The teachers would be correct if they specified their judgments to relate to the individuals' ability to do well on an intelligence test. However, if the teachers assume that, because the individuals have this IQ score, they are going to be good citizens, be good students, or even have the ability to reason at higher levels (in the moral development sense), then the teachers are assuming that decalage has occurred when it has not.

The notion of decalage is particularly relevant in schools today, where educators tend to look at only one aspect of an area and make generalizations. For example, if a child can decode a certain percentage of words, he or she may be placed in a particular reader with little attention paid to the other facets of reading, such as comprehension, that could possibly set up the child for failure. This is another instance of presupposing that decalage has occurred when it has not. Kohlberg (1973) asserted that "psychometric brightness heavily influences performance on pure tests of conservation of concrete reasoning, but is less determinative of the application of concrete reasoning to areas of causal thinking, concepts of dreams, social identities, and so on" (p. 32).

The implications of decalage are clear. Cognition (thinking ability) plays a major role in feelings. The more options and alternatives that children have, the more likely it is that they may be able to avoid prolonged periods of unhappiness and/or depression. Also, how children interpret events may determine their emotional state. Although a student may have the cognitive ability to reason morally, other factors may inhibit moral growth, such as lack of stimulation from and/or interaction with an environment that invites higher level reasoning (e.g., an "indoctrinative" environment). Also, some students do not possess the cognitive ability to reason at higher levels, but are expected to do so because of their chronological ages. In both cases, many teachers make the supposition that the students are capable of making proper decisions but choose instead to behave in an inappropriate manner. The moral development research suggests that this supposition may be faulty and that teachers may be requesting reasoning that these students are not capable of producing. These students may be operating from a limited viewpoint, which creates a hidden handicap. Research has supported the concept of decalage in that higher levels of cognition are *necessary but not sufficient* for a child to attain higher levels of moral development.

## Cognitive Stages

Because cognition plays so vital a role in promoting moral reasoning, the characteristics of the cognitive stages should be examined. Piaget (1952, 1963), through extensive research, developed the following four stages of cognition (see also Furth, 1970; Ginsburg & Opper, 1978):

1. *Sensorimotor* (before 2½ years of age)—Although children at this stage may begin to take the environment into consideration, they operate solely at the sensory level. This is the stage of action without thinking. Children explore through touch, taste, and smell. They may "know" certain things (e.g., parents) but not in any reflective manner. Movement that may take the form of a pattern actually does not have a logical sequence. These children are preoccupied with self.

2. *Preoperational* (2½ to 7 years)—This is also called the prelogical stage. Children begin to assimilate newfound knowledge, creating "new" thinking. Play is very imaginative, and as the stage progresses the child's preoccupation with self (egocentrism) lessens. Interaction with peers begins to appear at a rudimentary level. Drastic developmental changes occur during the latter part of this stage. Children's behavior is very similar to their speech development. They take only their own point of view, and are initially unable to take another's perspective (Duska & Whelan, 1975).

3. *Concrete operational* (7 to 12 years)—This is the first stage of operational intelligence. Children take their newfound knowledge from the preoperational stage and begin to apply it to life in a consistent manner. Children are able to look at a concrete problem and solve it (e.g., Piaget's famous conservation problem with different shaped beakers, each holding the same volume). However, conservation, classification, and seriation problem solving is limited to *real* (concrete) objects.

4. *Formal operational* (12 and up). This is the final stage of operational intelligence. Children not only have the ability to solve concrete problems, but now can transform such problems into abstract and hypothetical concepts provided they have had the concrete experiences. The children are able to work with such concepts as probable and improbable. Qualitative development reaches its highest level during the stage, after which quantitative (applying results to *new* problems) development can be attained (Clifford, 1981).

Higher levels of cognition are attained through the interactive process between the self and the environment. According to Piaget, cognition occurs through two processes inherent in the human species: *organization,* or the tendency to deal with information in some systematic manner, and *adaptation,* the tendency to adjust oneself to the environment. In the attempt to organize information from the environment, the individual mentally structures or represents relevant aspects of that information. These mental representations are termed *schemata.* For example, when a child first encounters a dog, certain attributes (e.g., furry, four legs, tail) are mentally represented.

Piaget also believed that the human species has a tendency to maintain a mental balance or *equilibrium,* analogous to the homeostasis that keeps biological processes in balance. There are two processes that may lead to a state of equilibrium in the individual: assimilation and accommodation.

*Assimilation* is the process of dealing with new information in terms of existing schema. Imagine the child who has a schema for "car" that includes wheels, movement, sound, and the label "car." One day while looking out the window, the child sees a sedan go by and he points and says "car." He has correctly assimilated the object into his existing framework. A little while later a truck passes by and the child again points and says "car." This time the child has incorrectly assimilated the object into his existing schemata. Eventually the child will understand that the truck, although similar to cars, does not fit into the car schema. When this understanding occurs, the child will be in a state of mental *disequilibrium* or imbalance. To achieve a state of equilibrium, he will have to modify his conception and develop a new schema. This process of modifying concepts based on new experiences is termed *accommodation.*

Thus, equilibrium is achieved through the processes of assimilation and accommodation. When there is a balance between assimilation and accommodation, the individual is in a state of equilibrium. When the individual interacts with the environment, the active processes of assimilation and accommodation occur again, creating disequilibrium (Hersh & Paolitto, 1979). Implicit in the concept of equilibrium is the belief that, if an individual leads a relatively uneventful life and is constantly facing situations that are familiar, little learning will be acquired.

It is the responsibility of the teacher to aid the student in the process of achieving equilibrium. This involves encouraging interaction with peers and the teacher as well as opportunity for introspection. Direct confrontation, rather than avoidance with conflict, is encouraged. Putting conflict aside may cause it to fester into a major problem. Furthermore, stimulation is necessary for progress through the cognitive stages. Piaget considered these same dynamics to be valid in his theory of moral judgment.

## Moral Judgment: Practice of Rules

To understand how children apply (*practice*) and understand the nature (*consciousness*) of rules, Piaget (1948) observed, questioned, and interacted with hundreds of Swiss boys while they played the game of marbles. Piaget chose marbles because the game has many similarities to a moral system. The game of marbles has rules that govern interpersonal relations, including such aspects as mutual respect of personal rights and respect of property (Duska & Whelan, 1975; Ginsburg & Opper, 1978). Also, the game was subject to little adult influence, because it was played almost exclusively by children and it was taken very seriously by them. Piaget observed the same children in many different situations. He probed them by asking such questions as "How do you play marbles?" and "Can you invent a new rule?" (Piaget, 1948). He would consciously make errors so that he could be corrected and appear as ignorant as possible in hopes that the boys would offer accurate information. When questioning children about why they would play by a particular set of rules, Piaget discovered that the answers given seemed unique to each age group.

As a result of his research, Piaget (1948) determined that boys passed through the following four stages in the *practice* of rules:

1. *Purely motor and individual* (before 2 years of age)—"The child handles the marbles at the dictation of his desires and motor habits" (p. 16). In this stage, patterns of play may emerge; however, there is little sense of obligation separating the concepts of rules and regularity. Obligation is not to society or to other individual(s), but to oneself.

2. *Egocentricism* (begins 2 to 5 years of age)—This stage is between purely individual and socialized behavior. The child begins to "play" with other children because that is what "others boys do." The child believes he is playing with another in the adult sense, and that he is cooperating with another individual. In reality, he is seeing only his own perspective. The child has little sense of competition, and it is quite possible for all players to win.

    Piaget observed and interviewed two boys who frequently played together. Each boy discussed the rules of the game separately with Piaget. Both boys had completely different conceptions of the game, yet they often "played together." The child in this stage still does not possess the ability to take another's role, because the self and others are the same to the child.

3. *Incipient cooperation* (begins 7 to 8 years of age)—A respect for peers begins to surface during this stage, and rules begin to regulate group behavior. Each child attempts to win the game and a concern for a mutual obeyance of the rules begins to form. However, rules are not completely understood at this stage, creating many conflicts among participants. Children in this stage *intend* to follow the rules, but can-

not because they cognitively do not understand all of the possible idiosyncrasies of the game.

4. *Codification of the rules* (begins 11 to 12 years of age)—At this stage, boys not only are cooperating under a given framework, but are often preoccupied with the legalistic structure of the rules. "Not only is every detail of the procedure fixed, but the actual code of rules to be observed is known to the whole society" (Piaget, 1948, p. 17). "What ifs" abound, and all possible resolutions are attempted. Piaget observed eight boys in this stage who were preparing a snowball fight. They began by "electing a president, fixing the rules of voting, then in dividing themselves into two camps, in deciding upon the distances of the shots, finally in foreseeing what would be the sanctions to be applied in cases of infringement of these laws" (p. 41).

The game of jump rope, played almost exclusively by girls, provides another example of Piaget's stages. Starting between the ages of 4 and 7, jump rope is played by girls who do not operate by any set of rules, although they think that they do. They are not concerned with winning the game, but only with having a good time. Although operating by a basic principle (to jump the rope), they usually make up their own rules as play progresses. Sometimes a girl breaks a rule to her advantage, initiating leadership, and the others go along with her because they are interested only in interacting with the group. To the followers, winning is "playing." During this period, the girls' patterns are fluid: They follow their own drives, they are sensitive to their own needs, and they create a world for themselves. As

### Window on Reality

A vivid example of Piaget's practice stages was presented when I participated in a student–faculty basketball game while teaching in a state reform school. Although the game of basketball requires individual skills, a measure of team cooperation also must be present for the game to be played successfully. The students probably possessed far greater individual skills than the teachers, but they lost repeatedly by lopsided scores. Normally, a student would throw the ball inbound and four staff members would converge upon him, leaving his teammates free of defenders. The student would rarely give up the ball, however, and would eventually lose it to one of the staff, who would loft the ball to a lone teacher standing around the students' basket who, after three or four attempts, would score a basket. The students' stage of practice was clearly *egocentric* even though they were early adolescents. One might suggest that it is the students' highly individualistic manner of practicing the rules that may have contributed to their being placed in a reformatory (see Hickey, 1972, for research regarding stage placement of youthful offenders and prison inmates).

the girls progress into the stage of incipient cooperation, they begin to socialize and become more knowledgeable about the nature of the game. Although they still make errors and repeats, they are fairly rigid with their perceptions of the exact nature of the rules. In the final stage, the girls make the game increasingly more difficult and more rule laden. Novices often find it impossible to comprehend what they are observing. Nevertheless, the girls' enjoyment of the game increases as it becomes more complex.

Although research has not found Piaget's four stages of the practice of rules to be clear-cut, the implications for education are evident. Are educators asking students to follow rules with respect to which they may be "developmentally delayed"? (Remember, the above stages are based on "normal" children.) One can only imagine what may be going through the mind of a first grader who is being lectured for inappropriate behavior. It is not unusual to hear teachers preach to students and demand that they understand. Setting rules is clearly difficult when students do not possess the cognitive or moral development to understand the behaviors that are required of them. Although students are expected to behave in a manner that is indicative of the behaviors of others who are of similar age, some students *simply may not possess the developmental skill to do so.* Such students are routinely punished for exhibiting behaviors that are representative of their developmental level—in this case, lower than their peers and not at their chronological ages. It is of little wonder that teacher and student reach a stalemate, and often feel frustration, in scenarios such as the following:

TEACHER: Why did you punch Bobby?

JOE: Because he called me a name.

TEACHER: Don't you know we don't fight in our school? (Rule)

JOE: (Silence)

TEACHER: I suggest that you sit here until you can answer my questions.

JOE: Oh yeah, well he called me a name!

In terms of Piaget's stages of the practice of rules, the teacher is trying to elicit rule understanding indicative of Stage 4: the codification of rules. The student is unable to respond to her questions and seems unable to understand that rules should be followed because of their "outside" influence. A more appropriate level of communication may be to attempt to have the student concretely empathize with the victim (Stage 2), perhaps by saying, "It hurts when you are hit or pushed to the ground." It seems imperative that educators become aware of the child's abilities with regard to the practice of rules.

224    Unit 2: Moral Development

## Exercise

Read the following case studies and place each student in one of Piaget's *practice* stages. Then create an educational activity that might encourage advancement for a student at each stage (i.e., an incipient cooperation exercise for an egocentric student).

1. Bob is a 17-year-old who is labeled emotionally disturbed and is employed in a work experience. His problem is his constant tardiness—he has a habit of strolling in late for work and after breaks. Bob really does not understand what the "big deal" is if he is 5 minutes late for work. His logic for his tardiness is that as long as he is on the job site, he is not tardy and he does not have to report to designated areas on time. He does not follow the rules, but he insists that he does.

2. Tracy, age 9, is on the playground during recess and observes another child throwing rocks. She walks over to the child and tells him he is not allowed to throw rocks on the playground (her teacher told her). Just as she finishes saying this, the bell rings to end recess. Tracy goes into school, running down the hall to her classroom.

3. Johnny, age 5, recently began kindergarten. Ms. Alford, his teacher, has noticed that Johnny very seldom considers the other children in his class. He shows no respect for the possessions of others, and is often overheard to say "it's mine," taking away things that other children are working on, as well as toys that other children bring from home.

4. Suzi is 12 years old and enjoys playing games with other classmates, but only on her terms. She is fairly competitive when playing a game. She also enjoys participating in any particular game offered. Suzi will challenge her classmates to a game, but only under her rules.

5. In a long lunch line, Jon's best friend Vinnie is among the first in line. Jon, standing at the end of the line, suddenly spots Vinnie near the front of the line and pushes his way to him and demands that he be given "cuts" because he is hungry and there may not be enough food to last until the end of the line is served.

It would seem that the goal in moral development, as in cognitive education, would be to present readiness exercises to the morally developmentally delayed child to stimulate growth. The examples of activities later in this chapter are presented so that the reader may be better able to understand the stages as well as to teach them. The use of these activities serves two purposes.

First, they provide "learning by doing" rather than "learning by lecturing" opportunities for the students. Most of the games are familiar to most teachers, yet their affective use is rarely explored. Second, the activities provide teachers with a starting point to teach moral judgment in the classroom, as well as allowing them to add activities already in their repertoire in a systematic fashion. It is strongly suggested that time be afforded for simulations because it is the "doing" that not only clarifies the concepts but also provides the teacher with the confidence to try the exercises in the classroom.

## Moral Judgment: Consciousness of Rules

Not only was Piaget interested in how children apply the rules, but he also tried to determine if they understood the nature of the rules. Their *consciousness* of the rules was arrived at by asking derivatives of three questions: Can rules be changed? Have rules always been the same as they are today? How did rules begin? He found that boys passed through the following three stages of consciousness:

1. *Premoral* (under 6 years)—Although children seem to be—and insist that they are—following rules, upon closer examination it is clear that they understand little. What they are doing instead is either imitating older children or adults or simply "following orders." Rules, usually unchangeable ones (e.g., bedtime, feeding, and "don't touch!"), are imposed upon the child at this stage. Hersh et al. (1979) suggested that "respect for rules" may more aptly be termed "fear." When asked why he follows a particular rule, a boy may reply, "Because my father told me I should." The child may bring these "shoulds" and "should nots" into the next stage.

2. *Moral heteronomy* (6 to 10 years)—The child begins to understand the notion of rules. He believes that rules are laws that are sacred and unchangeable. According to this child, *rules are rules* and one must not tamper with them even if the majority of the group wants change. This stage is characterized by an unusual amount of *adult constraint,* from parents as well as teachers. Adults often lay down directives, and more often than not add "no ifs, ands, or buts" or "because I said so!" Piaget suggested that the conflicts that arise may not necessarily involve following the rules, but rather cooperating with others who may be operating from a different set of rules. Therefore, each child behaves with a literal obedience to the rules.

    When asked how the game of marbles originated, the boys in this stage answered that the game was never played before an authority figure "made it up." Early in this stage children seem to accept changes if passed down from an authority figure. Piaget suggested that, because children never really know what the rules "are," they readily accept the changes as the rules themselves. Later in this stage, the child will not accept any change.

3. *Moral autonomy* (11 and up)—This child perceives rules as good for society and understands that they are changeable through consensus. To reach consensus, a level of mutual respect and cooperation must be present. Rules are no longer "forever," and are neither necessarily handed down by adults nor intrinsically "good" because that is what an adult may suggest. It is during this period when children spend increasingly longer periods of the day away from home and are exposed to different thoughts and opinions. They must either join a group or be isolated. This is evident in the conformity that is present in dress as well as behavior in students from middle school through college (see Sweeney & Zionts, 1987).

These stages present the educator with a more complete picture of the child's understanding of rules. Table 6.1 reviews both cognitive and moral judgment stages of Piaget's theory and research, and illustrates how each stage corresponds to particular age levels (see also Turiel, 1978).

## Perceptions of Intent

Piaget (1948) also was interested in how children thought about specific actions. He presented short dilemmas to children and asked them to respond "yes" or "no" to such questions as "Who was naughtier? Was Sue? Was Jim?" Younger children often looked at the results of the incident rather than the intent or motive of the perpetrator. If the character was helping to put away dishes and accidentally dropped nine of them, he was naughtier than one who may have purposely dropped only one (see also Piaget & Inhelder, 1969). Material consequences would therefore dictate whether an action is "good" or "bad." Follow-up research (Breznitz & Kugelmass, 1967; Costanzo, Coie, Grumet, & Farnell, 1973) has supported Piaget's claims.

Nelson's (1980) investigation questioned whether Piaget's method of determining right or wrong is adequate for all children. She found that the method of presentation (visual vs. aural) can significantly alter the statements given by preschoolers. This research adds credence to the notion that handicapped children may score lower on affective measures because of a weakness in the modality in which the diagnostic tool is presented.

## Activities for Elementary Students

The following activities are designed to have two purposes: (a) to enable the reader to apply the theory of Piaget and (b) to enable the reader to

## TABLE 6.1
### Piaget's Cognitive and Moral Judgment Stages

| | Moral Judgment Stages | |
|---|---|---|
| **Cognitive Stage (Age)** | **Practice** | **Consciousness (Age)** |
| Sensorimotor (birth–2½ years) | Purely motor and individual | Premoral (<6 years) |
| Preoperational (2½–7 years) | Egocentrism | Moral heteronomy (6–10 years) |
| Concrete operational (7–12 years) | Incipient cooperation | Moral autonomy (11 + years) |
| Formal operational (12 + years) | Codification of rules | |

understand that many of the most familiar games may have both practical and educational purposes and can serve to motivate and teach students with emotional and behavioral problems. Moral development may be stimulated in elementary school students through the use of such activities as Simon Says and Musical Chairs. A suggestion pertaining to all of the exercises for students operating at the egocentric level is to have everyone win the first time the exercise is done (e.g., have enough chairs for everyone on the first go-round in Musical Chairs). This enables all students to "win" and still play by the rules. The reader should remember that these exercises reflect stage placement and not necessarily age levels. Although the developmentally average child will probably reach the various stages in the time frame Piaget suggested, some older students may be on the egocentric level. Appropriate age levels and motor and skill abilities of the students should be considered when using these exercises.

### *Role-Playing: Stealing from Others*

**Scenario.** One student is assigned to play the role of Rick, a third grader who has trouble distinguishing between his possessions and those of his classmates. Rick takes objects that fulfill his immediate needs despite the problems he may cause his classmates or the rules of the classroom. Items Rick has taken include pencils, paper, candy, toys, and mittens. The most annoying flaw, as felt by his classmates, is when Rick resolutely denies such actions.

**Objectives.** At the end of the role-playing activity, Rick will verbally answer questions that indicate he has a firm grasp of the rules concerning stealing from others. He will acknowledge that he must consider others' wants and needs.

**Activity 1.** The first role-playing activity includes Rick and one classmate. The children role-play situations that are explained by the teacher. In one scene, a child steals Rick's lunch money. The other child needs it, but pretends he does not realize or consider that Rick will soon need the money. When Rick becomes aware of what is happening, he begins to question the other student, to no avail. This discussion or argument does not solve anything, so the teacher must intercede. Even after interrogation by the teacher, the child continues to deny taking Rick's money. The class should attempt to get feedback from Rick about his feelings and attitudes while experiencing being in the other person's shoes.

**Activity 2.** The second role-playing activity demonstrates one child borrowing from another. Pat needs lunch money because she forgot hers, so she asks Jeff for money. Jeff explains to her that he cannot give Pat all of his, but he will be glad to share and let her borrow some of his money. The teacher should make a point of mentioning how smoothly this activity went compared with the first. Again the class should get feedback from Rick about the activity.

**Evaluation of Activities.** The teacher should ask the children the following question: "What would you do if you needed a pencil and your neighbor had one sitting on his or her desk? Would it be best to steal it and hope nobody finds out, or would you ask to borrow or share it?" The teacher can ask the children to verbally express their feelings. The teacher should ascertain if all the children realize that they can receive what they need and want in a fashion that corresponds to the rules.

## Activities for Middle and High School Students

*Following Typing Directions.* In this exercise each student is given a sheet of typing directions consisting of a certain number of steps (e.g., line 1: space over 30 times, type 23 capital Xs; line 2: space over 28 times, type 27 capital Xs). Each step must be followed to get a correct finished piece. If all the steps are followed, the typed page should look like, for example, a historical figure. This exercise is representative of many others that can be used with a microcomputer or typewriter. The computer can even correct the work, depersonalizing the judging process.

*Puzzle Dot Game.* In this game each child is given four index cards with numbered dots that form geometric shapes (e.g., square, diamond, triangle). The object of the game is to connect the dots with either crayons or colored markers according to the given directions. After completing the index cards, the child can compare his or her geometric figures with those of classmates. The child's index cards should match those of classmates if the child correctly followed the rules of the game. If the child's cards differ, the teacher should point out why. The teacher could give a reward for correctly completed cards.

***Assembly Line.*** To introduce this activity, the teacher shows the class a movie or a filmstrip of assembly lines, and discusses how it takes teamwork and cooperation in following the rules to get a good finished product. The teacher explains that, although each person is an individual, he or she also may be an important part of a team. Each class member takes a number from a box for a position on the assembly line. Next, each person goes to the "assembly line" table where his or her number is placed. In a large class, more than one group may be used. On the tables are cards with directions that the students must follow to correctly construct their product. Also, a checklist is provided for them to determine whether they have all required materials. After they have read the directions, checked off their materials list, and turned in the list to the teacher, they should start to make their product. Each person is assigned a different task. It is important to stress that this is not a race and they should take their time and be neat.

For example, the class might make kites using the directions that follow. When the students are in place and have read their directions, checked off their materials, and turned in the list to the teacher, they may start the assembly line. The following numbers represent the students' assigned place in line.

1. Place the diamond model on top of the large piece of paper. Trace the diamond on the paper and cut it out. Pass the cutout to your left, and begin making more.

2. Tape the sticks to the four corners of the diamond. Pass the diamond to your left. Wait for the next one.

3. Take the long strip of cloth and tape it to the bottom of the diamond. Pass the kite to your left.

4. Take the short strips of cloth and tie them onto the long piece of cloth attached to the diamond. Pass the kite to your left.

5. Tie three precut strings to the top and bottom, and across the diamond (using a chart for help). Pass the kite to your left.

6. Tie the strings together in the middle of the kite (using a chart), and attach a long precut string to the middle knot. Pass the kite to your left.

7. Inspect the product. Use your checklist to examine the assembly of the kite. Are all the strings attached? Are the sticks taped? When you complete the checklist, sign your name and pass the kite and the list to your left.

8. Reread the checklist. If anything is not checked, such as "Are the sticks taped?" take the kite to the group that taped the sticks. If the checklist is complete, place the kite at the table labeled "Storage." Keep the checklist for your records.

***Understanding Rules.*** This exercise may also be used when first explaining classroom rules (see Chapter 4). The teacher begins class discussion by telling students that there has been an increase in classroom rule breaking. The teacher states that it is important that everyone understands the need for rules and asks what would happen if there were no rules.

The teacher suggests to the class that almost everything they do has a set of rules. Using the example of sports, the teacher asks a student to tell how many players one team can have on the basketball court at the same time, and writes the answer on the blackboard. The teacher asks additional prompting questions about playing basketball (possible answers are in parentheses).

1. Could I play in my street clothes? (No. You wouldn't look like everyone else on the team and you could get them dirty and torn.)
2. Could I play on the team wearing my high heels?(No. You might hurt yourself and would damage the floor.)
3. What would happen if I was dribbling the ball and you ran into me trying to get the ball away from me? (I would get a foul called on me and you would get a free shot.)
4. How many points do you get for throwing the ball in the basket? (One, two, or three.)
5. What happens when two people from different teams wind up with the ball at the same time? (The referee would call a jump ball.)

The teacher then notes that the purpose of basketball rules is to keep the game orderly, keep people from getting hurt, keep property from getting destroyed, and allow people to have a good time.

Following this example, the teacher makes the transition to classroom rules. Using the same procedure, the teacher asks a student to start listing some of the classroom rules, allowing other members of the class to volunteer. After the classroom rules have been written on the board, the teacher asks a student to come to the front of the room to lead an exercise. Telling the student that he or she is now the teacher, the teacher moves to the back of the room and begins to play rule-breaking situations with other students.

When the need for the rules is made clear, the teacher leads a closure exercise by recounting why the simulation began: There was a problem with classroom rule breaking. Thus, there was a need to review why there are rules and what would happen if there were no rules. The teacher elicits answers from the class to review the lesson (some students may not have any conceptualization of rules). Referring back to the example of basketball, the class reviews the rules of the game and what would happen if there were no rules: People would get hurt, property would be damaged, and the game would be chaotic. The same reasons exist for classroom rules: The class could become disorderly, students could be hurt, property could be damaged, and little learning would occur.

*Developing Rules.* A student operating at the incipient cooperation stage is placed with a peer who is in the genuine cooperation stage. Together they must devise a game complete with board, playing pieces, and rules. They must construct all the parts of the game and list all of the rules. The game is aimed toward youngsters in the lower elementary grades. The eventual goal would be for the "partners" to teach the game to two youngsters. To complete this assignment, the two students must be able to agree on how they should make up the game.

*Identifying Individual Feelings About Classroom Rules.* The objective of this activity, which takes about 30 minutes, is for each participant to be able to identify at least five classroom rules and discuss their possible classroom use. The teacher asks the participants to count off from 1 to 5 to establish five groups. The teacher then distributes a 3-inch by 5-inch card to each participant. Everyone in each group takes a turn by sharing something positive about a particular classroom rule. Next, the others in the group write a phrase on a sticky label about what the speaker has to share. The speaker tells the other group members a positive comment about the rules, presses the label on his or her card, and passes the card to the person on his or her left. As the card is passed, each person should tell the speaker the positive comment he or she recorded as the speaker was talking and press an additional label on the card. Continue this sharing until one card has been completed for each person. The teacher concludes the activity by indicating to the students that their participation in the activity will hopefully add to their understanding of the value of classroom rules.

# Implications of Moral Development to Special Educators

Students who have emotional and/or behavioral disorders typically have lower levels of reasoning (Swarthout, 1988). Moral development is beginning to be recognized in teacher training literature (Center, 1989; Coleman, 1992; Goldstein & Glick, 1987; Kauffman, 1993; Newcomer, 1993) as a theory that can provide teachers with the means to understand the reasoning ability of their students. This is particularly important when considering which affective intervention to utilize in the classroom.

As discussed, students operate at different levels of practice of and consciousness of rules. If teachers are to be more than reactive to disturbances when they occur, they must be aware of the level of moral development of their students. Often, however, "a teacher acts only if there is a threat to the control of the classroom—and even then, the action is typically to reprimand or to punish rather than to foster the moral growth of students through some kind of shared responsibility for making things better . . . While some teachers are unhappy about the way students treat others, while they are distressed about their lack of moral responsibility, they tend to see this as something to be endured. They do not see it as a problem to be solved" (Lickona, 1980, p. 54). Teachers' lounge conversations often contain phrases such as "moral decay" and "lack of sense" in reference to students, whether elementary or high school age (Jantz & Fulda, 1975; Mackey, 1973). Parents are often blamed for the students' lack of values, but, as Muss (1976) discovered, it is these same parents who feel poorly equipped to handle the responsibility of inculcating values on their own and want the school to do it for them (see also Gallup, 1981).

The implication of Piaget's work is that students do not exhibit moral growth in a vacuum (see also Hurt, 1977; Lickona, 1980). If it is the teacher's responsibility to promote moral development, it is the teacher training institutions' responsibility to enhance the moral maturity of their students—the future teachers—*before* they leave the university or college. As discussed later, this cannot be accomplished through the standard teacher-in-the-classroom role. Both teacher and student should be aware that the teacher cannot solely lecture his or her charges, whatever their ages, and expect growth, except in the time-honored ability to lecture!

If the goal of special educators is indeed to "mainstream" or "include" disturbed and disturbing children, the evidence presented suggests that the need to help children control their behaviors is of primary concern to teachers. Unit 1 presented a classroom rather than a student management program. Unit 2, however, suggests that there is an additional factor that teachers may have overlooked in the education of disturbed and disturbing students. This factor is students' inability to solve problems and resolve new conflicts. Pappanikou (1979) argued that, if the system from which he or she came has not been "mainstreamed," a student who enters a general education environment without the tools to recognize and solve conflicts that are tempting (e.g., skipping class with friends) or troublesome (e.g., the teacher does not give the immediate response that the student was accustomed to in the special education room) has little chance to succeed.

If the general education teachers have not modified their "system" to take into account childrens' handicaps, the chances are that students will get "mixed messages." Cooney (1977) noted that "one of the striking features of social interaction as compared with the physical world is the much greater complexity of the social feedback system. The physical world responds to the child and his/her actions in a relatively visible and uniform way" (p. 7). The special educator often tries to present a management system that is consistent in the same "relatively visible and uniform way."

However, the general education environment rarely provides this feedback, which may in turn create stress for the student. It is important that the students be presented with the skills to adequately "fit" into the general education environment. Their ability to assess situations and see beyond their own egocentric viewpoints must be promoted.

Chapter 1 contended that some schools have environments that are not conducive to accepting deviance (those that are unintentionally or intentionally disinviting). These "atmospheres," which differ from school to school, may transmit inconsistent signals to students. Democracy and student involvement are doctrines often espoused in junior and senior high schools; however, the "hidden curriculum" (Jackson, 1968) warns that democracy is fine as long as conformity, constraint, and subordination to the time-held truths are observed. The disturbed and disturbing students are unable to unfold the hidden curriculum and normally suffer because of their inability to do so.

An additional hidden curriculum is frequently found when rules are developed in the classroom. As mentioned in Chapter 4, some educators believe that students should develop classroom rules because they will then feel an obligation to follow them. However, if the students are operating at Piaget's egocentric or premoral stage of development, they may suggest rules that are clearly contradictory. Many of their "rules" will not be rules at all and, if installed, could lead to chaos. When this occurs, the teacher may "lead" the students to rules and regulations with which they feel comfortable, rules that *were always on the teacher's agenda* .

Although disturbed and disturbing students must contend with a sometimes confusing and not-so-open system, their difficulties may be compounded when they experience *temporary moral developmental or situational crises* and *lags in learning and social development* (Kohlberg, 1973). In other words, the problem may not be with the system, but rather with the students' lack of the skills needed to interact successfully with the system. One approach that teaches these skills is moral development training.

The teacher's role in implementing a moral development curriculum cannot be understated. Inherent in it is a commitment to help disturbed and disturbing students learn to reason in a more sophisticated fashion. This can be very threatening to some teachers because they must put aside their comfortable dictums stating, "Yours is not to reason why . . ." and "Do as I say . . . ." Also, the results of moral development training will not guarantee that the students will behave in a more appropriate fashion, but rather that they will understand the options available to them. The purpose of moral development training is to stimulate the student's reasoning to the next step of development rather than to supply information to be regurgitated at a later date (Kohlberg, 1973). Successful gains in moral development will generalize to academic areas where reasoning is valued, such as social studies, science, mathematics, and creative writing.

The research and methodology presented thus far falls short on two counts in providing a totally adequate program in moral development. First, Piaget's (1948) work concentrated primarily on the growth of boys into early adolescence; he did not include any data to suggest that growth occurs after early adolescence. Second, educators should be concerned not only with how students perceive and apply rules, but also with their reasoning. This latter shortcoming has been the foundation for much of the advancement in moral development theory and application by Kohlberg.

## Kohlberg's Theory of Moral Development

Kohlberg began his research on moral development in the mid-1950s, with his first major work being his doctoral dissertation in 1958. Kohlberg (1981) was influenced strongly by both psychology and philosophy, especially the work of Piaget, Baldwin, Dewey, Plato, and Mead. While he expanded upon the work of Piaget, he based his theory on Dewey's claim that "development is the aim of education," as well as on the Platonic view that the purpose of education is justice (Kohlberg, 1978b). Kohlberg believed that *structure,* or reasoning, is central to moral development and that *content,* or information, provides little knowledge about the individual. His dissertation methodology differed from Piaget's methodology in that his interviews were open-ended rather that forced choice (yes or no answers).

Kohlberg agreed with Piaget that individuals develop reasoning by progressing through a series of stages. Kohlberg's (1973) stages of development attempt to satisfy the following criteria with respect to this progression from one level to the next:

1. The change is irreversible. Once it has occurred the change cannot be undone, forgotten, or replaced under normal conditions.

2. The change is general over a field of responses and situations.

3. The change is a change in shape, pattern, or quality of response, not merely in the frequency of its correctness according to external criteria.

4. The change is sequential; it occurs in an invariant series of steps.

5. The change is hierarchical; that is, the later forms of response dominate or integrate the earlier forms. (p. 13)

To determine the stage structure, Kohlberg presented his subjects with hypothetical dilemmas and asked them to respond. Again, he was not interested in what (content) the subject thought, but rather with why and how (structure) the student arrived at his or her answer. His early data suggested six stages of moral development (presented later in the chapter).

It is important to note that Kohlberg *never intended* to suggest that if individuals reason at Stage 1 or 2, they do not act in a moral fashion (Gibbs, Kohlberg, Colby, & Speicher-Dubin, 1976). Many factors may influence a person's behavior, and to consider only one is simplistic and short-sighted. Furthermore, Kohlberg's cognitive theory of moral development is not a "personality"-oriented approach, nor does it encompass all that is intrinsic to moral development. There has been evidence to suggest that cognitive-moral development can stimulate other facets of development, much in the same fashion as Piaget's (1948) horizontal decalage. Kohlberg's (1973) model stresses:

1. Knowledge of the child's stage of functioning.
2. Arousal among children of genuine cognitive and social conflict and disagreement about problematic situations . . .
3. The presentation of modes of thought one stage above the child's own. (p. 9)

In this respect Kohlberg's model differs from the models of others who often have been included under the rubric of moral development (e.g., Bandura, 1977). His is simply one approach that has been effective in promoting the reasoning ability of students.

The cognitive-moral development process is enabled by teachers' presentation to their students of conflicts that revolve around 10 moral issues that Kohlberg suggested are universal (see Table 6.2). These issues may not be universal with regard to *content,* but they are with regard to *structure.* The 10 moral issues may surface in the classroom in many variations, such as films, television shows, real-life experiences, and, most commonly, hypothetical dilemmas. These dilemmas are short vignettes that elicit various levels of reasoning from the students. Enright's (1980) research suggests that, when presenting dilemmas, teachers should consider a five-step process: encouraging interaction, reflecting upon that interaction, reflecting on the reasoning behind the interaction, considering discrepancies between reasoning and action, and being exposed to stage thinking that is higher than that at which the students are presently operating. These steps emphasize both the nature of Piaget's developmental stages and Kohlberg's cognitive moral notion of structure. Chapter 7 further examines the development and application of hypothetical dilemmas.

# Review of Important Concepts

This chapter has suggested that the education of disturbed and disturbing children is incomplete if it relies solely on the behavioral approach presented in Chapter 5. If educators are committed to mainstreaming disturbing

**TABLE 6.2**
**Kohlberg's 10 Universal Moral Issues**

I. Punishment and Blame
Should someone be punished or not? Why?
What is fair punishment?

II. Property
Should someone give, take, or exchange property or not? Why?
What are property rights?

III. Affiliation Roles
Should someone help another or maintain the other's expectation in a personal relationship? Why?
What are the motives and obligations of a good family member or friend?

IV. Law
Should someone obey or maintain a law? Why?
What are the characteristics of a good law?

V. Life
Should someone save a life or not? Why?
What makes life valuable?

VI. Truth
Should someone tell the truth or allow the truth to be disclosed or not? Why?
What defines truth-telling and why is it valuable?

VII. Governance
Should someone obey or accept the authority of another person of a government or rule-making group? Why?
What are the characteristics of a good governor and a good citizen?

VIII. Civil Rights and Social Justice
Should someone violate or uphold the political, economic, and social rights of another person or group? Why?
What are the basic political, economic, and social rights?

IX. Sex or Eroticism
Should one have a sexual relationship or not? Why?
What is the nature of a good erotic relationship and why is it valuable?

X. Morality and Mores
Should one follow one's moral opinion or conscience when it conflicts with law, love, or self-interest? Why?
What is the nature of morality and what is the basis of its validity?

From "The Domain and Development of Moral Judgment: A Theory and a Method of Assessment" by J. Gibbs, L. Kohlberg, A. Colby, and B. Speicher-Dubin, in *Reflection on Values Education* (pp. 28–29) by J. Meyer (Ed.), 1976, Waterloo, Ontario: Wilfrid Laurier University Press. Reprinted by permission.

children, teachers must teach students to evaluate conflicts in an everchanging environment (i.e., the general classroom setting). My purpose here is not to discount the value of behaviorism, because it does provide the means to control aberrant behaviors in a controlled setting. Appropriate behavior is rarely rewarded in the regular setting as it is in the special setting. However, I propose that affective programming must be added to supplement the behavioral component.

Scharf (1978) examined three affective approaches (see Table 6.3) that suggest that moral development, rather than indoctrination or values clarification, can best satisfy students' needs. It is an approach that attempts to teach the individual how to dissect conflicts and make decisions. Next, the foundation of moral development theory as defined by Piaget and later by Kohlberg and his associates was presented. It should be remembered that neither Piaget nor Kohlberg suggested that moral judgment or cognitive-moral development constitutes moral education in total; rather, it is one important facet to be considered. Piaget's goal was to *stimulate further thought and research.* (An examination of Unit 2 in this text indicates that this modest goal was met.)

Piaget's study in Geneva has engendered two stage structures: *practice,* how individuals apply rules, and *consciousness,* how individuals perceive the nature of rules. Turiel (1969) suggested that these stages are more qualitative than quantitative in nature because it is very difficult to ascertain clear-cut stages. This may be the case, although research such as that discussed thus far presents at least correlative evidence of the stages. As reasoning progresses, adult constraint is lessened and cognitive maturity and social interaction increase. Research regarding the adult constraint factor has been less powerful than that regarding the latter two factors (Lickona, 1976).

Piaget claimed that children will progress through the stages if they have not been deprived of the proper environmental stimulation. Children do not tend to learn in a vacuum; they will not cognitively or socially develop by simply growing older without adult and peer stimulation. Supplementing his conclusions about stages of practice and consciousness are Piaget's observations of children's perceptions of intent. Again, there seems to be a developmental sequence of how children perceive the specific actions of others.

Piaget's work, although substantive, ignored the possiblity of further developmental process in adolescence and adulthood. He also paid little attention to the classroom implications of moral judgment. He did provide a solid framework from which Kohlberg and his associates developed, and continue to refine, the cognitive-moral development model. This model and its classroom implications and application are examined further in the remainder of this chapter and the next.

If special educators are to aspire to include disturbing and disturbed students in general education classes, they must examine their affective

**TABLE 6.3**
**Three Affective Approaches to Developing Appropriate Behavior**

|  | Indoctrination | Values Clarification | Developmental Moral Education |
|---|---|---|---|
| *What is right?* | Determined by societal and cultural norms. | Determined by individual through reflection on alternative value premises. | Determined by philosophic rightness. Either principle should be universally valid. |
| *How children learn or change moral ideas* | Through repetition, association, modeling, reward, and example. | Through self-analysis and awareness of implications of value choices. | Through conflict, dialogue, role-taking, and moral interchange. |
| *State of society* | Under threat, but capable to return to traditional values. | In state of more or less continual value flux. | While societal norms and mores are subject to change, moral principles are eternal. |

From "Creating Moral Dilemmas for the Classroom" by P. Scharf, in *Readings in Moral Education* by P. Scharf (Ed.), 1978, Minneapolis: Winston Press. Copyright by Winston Press, Inc., 430 Oak Grove, Minneapolis, MN 55403. Reprinted with permission.

programming used in the special classes (Gresham, 1982). Implicit in the mainstreaming and inclusion concepts is the idea that the "cured" (or accepted) students will now be able to cope with a modified general education program. The reality, however, is that the students most likely will be placed in an environment that is very similar to the one in which they failed in the first place and certainly very different from the consistent special education class from which they came. These students, successful where there are fixed environmental expectations, often fail in general education, perhaps because of their inability to analyze conflicts and attempt to resolve them under the system's "fluctuating" demands. This chapter has suggested that moral judgment or moral development training is one classroom curriculum that can increase the students' ability to reason. The approach of this training is clear, concise, and relatively simple to implement. The dilemmas provided in the next chapter allow the educator to immediately introduce moral development into the classroom.

The theory and research discussed in this book suggest that disturbed and disturbing students may benefit not only from a classroom management program, but also from one that increases the students' ability to cognitively react to conflicts. This thesis has important implications for how special educators are preparing students for general education classes. The remainder of this chapter further examines the theory of moral development as postulated by Kohlberg and his associates. Chapter 7 provides specific techniques to assess and program in the classroom.

An understanding of theory is extremely valuable when attempting to utilize *any* approach. Teachers sometimes consider the concept of learning in a rather narrow manner; that is, they feel that learning can occur only by means of techniques that can be brought into the classroom. While I wholeheartedly agree with the spirit of this conception of learning, I also think this view is shortsighted. Too often valuable interventions are attempted and then discarded as soon as implementation problems occur because "It doesn't work!"

The possible ramifications of this practice in the area of academics are startling. By the time some students reach high school, they have been exposed to more reading programs than their teachers. This could be due to teachers' changing programs as soon as the student encounters any difficulties. Many times problems can be alleviated if the teacher understands the theory and can identify and remediate possible difficulties. It is for these reasons that the reader is encouraged to carefully consider the precepts of moral development described in the following section.

# Research Generalizations

Fenton (1976) summarized conceptual generalizations of moral development theory. This section expands upon the work of Fenton to provide a framework for the reader. It should be noted that much emphasis is paid to generalization 1, which discusses the concept of stage development. I have added generalizations 12 and 13 to explore issues that Fenton had omitted.

## 1. People Think About Moral Issues in Six Qualitatively Different Stages in Three Levels of Two Stages Each.

Kohlberg, in his continuing work of analyzing both his research and the research of those following his approach, developed *three levels of moral judgment*. These are three broad categories that were originally divided into six specific stage descriptions. The first level, *preconventional* reasoning, is the level at which the individual has a very narrow view of society. Conformity to rules and regulations happens only because of fear of physical punishment; which may take the form of societal ("Be good, or I'll spank you") or of natural ("You will fall and hurt yourself") consequences.

An individual is on the preconventional level when "situations of moral conflict are seen as situations in which needs collide and are resolved either in terms of who has the most power in the situation . . . or in terms of simple individual responsibility for one's own welfare . . . except where bound by simple market-place notions of reciprocity" (Kohlberg & Hersh, 1977, p. 56). Rules are considered to be external and individuals are unaware that they have control over them. In fact, these individuals may be highly influenced by their environment. Kohlberg's (1976) findings suggest that the preconventional level describes most children under 9 years of age, some adolescents, and many adolescent and adult criminal offenders (see also Fodor, 1972; Ruma & Mosher, 1967).

*Conventional* reasoning is that level at which authority figures are still highly influential, but not necessarily from a "fear-of-punishment" perspective. Interpersonal relationships that involve pleasing parents, authority figures, or influential peers are integral to the conventional level. Identification with others (social groups) begins to be a priority at this level. The individual reasons from a "member-of-society" perspective and is attempting to conform to that society. Kohlberg (1976) reported that most adolescents and adults are on the conventional level.

The *postconventional* level is reached by only a minority of adults and usually only after age 20 (Kohlberg, 1976). People at this level have differentiated themselves from the rules and expectations of others and define their values in terms of self-chosen principles. These individuals reason on a "prior-to-society" perspective and are guided by moral principles that may or may not conform to those of society.

An examination of the three levels of moral judgment is presented in Table 6.4. Three perspectives of reasoning—(a) what is right, (b) reasons for upholding right, and (c) social perspective—are delineated. Kohlberg's six stages (Table 6.5) are empirically derived from these three levels of moral judgment. An understanding of these levels is important because the cognitive-moral development approach is based on them. There are certain conditions that Kohlberg and his associates claimed are mandatory in both the research and the implementation of this model.

The reader is encouraged to pay attention to the implications each stage has for the practice of classroom discipline. George (1980) suggested that specific interventions may be attempted with students who are on a particular stage (see also Zionts & Weddle, 1983). The success or failure of the interventions may be predicated on the appropriateness of the relationship of the reasoning behind the intervention to the students' level of reasoning.

*Stage 1* thinking contends that behaving or "doing right" is necessary to avoid physical punishment. As Hersh et al. (1979) pointed out, children at this level perceive only one consequence for misdeeds, and that is physical punishment. The children do not believe that their actions have a good or bad value; rather, they *result* in approval or disapproval from an authority or power figure. Not only is "doing right" an important concept, so too is "might makes right." George (1980), relating Stage 1 reasoning to classroom terms, perceives these students to be in preschool through Grade 2. They are generally students who "need to learn the basic habit pattern of classroom life. They need to learn it is right to listen to the teacher, to follow directions, to share, to ask questions and to adapt to routines" (p. 60). Characteristic to these tasks are activities that *must* be followed in most classrooms to *avoid* punishment.

## TABLE 6.4
### Three Levels of Moral Judgment

**A. Preconventional Level**

1. What is right? Right is usually following the rules. The rules, however, are literal. They are not understood in terms of the expectations of a society or of a notion of a good person. Bad is a label applied to an act without considering a person's motive. What is right is limited to following concrete rules or orders with power and punishment behind them; it is not defined in terms of the expectations and welfare of others. Where right is not a matter of obeying concrete rules or commands, it is a matter of serving interests of the self or those close to the self.
2. Reasons for upholding right: Reasons include self-interest, avoidance of punishment, deference to power, avoiding physical harm to others, and exchange of favors.
3. Social perspective. Right and good are seen from the point of view of one individual looking at other individuals or at the physical dimensions and consequences of rules and actions.

**B. Conventional Level**

1. What is right? Right means conforming to and upholding the rules, roles, and expectations of society at large, or conforming to the rules and expectations of a smaller group, like one's religious or political denomination. "Comforming to and upholding" rules and roles means more than just obedience; it means the inner motivation corresponding to the rules.
2. Reasons for upholding right: Reasons include approval and general social opinion, loyalty to persons and groups, the welfare of others and of society.
3. Social perspective: Right and good are seen from the point of view of a member of society or of a smaller group. The point of view is consciously shared with others. Individual or egoistic points of view are subordinated to the shared point of view.

**C. Post-Conventional or Principled Level**

1. What is right? Right is defined by general or universal human rights, values, or principles which society and the individual should uphold. While it is usually right to uphold the law because the law does protect human rights, violations of the law are justified where the law is not protecting human rights.
2. Reasons for upholding right: Reasons are essentially defined by a "social contract," the notion that by living in society you have made a generalized commitment to respect and uphold the rights of others (and the laws this entails) or by "principle," by commitment to moral principles which it is believed any moral person would perceive as rationally valid.
3. Social perspective: The perspective is prior to society. It is that of a rational individual defining values and principles prior to society or as a basis for defining a good society and committing himself to society.

From "The Domain and Development of Moral Judgment: A Theory and a Method of Assessment" by J. Gibbs, L. Kohlberg A. Colby, and B. Speicher-Dubin, in *Reflections on Values Education* (pp. 21–22) by J. Meyer (Ed.), 1976, Waterloo, Ontario: Wilfrid Laurier University Press. Reprinted with permission.

## TABLE 6.5
### Kohlberg's Six Moral Stages

| | Content of Stage | | |
|---|---|---|---|
| Level and Stage | What Is Right | Reasons for Doing Right | Social Perspective of Stage |
| **Level I—Preconventional** | | | |
| Stage 1—Heteronomous morality | To avoid breaking rules backed by punishment, obedience for its own sake, and avoiding physical damage to persons and property. | Avoidance of punishment and the superior power of authorities. | Ecocentric point of view. Doesn't consider the interests of others or recognize that they differ from the actor's; doesn't relate two points of view. Actions are considered physically rather than in terms of psychological interests of others. Confusion of authority's perspective with one's own. |
| Stage 2—Individualism, instrumental purpose, and exchange | Following rules only when it is to someone's immediate interests and needs and letting others do the same. Right is also what's fair, what's an equal exchange, a deal, an agreement. | To serve one's own needs or interests in a world where you have to recognize that other people have their interests, too. | Concrete individualistic perspective. Aware that everybody has his own interest to pursue and these conflict, so that right is relative (in the concrete individualistic sense). |
| **Level II—Conventional** | | | |
| Stage 3—Mutual interpersonal expectations, relationships, and interpersonal conformity | Living up to what is expected by people close to you or what people generally expect of people in your role as son, brother, friend, etc. "Being good" is important and means having good motives, showing concern about others. It also means keeping mutual relationships, such as trust, loyalty, respect, and gratitude. | The need to be a good person in your own eyes and those of others. Your caring for others. Belief in the Golden Rule. Desire to maintain rules and authority which support stereotypical good behavior. | Perspective of the individual in relationships with other individuals. Aware of shared feelings, agreements, and expectations which take primacy over individual interests. Relates points of view through the concrete Golden Rule, putting yourself in the other guy's shoes. Does not yet consider generalized system perspective. |

*(continues)*

**TABLE 6.5** (Continued)

| | | | |
|---|---|---|---|
| Stage 4—Social system and conscience | Fulfilling the actual duties to which you have agreed. Laws are to be upheld except in extreme cases where they conflict with other fixed social duties. Right is also contributing to society, the group, or institution. | To keep the institution going as a whole, to avoid the breakdown in the system "if everyone did it," or the imperative of conscience to meet one's defined obligations. (Easily confused with Stage 3 belief in rules and authority . . .) | Differentiates social point of view from interpersonal agreement or motives. Takes the point of view of the system that defines roles and rules. Considers individual relations in terms of place in the system. |
| **Level III—Postconventional, or Principled** | | | |
| Stage 5—Social contract or utility and individual rights | Being aware that people hold a variety of values and opinions, that most values and rules are relative to your group. These relative rules should usually be upheld, however, in the interest of impartiality and because they are the social contract. Some non-relative values and rights like life and liberty, however, must be upheld in any society and regardless of majority opinion. | A sense of obligation to law because of one's social contract to make and abide by laws for the welfare of all and for the protection of all people's rights. A feeling of contractual commitment, freely entered upon, to family, friendship, trust, and work obligations. Concern that laws and duties be based on rational calculation of overall utility, "the greatest good for the greatest number." | Prior-to-society perspective. Perspective of a rational individual aware of values and rights prior to social attachments and contracts. Integrates perspectives by formal mechanisms of agreement, contract, objective impartiality, and due process. Considers moral and legal points of view: recognizes that they sometimes conflict and finds it difficult to integrate them. |
| Stage 6—Universal ethical principles | Following self-chosen ethical principles. Particular laws or social agreements are usually valid because they rest on such principles. When laws violate these principles, one acts in accordance with the principle. Principles are universal principles of justice: the equality of human rights and respect for the dignity of human beings as individual persons. | The belief as a rational person in the validity of universal moral principles, and a sense of personal commitment to them. | Perspective of a moral point of view from which social arrangements derive. Perspective is that of any rational individual recognizing the nature of morality or the fact that persons are ends in themselves and must be treated as such. |

From "Moral Stages and Moralization: The Cognitive-Developmental Approach" by L. Kohlberg, in *Moral Development and Behavior: Theory, Research, and Social Issues* by T. Lickona (Ed.), 1976, New York: Holt, Rinehart & Winston. Reprinted with permission.

*Stage 2* reasoning suggests a more positive view of one's self and of others. Being physically punished is not necessarily a concern. Rather, the Stage 2 thinker attempts to negotiate the best arrangement with others by giving the least effort and may behave appropriately only to receive rewards. At this stage, the child is beginning to recognize that there are other people in society who should be taken into consideration. This is a major shift from Stage 1, which emphasized fear of corporal punishment and ramifications of disobedience to the teacher.

Discipline in Stage 2 tends to be in the form of behavior modification and contingency management, which both effectively deal with the notion of fairness (George, 1980). Furthermore, with behavior modification, the parameters of behaviors are clear and students can understand how reinforcement is rewarded. "The central value of Stage 2—authority—is relativized at Stage 2. An authority is like everybody else insofar as he has to play by the rules of the game, which are the rules of fairness" (Hersh et al., 1979, p. 69).

*Stage 3* marks the entrance to the conventional level. The individual wants to be accepted by others in society. To do so, the individual must take into account the expectations of others. It is not unusual for people to sacrifice what they desire for the good of the group. The individual considers not only the more overt forms of approval or disapproval, but also the more subtle aspects, such as "What does he *think* of me?" Mutual trust and commitment between parties are integral to this stage.

Gibbs (1979) suggested that there are two parts to Stage 3. Stage 3A thinking is concerned with gaining the approval of others "and role-stereotypical good conduct" (p. 93). The individual may progress to Stage 3B, "mutual good faith or understanding and universal caring" (p. 93). George (1980) asserted that most middle school and junior high school students are Stage 3 reasoners. A frequent discipline problem occurs when these once-obedient children may be more intent on gaining group approval than teacher approval. A common mistake by teachers is to discipline these students as one would elementary school students, ignoring the possible social embarrassment levied upon the youth. These teachers, either intentionally or unintentionally disinviting, may be experiencing only the *beginning* of their problems.

The *Stage 4* thinker is concerned not only with significant others, such as parents, teachers, and friends, but also with society as a whole. "Law and order" is a phrase often mentioned in connection with Stage 4, not in the sense of a police-controlled society, but rather in recognition of the need for common rules that meet the needs of most of the people. Thus, "the ability to take the perspective of the whole social system in contrast to the perspective of the immediate group, characterizes Stage 4. . . . It involves a greater cognitive ability, for one must keep in mind the interests of each constitutive group and compare them to the interests of the whole" (Hersh et al., 1979). It is obvious that when this is attempted with Stage 1,

2, and 3 thinkers, cries of "unfair" resound when individual rights must be compromised. The students in Stage 4 are generally in high school, although not all high school students reach this stage.

George (1980) suggested that an appropriate discipline or problem-solving approach for this level may be reality therapy (a cognitive therapy; see Unit 3). This approach emphasizes problem solving and the ability to choose among alternatives, taking into account the possible ramifications of decisions. However, if one subscribes to the theories postulated by Piaget and Kohlberg, it is evident that there are many students, especially those who are disturbed and disturbing, who are cognitively unable to reason at the level required by reality therapy. This has some important implications for teachers who are currently implementing reality therapy. Implicit in the use of this intervention is that it is appropriate for adolescents *regardless* of their ability to cognitively understand the process. One result may be that some educators are indiscriminately indoctrinating lower stage students to accept or reject the most "appropriate" alternative.

Students in Grades K through 12 are almost exclusively found in Stages 1 through 4. Whereas a Stage 4 person may be more concerned with obedience to a social law, a *Stage 5* individual may be concerned more with such issues as civil rights and social justice (Gibbs et al., 1976). In other words, Stage 5 individuals are concerned about the social utility of an act such as Martin Luther King's civil disobedience rather than about whether such an act is against the law. Although Stage 6 is included in Table 6.5, many of the concepts discussed in Stage 6 have become incorporated into Stage 5 because of the scarcity of research supporting placement in the structure of Stage 6.

The knowledge of stage and level differences is necessary if one is to apply moral development training. The age correlates discussed above are based on research data and do not necessarily hold in individual cases. How students reason, as determined by the structure of their statements, will define where they are placed along a continuum. That is, some 16-year-olds may reason at Stage 1 and some 10-year-olds may reason at Stage 3. One problem in trying to attach stage numbers to statements students may make is the tendency to concentrate on their content rather than their structure. If students can reason at a higher level, they also will understand the lower stage reasoning. Their stage position would be the highest that they consistently can comprehend.

## 2. The Most Reliable Way to Determine a Stage of Moral Thought Is Through a Moral Interview.

Fenton's (1976) second generalization is intended primarily for those who conduct research. The importance of diagnosis of the stages of students *by teachers* is discussed later in this chapter. This section considers the utility of Kohlberg's (1981) revised testing instrument. Kohlberg agreed with critics (Kurtines & Greif, 1974) that there were methodological problems with the *Structural Issue Scoring Test,* his first instrument for determining an individual's stage of moral thought. Implicit in the assignment of levels and stages is that scores tended to weight sociopolitical statements higher than interpersonal comments. This may have resulted in some populations scoring higher and others lower (Colby, 1978).

There are three parts to Kohlberg's (1981) research instrument: the standard moral interview, the interview, and the standard form scoring manual. Individuals are given only three dilemmas, as opposed to nine in the previous instrument, considerably shortening the diagnostic process. Each of the dilemmas measures a different concept, "one exhibiting a conflict between helping someone to enhance the quality of life, in violation of the law, versus obedience to the law; the second dealing with conflict between regard for character and conscience versus the meting out of retributive justice or punishment and deference; the third involving a conflict between the maintenance of a contract as opposed to the upholding of legitimate authority" (Kohlberg, 1981, pp. 9–10).

An attempt by Rest (1975) to assess stage placement suggested that there are other influences that may determine how an individual will reason, such as a friend's advice or the media. Rest's *Defining Issues Test* (DIT) gives the respondent alternative reasoning from which to choose, thus creating an instrument that is easier to standardize and implement. Research on cross-sectional populations (one-time testing of individuals of different ages) by Rest, Cooper, Coder, Masanz, and Anderson (1974) found the DIT to be correlated at 0.68 with Kohlberg's *Structural Issue Scoring Test,* not high enough to be considered equivalent to Kohlberg's test. Students who scored high on the DIT, however, also did well on Kohlberg's measure.

The moral interview may be considered as *one* reliable way to determine a stage of moral thought. Further consideration of Kohlberg's revised instrument as well as Rest's work should be made to efficiently and accurately identify stage placements for research purposes. Assessment is discussed in depth in Chapter 7.

## 3. A Stage Is an Organized System of Thought.

Kohlberg (1971) adopted Piaget's concept that stages are "structured wholes." In other words, the structure of any stage is a pattern of thinking and not specific information that the individual is thinking (content). The following examples indicate different stages:

> EMORY (AGE 6): I shouldn't steal, because if I do, my daddy will whip me, or worse I might even go to jail and be whupped there.

TIM (AGE 15): I shouldn't steal because if I do the police will catch me and throw me in jail where I will be beat up by prisoners.

MARY (AGE 15): I shouldn't steal because it is against the law. Laws are made to protect the rights of the members of our society.

The content of the statements of Emory, Tim, and Mary is acceptable and appropriate to the norms of society; however, Tim clearly demonstrates Stage 1 reasoning about why he should not steal, a reasoning that, in consideration of his age, suggests egocentrism and perhaps arrested moral development. In other words, in determining stages, the concern is with the process, not the product. Structure is important in teaching students with EBD because, although environments may change, levels of moral reasoning are normally consistent. By enhancing moral development, similar conflicts that occur in different environments may be better analyzed by the students.

## 4. An Individual Reasons Predominantly at One Stage of Thought and Uses Contiguous Stages as a Thinking Pattern.

Feldman (1986) proposed a five-phase process of how one progresses through stages. At the first phase, individuals have very little reasoning, if any, outside their primary stage. The next four phases entail a gradual to complete integration of reasoning at the next highest stage, when the process ideally will continue. Kohlberg (1969) also suggested that an individual reasons the majority of the time in one stage. However, lower stage reasoning also may occur, as well as reasoning one stage above the primary stage level (see also Kohlberg & Elfenbein, 1975). For example, an individual may reason 20% of the time in Stage 2, 60% in Stage 3, and the remaining 20% in Stage 4. As indicated in the discussion of generalization 6, individuals tend to reason mostly in one primary stage and its adjacent stages, rather than ranging two stages above or below that primary stage.

## 5. These Stages Are Natural Steps in Ethical Development, Not Something Artificial or Invented.

"Natural" in this sense implies Kohlberg's contention that there is a universality of stage sequence. Research studies by Kohlberg's doctoral students have suggested that the phenomenon of stage sequence occurs in Canada, India, Taiwan, Mexico, the United States, Israel, and Turkey (Kohlberg &

Turiel, 1971). The implication of this research is that the reasoning measured by Kohlberg transcends the rote learning of rules or particular cultural norms and mores.

## 6. All People Move Through These Stages in an Invariant Sequence, Although Any Individual May Stop at a Particular Stage.

Goldstein and Glick's (1987) review of the research led them to conclude that stage development is correlated with age. They were careful to warn that "it is important to recognize that individual differences exist, with some variation accounted for by such factors as socioeconomic status, intelligence, and education" (p. 107). In two studies conducted by Blatt and Kohlberg (1975), no individuals had skipped a stage during a 1-year period after training; however, many people had not advanced to what was thought to be the statistically age-appropriate stage. One reason for these age–stage discrepancies is the purported relationship between cognitive capacity and the ability to reason. Keasey (1975) found that concrete operational thought is necessary for an individual to reason at Stage 2 and formal operational thought is needed to reason at Stage 5 (see also Tomlinson-Keasey & Keasey, 1974). Research has tended to support a relationship between cognitive and moral development (Jantz, 1973; Kohlberg & Turiel, 1971; Langford & George, 1975). Kohlberg (1975) contended that cognitive development is a necessary *but not sufficient* condition for moral growth. He cited instances of very intelligent juvenile delinquents who nevertheless were reasoning at Stage 2. Ruma and Mosher (1967) found only 1 of 36 delinquents to be above Stage 3.

Another possible reason for age–stage differences may be a person's inability to role-take (Selman, 1976; Walker, 1980, 1988). Perry and Krebs (1980) tested individuals who were mentally retarded (mean IQ of 60) and found their lack of cognitive ability to be highly correlated with their inability to role-take and reason (see generalization 12 for a discussion on role-taking). Krebs and Gillmore (1982) contended that the "stages of role-taking and moral development should be more closely aligned than stages of moral development and cognitive development because the subject matter of role-taking and moral development is social in nature" (p. 884).

The results of this and other research indicate that, although growth in some areas for some people may be slower, educational methods have been devised to increase moral reasoning. Regardless of the speed of individuals' growth, the research of Walker and Taylor (1991) clearly "indicates that most individuals are reasoning predominately at a single stage, with smaller amounts of reasoning at adjacent stages. This is consistent with the cognitive developmental criterion of structure: that each stage represents a holistic structure and that subjects are either 'in' a stage or 'in transition' between stages" (p. 336). Again, the theory and research of Piaget, Kohlberg, and Selman suggest that one possible cause of retarded growth is the lack of stimulation in the environment to which the individuals are exposed.

## 7. People Can Understand Moral Arguments at Their Own Stage, at All Stages Beneath Their Own, and Usually at One Stage Higher Than Their Own.

Turiel (1966) exposed 44 seventh graders to reasoning below, above, and on the same level as their current moral reasoning. Presenting reasoning at one stage above was the most effective technique for growth, whereas teaching two stages above their ability was least effective. Furthermore, students tended to choose reasoning above their current stage rather than below it. This conclusion was supported by Rothman (1976), who found individuals at Stage 4 to be more influenced by plus-one stage reasoning than students at Stage 3, and by Lockwood's (1978) investigation, which suggested that Stage 2 subjects were more responsive to Stage 3 responses than to those illustrative of Stage 1 or Stage 4. Rest (1979) found, however, that adolescents could understand only reasoning on or below their stage level.

The teaching implications of moral development seem evident. A Stage 1 child who may think that stealing is wrong out of fear of being physically punished probably will not comprehend that stealing is against the law and, therefore, antisociety (Stage 4). The child *may* understand that the person she steals from would feel bad, just as she would if she were the victim (Stage 2). Kohlberg (1976) found that "Stage 2 children tend to reject Stage 1 advice because it is egotistical and ignores feelings; and Stage 4 . . . children in turn, tend to reject Stage 3 advice because it is based

---

### Window on Reality

A youngster had recently arrived at a reform school. During meals, he would eat only desserts. Various staff members tried to explain the nutritional value of eating the entire meal.

One staff member even brought in pictures of children who were in various stages of starvation. He implored, "Benji, look at these pictures. These children would love to eat the food that you are passing up." Benji looked up and passively said, "F———— 'em." Clearly, Benji was not motivated by the concerns or needs of others.

on personal feelings and relationships rather than upon moral rules" (p. 43).

In view of these findings, it is little wonder that one often hears of populations in various polls being against many of the concepts in the U.S. Bill of Rights or Constitution. Examining both documents in terms of stages, one finds that they contain Stage 5 concepts, which is reasoning two stages above that of most public school students.

## 8. Higher Moral Stages are Better Than Lower Ones.

In the statement "Higher moral stages are better than lower ones," "better" actually means "preferable" because the individuals at higher stages can analyze situations by understanding as many factors (self, others, society) as possible, and thus have more choices. Another facet of this concept is that of "hierarchical integrations," which suggests that thinking incorporates lower level reasoning and that, when given a choice, most people prefer higher stage thinking (Kohlberg, 1969). Furthermore, while the relationship between stage level and conduct is inconclusive, some strong evidence indicates that many students with EBD are operating at lower levels of reasoning (Bear & Richards, 1981; Thoma, Rest, & Barnett, 1986).

## 9. Stage Transition Takes Place Primarily Because Encountering Real-Life or Hypothetical Moral Dilemmas Sets Up Cognitive Conflict in a Person's Mind and Makes The Person Uncomfortable.

The focus on promoting moral growth has been to present dilemmas to individuals and challenge their thinking with conflicting reasoning that is one stage above their current level. Blatt and Kohlberg (1975) found significant growth of moral maturity of students in both religious and public school settings by using the challenging procedure. Berkowitz, Gibbs, and Broughton (1980) also found growth through the use of peer interaction. The stages of the individuals in this study were different. Students preferred reasoning one stage level higher than their own.

It is important to note that growth becomes evident upon the repeated challenging of the individual's reasoning, and this is a process that the individual internally undertakes. In other words, a *structural* change takes place when the individual thinks at a higher level that can be generalized to many situations. This process differs from indoctrinative education in which the student passively submits to different reasoning and is required to parrot another's beliefs.

## 10. Deliberate Attempts to Facilitate Stage Change in Schools Through Education Programs Have Been Successful.

Much research and thought have gone into attempts to transfer what appears to be a psychological theory into one with educational applications (Doris, 1978). In addition to their research conducted in classrooms, Kohlberg and his associates studied the growth of moral development in a women's correctional facility. They found that peers tended to have a profound influence on behavior, and that such an environment does not allow moral growth because of the few opportunities available for individuals to develop (Kohlberg, Kauffman, Scharf, & Hickey, 1975). The same criticism may be levied against some schools.

Kohlberg (1978a) suggested that moral development approaches be instituted in both prisons and schools, creating "just" communities. Moral development programs have been implemented in both these settings with positive results. Jennings and Kohlberg (1980) found that such an approach was successful with youthful offenders when compared with a behavior modification or a transactional analysis approach (see also Kohlberg & Higgins, 1987; Jennings & Kohlberg, 1983). Their "just community" offered:

1. A high amount of moral discussion and dialogue.
2. A high amount of resident power and responsibility for making rules, policies, and decisions.
3. A high amount of perceived fairness or concern about fairness in the institution. (p. 24)

Schonert and Cantor (1991) believed that alternative programs could hold much promise for students with EBD, although their research was inconclusive.

In the mid-1970s, Kohlberg developed a just community in a Cambridge, Massachusetts, public high school called the Cluster School. Learning that hypothetical dilemmas were irrelevant to many of the prisoners whom he had studied, Kohlberg increasingly used real-life issues that the students felt it was necessary to discuss. Wassermen (1976) noted that one of the most difficult tasks of implementing the approach was that "staff members tended to dominate discussions and to present reasoning which reflected their own concerns. They sometimes presented arguments based on Stage 5 reasoning which most students could not understand" (p. 206).

Of the four target areas of improvement in the Cluster School, three showed significant student improvement due to the moral development program design (Reimer, 1981). Student attendance, respect of property, and racial harmony made advances, but the prohibition of the use of drugs did not make any gains. In a comparison with other research, Reimer noted that more development in terms of quantitative stages was not present, but a greater proportion of subjects achieved some growth. Reimer concluded that one must belong to a social group in order to reach the conventional level because this provides a reference group from which to work.

Kohlberg (1981) revised his stage definitions to include the concept of community (Table 6.6). The reader should be aware that these revised stages are directly related to the stages that Kohlberg originally presented (see Table 6.5). It is particularly relevant for classroom teachers to consider these stages of collective values because it will allow them to assess the moral stages of both their classrooms and schools.

Considerable research has been done to measure the efficacy of moral development with "deviant" populations. Damon and Killen (1982) argued that "psychological inquiry has established that peers indeed can positively influence one another's psychological development in cognitive as well as moral spheres of growth" (p. 348). Moral development group training has been found to work with prison populations (Arbuthnot, 1984), juvenile delinquents (Fleetwood & Parish, 1976; Niles, 1986; Rosenkoetter, Landman, & Mazak, 1980; Wright, 1978), at-risk students (Brion-Meisels, 1979; see also Arbuthnot & Gordon, 1986) and students labeled learning disabled (Doerr, 1986). In summary, moral development can be "taught" under the correct conditions. Goldstein and Glick's (1987) review led them to conclude that:

(1) moral dilemma discussion groups can lead to significantly more moral growth (one-third to one whole stage increase over one semester) than in various control groups;

(2) this change occurs when a range of reasoning stages are represented in the classroom;

(3) the teacher must help the student probe his reasoning in an environment that promotes openness and trust;

(4) the moral discussion must create divided opinions and controversy among the students;

(5) the most effective Moral Education interventions occur with discussion of real dilemmas in the context of a "real" group (e.g., the classroom, the family); and

(6) delinquent individuals characteristically function at lower levels of moral reasoning than do nondelinquent cohorts, but can be trained to increase their levels of such reasoning ability as a result of participation in Moral Education. (p. 116)

## TABLE 6.6
### Kohlberg's Stages of Collective Normative Values and the Sense of Community

| Collective Normative Values | Sense of Community |
|---|---|
| **Stage 2** | |
| There is not yet an explicit awareness of collective normative values. However, there are generalized expectations that individuals should recognize concrete individual rights and resolve conflicts through exchange.<br><br>*Examples:*<br>1. Do not "rat" on another group member. Ratting or reporting another group member to authorities is disapproved of because it exposes the rule breaker to likely punishment.<br>2. Do not bother others. Live and let live.<br>3. Help others out when you want to. | There is no clear sense of community apart from exchanges among group members. Community denotes a collection of individuals who do favors for each other and rely on each other for protection. Community is valued insofar as it meets the concrete needs of its members.<br><br>*Example:*<br>The community is like a "bank." Members meet to exchange favors but you cannot take more than you give. |
| **Stage 3** | |
| Collective normative values refer to relationships among group members. Membership in a group implies living up to shared expectations. Conflicts should be resolved by appeal to mutual collective normative values.<br><br>*Examples:*<br>1. Members of group should be able to trust each other with their possessions.<br>2. Members of a group should care about other members of the group. | The sense of community refers to a set of relationships and sharings among group members. The group is valued for the friendliness of its members. The value of the group is equated with the value of its collective normative expectations.<br><br>*Examples:*<br>1. The community is a family in which members care for each other.<br>2. The community is honorable because it helps others. |
| **Stage 4** | |
| Collective normative values stress the community as an entity distinct from its individual members. Members are obligated to act out of concern for the welfare and harmony of the group.<br><br>*Examples:*<br>1. Individuals not only are responsible for themselves but share responsibility for the whole group.<br>2. Individuals should participate in the political organization of the group by making their opinions known and by being informed voters. | The school is explicitly valued as an entity distinct from the relationships among its members. Group commitments and ideals are valued. The community is perceived as an organic whole composed of interrelated systems that carry on the functioning of the group.<br><br>*Examples:*<br>Stealing affects "the community more than the individual because that is what we are. We are not just a group of individuals." |

From *The Meaning and Measurement of Moral Development* (p. 47), by L. Kohlberg, 1981 Worcester, MA: Clark University Press. Reprinted with permission.

## 11. Moral Judgment Is a Necessary But Not Sufficient Condition for Moral Action.

As Kohlberg (1981) suggested, moral judgment can indicate only if students know *what* to do, not necessarily if they *will* act in that manner (see also Locke, 1983). The aim, therefore, would be to increase their ability to reason. If students do not have the ability to "know better," they rarely will "behave better" unless they are in carefully controlled environments. The initial research by Hartshorne and May (1928–1930) revealed that, although children could repeat the rules they were given, they were unable to behave consistently in accordance with these rules. Blasi's (1980) review of 15 studies, as well as the research of Blatt and Kohlberg (1975) and Pittel and Mendelsohn (1966), led to the conclusion that moral judgment may differ from behavior.

As already mentioned, delinquents have been found to operate at lower levels of moral development. It should be remembered, however, that moral development is only one factor that may involve the personality and behavior (see Chandler, 1973). Arbuthnot and Gordon (1986) implemented a moral development program with groups of adolescents who were at risk for behavioral disorders (nominated by teachers) and found improved moral reasoning, as well as fewer discipline referrals, less tardiness, and improved academic performance. A 1-year follow-up indicated sustained improvement.

Cognition, role-taking ability, family background, intelligence, and the immediate situation may all influence action (Hains & Miller, 1980; Santrock, 1975). Ruma and Mosher (1967) found that delinquent boys expressed higher levels of guilt when they were higher stage reasoners; in other words, they had internalized perspective taking in a "positive" manner and not in the neurotic sense. Kohlberg (1970, 1975) found that the act of cheating was prevalent in all six stages, but was highly evident in Stages 1 through 4 and less so in Stages 5 and 6. Perhaps Miller and Aloise (1989) presented it best in their attempt to explain how preschool students may interpret events (dilemmas): "Very little is known . . . about young children's conceptions of how intentions, motivation, effort, etc., change as a result of events. [Also], the effect of a mental state on behavior is nearly always studied by requiring the child to infer the mental state from known behavior rather than to predict behavior from the known mental state" (p. 269). In summary, stage placement may only be considered a tentative indicator of behavior (see also Keasey, 1971).

## 12. There Is a Relationship Between Role-Taking and Moral Development

Inherent in the ability to progress past Stage 1 is the individual's growing expertise to role-take, or to take another's perspective. Kohlberg (1978b) insisted that role-taking is the bridge between the cognitive and moral development domains. Selman (1976) identified three structural aspects of role-taking:

1. The subject's own point of view.
2. The different viewpoints of each character in the dilemma.
3. The relationships among those varying perspectives. (p. 302)

Selman's (1977) research supported the contention that role-taking, or perspective-taking, as he described it, is a prerequisite to attaining a moral stage. Those individuals with problems in the moral and cognitive stages also appear to have difficulties in relating to peers. Research has supported high correlations between role-playing and chronological age (Selman & Byrne, 1974) and between role-playing and Piaget's cognitive stages (Walker, 1980). Dickstein and Warren (1980) found a role-taking deficit in young children with learning disabilities compared with "normal" children. Maccoby (1980) argued that much of the role-taking research on younger children may be underrated because the children may have difficulty verbalizing their responses.

Selman (1976) outlined the parallel relationship that social role-taking has with Kohlberg's moral development stages. His Stage 1 is labeled Social-Informational Role Taking; Stage 2, Self-Reflective Role Taking; Stage 3, Mutual Role Taking; and Stage 4, Social and Conventional System Role Taking. The questions presented after the following sample dilemma exemplify differences between the structure of role-taking (Selman) and that of moral reasoning (Kohlberg):

> Holly is an eight-year-old girl who likes to climb trees. She is the best tree-climber in the neighborhood. One day while climbing down from a tall tree, she falls off the bottom branch but doesn't hurt herself. Her father sees her fall. He is upset and asks her to promise not to climb trees anymore. Holly promises.
>
> Later that day, Holly meets Shawn. Shawn's kitten is caught up in a tree and can't get down. Something has to be done right away or the kitten may fall. Holly is the only one who climbs trees well enough to reach the kitten, but she remembers her promise to her father. (Selman, 1976, p. 302)

Role-Taking Questions:

1. Does Holly know how Shawn feels about the kitten?
2. How will Holly's father feel if he finds out she climbed the tree?
3. What does Holly think her father will do if he finds out that she climbed the tree?

4. What would you do in this situation?

Moral Reasoning Questions:

1. Should Holly rescue the kitten or should she keep her promise to her father? What is the right thing for her to do? Why?
2. Was it fair for Holly's father to ask her to promise never to climb trees? Why? Can you think of a promise that would be more fair to Holly?
3. Suppose that Holly's father asks her if she broke her promise; what should Holly say? Why?

The above examples of questioning (adapted from Hersh & Paolitto, 1979) clearly delineate the two approaches. The first set of questions attempts to have the students try to "put themselves in another's shoes." The second set reflects the students' ability to discern the conflict along the sequence supported by the research of Kohlberg. The reason to be cognizant of role-taking stages is that the students' ability to take the viewpoint of others seems to be clearly indicative of their ability to advance beyond Kohlberg's Stage 1. It is important to consider role-taking as another factor in the multifaceted concept of moral development.

## 13. There Are Criticisms of Kohlberg's Theory.

There have been criticisms of Kohlberg's theory, as one might expect with any developing theory. Kohlberg and his associates have carefully examined these criticisms and have in many cases reconceptualized some important segments of their theory of moral development. One critic, Fraenkel (1976), questioned Kohlberg's claim that there is universality of his stages. Fraenkel suggested that the samples of the various cultures researched were rather small. Also, Fraenkel wondered how one "proves" that higher level reasoning is better than lower level reasoning. Finally, Fraenkel questioned how a teacher can promote moral growth by presenting reasoning one stage above the student's reasoning if, in fact, the teacher does not possess that same level of reasoning (i.e., Stage 5 is purported by Kohlberg to be attained by only a minority of adults).

The concepts of Kohlberg's original Stages 5 and 6 (postconventional morality) have been questioned by Gibbs (1977), Peters (1975), Phillips and Nicolayev (1978), and Wonderly and Kupersmid (1980). All of the above except Phillips and Nicolayev found empirical support for Stages 1 through 4, but had extreme difficulty in accepting Stages 5 and 6. As a result of these criticisms, Kohlberg eliminated Stage 6 as a possible attainment level.

Much of the above criticisms has been generated from Kurtines and Greif's (1974) detailing of the methodological problems of Kohlberg's testing instrument. Interestingly, Kohlberg (1981) did not perceive his original procedure as a test in itself. The work of Colby (1978) and Colby, Kohlberg, Gibbs, and Lieberman (1980) has generated a testing measure that attempts to take into account the other issues raised by Kurtines and Greif.

Another criticism levied against both Piaget and Kohlberg is that most of their research that determined stage structures had been conducted on male populations. Gilligan (1977) argued that there may be a different construction of reality for females that is just as intricate as that for the male population. Males may have a "justice" orientation and females a "care" orientation because of their socialization (Gilligan, 1982). She suggested that the female differences have been defined by most male developmentalists as either "deviant" or "deficient." Baumrind (1986) also believed that there are different social aspects that affect men and women and that these aspects may result in differential assessment. This was further supported by Santilli and Hudson (1992), who found that an "interesting pattern was found in the gender differences in social perspective-taking. While females demonstrated higher proportions of Level 2 perspective-taking prior to training, males significantly increased their posttraining performance to a level comparable to the females. These findings suggest that males may not possess equivalent perspective-taking competence, relative to females, but may acquire equivalent ability as a function of training" (p. 157). Walker's (1989) and Walker, de Vries, and Trevethan's (1987) research refuted Gilligan's claims, however, when they found that "there was no difference between the sexes in response scores among younger children, and high school boys had higher scores than girls. . . . However, congruent with her notions, women had higher scores than men. Also, a sex-related pattern in orientations was not found for most of the standard dilemmas, although females had higher response scores than males on two of nine dilemmas" (p. 856).

Moral development has also been criticized by Maag (1989), who suspected that "students who lack the prerequisite skills to behave prosocially/promorally probably would benefit more from the behaviorally-oriented social skills training than the cognitive-oriented approach indicative of moral reasoning training" (p. 100). Maag is correct if one wants only a "quick fix." Moral development is not a quick fix. The benefits, as with all kinds of development, appear to be real and long lasting. Perhaps, however, they may be most effective when paired with social skills training (see also Blackney & Blackney, 1991).

Many of these criticisms do have validity. However, they have helped strengthen Kohlberg's theory rather than weaken it, because they have prompted researchers to reexamine and in some cases revise and improve earlier claims (Ericson, 1979; Selman, 1976).

## Summary and Conclusion

The purposes of this chapter were twofold. The first was to present a rationale for the use of moral development with students who have EBD. A brief comparison with values clarification and indoctrinative education was made to illustrate other attempts to help students learn about themselves and their relationships to others. Piaget's approach to the understanding and application of rules (moral judgment) and their implications was presented.

Second, Kohlberg's research and theory were presented to explain how individuals reason. An understanding of the reasoning process will allow teachers to better interact and plan for their students. The next chapter demonstrates methods that can enable students to reason at higher levels, which hopefully will lead to better mental health and behavior.

# 7

# Moral Development: Application in the Classroom

The theory and research discussed thus far in this text have stressed the necessity to provide moral development curricula to disturbed and disturbing students. Both individual and educational system implications of moral development have been examined. This chapter presents the theory and assessment procedures that I believe are necessary to implement moral development curricula in the classroom. Because of the nature of special education practices regarding the rights of students and their parents, the issue of assessing individual stage placement is addressed. A moral development program is presented, as well as the importance and application of assessment. A step-by-step presentation that will enable the reader to implement moral development is detailed. Examples of the types of dilemmas that teachers can use in their classrooms are presented.

## Assessment

To adequately use assessment procedures in the classroom, educators should attempt to understand what the environmental influences of the community and school are and how potentially inviting they are to moral development. For example, a potential problem with regard to the measurement of moral development and students with emotional and behavioral disorders (EBD) is that one needs to take into consideration the level of the students' interpersonal skills (Santilli & Hudson, 1992). Managing one's classroom is an arduous task in itself, and it would be foolhardy to suggest that the nature of the school does not have an impact on the classroom. Consequently, assessment must begin with the school.

The research and literature regarding "moral atmospheres" to date has been only suggestive. The work of Kohlberg, Kauffman, Scharf, and Hickey (1975) in institutions and schools offers a framework from which to begin. Before assessment in the classroom, the educator should be able to ascertain if the school, community, and/or family provide:

1. A situation where seeing things from other people's points of view occurs and is encouraged.

2. An environment where logical thinking [rather than the parroting of rules] is encouraged.

3. An environment which gives the individual responsibility to make moral decisions and to influence his moral world.

4. Exposure to conflict in reasoning [as opposed to sheer emotional conflict] about moral decisions.

5. Exposure to individuals at a stage higher than one's own.

6. Exposure to a just environment. (pp. 256–257)

Analyzing the school, family, and/or community will allow the teacher to be aware of the support, or lack of support, that can be counted upon. Obviously, the above criteria cannot, in most cases, be evaluated on a clearcut yes or no basis. However, by utilizing a Likert-type, 1 (*never*) to 5 (*always*) continuum for each of the above statements, a clearer picture of the environment may prevail, perhaps aiding in uncovering a school's "hidden curriculum."

Although the above criteria allow the educator to begin to assess the school environment, there remains a controversy as to whether it is necessary to determine the stage reasoning of specific students in the classroom. Two opposing arguments have surfaced with regard to the need for assessment in the classroom: "to assess" or "not to assess." Kohlberg (1971) contended that the original purpose of his work was for research and not for direct use in the classroom, yet Lickona (1977a) argued that stage placements of students should be known in order for a moral development curriculum to be implemented properly.

One should remember that implicit in the definition of any developmental theory is the fact that the stages are determined using normative data. As an example, the average 9-year-old may be expected to reason at Stage 2. Theoretically, however, approximately half of the population may be developmentally advanced and the other half may be developmentally delayed.

Arbuthnot and Faust's (1981) review of research data suggests that most 5- to 8-year-olds are at Stage 1 most of the time; that 9- to 11-year-olds are probably equally divided between Stages 1 and 3, with most in Stage 2; that 12- to 14-year-olds are primarily in Stage 3, with a few in Stage 1, more in Stage 2, and some in Stage 4; and, interestingly, that approximately the same breakdown occurs with 15- to 17-year-olds, although there are fewer Stage 1 individuals and a few more Stage 4 reasoners.

Students with EBD may be at a lower stage of moral development than their nondisturbing peers. Although the common factor of age in determining stage levels has little meaning to special educators, knowledge of the milestones in moral development will give these educators a proper perspective in determining appropriate moral developmental goals and objectives. An ability to assess, while not necessarily a prerequisite to implementing moral development, will add depth to the educators' working knowledge of the curriculum. An awareness of the students' stage levels will allow facilitators to expose the individuals to varying degrees of reasoning more appropriately.

The purpose of assessment is to gather information on students' primary stages of moral development for future program implementation. The process of assessment is *not* to try to facilitate or promote stage growth, but simply to observe interactions and the structure underlying those interactions. The following techniques are provided to help the teacher to arrive at the students' approximate stage levels.[1] It is highly recommended that these techniques be integrated with the theory presented in this unit.

## Types of Assessment

***Individual Assessment.*** Individual assessment generates information about the student's moral self-perception. The teacher can observe the student in class, in the playground, in the cafeteria, or in the hallways. The teacher can try to encourage didactic discussion with the student by asking such questions as:

1. How did/do you feel when _____? Why?
2. Why did/didn't you think _____ was unfair/fair? (bad/good?) (wrong, right?)
3. How did you come to the decision to _____?
4. Why are you upset about _____? Yes, that is what happened, but why are you upset?

---

[1] I express gratitude to Suzanne Goulet, a special educator from Alpena, Michigan, for assistance in developing some of the activities presented in this section.

5. Is that a fact? Why?
6. Explain to me why you did this.
7. Why should that have happened?

***Impersonal Assessment.*** Impersonal assessment generates information about the student's perception of other people's morals. The teacher can observe the student before, during, and after academic lessons. At appropriate times, the teacher can ask questions such as the following:

1. Do you agree/disagree with what happened to _____ in the story? Why?
2. What would you have done in that situation? Why?
3. Why do you think _____ acted that way?
4. Why are you doing this assignment?

***Group Discussion of Dilemmas.*** The assessment process can take place with the entire class or in a small group setting; an audiotape may be helpful. Solving dilemmas is *not* the concern in assessment. The teacher should try to elicit ideas from the group about a real-life dilemma. If prompting is needed, the teacher may want to ask:

1. Did anything different happen on the bus today?
2. Did anyone watch television last night? What happened? Why did you think it should have/should not have happened?

The teacher should encourage a free and open discussion about the dilemma, probe for justification of the content, and ask clarifying questions in an attempt to arrive at the *structure*.

## Nine Assessment Techniques

The following techniques can be used by teachers to determine students' moral reasoning stages.

1. *In attempting to gather information that may be helpful, the teacher should try to sample the student's moral reasoning in as many settings as possible.* What is the student's reasoning in group discussions, as well as in real-life (on-the-spot) conflicts in various classrooms, on the playground, or in the lunchroom? Does the student use different reasoning with authority figures (parroting adult dictums) than with peers? This may more accurately reveal the individual's *own* thinking, as discussed in Chapter 6 in the section on Piaget's (1948)

research. This concept corresponds to the "setting" element of Wood's (1979) definition (see Unit 1).

2. *To accurately evaluate reasoning, the teacher should have a "checks and balances" system.* The teacher should use simple, nonthreatening listening checks with students. In other words, without probing or interrogating, the teacher can simply ask the learner if the teacher's interpretation of the student's reasoning is correct. This directness may save valuable time that the teacher may otherwise use in delving into what the student *meant* by particular statements. Second, if other individuals are present who are versed in moral development, the teacher can ask them to observe and try to ascertain stage placement to see if there is agreement. Another technique would be for the teacher to write down or tape the reasoning and see if other teachers can agree as to the stage reasoning of the statements.

3. *The teacher should attempt to observe over many days and different times of the day.* This is to ensure that the primary reasoning stage is consistent and not due to a particularly good or bad day or a unique event.

4. *The teacher should record reasoning statements as quickly as possible.* This aids in charting the frequency of reasoning as well as maintaining accurate recordings of statements. People's perceptions of statements may change over time.

5. *The teacher should record students' exact statements.* By listening carefully and objectively, the teacher may find statements that are incongruent with a student's actions and the teacher's beliefs. Many times students' reasoning is not related to their acts, and it is tempting to suggest that "evil-doers" (delinquents, etc.) are lower stage reasoners.

6. *The teacher should look for the structure and not the content of the students' statements.* Implicit in this statement is the fact that there is no right or wrong answer to reasoning. Again, a student may have a very high-level type of reasoning and yet behave inappropriately.

7. *The teacher should understand that eliciting structure can be a very difficult task.* Although many students may gladly offer their reasoning, many others are less likely to be accommodating. In other words, students who are talkative may provide plenty of content with very little structure, and those who are reticent may offer little content or structure.

8. *Assessment should be an ongoing process.* Upon arriving at appropriate stage-level placements, the teacher should be aware that changes may indeed occur. The teacher should continue to observe students for consistency to their answers over time.

9. *Development goals and objectives should be placed in each student's Individualized Education Program (IEP) to ensure continuity in affective programming.* Moral development curricula can be an integral component in both cognitive and affective growth. Goals and objectives

that focus upon such behaviors as interaction, cooperation with others, and the ability to make inferences are all commonly cited as problem areas for many special education students. These goals belong in the IEP and may be "measured" along a continuum from "needs to improve" to "consistently in evidence."

## Arguments For and Against Assessment

Two opposing arguments have surfaced with regard to the need for assessment in the classroom. Napier (1976, 1978) argued that most teachers are unable to accurately evaluate students according to Kohlberg's system. Napier (1979) further contended that it is the process of moral development, including any possible communication problems such as listening and responding, that should be analyzed and diagnosed. Conversely, Galbraith and Jones (1976), Hall and Davis (1975), and Hersh, Paolitto, and Reimer (1979) suggested that assessment is not necessary to implement an effective moral development curriculum. These authors proposed that, because most groups are heterogeneous with regard to stage levels, the students will "naturally" be exposed to higher stage reasoning. It is the teacher's responsibility to facilitate and point out the difference in reasoning rather than to prescribe appropriate reasoning for individual students. However, this rationale may not be the case in classes of disturbed and disturbing students, which may comprise entirely Stage 1 and 2 reasoners or may contain an occasional student who is two or more stages above the rest of the class.

Implicit in Kohlberg's work is the fact that a particular behavioral/affective intervention may be more appropriate for certain stage-level students (behavior modification for Stages 1 and 2 or cognitive-behavior therapy for Stages 3 and 4) and that, for a teacher to successfully employ these interventions, an appropriate (moral) evaluation may be beneficial. If teachers choose not to assess, they may be overlooking the individual needs of some students.

Another argument in favor of an ongoing assessment process is that it provides the teacher with a means for updating and documenting student progress. However, assessment can be useful only when it generates programming. It should *never* be used as evidence for labeling students as emotionally disturbed.

# Review

The previous chapter and this one are inextricably linked. To assess and apply moral development well, the teacher must understand its concepts. One should remember that Kohlberg contended that most conflicts are based on variations of 10 moral issues and that the reasoning behind students' stands on these issues is of primary importance. Through extensive research, both longitudinal and cross-sectional, Kohlberg originally arrived at three levels consisting of two stages each to help explain moral development. Later, Kohlberg (1981) revised the theory to include only five stages.

The concept of stages as "structured wholes," in that individuals tend to reason primarily at one stage, has been discussed. Integral to this concept is that these stages are not fabricated, but are clearly natural, universal steps through which people progress in an invariant fashion, although growth may be halted at any one stage. Correlates to moral development such as cognition and role taking help one understand the theory in broader terms. Many different possible influences on moral growth, such as Piaget's horizontal decalage, should be considered. People tend to understand and accept reasoning that is on their stage level or at one above and, although they may understand lower level reasoning, they are apt to reject it. Closely related to this is the notion that higher stage reasoning is more desirable than lower stage reasoning because it provides varied options for analyzing a problem.

Kohlberg and Piaget agreed that learning is achieved through conflict (disequilibrium) and resolution of that conflict (return to equilibrium). Although Kohlberg originally suggested the use of hypothetical dilemmas to promote growth, he has since recognized the value of bibliotherapy and real-life dilemmas.

Probably most important and relevant to educators is that many successful attempts have been made to promote moral growth in schools and in correctional institutions. Also, a plethora of classroom methods and techniques for developing moral growth have been generated, which will be detailed later. Moral judgment is not, and will not be, *the* panacea for disturbed and disturbing youth. However, it provides a means for students to indeed "know better" before they take action on a conflict or dilemma. One such way to help students develop this ability is to have them stand in another's shoes, that is, to role-take. It has been found that the ability to role-take is highly correlated with moral growth.

Kohlberg's theory of moral development has not been without its critics. However, Kohlberg and his associates have in many instances taken this criticism constructively and subsequently have revised portions of the theory. In fact, Kohlberg recognizes that he may have been somewhat naive to suggest that teachers should be interested *only* in structure, because indeed information is required if a student is going to at least "handle" the constraints of the system. Specific assessment procedures have been included in this text to help the teacher begin implementation of moral development. The evidence (and my own bias) tends to indicate the need to understand and assess the developmental levels of students.

# MORAL DEVELOPMENT PROGRAM: DISCUSSIONS AND DILEMMAS

The theory and research discussed in this unit has stressed the necessity for educators to provide moral development curricula in their classrooms. The work of Piaget, Kohlberg, and their associates indicates that moral development is one means to increase the reasoning ability of students. This ability will allow students to better examine conflicts and choose from among the available alternatives, a skill that is requisite to successful integration into the regular classroom setting. The purpose of this section is to provide the techniques to adopt and integrate a moral development program into the school day.

The theory of moral development purports to help students learn to become what Garrod and Bramble (1977) called "autonomous decision makers." Although many other personality factors may come into play, individuals who cannot look beyond their own egocentric needs have little chance of succeeding in the mainstream, whether that be the regular classroom setting or the daily rigors of life. Therefore, the goal of moral educators is to help students grow beyond their egocentrism and move toward relating to their community, and eventually to society as a whole (Lickona, 1977b). The process of promoting moral development is achieved through recognizing the cognitive side of morality, attempting to understand both the structure and the content of reasoning, and understanding that structure is developmental in nature and can be nurtured through an interactive environment (Colby, 1978). Furthermore, a moral development curriculum can foster an atmosphere that allows the consideration of the viewpoint of others (role or perspective taking).

Integral to any moral development program is confronting students with new, higher stage reasoning that differs from their present viewpoints. Paolitto (1977) suggested that the teacher's role is to "(a) create 'conflict'— the type of conflict which facilitates cognitive structural change in students—and (b) stimulate students' ability to take the perspective of others beyond themselves" (p. 75). An environment should be created in which students feel free to interact with each other. This environment will be the marketplace for discussions revolving around moral issues. In other words, *moral development cannot be taught through lecture of its concepts.* Students will have the opportunity to use their reasoning and have it accepted by others. They will also be exposed to the reasoning of (Galbraith & Jones, 1977). Again, it is through this interactive process that the students may increase their moral growth.

Special educators may have difficulty instituting a moral development program in their classrooms. One reason is that their students may be limited in how well they communicate the knowledge that they possess. One only has to examine the research on preschoolers that indicates they know "more about the psychological world of thinking, perceiving, attending, remembering, and feeling than was apparent from earlier investigations" (Miller & Aloise, 1989, p, 264). Also, much to the frustration of their teachers, disturbed and disturbing students often claim that what the teacher and their peers perceive as moral dilemmas are really "no problem" to them. These beliefs may be due to two conditions: (a) the students are at lower stages of reasoning and there are no problems as long as their needs are met, or (b) they have had a life of doing (following) whatever their peers desire and/or having authority figures make decisions and solve conflicts for them. Although it is tempting to allow passive, subordinate, well-behaved students to continue reasoning at lower stage levels, the reality is that the general education environment and the real world are rarely without conflicts, which can almost guarantee frustration and failure to students without the ability to reason at higher levels. This is a goal of most teachers who realize that someday these students will have to reason for themselves and be able to decide their long-term goals in a manner that is not detrimental to others.

The following cautions should be heeded before moral development application techniques are presented (Hersh et al., 1979; Lickona, 1977a):

1. Moral development, although "easy" to implement, requires time before growth occurs.

2. Moral development takes practice before the students and teacher feel comfortable.

3. Moral growth may not lead to moral behavior, although research suggests that it may be a prerequisite.

4. Saying the "right things" may only reflect content attainment and not structural growth.

5. Labeling students as "stage thinkers" prevents the teacher from understanding the multidimensionality of students.

6. Moral development is only one facet of the student's personality.

These cautions are outlined to help the reader avoid making careless assumptions. A moral development curriculum can be an important part of the educator's programming when it is taken in the proper perspective.

The remainder of this chapter is divided into two sections: (a) preparing for moral discussions and (b) types of moral dilemmas. The first section is intended to examine the factors necessary to implement a moral development curriculum. The final section presents format and content that can be introduced during group sessions, including both hypothetical and real-life dilemmas.

# Preparing for Moral Discussions

To systematically implement a moral development program, the teacher should consider six factors, which may vary with regard to the composition of each environment. These factors include:

1. The *organization,* including designing group rules, length of discussions, class size, and physical arrangement.
2. The *teacher's role,* assuming behaviors that will help facilitate sessions.
3. *Initiating group discussions,* including warm-up exercises, and developing a vocabulary that is common to the group.
4. *Presenting the dilemma,* utilizing clarification, listening checks, and brainstorming techniques.
5. *Asking appropriate questions,* such as the issue-related probe, role-switch probe, and universal consequence probe.
6. *Avoiding potential problems* by analyzing insensitive participation, overactive or underactive participants, negative attitudes, bored group members and stagnant groups, problematic leadership styles, and ineffective education groups.

## Organization

Before commencing group discussions, the teacher may find it helpful to have students review the rules of the classroom aloud. As mentioned in Chapter 5, when there is a break in the routine, many students will not know how to handle the situation. The teacher may want to have special rules for group discussions, such as the following:

1. *Students must respect peers.* This may already be a rule in the classroom, but reinforcement is needed because of the different setting. Listening intently, speaking only when a peer has finished speaking, and accepting a peer's input are behaviors that show respect. Teachers should remember that this may be the first time that students will be sharing their personal thoughts.
2. *Participation is voluntary at all times.* The students may leave group discussion at any time and return to their schoolwork.

As with the rules in the normal classroom routine, the teacher must consistently support these rules and, when necessary, apply the appropriate contingencies (which should already have been presented to the students).

Another facet of organization to consider is the size of the group, which varies according to the number of students with which the educator can work with ease. Hophan (1977) tried groups of 3, 6, and 12, and found groups of 6 to be the most workable for her. Others have suggested that with proper planning moral development curricula can be utilized with a class of 25 students. Adams (1977) suggested three ways to divide the class for discussion purposes:

1. Divide groups into those who support the same side of an issue (the groups can be divided to limit sizes). Have the students list their reasons for support.
2. Same as above, but have the students list reasons for supporting the opposite belief.
3. Heterogeneously group the students and have them debate the issues.

If the whole class is in agreement about the issue, change the content to enhance the conflict. Adams suggested that a 50–50 split is needed for effective discussion, whereas Galbraith and Jones (1976) believed a 70–30 split can work. A predesigned split may not be necessary, although it certainly is desirable, because the structure or reasoning behind the content (agreement or disagreement) may often be very different.

The amount of time devoted to class discussion differs with regard to age, development levels, and teacher structure. Lickona (1977b) found that teachers generally set aside about 20 minutes at the end of the morning and, in some cases, in late afternoon. With the advent of mainstreaming and inclusion, the full-time student in special classes is a rarity. Therefore, the special education teacher in either environment may choose to implement the approach 2 or 3 days a week during different times of the day so that each student is exposed to discussions for at least 40–60 minutes per week. Whatever time period the teacher chooses, it should become part of the classroom routine rather than something "special."

The physical classroom arrangement can be a crucial factor in ensuring the flow of class discussion. Two commonly used designs are the horseshoe and the circle. If the educator has adopted the classroom design recommended in Chapter 5, the table in the back of the room can provide the means for small group interaction and still allow the teacher to observe those students who are working independently at their desks. Any type of special physical arrangement for discussions has the added benefit of allowing the students to get out from behind their desks and interact with each other in a more comfortable manner.

## Teacher's Role

Beyer (1976) suggested that "Teachers have two main tasks: to promote student-to-student interaction, and to keep the discussion a moral discussion"

(p. 198). To promote discussion, the teacher should attempt to provide an "inviting" classroom atmosphere. Trust can be attained only when there is a constant expectation of having one's beliefs accepted. The students should be able to expect reactions from the teacher that are fair to all involved. Students realize that, as humans, teachers are fallible; however, by perceiving teachers' striving to be consistent, students may begin to realize that inconsistencies do happen but are not the norm (at least in this particular setting), and trust may begin to surface.

The teacher should attempt to keep within the allotted time constraints of the classroom. As the discussions grow and become exciting, the temptation may be to "let it go" for a few more minutes. Unfortunately, this attitude interferes with the simultaneous long-term goals of the students to attain the academic skills that they need.

Griese (1977), an elementary school teacher, found that during the initial group sessions she tended to dominate the discussions and perhaps instill her values. She stressed that, although group meetings were difficult in the beginning, she was surprised at how little she had to participate in later classroom discussions. In other words, when the students began to understand and solve problems on their own, and were encouraged to do so, they seized the opportunity.

Hophan (1977) was more specific with the problems she had in leading class discussions:

1. Like many people, I have fixed values, and my questioning techniques made clear my feeling that I had the "right" answer and we were just playing a game to see who could guess what it was. I became aware of voice tones and facial gestures that slanted even the ready-made questions in the manual.
2. I had perpetuated the subtle and unspoken belief that I am the sole source of wisdom. The children spoke only to me, and in response to my questions.
3. I was unable myself to see a moral dilemma from many points of view. I could not grasp all the possible implications. Therefore, my questions dealt with only the most obvious problems, and I was unable to keep discussion going for any length of time.
4. I gave subtle approval to those who responded in ways that showed higher stages of reasoning. I spoke to them more often, even calling on them to reply when no one was volunteering.
5. Since I truly felt that there was a right solution, I dragged discussion along and prompted the leaders to give me that solution. At that point we concluded the discussion, leaving the children with no conflict at all. (pp. 37–38)

Hophan's statements provide much food for thought because some difficulties may be virtually impossible to solve. As Hersh et al. (1979) suggested, "even if we worked hard to eliminate verbal style and vocabulary that communicate praise or blame, we still have a vast repertoire of gestures, facial expressions, and tones of voice that convey our personal reactions to what students say" (p. 176). Some teachers find it difficult to avoid negating the comments of a student who reasons at a lower stage, especially when it is clearly not the choice of the majority of the students. Again, these students must feel comfortable in the group if they are to be active members.

Kohlberg and Higgins (1987) suggested that the following conditions for moral growth are enhanced when the teacher acts as a process facilitator:

1. *Role Taking.* The teacher should encourage students explicitly to consider the feelings and points of view of the other students discussing the dilemma and of the staff, the administration, or community figures. This may extend to actual role playing of reactions in another's place.
2. *Considering Fairness.* The teacher should raise issues of fairness in student or staff discussions of a dilemma or in community meetings.
3. *Treating Decisions as Moral* (*moral* includes but is more extensive than *fairness*). *Moral* is distinguished from the pragmatic, the legal, or the procedural. The teacher should focus the discussion on the moral issues of the decision.
4. *Exposure to Cognitive-Moral Conflict.* The teacher should highlight or encourage higher-stage reasoning or articulate it himself or herself. (p. 122)

## Initiating Group Discussions

The teacher should not attempt to rush into meaningful conflict and dilemma solving in the earliest meeting(s). Some educators who normally permit little interaction in their classrooms expect students to participate spontaneously in open discussions, and are surprised to find reticent students. Teachers also may be surprised to find that some students who have been in the same classes together for years have rarely spoken to each other.

One approach to breaking the ice is simply to have the students give their names and perhaps tell something about themselves. This process allows the teacher to observe how comfortable or uncomfortable students may be in a group. Some students can hardly wait to participate and others will talk into their shirts. An effort should be made to make these latter students as comfortable as possible. Teachers should remember that the behavior of quiet students is attributed to any number of circumstances: shyness (especially in new experiences), fear of giving the wrong statement, or not knowing how to respond (the student may never have been asked to participate in class). One way to respond to quiet or shy students is to have them work together in small groups. Let them work collaboratively to define their positions regarding the dilemma.

The teacher should not press uncomfortable students into participating because some students may need more time to become acclimated to the new experience of sharing. One method of inviting these students is to ask them to respond to general questions about television shows, movies, or music. Hall (1979) commented that students may wish to present their memories of certain personal experiences in which they felt they were wrongly treated, rewarded, or punished.

Integral to the smooth running of class or group discussions is having all participants operating from the same frame of reference. A vocabulary lesson that incorporates terms and concepts that will be used during moral development sessions can facilitate the meetings. Elementary vocabulary words should include *good–bad, approval–disapproval, fair–unfair, selfish–sharing, punishment–reward,* and *obey–disobey.* Middle and high school vocabulary words should include *reasoning, rational, values, justice, society, peers, conventions, conscience, relationships, conformity, opinions,* and *fact.* A pretest of the elementary words would be recommended for the older students. Once the vocabulary words are chosen, the educator should:

1. Begin with one concept.

2. Brainstorm and compile the various possible meanings.

3. Ask students to give explanations (personal experiences, role playing, and pictures can be used).

4. Put concepts on index cards for future reference (student-made bulletin boards are excellent reinforcing ideas).

5. Be aware of dilemmas and conflicts that may surface during the activity and use them.

## Presenting Moral Dilemmas

When the previously discussed conditions have been taken into consideration, the teacher may prepare to present the moral dilemmas. The type of dilemma chosen will be dictated by the group's progress, goals, and constitution. Niles (1986) believed that "the realization of the link between moral reasoning and behavioral choice is dependent on many variables including the social context of the choice situation; therefore, real-life, situation-specific dilemmas may be critical in promoting the transition from reasoning structures to behaviors. Research with this type of dilemma has not been undertaken" (p. 49). As previously mentioned, the teacher should go over group rules, stressing that positive or negative feelings should not be associated with any group member's responses. The student should not have to feel apprehensive about the possibility of being ridiculed. In Mosher and Sullivan's (1976) study with an adolescent population, attendance and participation were the only requirements of the course, not right or wrong answers.

The dilemmas could be presented in movies, filmstrips, newspaper articles, handouts, real-life episodes, picture cards, or puppet shows (Galbraith & Jones, 1976). It is important that the dilemmas be relatively easy to understand, be open-ended, and have at least two possible positions. Scharf, McCoy, and Ross (1979) suggested that dilemmas involving peers, parents, or self should be used before those involving historical or societal problems. Three important and closely related skills will facilitate the presentation of dilemmas: clarification, listening checks, and brainstorming.

*Clarification* allows the teacher to carefully delineate the dilemma. The teacher should specifically discuss the facts of the dilemma and present the sides of the issue. Clarification is not an opportunity for teachers to instill their own values. One clarification method is to list all of the dilemma's facts either on the chalkboard or on dittos. The use of the vocabulary lesson is helpful because language and terms may often cloud the meaning of a dilemma. Another technique is for the teacher to role-play or take a position on a dilemma to make the character's problem clearer to the students.

*Listening checks* help to make sure students are following the dilemma and can understand particular statements. Teachers can conduct listening checks by asking students to restate the problem and state the possible conflicts. Listening checks can include questions such as, "Can you tell me what just happened to [the main character]?" or "What happened after . . . ?"

*Brainstorming* serves two functions: (a) It expands upon listening checks and clarification in that it helps the teacher keep aware of how well the students understand the problem, and (b) it provides a means to generate many different reasons, and stage levels of reasons, in a quick and creative manner. When brainstorming, all ideas are accepted even when they are similar to previously stated reasons. The students are encouraged to say whatever comes into their minds, and the discussion should move at a quick pace. One purpose of the brainstorming process is to let other people's comments create new ideas (Hall, 1979).

Brainstorming concentrates on the reasoning, not the content, of the dilemma. When a dilemma is unclear, students tend to argue about facts rather than concentrate on reasoning (Beyer, 1976). Teachers should use listening checks and clarification to refocus on the discussion and deal with the reasoning. Teachers should refrain from offering alternate reasoning because it may tend to be perceived as the "right" answer. Dilemmas are potentially very powerful tools that could be incorrectly used for indoctrinating values (Adams, 1977). However, if a dilemma does not yield divergent reasoning, the teacher may want to make the story more complicated by changing an element, such as, "Well, what do you think would happen if the main character was physically impaired or mentally retarded?"

## Questioning Techniques

To successfully conduct moral discussions, teachers must practice appropriate questioning techniques. Many disturbed and disturbing students have rarely been asked to express their opinions about anything, let alone conflicts. It is important that the teacher invite participation rather than disinvite (whether intentionally or unintentionally) reasoning. This is attempted by asking open-ended instead of forced-choice (yes or no) types of questions. Teachers can encourage student participation by asking questions such as the following: Why? What do you think about . . . ? What do you think the problem is? Why did the main character do . . . ? Why is the action wrong? What is the conflict between the son and the father? Is this relationship important to our society? Why? Galbraith and Jones (1976) listed three types of classroom questioning:

1. *Issue-related probes.* The teacher helps the students see the relationship of a dilemma to one of Kohlberg's 10 moral issues. This promotes clarification of the dilemma and allows the students to center upon a particular concept.

2. *Role-switch probes.* The teacher encourages the students to take the perspective of a character in the dilemma. This allows the dilemma to become more vivid to the students.

3. *Universal consequence probes.* The teacher encourages the students to see society's viewpoint of the character's actions. "What would happen if everyone did what the character did?"

The probes allow the teacher to diagnose the structure of the discussion. A common error that teachers should try to avoid is superficially discussing a particular issue before all aspects are covered. The teacher should attempt to view as many sides of the dilemma as possible by using the above probes. Another technique used to examine reasoning is referring to the history (of reasoning) of the group or individual. This is done by comparing the present reasoning of the group with earlier discussions. This permits the students to observe changes in their own reasoning (Hersh & Paolitto, 1979).

Questions may also be encouraged by the comparison of the groups themselves (see the previous section titled Organization). Grouping the students according to how they reason may help them to clarify their own rationales. The teacher can aid this process by summarizing the reasons stated so that the students can verify whether their intent is being expressed.

Teachers may be tempted to use "implosion" techniques in the classroom. This occurs when the teacher bombards students with questions and reasoning that are two or more stages above their levels in hopes of raising their stage placement. This generally results in frustration for both teacher and students. Teachers need to remember that development is a slow and difficult process that will not occur overnight.

Teachers may find it helpful to audiotape or videotape the class discussions. This serves three purposes: (a) It allows the teachers to critique their own performance; (b) it permits the teacher to pick up reasoning that may have been overlooked; and (c) some students may find being on videotape an event in itself, which will increase their motivation to participate. Figure 7.1 provides guidelines, developed by Beyer (1976), that may be followed for conducting moral discussions. Each of the tasks is either self-explanatory or has been discussed in the prior text.

## Preventing Problems

No matter how carefully the teacher prepares for the moral discussion sessions, problems are bound to occur. One such problem is that peer pressures may place a less than subtle "lid" on conversations—it may not be considered "cool" to be open and honest. One way to combat this is to present hypothetical dilemmas before real-life conflicts are attempted. Initially, moral growth may be painful, especially when long-held beliefs are brought into question. This can be approached only in a classroom atmosphere that the students perceive as accepting. Arbuthnot and Faust (1981) pinpointed seven possible problems that may arise during discussion:

1. *Insensitive participation.* This should be handled in a preventative manner by structuring rules to avoid ridicule-inducing situations. Whenever verbal attacks occur, steps should be taken immediately to stop them. This may require the teacher to be directive or indoctrinative. Whatever "damage" is created by the teacher's actions is minor compared with possible effects that ridicule may have on the student who is being ridiculed.

2. *Overactive participant.* There are two types of overactive participants. One type may be contributing meaningfully to the discussion, but simply talks too much. A gentle private talk with these students may decrease their frequency of participation. The second type is most likely egocentric. These students want to be the center of attention and have everything revolve around them. Such students may not be aware that they are monopolizing the discussion. The teacher

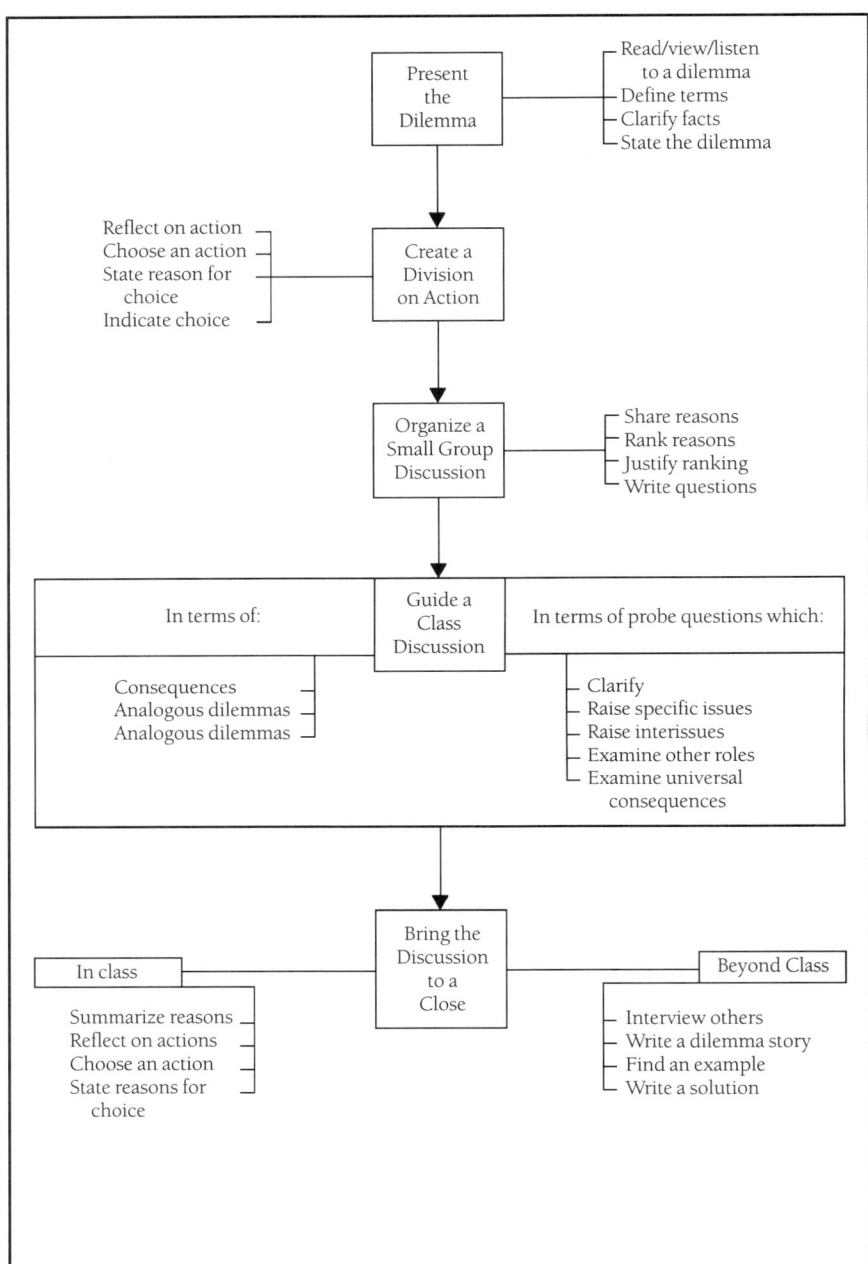

**FIGURE 7.1.** Flowchart of a strategy for guiding moral discussions.

From "Conducting Moral Discussions in the Classroom" by B. K. Beyer, 1976, *Social Education, 40,* pp. 194–202. Copyright 1976 by the National Council for the Social Studies. Reprinted with permission.

must let them know that others must participate in the group, and that, if this is to occur, they must be quiet. Initially, gentle hints should be attempted with the teacher becoming more forceful later if necessary.

3. *Underactive participant.* This type of student may cause undue stress on the teacher. Although they may not choose to participate in an obvious way, some underactive students will still be growing morally. Moral development is an internal process that promotes cognitive dissonance (disequilibrium). Active participation may *not* be necessary to progress. It may take time to discriminate between the student who is turned off and one who is simply quiet.

4. *Negative attitudes.* Many students bring their negative feelings to any activities. This may be due, in part, to parental attitudes: Parents may stress that moral development is useless and that teachers should be devoting all of their energy to the three Rs, or more simply they may have negative feelings regarding school. The students may also perceive realistic or imagined negative attitudes from their peers. Each of these cases should be considered separately because the causes of the attitudes differ; students whose attitudes are caused by negative parental or (actual) peer attitudes are the most difficult to integrate into discussion. It is suggested that these students be allowed to join the group if they can follow the rules (no ridicule, respect for peers, etc.). Hopefully, they will learn to see the classroom discussion period in a better light. As with the other students, they always have the option to return to their seats to do other classwork.

5. *Bored group members and stagnated groups.* This problem may be due to situations that the teacher can avoid with careful observation and planning. The teacher should not present the dilemmas in the same manner each time. Also, dilemmas that discuss the same issues may lead to redundancy in student arguments and should be avoided. If the group reasons on the same stage level, it may require much harder work for teachers because *they* have to produce the higher level reasoning that the group is unable to develop. Finally, group members may become bored if reasoning is presented that is constantly two stages above or two stages below their current level of reasoning. A restructuring of the group may become necessary to ensure stimulation of these students.

6. *Problematic leadership styles.* If group discussions are not progressing in a fashion suitable to the teacher, an assessment of that group by audiotape or videotape may be helpful. Common problems are that the teacher talks too much, tends to drill students using higher level reasoning, and asks inappropriate questions (forced-choice, poor use of probes).

7. *Ineffective education groups.* Teachers may question whether the groups are a waste of time if little behavioral progress is observed.

Keeping in mind that development is a slow process, teachers may want to check their perceptions by getting feedback from their students, receiving evaluations from observers, comparing recordings from different dates, and reviewing written records of the group.

These summaries of the major problems teachers may face in conducting classroom discussions are useful in *any* group situation (see the following unit on rational-emotive therapy). Awareness of these potential dangers may allow an unintentionally disinviting teacher to become intentionally inviting. Although problems will frequently arise no matter how carefully one plans, it is the reaction to these problems that can make or break discussion groups. Also integral to the smooth running of moral discussions are the moral dilemmas themselves.

# Types of Moral Dilemmas

Moral dilemmas may take many forms and each has a justification for classroom use. They may represent hypothetical, real-life, or academic content areas. The final section of this chapter examines each of these forms, presents the pros and cons of their use, and provides examples of each for classroom use.

Before deciding upon specific dilemmas, the teacher should determine issues that are appropriate to the students. The issues should be understood by all participants. By definition, dilemmas are issues that have at least two reasonable sides. They should be thought-provoking and, if possible, should focus on a particular stage level. In other words, dilemmas revolving around the civil rights of African Americans may be appropriate for Stage 3 or 4 reasoners, whereas those concerned with individual rights, including stealing, cheating, and fighting, may be more appropriate for reasoners in Stages 1, 2, and 3. Dilemmas dealing with parents and teachers may be more appropriate for students at Stages 1, 2, and 3, and relationships to peers and society for students at Stages 2, 3, and 4. Individuals will be "asked to determine which action the characters in the story should take and why. Through a series of probe questions, it is believed that the participant's decision-making processes concerning the resolution of these dilemmas as they relate to specific moral issues (e.g., value of human life, laws and rules, punishment and justice, truth and contract, property rights) can be ascertained" (Goldstein & Glick, 1987, p. 98).

Galbraith and Jones (1976) contended that each dilemma should include the following elements: (a) a *focus* on students' lives, course content, or societal concerns; (b) a *central character* about whom the students make particular judgments on what the character should do; (c) a clear *choice* of alternatives; (d) one of the *moral issues* discussed in Chapter 6; and (e) a *"should" question* to help the discussion center on structure rather than content.

## Hypothetical Dilemmas

Hypothetical dilemmas invite discussion without requiring the students to "disclose" their personal feelings. Many hypothetical dilemmas reflect conflicts that are similar to real-life dilemmas (Hersh & Paolitto, 1979), thus allowing students to make generalizations about the hypothetical dilemma and their own conflicts.

The following hypothetical dilemma is a sample from the hundreds that are commercially available. Other sources, such as popular songs, contain dilemmas. Teachers should pay particular attention to the *structure* in the following exercise, because it may be useful for presenting subsequent dilemmas, as well as for modifying vignettes from other types of books (e.g., values clarification texts). The reader is encouraged to use the questions as a model for devising questions for other dilemmas.

---

### Mrs. Bartholomew and Her Regular Customers

Mrs. Bartholomew had owned and operated a local gas station for almost 20 years. She had built the small business slowly and often had trouble competing with the large, company-owned stations in the area. She did manage to make enough money to raise her family and support her husband, who was an invalid. Her small station thrived mostly because she had old-time regular customers. However, a gasoline shortage threw everyone into a panic—everyone needed gasoline badly.

Mrs. Bartholomew felt that her regular customers had been loyal to her for years (even when her gas was 2 or 3 cents higher than other stations) and that they deserved her loyalty now. Mrs. Bartholomew also feared that she would lose the regular customers if she couldn't provide them with gasoline. She decided to sell gas only to her regular customers.

People began pulling into her station with their tanks almost empty asking to buy gas. They were not regular customers so she refused to sell to them. One woman told Mrs. Bartholomew that the "regular-customer" policy was against the law and that she intended to report her. Other customers argued that the policy was unfair and that she should treat everyone equally.

*(continues)*

**Dilemma** (Continued)

Should Mrs. Bartholomew sell gas to everyone or only to her regular customers?

## TEACHING PLAN

*Part I: The Original Dilemma*

Distribute a class handout that tells the story of Mrs. Bartholomew and her regular customers. Make sure that the students understand the terminology in the dilemma and can state the nature of the dilemma that Mrs. Bartholomew faces. Determine by a show of hands or in some other way how the class feels about whether Mrs. Bartholomew should sell gas to everyone or only to her regular customers.

*Part II: Alternative Dilemmas*

If the class agrees that Mrs. Bartholomew *should* sell gas only to her regular customers, one of the following alternative dilemmas can be used to provoke disagreement:

1. Mrs. Bartholomew was told that she could be sued for her regular-customer policy.

2. The regular-customer policy had caused a lot of trouble. Several fights had started. One of her attendants had been cut by glass when a brick went through her plate window, several tires had been stolen from her display case, and a child was almost hit by a car that went speeding out of her station when she told the driver about the policy.

If the class agrees that Mrs. Bartholomew *should not* sell gas only to her regular customers, one of the following alternative dilemmas can be used to provoke disagreement:

1. Many of Mrs. Bartholomew's regular customers had asked her to save gasoline specifically for them and had indicated that if she could not, they would take their business elsewhere.

2. Mrs. Bartholomew had signed an agreement with most of her regular customers promising to sell them all the gasoline they wanted.

*Part III: Probe Questions*

1. Is it fair for a businessperson to make special deals for certain people or old-time customers? Why or why not?

*(continues)*

**Dilemma** (Continued)
2. Is it right for Mrs. Bartholomew's regular customers to expect her to give them special treatment?
3. Should there be a law prohibiting gas stations from selling gas to their regular customers first? Why?
4. If the attendant knows that there is a law against selling to special customers, should he report Mrs. Bartholomew to the authorities? Why or why not? Should someone else report her?
5. From the point of view of a regular customer, is Mrs. Bartholomew's policy fair? Why?

## A ROLE-PLAYING GROUP STRATEGY

A strategy that works particularly well with this story involves a role-taking situation. If your class is divided somewhat evenly over the final question in the story (e.g., 14 students say that Mrs. Bartholomew should sell to everyone and 19 say that she should stick to her regular-customer policy), break the class into four groups, two groups representing each position. Ask the groups to discuss among themselves the reasons for their position. While the small groups meet, move to each group and give the following tasks:

Group 1 (sell to everyone)—Tell this group to select two or three people who will take the role of customers seeking gas at Mrs. Bartholomew's station (they are not regular customers, however). The rest of the group should help these individuals prepare the reasons they will use to try to convince Mrs. Bartholomew to sell them gasoline.

Group 2 (sell to everyone)—Same task as above.

Group 3 (regular-customer policy)—Ask this group to select two or three people who will take the role of regular customers who arrive at Mrs. Bartholomew's for gasoline. The entire group should help them prepare to discuss the policy with the others who also come for gas.

Group 4 (regular-customer policy)—Ask this group to select three individuals to take the following roles: Mrs. Bartholomew (or her oldest son); a cousin of the family who works at the station; and a young high school student who works at the station. The group should help these people prepare to defend their regular-customer policy.

Begin the role-taking session by asking the participating customers to line up their chairs or desks as if they were in a line waiting to get to the pumps. Ask

(continues)

**Dilemma** (Continued)

Mrs. Bartholomew and the attendants to stand (the rest of the class can sit on the periphery of the station setting). Suggest to the class that Mrs. Bartholomew and the cousin are busy pumping gas and that the other attendant is walking from car to car identifying the regular customers. Instruct the attendant to ask any others waiting in the line to pull out and go to some other station.

Sit down and watch the discussion as Mrs. Bartholomew and the service station crew try to convince people who are waiting for gasoline to leave the line. Eventually draw the students on the outer circle into the discussion and focus on the issues involved in the dilemma story.

From *Moral Reasoning: A Teaching Handbook for Adapting Kohlberg to the Classroom* (pp. 141–147) by R. E. Galbraith and T. Jones, 1976, Minneapolis: Greenhaven Press.

---

## The Salesman's Dilemma

Rick owns a car dealership and recently hired Sam. Sam had been unemployed for 6 months and during that time his wife had been very ill, incurring many medical bills. Sam is very hard-working and was extremely grateful for the opportunity to work for Rick.

One day Rick told Sam that a couple was in the process of purchasing a car for their teenage daughter to commute to and from college, which was 50 miles away. Rick instructed Sam to finish the deal because he was going to take the rest of the day off. After Rick left, the man and woman arrived to buy the car. Coincidentally, Sam knew the couple. In fact, they were close friends with his parents. He also realized that the car they had decided to buy was going to need some major repairs before too long. Sam knew that Rick was aware of this problem. What should Sam do? Remember that:

1. Sam desperately needs this job.

2. The couple went to Rick's dealership because they had heard that Sam worked there and thought they would be treated fairly.

3. Sam's wife may soon need major surgery that is covered by his job benefits.

4. The car is dangerous.

5. Sam will probably be fired if he loses this deal.

### QUESTIONS

1. What do you think that Sam should do? Why?

*(continues)*

> **Dilemma** (Continued)
> 2. What are Sam's alternatives?
> 3. Do you think *not* telling the couple is like not telling the truth? Why?
> 4. What do you think would happen if most businesses were run like Rick's?
> 5. What about the phrase "Buyer Beware"? Should Sam feel responsible for the car?
> 6. Does it make a difference that Sam knows the couple? Why?

## Hypothetical Classroom Dilemmas

The following dilemmas represent situations common to the classroom. Examples are given for elementary, middle, and high school students. Further examples may be found in Blatt, Colby, and Speicher (1974) and Scharf et al. (1979).

> ### Elementary School: Accidental Injury
>
> A girl was about to sit down on her chair; as she was sitting down, a boy removed the chair from behind her. He did not mean to do her any harm, but wanted to get her attention. The girl fell to the floor and broke her back.
>
> **QUESTIONS**
> 1. Is the boy responsible for breaking her back? Why or why not?
> 2. People often joke around and occasionally someone gets hurt. When do you hold the person responsible for consequences of an accident? What if someone was injured in a baseball game?
> 3. Would it be right for the girl's parents to sue the boy's parents? Why or why not?
> 4. Are parents responsible for the behavior of their children? Why or why not?
> 5. What is negligence? Are people responsible for damage only when they have been negligent? Why or why not?
>
> From *Hypothetical Dilemmas for Use in Moral Discussion* by M. Blatt, A. Colby, and B. Speicher, 1974, Cambridge, MA: Moral Education and Research Foundation. Copyright 1974 by Moral Education and Research Foundation. Reprinted by permission.

## Middle School: Larry's Dilemma

One of Larry's school friends, Richard, was planning a party at his house. Larry's parents had made the rule that Larry wasn't allowed at someone's house unless their parents were home. Richard told Larry that his (Richard's) parents were going to be home during the party. After Larry's parents dropped him off at the party, Larry found out Richard's parents were not home. He really wanted to stay, because he knew he'd have a good time. His friends told him he would be a "baby" if he left, yet he had promised his mother and father that Richard's parents would be home. What should he do?

### QUESTIONS:

1. What are some factors Larry should take into consideration before deciding to stay or go: the number of people at the party? the planned activities?
2. What types of things could go wrong at the party?
3. What if Richard's parents know he's having the party and gave him permission?
4. What if Larry's parents have always been overly strict and often unreasonable?
5. What if Larry's parents have always been fair and understanding and discussed the rule with Larry before they made it?
6. Should you always obey your parents no matter what, or are there times it might be right to disobey?

If students agree Larry should leave, pose the following:

1. Suppose Larry's parents decide Richard's parents should be told about the party; wouldn't Larry risk getting everyone in trouble and possibly risk losing a lot of friends?
2. Suppose Richard tells Larry not to worry because Richard's older brother (age 18) has stayed home to supervise the party.

If students agree Larry should stay, pose the following:

1. Suppose the party goers are planning to take rides with Richard's older brother on his motorcycle.
2. Suppose Larry's parents know Richard's parents and there's a possibility that they all might find out the truth later.

From "Building Moral Dilemma Activities" by D. Adams, 1977, *Learning, 5,* pp. 44–46. Reprinted with permission.

# Middle School: Laetrile

You wouldn't think that apricot pits could cause arguments and problems, but they have. People are really arguing about a drug called Laetrile, which is made from crushed apricot pits. The people who sell and support the use of Laetrile say that the drug helps to prevent cancer, to treat cancer, and to relieve the pain of cancer.

Laetrile is not allowed in many states, yet thousands of people still use it. It's smuggled into the United States from other countries. The Food and Drug Administration won't allow Laetrile to be made in this country because the law says that people cannot use a new drug until it's been proved to work and be safe. While Laetrile hasn't been found to hurt anyone, no study has proved that it cures or prevents cancer. Officials of the American Cancer Society and the National Cancer Institute say that Laetrile is a fraud and believe that people who use Laetrile won't look for proper medical treatment. Most doctors don't think the drug should be used.

People who want Laetrile allowed say that since it doesn't hurt anyone there's no reason to stop people from using it if they want to. They feel that they have the right to choose how to be treated. They say that making Laetrile illegal limits their freedom of choice.

People who don't want Laetrile legalized feel that people who use it are only hurting themselves, and that those who sell it are taking advantage of others. They tell of cases in which people who have had a 65 percent chance of being cured by surgery have taken Laetrile instead and then died.

## QUESTIONS

1. What's the problem here?

2. Is it right or wrong to keep the use of Laetrile illegal? Why?

3. What's the best reason you can think of for keeping Laetrile illegal?

4. What's the best reason you can think of for making Laetrile legal?

5. Does the government have the right to ban things it thinks can harm people? Why or why not? Should people be able to make up their own minds in situations like these? Why or why not?

6. Many people feel that cigarettes and alcohol are harmful. Should these be made illegal? Why or why not? What do you think would happen if cigarettes and alcohol were made illegal?

From *Growing up Moral: Dilemmas for the Intermediate Grades* by P. Scharf, W. McCoy, and D. Ross, 1979, Minneapolis: Winston Press. Copyright 1979 by Winston Press, Inc. Reprinted with permission.

## High School: Bulimia

Janet and Belinda had been best friends for many years and they shared many secrets. They often slept at each other's home. They were of average weight and in good health. They liked to do many of the same things. Both girls dreamed of being fashion models. They collected fashion magazines and each had their favorite models. They knew that most models were very thin and they resolved to lose weight before graduation. Unfortunately, Janet couldn't lose any weight. Perhaps their pizza and junk food binges were the cause. Belinda, however, began to lose weight at a very fast pace. Janet couldn't understand how Belinda was losing so much weight, as they both ate the same junk food.

One evening at a sleep-over, Janet learned how Belinda was losing weight. They had just finished eating a quart of ice cream. Janet walked by the bathroom and heard Belinda vomiting. She asked Belinda if she was ill, and Belinda replied, "No, this is how all of the models stay thin!" Janet knew that Belinda could get very sick from this and warned her about it. Belinda told Janet that if she told anyone about her, she would never speak to her again. It was none of her business.

### QUESTIONS

1. Should Janet let someone know about Belinda's problem?
2. Should Janet mind her own business and continue being Belinda's friend?
3. How would Belinda feel if Janet had the same problem?
4. What would you do if your best friend had this problem?
5. What would you want Janet to do if you were Belinda?

From *Growing up Moral: Dilemmas for the Intermediate Grades* by P. Scharf, W. McCoy, and D. Ross, 1979, Minneapolis: Winston Press. Copyright 1979 by Winston Press, Inc. Reprinted with permission.

## High School: Adult Retarded People

A psychologist who was interested in the plight of adult retarded people established a community for them. He provided them with jobs and other facilities in order to allow them to maximize their potential abilities. After the community was established, the psychologist faced a new problem.

*(continues)*

> **Dilemma**  (Continued)
> Some of the people in the community became interested in getting married to each other.
>   The psychologist knew that one of the main causes for mental retardation was genetic abnormality. These genetic abnormalities are transmitted by heredity from the parents to their children. The chance that a child will be retarded is extremely high if his or her parents are retarded.
>   Some people argue that retarded people should not be permitted to get married or have children. These people claim that retarded children do not have the potential of living full and useful lives. Furthermore, retarded children have to be taken care of, and in most cases they have to be supported by the state. Therefore, the care of retarded children places a heavy drain upon the resources of the state and the taxpayers.
>
> **QUESTIONS**
>
> 1. Should there be a law which prohibits retarded adults from getting married and having children? Why or why not?
>
> 2. Some people would argue that prohibiting retarded people from getting married and having children is unconstitutional. Why do they think that way? How would this be unconstitutional?
>
> 3. Which do you think is more important, guaranteeing each person the right to get married and have children or the consequences to society and to resources of the state and taxpayers if the number of retarded persons is permitted to increase?
>
> 4. What solution could you offer in this situation?
>
> 5. Suppose you have a retarded son or daughter. Would you want your child to get married if you thought your grandchildren would be retarded?
>
> From *Hypothetical Dilemmas for Use in Moral Discussion* by M. Blatt, A. Colby, and B. Speicher, 1974, Cambridge, MA: Moral Education and Research Foundation. Copyright 1974 by Moral Education and Research Foundation. Reprinted with permission.

## Real-Life Dilemmas

Although hypothetical dilemmas may stimulate student interest and discussion, they may not allow students to use their skills with regard to real-life dilemmas. A valuable source of dilemmas is the many real-life situations that confront students daily. Fraenkel (1976) suggested that these dilemmas may be interpersonal and intrapersonal in the elementary grades, slowly progressing to conflicts that revolve around the school, community, and public law. Remembering that all dilemmas should contain the elements mentioned by Galbraith and Jones (1976) and involve issues that are relevant to the students, the teacher can generate a real-life dilemma by posing such questions as the following:

1. Tell us exactly what the problem is?
2. Can someone tell us one reason for doing what Joe wants to do?
3. Can someone tell us one reason for not doing what Joe wants to do?
4. Was the principal fair (unfair) to Joe? Why or why not?
5. How could the principal have been fair?
6. Should all rules be fair?
7. Can a rule be fair to Bob and not to Joe?

List the answers on the board, using listening checks, clarification, and brainstorming techniques.

Newspapers and textbooks can be timely resources because each day they contain many dilemmas that can easily be adapted for classroom use (Scharf, 1978). The following lesson, designed by Galbraith and Jones (1976), is an excellent example of using newspaper articles.

---

### Middle School and High School: Mercy Death

Situations involving moral issues surround us. Articles in newspapers, programs on television, and events in our community confront us with real-life moral dilemma stories. This newspaper story appeared in the *Pittsburgh Press*:

*Man Charged in Wife's Mercy Death*—Pontiac, Michigan (UPI)

Robert Waters told his wife of 40 years he loved her, then kissed her goodbye; minutes later, she was dead.

Waters, a 65-year-old former high school principal, has been charged with manslaughter in the November 13 death of his wife Kathleen. He pleaded innocent and was released on bond.

Police said Waters was responsible for his wife's death because he helped her get into a motor-running auto in the couple's garage, then closed the door. Waters said his wife was despondent because of failing health and wanted to commit suicide. He said he could not talk her out of it.

*(continues)*

**Dilemma** (Continued)

"In the car he asked her if she was sure this was what she wanted," Oakland County Prosecutor L. Brooks Patterson said. "She said yes," Patterson said. "And then she said to kiss her goodbye and they expressed their love for one another. And then he got out of the car."

Mrs. Waters died of carbon monoxide poisoning. Waters pleaded innocent to a charge that he did willfully, feloniously, negligently and knowingly, but without malice or premeditation, kill and slay Kathleen Waters.

"This couple was very close," Patterson said. "But I am a servant of the law and am obliged to carry it out."

Many people have discussed whether Mr. Waters should be punished for helping his wife commit suicide—or killing her (as some people insist).

- Some people say, "Let him go free."

- Some say Mr. Waters should get at least a 2-year prison sentence.

- Others say that Mr. Waters should get a 10-year prison sentence for taking a life.

Which statement do you agree with?

## TEACHING PLAN

### Part I: The Original Dilemma

Distribute a class handout that describes the incident. Make sure that the students understand the terminology in the dilemma story. Determine how the class responds to the three statements about what should happen to Mr. Waters. If the class members disagree about the statements, you may select a particular small group strategy and ask the students to prepare a full class discussion of the action that should be taken in regard to Mr. Waters.

If the class agrees on what should happen to Mr. Waters, use one of the following alternatives of the dilemma story.

### Part II: Alternative Dilemmas

If the class agrees that they *should* let Mr. Waters go free, use the following alternative:

What if Mr. Patterson, the prosecutor, established that Mr. and Mrs. Waters had not been very close for several years and that their marital problems had something to do with Mrs. Waters's depression.

*(continues)*

> **Dilemma** (Continued)
>
> Yes, she was in ill health, but that was not the only reason for her desire to commit suicide. Should Mr. Waters still go free?
>
> If the class agrees that Mr. Waters *should not* go free, use the following alternative:
>
> What if Mr. Waters's attorney could establish that Mrs. Waters was dying from a very painful and rare disease? The disease had no known cure, and Mrs. Waters wanted very much to die peacefully, without the trauma of many months in a hospital. Should Mr. Waters still be punished?
>
> *Part III: Probe Questions*
>
> 1. Does a person have the right to decide when he or she will die?
> 2. Do you think Mr. Waters had an obligation to honor his wife's wish to commit suicide?
> 3. Should a person suffering from a terminal and painful illness be allowed to end his or her life when he or she chooses?
> 4. Should society try to prevent suicides? Why or why not?
> 5. Should an individual be punished for not preventing a suicide? Why or why not?
>
> Adapted from *Moral Reasoning: A Teaching Handbook for Adapting Kohlberg to the Classroom* by R. E. Galbraith and T. Jones, 1976, Minneapolis: Greenhaven Press.

## Academic Content Dilemmas

Moral development dilemmas are also applicable to the course content found in most classrooms. It has been suggested that dilemmas are natural curriculum aids in such varied areas as drug abuse (Riggs & Evans, 1979), social studies, English, math, guidance (Galbraith & Jones, 1976), and children's literature (Garrod & Bramble, 1977; Hoskisson & Biskin, 1979; Pillar, 1976).

Moral development exercises can also be used to motivate students in creative writing. Students can develop their own dilemmas (either fact or fiction) that, if "good," can also be presented in future classes. Educators' time may be needlessly spent on developing dilemmas, and the students' dilemmas are often more interesting and relevant than most teacher-created dilemmas.

Garrod and Bramble (1977) suggested that the characters in literature offer many personal dilemmas. Students can role-play the characters themselves and be encouraged to accurately perceive the characters' attitudes and values. Garrod and Bramble presented the following as an example of integrating moral development and the story of Huckleberry Finn.

## Friendship: Huckleberry Finn

Chapters 14–16: This section is one of the meatiest in the book. Chapter 15 finds the companions separated in the fog and then reunited. The trick that Huck plays on Jim backfires and reveals a new dimension—a new depth—to the friendship. Huck says: "It was fifteen minutes before I could work myself up to go and humble myself to a nigger; but I done it, and I wasn't very sorry for it afterward, neither."

### SUGGESTIONS FOR EXERCISES

Invite students to explore Huck's reasoning during the fifteen minutes he spent making up his mind to apologize; then have them write a script, with imaginary dialogue, detailing the various arguments and counter-arguments which culminate in the apology.

### SUGGESTIONS FOR STUDY QUESTIONS

1. Why is Huck so surprised by Jim's indignant response to his innocent joke?
2. Why does it take Huck a full fifteen minutes of internal debate before he can bring himself to apologize?
3. What considerations hold him back?
4. As a friendship deepens, does the obligation to apologize for unkind or thoughtless acts or words become greater or lesser, or remain constant?
5. Discuss the development of Huck's role-taking ability by comparing the time where he doesn't apologize (the snake-skin incident in Chapter 10) with the time that he does (after the separation in the fog).

Chapter 16 deals with the first of two major moral crises that confront Huck (the second one arises in Chapter 31). Huck's dilemma involves the conflict between his friendship for Jim, and his perceived obligations to society (and to Miss Watson in particular). His reasoning resolving this dilemma is beautifully presented in the middle of the chapter, and it's a classic example of Stage 2 instrumentalism: doing "whichever comes handiest at the time."

### SUGGESTIONS FOR STUDY QUESTIONS

6. What factors influence Huck's initial decision to turn Jim over to the authorities?

*(continues)*

> **Dilemma** (Continued)
> 7. What considerations encourage him to change his mind when he decides to lie to the bounty hunters?
> 8. Isn't it wrong to lie to them? Is it wrong to lie under all circumstances?
> 9. What are the moral implications of the rule Huck embraces when he decides that in the future he will do "whichever comes handiest at the time?" How does this rule solve the problem of right and wrong for Huck?
>
> From "Moral Development and Literature" by A. C. Garrod and G. A. Bramble, 1977, *Theory into Practice, 16,* p. 108. Reprinted with permission.

## Summary and Conclusions

This chapter provided the reader with the techniques necessary to introduce moral development into the classroom. Cautions that should be attended to before assessing and utilizing the curriculum were reviewed. For example, teachers should be aware that moral development is not a "quick and easy" process and that it is easy to confuse the concept of content with that of structure. A step-by-step model of preparing for moral discussions also was presented. This included the need for organizing the sessions with regard to such factors as group size, length of discussion, implementing group rules, and designing the physical arrangement of the session.

Understanding the teacher's role in facilitating the discussions is integral to a successful moral development lesson. Although this role necessarily includes implementing the above-stated factors of organization, it also may mean assessing the teacher's ability to increase student participation and accept values that are different from his or her own. Furthermore, it was noted that, if all parties are using the same vocabulary, unnecessary confusion may be avoided. An exercise to implement this procedure was provided.

Additional teacher skills that may enhance the presentation of dilemmas include the use of clarification, listening checks, and brainstorming. These skills will better enable teachers to focus on such questioning techniques as the issue-related, role-switch, and universal consequence probes.

There are apt to be problems with any classroom discussion. Seven specific problems and solutions were discussed: insensitive participation, overactive and underactive participants, negative attitudes, bored group members and stagnated groups, problematic leadership styles, and ineffective education groups. The three types of moral dilemmas that can be presented in the classroom are hypothetical, real-life, and academic content dilemmas. Examples of each of these types of dilemmas with specific probes were provided to acquaint the reader with the available resources for introducing moral development to students. These examples were not intended to be inclusive; the teacher's creativity may certainly broaden the dimensions of how a dilemma can be introduced.

Detailed attention was paid to the practice of assessment, a controversial aspect of moral development. Types of assessment and techniques to implement them were presented so that teachers can ascertain the specific level of reasoning of their students. The famous "Heinz Dilemma" was given so that the reader could apply his or her own assessment and moral development background.

The introduction of moral development discussions into the classroom routine can have many positive and long-lasting effects. Besides increasing the students' reasoning ability, the discussions and exercises can enhance communication skills, creativity, and an understanding of others. Furthermore, this curriculum can easily be integrated into the academic content areas, making them more stimulating and enjoyable.

# Unit 2 References

Adams, D. (1977). Building moral dilemma activities. *Learning, 5,* 44–46.
Arbuthnot, J. (1984). Moral reasoning development programmes in prison: Cognitive-developmental and critical reasoning approaches. *Journal of Moral Education, 13,* 112–123.
Arbuthnot, J. B., & Faust, D. (1981). *Teaching moral reasoning: Theory and practice.* New York: Harper & Row.
Arbuthnot, J., & Gordon, D. A. (1986). Behavioral and cognitive effects of a moral reasoning development intervention with high-risk behavior-disordered adolescents. *Journal of Clinical and Consulting Psychology, 54,* 208–216.
Bandura, A. (1977). *Social learning theory.* Englewood Cliffs, NJ: Prentice-Hall.
Baumrind, D. (1986). Sex differences in moral reasoning: Response to Walker's (1984) conclusion that there are none. *Child Development, 57,* 511–521.
Bear, G. G., & Richards, H. C. (1981). Moral reasoning and conduct problems in the classroom. *Journal of Educational Psychology, 73,* 664–670.
Berkowitz, M. W., Gibbs, J. C., & Broughton, J. M. (1980). The relation of moral judgment stage disparity of developmental effects of peer dialogues. *Merrill-Palmer Quarterly, 26,* 341–357.
Beyer, B. R. (1976). Conducting moral discussions in the classroom. *Social Education, 40,* 194–202.
Blackney, C. D., & Blackney, R. A. (1991). Understanding and reforming moral misbehavior among behaviorally disordered adolescents. *Behavioral Disorders, 16,* 120–126.
Blasi, A. (1980). Bridging moral cognition and moral action: A critical review of the literature. *Psychological Bulletin, 88,* 1–45.
Blatt, M., Colby, A., & Speicher, B. (1974). *Hypothetical dilemmas for use in moral discussions.* Cambridge, MA: Moral Education and Research Foundation.
Blatt, M., & Kohlberg, L. (1975). The effects of classroom moral discussion upon children's level of moral judgment. *Journal of Moral Education, 4,* 129–161.
Breznitz, S., & Kugelmass, S. (1967). Intentionality in moral judgment: Developmental stages. *Child Development, 38,* 469–479.
Brion-Meisels, S. (1979). Reasoning with troubled children: Classroom meetings as a forum for social thought. *Moral Education Forum, 4*(4), 17–23.
Campagna, A. F., & Hunter, S. (1975). Moral judgment in sociopathic and normal children. *Journal of Personality and Social Psychology, 31,* 199–205.
Center, D. B. (1989). *Curriculum and teaching strategies for students with behavioral disorders.* Englewood Cliffs, NJ: Prentice-Hall.

Chandler, J. J., Greenspan, S., & Barenboim, C. (1974). Assessment and training of role-taking and referential communication skills in institutionalized emotionally disturbed children. *Developmental Psychology, 10,* 546–553.

Chandler, M. J. (1973). Egocentrism and antisocial behavior: The assessment and training of social perspective-taking skill. *Developmental Psychology, 9,* 326–332.

Clifford, M. M. (1981). *Practicing educational psychology.* Boston: Houghton Mifflin.

Cohen, A. K. (1955). *Delinquent boys.* New York: Free Press.

Colby, A. (1978). Evolution of moral-developmental theory. *New Directions for Child Development, 2,* 89–104.

Colby, A., Kohlberg, L., Gibbs, J. C., & Lieberman, M. (1980). *A longitudinal study of moral judgment.* Unpublished manuscript, Harvard University, Cambridge, MA.

Coleman, M. C. (1992). *Behavior disorders* (2nd ed.). Boston: Allyn & Bacon.

Cooney, E. W. (1977). Social-cognitive development: Applications to intervention and evaluation in the elementary grades. *The Counseling Psychologist, 6,* 6–9.

Costanzo, P. R., Coie, J. D., Grumet, J. F., & Farnell, D. A. (1973). A reexamination of the effects of intent and consequences on children's moral judgments. *Child Development, 44,* 154–161.

Cowan, W. A. (1978). *Piaget: With feeling.* New York: Holt, Rinehart & Winston.

Damon, W., & Killen, M. (1982). Peer interaction and the process of change in children's moral reasoning. *Merrill-Palmer Quarterly, 28,* 347–367.

Denno, D. (1979). Moral development and treatment potential of youths under age eighteen. *Adolescence, 14,* 399–409.

Dickstein, E. B., & Warren, D. R. (1980). Role-taking deficits in learning disabled children. *Journal of Learning Disabilities, 13,* 378–382.

Doerr, A. M. (1986). How learning disabled adolescent boys make moral judgments. *Journal of Learning Disabilities, 19,* 160–164.

Doris, D. A. (1978). Teaching moral education: Principles of instruction. *Peabody Journal of Education, 56,* 33–44.

Downey, N., & Kelley, A. V. (1978). *Moral education: Theory and practice.* London: Harper & Row.

Duska, R., & Whelan, M. (1975). *Moral development: A guide to Piaget and Kohlberg.* New York: Paulist Press.

Enright, R. D. (1980). An integration of social cognitive development and cognitive processing: Educational applications. *American Educational Research Journal, 17,* 31–41.

Ericson, D. P. (1979). Response to Phillips and Nicolayev: Kohlberg's "Research Program." *Educational Theory, 29,* 345–347.

Feldman, D. H. (1986). How development works. In I. Levin (Ed.), *Stage and structure: Reopening the debate* (pp. 284–306). Norwood, NJ: Ablex.

Fenton, E. (1976). Moral education: The research findings. *Social Education, 40,* 188–193.

Fleetwood, R. S., & Parish, T. S. (1976). The relationship between moral development test scores of juvenile delinquents and their inclusion in a moral dilemma discussion group. *Psychological Reports, 39,* 1075–1080.

Fodor, E. M. (1972). Delinquency and susceptibility to social influence among adolescents as a function of moral development. *Journal of Social Psychology, 86,* 257–260.

Fraenkel, J. R. (1976). The Kohlberg bandwagon: Some reservations. *Social Education, 40,* 216–222.
Furth, H. G. (1970). *Piaget for teachers.* Englewood Cliffs, NJ: Prentice-Hall.
Galbraith, R. E., & Jones, T. (1976). *Moral reasoning: A teaching handbook for adapting Kohlberg to the classroom.* Minneapolis: Greenhaven Press.
Galbraith, R. E., & Jones, T. (1977). Teaching for moral reasoning in the social studies: A research report. *The Counseling Psychologist, 6,* 60–63.
Gallup, G. (1981). The 13th annual Gallup Poll of the public's attitudes toward the public schools. *Phi Delta Kappan, 63,* 33–47.
Garrod, A. C., & Bramble, G. A. (1977). Moral development and literature. *Theory into Practice, 16,* 105–111.
George, P. S. (1980). Discipline, moral development, and levels of schooling. *Education Forum, 45,* 57–67.
Gibbs, J. C. (1977). Kohlberg's stages of moral judgment: A constructive critique. *Harvard Educational Review, 47,* 43–61.
Gibbs, J. C. (1979). Kohlberg's moral stage theory: A Piagetian revision. *Human Development, 22,* 89–112.
Gibbs, J., Kohlberg, L., Colby, A., & Speicher-Dubin, B. (1976). The domain and development of moral judgment: A theory and a method of assessment. In J. Meyer (Ed.), *Reflections on values education.* Waterloo, Ontario: Wilfrid Laurier University Press.
Gibbs, J. C., Widaman, K., & Colby, A. (1982). *Social intelligence: Measuring the development of sociomoral reflection.* Englewood Cliffs, NJ: Prentice-Hall.
Gilligan, C. (1977). In a different voice: Women's conceptions of self and morality. *Harvard Education Review, 47,* 481–517.
Gilligan, C. (1982). In a different voice: Psychological theory and women's development. Cambridge, MA: Harvard University Press.
Ginsburg, H., & Opper, S. (1978). *Piaget's theory of intellectual development* (2nd ed.). Englewood Cliffs, NJ: Prentice-Hall.
Goldstein, A. P., & Glick, B. (1987). *Aggression replacement training.* Champaign, IL: Research Press.
Gresham, F. M. (1982). Misguided mainstreaming: The case for social skills training with handicapped children. *Exceptional Children, 48,* 422–433.
Griese, R. (1977). Responsibility: The 4th "R." In J. Lickona (Ed.), *The mini-book* (No. 5): *Moral development in the classroom* (pp. 20–27). Cortland, NY: Project Change, State University of New York.
Hains, A. A., & Miller, D. J. (1980). Moral and cognitive development in delinquent and non-delinquent children and adolescents. *The Journal of Genetic Psychology, 137,* 21–35.
Hall, R. (1979). *Moral education: A handbook for teachers.* Minneapolis: Winston Press.
Hall, R. T., & Davis, J. U. (1975). *Moral reasoning in theory and practice.* Buffalo, NY: Prometheus Books.
Hartshorne, H., & May, M. (1928–1930). *Studies in the nature of character* (Vols. 1, 2, and 3). New York: Macmillan.
Hersh, R. H., & Paolitto, D. P. (1979). The teacher as moral educator. In T. C. Hennessy (Ed.), *Value/moral education: The schools and the teachers.* New York: Paulist Press.

Hersh, R. H., Paolitto, D. P., & Reimer, J. (1979). *Promoting moral growth: From Piaget to Kohlberg.* New York: Longman.

Hewett, F. M., & Taylor, F. D. (1980). *The emotionally disturbed child in the classroom: The orchestration of success* (2nd ed.). Boston: Allyn & Bacon.

Hickey, J. (1972). *The effects of guided moral discussion upon youthful offenders' level of moral judgment.* Unpublished doctoral dissertation, Boston University.

Hophan, P. (1977). Learning to lead moral discussions: It takes a lot of slow to grow. In J. Lickona (Ed.), *The mini-book* (No. 5): *Moral development in the classroom* (pp. 37–40). Cortland, NY: Project Change, State University of New York.

Hoskisson, K., & Biskin, D. S. (1979). Analyzing and discussing children's literature using Kohlberg's stages of moral development. *The Reading Teacher, 33,* 141–147.

Hurt, B. L. (1977). Psychological education for teacher education students: A cognitive-developmental curriculum. *The Counseling Psychologist, 6,* 57–60.

Jackson, P. (1968). *Life in the classroom.* New York: Holt, Rinehart & Winston.

Jantz, R. K. (1973). An investigation of the relationship between moral development and intellectual development in male elementary school students. *Theory and Research in Social Education, 1,* 75–81.

Jantz, R. K., & Fulda, T. A. (1975). The role of moral education in the public elementary school. *Social Education, 39,* 24–28.

Jennings, W. S., & Kohlberg, L. (1980). *Effects of just community programs on the moral level and institutional perceptions of youthful offenders.* Unpublished manuscript, Harvard University, Cambridge, MA.

Jennings, W. S., & Kohlberg, L. (1983). Affects of a just community programme on the moral development of youthful offenders. *Journal of Moral Education, 12*(1), 33–50.

Kauffman, J. M. (1981). *Characteristics of children's behavior disorders* (2nd ed.). Columbus, OH: Merrill.

Kauffman, J. M. (1993). *Characteristics of emotional and behavioral disorders of children and youth* (5th ed.). New York: Merrill.

Keasey, C. B. (1971). Social participation as a factor in the moral development of preadolescents. *Developmental Psychology, 5,* 216–220.

Keasey, C. B. (1975). Implications of cognitive development for moral reasoning. In D. J. DePalma & J. M. Foley (Eds.), *Moral development: Current theory and research.* Hillsdale, NJ: Erlbaum.

Kohlberg, L. (1969). Stage and sequence: The cognitive-development approach to socialization. In D. A. Goslin (Ed.), *Handbook of socialization theory and research.* Chicago: Rand McNally.

Kohlberg, L. (1970). Stages of moral development as a basis for moral education. In C. Beck & E. Sullivan (Eds.), *Moral development and moral education.* Toronto: University of Toronto Press.

Kohlberg, L. (1971). From is to ought: How to commit the naturalistic fallacy and get away with it in the study of moral development. In T. Mischel (Ed.), *Cognitive development and epistemology.* New York: Academic Press.

Kohlberg, L. (1973). The concepts of development psychology as the central guide to education: Examples from cognitive, moral and psychological education. In M. Reynolds (Ed.), *Psychology and the process of schooling in the next decade: Alternative conceptions.* Minneapolis: University of Minnesota.

Kohlberg, L. (1975). The cognitive developmental approach to moral education. *Phi Delta Kappan, 56,* 670–677.
Kohlberg, L. (1976). Moral stages and moralization: The cognitive-developmental approach. In T. Lickona (Ed.), *Moral development and behavior: Theory, research, and social issues.* New York: Holt, Rinehart & Winston.
Kohlberg, L. (1978a). The moral atmosphere of the school. In P. Scharf (Ed.), *Readings in moral education.* Minneapolis: Winston Press.
Kohlberg, L. (1978b). Revisions in the theory and practice of moral development. *New Directions for Child Development, 2,* 83–87.
Kohlberg, L. (1981). *The meaning and measurement of moral development.* Worcester, MA: Clark University Press.
Kohlberg, L., & Elfenbein, D. (1975). The development of moral judgments concerning capital punishment. *American Journal of Orthopsychiatry, 45,* 614–640.
Kohlberg, L., & Hersh, R. H. (1977). Moral development: A review of the theory. *Theory into Practice, 16,* 53–59.
Kohlberg, L. & Higgins, A. (1987). School democracy and social interaction. In W. M. Kurtines & J. L. Gewirtz (Eds.), *Moral development through social interaction* (pp. 102–128). New York: Wiley.
Kohlberg, L., Kauffman, K., Scharf, P., & Hickey, J. (1975). The just community approach to corrections: A theory. *Journal of Moral Education, 4,* 243–260.
Kohlberg, L., Selman, R. K., & Lickona, T. (1972). A strategy for teaching values. In L. Kohlberg, R. K. Selman, & T. Lickona (Eds.), *First things: Values.* New York: Guidance Associates.
Kohlberg, L., & Turiel, E. (1971). Moral development and moral education. In G. Lesser (Ed.), *Psychology and education practice.* Chicago: Scott, Foresman.
Krebs, D., & Gillmore, J. (1982). The relationship among the first stages of cognitive development, role-taking abilities and moral development. *Child Development, 53,* 877–886.
Kurtines, W., & Greif, E. B. (1974). The development of moral thought: Review and evaluation of Kohlberg's approach. *Psychological Bulletin, 81,* 453–470.
Langford, P. E., & George, S. (1975). Intellectual and moral development in adolescence. *British Journal of Educational Psychology, 45,* 330–332.
Lewis, F. W. (1979). What the value/moral educator can learn from Piaget. In T. C. Hennessey (Ed.), *Value/moral education: The schools and teachers.* New York: Paulist Press.
Lickona, T. (1976). Research on Piaget's theory of moral development. In T. Lickona (Ed.), *Moral development and behavior.* New York: Holt, Rinehart & Winston.
Lickona, T. (1977a). Creating the just community with children. *Theory into Practice, 16,* 97–104.
Lickona, T. (1977b). How to encourage moral development. *Learning, 5,* 37–43.
Lickona, T. (1980). Preparing teachers to be moral educators: A neglected duty. *New Directions for Higher Learning, 3,* 51–64.
Locke, D. (1983). Doing what comes morally: The relation between behavior and stage of moral reasoning. *Human Development, 26,* 11–25.
Lockwood, A. L. (1978). The effects of values clarification and moral development curricula on school age subjects: A critical review of recent research. *Review of Educational Research, 48,* 325–364.
Maag, J. W. (1989). Moral discussion group interventions: Promising technique or wishful thinking? *Behavioral Disorders, 14,* 97–105.

Maccoby, E. E. (1980). *Social development: Psychological growth and the parent–child relationship.* New York: Harcourt, Brace, Jovanovich.

Mackey, J. A. (1973). Moral insight in the classroom. *Elementary School Journal, 73,* 233–238.

Miller, P. H., & Aloise, P. A. (1989). Young children's understanding of the psychological causes of behavior: A review. *Child Development, 60,* 257–285.

Morse, W. C. (1977). The psychology of mainstreaming socio-emotionally disturbed children. In A. J. Pappanikou & J. L. Paul (Eds.), *Mainstreaming emotionally disturbed children.* Syracuse, NY: Syracuse University Press.

Mosher, R. A., & Sullivan, P. R. (1976). A curriculum in moral education for adolescents. *Journal of Moral Education, 5,* 159–172.

Muss, R. E. (1976). Kohlberg's cognitive developmental approach to adolescent morality. *Adolescence, 11,* 39–59.

Napier, J. (1976). The ability of elementary school teachers to stage score moral thought statements. *Theory and Research in Social Education, 4,* 39–56.

Napier, J. (1978). Experiments in the validity of preservice teacher stage scoring of moral thought statements. *Educational and Psychological Measurement, 38,* 575–587.

Napier, J. (1979). Stage scoring moral judgments as a teacher task in "Kohlbergian" programs. *Journal of Social Studies Research, 3,* 24–28.

Nelson, S. A. (1980). Factors influencing young children's use of motives and outcomes as moral criteria. *Child Development, 51,* 823–829.

Newcomer, P. L. (1993). *Understanding and teaching emotionally disturbed children and adolescents* (2nd ed.). Austin, TX: PRO-ED.

Niles, W. (1986). Effects of a moral development discussion group on delinquent and predelinquent boys. *Journal of Counseling Psychology, 33,* 45–51.

Paolitto, D. P. (1977). The role of the teacher in moral education. *Theory into Practice, 16,* 73–80.

Pappanikou, A. J. (1979). Mainstreaming. *Teacher Education and Special Education, 2,* 51–55.

Pappanikou, A. J., & Paul, J. L. (1977). *Mainstreaming emotionally disturbed children.* Syracuse, NY: Syracuse University Press.

Perry, J. E., & Krebs, D. (1980). Role-taking, moral development and mental retardation. *Journal of Genetic Psychology, 136,* 95–108.

Peters, R. S. (1975). A reply to Kohlberg, "Why doesn't Kohlberg do his homework?" *Phi Delta Kappan, 56,* 678.

Phillips, D. C., & Nicolayev, J. (1978). Kohlbergian moral development: A progressing or degenerating research program? *Educational Theory, 28,* 286–301.

Piaget, J. (1948). *The moral judgment of the child* (M. Gabain, Trans.). Glencoe, IL: Free Press.

Piaget, J. (1952). *The origins of intelligence in children.* New York: International Universities Press.

Piaget, J. (1963). *The child's conception of the world.* Paterson, NJ: Littlefield, Adams.

Piaget, J., & Inhelder, B. (1969). *The psychology of the child.* New York: Basic Books.

Pillar, A. M. (1976). Using children's literature to foster moral development. *Reading Teacher, 33,* 148–156.

Pittel, S. M., & Mendelsohn, G. A. (1966). Measurement of moral values: A review and critique. *Psychological Bulletin, 66,* 22–35.

Raths, L. E., Harmin, M., & Simon, S. B. (1966). *Values and teaching.* Columbus, OH: Merrill.

Reimer, J. (1981). Moral education: The just community approach. *Phi Delta Kappan, 62,* 485–487.

Rest, J. (1974). Developmental psychology as a guide to value education: A review of "Kohlbergian" programs. *Review of Educational Research, 44,* 241–259.

Rest, J. R. (1975). Recent research on an objective test of moral judgment: How the important issues of a moral dilemma are defined. In D. J. DePalma & J. N. Foley (Eds.), *Moral development: Current theory and research.* Hillsdale, NJ: Erlbaum.

Rest, J. R. (1979). *Development in judging moral issues.* Minneapolis: University of Minnesota Press.

Rest, J., Cooper, D., Coder, R., Masanz, J., & Anderson, A. (1974). Judging the important issues in moral dilemmas—An objective measure of development. *Developmental Psychology, 10,* 491–501.

Riggs, R. S., & Evans, D. W. (1979). Child abuse prevention—Implementation within the curriculum. *The Journal of School Health, 49,* 255–259.

Rosenkoetter, L. I., Landman, S., & Mazak, S. G. (1980). Use of moral discussion as an intervention with delinquents. *Psychological Reports, 46,* 91–94.

Rothman, G. R. (1976). Influences of moral reasoning of behavioral choices. *Child Development, 47,* 397–406.

Ruma, E. H., & Mosher, D. L. (1967). Relationship between moral judgment and guilt in delinquent boys. *Journal of Abnormal Psychology, 72,* 122–127.

Santilli, N. R., & Hudson, L. M. (1992). Enhancing moral growth: Is communication the key? *Adolescence, 27,* 145–160.

Santrock, J. W. (1975). Moral structure: The interrelations of moral behavior, moral judgment, and moral affect. *The Journal of Genetic Psychology, 127,* 201–213.

Scharf, P. (1978). Creating moral dilemmas for the classroom. In P. Scharf (Ed.), *Readings in moral education.* Minneapolis: Winston Press.

Scharf, P., McCoy, W., & Ross, D. (1979). *Growing up moral: Dilemmas for the intermediate grades.* Minneapolis: Winston Press.

Schonert, K. A., & Cantor, G. N. (1991). Moral reasoning in behaviorally disordered adolescents from alternative and traditional high schools. *Behavioral Disorders, 17,* 23–35.

Selman, R. L. (1976). Social-cognitive understanding: A guide to educational and clinical practice. In T. Lickona (Ed.), *Moral development and behavior: Theory, research, and social issues.* New York: Holt, Rinehart & Winston.

Selman, R. L. (1977). A structural-developmental model of social cognition: Implications for intervention research. *The Counseling Psychologist, 6,* 3–6.

Selman, R. L., & Byrne, D. G. (1974). A structural-developmental analysis of levels of role-taking in middle childhood. *Child Development, 45,* 803–806.

Swarthout, D. W. (1988). Enhancing the moral development of behaviorally/ emotionally handicapped students. *Behavioral Disorders, 14,* 57–68.

Sweeney, M. M., & Zionts, P. (1987). The "second skin": Perceptions of disturbed and non-disturbed early adolescents on clothing, self-concept and body image. *Adolescence, 24,* 411–420.

Thoma, S., Rest, J., & Barnett, R. (1986). In J. Rest (Ed.), *Moral development: Advances in research and theory.* New York: Praeger.

Tomlinson-Keasey, C., & Keasey, C. B. (1974). The mediating role of cognitive development in moral judgment. *Child Development, 45,* 291–298.

Turiel, E. (1966). An experimental test of the sequentiality of developmental stages in the child's moral judgments. *Journal of Personality and Social Psychology, 3,* 611–618.

Turiel, E. (1969). Developmental processes in the child's moral thinking. In P. H. Mussen, J. Langer, & M. Covington (Eds.), *Trends and issues in developmental psychology.* New York: Holt, Rinehart & Winston.

Turiel, E. (1978). Social regulations and domains of social concepts. In W. Damon (Ed.), *New directions in developmental psychology: Vol. 1. Social cognition.* San Francisco: Jossey-Bass.

Walker, L. J. (1980). Cognitive and perspective-taking prerequisites for moral development. *Child Development, 51,* 131–139.

Walker, L. J. (1988). The development of moral reasoning. *Annals of Child Development, 5,* 33–78.

Walker, L. J. (1989). A longitudinal study of moral reasoning. *Child Development, 60,* 157–166.

Walker, L.J., de Vries, B., & Trevethan, S. D. (1987). Moral stages and moral orientations in real-life and hypothetical dilemmas. *Child Development, 58,* 842–858.

Walker, L. J., & Taylor, J. H. (1991). Stage transitions in moral reasoning: A longitudinal study of developmental processes. *Developmental Psychology, 27,* 330–337.

Wasserman, E. R. (1976). Implementing Kohlberg's "Just Community Concept" in an alternative high school. *Social Education, 40,* 203–207.

Wonderly, D. M., & Kupersmid, J. H. (1980). Prompting postconventional morality: The adequacy of Kohlberg's aim. *Adolescence, 15,* 609–631.

Wood, F. H. (1979). Defining disturbing and disturbed behavior. In F. H. Wood & K. C. Lakin (Eds.), *Disturbing, disordered, or disturbed? Perspectives on the definition of problem behavior in educational settings.* Minneapolis: Department of Psychoeducational Studies, University of Minnesota.

Wright, I. (1978). Moral reasoning and conduct of selected elementary school students. *Journal of Moral Education, 7,* 199–205.

Zionts, P., & Weddle, C. (1983). Understanding the relationship between cognitive development and classroom management decisions. In R. B. Rutherford, Jr. (Ed.), *Monograph in behavior disorders: Severe behavior disorders of children and youth* (Vol. VI). Reston, VA: Council for Children with Behavior Disorders.

# UNIT 3

## Rational-Emotive Therapy in the Classroom

This text has concentrated primarily on classroom interventions for children who cognitively cannot or have not been taught to understand the how and/or why of their behaviors and feelings. Unit 1 was concerned with the ecological management of children in which there are concerted efforts of the individual, classroom, school, and/or community to suppress or encourage particular behaviors. The contention of Unit 2 was that special educators should better prepare their students to assess and perhaps solve problems outside of the structured special education environment. Unit 2 presented the theory and practice of moral development, which may promote an interactive classroom from which the child may grow and develop. Unit 3 offers a methodology that could be interpreted either as the natural extension of Units 1 and 2, or as an intervention itself.

Clearly, those teachers who solely implement the methods discussed in Unit 1 will be serving adequately the vast majority of the special education population. This philosophy, however, is one of preventing and managing surface behaviors. The contention of Unit 2 is that there are some students who will not react favorably to the techniques in Unit 1 and, more important, who seem to have difficulty generalizing their "learned" behaviors to other settings. It was suggested that this failure may be due to the inability to reason at higher levels, which seems to be a prerequisite for problem solving. Unit 2, therefore, examined the cognitive or internal processes that may promote or prevent disturbances.

Unit 3 assumes that most students above the fourth-grade level have progressed through the lower reasoning levels discussed in Unit 2. These students are in the position to solve their own conflicts through rational-emotive therapy (RET), a logico-scientific method that is relatively simple to understand. The approach discussed in this unit assumes that an interactive environment, such as the one discussed in Unit 2, is present. RET gives the teacher and students a specific process, which, if followed, can alleviate severely disturbed and disturbing feelings.

In a developmental manner, rational-emotive therapy asserts that, once children have the ability to demonstrate higher level reasoning (Kohlberg's Stages 2–4, Piaget's formal operations), disturbances may be minimized and/or alleviated if the children are taught to discover that their disturbances may be due to their mistaken interpretations of or overgeneralizations of learned philosophies. Furthermore, proponents of this therapy maintain that, once students are made aware of this thinking process, they must practice behaviors that are more congruent with their new knowledge about themselves.

Three emphases of RET are discussed as they pertain to education: (a) the personal utility of the philosophy and practice of RET for teachers (Chapter 8); (b) the utility of RET as an intervention for alleviating the emotional disturbance of students (Chapter 9); and (c) the utility of RET as a preventive mental health program in the classroom (Chapter 10). Chapter 8 examines the theory of rational-emotive therapy and briefly outlines two similar perspectives, both of which fall under the rubric of cognitive behavior therapy. The purpose of this chapter is to investigate the relationship between the internal (cognitive) and external (behavior) aspects of disturbance.

Chapter 9 provides the methods necessary to apply RET as a classroom intervention. The implementation of RET as an individual counseling technique and as one that facilitates group problem solving is presented. Examples of RET as a preventive mental health curriculum are furnished in Chapter 10. This allows teachers who are utilizing RET as a counseling intervention to supplement their sessions with reinforcing content. Furthermore, it gives the educator who feels uncomfortable "therapizing" in the class, and yet who agrees with the principles of RET, the means to present it in a noncounseling manner.

# 8

# Rational-Emotive Therapy in the Classroom: Theory

This chapter examines rational-emotive therapy (RET) and its relationship to the more general category of cognitive behavior therapy (CBT). Two strands of CBT that have been influenced by RET and that offer useful techniques for the classroom are explored. The theory of RET is discussed, specifically a delineation of its personal use to the teacher, its value as a classroom intervention (Chapter 9), and its merits as an affective curriculum (Chapter 10). Before beginning this discussion, however, the teacher must consider not only the notion of choosing which intervention to use but also the importance of choosing an intervention.

## Choosing an Intervention

One of the most important decisions that teachers need to make is the choice of a particular intervention to use with and for their students. It is not unusual for teachers to claim that they are "eclectic," that is, that they take a little from one theory and a little from another. When teachers employ a hodgepodge of tricks and methods, they rarely know when and how to remediate if a problem occurs. Instead, they simply look for another trick from their repertoire. These tricks, however, are often integral components of a complicated theory. Rather than simply using techniques, teachers should adopt a theoretical rationale that allows them to know how, when, and where to intervene with students. Ginter (1988) said it best when he contended that "therapy cannot exist without theory" (p. 3).

> **Window on Reality**
>
> Much of the content in Unit 1 was devoted to the importance of understanding what type of teacher one is and the type of teacher one aspires to be. In choosing an intervention, a teacher should understand his or her basic philosophy of life, and, consequently, of education and deviance. Upon reading this paragraph, one may be struck with its "loftiness." However, it is all too frequent that teachers who are psycho- dynamically or affectively oriented will attempt and fail to implement a rigid behavioral program.
> Similarly, teachers with behavioral orientations are extremely uncomfortable with the concept of classroom counseling (reality therapy or life space interview). Therefore, it makes sense that educators should choose an intervention that is philosophically aligned with their beliefs.

The temptation to use the trick approach is high, especially because only the rare university or inservice program gives teachers or teacher trainees the necessary depth of any one approach. This lack of in-depth training led Hurt (1977) to observe that, rather than using what was taught in the university classroom, his "pre-service teachers tended to revert to their more natural style of communication, namely providing enormous amounts of direct advice and ignoring feelings and non-verbal messages from the role play teacher–client" (p. 57).

Weinrach's (1991) personal revelation might best explain the need for teachers to adopt a theory: "Without a good theory, I have no road map. Without road maps, mental health counselors either do not know where to go or do not care where they end up" (p. 375). He chose RET (see below) because he viewed it as comprehensive (rather than eclectic) and because it was the closest theory to his own philosophy of life.

Choosing a theory and its subsequent intervention(s) is not the answer to all of one's problems. It is merely a framework from which to begin. Muran (1991) supported this notion by suggesting that "the real world, unlike the model, is far too complex to be explained thoroughly by a theory. It is important to realize how limited a scientific model truly is and what is its true purpose" (p. 400).

# Cognitive Behavior Therapy

Cognitive behavior therapy was developed mainly by psychologists to meet more effectively the needs of their clients. These psychologists realized that, as the pure psychoanalytic approach was imperfect, so too was the sole use of behavior modification. Cognitive behavior therapy, therefore, combines how an individual thinks (the internal process) and how an individual exhibits behaviors (the external process). The comprehensive nature of CBT is well suited for teachers. Meichenbaum and Cameron (1974) pointed out that, if psychologists can influence cognitions and behaviors of their clients with relatively little exposure, one can speculate on the more pervasive influence that teachers, who are with students most or all of the day, might have on their students. Although the research on CBT in the schools is relatively new, cognitive-behavioral intervention programs have demonstrated positive results in the public schools (Zelie, Stone, & Lehr, 1980). Furthermore, they seem to work regardless of the socioeconomic status of the students (Braswell, Kendall, & Urbain, 1982).

Two theories that are commonly associated with CBT and that have strong educational implications are cognitive therapy and cognitive behavior modification. Aaron Beck (1976), the leading proponent of cognitive therapy, argued that "the individual's problems are derived largely from certain distortions of reality based on erroneous premises and assumptions. These incorrect conceptions originated in defective learning during the person's cognitive development" (p. 3). He believed that students' problems are due to their misinterpretations of actual occurrences. For example, if a teacher tells the class that a special field trip had been canceled, the following reactions may occur:

- What a horrible teacher! She's always taking away privileges. I'm mad! I hate her!
- Boy, we must have done something really wrong. We are a pretty bad bunch of kids. I'm so sad.
- Why does this always happen to me? I was looking forward to this trip. Nothing goes the way I want it to! I'm really upset!
- Who cares about a dumb field trip? What a bunch of geeks!

The "stimulus" was the same for each individual, yet each individual perceived the statements in a different manner. If the perceptions result in extremely negative emotions, counseling may be desirable. Beck argued that most psychodynamic therapies ignore the individual's conscious thoughts that occur immediately after encountering a stimulus. People are accustomed to "speaking to themselves" in one way and to others in different ways. These thoughts are categorized as automatic. In most cases, automatic thoughts are falsely considered by individuals as those that occur "without any prior reflection or reasoning and they impress him as plausible and valid" (Beck, 1976, p. 237). There are two types of negative automatic thoughts: (a) direct thoughts, which are tangible distortions of reality (e.g., the perceived event did not occur), and (b) illogical thoughts, which are inappropriate, destructive inferences or conclusions from events that did occur.

Cognitive therapy involves a focused awareness of cognitions or thought processes as they relate to self-defeating feelings and behaviors. It relies upon the use of verbal and rational abilities to solve problems. Accurate perceptions are those that can be verified as factual, such as "Bob called me a jerk." Inaccurate perceptions are those that are based almost purely upon conjecture, such as "Bob called me a jerk and therefore I must be one!"

Beck suggested that, by helping individuals identify their faulty perceptions as such, more accurate ones may be learned. The purpose of cognitive therapy is to help students understand the nature of their inaccurate perceptions and learn to restructure them so that they will not cause emotional distress. Simply stated, cognitive therapy is an intervention that stresses common sense.

Beck (1976) contended that the individual progresses through four steps when experiencing cognitive therapy: "First, he has to become aware of what he is thinking. Second, he needs to recognize what thoughts are awry. Then he has to substitute accurate for inaccurate judgments. Finally, he needs feedback to inform him whether his changes are correct" (p. 217). Didactic methods are especially effective as a means to maintain the newer, more productive thoughts, feelings, and behaviors. Cognitive therapy differs from the more common behavioral and psychoanalytical theories in that it takes into account the individual's conscious thoughts following a stimulus, which in turn leads to an emotion. This is different from behavior theory, which maintains that emotions immediately follow the stimulus, and psychoanalytic theory, which purports that emotions are due primarily to unconscious thoughts.

Donald Meichenbaum (1977a), a psychologist and researcher, attempted to combine the theory of conscious thoughts with behavior modification. Acknowledging the influence of Ellis, Beck, and the Russian psychologists Luria and Vygotsky, Meichenbaum developed an intervention using teacher-directed conscious thoughts with students who are disturbed or who use faulty logic in attempting academic tasks. This approach, cognitive-behavior modification (CBM), attempts to progress from the presentation of the teacher's external conscious thoughts to the students' thoughts, which in turn result in the exhibition of appropriate behaviors. Reinforcers are used to motivate the student to learn the cognitions necessary to facilitate these behaviors. CBM has been found to be effective on measures of cognitive impulsivity, performance IQ, motor ability, and self-control (Meichenbaum & Goodman, 1969, 1971).

Meichenbaum's (1977a) interpretation of CBM includes the implementation of three phases of intervention. *Self-observation* is the first phase in which the students become observers of their own behavior. As in cognitive therapy, the goal is to increase their awareness of conscious thoughts and behavior so that they can then conceptualize their problems. Integral to both CBM and cognitive therapy is the concept that the conscious thoughts that cause emotional disturbance must be altered or restructured to more reality-based thoughts. This reconceptualization or awareness process may become the intervention itself. Meichenbaum would contend that specific behavioral changes must result for the intervention to be judged truly effective.

*Incompatible thoughts and behaviors* is the second phase of CBM, in which the formation of "new" conscious thought is developed. The new thoughts pave the way for developing new behaviors. The actual manifestations of these new behaviors are not present during this phase.

The third phase, *cognitions concerning change,* "is concerned with the process of the client's producing new behaviors in his every day world and how he assesses (or what he says to himself about) the behavioral outcomes" (Meichenbaum, 1977a, p. 225). After demonstrating new behaviors, the students receive positive reinforcers. It is important that teachers keep in contact with individuals during this phase to check their interpretations of the reactions of others to their new behaviors. Thus, CBM integrates Beck's cognitive therapy and behavior modification.

Cognitive behavior modification has been effective in aiding students with specific academic tasks (Hall, 1980; Meichenbaum & Asarnow, 1979) and behaviors (Kneedler, 1980; Meichenbaum & Genest, 1980). Camp and Bash (1981) developed a *Think Aloud* curriculum for primary-grade students that is representative of cognitive behavior modification (see Chapter 5 for a brief description of this process). However, generalization of student improvement resulting from CBM has yet to be consistently in evidence. This means that, once students successfully changed cognitions on one task, they may have to be retaught similar cognitions to complete other skills. Furthermore, CBM has been criticized as being indoctrinative, in that it force feeds students with conscious thoughts rather than concentrating on helping them do it for themselves (Ellis, 1977g).

In summary, cognitive therapy, as conceived by Beck, contends that, through the restructuring of thoughts and the disputation of the students' invalid perceptions, disturbances may subside. This process clearly focuses on the internal (cognitive) aspect of personality change. Meichenbaum has attempted to combine the internal and external (behavioral) processes by suggesting that, for disturbance to be truly remediated, new behaviors must occur along with the cognitive restructuring. In CBM, reinforcers should be used to promote these new appropriate behaviors. Schwartz (1982) called for a unified approach to helping individuals with their problems, combining cognition, behavior, and affect. One theory that utilizes each of these areas is rational-emotive therapy (RET).

# Rational-Emotive Therapy

Rational-emotive therapy is both a unique philosophy of life and an effective intervention for reducing intense emotional feelings and behaviors. Conceived by Albert Ellis as a clinical technique, it also has developed into a practical classroom tool for the prevention and remediation of emotional or behavioral disturbances (EBD). RET integrates the cognitive, behavioral, and emotional aspects of personality and suggests that all three must be regarded in order to modify disturbance (Ellis, 1977a). It has recently received attention in the professional training literature for teachers of students with EBD (Center, 1989; Coleman, 1992; Dice, 1993; Hughes, 1988).

Rational-emotive therapy is a theory and strategy that may be used to help individuals combat extremely negative feelings and behaviors. Although RET and CBT have many similarities, the major difference is the use of behavioral and emotive modes to affect the individual's cognitions. RET examines the basic philosophical underpinnings of human nature. This is reflected in the acceptance of rational, preferential, flexible, and tolerant philosophies as opposed to irrational, rigid, intolerant, and absolutistic philosophies (Ellis & Dryden, 1987). RET is behavioral, but only in that it employs "behavioral techniques mainly as a means of abetting deep-seated philosophical changes rather than mainly as symptom-removal methods" (Ellis, 1973a, p. 8).

The purpose of RET is to help students learn to deal with serious emotional problems. "RET is not designed to help . . . solve current presenting practical problems, but rather to reduce extreme levels of (anger) rage, anxiety, and feeling down (depression) which prevent the young person—or make it harder—from figuring out how to overcome a specific problem" (Bernard, 1990, p. 295). Nondisturbed emotions are characterized by annoyance, aggravation, and disappointment. Furthermore, RET "posits qualitative differences between disturbed or inappropriate emotions and non-disturbed, appropriate emotions. Non-disturbed, appropriate emotions lead to functional behavior" (DiGiuseppe & Bernard, 1990, p. 270).

RET can be used for personal and professional growth, as a classroom therapeutic intervention, or as a problem-solving intervention. It has been found to be effective in helping students work on their emotional and behavioral problems through the use of teacher–student or teacher–group "counseling" and/or structured classroom lessons. RET can be effective as a mental health program for both teachers and their students. As presented in Chapter 2, many teaching-related pressures can result in educator stress or burnout. By implementing RET in the classroom, teachers learn to identify and work on their own feelings and beliefs that may be contributing negatively to their own mental health and, ultimately, their classroom teaching. Also, implementation will serve as reinforcement of RET principles.

RET embodies psychology, philosophy, and education. It is psychological in that it examines how thoughts cause emotional problems; it is philosophical in that it suggests that the individual's view of life strongly influences emotions; and it is educational in that it provides a model that shows how people can manage their problems. This chapter and the next focus on the theory and practice of RET so that it may be utilized for the first two purposes, and Chapter 10 provides the lessons and techniques necessary to implement an affective education program.

## Psychological Foundations

Rational-emotive therapy evolved in the mid-1950s from traditional psychotherapy. Many theories of psychology are embodied in RET. Cognitive therapy, behavior modification, and even humanistic psychology are all integral to the theory of RET. Ellis believed that traditional psychotherapy is inefficient because of the amount of time spent helping clients achieve "insight" into their problems. Uncovering the insight is not only a long and often drawn-out process, but once it is achieved, much effort still must be devoted to working on the clients' specific problems. Ellis was not sure the insight gained enabled his clients to be more effective in problem solving (Ellis, 1962). He became, therefore, much more involved in guiding his clients by questioning their current thoughts instead of allowing them to ramble with the hope that they would eventually discover their problems.

Ellis began to implement what he described as an "active-directive" approach, in which he verbalized to his clients what he thought to be the inevitable insight. He found this method to be more effective and more efficient than his previous practice, yet few of his clients were actually being cured. "I began to see that insight alone was not likely to lead an individual to overcome his deep-seated fears and hostilities; he *also* needs a large degree of fear- and hostility-combating *action*" (Ellis, 1962, p. 10). Next, Ellis attempted to have his patients try the behaviors that they were avoiding.

Ellis (1973b) readily admitted that RET overlaps with many theories such as Adlerian, except for its stress on childhood and the importance of the therapist–client relationship; Jungian, except for its stress on unconscious dreams and fantasies; Rogerian, but only in the way the therapist holds the client in "full acceptance or tolerance"; and behavior modification as espoused by Eysenck, Skinner, Bandura, and Meichenbaum. In other words, although Ellis initially labeled his approach rational therapy, he implemented aspects of many theoretical perspectives.

Rational-emotive therapy attempts to discard psychoanalytic jargon. In an attempt to demystify therapy, most of its terms are in layman's language. As with Beck's cognitive therapy, an interpretation of the past is ignored because the disturbed individual is viewed as disturbed not by past experiences, but by his or her misinterpretations of those events. Furthermore, the notions of exploring the unconscious or the id are disregarded. RET is a unified approach of cognition, behavior, and affect used in combination to attack emotional problems (Ellis, 1973b, 1991; Schwartz, 1982). Thus, RET may be perceived as having philosophical and educational bases rather than a medical foundation. This educational orientation is evident upon examination of the integration of philosophy with psychology as presented in the principles of RET, which are listed later in the chapter.

## Philosophical Foundations

A basic theoretical assumption of RET is that human beings, as opposed to other "life forms," are uniquely rational. People have the ability to reason, to think clearly, to discover alternatives, and to solve problems. Although people do indeed have such abilities, they also have the ability to think in an irrational manner, to be confused, to be narrow minded, and to not solve problems. Those who strongly demonstrate these latter abilities are generally more susceptible to emotional upset.

Epictetus, a first-century philosopher, is quoted often by Ellis: "What disturbs people's minds is not events but their judgments on events" (Ellis, 1977c, p. xv). This is clearly a departure from the current beliefs of most people. Many people believe that events *cause* emotional upset. For example, a teacher may consider an event such as being unable, after many attempts, to help a student progress to be a "good" justification for anger, frustration, or depression. Not all people, however, perceive the same events as equally devastating. Those who perceive these events as devastating may feel very angry, whereas others who perceive the events as unfortunate may feel only annoyed. Simply stated, events contribute to a person's feelings, but the feelings themselves are a result of interpretations or perceptions. Feelings, therefore, are for the most part caused by thinking, not by events.

RET involves a rather nontraditional yet commonsense approach to explaining how emotional problems occur. Many people have been raised to believe that when something bad happens, the natural consequence of that bad event is a bad consequence—as if there is an uncontrollable cause–effect process at work. To believe that bad consequences *must* accompany difficult situations negates one important component of human nature: the ability to think.

The central premise of RET is that feelings are not caused by things, but rather by a person's perceptions of those things. For example, individuals may have many different reactions to the same event. Some individuals might react similarly, whereas others might react in a markedly different manner. If one person perceived an event to be disappointing, the subsequent feelings would probably be manageable. If another perceived that same event to be devastating, then more harmful feelings might result. People who think irrationally tend to think that way as a habit. Their "disturbed emotions are mediated by absolutistic, rigid, demanding irrational thoughts" (DiGiuseppe & Bernard, 1990, p. 271).

Thoughts and feelings are closely related. A central theme of RET is that thinking actually causes most feelings. If people think an event is pleasurable, they feel good. If people think that something is obnoxious, they feel bad. In other words, people feel what they think. The fact that not all people think the same about a particular event explains why all people do not have the same feelings about the same event. For example, one teacher of a student with EBD reported that she becomes extremely angry and frustrated when the student uses profanity. Another teacher of the same student commented that the profanity does not bother her very much; it is merely another inconvenience with which she must deal during the day. As explained later in this chapter, the first teacher might be experiencing *irrational* thinking, which, in fact, is a dysfunctional thought process. Irrational thinking may take the form of unrealistic demands, overgeneralizations, exaggerations, and unvalidated assumptions.

Meanwhile, the second teacher does not appreciate the profanity. However, instead of believing (thinking) that the student *must not* use profanity, she *wishes* that the student would not use profanity, but knows that, given his condition (or upbringing), it is unrealistic to expect him to stop using profanity without training or other interventions. Although this type of thinking makes sense, it is contrary to the way most people were raised. Many people are taught that it is not their fault if others treat them badly and that anger is a "natural" reaction to this occurrence. There is little doubt that many people think and approach problems in a particular way. The theory of RET is that, with hard work, people can learn to think in new ways in order to manage their unfortunate realities. This new thinking will thus create new feelings. "If children are more able to control their dysfunctional emotional reactions, they are in a far superior position to take constructive action to change things" (Bernard & Joyce, 1984, p. 174).

Although RET recognizes that other influences, such as the environment (peers, authority, relationships, media, organizations) or biophysical constitution (heredity, genes), might also contribute to problems, the philosophy of RET places faith in people's ability to learn how to think in a clear, rational manner despite these influences (Ellis, 1979). A clear-thinking person is less prone to emotional disturbance, and the ability to think clearly can be learned. Furthermore, as individuals become able to think in a more rational manner, they would be expected to behave in a more rational manner. "Emotional disturbances, such as intense anxiety and hostility, largely (but not completely) stem from distorted human perceptions and irrational thinking and can largely with hard work be alleviated by profound cognitive changes"

> ### Window on Reality
>
> The theory of RET suggests that the same stimulus will generate different consequences by different people. Ask an entire class to imagine that they receive an electric shock while sitting on their chairs. Have each student describe his or her initial *physical* reaction to the shock (most answers will probably be similar due to the pain of the shock) and then to imagine what emotions he or she will have 5 minutes after receiving the shock. What statements are students saying to themselves? Compare statements of at least 4 individuals. Different emotions such as anxiety, fear, anger, or maybe even sadness may surface. This may be due to the different thoughts (cognitions) that each student processed during the 5-minute period.
> For example:
>
> Anxiety: Did I do something wrong? Will I be shocked again? It would be terrible if I get shocked again?
>
> Fear: Boy, that hurt. I could not stand it if it happens again. Will it be worse next time?
>
> Anger: Who does that teacher think he is to shock us! This is education? If he does it one more time, I am going to punch his lights out!
>
> Sadness: He's right to shock us. Life is miserable. I'm a rotten person; I deserve this and worse! This pain is and always will be unbearable.
>
> Each of these four emotions is the result of sustained thinking about the same stimulus: the electric shock. The responses quite obviously differ greatly across individuals. This is in contrast to the dictums of behavior therapy, which contends that given a stimulus, similar responses will occur. RET questions the stimulus–response model by providing evidence that emotions may differ even when the individual is exposed to the same stimulus.

(Ellis, 1984, p. 216). However, for people to behave better and in a consistent manner across settings, it is necessary for them to have the necessary philosophical and psychological repertoire. As Bernard and Joyce (1984) suggested, "We believe that a psychological model of maladjustment will have to be primarily cognitive or behavioral, and not both. We therefore choose to embrace a cognitive model which employs behavioral methodologies to test its theoretical propositions and principles" (p. 21).

Proponents of rational-emotive therapy argue that, when the process and practice of irrational thinking is combated, then long-lasting rather than symptomatic change can occur. The following principles of human behavior, as presented by Ellis and Dryden (1987), lay the foundation for RET:

1. Virtually all humans, including bright and competent people, show evidence of major human irrationalities.

2. Virtually all the disturbance-creating irrationalities (absolutistic shoulds and musts) that are found in our society are also found in just about all social and cultural groups that have been studied historically and anthropologically.
3. Many of the irrational behaviors that we engage in, such as procrastination and lack of self-discipline, go counter to the teachings of parents, peers, and the mass media.
4. Humans—even bright and intelligent people—often adopt other irrationalities after giving up former ones.
5. People who vigorously oppose various kinds of irrational behaviors often fall prey to these very irrationalities. Atheists and agnostics exhibit zealous and absolutistic philosophies and highly religious individuals act immorally.
6. Insight into irrational thought and behaviors helps only partially to change them. For example, people can acknowledge that drinking alcohol in large quantities is harmful, yet this knowledge does not necessarily help them abstain from heavy drinking.
7. Humans often return to irrational habits and behavioral patterns even though have often worked hard to overcome them.
8. People often find it easier to learn self-defeating than self-enhancing behaviors. Thus, people very easily overeat but have great trouble following a sensible diet.
9. Psychotherapists [and teachers!] who presumably should preferably be good role models of rationality often act irrationally in their personal and professional lives.
10. People frequently delude themselves into believing that certain bad experiences (e.g., divorce, stress, and other misfortunes) will not happen to them. (pp. 6–7)

## Educational Foundations of RET

Both psychological and philosophical principles are embedded in RET. It encourages self-interest, the acceptance of self and others, commitment, acceptance of uncertainty, tolerance, risk-taking, self-direction, and nonutopianism (Ellis, 1980). It is important to note that RET does not stress the elimination of all emotions. It simply tries to help individuals avoid highly disturbing and/or long-term negative behaviors by promoting the use of the full complement of tools (cognitions, emotions, behaviors) available to attack them.

The educational philosophy of RET is similar to that of the classroom management schema presented in Unit 1. Prevention, as well as the reaction to problems of students, is stressed. RET is not a "cure" (see Chapter 2 discussion on remediation), because cure implies that individuals will not slip back into their previously negative or disturbed or disturbing behaviors. People *can* and *do* make errors, and teachers and students *are* people. It is because of this lack of a magical cure that RET attempts to teach individuals to help themselves. Ellis (1991) agreed with Piaget (see Chapter 5) that people learn by actively interacting with their environments and with Skinner's behavioral theory, although the latter contended that the "principle of reinforcement often seemed to imply that people are passively reinforced in both a positive and negative manner" (Ellis, 1991, p. 19). As explained in this chapter and the next, for RET to work, an active teacher–student collaboration is needed, which involves the use of scientific disputation, rational coping statements, referenting methods, hard work, humor, in vivo desensitization, and positive and negative reinforcement.

## Eight Basic Concepts of RET

Ellis (1973b) explained the philosophy of RET by organizing them among eight concepts. A clear understanding of these concepts is prerequisite for implementation of RET.

1. *"Man is born with a potential to be uniquely rational and straight thinking as well as a tendency to be a uniquely irrational and crooked thinking creature"* (Ellis, 1973b, p. 171). Ellis conceded that biological malfunctions may contribute to emotional disturbance, but it is the thinking process that *maintains* the disturbance. Ellis (1980) contended that humans worldwide tend to exhibit problem behaviors despite their intelligence, demonstrate the inability to change once they have insight into their problems, and, if they do "change," frequently fall back to their previous self-defeating behaviors.

In other words, "RET accepts the (innate) human tendencies to partially construct (and reconstruct) personal and social reality, to partially construct (and reconstruct) preferences and goals about these realities, and to partially construct absolutist musts and demands about the (accepted and constructed) realities and preferences" (Ellis, 1992, p. 451).

2. *"Man's tendency to irrational thinking, self-damaging habituations, and intolerance is frequently exacerbated by his culture in general and his family group in particular, especially when he is a child and most vulnerable to outside influences"* (Ellis, 1973b, p. 171). The fact that a child's environment may have a deleterious effect on his or her development has been documented (Algozzine, 1977; Apter, 1981; Mercer, 1975; Rhodes & Paul, 1978). During childhood, a student may find himself in "a poor training ground without preparation for the kind of thinking, emoting and acting that he will have to do if he is to live sanely as an adult" (Ellis, 1962, p. 381). The the-

ory of RET recognizes that the environment does not play a passive role in development; rather, it is constantly bombarding individuals throughout their lives with often unhealthy and negative ideations. An example of this is popular music. Protinsky and Popp (1978) found that over 80% of the "Top 100" country and popular songs contained such irrational ideas as the notion that "if you don't love me, I am worthless and probably should die." The amount of time impressionable youths listen to and the degree to which they internalize these lyrics can only be speculated.

3. *"Man tends to perceive, think, emote, and behave simultaneously and interactionally. He is, therefore, at one and the same time, cognitive, conative and motoric"* (Ellis, 1973b, p. 171). RET encompasses more than simply the cognitive aspect of emotional disturbance because individuals communicate in a varied and complex manner that is neither purely cognitive nor purely emotive. Consider the following vignette:

> Dave has been causing problems for Ms. Smith all year and has been trying to earn behavior points for 5 days. His "prize," conceived by the social worker and Dave's dad, is a weekend camping trip with his father. Ms. Smith feels that it is very important for Dave to be with his father, yet is fully aware that if Dave misbehaves, the trip will be canceled. At lunch, after Dave is called an obscenity by a peer, a shoving match evolves. Ms. Smith is faced with a dilemma, which she resolves by having Dave promise that he will not fight again and he will stay after school twice the next week. When questioned by the lunch monitor, Ms. Smith replied, " Well, it was one of those situations when my head told me to follow through with our contract, and my heart told me to let Dave go camping with his father. After all he was trying so hard!"

People often claim that they act with their "hearts" rather than their "heads," suggesting that affect overpowers reasoning ability. Teachers often use this as an excuse for their inconsistency in enforcing rules. The theory of RET argues, however, that teachers think and act with their heads rather than their hearts. Emotion and cognition in such instances are not separate processes, but the same process. It can be argued that one's heart biologically does not send cognitive impulses to the brain. In most cases, however, feelings are a result of cognitive, conative, and motoric processes. To effectively combat emotional disturbance, each of these must be confronted.

4. *"Highly cognitive, action-directive, homework-assigning, and discipline oriented [approaches] are likely to be more effective [than traditional psychotherapy], usually in a significantly briefer period of time . . ."* (Ellis, 1973b, pp. 171–172). This concept reflects RET's rejection of traditional psychotherapy as an inefficient and often unsuccessful means for effecting behavioral change. Closely tied to concept 3, this suggests that, to effectively remediate emotional disturbances that are due to cognitive, conative, and

motoric processes, one cannot fix only the cognitive, conative, or motoric areas and expect success. RET is a carefully integrated approach with the goal of combining these processes. This is why RET has been found to be effective in many instances after a relatively brief exposure (Ellis & Abrams, 1978).

    5. *"The rational-emotive therapist does not believe that a warm relationship between counselee and the counselor is either a necessary or a sufficient condition for effective personality change"* (Ellis, 1973b, p. 172). Although Ellis or any other practitioner of RET would hardly suggest alienating the counselee, this concept addresses the oft-quoted "unconditional regard" that Rogers (1969) suggested that teachers should have for their students. The theory of RET asserts that unconditional regard can validate inappropriate beliefs and behaviors to the counselee. Instead, the teacher who practices RET holds individuals in unconditional acceptance, yet will not accept their maladaptive, disturbed behaviors or beliefs. A primary goal of special education teachers is to teach their students to interact with peers and other teachers. Unfortunately, special educators sometimes tend to teach students to respond only to them, creating a "beautiful, warm relationship." This alone will not adequately prepare the students to deal with those persons who do not hold them in such high positive regard (e.g., some of their teachers in general education settings).

    6. *"Like the behavior modification therapist, the rational therapist uses a variety of techniques with his client: including roleplaying, assertion training, desensitization, humor, operant condition, suggestion, support . . ."* (Ellis, 1973b, p. 172). These techniques allow teachers to use as many methods as possible in order to help students rather than sticking dogmatically to one particular approach. Chapter 9 will detail the many of these procedures.

    7. *"RET holds that virtually all serious emotional problems with which humans are beset directly stem from their magical, superstitious, empirically unvalidatable thinking . . ."* (Ellis, 1973b, p. 172). Emotional problems may take the form of irrational beliefs that are due to "exaggeration, oversimplification, overgeneralization, illogic, unvalidated assumptions, faulty deductions, and absolutistic notions" (Walen, DiGiuseppe, & Wessler, 1980, p. 2). Examples include the idea that, if a student hits an authority figure once, he is labeled violent throughout his school career; or if someone drinks, she is considered a drunk; or if someone does "something crazy," others will consider him crazy (Ellis & Harper, 1975). To dispute such ideas, the individual is simply asked to prove their validity. In other words, the logico-scientific approach of RET attempts to teach students how to analyze a particular situation and supply evidence or proof to support their thinking.

    An underlying principle of RET is that humans think about their problem in much the same way as scientists would. DiGiuseppe (1986) suggested that "people formulate theories about important life events that are problematic and require practical solutions. Such theories about life events are used to help the person maneuver through the world" (p. 634). The scientific model "defines the way [an individual] looks at problems; what hypotheses are considered acceptable or plausible; and what sets of data are relevant to the problem. According to the [scientific] model, disputing the cognitions at the inferential level is equivalent to once having deduced a prediction or hypothesis from the paradigm or scientific theory" (DiGiuseppe, 1986, p. 636).

8. *"Rational-emotive psychology asserts that ordinary psychological insight does not lead to major personality change"* (Ellis, 1973b, p. 173). Achieving an understanding of one's problem certainly does not guarantee the possession of the tools or even the desire to change. Changing emotions and/or behaviors is very hard work and requires an active commitment to change by the student. No magic will automatically convert cognitive insight into behavioral change. Furthermore, RET is dramatically opposed to traditional psychotherapy, which purports to help individuals live with ill-founded philosophies rather than dispute them as irrational. Again, the difference, according to Ellis (1973b), between RET and psychotherapy is that the latter helps the individual "feel better," whereas the former helps the individual "get better."

## RET Terms and Definitions

One of the attractions of RET is the lack of scientific, psychological jargon. Nevertheless, it is a theory that contains ideas and terms that definitely differ from those of everyday language. The following concepts are integral to understanding and implementing RET:

*Disturbed feelings and behaviors* are those that are so intense that individuals are prevented from meeting their goals. Disturbed feelings and behaviors can also be described as extremely negative, harsh, and distressing.

*Undisturbed negative feelings and behaviors* are those that allow individuals to meet their goals. "Emotions such as mild anxiety, irritation, and annoyance may stimulate . . . efforts to solve [a] problem or make reasonable preparations for the future" (Kranzler, 1974, p. 6).

*Rational* thinking is clear, sensible, responsible, and congruent with one's long-term goals (Ellis, 1980). Synonyms of rational are responsible, moral, and sensible. When people are rational, they are more able to attend to their long-term goals. Rational long-term goals include:

1. accepting what actually exists in the "real" world,
2. trying to live amicably in a social group,
3. relating intimately to a few members of this social group or community,

4. engaging in productive and enjoyable work,
5. participating in selectively chosen recreational pursuits (ranging from sports to arts and sciences). (Ellis & Abrams, 1978, pp. 36–37)

Furthermore, a rational belief is empirically verifiable when "(a) regardless of circumstances, it leads to action that is likely to preserve the individual's life; (b) it leads to action that is likely to most efficiently achieve the individual's personally defined goals; (c) it tends *not* to result in significant personal, emotional, or environmental conflict" (Maultsby, 1970, p. 9).

It is crucial to note that rational does not have the same definition as logical. It may be logical for individuals to demonstrate self-defeating behaviors. For example, if a student screams at a teacher who is blatantly unfair and discriminatory, his long-term goal of passing that class may be jeopardized. A rational response is to be aggravated, annoyed, and upset at the teacher's behavior, but to remain silent so that the long-term goal could be achieved. Individuals who think rationally exhibit the following psychological characteristics: self-interest, social interest, self-direction, high frustration tolerance, flexibility, acceptance of uncertainty, commitment to creative pursuits, scientific thinking, self-acceptance, risk-taking, long-range hedonism, nonutopianism, self-responsibility for their own emotional disturbance (Ellis & Dryden, 1987).

*Irrational thinking* is that which interferes with achieving one's long-term goals. Irrational beliefs are not empirically verifiable. They "(1) . . . go beyond the data at hand; (2) . . . tend to sabotage the person's goal; and (3) . . . are held with absolute conviction" (Ellis & Dryden, 1987, p. 13). Furthermore, the intense emotions that may accompany irrational beliefs result from inconsistency in how one evaluates, generalizing from a few particulars, viewing feelings as facts, viewing memories as present-day realities, perceiving remote possibilities as imminent probabilities, and expecting immediate or rapid change (Goodman & Maultsby, 1978).

These terms are applied in the context of the RET model. The model explained in the following section can best be understood not only as a theoretical perspective, but as having practical applications as well.

# The RET Model

Although the theory of RET is relatively simple to understand, the RET model, sometimes called ABC(DE), is a difficult process for many people to practice effectively without having instruction and feedback from qualified professionals (Harris, 1977). To better conceptualize how internal statements make one disturbed, Goodman and Maultsby (1978) developed the following evaluation of self-communication to differentiate between the rational behavior therapy (RBT; Maultsby's version of RET) concept of how one speaks to oneself and the "popular" concept of self-communication:

| Self-Communicating Using RBT Concept | Self-Communicating Using Popular Concept |
|---|---|
| 1. *I upset myself* about the event. | 1. *"It"* (the event) upset me. |
| 2. *What am I thinking* that is causing me to upset myself? | 2. *It's normal to be upset* in this horrible situation. |
| 3. *How can I correct* my faulty thinking so I will stop upsetting myself? | 3. I'm so upset I *can't* do anything. |
| 4. *What can I do* to change the situation? | 4. I sure *hope* "things get better soon." |

The popular concept, one that is accepted and supported by much of society, clearly places responsibilities for happiness or hopelessness on external sources. Negative events lead directly to consequences (terrible feelings or behaviors). The use of RET allows people to assume internal responsibility for these feelings and behaviors by changing their type of self-communication, or their belief system.

To combat the irrational ideas that may be contributing to emotional disturbance, Ellis devised the ABC technique of therapy. The ABC model stands for the specific elements of an emotional problem as identified in RET theory: the Activating event (A), the irrational and rational Belief systems (B); and the emotional or behavioral Consequences (C). Changing irrational thinking to rational thinking is accomplished through Disputation (D). Finally, the new feeling or behavior change is called the Effect (E).

## Activating Event (A)

The *activating event* is the negative stimulus that is believed by disturbed individuals to cause emotional upset. The A may be real or imagined. In other words, witnesses may confirm that an event actually occurred. Conversely, individuals may report a highly biased, imaginative version of an event. Regardless of the event's factual basis, the important concept to understand is that the individuals have the perception that the activating event is causing distress.

## Consequences (C)

The feelings and/or behaviors that some regard as the result of the activating event form the C part of the ABC model, or the *consequence(s)*. The consequences that are of concern in this text are those that are so severe that they prevent people from meeting their goals (see the previous definition of disturbed feelings and behaviors).

People who are distressed refer to such feelings as anger, as opposed to aggravation; depression, as opposed to sadness; frustration, as opposed to annoyance; and fear, as opposed to apprehension. As a result they may engage in a variety of behaviors, such as eating too much or too little; sleeping too much or too little; and/or an inability to concentrate.

Again, many people believe that when something bad happens to them, the natural reaction is to feel bad. They believe that it is not their fault when others treat them unfairly or badly, and that the blame lies elsewhere. Other people may not react in the same manner. They may not like it when they are treated badly, but they do not waste time and effort blaming others for their feelings. To recognize these disparate responses is to acknowledge that there is rarely only one natural reaction to a given situation. These different reactions constitute the major component of the ABC model, the belief system (B). Belief systems are perceptions or reactions to activating events.

## Belief Systems (B)

One way of understanding the concept of *belief systems* is to think of them as organized patterns of thought. There have been hundreds of belief systems identified that create feelings. However, people tend to use the same belief system when they are confronted with a wide range of activating events. These belief systems take the form of self-talk, the specific things that people say to themselves that create their feelings. Beliefs are "(a) thoughts an individual is thinking and is aware of at a given point in time about A; (b) thoughts about A that the individual is not immediately aware of; and (c) more abstract beliefs that the individual may hold about A in general" (Bernard, 1980, p. 3).

For example, some individuals report that they become angry, depressed, or frustrated because of their inability to complete assignments. RET asserts that the inability to complete the specific task is not what actually caused the reaction to the assignment. The probability is high that these individuals react in a similar fashion (anger, depression, or frustration) to other activating events that they cannot control. A belief system is a series of personal evaluations, and evaluations are perceptions of events. An objective, factual description of an event is not an evaluation. "I cannot do this assignment" is a description of an event. Evaluations may be rational or irrational. A rational evaluation would be, "I cannot do this assignment. That's too bad. I'll ask my teacher for help."

Negative statements that are exaggerations of reality tend to be irrational. An irrational evaluation would be, "I cannot do this assignment and that's terrible! It's driving me crazy! I know I won't be able to sleep tonight!" As mentioned above, rational thinking can enable individuals to reach their goals (be uncomfortable with failure, sleep at night), whereas irrational thinking prevents individuals from reaching their goals (while they experience anger, frustration, loss of sleep). Depending upon which RET source one reads, there are normally between 3 and 14 irrational ideologies to which people are subject (Ellis, 1962, 1973a, 1973b; Ellis & Abrams, 1978; Knaus, 1974). Actually, Ellis (1977e) claims to have identified some 259 irrational beliefs (personal communication, Ellis, 1981). For practical purposes, it might be helpful to concentrate on Ellis's (1977e) three basic irrational ideologies. Some major subideas are included to allow the reader to understand the scope of each ideology:

*Ideology 1:* I must do well and win approval for my performances, or else I rate as a rotten person.

   a. I must have sincere love and approval almost all the time from all the people I find significant.
   b. I must prove myself thoroughly competent, adequate, and achieving or at least have real competence or talent at something important.
   c. My emotional misery comes almost completely from external pressures that I have little ability to change or control; unless these pressures change, I cannot help making myself feel anxious, depressed, self-downing, or hostile.
   d. If events occur that put me in real danger or that threaten my life, I have to make myself exceptionally preoccupied with and upset about them.
   e. My past life influenced me immensely and remains all-important because if something once strongly affected me it has to keep determining my feelings and behavior today; my early childhood gullibility and condition ability still remains; and I cannot surmount it and think for myself.
   f. I must have a high degree of order or certainty in the universe around me to feel comfortable and to perform adequately.
   g. I desperately need others to rely and depend upon; because I shall always remain so weak, I also need some supernatural power on which to rely, especially in times of severe crisis.
   h. I must understand the nature or secret of the universe in order to live happily in it.
   i. I can and should give myself a global rating as a human, and I can only rate myself as good or worthy if I perform well, do worthwhile things, and have people generally approve of me.
   j. If I make myself depressed, anxious, ashamed, or angry, or I weakly give in to the feelings of disturbance that people and events tend to

make me feel, I perform most incompetently and shamefully. I must not do that, and I amount to a thoroughly weak, rotten person if I do.

k. Beliefs held by respected authorities or by my society must prove correct and I have no right to question them in theory or action; if I do, people have a perfect right to condemn and punish me, and I cannot bear their disapproval.

*Ideology 2:* Others must treat me considerately and kindly, in precisely the way I want them to treat me; if they don't, society and the universe should severely blame, damn, and punish them for their inconsiderateness.

a. Others must treat everyone in a fair and just manner; and if they act unfairly or unethically they amount to rotten people, deserve damnation and severe punishment, and the universe will almost certainly see that they get this kind of retribution.

b. If others behave incompetently or stupidly, they turn into complete idiots and ought to feel thoroughly ashamed of themselves.

c. If people have the ability to do well but actually choose to shirk and avoid the responsibilities they should accept and carry out, they amount to rotters and should feel utterly ashamed of themselves. People must achieve their full potential for happy and worthwhile living, else they have little or no value as humans.

*Ideology 3:* Conditions under which I live must get arranged so that I get practically everything I want comfortably, quickly, and easily, and get virtually nothing that I don't want.

a. Things must go the way I would like them to go, because I need what I want; and life proves awful, terrible, and horrible when I do not get what I prefer.

b. When dangers or fearsome people or things exist in my world, I must continually preoccupy myself with and upset myself about them; in that way I will have the power to control or change them.

c. I find it easier to avoid facing many of life's difficulties and self-responsibilities than to undertake more rewarding forms of self-discipline. I need immediate comfort and cannot go through present pain to achieve future gain.

d. People should act better than they usually do; and if they don't act well and do create needless hassles for me, I view it as awful and horrible and I can't stand the hassles that they then create.

e. Once handicaps exist in my life, either because of my hereditary tendencies or the influences of my past or present environment, I can do practically nothing to change them; I must continue to suffer endlessly because of these handicaps. Therefore life hardly seems worth continuing.

f. If changing some obnoxious or handicapping element in myself or my life proves hard, that difficulty ought not exist. I find it *too* hard to do anything about it; I might as well make no effort, or very little effort, to change it.

g. Things like justice, fairness, equality, and democracy clearly have to prevail; when they don't, I can't stand it and life seems too unbearable to continue.

h. I must find correct and practically perfect solutions to my problems and others' problems; if I don't catastrophe and horror will result.

i. People and external events cause practically all my unhappiness and I have to remain a helpless victim of anxiety, depression, feelings of inadequacy, and hostility unless these conditions and people change and allow me to stop feeling disturbed.

j. Since I managed to get born and now remain alive, my life has to continue forever, or just about as long as I want it to continue. I find it completely unfair and horrible to think about the possibility of my dying and no longer having any existence.

k. As long as I remain alive, my life has to have some unusual or special meaning or purpose; if I cannot create this meaning or purpose for myself, the universe or some supernatural force in the universe must give it to me.

l. I can't stand the discomfort of feeling anxious, depressed, guilty, ashamed, or otherwise emotionally upset; if I really went crazy and wound up in a mental institution, I never could stand that horror and might well have to kill myself.

The derivatives of these irrational beliefs involve thinking in the following patterns (Ellis & Dryden, 1987):

1. *All-or-none thinking:* "If I fail at any important task, as I *must* not, I'm a *total* failure and *completely* unlovable!"

2. *Jumping to conclusions and negative non sequiturs:* "Since they have seen me dismally fail, as I *should* not have done, they will view me as an incompetent worm."

3. *Fortune-telling:* "Because they are laughing at me for failing, they know that I *should* have succeeded, and they will despise me forever."

4. *Focusing on the negative:* "Because I *can't stand* things going wrong, as they *must* not, I can't see any good that is happening in my life."

5. *Disqualifying the positive:* "When they compliment me on the good things I have done, they are only being kind to me and forgetting the foolish things that I *should* not have done."

6. *Allness or neverness:* "Because conditions of living ought to be good and actually are so bad and so intolerable, they'll *always* be this way and I'll *never* have any happiness."

7. *Minimization:* "My good shots in this game were lucky and unimportant. But my bad shots, which I *should* never have made, were as bad as could be and were totally unforgivable."

8. *Emotional reasoning:* "Because I have performed so poorly, as I *should* not have done, I feel like a total nincompoop, and my strong feeling proves that I *am* no damned good!"

9. *Labeling and overgeneralization:* "Because I *must* not fail at important work and have done so, I am a complete loser and failure!"

10. *Personalizing:* "Since I am acting far worse than I *should* act and they are laughing, I am sure they are only laughing at me, and that is *awful.*"

11. *Phonyism:* "When I don't do as well as I *ought* to do, and they still praise and accept me, I am a real phony and will soon fall on my face and show them how despicable I am!"

12. *Perfectionism:* "I realize that I did fairly well, but I *should* have done perfectly well on a task like this and am therefore really an incompetent!" (pp. 15–16)

The following examination of these internal statements indicate that, whereas rational beliefs are wishes and preferences, irrational statements tend to be absolutistic demands. Specifically, these statements can fit into one of the belief systems described in the following paragraphs

*Awfulizing statements* tend to take a negative event and exaggerate it so that it becomes a catastrophe. Uncomfortable thoughts include "It's terrible," "It's awful," "It's the worst thing that could possibly happen," or "I can't stand it," and can lead to extreme unhappiness.

The *demanding shoulds* include unwritten laws of behavior that people have of individuals who occupy the roles of parents, teachers, students, friends, and so forth (see Ellis, 1977b). Horney (1950) wrote of the "tyranny of the should," which "leaves us with the impression of demands on self which, though understandable, are altogether too difficult and too rigid" (p. 65), paving the way for failure. People ignore the reality of the situations that make their shoulds implausible. Horney suggested that the drive to arrive at one's "shoulds" can also create emotional disturbance.

Vertes (1971) examined the semantic properties of the irrational should, which may be summarized with the following four questions:

1. Am I absolutizing? Do I feel that someone ought to love me or am I simply looking at his behavior to see what indications I can get that he may or may not?
2. Do I have something riding on the outcome? Do I base my self-worth on the fact that someone may or may not love me, and I feel the loss of self-esteem when he doesn't?
3. Am I blaming? Do I believe that I have done something wrong or the other person has when I am not completely loved by him?
4. Do I expect immediate change? (p. 25)

These questions, if answered in a positive vein, reflect demands on other individuals that may be preferable for the person making them, but are rarely attainable due to their unrealistic nature.

Closely related is the self-made *categorical need* that some people hold. "I must get an 'A' on the test," "I need to be loved," or "I need a boyfriend" may surely be highly desirable preferences but are hardly environmental or biological "needs," as many human beings have been known to lead quite satisfying lives without grades of A, without being loved, or without having a boyfriend–girlfriend relationship. RET encourages being concerned about such issues if one chooses but not to be consumed by them, because if the end result is not to one's liking, the person consumed may react in an irrational manner.

Another belief system that contributes to disturbances suggests that life *must* be easy and comfortable and that, although change may be a goal, it is too difficult to achieve. The individual with this belief has *low frustration tolerance*. In a society that simplifies the remediation of most ills into easy 5-minute interventions (ranging from weight loss to curing mental illness), it does not stretch the imagination to contemplate where this type of thinking may originate. Rational-emotive therapy does not purport to be an easy cure. It takes hard work to change (or unlearn) behaviors, and this fact is reinforced throughout group and individual sessions.

*Rating of self or others* is considered unhealthy because, if people continue to value themselves highly for the success they are having, they most likely will *devalue* themselves when things go poorly. Ellis (1973a) would contend that evaluations are time-consuming and are rarely an accurate gauge of one's performances. It is these (mis)interpretations that can also generate disturbance. Ellis (1977c) contended that "the core of rational-emotive therapy consists of teaching the client that no one is to be blamed, condemned or moralistically punished for any of his deeds, even when he is indubitably wrong and immoral, because he is a fallible human being and can be accepted as such even when he makes serious blunders and commits crimes" (p. 222).

It should be stressed that, while not evaluating others and simply accepting them as people, one can still reject their maladaptive behavior.

RET thus distinguishes between (a) acceptance of self and others and (b) self-concept by noting the following (Ellis, 1977c):

1. Self-rating only works well when one has many talents and few flaws; but statistically speaking few are in that class.

2. Self-appraisal almost inevitably leads to one-upmanship and one-downmanship. If one rates himself as being "good," he will usually rate others as being "bad" or "less good."

3. Blaming or praising the whole individual for a few of his acts is an unscientific generalization. (p. 103)

The ability to accept oneself and others, even though maladaptive and obnoxious behaviors are exhibited, is integral to RET. Demanding perfection is rarely obtainable and often is self-defeating.

In summary, whereas rational beliefs are wishes and preferences, irrational beliefs tend to absolutistic demands. Rational beliefs are ideas or perceptions about events that are healthy and do not impair the quest to meet long-term goals (Ellis, 1980). Rather than catastrophizing about events, rational beliefs attempt to put them in perspective. Statements that represent rational beliefs include "I would prefer to win the game," "It's unfortunate that I lost my job," and, "It's irritating when he calls me a name."

Irrational beliefs are ideas or perceptions that give rise to emotional upset. These irrational beliefs are due to exaggerations of activating events into internal statements that limit one's effectiveness. Inappropriate feelings such as anger, depression, or extreme anxiety are the result of subscribing to irrational beliefs. These feelings may prevent individuals from reaching goals by developing poor health habits, such as improper eating and sleeping (too much or too little), aggressiveness, or withdrawal. Consider the following irrational belief variations of the rational belief statements listed above: "I must win the game," "I can't stand the fact that I lost my job; it's the worst thing that could ever happen," and, "He made me upset when he called me a name."

## Disputation (D)

If it is irrational thinking that creates emotional upset, then it follows that people would feel better if they learn to think rationally. *Disputation,* the D of the ABC technique, is the process whereby irrational thinking is attacked for its veracity; that is, the thinking that is causing feelings is challenged cognitively or behaviorally to demonstrate that it is unfounded and cannot be proved. The goal of disputation requires the individual to think as follows:

1. If I am upset, I am largely responsible.
2. There is something about what I am saying to myself and how I am evaluating this situation that is causing me to be overly upset.
3. I had better be prepared to accept another point of view about what is going on.
4. And I had better be prepared to question my thoughts and beliefs about the world and not rigorously hold on to those (whatever they might be) that do not have any relationship with reality (and particularly with my goals). (Bernard & Joyce, 1984, p. 81)

A crucial principle of RET is that irrational beliefs are exaggerations and untrue and do not reflect common sense. The goal of Disputation, therefore, is to minimize the exaggerated irrational statements by making them relative to other "life" occurrences, such as in the following examples:

- Is your failure to understand the assignment the worst thing that could happen to you?
- Does your failure to understand the assignment make you a failure as a person?
- Can you prove that you must understand everything and be achieving at everything that you do?

In most cases, irrational beliefs are highly secular. They are opinions, albeit influenced by the environment or perhaps one's biological constitution, that are individualistic and do not represent fact. Simple awareness of the beliefs as perceptions that influence the consequences is usually not enough to enable the individual to change irrational beliefs into rational beliefs. The process used to counteract the irrational beliefs is disputation, which normally encompasses the following three insights (Ellis, 1977d):

> *Insight number 1* occurs when the clients see that their present neurotic behavior has antecedent causes.
>
> *Insight number 2* . . . takes place when the clients come to understand that the reason why the original causes of their disturbances still upset and disorganize them is because they still believe in and endlessly keep repeating to themselves, the irrational beliefs that they previously acquired.
>
> *Insight number 3* . . . is the full acknowledgment by the client that there is probably no other way for him to overcome his emotional disturbance but by his continually observing, questioning and challenging his own belief systems, and his working and practicing to change his own irrational philosophic assumptions by verbal and motor counter-propagandizing. (pp. 190–191)

## Effect (E)

The final component of the ABC technique is *effect* (E)—that is, how the new rational thinking is generated into a new behavioral or cognitive effect. Simply recognizing that beliefs are distorted does not necessarily guarantee that change will occur. The reader may perceive the similarities between this concept and the levels of moral development and moral behavior ("necessary but not sufficient") discussed in Unit 2. Effect, therefore, is the bottom line of the ABC practice of RET: How has the problem been disputed and where is the effect in evidence? There may be an incongruence between the student's behavior and the newfound rational belief. That student may still act irrationally because "it is too difficult to change even though I know I should" (low frustration tolerance). Behavior modification techniques, such as reinforcement or response cost measure, may be warranted at this time.

The effect component of the ABC model is the commitment to change negative feelings. This commitment is demonstrated by the hard work and practice needed to make the desired change. "The main way RET accomplishes the goals of the final stage of therapy is through *homework*. Once the young client accepts the possibility and desirability of change, the practitioner has sufficient leverage to 'request' that the client 'does one or two things between sessions'" (Bernard & Joyce, 1984, p. 251). Maultsby (1971) reported that 85% of his clients who were successful with RET admitted that homework significantly helped them.

Behavioral principles such as positive reinforcement can often be used to help ensure that realistic self-talk is practiced. That is, rewards or

---

### Exercise 1

The teacher can check for students' understanding by asking the following questions:

1. What criteria do you employ to determine whether a person's philosophy of life is rational? How does the philosophy differ from RET?

2. Review the list of irrational beliefs. Which of them do you use (at least occasionally)? In particular, cite those that are related to your experiences as a student, teacher, friend, and so forth.

3. Do you agree with the idea that "One does not need love and acceptance from others?" Is it realistic to teach techniques of enjoying life without feeling loved? Why or why not?

4. Which of the irrational beliefs do you believe are most commonly held by others?

punishments are applied when the self-talk is used or not used. RET ends when students can "(1) acknowledge that they experience 'inappropriate' negative emotions and act dysfunctionally when they do; (2) detect the irrational Beliefs that underpin these experiences; (3) discriminate their irrational Beliefs from their rational alternatives; (4) challenge these irrational Beliefs; and (5) counteract them by using cognitive, emotive, and behavioral self-change methods" (Ellis & Dryden, 1987, pp. 60–61).

## Elegant and Inelegant RET

Since its conception, RET has emerged in two basic forms, elegant and inelegant (sometimes called preferential and general). In its inelegant form, RET is very similar to Beck's cognitive therapy. Beck (1970) contended that RET and cognitive therapy are essentially the same. Both approaches differ from psychoanalysis and are similar to each other in the following ways:

1. Both are more structured than psychotherapy. Diagnosis and programming are circumscribed rather than operating with open-ended goals.
2. Both look at the "overt symptom or behavior problem, such as a particular phobia, obsession, or hysterical symptom" (Beck, 1970, p. 185), rather than at unfolding subconscious thoughts.
3. Neither deals substantially with the past, either in reconstructing the past or in attaching blame.
4. Both exclude "traditional psychoanalytic assumptions such as infantile sexuality, fixations, the unconscious and mechanisms of defense" (Beck, 1970, p. 185).
5. Both may be perceived as optimistic, in that they believe that people have the ability to solve their emotional disturbances.
6. Although both attack the problem somewhat differently, it is with the recognition of conscious thoughts that both agree.

*Inelegant RET* is actually symptom removal, implemented by changing the interpretations of particular stimuli that are upsetting the student. Vernon (1990) suggested that inelegant RET (she called it "practical") was similar to applying a Band-Aid. If the individual's problems persist, the need exists for elegant (or "psychological") interventions. Ellis (1980) recognized that RET in its inelegant form has limitations with regard to generalizability. Consequently, he emphasized the therapeutic preference of RET in its elegant form. *Elegant RET* stresses the behavioral generalization of a restructured belief system (conscious thoughts). It suggests that disturbance is due to one's philosophy of life or the subscription to irrational beliefs. The following are the precepts of RET in its elegant version:

1. It especially (but never solely) stresses the achievement of a profound cognitive or philosophic change in clients' basic assumptions . . .
2. It strives when feasible for an elegant therapeutic solution to emotional disturbance rather than for a mere symptom removal . . . that will help them cope with and eliminate new symptoms if and when they arise and help them to prophylactically ward off or minimize their chances of creating new emotional disturbances in the future.
3. It holds that cognitions do not by themselves cause "emotional" disturbances . . .
4. It hypothesizes that changes in cognition . . . usually (not always!) require considerable behavioral practice . . .
5. It views most clients as having powerful (though hardly unlimited) capacities to significantly change their own dysfunctional thoughts, emotions and behaviors . . .
6. It strongly encourages . . . the use of the scientific, logico-empirical method by both therapists and clients. (Ellis, 1977g, pp. 74–75)

Elegant RET attempts to help people "get better" rather than only "feel better." The purpose of elegant RET is to help students deal with future "terrible" activating events so that future disturbance is prevented.

For example, consider the following difference between inelegant and elegant RET: Suppose Karen, a second grader, comes into the classroom crying that "Dennis called me a jerk!" The teacher immediately soothes her and gives her a hug, and perhaps yells at Dennis. Two days later Karen is again crying that "Caroline called me a creep!" This scenario becomes almost a daily routine. The teacher is applying inelegant RET, as she is attempting to change the events by yelling at the boys and also to change Karen's feelings by "taking care of her." The teacher wants Karen to believe her rather than the boys. If the teacher chose to employ elegant RET, she would have taught Karen that her essence and her feelings should not be affected in a negative way because of the "opinions" of others ("Sticks and stones . . ."). When this concept is learned, Karen can use this new way of thinking in a variety of environments.

Again, inelegant RET (simple problem solving) may be appropriate in some instances. Ellis and Dryden (1987) have argued that time and effort will be better used if specific philosophic change is achieved by teaching students how to moderate such emotions as depression, anger, anxiety, and guilt into sadness, annoyance, concern, and regret.

## Irrational Beliefs of Teachers

Another aspect of RET that the educator may wish to examine is the relationship of the ABC theory to the profession of teaching. As mentioned earlier in this chapter, one of the most beneficial aspects of RET is its usefulness as a personal and professional mental health program. Research has suggested that teachers, as professionals, may posses a variety of irrational beliefs that can lead to stress or burnout (Forman, 1990; Forman & Forman, 1980; Grieger, 1972; Zionts, 1981).

It should have been clear, upon reading Chapter 4, that inappropriate classroom behaviors are often a shared responsibility. Forman (1990) argued that "certain teachers, given their personality, are likely to bring irrational attitudes to their teaching environment and that these attitudes will lead them to experience teaching demands and threats as more emotionally stressful than those teachers who confront the same teaching stressors from a more rational perspective" (p. 317). Bernard and Joyce (1984) identified irrational beliefs (all derivatives of the major three ideologies discussed previously) that teachers may use:

1. I must have constant approval from students, other teachers, administrators, and parents.
2. Events in my classroom should always go exactly the way I want them to.
3. Schools should be fair.
4. Students should not be frustrated.
5. People who misbehave deserve severe punishment.
6. There should be no discomfort or frustration at school.
7. Teachers always need a great deal of help from others to solve school-related problems.
8. Those who don't do well at school are worthless.
9. Students with a history of academic or behavioral problems will always have problems.
10. Students or other teachers can make me feel bad.
11. I can't stand to see children who have had unhappy home lives.
12. I must be in total control of my class at all times.
13. I must find the perfect solution to all problems.
14. When children have problems, it's their parents' fault.
15. I must be a perfect teacher and never make mistakes.
16. It's easier to avoid problems at school than to face them.

Each of these 16 beliefs is irrational only when it causes major emotional upset.

The following actual quotes by teachers are not unusual. While reading them, the reader should assess with which of the previous beliefs the statements fit.

> I think it's awful when students cuss in my class even if that's how they speak in their homes, because in my class they should show respect and use proper language.

Note that the teacher is awfulizing the situation: "It's *awful* when students misbehave in my classroom; they *should* show respect!" Disputations of these thoughts include: Why should they? Why should students automatically learn two different sets of behavior, one at home and one at school? Most students who are disturbed do not behave differently in the two settings. For example, a teacher reported that "Doug chooses to swear at school and not at home." When asked how she knew this, she replied "I asked him and he said that if he swears at home he gets 'slapped in the face.'" This indicates that Doug does indeed swear at home. Regardless, it certainly would be *preferable* if students did not curse in class. However, to demand that they not curse and to get angry about it will rarely alleviate the situation. Besides, if students with EBD should not act disturbed, it is pointless to label them as disturbed.

Closely aligned to this type of thinking is the belief that students should know better:

> He's bright and he seems like a nice boy. He should know better than to behave in such a manner.

The underlying assumption is that intelligent students cannot and should not be disturbed. It is clearly an assumption that cannot be validated because there are intelligent disturbed people.

A different type of attitude that some teachers possess is that students should always be successful in their work:

> I believe that success breeds success, and that children should never be frustrated.

Two irrational beliefs are tied to this statement: (a) the absolute *never* may suggest that, if students are frustrated, something terrible will happen, and (b) frustration *should not* exist in education. However, frustration does exist not only in education but also in life. To shield special education students from frustration is to render them unmainstreamable. There is frustration in a classroom of 28 students when a question is not immediately answered, and students probably will be better prepared if they learn to cope with and accept frustration in the special education setting. Informal discussions with children about their feelings are often avoided because questions and comments cannot be predicted.

Sometimes irrational thinking may prevent teachers from attempting lessons that may be beneficial to both the class and the teacher:

> I am often guilty of being unwilling to try something new for fear of failure.

This statement expresses an attitude of perfectionism:

> Things must go perfectly in my classroom or it would be terrible, and I would be a terrible teacher!

Again, RET does not suggest that teachers should not prepare adequately for lessons and strive to do the best job possible. Instead, it stresses that teachers are not failures if their lessons are less than they desire. Stagnation in lesson planning often occurs when teachers are afraid to try something new because there is a chance that something "wrong" will happen. It would not be surprising if these teachers resort to the use of safe ditto/workbook assignments.

Closely related to the above example is the teacher who ruminates about making a mistake in judgment:

> Sixteen years ago I had to spank a child for belligerent behavior.... After the event, I kept saying to myself, you should have had more control. You should have had more patience. You should have handled the situation differently.... What if his parents report me to the principal? What if they sue me? Will I lose my job? I was a nervous wreck for a long time.

Note the "should" in this teacher's statement. The first half of the quote commiserated about her perceptions of an incorrect behavior. The second half of the quote catastrophized the situation into fear of the unknown, or anxiety. Both types of thinking were counterproductive to her goals: effectively managing the classroom ("I'll think of alternatives for the next time this occurs") and teaching ("I'll tell the principal if I spank any child so we can be adequately prepared if something does happen").

The example statements are representative of common irrational beliefs of teachers and are certainly not inclusive. As explained earlier in this chapter, these beliefs may be disputed through the use of RET. This is especially pertinent to teachers of students who are disturbed and disturbing, because they are frequently called upon to offer advice to their peers who have students who act out.

Teachers may act in an irrational or inconsistent manner as a result of their belief systems, and these actions may engender disturbing behavior in their students. Forman and Forman (1980) found that teaching RET to teachers was a very effective consultative tool because teachers seem to possess many additional irrational beliefs, such as self-damning, poor me's, misinterpreting events, worrying about gaining approval, having problems that drive them crazy, and establishing "shoulds" regarding students, parents, peers, and administrators. Forman and Forman found RET inservice training to result in significantly less irrational thinking in teachers. I have found similar results to be sustained over a 5-month period (Zionts, 1981).

Even teachers trained in the principles and techniques of RET are not always going to be rational. Ellis (1972) observed that teachers trained in RET often acted in a disturbed manner when their RET lessons did not "come off as planned" or when their own behaviors were sometimes irrational. Forman's (1990) RET stress management program emphasized an educational phase (teaching the concepts of RET), skills acquisition (relaxation and rational restructuring), and an application phase. Exercise 8.2 illustrates some of the common irrational beliefs of teachers. As explained earlier in this chapter, these beliefs may be disputed through the use of RET. This is especially pertinent to teachers of disturbed and disturbing students.

---

### Exercise 2

1. Reread the quotes by the teachers in this section and determine if other irrational beliefs are stated. Consider the following statements and relate them to the quotes:
   It's all his fault.
   I'd be a fool if I tried that.
   Bobby shouldn't have done that.
   He's stupid.
   I can't stand this class.
   How *can* I be positive? I am absolutely *sure* that I will fail.
   There *must* be a way for me to succeed!
   I might not do well.

2. List the belief system that would be more rational than those statements that are irrational.

3. List other irrational belief statements that teachers may have and compare them with your peers. Attempt to dispute them.

---

# Application

Two of the most damaging emotions that can be experienced are anger and frustration. They are damaging because they interfere with the educator's long-term goals of creating an active, loving, exciting, and enriching learning environment for students. Once a self-defeating feeling (behavior) is exhibited, it is extremely difficult to regain the composure necessary for achieving one's goals.

A number of events seem to lead individuals to feel extraordinarily upset under any circumstances, let alone with the arduous task of continually dealing with an individual who is handicapped. Educators report that the following are only a few of the things that make this relationship difficult: family members who do not understand the teacher's situation, lack of support from administration, bad behavior of children, teacher's inability to help certain youth, people who do not care, lack of student progress, and caregivers who are unprofessional. These problems can be debilitating if a person's self-talk is unrealistic. The following are descriptions of how Frank, and later Susan, used the ABC model to deal with their problems.

## Frank's Problem: Dealing With a Lack of Support

Frank is a special education teacher who works with students with severe handicaps. He is considered to be quite good with his students, and has been highly evaluated by his superiors. During the previous school year, Frank's principal, Mr. Smith, placed three students over the state limit into Frank's special education setting. The additional students placed an unfair burden on Frank, and this was detrimental to the students' education. Frank protested, and Mr. Smith promised that if Frank did not "make waves," he would hire another special education teacher, resulting in underenrollment for Frank the next year. Frank agreed not to cause any problems.

This next year came, and Frank's class was again three students over the maximum. Frank complained to Mr. Smith. Mr. Smith said funds could not be found, and said to Frank, "Since you did such a nice job last year with your class size, I didn't think it would be a problem this year." Frank reminded Mr. Smith of their agreement. Mr. Smith's response was to tell Frank to stop whining, and if he did not like his job, he could look for another one. He also reminded Frank that he agreed to the extra numbers the previous year ("Nobody put a gun to your head"). Frank became extremely angry. He could not concentrate on preparing his lessons and he found himself short-tempered with his students and family. He could not sleep well. He began to consider quitting his job.

***Activating Event (A).*** (What happened?) "Mr. Smith broke an agreement with me. He promised to reduce my class size. Heck, I wouldn't even mind if he just lowered it to meet the state regulations."

***Consequences (C).*** (What emotions or behaviors do you want to change?) "Anger. Also, resentment, frustration, and depression." [Frank chose to work on anger.]

(How does the feeling affect you?) "I can't sleep . . . can't concentrate. I feel like hitting Mr. Smith or telling him what a creep he is. It seems like I lose my temper too quickly with my students. I'd rank my anger at 90 out of 100. I'm losing it, and this is just not like me."

(How do you want to change this feeling?) "This is tough. I know I'm right. I just can't do anything because of these feelings. I would like to be able to control myself. I don't want to stop caring about this, but I'm also not getting anything done and I'm being a jerk with my students and family. They don't understand me."

**Belief System (B).** (List the self-talk that makes you angry.) "The jerk lied to me. He has no right to do that! Principals shouldn't do that! I'm going to do what I can to get that bum fired! Poor me. I can't stand this job anymore." (Not appropriate for this problem! Does this statement make you angry or depressed?) "Everybody should stand up and support me on this one! They don't care and they deserve what they will get." (No realistic beliefs were given by Frank.)

(What system is used?) "Demanding. Some rating, but primarily demanding."

**Disputations (D).** (Give evidence that your beliefs are true.) "How provable is it? Well, he did lie to me. I guess others have lied to me before and I've handled it. I realize that people do lie, even educators! I wish they wouldn't, but that's the way it is."

"Principals are people, and many people do look out for their best interests. I don't know why I let him sucker me. He's done it before. I'd prefer that he be honest."

"Maybe he was looking out for his own best interests, maybe even the students'. I wish he knew a better way to communicate, even though I know that he's always been this way."

"It would be nice if he would uphold his end of the bargain, because I upheld mine. Unfortunately things don't always work out that way."

"Even though he could have acted differently, I really have little evidence that he should have. I don't know his pressures. Maybe he was telling me the truth, and he simply doesn't have the communication skills to effectively tell me, and don't I know that!"

"I guess I'm really asking him to be a better person because I want him to be one. Sounds like I'm doing the same thing he's doing. Maybe I can't have what I want all of the time, even though this was promised!"

"I could probably get others to agree that I was wronged. Yet, does that prove it without a shadow of doubt?"

"I could probably be reasonably happy in my job with the extra kids. If I can't be happy, I might look for another job. What choices do I really have? To let him destroy my home life and job, or for me to tolerate his behavior?"

"My anger is not getting me what I want! My job and relationships are suffering. Mr. Smith is avoiding me. In fact, if I get my way through a demonstration of anger power, he just might figure out a way to get back at me!"

***Effect (E).*** (How am I going to make needed changes?) "I am going to try to accept my principal's dishonesty. I do not like it, but I do like my job and this community. His lies are really only an annoyance. I am going to try different avenues, in an assertive yet nondemanding way, to have my class size lowered." (*Note:* Frank is not trying to get the activating event altered.)

"The next time he lies, I am not going to be surprised. I will simply not react with great expectations to his statements. I will try to avoid future agreements with him. If I fail to accept his dishonesty and get angry with him again, my punishment (because I am not practicing my rational thing) will be to ask him if there are any committees or extra work he would like me to do for him."

## Susan's Problem: Inability to Help Certain Youth

Susan has been attempting to help Joe, a student with severe emotional disturbance, to learn some simple communication skills using a new program. The program involves training gestures that will allow Joe to make some of his needs known. Joe seemed to be fairly successful in learning the program, but he continually regressed, sometimes to the point of losing all of his skills. Susan feels that she cannot work with Joe; no matter what she tries, her efforts result in failure. She is very distressed with her inability to solve this dilemma.

***Activating Event (A).*** (What happened?) "Joe is just a constant failure. He cannot learn to communicate. No matter what I have tried, he still fails to learn."

***Consequences (C).*** (What emotions or behaviors do you want to change?) Frustration. [Susan had only one feeling about the event.]

(How does the feeling affect you?) "I find myself spending too much time trying to solve this puzzle. I find myself wanting to avoid Joe. This is affecting my work, my family members, my social involvements, even my job."

(How do you want to change this feeling?) "I would like to lower my frustration. I want to be able to continue working with Joe, and regain perspective on the other aspects of my life."

**Belief System (B).** (List the self-talk that makes you frustrated.) "I can't stand the fact that he isn't learning from me. This is the worst thing that has happened to me. Maybe he needs a better teacher. He should know how to communicate by now! Everyone can learn. There must be a way for me to reach him."

(What System is used?) "Awfulizing, demanding, and rating."

**Disputations (D).** (Give evidence that your beliefs are true.) "First and foremost, I seem to be telling myself that Joe, a boy with severe EBD should know better! Common sense would indicate that, if he did know better, he wouldn't be handicapped! I'm not accepting conditions the way they are."

> "I seem to be putting an awfully big responsibility upon myself. I would certainly prefer to be successful in all of my endeavors, but it seems grandiose to expect that I am some sort of superteacher."
>
> "I know from my experiences, and the experiences of others, that everybody doesn't learn at the same speed or by using the same program."
>
> "This is really an unfortunate time that I am going through, but it certainly isn't the worst thing that has ever happened to me."
>
> "There might be (not necessarily is) a way to teach Joe. I am going to continue to try."
>
> "Joe isn't doing this 'to me,' but rather this situation is occurring because he can't help it."

**Effect (E).** (How am I going to make these changes?) "Even though it is frustrating for me to watch Joe slip each time, I will try to be more tolerant and accepting of him and myself. Since my goal is to teach Joe, my previous unrealistic feelings were only getting in the way of that goal (which may never be met). As a punishment if I find myself getting very frustrated again, I will invite my in-laws to my house for Thanksgiving. However, if I can manage my frustrating feelings, I will go buy that sweater that I have been admiring, but have been reluctant to buy!"

## Efficacy of RET with Children

Before reviewing investigations that have utilized RET or have compared RET's effectiveness with other interventions, it should be stated that research conducted on the successes or failures of *any* psychotherapeutic method is questionable. Methodology is often weak, nondisturbed populations such as college students (the most studied group after white rats) are often used, and the lack of any longitudinal data is alarming. Furthermore, control groups are often absent, and the primary researcher is often the tester. Therefore, the research cited in this section must be considered to be merely suggestive at best.

Ellis (1977f) reviewed over 600 research investigations in an article written to support both RET and cognitive behavior therapy (this article is criticized later in this chapter). Ellis included cognitive behavior therapy because of his belief that much of it is synonymous with RET, especially its inelegant form. Over 90% of the research cited by Ellis was supportive of RET and CBT. Other reviews have supported use of RET with adults, including that of Hobbs, Moguin, Tyroler, and Lahey (1980), who found that "in some cases, rather dramatic change has been demonstrated in problem behaviors, whereas in other instances, treatment appears to increase skills that are useful only in relatively contrived contexts" (p. 162). Ellis would suggest that the former studies were elegant and the latter inelegant.

Remarkably little research has been done on the use of RET with children and youth. Perhaps this has to do with the difficulty of using "therapies" with this population. Rossi (1977) suggested that working with children and youth presents unique challenges to counselors and therapists. In RET, the teacher "is faced with the task of not only helping children change their thoughts but of teaching them how to think" (p. 22). He contended that students tend to think in a concrete manner, making it difficult for them to generalize and understand the consequences of their behavior. He did find that many students can generalize and understand things that are not personal to them.

Ellis (1973c) did not claim that RET is effective with all populations. As with other therapies, it works best with those who have minor emotional disturbances that are manifested with only one symptom. Smith and Glass (1977), in a meta-analysis of RET and other psychotherapeutic approaches, found RET to be an effective counseling and therapy technique. It should be mentioned, however, that because of the above-stated difficulties of research in this area and the many dimensions of personality, the authors questioned the supremacy of any intervention.

When to utilize RET has also drawn some discussion. In a review of various theories, Livneh and Sherwood (1991) concluded that Rogerian-type theories might be more helpful to students who are dealing with the onset of physical disabilities and RET and other cognitive theories might be more helpful with adaptation to society. Ellis and Abrams (1978) found RET to be a helpful therapy with those persons who possess a permanent disability, such as a physical handicap or a disease. For example, a person may actually become disturbed not because of his or her inability to walk, but because of a belief that "it shouldn't have happened to me" or that "it is the worst thing that could ever have happened to me." The actual disability may contribute to the disturbance, but it is the individual's belief systems that cause the disturbance. RET attempts to teach individuals to accept themselves with their handicaps.

Furthermore, as is the case with most other cognitive therapies and psychotherapies, RET has had little effectiveness with "individuals who are completely out of contact with reality such as catatonic or regressed schizophrenics, who are in a highly manic state, who are seriously autistic or brain injured, and who are in the lower ranges of mental retardation" (Ellis, 1973c, p. 191). The techniques described in Chapter 4 may be more appropriate for some of these individuals.

Although RET research subjects have included students who were at risk and who had learning disabilities and/or EBD, most efforts have been with "normal" students. Knaus (1977) reviewed mostly unpublished master's theses and doctoral dissertations on RET and found RET to be effective in enhancing self-esteem, reducing test anxiety, building tolerance of frustration, reducing anxiety and neuroticism, increasing school attendance, reducing subject failures, and promoting the display of more appropriate classroom behaviors. Hajzler and Bernard's (1991) review of the research indicated that, when the length of treatment in investigations was at least 12 hours long, there were significant reductions in irrationality (as measured on tests), neuroticism, and trait anxiety (as measured on scales), as well as increases in self-esteem (as measured on inventories). RET was more effective and efficient when specific problems were identified.

Hooper and Layne (1985) presented 1 hour of RET training per week for 6 weeks to 586 fifth- to seventh-grade students from 14 schools in Kentucky. The students who were trained responded in a significantly more rational manner on a questionnaire than did the control group. Thus, the content of RET was learned in a relatively short time. In another study, adolescents with EBD were presented with RET for 40 minutes a day, 3 days per week for 10 weeks, and increased their understanding of RET concepts, decreased their irrationality, and increased their time competence (Patton, 1985). Self-concept research using RET has been found to be successful with junior high school females (Cangelosi, Gressard, & Mines, 1980) and with sixth-grade students (Knaus & Bokor, 1975). It should be noted that, although these students were able to respond better after treatment on self-report inventories and content questionnaires, their subsequent behaviors did not change. Wasserman and Vogrin (1979) conducted a study on 27 children with EBD. These children who attended a mental health center reported less irrational beliefs and more internal locus of control, and were found to be more creative and more likely to take initiative. Again, their inappropriate behaviors did not change because of the treatment, although their behaviors did improve with age. Their intelligence levels were not related to their subscription to irrational beliefs.

Warren, Smith, and Velten (1984) found that the use of RET was successful in reducing anxiety with the general population of junior high school students. Boys with learning disabilities who were exposed to RET training twice a week for 12 weeks increased their internal locus of control, lowered their anxiety, and increased their self-esteem. The training was designed:

1. to learn ABC format of RET
2. to acquire basic problem-solving skills
3. to demonstrate that feelings are influenced by thought
4. to understand that feelings are not expressed in identical ways
5. to provide for transfer of learning by encouraging students to test in various life situations the principles being learned
6. to develop rational coping strategies
7. to learn concretely and accurately how to express feelings and not to speak in generalities
8. to give support, empathy, and encouragement to others in the group
9. to learn to dispute irrational thoughts (p. 897)

Harris (1976) conducted a comparative study with RET and the Human Development Program (known as the Magic Circle) with fifth and sixth graders. The RET students exhibited more rational beliefs than the Human Development group or a no-treatment control group. DiGiuseppe and Kassinove (1976) met with fourth graders who were given RET training once a week for 15 weeks. They found that the students scored higher on two RET inventories, the *Junior Eysenic Personality Inventory,* and the trait anxiety scale of the *State-Trait Anxiety Scale for Children,* when compared with groups receiving psychodynamic programming and health classes. The higher results on the latter two instruments were significant, suggesting that perhaps RET does lead to generalized adjustment.

Although no longitudinal research has been published, two cross-sectional investigations have yielded some interesting information about the efficacy of RET. Kassinove, Crisci, and Tiegerman (1977) found that older children were more rational, although most students ($n = 435$, fourth through eighth graders) subscribed equally to the irrational belief that "others are responsible for our own unhappiness." Seventh- and ninth-grade boys were found by Spirito and Erickson (1979) to be similar in their belief systems, and twelfth graders were found to be more likely to be irrational, especially in the areas of blaming and the inability to control their own emotions.

Raynor (1992) worked with three "angry" 7-year-old children who were in a hospital classroom setting. She divided her sessions into Getting Acquainted, Showing How You Feel, Expressing Anger, Seeing Problems from Another Point of View, (dealing with) Name Calling and Teasing, and Talking to Yourself and How You Feel. Her experiences led her to conclude that "these children were able to recognize their own thinking patterns and to show problem-solving abilities in role playing situations that involved anger" (p. 14).

Using a different approach, DiGiuseppe (1975) taught the RET ABC model to children, who first learned to express both the activating events and the consequences. Next, the concept of belief systems was explained. The activating events were role-played, and when the conflict surfaced, the rational belief was verbalized. Then, DiGiuseppe and the student reversed roles, with the student verbalizing the rational beliefs both overtly and then covertly. Reinforcement was offered upon the successful completion of the exercise. Results of two clinical case studies were positive.

Early research using inelegant RET by Meichenbaum and Goodman (1971) and Meichenbaum and Cameron (1974) suggested that specific academic skills could be taught to children first by "thinking out loud" and second by "talking to yourself." DeVoge (1974) used a methodology similar to that of Meichenbaum. He gave rewards to active participants (8–13 years old) in a state hospital therapy group. Although the results were primarily anecdotal, and there was no mention of the number of subjects, those in the RET group were reported to be "consistently less upset by frustrations, personal rejections, and failures" (p. 26).

Although the research conducted thus far is clearly supportive of the use of RET with schoolchildren, RET may not be effective with all populations. As with other therapies, RET works best with those who have minor emotional disturbances that are manifested with only one symptom. It is encouraging to note that RET is one of the few psychodynamic approaches whose validity has been documented in the investigative research, but when research is reviewed, caution is key before the reader uses the word "proves." Longitudinal research is still needed to examine the long-term utility of RET.

# Criticisms of RET

To consider the use of RET in the classroom, one should be aware of both its strengths and its weaknesses. The chapter thus far has concentrated on the utility of RET; this section presents some of the common concerns about the theory. Perhaps the biggest criticism of RET is related to the assessment process. The assessment of students, especially in research investigations, most frequently uses inventories or scales to determine the relationships of irrational beliefs and various types of emotional and behavioral disorders. Malouff and Schutte's (1986) review suggested that scales do not serve this purpose well except to measure irrational beliefs as a single construct (see also Malouff, Valdenegro, & Schutte, 1987; Robb & Warren, 1990; Shorkey & Whiteman, 1977; Smith, 1982). However, Smith and Zurawski (1983) found RET inventories to be highly correlated with anxiety scales. The most consistent problem with RET devices lies in their inability to differentiate among beliefs, feelings, and behaviors. For example, Woods (1992) found that eight experts could agree on only 47 of 100 items as belonging on the *Jones Irrational Beliefs Test.*

RET has been questioned on both psychological and philosophical fronts. The Ellis (1977f) article cited above, which reviewed supportive research of RET and CBT, has been criticized by both Evart and Thoreson (1977) and Mahoney (1977) in that it reported only favorable results and that many of the hypotheses of RET are shared by virtually all therapies. Ellis (1977g) agreed with Evart and Thoreson and suggested that the commonality is a strength of RET. (Those authors did find RET's clinical evidence to be encouraging.) Meichenbaum's (1977b) criticisms were similar, although he admitted that RET strongly influenced his own work on cognitive behavior modification. He argued that some of the research listed by Ellis was methodologically unsound and should have been omitted from the review. He also suggested that there is a need to distinguish between the therapeutic procedures of RET and "the more complex demand of explaining the origin and maintenance of maladaptive feelings, thoughts, and behaviors" (p. 44).

Saltzberg and Elkins (1980) addressed the following common criticisms of RET:

> *RET is too confrontational.* Yes, but only to the beliefs that are disturbing the person and others, never directly to a person's attributes.
>
> *The RET relationship is unequal.* Right! The teacher–student relationship is just that . . . not one of peer friendship. Unequal does not mean unfair, undemanding, or punitive.
>
> *RET therapists do not build relationships.* Empathy is integral to RET; sympathy is not. Sympathy justifies or lends credence to the "poor-mes." The goal of RET is not to meet the student's needs in a "group," but in life (at least in regular classrooms).
>
> *RET neglects emotions.* Only harmful emotions are discouraged.
>
> *RET forces values on clients.* RET is not concerned with the choices made by the students. Instead, it is concerned that choices are congruent with their long-term goals, and that the rights of others are respected.
>
> *RET is not compatible with religion.* Only that religion (or part of one) that is harmful to the emotional health of the student.

*RET only disputes irrational beliefs.* RET does include skill training and does not end with cognitive disputation.

*RET is too simple.* Simple to understand perhaps, but certainly not simple to implement (see Harris, 1977, and Chapter 9).

*RET is too limited in its techniques.* RET is very eclectic in its approaches. Rational-emotive imagery, in vivo homework, and role playing are just a few of the many modes one can utilize as a practitioner.

Young (1979) added the following three criticisms and his responses to them:

*RET promotes complacency.* No, instead it encourages individuals to energetically combat and solve their problems. It tries to teach students not to be disturbed when they don't reach their goals. This is not the same as learning to be void of all emotions, simply those that are debilitating.

*RET encourages self-centeredness.* RET maintains that concern about the welfare of others and not impinging on their rights is integral to its position.

*RET is a cop-out.* Although RET recognizes that humans are fallible, its dictums also encourage people to "energetically combat and solve problems."

# Summary and Conclusions

This chapter has examined the theory of rational-emotive therapy. Initially, two cognitive theories that are encompassed in RET were discussed. The theory of cognitive therapy suggests that individuals become disturbed because of their faulty interpretations of events and that, by proving them to be faulty, the person may become less disturbed. Cognitive behavior modification contends that children can change faulty cognitions both affectively and academically through behavior modification techniques. Next, rational-emotive therapy was presented as a cognitive-behavioral intervention that has been integrated into school programs. It has the following three uses to educators: (a) for personal and professional growth, (b) as a classroom or student intervention, and (c) as a preventive mental health curriculum.

The concepts and goals of RET include the following principles as elucidated by Morris and Kanitz (1975):

1. RET does not pretend to be effective with all types of clientele.
2. The irrational and illogical ideas, beliefs, and values which RET delineates as prevalent in Western Man do seem to be present in most disturbed and dysfunctional clients.

3. RET has aided the field of psychotherapy in furthering its understanding of the relationship between feeling (emotion) and thinking (cognition).
4. Although RET stresses cognition, it does not, as many believe, neglect the emotions.
5. RET admits that the essence of efficient therapy is the changing of attitudes and irrational value beliefs. (pp. 35–36)

Although Morris and Kanitz discussed RET in psychological terms, clearly it also has far-reaching educational implications. RET offers techniques that educators may use as problem-solving interventions. This would entail an understanding of the concepts of rational and irrational, the four types of internal statements, and the ABC theory.

The ABC theory concretely illustrates that it is not activating events (As) that cause disturbances (consequences, or Cs), although they may contribute to them. Rather it is one's inaccurate perceptions (beliefs, or Bs) of those events that cause disturbances. To change those perceptions through disputation (D), a cognitive and ultimately behavioral restructuring (the effect, or E) may occur. Therein lies the difference between elegant RET, which is changing one's philosophy about events, and inelegant RET, which is temporarily changing events or feelings.

Irrational ideas of teachers and the efficacy of RET with children in school were discussed to further enable educators to understand how RET may apply to their professional lives. Finally, some common criticisms of RET and rebuttals to them were examined to help answer any questions that the reader might have.

# 9

# Rational-Emotive Therapy as an Intervention

This chapter explores the use of rational-emotive therapy (RET) as a classroom problem-solving intervention. The techniques needed to begin using RET in the classroom are presented. Inherent in this discussion is RET's utility *both* as a personal, professional intervention and as a tool to help students reduce their disturbances. The actual practice of its principles and techniques allows teachers, whether working with individuals or with groups, to actively dispute the irrational beliefs that may be causing emotional problems. Consequently, RET encourages teachers to be more accepting of themselves and others and to perceive obnoxious events not as catastrophes and personal affronts, but as occurrences that can be endured. Chapter 10 provides the teacher with sample lessons and resources needed to begin to integrate RET as an affective curriculum. These lessons can be used separately, or as part of the teacher's academic curriculum.

## The Teacher's Role in RET

Implementing RET as an intervention may very well require that teachers assume a different role from the usual provider of instruction. The following sections explore some of the behaviors that teachers need to demonstrate to be successful at implementing RET in the classroom.

## Assume the Role of a Classroom Counselor

For many teachers, the term *therapist* has negative connotations. Therapist or therapy may imply a clinical setting where the teacher attempts to "get inside the student's head." Some teachers believe that they should not be concerned with the feelings and beliefs of students, but rather with their observable behaviors. Although observable behaviors are certainly important, internal factors also need to be considered. To do so, the teacher may need to undertake emotional instruction or classroom therapy. Classroom therapy seems to be within the job description of special educators who work with disturbed and disturbing students.

As mentioned in Chapter 8, many RET educators exhibit different personal styles. Although many different styles can facilitate the RET process, specific behaviors can enhance the efficiency of the sessions. In other words, different approaches by the same educator may be necessary. For example, Meichenbaum and Cameron (1974) suggested that teachers who respond to younger children in a playful manner are more likely to elicit student responses. Other ways that teachers can establish rapport with students is to speak to them on their own level, use humor, talk about how actions defeat their goals, use concrete examples, or use self-disclosure (Bernard & Joyce, 1984; Wagner & Glicken, 1966). To conduct rational-emotive therapy in the classroom, the teacher should exhibit the following teacher characteristics:

## Teach RET Concepts

The RET educator needs to be able to explain to students the process of RET, the ABCs, and rational and irrational beliefs. There is a fine line between giving informative mini-lectures and continually giving advice and answers to students. RET is intended to be a joint problem-solving venture.

## Demonstrate Empathy

One of the key impressions that teachers should attempt to communicate is empathy. Walen, DiGiuseppe, and Wessler (1980) defined empathy as "the ability to perceive accurately what another person is experiencing, and to communicate your perception" (p. 18). *Empathy is not the same as sympathy.* Sympathy implies that the listener is accepting the individual's statements as facts, which, in turn, reinforces his or her misery. Empathy implies acceptance of the individual, with the teacher trying to convey that "I accept you no matter what stupid thing you've done or way you're acting; what I don't accept is the fact that you cannot change that way of acting, and I'll do my best to help you in that regard" (Grieger & Boyd, 1977, p. 55).

The empathizing teacher may agree that "the situation is bad . . . but it is not the worst that *could* happen." The sympathizing teacher may support the students, and their disturbed or disturbing thinking, by commenting, "That's terrible. I know how you *must* feel!" or "You must feel terrible for getting a failing grade." The first teacher's statement emphasizes acceptance, whereas the second teacher's statement suggests that human worth is inextricably attached to one's behavior. Although individual acts may be judged as good or bad, to label people by their acts would be to arrive at faulty and careless generalizations.

Demonstrating empathy and not sympathy does not mean that the teacher cannot communicate warmth. Walen et al. (1980) suggested that warmth can be expressed "by carefully attending to the client's behavior, by frequent questions for clarification or therapeutic intervention, by recall of personal details about the client and his or her problem, by use of gentle humor and by quick, active attempts to help the client solve difficult issues" (p. 30). Warmth is interpreted as earnestly trying to help students solve their problems. This can be achieved by using listening checks and defining terms.

***Use Listening Checks.*** One way teachers can express warmth and empathy is by trying to enable students to communicate their thoughts in a clear manner. Clarification of students' statements communicates to them that group members care by checking how reliable their own listening skills may be, as well as by checking with the students to see if they said what they actually meant to communicate.

***Define Terms.*** Another type of clarification is the procedure of defining terms (Grieger & Boyd, 1980). This is especially useful when the students communicate in cultural dialects, slang, or age-related language. Teachers need to ask the students to define what they mean when they say, for instance, "it's bad" or "I'm bummed."

## Use the Active-Directive Approach

Ellis (1962) suggested that initial sessions should be similar to the client-centered approach, which is warm, permissive, supportive, and passive. During these sessions, students should be introduced to the concepts of RET and the behaviors that will be required of them. Later, the typical RET session may be described as *"active-directive."* Teachers and groups work vigorously because many students (and teachers) have practiced irrational thinking and behaviors for most of their lives. To expect students to change radically their thinking quickly because of arguments "that clearly make sense" to adults or other advice-givers is not realistic.

The educator who implements RET actively confronts students who are dishonest and waste time (Ellis, 1962). The direct confrontation may contribute to uncomfortable feelings for the teacher who considers the student–teacher relationship to be the most important variable of education. Ellis (1977c) suggested that it is the students' relationships with peers, community, and other teachers that are *normally* more important to school functioning than relationships *only* with the RET educator.

The RET educator is *active* and *directive* in addressing irrational thinking. Evasions are quickly identified as such and the student is brought back to task. Evasions in RET are similar to those often found in classrooms. Students may expand upon irrelevant information or comment that "I'm dumb" or "I'm a failure" in hope of changing the thrust of the discussion. Pacing questions is vital in avoiding evasions. This may require interrupting students in the middle of long-winded monologues if they are imploding extraneous information. Pertinent questions can help the students focus on their problems.

Although positive student–teacher relationships are desired, the active-directive approach may result in some uncomfortable moments. Sometimes, students will evade difficult problems by verbally attacking the teacher in an attempt to change, temporarily, the focus of attention. The teacher should attempt to stay on task during these moments because the students always have the option to discontinue if they so choose.

## Give Homework

It is important for teachers to convey to students that RET is not a process that occurs only during the school day. Homework is a necessary component of RET. As explained in a later section, homework should be assigned after each session so that the students can continue their work.

## Stay Focused

Communication is a two-way process. After asking a question, the teacher should attempt to get a direct answer to it, gently guiding the student back to the question if necessary. When using the ABC model, teacher and students should focus on each area (e.g., A) until both understand that area well. Going back and forth (e.g., A to C to A to B to A) can become very confusing for all involved.

## Concentrate on the "Here and Now"

As teachers inaugurate RET, differences in the sessions, when compared with traditional problem-solving attempts, become evident. Rarely will RET educators spend time trying to link past events to the student's present state of mind. Ellis (1977c) suggested that it is the individual's interpretations of events ("My teachers *should have* treated me better") that create the disturbance, not the events. Attempting to keep the discussion in the present is a very difficult task because many people believe that their problems are rooted in the past. If students dogmatically use past events as excuses for their behavior, the teacher may explain that (a) others have probably experienced similar events and are not necessarily in the same emotional state, and (b) the options that the students have are to ruminate about the past forever and stay disturbed or to try to minimize past events and accept reality as it presently exists.

For RET to be successful, cooperation between the teacher and the students must be present. The student with a problem must desire emotional or behavioral change because RET is not intended to be indoctrinative. Although teachers may set standards for appropriate behaviors in the classroom, which include rewards and consequences, they should not preach how and what to think.

# The Students' Role in RET

The most crucial new role that students may assume in RET is that of decision maker. The RET process allows students to decide if they want to change the reasons or the illogical thinking that contributes to maladaptive reactions. The following behaviors are integral to the success of students in this role.

## Work Hard

Students need to learn that behavioral and emotional change is a difficult process. Some believe that, if they disclose their problems, especially for the first time, then there should be an instant cure. If the cure is not quick and easy, especially after a painful disclosure, the student may stop trying to change (Grieger & Boyd, 1980). Individuals need to be continually reinforced and reminded of the difficult task that they are undertaking.

Closely related to the need to focus on hard work is the concept that continuous work is needed. Some students believe that, after a helpful session, all of their problems will be solved. The problem with this assumption is that RET is not a *cure;* rather, it is a means to change very disturbed feelings, which occur occasionally in most humans, into mildly disturbed feelings. The concept of cure implies that the problem will cease to exist, which is most likely a faulty assumption. RET suggests that humans, being fallible, do tend to slip back into their previously learned irrational behaviors.

## Be Honest

RET participation is voluntary, which should encourage students to be as honest as possible with both the teacher and the group. Some students may be dishonest, however, to gain the approval of others, thus satisfying one of their "requisites" of life.

## Demonstrate Respect

The role of the student in moral development meetings is also pertinent to RET. Students need to demonstrate respect for others, acceptance of others' personhood (not necessarily of their ideas), and the ability to follow group decorum. When a student assumes the role of leader, which should be encouraged, the student should attempt to demonstrate behaviors described in the previous section (Teacher's Role in RET).

## Achieve Independence

One of the most important goals of RET is to train students to think rationally and meet their individual goals without the aid of the teacher or group sessions. Students can learn to apply the process on an individual and private basis.

# Instituting RET

Once the teacher and student roles are defined, the RET process may begin. The following steps will help the teacher implement a classroom RET program.

## 1. Set Ground Rules

Before attempting RET group sessions, the teacher should reread the Initiating Group Discussions section of Chapter 7. When introducing the class to RET as an intervention technique, the teacher should stress that emotional and/or behavioral change will occur only if the individual desires it. The teacher should then determine what the students want from the session by discussing their behavioral and emotional goals. Throughout the intervention process, especially during stressful and difficult moments, the teacher needs to check on and reinforce the individual's motivation. This type of preparation and the organization of the RET discussions play an important role in ensuring serious and productive meetings. RET sessions are intended to help students solve their own problems. These meetings are not intended to be "bull" sessions where the students may complain about everything. RET problem solving is difficult and active work, involving concepts that should be made clear to the participants.

**Teach RET in Groups.** Group problem solving is efficient. More than one student will benefit not only from the process but also from the understanding that others have significant and maybe similar problems. Group meetings battle what Protinsky (1976) described as the "person fable," in which an individual believes that his or her problems are unique, and the "imaginary audience," in which the person believes that others hold the same beliefs about him or her. Other benefits of group meetings include the peer pressure of having to do the (sometimes difficult) RET homework assignments, learning to be accountable to others, and the observation that their peers are attempting to do the homework. Also, as the number of active participants increase, so does the number of possible resolutions that can be generated.

Consequently, group sessions tend to promote information that is germane to the students. Discussions, rather than lectures, are the mode of interaction; thus, such communication skills as listening, expressing oneself, and language development are promoted. Furthermore, social interaction that includes respecting the rights of others to speak is enhanced. Finally, creative thinking, through the disputation of irrational beliefs, is encouraged.

Teachers should monitor group interactions to assure that it is the irrational beliefs that are being attacked, and not the students who believe them. Another potential problem of group meetings is an implosion of disputes by members that may create confusion for the students. Each individual dispute should be thoroughly explored. Sometimes, students may quickly perceive the irrationality of a belief without the need to be exposed to every possible dispute. Another result of implosion is that some students may passively accept the bombardment and state that they agree with the disputations, yet never truly understand the implications.

Some students may not respond in a positive manner to group sessions. They may be reluctant to disclose their problems in a group, preferring one-to-one interaction. Wilson and London (1977) further suggested that some teenagers may feel uncomfortable with self-disclosure. Hypothetical dilemmas similar to those discussed in Chapter 7 can be presented, with the students applying the appropriate ABCs. Ice-breaking activities, such as relaxation exercises (e.g., yoga), may help create a sharing atmosphere.

There are many topics that the teacher may wish to explore if none of the students care to share a problem. Suggested global topics include dating and sex, separation from parents, occupational goal setting, and lifestyle conflicts (Wilson & London, 1977). Specific conflicts such as incidents on the playground or bus may also be discussed. The teacher's self-disclosure of personal problems may also encourage participation (not to mention trust).

***Regularly Schedule Sessions.*** In Chapter 5, the importance of scheduling daily activities was discussed. It is crucial that the teacher maintain schedules for RET sessions as rigorously as for English or mathematics lessons. If the teacher has the same students for the entire day, one or two RET sessions per day, perhaps at the beginning and end of the day, could give the students the time and continuity needed. If the students are with the teacher for 1 or 2 hours daily, two or three times a week could suffice. Sessions should last 20 minutes and, as explained later, should have a well-structured beginning, middle, and end. Finally, a maximum of six to eight students should be in each group for management and comfort purposes.

***Discuss Group Rules.*** While the basic classroom rules should still be followed, additional guidelines should be instituted:

- Group participation should be voluntary. (If students do not want to participate, the teacher should supply other affective curricula that they can use at their desks.)
- Students must respect peers. (It is appropriate for students to actively dispute ideas, not each other.)
- Confidentiality must be respected. (What is discussed in the group, stays in the group.)

***Keep Records of Sessions.*** The teacher should maintain a large notebook in which he or she records all the information that is given for each discussion. A sheet of paper divided into three columns, labeled A, B, and C, is used to list statements given as the class works through the RET process. The actual statements given by students often serve as "eye-opening" experiences. On subsequent pages, the teacher can list all of the techniques employed. Some of the techniques described in this chapter can be used for specific purposes, such as understanding an A or a C. Other techniques, such as the Feelings Thermometer (Technique 5), may be referred to throughout the session. Teachers may want to audiotape or videotape RET sessions to serve as a learning tool.

## 2. (Re)introduce RET

Once change goals have been identified, (re)orient the students about RET and ABC theory. Chapter 9 is designed for this specific purpose. Chapter 10 provides lessons that will help teach the RET concepts. Additionally, the teacher should recommend readings periodically.

## 3. Discuss the Nature of Change

Before determining the nature of the students' problems, the teacher and the class need to discuss the complexity and difficulty of change. Implicit in this discussion is the notion that individuals usually have to work hard to change disturbed emotions or behavior. One technique to reinforce this concept for students is to have an in-depth exploration of Lazarus and Fay's (1975) "myths about change" during the first group sessions. The teacher can ask the students to list the pros and cons of each of the following myths:

1. If you have knowledge and understanding—in other words, if you know why you are the way you are, or why you do the things you do, or why you feel the way you feel—then you will change.
2. If you don't know the reasons behind your behavior, you won't change.
3. It takes a long time to change. After all, you've had problems for a long time.
4. If you can change fairly quickly, it is superficial and it won't last.
5. It is frequently impossible to change. "This is the way I am, and this is the way I'll always be."
6. [Because I am this old] . . . it is too late to change. (pp. 18–19)

Lazarus and Fay noted that passive efforts such as only listening or reading will rarely yield change. They identified four conditions of change: identifying something as a problem, accepting the possibility that something can be done about it, expressing a desire to change, and making an effort to change. If the above concepts are understood by both the teacher and the students, implementation of RET may continue.

## 4. Briefly Identify Activating Events and Consequences

The actual initiation of problem solving begins with the identification of any feelings or behaviors (the C or consequences) that one of the students would like to change, or to identify an occurrence (the A or activating event) that a student believes to be the cause of his or her emotional problems. RET can begin with either an A or a C. Once an A has been identified, the C should be determined. If a C surfaces first, the students should attempt to recognize the A. Questions that can be asked to elicit an A or C include the following:

- Does anybody have a feeling or a problem that you would like to work on?
- Did anything happen recently that made you go out of control?
- Does anybody feel so angry, sad, or frustrated that you lose control and don't do as well as possible?

Regardless of what questions the teacher asks, the students may respond with either an activating event or a consequence. If the student gives a C, the teacher asks for an A. At this point, it is appropriate for students to give brief responses. If the student gives a C, the teacher attempts to get an A by asking the following questions (Grieger & Boyd, 1980):

- Under what circumstances do you have upset feelings?
- Describe the events that led to those feelings.
- Tell me how you felt in those situations; put words to your feelings.
- Feeling that way, how did you act? What did you do?
- What was going through your mind? What were you thinking when you began to feel that way?

Identifying the activating or obnoxious event is usually not difficult. The teacher tries to have the students identify what they thought caused their disturbed feelings. One technique that can help students recall the activating event (A) is the Camera Check (Technique 1). A potential problem, however, is determining the difference between the facts and the opinions, or between the confirmable reality and the perceived reality. "*Perceived reality* (or opinions) is reality as clients describe it and as they presumably believe it to be. *Confirmable reality* (or facts) refers to social consensus of what has happened" (Walen et al., 1980, p. 37). An example of an attempt to identify the **A** follows:

TEACHER: When exactly do you have these feelings of anger?

CHARLIE: Are you kidding? All of the time! Whenever I walk into her room. Everyone knows she is the worst teacher in this school.

TEACHER: You seem to be very angry. Do you actually feel this way all the time in her classroom?

CHARLIE: Well, not all the time. Only when she acts like a jerk.

TEACHER: When does she act like a jerk?

CHARLIE: When she yells at us to keep quiet.

The teacher in the above dialogue is sorting out and unscrambling the message transmitted by the student to narrowly define the activating event (A).

### Technique 1. The Camera Check

Maultsby's (1975) technique for clarifying the activating event is the Camera Check. The teacher asks the student, "If you had filmed a movie (or videotape) of the incident, what exactly would I see?"

Some students have difficulty specifying exact events. One method to aid in this process is to ask the students to keep journals (Technique 2) in which they will transcribe the incidents of the day. Listening checks and clarification techniques are also quite useful. These methods are represented by such comments as "Are you sure this is what is upsetting you?" "I'm confused; what exactly is bothering you?" or simply "What causes these painful emotions?" Some students may come into the class shouting the events (e.g., "Do you know what the stupid teacher did today? He . . ."). If the A is the first piece of information offered, the next step is to identify the emotional or behavioral consequences, or the C.

### Technique 2. Keep a Journal

Responding to spontaneous questions can be difficult under the most benign situations. Answering during times of tension can be overwhelming. Having students keep journals can be effective for the purpose of allowing them to record their thoughts as they happen or as they remember them.

## 5. Determine the Seriousness of the Problem

A critical point to remember is that RET is for individuals who have emotional or behavioral problems that are so extreme that they are interfering with their lives. Sometimes, students experience obnoxious events and are negatively affected by them, yet their goals are not impaired. For example, even though a student believes that she is being humiliated by a teacher and the consequence is annoyance, the student may still be able to learn in the classroom, be kind to others, and function appropriately. In other words, feeling upset is appropriate and is a sign that the student is capable of dealing with negative events. To determine if the RET process should continue, the teacher can ask:

- How are your feelings getting in the way of your goals?
- How are your feelings preventing you from doing what you need to do?

If the feelings are bad but not severe, then the process should be gently stopped. For example, "Maria, given that your teacher said those things to you, it would seem that your feelings of sadness are appropriate. You should be congratulated for handling them in a way that will allow you to stay in that classroom and learn."

If the problems are getting in the way of the student's goals, the next step of RET should be initiated. During this part of the process, the teacher should confirm the student's intentions to continue the hard work that will be necessary for change.

## 6. Understand the Activating Event

The purpose of Step 6 is to expand on the information received in Step 4. It is important for the teacher, the student with the problem, and the other students to fully understand the A (the teacher may need to review the activating event section in Chapter 8). Again, the A is what the individual *believes* has caused the problem. The student believes that the event, thought, inference, image, sensation, or behavior actually happened (regardless of whether it did). The A should be given in observable terms.

Specific questions that can be asked to attain the A include:

- What happened?
- Under what circumstances do you have upset feelings?
- Describe the events that led to those feelings.
- What was going through your mind that caused you to feel this way?
- I'm confused. Can you help me understand what exactly is bothering you?
- Can you give me some recent examples?

Occasionally, students will give rather vague interpretations of their activating events. The teacher then should ask more specific questions such as the following: "What about (school, your mom, your friend) gets you so mad?" One helpful technique is for the teacher to ask the other students if they understand the activating event. If not, they should be given the opportunity to ask their own A questions. It is crucial that the teacher stay focused and not allow any questions that do not pertain directly to the A. A frequently used reminder, such as "Does your question relate to what actually happened?" should be used.

Verbal discussions may not work with all students. Other ways to encourage communication should be attempted, including use of Techniques 1, 2, and 3.

Because RET differs from most counseling or problem-solving procedures, pitfalls are likely to occur, especially for the novice. Dryden and DiGiuseppe (1990) listed the following suggestions to avoid pitfalls:

- *Do not obtain too much detail about the A.* Understand the A and move on. Too much information may serve as an incorrect reinforcer. That is, the A is actually causing the problem.

- *Discourage the student from describing the A in vague terms.* Rather than accepting that "My mother hates me," try to encourage something observable such as "My mother called me a jerk."

- *Discourage the student from talking about several As at one time.* Tell the student that you need to hear about the A that is related to the above-mentioned C. Hopefully, you will have time later to deal with the other feelings.

### Technique 3. Role-Play

Some students find it difficult to verbally express themselves. The teacher can ask such a student to remember what happened and act out the incident. The teacher or other students may assume the roles of others in the role-play vignette. Role reversal is another type of role-play. The student and a peer (or teacher) reverse roles and role-play.

## 7. Understand the Consequence

Once the student has given a brief description of the feelings or behaviors that are causing problems, the goal is to define and fully understand the consequence (C). Each member of the group attempts to comprehend virtually every facet of the consequence. To enable the student to accomplish this step, the teacher asks the student to:

- List all of the consequences that followed the activating event.
- State how he or she felt after it happened.
- Choose from the Feelings and Behaviors List how he or she felt (see Table 9.1).

Should the verbal approaches fail or render incomplete responses, Techniques 1 through 4 may be used. An example of a dialogue in which a teacher attempts to help a student identify her feelings follows:

TEACHER: Can you tell me how you felt when Bobby said that about you?

POLINA: It was terrible! Awful!

## TABLE 9.1
### Feelings and Behaviors List

| Anger | Sadness | Cheated |
|---|---|---|
| Lying | Guilt | Avoid responsibility |
| Jealousy | Shame | Outraged |
| Bordeom | Anxiety | Undereating or overeating |
| Frustration | Hopelessness | Procrastination |
| Stress | Enraged | Take drugs/alcohol |
| Furious | Blue | Demand attention |
| Rejected | Despondent | Unhappy |
| Depressed | Alienated | Persecuted |
| Harassed | Annoyed | Abandoned |

TEACHER: Perhaps, but can you tell me how it feels?

POLINA: He shouldn't have said that! He is supposed to be a friend of mine!

TEACHER: Perhaps, but does that make you feel angry? Sad? Hurt?

Note that Polina's actual feeling had yet to be expressed. With the latter question, the teacher gave the student options from which to choose.

Students may name two different feelings for the same event: "I am sad" and "I am angry." *Different Cs are actually different problems* (e.g., sadness and anger). If two feelings are given, the teacher should ask which of the two problems the student would like to work on. The reason that two problems may be attached to the same event is because the student may have a different belief system (cause of disturbance) for each feeling.

Emotional or behavioral consequences generally are easy to identify. Often the students will volunteer or exhibit their feelings. Again, clarification and checking with the students about perceptions are necessary. For example, some teachers believe that students are expressing feelings through various aspects of body language such as tense facial manifestations or a closed stance. The teacher can validate these observations by asking questions such as, "Your face seems tense. Are you? About what?" It may be the session, rather than the recollection of unpleasant events, that is contributing to tenseness.

### Technique 4. Rational-Emotive Imagery

This technique may be used to help the student, teacher, and group understand the A, B, C, and D of RET. Based on the premise that some students will find it difficult to cognitively understand how RET works in practice, rational-emotive imagery (REI), as described by Grieger and Boyd (1980), allows the student to practice the ABCD routine. Maultsby (1977) contended that most irrational thinkers actually are practicing REI in an irrational manner. When attempting to understand the A, the teacher asks the student to visualize (often with eyes closed) the activating event as closely as possible. Next, the student attempts to recall his or her feelings both cognitively and emotively. During the D, the student tries to moderate the emotions being experienced. Maultsby (1971) described the results of REI: "a) [Students] efficiently decondition themselves to the most important external stimuli which are usually eliciting the major parts of their undesirable emotional responses; b) They create mental frames of reference for successfully behaving rationally, thereby increasing the probability of actually behaving in that rational behavior in the future; and c) Regular REI efficiently enables patients to learn 'self-talk' [think] rationally as easily and as reflexively or naturally as they were irrationally doing prior to RBT" (p. 19).

It is important at this time for the teacher to ask the students how they visualized or changed their emotions. Meichenbaum and his associates (see Chapter 8) suggested that some students may be unable, due to their youth or intellectual deficits, to cognitively change emotions. The teacher may choose to "think out loud" for the student until the appropriate self-talk is learned.

In summary, before proceeding to the next step, the following should be accomplished:

1. *The student chooses the consequence that he or she would like to work on.* Because people may experience a variety of feelings after a stimulus occurs, the student should choose the feeling he or she wants to moderate.

2. *The student, teacher, and class elaborate on the dreaded C.* All facets of the consequences should be understood before the process continues. The most obvious and direct questions to ask are:

   - How bad is the feeling?

   - What are the consequences of feeling this way?

   The Feelings Thermometer (Technique 5) is a powerful and highly recommended procedure that allows the student to visualize his or her feelings. All students should be given an opportunity to clarify and understand the individual's **C**.

3. *The teacher may need to encourage the class to persevere.* Occasionally, a display of emotions may surface during the sessions. Although students realize that they may stop at any time, it is important to continue with the session. The teacher should ask students exactly what they are feeling (the C) and what is upsetting them (A). The teacher

must not stop the session for the students and should avoid communicating that they "shouldn't" be getting upset (even though the process can be very upsetting).

### Technique 5. Feelings Thermometer

The teacher asks the student to provide a number or to point to a position on the scale that communicates the strength of his or her feelings. The value of 0 means "no feelings" and 100 means the most intense feelings a human can experience. The teacher asks the student to clarify what the number means, or what effects are attached to it, and how feeling that intense gets in the way of their goals.

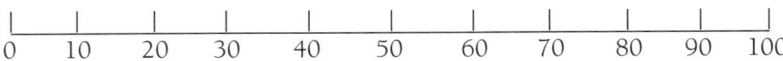

4. *The teacher should avoid C pitfalls.* Dryden and DiGiuseppe (1990) cautioned that the leader should do the following to avoid confusing the student and the group:

- *Make sure that the C is a feeling rather than a description.* "I feel angry" is an expression of a feeling. People may have different feelings (frustration, anger, sadness) when they feel cheated, for example.

- *Clarify vague feelings.* Upset, bad, and lousy are all general feelings. Try to have the student expand and communicate what those general feelings actually mean to the student.

- *Do not ask questions that reinforce the assumption that A causes C.* "Novice RET therapists frequently ask their clients, 'How does the situation make you feel?' An alternative question that does not imply that A causes C is 'How do you feel about the situation?'" (p. 22).

## 8. Set a Realistic Goal

The next step is for the teacher to ask the student to establish a goal. For example, the teacher might say, "You are feeling angry. How would you like to feel?" This is another chance to get a commitment from the student. Again, the goal should pertain to changing C, not A, as it is very difficult to change others or other things. The teacher can refer to the questions asked in number 4, such as "what feelings and behaviors would you like to change?" The Feelings Thermometer (Technique 5) is again helpful at this point. The teacher then reviews the student's original remarks about the feelings and how they get in the way of the student's goal. A crucial step is to ask the student to point to the number that reflects the intensity of feelings or behaviors that will allow the student to reach the goal. This activity restates the student's commitment to change. Questions that may help set up long-term goals include:

- What else could be meaningful despite . . . ? (This acknowledges the student's diminished happiness while still communicating the desire to make life at least somewhat happy.)
- How will [this event] destroy your world? (To reach this answer, the student can survey the satisfying events in his or her life. The teacher should attempt to understand the student's fields of interest.)
- What good things can you do if [the event] occurs?
- What good things still can exist despite the existence of the awful event?

One of the more common pitfalls during this step is to accept a dichotomous statement, such as "I feel horrible and my goal is to feel wonderful." This is a pitfall because it is unrealistic and probably inappropriate for one to feel terrific about an obnoxious, annoying event. The following vignette offers an example:

> EMILY: I am very angry that I have to study hard. It is much easier for my friends.
>
> TEACHER: How would you like to feel about it.
>
> EMILY: Happy.

It is unrealistic for most people to feel *happy* about studying harder than others. A more sensible goal for Emily would be to feel annoyed or at least uncomfortable and accept the fact that she has to expend more effort on studying. If the goal of "happy" is accepted, failure is almost ensured. An analogy to realistic goal setting is when extremely overweight people set target weights of 50 to 100 pounds lower than their current weight. When their goals are not reached quickly, they stop dieting. Dryden and DiGiuseppe (1990, p. 28) listed other ways for teachers to avoid pitfalls:

- Do not accept the wish to experience less of an inappropriate negative emotion. For example, "less angry" still implies anger. A more appropriate goal is to replace anger with annoyance or concern.
- Do not accept goals indicating wishes to feel neutral, indifferent, or calm about events for which it would be rational to feel an appropriate negative emotion.

## 9. Determine Elegant or Inelegant RET

Once the feelings (C) are known and the "what happened" (A) is determined, traditional problem-solving techniques are used to change the event ("Let's get you out of that situation") or to change the feeling ("Come on, let me give you a hug; you're a terrific person"). Unpleasant events may be altered or avoided to prevent the disturbed feelings from recurring. This type of problem solving, as discussed in the previous chapter, can be described as inelegant RET. RET asserts that these changes do not encourage long-term growth, however, because the student's problem lies in beliefs about the events. When similar events occur, the student will probably react in the same disturbed manner to them. The process of attacking the irrational belief system is integral to elegant RET.

## 10. Understand the Belief System

Although it may seem incongruent to progress from A to C or C to A in an ABC theory, the contention of RET is that only rational human beings can readily identify the belief system, or B, that is causing their unhappiness. Most individuals assume that feelings are caused by an event, rather than by beliefs about the event. The following subsections describe what the teacher can do to help students understand the B part of the theory.

***Teach (reteach) the Relationship Between B and C.*** Using a mini-lecture, the teacher explains the ABC model. The content in Chapter 8 and the lessons in Chapter 10 may assist in this area. RET's entire philosophy is to teach students to become independent problem solvers. For students to achieve this goal, they need to understand the reasons why intense emotional problems occur (from perceptions, not the event).

In one mini-lecture, for instance, the teacher could explain that, although many people believe that events (A) cause emotional or behavioral consequences (C), RET argues that it is the beliefs (B) about those events that determine the emotional or behavioral outcomes. For example, the failing of a math test may generate depression, anger, or guilt (all irrational Bs), or concern, annoyance, or minor frustration (all rational Bs). If individuals believe that they *are* their grades, it is easy to see how they may become depressed and/or guilty. Students may become angry if they believe that their teacher unfairly graded them or that the test itself was poorly constructed. If, however, individuals realize that test scores are not, in fact, their "being," that the test did seem a little erratic, and that, despite studying long and hard, little can be accomplished by being depressed, angry, and guilty, then the rational emotions of concern, annoyance, and minor frustration may surface.

There are many types of irrational Beliefs, with the non sequitur being among the more prominent. In that irrational Bs are distorted perceptions or incorrect self-talk, the non sequitur is a prime example of how irrational ideas are promoted in this society (Goodman & Maultsby, 1978, pp. 47–48):

| Just because . . . | Doesn't mean that . . . |
|---|---|
| you've been insulted | you need to get angry |
| you haven't accomplished something | you can't do so |
| you make many mistakes | you are a louse |
| someone behaved poorly in the past | he will always do so in the future |
| having to wait in line is annoying | it is terribly irritating, even unbearable |
| a lot of bad things have happened to you in the past year | you are the original hard luck kid and always will be |

**Educational correlates could include:**

| | |
|---|---|
| You get an F on a test | you are a failure |
| A peer calls you a jerk | you are one |
| A student acts like a devil | he is one |
| You get frustrated | you have to kick chairs, scream, mope about, etc. |

It is often very difficult to convince people who subscribe to these beliefs that their thoughts are irrational, because they tend to believe this type of reasoning to be part of human nature and societal standards. The teacher can help students understand that their beliefs are irrational by requesting them to provide evidence to support the validity of the statements.

***Detect Self-Talk.*** The belief system is the key to elegant RET and is a crucial component of the assessment process. Beliefs are statements that people say to themselves, sometimes called self-talk, and that determine how the people feel about events. Specific questions that can be asked to elicit students' belief systems include "What are you saying to yourself when the A happens?" or, following role-play (Technique 3), "What were you thinking during the role-play?"

Diagnostically, the educator should try to place the self-talk into one of these categories: self, others, or world. This allows a focusing on the specific belief that the student is holding. An example of detecting the B follows:

> TEACHER: What did you tell yourself when you received a "D" on the test?
>
> PATRICK: I couldn't believe it.
>
> TEACHER: Is that all you said?
>
> PATRICK: No. It should have been an "A" or at least a "B." I worked hard and I deserve an "A." The teacher (other) is an unfair jerk!

Beliefs tend to surface through phrases, sometimes called buzzwords, such as, "I can't stand it," "I must," "they should," "it's awful," and/or "I'm a no-goodnik." Individuals beginning to use the ABC process tend to search only for the buzzwords and immediately try to dispute them. These buzzwords, however, are only symptomatic of a student's overall problem. A pattern often emerges of generalizing the particular buzzword, such as "should," to behaviors or beliefs that tend to be consistent, such as the demanding of others, *not only in one particular instance, but also in other situations.*

***Generalize the Self-Talk into Belief Systems.*** When R. Wessler (personal communication, 1981) gets a B statement, she continues to explore the irrational reasoning. Probes she uses to generalize the B include "Why must you?" and "Why should you?" In other words, she attempts to have the student elaborate on the belief system. Two types of belief systems—rational and irrational—may be attached to any event. The former is relativistic, whereas the latter tends to be absolutistic. Rational beliefs tend not to result in harmful emotions that impede goal attainment, whereas irrational beliefs can be easily disproved and impede goal attainment, leading, perhaps, to harmful emotions. Rather than stopping at one irrational belief, the teacher and students need to explore other alternatives because additional irrational beliefs may surface. Both irrational and rational beliefs should be listed. The students should be asked whether they believe any irrational beliefs more strongly than others.

One problem that may arise, especially with students who are familiar with RET, is the tendency for them to minimize their true feelings, avoid buzzwords, and give a rational belief. If this is suspected, the teacher needs to keep exploring with the students to ascertain if the problem still exists, using such comments as:

- If you are only annoyed, why can't you sleep?
- It sounds as though it feels stronger than *that.*
- There seems to be a confusion between your C and your **B**.

***Stay Focused.*** During this step, teachers may lose their focus. For example, a student may say he feels angry and depressed about a particular **A** and may choose to work on depression. When sharing his self-talk, he may express anger statements. At this time, the leader or another student needs to remind the student that his self-talk is accurate, but it relates to his feelings of anger. The teacher should ask, "And what do you say to yourself when you get depressed?"

Occasionally, the student will use synonyms for buzzwords:

**BARRY:** He could have been nicer to me.

**TEACHER:** Yes, I suppose that's true. However, when people *could* act in ways other than what we desire we rarely get as angry as

|         | you are right now. "Could" allows for people to behave as they please. |
|---------|---|
| BARRY:  | Oh yeah, well, he could have been nicer because I was nice to him! |

Barry is probably upset due to his demanding (shoulding) that his friend act "nice" to him, *especially* since he was nice to his friend.

Educators who often practice RET become quite proficient in identifying the B. There is a tendency for some educators to do all the work for the students, even to the extent of giving them the irrational beliefs. This practice is particularly common when students make comments that seem to stop short of expressing the entire belief. Encourage as much student input as possible:

| BRADLEY: | The teacher yelled at me again! |
|----------|---|
| TEACHER: | And . . . ? |
| BRADLEY: | Just because I was talking, she yelled! |
| TEACHER: | Therefore, she . . . |
| BRADLEY: | She's a rotten teacher! |
| TEACHER: | Because . . . ? |
| BRADLEY: | Teachers shouldn't yell at their students! It's not fair. I wasn't doing anything to her. |

Notice that the teacher is simply inviting Bradley to finish his thoughts.

Another type of communication that is usually indicative of irrational beliefs is the use of rhetorical questions: "How could this happen to me" may mean "It shouldn't happen to me!" "What's the use anyway?" may mean "I'd fail and I must be competent." "Do you mean I have to put up with this?" may mean "It's too hard and life should be easier." Again, by questioning and exploring the questions, irrational beliefs may emerge.

Generalizing the belief cannot be overemphasized. If the belief is specific only to one situation, there is a temptation to solve only the A, or to help the student "feel better" rather than "get better" (Ellis, personal communication, 1981). The RET educator should attempt to identify a consistency in students' thoughts, feelings, and behaviors throughout the year.

***Examples of RET Diagnoses.*** Many types of generalized feelings that are common in the classroom are often used when describing or classifying disturbed and disturbing students. These feelings include anger, depression, anxiety, guilt, and shame. The following are brief RET interpretations of these feelings (irrational beliefs). RET disputations of these feelings are presented in the following section.

*Anger* describes a student's feeling that usually is accompanied with destructive (to self, others, or inanimate objects) behaviors. One RET interpretation of anger may be that the student has a perfectionistic attitude. The student demands that others behave in a particular manner, or that tasks be performed *exactly* as intended. Another possibility is that anger is caused by low frustration tolerance: "Things shouldn't be this hard!" The following is an ABC diagram of anger:

| A | B | C |
|---|---|---|
| He is not a "good" teacher. | He should live up to my expectations. He's awful for *not* living up to my expectations. He should be fair. | Anger |

*Depression* may result because of self-blame due to the student's perceived inadequacy. "Poor me," "This could only happen to me," and "I need this to happen for me to be happy" are irrational beliefs representing depression. Students believe that, if they are not perfect, or at least adequate, in performing acts that they deem important, they will be miserable human beings and have the "right" to be upset. The following is an ABC diagram of depression:

| A | B | C |
|---|---|---|
| Nobody likes me. | Poor me. I can't stand it. It's awful. | Depression |

*Anxiety* is probably due to a student's catastrophizing about an event of fear of what will happen. In most cases, the student is exaggerating beliefs or fears. This is especially evident before students take quizzes or tests, as depicted in the following diagram:

| A | B | C |
|---|---|---|
| I'm worried about the test. | I must do well on this test or I am a failure. | Anxiety |

Finally, the feelings of *guilt* and *shame* are often used interchangeably. RET distinguishes between them by defining guilt as a feeling that occurs when students believe they are doing, or have done, something blameworthy, and that they should be forever blamed and punished for the act. Shame may be a similar perception; the difference is that the student is concerned with others' perceptions of the act. The following are ABC diagrams of shame and guilt:

GUILT

| A | B | C |
|---|---|---|
| Not doing the right thing for *me*. | I mustn't do *that*. I'm a horrible person if I do. | Guilt |

SHAME

| A | B | C |
|---|---|---|
| Public mistake | I must have other people's approval. I need approval; if not, I'm a horrible, worthless person. | Shame |

The student who is guilt-ridden would still feel terrible, even if nobody knew or could possibly find out about the act. The student who feels shame is preoccupied about any possible social ramifications. A question to differentiate the two may be, "Would you still feel guilty if nobody found out that you failed the test?" If the answer is affirmative, the student feels guilty; if negative, shame is probably the feeling.

If the feelings are properly diagnosed, the disputation process may be facilitated. Each feeling has a distinct belief system, which, if identified in the assessment process, can lead to a more efficient remediation. Again, each ABC is *one* problem. When disputations of irrational beliefs are unsuccessful, it is usually due to the therapist's vague understanding of the ABCs.

## 11. Dispute Irrational Beliefs

Once the ABCs have been determined, the teacher and the group attempt to dispute the student's irrational belief system. Disputation is intended to help the individual understand the relationship between irrational thinking and its consequences. Disputation is a cognitive process that usually involves some form of questioning. The idea is to try to have the student *prove* that his or her irrational beliefs are really rational beliefs. Criddle (1974) contended that challenging the individual's irrational belief system "is the leading step to permanent change.... This is done by questioning, asking for evidence, applying logic and the scientific method of thinking to one's ideas, and then replacing the illogical ideas with rational, logical ones" (p. 9). This is more complicated than enabling the student to recognize that thoughts or behaviors are "irrational."

Dryden and DiGiuseppe (1990) summarized four disputing tactics that can be used to help students recognize their irrational beliefs and then replace them with rational beliefs. These tactics are the Socratic Style of asking questions, the Didactic Style of using mini-lectures to give the students explanations, the Humorous Style of using gross exaggerations of statements, and the Self-Disclosure Style of using oneself as an example. Although too much usage of any of these tactics may lead to a loss of effectiveness, the reader should be cautioned especially regarding the use of humor. Some students may lack a sense of humor and may interpret the teacher's attempts as ridicule. The teacher should use listening checks with them to ensure that his or her intentions are being understood.

***Attacking Irrational Belief Systems.*** The process of disputation is facilitated when the belief system has been clearly identified. Dryden and DiGiuseppe (1990) identified the goals of disputing that can be achieved by vigorously attacking the students':

- *Musts:* There is no evidence to support individuals' absolute demands. Evidence does exist for their preferences.
- *Awfulizing:* Defining anything as 100% awful is nonsense; all experiences lie within a 0% to 99.9% range of badness.
- *I-can't-stand-it-itis:* Students will always be able to stand what they think they can't, and may even find *some* happiness in their lives, even if the dreaded "A" continues.
- *Damnation:* This concept is illogical and invariably leads to emotional upset. The fact is that the students, their "others," and the world, for that matter, are fallible. When this is understood, acceptance and dislike instead of damnation can take place.
- *Always-and-never thinking:* "It is most unlikely that the (student) will always be rejected or never succeed in doing well. He is not intrinsically unlovable, nor a total failure" (p. 42).

In summary, there is only one correct answer to any dispute: There is no evidence to support irrational thinking. There are many different ways to attack irrational beliefs, such as asking questions ("Why must your mother be the best in the world?"), using mini-lectures, and using humor ("You absolutely, totally can't be happy unless you are terrific with everything that you do? What about us fallible people? Are we doomed to misery because we can never beat you?"). The use of many of the techniques presented in this chapter may provide students with a clear understanding of their irrational thinking.

Understanding and adaptation of rational principles are often two different concepts. A disputation may be "very clear" to the students, yet they may continue to behave in a destructive manner. This may be because of "conflicting ideas [and emotions], and [because] the well-used, well-established ideas are much stronger than the newly acquired rational ideas" (Criddle, 1974, p. 8). Intelligent students may quickly understand the rational reasoning, but may not be convinced that it applies to their individual problems.

The novice RET educator will sometimes vigorously attack obviously irrational beliefs. It is important not to negate the feelings of students during the disputation process, but to acknowledge their diminished happiness. Although their beliefs may seem to be irrational, their feelings are probably real. Negating feelings can impede the RET sessions. The objective of disputation is to minimize the harmful feelings; in other words, students need to learn that *bad* things do happen and nobody is trying to change the event, merely the reactions to *badness*. Again, the goal is not to feel good about bad events, merely less awful or bad. Disputation in elegant RET is *not* intended to make the A disappear, but to help the student learn how to accept it and try to methodically change it if possible.

The area of accepting events is what differentiates RET from other counseling interventions. Rather than spending time disputing the accuracy of the A (if that can be possible), a RET approach would be to ask, "What if it *is* true? What is the worst that can happen? Assume that you are never going to pass mathematics. Why is it so *awful* when you don't pass a test" (see Technique 6). The objective of this type of disputation is to demonstrate to the student that, although it is uncomfortable to fail the test, it is probably not terrible.

Everybody involved in this process needs to stay focused. Dryden and DiGiuseppe (1990) suggested that it is crucial to be persistent in the disputation process by focusing on (a) irrationality—even though students want something to happen (very much), it does not follow that it will happen; (b) empiricism—people cannot get what they want if they are not getting what they want; and (c) pragmatism—determining what the consequences of self-talk are besides emotional distress.

### Technique 6. What Is the Worst that Can Happen?

Some students rather dogmatically contend that failing a test is *the worst* thing that could happen. Again referring to Technique 5, the teacher can ask the student to rate the strength of their feelings about failing the test using the scale. Students often will place a finger on 100. Next, the teacher can state an obnoxious event and have the student rate them both. This demonstrates that the seriousness of the student's reactions to the A is only relative to other things that can happen. The following disputation is an example:

DON: This is absolutely the worst thing that can happen to me (pointing to the number 100).

TEACHER: What if you failed all of your classes?

DON: Then it would be off the scale!

TEACHER: That's cheating. You can't go off the scale.

DON: Well, I guess that failing all of my classes would be number 100.

TEACHER: And where would failing only math be located?

DON: Around 80.

TEACHER: And what if you . . .

The teacher can add events that may be more obnoxious to the student in order to relativize the "terribleness" of the original problem.

### Technique 7. All or Nothing

Another technique that may be used to minimize the perceived "terrible" events is to explain to students that it is one's highly individualized particular belief system that causes harmful feelings. "How would 100 people react if they failed this test? Would they be equally upset?" If the students agree that many of the 100 people would react in different ways, it may become evident that what really causes the different reactions is each individual's self-talk about failure.

### Technique 8. Time Projection

Referring back to Technique 1, the teacher can ask the student to imagine "how you think you will feel about this event a week from today." The teacher can further inquire why the harmful emotions will probably subside after a week: "What do you say to yourself during the week?" The purpose of this technique is to actively demonstrate to the student that problems are often caused by catastrophizing immediate events and, over time, the intensity may subside.

### Technique 9. Bad Banana

The teacher asks the students to pretend that they are very hungry. As they unpeel a banana (the only food in town), they find that a small piece on the end of it is bad. What do they do next? Most students will take off the bad piece and still have a pretty good banana. The analogy of what occurs when someone does something "bad" should be presented: Is a person all bad because of one bad incident?

### Technique 10. Bibliotherapy

RET acknowledges the environmental and societal influence of irrational beliefs. For example, students are led to believe through songs, books, and magazine articles that love is the only important need that people must possess. One method of combating this type of "irrational propaganda" is to suggest readings with rational themes, such as self-acceptance, self-discipline, and overcoming past influences. Lesson 28 in Chapter 10 lists some appropriate supplemental RET resources. One excellent book, *A*

*New Guide to Rational Living,* written in layman terms by Ellis and Harper (1975), gives a "self-help" approach to RET. It attempts to clarify RET with such chapter headings as You Feel the Way You Think, Feeling Well by Thinking Straight, How You Create Your Own Feelings, and Thinking Yourself out of Emotional Disturbances.

Music is also an effective tool to illustrate irrational beliefs. Popular songs often contain many thoughts that exemplify irrational notions. These songs can be brought to class and discussed to illustrate how the individuals perceive themselves to be feeling. The songs can also be used when teaching RET as an affective curriculum (see Lesson 27 in Chapter 10).

### Technique 11. Shame Attacks

Many people are overly disturbed because of a fear that other people will disapprove of their actions. The purpose of shame-attacking exercises is to actively demonstrate to the student that, in most instances, few people actually are concerned about the acts of others, and very rarely will these acts result in physical harm. These exercises may be sequential (e.g., for a student who is afraid to date, suggest that he first say "hello" to a girl and then progress) to virtual immersion (e.g., suggesting that the student ask a girl out for a date to a shopping center).

Students and adults are often reluctant to ask peers for a date because they are afraid to be turned down and are equally reluctant to take tests for fear that others will ridicule them if they fail. Shame-attacking exercises illustrate that, even if one is turned down or ridiculed, few harmful effects will result from external sources. Of course, as described above, the individuals may choose to make themselves miserable by down-rating their personhood.

Shame-attacking exercises should be regularly assigned by the teacher. They *should not* interfere with the student's long-term goals, and the student should agree to the assignment. Exercises for students include:

- Calling out the time at a shopping mall
- Wearing silly clothing
- Calling out the floors in an elevator
- Asking 10 peers out for a date
- Deliberately throwing gutterballs in a bowling match
- Bringing a sack lunch to a fast food restaurant
- Going to a movie alone

None of these assignments interfere with classroom or societal rules. In-class assignments, such as raising one's hand three times during class, may also be given. Other in-class assignments include:

Asking one question of another student

Starting a conversation with someone you do not know

Speaking to or greeting verbally two people

Disagreeing with a statement made by a class member

Stating at least one opinion about something being discussed.
(Paris & Casey, 1979, p. 83)

***Sample Disputations.*** Disputations are often used for particular irrational beliefs. As RET educators are exposed to different situations, recall of disputes often becomes a more efficient process. This section presents some verbal disputes for the familiar irrational beliefs that were previously examined. Sample dialogues will be explored, as well as additional disputation methods.

A common and relatively easy irrational belief to dispute is anger. Although having a temper tantrum may be cathartic (feel good), few benefits usually result. People rarely change their behaviors, even when anger is justifiable, except perhaps for short periods of time. Effective disputes, such as the following, attempt to question *why* someone else should behave in the manner that the student demands.

TEACHER: So, you are angry at your teacher?

MOLLY: Yes! She gave me a lousy test.

TEACHER: What was so lousy about it?

MOLLY: There were a lot of unfair questions.

TEACHER: Yes?

MOLLY: Well, teachers shouldn't be unfair!

TEACHER: Why not?

MOLLY: Because they are not supposed to be unfair.

TEACHER: Who says so?

MOLLY: Everyone knows this!

TEACHER: Does this mean that *all* teachers should always be fair?

MOLLY: Yes. That's their job.

TEACHER: Are all teachers fair or, for that matter, are all students, policemen, parents, or principals always fair?

MOLLY: No, they're not! And that's what's wrong with this world!

TEACHER: Does everyone think that all of these people—and your teacher—are unfair?

MOLLY: No, I suppose not.

TEACHER: So these people should be fair only to you all of the time?

MOLLY: No . . .

TEACHER: Are you always fair?

MOLLY: No, but I try to be.

TEACHER: And if you're not fair, should I be very angry with you?

MOLLY: You're trying to confuse me!

TEACHER: Okay, then let me try to summarize. You are angry with your teacher?

MOLLY: Yeah.

TEACHER: And teachers cannot be unfair to you?

MOLLY: Right!

TEACHER: Let us assume that the teacher was unfair to you.

MOLLY: I knew I was right!

TEACHER: And how is getting angry helping you?

MOLLY: What do you mean?

TEACHER: If your teacher was unfair, either by accident or on purpose, is it fairly safe to say that the questions will remain unchanged and you will still fail the test?

MOLLY: Yeah.

TEACHER: Then why be angry about something that is a fact?

MOLLY: Well, it shouldn't be a fact!

TEACHER: But it is. And many times people become upset needlessly over things that they can't change.

MOLLY: So you're saying that I have no right to be angry about this unfair test?

TEACHER: You have a right to feel any way you wish. It seems, however, your *choice* is the real issue. Do you want to remain angry over something that you can't change?

MOLLY: That is kind of stupid, isn't it?

TEACHER: Yes, that is a stupid thought. Many of us sometimes have stupid thoughts, although it hardly makes us stupid. Can you think of other instances in which you become angry about things?

Although the teacher was originally attempting to dispute the student's notion that people can't be unfair, especially to her, the teacher was circling the issue without confronting the student and asking, "Why can't people be unfair?" Unfortunately, unfairness is a part of life and being upset about it rarely changes matters. An effective dispute for people who become extremely upset about events is "Tough Luck!" or "Too Bad!" In other words, "That's the way things are and may remain. Things are tough, but not awful!"

Molly is demanding that her teacher act as she expects. Although it is desirable for the test to be fair, it would be practically impossible for it to be totally "fair" to everyone. The teacher responded in a positive manner when Molly said she was confused. The teacher did not try to dispute the **A,** and instead questioned the utility of being angry. When Molly agreed, the teacher continued the disputation of the belief by asking for other instances of when Molly is angry about things that cannot change. This reinforces the notion that Molly's problem is demanding that people behave in an appropriate manner (according to her definition) rather than one teacher being unfair. Recognizing anger is different from dwelling on it.

Another common irrational belief of students (and teachers) is that of *having* to be competent and achieving in *everything* one attempts. Ellis and Harper (1975) disputed this by suggesting that hardly anyone can be competent in everything and, even if possible, by questioning whether achieving makes someone a better person. The authors argued that, although achievement may bring just rewards, a fanatical devotion to achievement may result in depression or anger if there is failure. This particular "need" may demonstrate a desire to be better than others rather than a desire for self-growth. Effective disputations regarding the need to be competent and achieving, such as the following, expand upon the notion that human beings are fallible and that there are few, if any, superhumans.

KELLY: Well, I understand that it's okay for *others* not to get all "Bs" on their report cards, but I have *my own standards.*

TEACHER: (in an exaggerated manner) Well, thank you for letting us be merely human!

KELLY: What do you mean?

TEACHER: It's okay for *you* to be better than us, but you understand that we slobs can make mistakes.

KELLY: But that's not what I said.

TEACHER: What, then, makes you so special that you have special standards? And, more important, why are those standards so special that you become so miserable when you can't reach those standards?

The teacher is attempting to bring two points into focus: (a) that most human beings are imperfect, and (b) that special standards may be acceptable unless harmful emotions accompany the failure to meet those standards. A frantic need to succeed (e.g., being the first person to complete a test) may create mistakes in communicating information that the student really does know.

Many people who believe that they *must* succeed only attempt tasks at which they feel confident. This practice can severely restrict the experiences to which individuals are exposed, especially if mediocrity is also disdained. Disputing this belief can include the following ideas:

1. He should try to *do,* rather than kill himself trying to *do well.* He should focus on enjoying the process rather than only the *result* of what he does.

2. When he tries to do well, he should try to do so for his own sake rather than to please or to best *others.* He should be artistically and esthetically, rather than merely egotistically, involved in the results of his labors.

3. When, for his own satisfaction, he tries to do well, he should not insist on his always doing *perfectly* well. He should on most occasions strive for *his* best rather than *the* best. (Ellis, 1962, p. 63)

The theme of the above disputes is that it is rational to be concerned about achievement. To be consumed by success, however, is probably irrational because of the harmful emotions that usually accompany failure.

Periodically, students may manipulate the principles of RET, which contend that people are not failures if they do not succeed in everything they attempt. To avoid misinterpretations, the facilitator should stress the concept of responsibility to the student:

TEACHER: What are you doing tonight, Gene?

GENE: I am going to a concert.

TEACHER: But what about your test tomorrow?

GENE: That's okay, man. I'm fallible. I know RET. It's okay if I fail a test or two. That doesn't make me a rotten person!

Gene is ignoring his long-term goals and manipulating the theory of RET to attend the concert. His previously stated goal was to pass the test and, by going to the concert, this goal probably will not be met. RET stresses these long-term goals and is *not* an excuse for "irresponsible" short-term pleasures.

Although anxiety may surface for any number of reasons, it frequently occurs in disturbed and disturbing students prior to taking quizzes or tests. "Test anxiety is generally defined as an inability to think clearly in spite of adequate preparation, and is usually independent of a realistic appraisal of one's ability" (Oliver, 1975, p. 6). Irrational beliefs that may accompany test anxiety are fear of failure, self-downing, perfectionism, need for approval, and low frustration tolerance. Technique 12 can be used to battle negative self-rating, which creates anxiety.

### Technique 12. Loaf of Bread

This is similar to the Bad Banana technique, with a particular focus on minimizing the negative self-rating thinking that creates anxiety. Again, the concept to communicate to the students is that any behavior is only a small indicator of one's essence. For example:

EMILY: I haven't slept well for 2 weeks. I'm really worried about Friday's test.

TEACHER: What exactly are you worried about?

EMILY: I just know it is going to be difficult, and I'll probably fail. Failing would be just intolerable!

TEACHER: Intolerable?

EMILY: Well, probably not intolerable. It would just prove that I'm a dumb jerk.

TEACHER: And failing a test makes you a dumb jerk?

EMILY: Sure, especially since all of my friends get passing grades.

TEACHER: How do you feel when you are a "dumb jerk"?

EMILY: Terrible. I go home and cry. Then I usually get high.

TEACHER: Get high?

EMILY: Yeah. On weed (marijuana).

TEACHER: You mean to tell me that when you do one thing wrong like failing a test, you become a dumb jerk?

EMILY: You said it!

TEACHER: Let's pretend that we just experienced a nuclear holocaust and you were the only person who lived. When you emerged from your shelter, you are starving for food. You find a loaf of bread that has a little piece of mold on the edge. What do you do?

EMILY: Why, I scrape off the mold and eat the rest of the bread.

TEACHER: But doesn't a piece of mold make that whole bread moldy?

EMILY: No, of course not.

TEACHER: Well, if you believe that about bread, why don't you believe it about yourself?

EMILY: What do you mean?

TEACHER: You claim that just because you do one thing wrong, like failing a test, your whole personhood changes into a dumb jerk. Yet, failing that test may be perceived as being a piece of mold.

EMILY: You mean that just because I do one thing wrong, I'm not a moldy bread?

TEACHER: (laughing) I guess that's it. Also, how is worrying to the point of not sleeping helping you study for this test?

EMILY: I guess it's not.

The teacher in the dialogue focused on Emily's self-downing. She attempted to dispute the notion that the feared event, failing a test, will make Emily a dumb jerk. By using an analogy that Emily could understand, the teacher stressed the concept that individuals are complex and that catastrophizing one act into a poor self-rating is probably faulty reasoning. The teacher did not try to change the A by suggesting that Emily probably will pass the test.

Oliver (1975, p. 9) contended that there are two common irrational beliefs that must be disputed with test anxiety: (a) "I have always been anxious when taking tests; therefore I will always be anxious" and (b) "to give up test anxiety means to give up caring about the outcome." The first irrational belief indicates that behavior is predetermined or environmentally determined and is impossible to change. Students may be reminded that, according to the theory of RET, both biological and environmental influences may contribute to behaviors; however, there is no evidence that these influences are causes that cannot be altered. Although changing long patterns of behavior can be stressful, change is possible because behaviors are not fixed. The second irrational belief contends that anxiety must be present in order to achieve. Although some people find anxiety beneficial, the RET educator is concerned with the degree of anxiety that interferes with reaching the long-term goals. The educator should dispute the irrational beliefs that cause extreme worry about the test, so that the student's goals may be effectively reached.

Extreme anxiety or worry is rarely beneficial to students because it may ultimately limit their effectiveness in taking tests. Furthermore, worrying will not ward off the dreaded event and will probably interfere in other facets of life. Finally, anxiety about certain outcomes can decrease individual risk taking, such as in making new friends or enrolling in difficult courses.

Closely related to the latter disputations of test anxiety is the irrational belief that demands the need for approval. Students often behave in a manner that they perceive will generate approval from peers, teachers, and/or parents. Although it is appropriate to care about being approved and to attempt to behave in a manner to gain approval, it is not rational to berate oneself if that approval is not found. Students claim that their feelings can be "hurt" by an uncaring peer. RET theory argues that the only way a student can be hurt is by physical harm. Technique 13 can be used to combat the irrational need for approval.

### Technique 13. Trust Me

One way to combat the self-talk that centers on the need to be accepted by others is to bring to students' attention that they can make decisions about who can influence them. This technique has the teacher making an obvious attempt at fooling a student. The student is reminded that she can make a sensible decision, despite the influence of another person.

KATIE: Fred called me a dumb jerk. I hate him!

TEACHER: What are you feeling right now?

KATIE: Actually, I'm quite sad. How could he call me such a name? I thought he was my friend.

TEACHER: I'm a bit confused. You are sad because your friend called you a dumb jerk?

KATIE: Yes, sad and hurt.

TEACHER: What if I said you were a smart kid?

KATIE: Huh?

TEACHER: Would you believe me if I said you were a smart kid? You seem to believe Fred. Would you believe me?

KATIE: I suppose so . . . But, I also believe Fred!

TEACHER: (taking out an ordinary pencil) This is a magic pencil. I will let you have it for one dollar.

KATIE: NO WAY!

TEACHER: Why not?

KATIE: That's a regular pencil. It's not magic, and it's surely not worth a dollar!

TEACHER: But, I'm telling you it's worth a dollar.

KATIE: Well . . . I don't believe you.

TEACHER: What if Fred agreed with me?

KATIE: I wouldn't believe him either.

TEACHER: Then why would you believe him when he called you a dumb jerk?

KATIE: I don't know.

TEACHER: I don't know either. But I do know that you feel sad because you *chose* to believe him *and* you still have your dollar because you *chose not* to believe me. It is what you choose to believe that makes you unhappy, not merely what other people say to you.

The teacher is actually expanding upon the rhyme "Sticks and stones will break my bones, but names will never hurt me." Instead of lecturing the student, the teacher actively involved the student in the disputation process.

Ellis and Harper (1975) argued that to demand that everyone approve of you is perfectionistic and virtually impossible. They contended that "If you *always* need love, you must always appear distinctly lovable . . ." (p. 92). This would include demanding that people approve of you even when you act, as most people sometimes do, in a bizarre manner. A dispute that I commonly use with students who need to be popular with everyone is, "I'm the type of person who hates those students whom everyone likes. It is impossible for you to get what you want, because when all the other students like you, I won't like you at all! I believe that there's got to be something wrong with you!"

Also, does this dire need suggest general approval or approval for *each* act? In other words, how much love and approval does the individual need, and for how long? Finally, the time and effort needed to win the approval of everyone will certainly prevent most people from being actively involved in their own personal activities. Ellis and Harper (1975) suggested that "When you free yourself from your demands that you receive love, you can better love!" (p. 95).

### Technique 14. Rational Role Reversal

One technique that can be used to generate disputations with students who intellectually argue with the teacher (for the sake of arguing) is rational role reversal (RRR) (Kassinove & DiGiuseppe, 1975). In RRR, the teacher exchanges roles with a student, who is supposed to offer disputations to the "new" student. This method can also be extended through short plays, to be role-played, that are written or dictated by the students involved. A variation of RRR is to ask the students what advice they would give to their friend who had the same problem. This type of perspective taking depersonalizes the problem for the students, perhaps allowing an objective view of the issues involved.

To summarize, the goal of disputation is to help students cognitively and/or behaviorally understand how their thinking and perceptions are causing emotions that prevent them from attaining their goals. The arguments presented above are representative of the many variations that can be used with a group. Disputes may include the following concepts: everyone makes mistakes; no one is perfect; mistakes do not change a person's good qualities; a person is not the same as his or her performance; people are not bad because they make mistakes; people who make mistakes do not deserve to be blamed and punished; and the reason why people make mistakes are (a) lack of skill, (b) carelessness or poor judgment, (c) not having enough information, (d) tiredness or illness, (e) difference of opinion, and (f) irrationality (Bernard & Joyce, 1984, p. 241). To cognitively understand during the group sessions why students are thinking or acting in a disturbed manner is only one facet of RET. The new rational thinking must also be exhibited outside of the comfortable confines of the special education setting. This can be accomplished by exposing the students to the other modes of disputation.

## 12. Practice the Effect

Some students will rarely change behaviors simply because they have suddenly "gotten the point" that their previous beliefs were irrational. For example, some students may understand that it is okay to fail tests (if effort was given), yet will continue to skip classes. The most important component of RET is that of effect (E), or the adoption of new feelings and behaviors that are congruent with rational thinking. This can be accomplished through reinforcers and maintained by continual and then intermittent homework.

Reinforcement techniques should be included when assigning RET work. Rewards such as those described in Chapter 4 may be used. Although students may understand that the homework is beneficial, additional motivators (e.g., check marks, getting to erase the chalkboard) for completing the assignment may prove to be necessary.

Ellis (personal communication, 1981) suggested that aversive consequences can also be quite effective, especially with adults. He had individuals agree to send money or write laudatory letters to obnoxious people or groups if they failed to attempt an assignment.

## 13. Homework

Teachers often tell their students to think about their newfound knowledge "at home tonight" or "when the same crisis occurs." As with *all* homework that the teacher assigns, RET homework must be clearly understood by the student. The teacher should be cautious not to assume that students understand the assignment simply because they can repeat the directions. Homework should be checked as soon as possible after completion. Some examples of homework that will reinforce RET concepts include:

1. Practice of behaviors role played and rehearsed with the practitioners such as verbal assertion and extinction.

2. Writing down upsetting thoughts young clients have during practical problem solving.

3. Trying out alternatives generated during practical problem solving.

4. Asking other people to write down positive things about the young client. This is especially useful for negative clients. (Bernard & Joyce, 1984, p. 255)

Two worksheets (Ellis & Harper, 1975; Zionts, 1983, 1993) have been developed that structure the outside-of-classroom learning. Both of these formats can be periodically assigned, especially following a group session. Zionts's (1993) *Rational-Emotive Education Worksheet–R* typifies the familiar ABC schemata. This form offers a systematic approach for disputing irrational beliefs as soon after the consequence (C) or event (A) as possible (see Figure 9.1). As with homework required in the academic areas, RET homework is assigned and should be followed up by the teacher. This

---

*Consequences*

List an emotional or behavioral consequence that *you* would like to change. Remember this consequence is usually of an overwhelming nature. It is one that is "getting in your way" of meeting your long-term goals.

Describe the nature of the emotion or behavior. What does it *do* to you? How does it affect you?

*Activating, obnoxious, extremely negative event*

Explain the event that contributes to the consequence. If there are *many* events, discuss one of them. Be precise.

*Belief System*

What do you say to yourself during or after the event occurs? (e.g., "He shouldn't be doing that!" or "I respect; he must respect me!")

*Disputation*

What proof exists that your self-talk is true. Provide all evidence.

---

**FIGURE 9.1.** Rational-Emotive Education Worksheet–R.
From *Rational-Emotive Education Worksheet–R* by P. Zionts, 1993, Mt. Pleasant, MI: RETCO. Reprinted with permission.

communicates to the students the importance of working on feelings and behaviors both at home and in the classroom.

Knaus and Wessler (1976) asserted that rational-emotive problem simulation is a technique that "consists of therapists creating conditions in the therapy session similar to those the client ordinarily encounters and finds troublesome in everyday life" (p. 8). Cues and appropriate statements are given to help the student deal with obnoxious stimuli. The student can orally practice these statements and then apply them (see also Camp & Bash, 1981; Meichenbaum, 1977a). As with the written homework forms, this type of assignment may be regularly assigned.

## 14. Working with "Difficult Customers"

Although RET is relatively simple to understand, common problems tend to surface. Some of these problems may be due to what Ellis (personnal communication, 1982) frequently called "difficult customers." Others may be due to a neglect of mutually established goals. Still other problems occur when students believe that behavior and feeling changes should be quick and easy. Walen et al. (1980) labeled this type of impatience as the "it's-not-working" syndrome, which is similar to low frustration tolerance. The students and group should review the concepts of RET. Change is difficult and may be a long and hard process. By working and disputing their irrational belief systems and by adopting a rational philosophy of life, students may develop new patterns of behavior.

Closely related to this problem is that of students becoming very upset if they slip back to their old behaviors. One way to prepare for this eventuality is to ask the students, "What is going to happen the next time you get angry? How soon do you think it will be?" Integral to the philosophy of RET is that human beings are fallible, and being upset because of this fallibility is ensuring the likelihood of emotional disturbance. Instead, when mistakes are made, students should consider them as such and attempt to exhibit the appropriate behaviors.

Another problem occurs when students realize that they *do* feel better after they have a tantrum. They have been taught that such a release may actually be healthy. This ignores the reality that frustrations and problems frequently recur and little resolution may be found in cathartic explosions.

Walen et al. (1980) identified four types of "difficult customers." The *argumentative* students are those who disagree with everything that is said. One technique with these students is to agree with their arguments, "You're right! You are a jerk for doing that! What do *you* think is the way to solve this problem?" The "*yes, but*" students are those who seem to be agreeing with the disputation, but always have a rejoinder. "Yes, but" actually means "no," except the students are trying to blunt the perceived attack. Furthermore, these students may not want to change their behaviors and this could be their means of communicating their reluctance. The *intellectualizing* students attempt to use circuitous arguments to confuse the issue. These students can generate much difficulty in group sessions, especially for the novice RET educator. Homework assignments and disputations are termed by these students as a "waste of time" or "silly." One way to dissuade these students is to refer them back to their previously stated goals of behavior change. Finally, students who are *"intellectually limited"* may be aided by techniques involving rational-emotive imagery (e.g., "drilling" the concepts), rote learning, and cognitive-behavior modification.

Even if students are effectively taught to moderate their emotions, the activating events that originally contributed to their being disturbed may continue. Although RET suggests that, by moderating emotions, students will be able to more effectively change the A, there will be instances in which that will not be possible. Ellis (personal communication, 1981) contended that, if the As are indeed obnoxious facts of life, decisions should be based on the pros and cons of continuing the situation.

## 15. Avoid Common Teaching Errors

RET educators can often be unintentionally disinviting during the group sessions. This disinviting behavior is probably very similar to the manner in which these teachers interact with their students during the entire day (Grieger & Boyd, 1980). Probably the most prevalent error made by RET teachers is lecturing. Some teachers talk too much and do not allow the students to work out their problems for themselves. Students may become passive and actually give little input to the session. Verbal instruction of short duration is fine; however, lengthy diatribes tend to bore students.

Closely related to lecturing is philosophizing. Teachers, especially those who are particularly enamored with RET, tend to extol the virtues of the principles of RET through the use of analogies and abstract theoretical concepts, ignoring the students' needs. Other group communication errors include asking too many questions during too short a time period. The exact nature of the questions may also be troublesome (Walen et al., 1980). Irrelevant ("What's new?"), rhetorical ("Where's that going to get you?"), and "why" questions often impede the smooth flow of the group process.

It is important for the teacher to practice the principles of RET, especially during the sessions. Practice includes remembering that students are fallible and that they will often attempt to be rational and fail. Teachers sometimes demand immediate perfection from both students *and* themselves. RET specifically suggests that the teacher has the right to make errors, *especially during the sessions*. If the session becomes "blocked," the teacher should accept that fact, communicate to the class that "we seem to be stuck," and either ask for help from the students or tell the students that the teacher needs to do homework, refer to references, and tackle the problem again tomorrow.

The novice RET educator may also unintentionally ignore the elegant goals. That is, the session may focus on changing the event or changing the person's feelings. Although these are certainly individual goals, the ultimate goal of RET is to change the belief system that is causing the disturbing feelings about the event.

## Summary and Conclusions

This chapter has focused on techniques for utilizing rational-emotive therapy as a classroom intervention. Some of the unique aspects of RET discussion groups, with regard to communication skills and student interaction, were outlined. The major emphasis was that problem solving is a difficult process and a commitment to "work hard" must be present from both the students and the teacher.

The teacher's role as facilitator also may differ from commonly accepted behaviors. Although no one specific attribute ensures success, the following teacher behaviors seem more effective than others: communicating empathy and warmth, being active-directive, and persistently staying on task (i.e., focusing on the problem). Students may, for the first time in their lives, be taking the responsibility for changing their own feelings and behaviors. They may be attempting new behaviors, being honest, and helping others change their irrational belief systems.

The remainder of the chapter explained the implementation of the ABC process. Techniques for identifying events (A) and understanding the nature of emotional or behavioral consequences (C) were outlined. In RET terms, A and C alone are *not* the student's problem. Identifying the irrational belief system will expose the self-talk that is causing the disturbance. Furthermore, integral to elegant RET is the disputation or restructuring of this irrational belief system. This allows the student to explore in a rational manner other conflicts that may be encountered. Specific techniques for the identification and disputation process included sample dialogues, common disputations, individual RET activity forms, and RET bibliotherapy. Next, the need was discussed for reinforcement to ensure that students' newfound knowledge regarding the reasons for their disturbance are acted upon. This is the effect (E) of the ABC process. Finally, methods of working with problem students or "difficult customers" were presented. These techniques, coupled with some relatively common teacher errors, may help to prevent early implementation difficulties.

# 10

# Rational-Emotive Therapy as a Mental Health Curriculum

The focus of Unit 3, thus far, has been on the theory of RET and its use as a classroom counseling intervention. This chapter presents lessons that can be used to teach the concepts of RET. The lessons are not intended to be comprehensive; other resources are recommended so that teachers can have access to a well-rounded rational mental health curriculum. Teaching RET in this manner leaves the decision to the students whether to adopt its philosophy and principles. The exercises presented in this chapter are only a sampling of the many available to reinforce the theory of RET. In fact, during the past two decades, a variety of texts have been published that provide examples of RET lessons (Anderson, 1981; Gerald & Eyman, 1981; Knaus, 1974; Vernon, 1989a, 1989b). However, an extensive knowledge and possibly RET training seem necessary if the educator chooses to use many of these texts. The purpose of this chapter is to provide teachers a more structured foundation from which to work.

Another benefit of RET lesson plans is that they provide "RET readiness" skills to students who are not developmentally ready, either cognitively or affectively, for RET counseling. DiGiuseppe (1990) contended that, although rehearsal of self-instructional statements and social skills training is appropriate for these students, they also need to learn about their thoughts and feelings.

Whereas Chapter 7 on the application of moral development specifically delineated exercises as having grade-level equivalents, this chapter views the understanding of RET as having developmental sequence.

Bernard and Joyce (1984) provided an excellent outline of concepts that would teach the content of RET (see Appendix 10.1).

Because of space limitations, the lessons provided in this chapter progress from (a) an introduction to RET to (b) the ability to identify and understand feelings to (c) an awareness that feelings are a result of beliefs regarding events to (d) recognizing the total RET process that includes both theory and techniques.

# Step 1: Introduction to the RET Process

It has been well documented that the use of anticipatory sets can motivate students to learn. Although the teacher's excitement about RET can serve this purpose, a "challenge" lesson such as the one presented by Gerald and Eyman (1981, pp. 1–4) can create much interest. The story of Ralph the Ram, presented in Lesson 1, allows students to see that people have different opinions about "facts." The elaborations of Gerald and Eyman's exercise provides the opportunity for active class participation.

### Lesson 1. The Fable of Ralph Ram

In this fable, eleven characters hear Ralph Ram say the same thing at the same time, but they respond with eleven different ways of thinking and feeling.

Ralph Ram was shouting at the flock: "It's time for us to take a stand on our two hind hoofs. Why should we follow the flock all the time? We're tired of it. We need something more than the boring life of a barnyard sheep—more than following the same old paths around the farm with the shepherd watching everything we do and the dog nipping at our heels all the time. We want freedom to roam, to explore, to experience. We want to know life the way a snake, a fox, a moth, a bat, a gnu knows it!"

"Baa-a-a-a-n that ram!" one sheep yelled.

"Baa-a-a-a-ck him up!" others shouted.

"Are you sheep or are you lemmings?" Ralph asked.

A hush fell over the flock. All the sheep—rams and ewes alike—considered what Ralph had said. Some spoke out loud about their *thoughts* and *feelings*. Others talked silently to themselves, like Great-Grandma Sheep. She said to herself, "That young whippersnapper is something else. He thinks he's the only one who ever came up with an original idea. I had those same radical thoughts thirty years ago. But I found out mighty soon they wouldn't work. They couldn't work then and they won't work now." She felt *superior*.

Brother Sheep shouted, "Wow, hey sheep, what's happening? We finally got a brother who got enough horns to say what's got to be said. Animals of the farm unite! Brave Ralph Ram, you are my main Ram!" He felt *excited*.

May Ewe thought, "That Ralph's just the most handsome and intelligent young sheep I've ever met. Every word he says makes my wool curl up real tight." She decided she was feeling *love*.

Shirley Sheep, Ralph's mother, mused, "I don't quite understand what my Ralphie is saying or what it all means for us sheep, but he's my son and I'm for him and everyone's listening to him." She felt *proud*.

Waldo Ram told himself, "Ralph's a nice guy but he sure is naive. The people that run this place will make lamb chops out of him. Forget it! I'm on good terms with the shepherd and I plan to keep things that way." He felt *aloof*.

Cherie Sheep had been deep in thought. Now she said out loud, "That Ralph, he's so good. He's always willing to take a stand even if people make fun of him—even if there's danger! But why is it necessary to take such risks? Oh, why can't the world be different?" She felt *sad*.

Other farm creatures heard Ralph's words and had their own reactions.

Gene the Shepherd thought to himself, "This sheep is a wise guy. Why did I ever get into this kind of work? I should've listened to my father and been a windmill repairman." He felt *miserable*.

Gilbert Fox, lying quietly in his lair, thought, "What a fool that sheep is! This is finer than my fondest dreams . . . silly, defenseless sheep roaming alone through the countryside waiting—no, begging—to be picked off one by one." He felt *thrilled*.

Connie Collie sighed, "Oh, boy! Just when I've got all the strays in line, this troublemaker comes along to ruin the whole plan. If I can't keep these sheep under my paw, I'll lose my job." She felt *disgusted*.

Syd Citizen proclaimed, "What? Sheep on the loose? In our community? Why, before long, sheep will be shedding everywhere. They'll stop traffic. They'll tramp on the flowers. We won't be able to control anything. The place will never be the same!" He felt *afraid*.

Golda Goat jumped for joy as she said, "It's about time! I left the herd years ago and I never could understand how those sheep could stay in line. Maybe now I can teach them a thing or two about independence." She felt *smug*.

Well, there it is. You've read the fable. Do you see Ralph as a whippersnapper? brave? intelligent? handsome? naive? good? a wise guy? a fool? a troublemaker? something else? All of those words were used in the story to tell what Ralph "is." But they are merely opinions. They may be biased and some (e.g., intelligent and a fool) are outright contradictions. The only thing we know for sure about Ralph from this fable is that he's a ram who tells the sheep in his flock to take a stand for independence. What Ralph does can be observed by everyone. What Ralph "is" remains a matter of opinion.

What caused Brother Sheep's excitement? Waldo Ram's aloofness? Connie Collie's disgust? Each of them very likely would say, "Ralph Ram and what he said." But how could that be true, when Ralph Ram spoke and acted the same way for everyone to hear and see? Something else was happening because, when each character saw Ralph and heard what he said, each had a very different reaction. Each felt a different emotion ranging from love and pride to fear and misery.

Why?

Because all of the animals and people told themselves something different, and this something that they told themselves—a thought or belief—caused the various feelings to occur. Suppose May Ewe told herself, "This sheep is a wise guy." Or said, "He'll get us all into trouble and that will be just terrible and I can't stand it!" Instead of falling in love with Ralph Ram, she might feel terror—even though everything Ralph Ram said and did remained the same. The only different thing would have been what May Ewe told herself.

What you tell yourself affects your feelings. You can make yourself happy. You can make yourself angry or sad.

# Step 2: The Ability to Identify and Understand Feelings

Before an educational plan for implementing RET is utilized, it is recommended that special educators determine if their students have a clear understanding of the definition of "feelings" as it pertains to RET. Feeling is an abstract term that may be confusing to many people. Adults, in fact, are often at a loss to express how they feel. Lessons 2, 3, and 4 will help students understand RET vocabulary and explore their feelings.

### Lesson 2. Developing a RET Vocabulary

Vocabulary lists can include terms of feeling such as *angry, happy, proud, scared, embarrassed, nervous, guilty, sad, anxious, grumpy, disappointed, hurt, curious, upset, frustrated, shocked,* and *apathetic.* These feelings may be defined through brainstorming, role-playing, poetry, and bibliotherapy. One familiar technique is to have the students periodically complete statements such as the following:

I feel . . .

I get angry when . . .

Whenever my mother . . . , I get upset.

When I am alone in the house, I feel . . . .

A variation of this exercise is to have three faces (see Figure 10.1) exhibiting positive, neutral, and negative feelings from which the student may choose the appropriate feeling.

Some students may continue to have difficulty understanding these concepts. An additional approach would be to differentiate between feelings as they relate to the senses and as they relate to emotions. Exercises

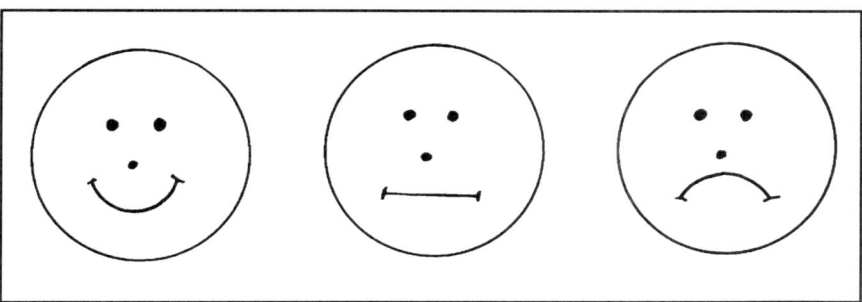

**FIGURE 10.1.** "Feelings" faces: positive, neutral, and negative.

illustrating senses (smell, touch, sight, etc.) could be presented and discussed. For example, the notion of physical pain can be examined using pictures exhibiting injured people as well as some causes of pain (matches, glass, getting fingers caught in a door, etc.). Other types of physical pain such as headaches can also be discussed. These concepts should be clearly taught in a step-by-step sequence.

Upon completion of these exercises, the teacher should introduce the concept of feelings as emotions. Pictures from magazines can be used for students to identify such feelings as happy, sad, and angry. The students can explain to the group why they believe the labeled feeling is appropriate for each picture. This allows them to form judgments, share their thoughts with their peers, and become aware of the feelings of others.

### Lesson 3. Exploring Different Feelings

The purpose of this lesson is to help students recognize that there are many feelings and words that may be used to describe feelings that they have or that they might see others experiencing. When given a picture, the students will label an emotion that the character (or scene) demonstrates. The students will be given alternative possibilities that are also acceptable.

**ACTIVITY 1.** The teacher discusses with the students a variety of "feeling" vocabulary words and their (possible) meanings. Suggested words include *pleased, discouraged, cheerful, upset, lively, glad, jealous, bored, curious, frustrated, nervous, silly, grumpy, frightened, embarrassed, lazy,* and *proud*. The teacher then asks, "Can anyone define or act out one of the feeling words I've written on the board?" and "How easy is it to determine what a person is feeling? Do we all have the same definitions of a particular feeling?"

**ACTIVITY 2.** The teacher distributes several magazines to each group of four to five students and instructs them to find pictures in the magazine that represent at least 10 feeling words that they know. Each picture should have a feeling word neatly attached to it (using glue or tape). The students then prepare a collage of the pictures, which they share with and explain to the class. The teacher should accept any picture as long as the students can give reasoning for their choice (e.g., a picture of a child in a dark room may be used to represent *frightened*).

For homework, the students can retrieve two pictures from home or from magazines borrowed from the classroom and label them with two different feelings. They can provide written or verbal explanations of how the different feelings might occur.

A variation of this exercise is for the teacher to give all groups (or individuals) the same pictures to develop their own descriptions of feelings. A comparison of the collages might follow. Another variation is for the teacher to present one of the pictures and ask students to write a short story that would explain the person's feelings. The teacher may need to begin the story to get the students started (Zionts, 1992b).

### Lesson 4. Feelings Charades

In this exercise, each student is requested to exhibit a particular feeling, and classmates attempt to correctly identify the feeling. Usually, students guess different feelings from the one being demonstrated, reinforcing the RET notion that it is very difficult to accurately perceive events.

Understanding the varying *degrees of emotions* is also a crucial aspect of RET. This exercise allows students to explore the different emotive meanings inherent in particular feelings. The teacher asks small groups of students to explore the words that describe degrees of a certain feeling. Each group makes up a chart that shows several different emotions in at least three degrees, such as the following:

| First degree | Second degree | Third degree |
| --- | --- | --- |
| frightened | panic-striken | terrified |
| irritated | provoked | aggravated |
| contented | relaxed | drowsy |
| happy | delighted | ecstatic |

Responses will vary from group to group. Not all students will have the same vocabulary development, and not all students will choose the same words for different degrees. The teacher should encourage their differences. Students also can be asked to discover the words authors use to indicate different degrees of emotions in order to create the moods of a story (Castillo, 1978, pp. 207–208).

In summary, a prerequisite to understanding the theory of RET is an understanding of the concept of feelings. The exercises presented are only a limited sample of the affective curricula that enable students to explore feelings.

# Step 3: Feelings Are the Result of Beliefs About Events

Integral to RET is the notion that feelings are relative phenomena. The purpose of the following exercises is to demonstrate to students that events may be interpreted differently by people, and that the personal reactions, not the event itself, cause the disturbance. Many of the activities in this chapter have been field tested and can be integrated into the general classroom. Not only do these activities address RET concepts, but they also involve language arts, social studies, science, and mathematics (Zionts, 1992c).

The theory of RET supports the belief that people distress themselves because of their inability to view a situation in a reality-based manner. Some people cannot distinguish between a fact (something that can be verified by others) and an opinion (something that might result in different evaluations by different people). Also, emotional problems are caused by one's internal philosophies or belief systems. These belief systems can be found by examining what people are actually saying to themselves (or thinking) about negative events. Lessons 5 through 18 illustrate that many "facts" are indeed "opinions," and are designed to help individuals identify the types of thinking that can cause harmful feelings or behaviors.

### Lesson 5. The Difference Between Facts and Opinions

The purpose of this exercise is to help individuals understand the difference between facts and opinions. First, the teacher should give the students definitions of the term *fact,* using a dictionary definition such as the following: something that has actual existence; an actual occurrence; and a piece of information having objective reality. In other words, people can see a fact and agree upon its presence. Next, the teacher defines the term *opinion:* a view, judgment, or appraisal formed in the mind about a particular matter. Other words that are similar in meaning are *conviction, belief,* and *sentiment.* The teacher can explain how some people perceive their beliefs to be facts, yet because of differences from beliefs of others, they are in actuality opinions. A belief that is widely held, such as opposition to murder, is only an opinion because other people and cultures believe murder can be appropriate.

Then the students and teacher should brainstorm facts and opinions. Such concepts as friendly, mean, and grouchy are merely opinions, and such concepts as height, weight, points scored on a test, hair color, and names are facts. For example, I weigh 180 pounds. Am I fat or thin? It depends on your values and maybe whether I am sitting next to somebody who weighs 300 pounds!

After the discussion, the teacher can ask students to identify the following sentences as facts (f) or opinions (o).

1. Marie is a girl. (f)
2. Marie is pretty. (o)
3. Marie was born in 1975. (f)
4. Marie is intelligent. (o)
5. Marie is young. (o)
6. Marie is not very good in math. (o)
7. Girls are not very good in math. (o)
8. Marie weighs 100 pounds. (f)
9. Marie is a good dancer. (o)
10. Girls are good dancers. (o)

For homework, the teacher may assign students to write two facts and two opinions about themselves.

### Lesson 6. That's a Fact!

The purpose of this exercise is to help individuals understand that people may have different feelings when experiencing the same event. The students are asked to identify a variety of feelings that might result from being exposed to different events. It is recommended that this lesson be presented over a period of days so that this concept can be reinforced.

The teacher begins by discussing the concept that events are facts, yet peoples' reactions to them are opinions. For example, "This test has 20 questions on each of the chapters" is a fact; how one feels about that fact is an opinion. A movie is a series of facts, yet some people like what happened and others may not. Theses perceptions result in differing feelings as well.

Next, the teacher presents different events to the students and asks the students to react to them. The teacher may want to have students write or talk about reactions, or have them discuss briefly in pairs before sharing with the group. If there is little trust in the group, the teacher may want to have students hypothesize how and why "others" might feel. One possible topic is the assassination of Martin Luther King, Jr. The students can describe how they think various people felt (civil rights leaders, racists, etc.).

Then the teacher arranges the following events and asks the students to list at least two possible responses. Experiencing and responding to these events will have more powerful results than simply discussing them.

1. Have somebody run in and out of the class with a mask, generally disrupting things. Ask the group to report what happened and how they felt.

2. Act angry about their poor achievement.

3. On the day of a test, tell the students that you did not have time to prepare it and that it is rescheduled for next week.
4. Give students a surprise quiz on information that you have not yet discussed.

For homework, the students can be asked to list one event per day in a journal. Days or weeks after they have recorded their feelings about the events, the teacher can ask them how they feel about those same events. The feelings will probably be different (Zionts, 1992).

### Lesson 7. Perceived Reality Versus Objective Reality

This lesson is a short example of how people may sometimes inaccurately perceive stimuli that seem relatively simple to understand. The teacher asks the students to memorize the following expressions as quickly as possible:

| A bird | is worth | A stitch in |
| in the | two in | in time |
| the hand | in the bush. | saves nine. |

When they are confident that they know them, the teacher covers the expressions with a piece of paper. Many students, in their haste, will ignore the words that are repeated, even though they are "sure" they know the answer. The teacher can address the fact that these students may, in fact, be changing the reality to fit their own sense of order, or "the way they think it *should be.*"

### Lesson 8. Sifting Facts from Opinions

Sifting facts from opinions reinforces the idea that it is extremely difficult to differentiate between confirmable reality (fact) and perceived reality (opinion). Ask the students to read the following passage and respond to the statements:

On Tuesday, October 9th, I got a call from Lorraine Callahan inviting me to a party at her house the following Saturday. I didn't really want to go, so I told her I was busy. On Thursday I ran into Willie Mason at the Country Corner Shopping Center and he asked me if I wanted to go to a party with him. I said I did but I didn't get any details because he had to leave. When he called me Saturday morning, he told me that the party was at the house of someone he had just met and he couldn't remember her name. When we got there, it turned out to be Lorraine Callahan's.

Now, read each of the following statements. If you are absolutely sure a statement is true, circle the T. If you are absolutely sure it is false, circle the F. Otherwise circle the question mark (?).

? T F 1. The person speaking is female.
? T F 2. Lorraine and the person speaking are good friends.

? T F   3. Lorraine was planning a big party.
? T F   4. The person speaking doesn't like Lorraine.
? T F   5. Lorraine's parties are dull.
? T F   6. Lorraine is a teenager.
? T F   7. The person speaking is honest.
? T F   8. The person speaking said (s)he didn't want to go to the party.
? T F   9. The person speaking had planned to do something on Saturday.
? T F  10. Willie Mason and the person speaking often go shopping.
? T F  11. Willie Mason is male.
? T F  12. There are often parties at Lorraine Callahan's.
? T F  13. The person speaking likes parties.
? T F  14. Willie was shopping when the person speaking met Willie.
? T F  15. Willie invited him or her to a party.
? T F  16. Willie is always in a hurry.
? T F  17. The person speaking accepted the invitation.
? T F  18. Willie and Lorraine had just met.
? T F  19. The person speaking and Willie went to the party together.
? T F  20. The person speaking was surprised and embarrassed to see Lorraine.

The teacher then says the following: Here are the correct answers. 1. ?, 2. ?, 3. ?, 4. ?, 5. ?, 6. ?, 7. ?, 8. T, 9. ?, 10. ?, 11. T, 12. ?, 13. ?, 14. ?, 15. T, 16. ?, 17. T, 18. ?, 19. ?, 20. ? Some of you are probably confused now. You may have been *SURE* that number 7 was false. After all, the person speaking did not tell Lorraine the truth. But all we can say for sure is that the person speaking did not communicate honestly in this situation. A little clearer? Now, look back over the story and see if you can decide why the correct answers were as I gave them. Discuss them with your classmates.

1. ? Maybe. Maybe not. We can't be sure.
2. ? Same as number 1.
3. ? Same as number 1.
4. ? Same as number 1. Maybe (s)he likes Lorraine, but just doesn't want to go to this party.
5. ? Same as number 1.
6. ? Same as number 1.
7. ? Same as number 1.
8. True. The person speaking said it.
9. ? The speaker said so, but whether (s)he did or not is unknown.
10. ? Same as number 1.
11. True. The story says "he had to leave."
12. ? Same as number 1.
13. ? Same as number 1.
14. ? Same as number 1. Maybe he was working there.
15. True.
16. ? Same as number 1.

17. True.
18. ? We know that Willie said it, but do we know that it is true?
19. ? Same as number 1. They both got there, but did they go together?
20. ? Same as number 1.

Hopefully, upon completion of this exercise, the students will be able to understand that events are not always what they seem to be (Gerald & Eyman, 1981, pp. 15–16).

### Lesson 9. InterpRETations of Events

This is another exercise designed to generate different answers to the same questions. The teacher shows students pictures of scenes depicting children in different situations. For example, one picture may be of a child holding a baseball bat with a broken window in the background. The teacher asks the students what happened in the picture. Students can either write a story or give their answers orally. The students then talk about the stories and discuss how the interpretations differ. Next, the students can compare the feelings they had when they saw the broken window with the possible feelings of the owners of the window. The teacher stresses that the different feelings are the result of the same event.

### Lesson 10. Feelings Thermometer

This technique, which was used in Chapter 9 as a counseling technique, can also be used to illustrate the fact that people react to events in different ways and that the same event can be positively or negatively perceived. By recognizing this occurrence, students can challenge their irrational thoughts of externally caused misery.

The teacher provides each student with two paper "thermometers" that show the ranges of several emotions and can have the "temperature" adjusted by the student. The students are asked to show what degree of emotion they would feel based on an event the teacher reads from a pile of situation cards. Cards may include such events as:

- Your sister wants to watch [a popular show] on television.
- You have to take a week off from school to go to Florida with your family.
- The teacher didn't call on you.
- You must go visit your grandpa.
- Your allowance has been changed to 50 cents a week.

The teacher emphasizes the fact that each person has different opinions about "positive" and "negative" events. Students with opposite responses can be asked to explain why they selected their "degree" on their thermometers.

Closely related to the misinterpretation of events is the irrational belief that other people can cause the unhappiness of others. Lessons 11 and 12, adapted from Gerald and Eyman (1981), examine the literal translations of statements that students claim can cause "hurt" feelings.

### Lesson 11. Who Causes Your Feelings?

The teacher asks the students to translate the following statements into far-fetched but accurate ones:

He really upsets me.

She makes me angry.

My mother makes me feel very guilty.

I can't go to school because of that teacher.

Every time I'm with my sister she makes me so depressed I can't eat.

My friend Geri really makes me laugh.

You made me love you.

I can't stand him.

She makes me feel like a nobody.

My girlfriend makes me feel like a real man.

Did any of those statements stump you? (Gerald & Eyman, 1981, pp. 58–59)

Next, the teacher presents the students with some "good news" and "bad news" and asks the students to complete each sentence by describing a condition or set of conditions that could explain why they are glad and not upset about the stated fact.

1. I came in last in the race and I'm glad because _____.

2. I got a cold and I'm really glad because _____.

3. I have no money, nowhere to go, and nothing to do this evening and I'm glad because _____.

4. The utilities company turned off our electricity and gas and I'm glad because _____.

5. My best friend moved a thousand miles away and I'm glad because _____.

6. It's pouring outside and we're home alone. Our TV is broken, someone stole our radio, our record player doesn't work, the library is closed, all of our games are in school, the phone is out

of order, the newspaper company is on strike, the dog chewed up all of our magazines, we've read every one of our books, and I'm really glad because _____.

Next, the students are asked to complete each of the following sentences by describing a condition or set of conditions that could explain why they feel sad and not pleased about the stated fact.

1. I received the highest grade in my geography test and I'm sad because _____.

2. I won the grand prize in the sweepstakes contest and I'm sad because _____.

3. I was asked to go to the party with the most popular boy (or girl) in the school and I'm sad because _____.

4. I earn a very good income, own two expensive cars, have a twelve-room mansion, and am sad because _____.

5. My picture and a very nice story about me appeared in the city newspaper today and I'm sad because _____.

6. My sister just had a baby and I'm sad because _____.

Perhaps students find it a little clearer now that they have the ability to control what they feel (Gerald & Eyman, 1981, pp. 59–60).

### Lesson 12. The Feelings Hurters: Killer Statements

This exercise is a variation of the concept illustrated in Gerald and Eyman's (1981) Who Causes Your Feelings? Killer statements may be made by peers, parents, or teachers and, whatever the intention of the speaker, may result in hurt feelings (note the similarity between these statements and those of the uninviting teacher described in Chapter 2). Examples of killer statements are:

You gotta be kidding!

Are you serious?

Do you know how difficult that is going to be?

Students can brainstorm all of the killer statements that they know. Next, the teacher can ask them to keep a 24-hour journal of all of the killer statements that they hear.

### Lesson 13. Make Me

This activity, created by Castillo (1978), helps illustrate the real and imagined influence that people think others have on them. The lesson is designed to help clarify the roles of responsibility within a classroom. If the teacher has a drained, heavy feeling after being with the class for only an hour and feels as if he or she has been trying to push a huge boulder up a steep hill, a game of "Make Me" may ease the tension.

The teacher asks, "What do I make you do?" and lists all the students' responses on the blackboard so that everyone can see the list. The teacher must not judge the responses or start justifying behavior. Once the list is complete, and it may be enormous, the teacher sits with the group and everybody looks at the list. Although nothing may seem to be happening, the teacher must wait. The following is an example of what could happen:

One boy, Jeff, begins to chuckle. Others join in. Soon most of the group is laughing and shaking their heads. With such a list in front of them, everyone sees how absurd it is to expect one person to make them do all those things. Jeff then goes to the blackboard, takes the eraser, and says, "I said you make me do this but I can really do it for myself, so I'll take it off." He then erases his own statement and returns to his seat. Another student follows his example. In each case the student says, "I can take this." At the end some things remain on the board. The class then talks together about how to help the student who still feels there are certain things he or she has to be "made" to do. Each student then offers what he or she feels he or she can realistically do to help out in those situations. One girl leaves her statement, "You make me do spelling." Another student offers to give her advance notice that it is going to be time to work on spelling so she can be prepared. The boy who sits next to her says he will get the materials needed for both of them, and then continues by saying, "You'll just have to do the rest yourself!" (Castillo, 1978, pp. 99–100).

### Lesson 14. The Shoulds of Society

This lesson teaches that many common irrational beliefs are promoted by society. Perhaps the most guilty party of propagandizing "shoulds" is advertising in the media. For example, Madison Avenue commercials contend that everyone should use deodorants to be popular or wear a particular pair of blue jeans to attract the opposite sex.

The teacher asks the students to list each commercial observed during an hour of television viewing and list the message that is being communicated. This exercise can also be done using the radio or teen magazines, or a teacher-prepared videotape or audiotape for the entire class to analyze.

### Lesson 15. Catastrophizing or Awfulizing

This exercise aids the students in understanding their tendency to exaggerate their perceptions of events. The students are asked to describe briefly situations that they consider unpleasant. Each student lists 10 unpleasant things and ranks them from *most unpleasant* to *least unpleasant*. (The lists might include statements such as the following:

going to the dentist, not being able to own a dog, not passing the fifth grade, sleeping in the dark, being punished by Dad, not being allowed to ride my bike, having to stay in on Saturdays, not having enough food packed in my lunch, having to stay in class while everyone is in the schoolyard, taking a test.)

To emphasize that people have different opinions about what is unpleasant and that people may rate the same situations differently, the teacher may want to have students exchange papers a few times to read each other's lists, or may call on a few students to read their lists aloud. After a reasonable sample has been read, the teacher asks the students if any of them had identical lists in the same order and why they think their lists were not the same.

The teacher chooses a few items that appear on several lists and asks the students to expand on their statements about these items. Responses are likely to vary:

1. I don't like going to the dentist. Sometimes I have to have fillings and it hurts. I wish I didn't have to go at all.

2. I can't stand going to the dentist. It might hurt. I'd rather let my teeth rot and fall out.

3. Going to the dentist is awful. I'd rather be dead than have a dental checkup.

4. Not being able to have a puppy is a disappointment. Mom says that the apartment doesn't permit them. I wish we could move.

5. Not having a puppy is terrible. I can't stand the idea that some children can have them and I can't.

6. Not having a puppy is worse than having no friends. It's terrible to be without a dog.

The teacher should draw attention to the similar unpleasant situations. In the above examples, the first three items have the same unpleasant situation, as do the last three items. What is different about the related unpleasant situations (the way they are viewed, the statements made about them)? Which of the statements show that the unpleasant situation has been accepted and that the individual has upset himself or herself about it? (In the above examples, 1 and 4.) If the students have written the statements on paper, the teacher can have them underline words such as *awful, can't stand,* and *terrible;* if the statements are on the board, the teacher can underline these words. Then the teacher reminds the class that the unpleasant situations were a matter of opinion—some people agreed and some people disagreed; neither were right or wrong.

The teacher asks for a definition of an unsound or irrational assumption. Then the teacher explains that the words *awful, terrible,* and *can't stand* are based on irrational assumptions, and that by telling oneself that something is terrible or awful, the person is taking for granted that the situation is *awful.* The teacher tells the class that the tendency to think of things as terrible, awful, or something the person cannot stand is called "awfulizing" (or catastrophizing, depending on age and maturity level).

To show the students that some situations may actually be disastrous, the teacher needs to discuss major catastrophes. The teacher can begin by asking the class what are man's basic needs (food, clothing, shelter, some kind of stimulation). The students can be asked to give examples of incidents they have viewed on TV in which people were victims of starvation, violent crimes, war, or natural catastrophes such as floods and volcanoes. The teacher establishes the fact that, in the examples given, people were deprived of their basic needs or their right to live; these are highly unfortunate incidents or catastrophes.

Then the teacher asks the students to think about ways to challenge their irrational beliefs that some unpleasant situations are awful or terrible catastrophes. One useful technique is to have them diagram an ABCD or HTFR (see Lessons 10.19 and 10.20) on one of the examples used that clearly contained irrational assumptions about "awfulness." Each student can do two diagrams: one as the person who actually had those ideas and one as a person who had a more realistic outlook. The teacher than calls on students to read the two diagrams aloud or write them on the board. While going over the diagrams, the teacher emphasizes that the challenging questions are "*What* is really that awful about this situation" and "*Who* is making it awful?" (Knaus, 1974, pp. 52–53).

### Lesson 16. I Yam What I Yam and That's All That I Yam!

One of the most difficult of the irrational beliefs for students to dispute is the constant rating of oneself. RET argues that it is very difficult, if not impossible, for one to accurately rate oneself. The purpose of this exercise is to have the students rate everything they can about themselves. Almost every student will omit some categories, such as interpersonal relationships with significant and insignificant others, their many roles, and their beliefs about their physical attributes. The teacher should promote discussion regarding not only the accuracy of the ratings, but also the amount of time necessary to begin assessing oneself.

### Lesson 17. It's Awful! It's Terrible! How Horrible!

The purpose of this lesson is to help individuals identify and understand how the three words *awful, terrible,* and *horrible* can contribute to negative feelings. The teacher writes the three words on the board and asks the students to generate (by brainstorming) definitions for each. As students talk, the teacher writes on a paper any personal anecdotes that may surface, but does not put them on the board. Next, the teacher asks the students to find these words in the dictionary and to compare the dictionary definitions with their definitions. For example, the word *awful* is defined as "filled with awe" or "extremely disagreeable or objectionable." Is that the definition that the class can agree upon? (This activity is designed to arrive at a common definition. The teacher should prevent the class from making the task more difficult by going off on tangents; hence, the writing down of different experiences.)

The next task is to have students share experiences or simply give statements that are awful, horrible, or terrible. The teacher may use those from the list generated in the activity described in the previous paragraph. Then the students role-play how they felt or would feel if they said those statements. The teacher asks the students if their true feelings are clearly communicated by what they said. For example, is it truly awful that they failed the test? The students then role-play the same event with a different word, such as "disappointing" ("I am disappointed that I failed the test" rather than "It is awful that I failed the test"). The class discusses how different feelings evolve from different choices of words. (If some students argue that "It is awful to fail a test," the teacher should accept their input. If the students have completed the facts versus opinions exercises, the teacher should gently ask the student if that awfulness is a "fact" or "opinion.") Again, the teacher should keep the students focused on this lesson by asking questions such as "Does one feel less 'awful' if one uses the word disappointed?" "Can these words make us feel worse?"

The teacher then asks students to list under the headings "awful," "terrible," and "horrible" words that are less extreme. Rather than approving their choices on questionable answers, the teacher should have them role-play what they mean. They may choose an extreme word "distressing" but actually mean "disappointing." After the role-play, the teacher should claim to better understand what the student meant, but explain that the common usage of "distressing" is much more serious.

For homework, the teacher can give students a sentence containing the word "awful," "horrible," or "terrible" and have them write a sentence expressing a different feeling. Alternatively, students can be asked to bring in magazine pictures of "awful" and "not-so-awful," which can also be used to reinforce facts versus opinions (Zionts, 1992e).

### Lesson 18. Tolerating Frustration

Created by Vernon (1989b, p. 127), this lesson was developed to teach students techniques for tolerating frustration. First, the teacher asks the students to explain the meaning of *frustration* ("a sense of dissatisfaction resulting from unresolved problems or unfulfilled needs") and to identify in writing two examples of things that are or have been frustrating to them. Examples include learning to do something new, trying out but not making a team, struggling with difficult homework assignments, and having a conflict of interest with parents or friends. After the students share their examples, the teacher introduces the idea of using *self-talk* to deal with frustration. The teacher might say, for example, "If you are learning to do something new, you can tell yourself you can't expect to know how to do it the first time and that doing it doesn't have to be easy. In trying out but not making a team, you can tell yourself that not being chosen doesn't mean you are no good, that not everyone makes it, or that maybe it's better to try and not make it than not to try at all."

Students then are paired up to discuss self-talk that they could use to deal more effectively with their own frustrating situations. They share examples with the larger group.

The teacher can then promote discussion by asking the following questions:

1. What is self-talk? How does it apply to frustration?
2. Do you ever experience frustration? Under what kinds of circumstances?
3. Have you ever used self-talk in dealing with your own frustrations? If so, how did it work?
4. Does it seem useful to apply self-talk to your frustrating situations? If so, do you anticipate any problems in executing the process? What do you think will be the result?

Self-talk is an essential tool for dealing with frustration. Emphasizing the irrational beliefs that underlie frustrating situations will help students begin to ask the challenging questions needed to cope.

In summary, the examples in Step 3 attempt to actively demonstrate to the students that most perceptions of events are relative to the individual student. If a student becomes disturbed about an event, these exercises (and RET) suggest that it is because the student chooses to be disturbed. Again, they are merely representative of the types of lessons that could be generated.

# Step 4: Recognizing the Total RET Process That Includes Both Theory and Technique

The final step in the RET curriculum is to demonstrate the ability to personally utilize RET as a preventative mental health alternative. This can be accomplished through a variety of methods, such as the teaching of ABC theory, creative writing, debates, song and poem composing, and bibliotherapy. The ABC theory, including the irrational beliefs and the RET buzzwords as presented in Chapters 8 and 9, can be taught to the students.

This step teaches students that it is necessary to understand fully one's problems before it is possible to begin to work on them. Many times problem solving is attempted in a rather haphazard manner. The following lessons teach students how to more fully understand the breadth of the problem.

### Lesson 19. Knowing Your ABCs

The goal of this lesson is to help students understand the three components of a problem. When given a problem (or potential problem), students will learn to attach statements and feelings to the appropriate categories.

**ACTIVITY 1.** On a chalkboard, the teacher writes the letters A, B, and C as headings of three columns. Then the teacher says: Today, I am going to explain a way to more clearly understand our problems. It is called the ABC model. Each of these three letters has a different meaning. Letter A means the "activating event" or the thing that we think is bothering us. An activating event can best be determined by asking the question, "What happened?" For example, on my ABC diagram, the activating event or A is that [write on the board while speaking] I didn't have time to correct all of the math tests last night. [The teacher can substitute a problem he or she is currently experiencing.]

| A | B | C |
|---|---|---|
| I didn't have time to correct all of the math tests last night. | | |

After I write down my A, I think about how I feel about it. If I didn't feel poorly about the A, then it wouldn't be a problem. Therefore, the C, or consequence, is a feeling or emotion that I want to change. With this particular case, I had four different feelings about not having time to correct the tests. It's easy to see how confused we can sometimes feel when there is more than one feeling involved. After I list the feelings under the C, I choose the one that is bothering me the most. I put a star in front of it. As you can see, I want to work on my feelings of frustration.

| A | B | C |
|---|---|---|
| I didn't have time to correct all of the math tests last night. | | *frustrated<br>sad<br>angry<br>disappointed |

Last, I write down my self-talk, or what I am thinking about the A when I get frustrated. This is a very important part of the exercise, because I might write down other kinds of thinking, like when I get sad or angry. The B section is only for our thinking about the feeling with which we want to work, in this case my frustration. I had a lot of thinking about the A.

| A | B | C |
|---|---|---|
| I didn't have time to correct all of the math tests last night. | I should have more time to do this!<br>I should be a better teacher! | *frustrated<br>sad<br>angry<br>disappointed |

For the time being, consider the above ABC model. Answer the following questions:

1. What is making me frustrated, the A or the B?

2. Can I be frustrated without the B part? How?

3. Could there be other Bs or Cs? Name them (see Supplemental Activity).

**ACTIVITY 2.** The teacher says: Let's try another situation. I will read a statement. You complete an ABC diagram. [Have the students complete an ABC diagram that leads to a neutral or happy feeling, so that you can point out later that rational thinking can lead to neutral or happy feelings.]

You are all required to write a report concerning an item in the news that will be given orally tomorrow to the class. Your grade will depend on how well you do on the oral presentation. Everyone else's grade will depend upon how well they give you positive and negative feedback.

**SUPPLEMENTAL ACTIVITY.** If the students can identify rational and irrational statements, the teacher may want to have them briefly label the B statements (with rationale), as in the following example:

| A | B | C |
|---|---|---|
| I must present an oral report. | I will mess up, look stupid, and be stupid. I won't do it. | *nervous scared dumb |

The B statement is irrational. If one messes up or does not do well on a particular assignment, it does not mean that the person is dumb.

| A | B | C |
|---|---|---|
| I must present an oral report. | Everyone has to do it, so they'll know how I feel. If I don't do it, I'll fail. So what the heck! | *a little nervous |

This B statement is rational. Although it can be scary talking in front of the entire class, that is not a reason not to do it (Zionts, 1992g).

### Lesson 20. Happening–Thought–Feeling Reaction

Knaus (1974) devised the *Happening–Thought–Feeling Reaction* (HTFR) diagram so that students can make "concrete" the theory that feelings are generated from thoughts (beliefs) rather than happenings (activating events). The teacher begins the lesson by drawing an HTFR diagram on the board, using an example from experience or the following:

| Happening + | Thought = | Feeling | Reaction |
|---|---|---|---|
| Late for school because of heavy traffic. | Hope someone is covering the class. It bothers me that I have to be delayed this way. | Frustrations, Mild tension | Tried to hurry to class once I parked the car. |

The day after the class has as the homework assignment to write down their thoughts when they were angry, frustrated, and so on, the teacher should ask if any of the students wrote about fear experiences. The teacher asks those students to read them aloud. (If none were fear experiences, the teacher asks about other emotions so that it is possible to get several points of view on one emotion.)

The teacher encourages discussion of the examples read aloud by asking questions such as the following: Why do you think [student's name] and [another student's name] were afraid [angry, frustrated]? What was each of them thinking that made them feel that way? What did each of them do? Volunteers with the same emotions can be asked to add their data to the charts. The following are more examples:

| Happening | + Thought = | Feeling | Reaction |
|---|---|---|---|
| Lost father's car keys. (George) | He's going to be angry and he will punish me. That would be awful. | Fear and anxiety | Didn't tell him. |
| Speaking in front of class. (Mary) | I would make a mistake, be laughed at, be a fool. | Anxious Frightened | Avoided class. |
| Nearly hit by car. (Donald) | Danger! Later thought, "That I would try to be more careful." | Fear, then relief | Took time to calm down. |

If students have difficulty sorting the data for the diagram, the teacher should offer assistance or ask volunteers to help.

For homework, the teacher assigns the students to do an HTFR diagram on their feelings about getting up in front of the class and discussing an item reported in the news (Knaus, 1974, pp. 21–22). Upon completion of the homework assignment, the class may decide to personalize a HTFR diagram.

A practical application of this tool was presented by Darwin (personal communication, 1980), who used it to help her students gain more confidence in their approach to tasks. First, the teacher asks the students to complete a HTFR diagram with the following happening "Having an assignment that looks difficult":

| Happening | + Thought = | Feeling | Reaction |
|---|---|---|---|
| Having an assignment that looks difficult. | It looks too hard. I can't do it. I will fail, it will mean I'm stupid. I won't finish my work on time. It isn't fair. | Fear Anxiety Feels inferior | Becomes fidgety, Starts "fooling around" Complains to teacher about assignment. |

Second, the teacher has the student challenge the irrational beliefs stated in the diagram and talk about more rational ways of thinking. For example, "Maybe if I tried I could do it. It might not be as difficult as it looks. If I make a mistake, it won't mean that I am dumb. Everyone makes mistakes." The teacher points out that self-questioning will help change irrational beliefs people have about things.

Third, the teacher asks the student how he or she can change the behavior. For example, after receiving an assignment, the student could try to do it before concluding that it is too difficult. The student could read the directions carefully, maybe two times, and think about them carefully. Finally, the student makes a new HTFR diagram using the rational thoughts and feelings discussed above. A homework assignment for this lesson would be to have the student complete a HTFR diagram on (nonacademic) tasks that are assigned at home.

Supplementary activities for this lesson can include using scales to visualize the degree of fear, anxiety, and frustration involved with assigned tasks. Also, the teacher can ask the student to make HTFR diagrams on different types of assigned tasks (reading, spelling, math, English, etc.) and then compare them to see which ones cause the most anxiety and frustration.

### Lesson 21. Rational Versus Irrational Beliefs

The objective of this lesson is to help the student learn to distinguish between rational and irrational beliefs (Vernon, 1989a, p. 203). Beliefs are irrational if they are demanding, absolutistic, or overgeneralized. For instance, although it would be preferable for most people to be nice to us most of the time, it is impossible for *all* people to be nice to us *all* of the time. Understanding the difference between rational and irrational thinking will enable students to recognize patterns in their own lives.

The teacher does the following:

1. Introduce the activity by writing the words *rational* and *irrational* on the chalkboard. Explain that irrational beliefs do not make good sense, whereas rational beliefs do. For example, demanding that your mother fix fried chicken every Sunday is irrational; merely wishing that she would but realizing that she may not is rational. Believing that everyone in the school is mean is irrational; realizing that only one or two people act mean some of the time is rational.

2. Discuss why the following statements are irrational beliefs.
   I must be perfect.
   Everyone should always like me all of the time.
   I can't help the way I feel; it's someone else's fault if I'm unhappy.
   It's awful if everything doesn't always go the way I want it to.
   I shouldn't have to work too hard at anything.
   I can't make mistakes.
   I can't stand to be criticized.
   Everyone and everything in this world should be fair.

3. Divide the students into two teams; then appoint one player per team to be the captain. Give each team a Rational or Irrational Beliefs List (Table 10.1). The game proceeds as follows: The captain of Team 1 reads the first statement on the list to his or her first player, who decides

## TABLE 10.1
### Rational or Irrational Beliefs List

1. I've never had any friends.
2. No one ever asks me to go anywhere.
3. I wish I could have a new stereo.
4. If I can't go to the skating party, I'll die.
5. If she is really my friend, she should always sit by me and not by other kids.
6. My parents never let me do anything.
7. It would be nice if he would invite me to stay overnight, but just because he hasn't, that doesn't mean he doesn't like me.
8. I'm such a terrible basketball player. If I go out onto that floor, everyone will laugh and make fun of me.
9. If I make a mistake on this test, it doesn't mean I'm a dummy.
10. Everyone should say nice things to me.
11. I wish I had more friends.
12. If I have to sit next to him, I might as well quit school.
13. I really don't like her, but if I have to be her partner I guess I can stand it.
14. Just because I lost in arm wrestling, everyone is going to make fun of me and call me a wimp.
15. If my mom yells at me, it just means she's had a bad day, not that she doesn't love me.
16. There's no way I can wear my sister's hand-me-down clothes to school. Everyone will make fun of the way I look.
17. If I have to be in a class with those kids, I might as well quit school.
18. I would like to go skiing over spring break like some of the others kids, but I understand my parents can't afford it.

*Rational or Irrational Beliefs Answer Key:* 1. Irrational, 2. Irrational, 3. Rational, 4. Irrational, 5. Irrational, 6. Irrational, 7. Rational, 8. Irrational, 9. Rational, 10. Irrational, 11. Rational, 12. Irrational, 13. Rational, 14. Irrational, 15. Rational, 16. Irrational, 17. Irrational, 18. Rational.

whether the statement is rational or irrational. If the player is correct, he or she remains standing. If not, the player sits down. Team 2 then gets a turn. The captain of Team 2 reads the next statement to the first player on his or her team. That player says whether the statement is rational or irrational, and sits down if that response is incorrect. The teams continue to take turns and team captains allow members to respond in order until all questions have been answered. At the end of the game, the team with the most players still standing is the winner.

To encourage discussion, the teacher asks the following questions:

1. Was it difficult to distinguish between rational and irrational thoughts? Were some more difficult than others?
2. How would you explain to someone the difference between these two kinds of beliefs?

3. Do you tend to have more rational or irrational thoughts?
4. What kind of irrational beliefs do you have? Share examples.

### Lesson 22. Copping Out

This activity, designed by Vernon (1989b, p. 121) for ninth and tenth graders, is intended to help students recognize avoidance or cop-out behaviors, to take personal responsibility for their own behaviors, and to recognize the unhealthy pattern and effects of avoidance.

The teacher does the following:

1. Explain that a cop-out is when you refuse to take responsibility for yourself and blame others for what happens. Examples might include blaming your coach because you did not get to start on the team, your parents for grounding you if you got home late, or your friend for ruining your day. Cop-outs represent irrational thoughts because you usually want to change the other person rather than take personal responsibility.

2. Avoidance behaviors can involve procrastination, in which you put off doing something because you feel uncomfortable about it or may not want the hassle of doing it. Avoidance may also include behaviors such as ignoring certain people because you do not want to face them, or drinking too much to avoid facing a painful or tough situation.

3. Invite students to brainstorm personal examples of avoidance or cop-out behaviors.

4. Share examples in small groups of four to five participants.

To encourage discussion, the teacher can ask the following questions:

1. Was it difficult to think of examples of avoidance or cop-out behaviors?

2. Do you think avoidance or cop-out behaviors are healthy or unhealthy?

3. How can you recognize cop-out or avoidance behaviors in your own life?

4. What would you like to do about these kinds of behaviors?

5. Do you know others who exercise lots of cop-out or avoidance behaviors? How do you see this affecting their lives? Do you think these behaviors are good?

### Lesson 23. The Consequence of Failure Is Death!

The purpose of this lesson is to help individuals identify and understand how thoughts (or beliefs) contribute to negative feelings. At the end of the lesson, when given a sentence using exaggerated feeling words (e.g., "awful" or "I can't stand it"), the student will be able to identify these words and replace them with more factual meanings.

The teacher has the group role-play the following situation using puppets or students.

JOE: What seems to be wrong? You look pretty upset.
SALLY: I have so much homework from my classes. I don't know how I'll ever get it all done! This is just awful! It's all due tomorrow!
JOE: I know. I have a lot to do, too. I guess I'm going to be pretty busy tonight.
SALLY: I just can't stand all of this pressure! Teachers should be fair. They just don't understand how much we have to do! They shouldn't give us all of this work to do!
JOE: Just do the best you can and try not to spend a lot of time worrying about it.
SALLY: Not worry?! I have to do well in school. I have to make good grades. This is so unfair! Teachers should go easier on us. I wanted to go to the movies tonight. Now I have to do homework. I need to finish it all.
JOE: I'm sure you'll get it done.
SALLY: What do you know? I have to get it done! I have to get a good grade on my math to make up for yesterday's homework! I didn't get that all done and it was just awful! I am a failure. I can tell the teacher hates me. I can't stand the fact that she hates me.
JOE: Uh-Huh. Yeah. Well, I have to get going now. See you later.
SALLY: Where are you going? Boy, what a friend you are! You hate me too. Get lost!!

Following the role-play, the students should identify the exaggerated statements. Why are they exaggerated? What would Sally say if she was more realistic in her thinking? Then they should discuss the actions and reactions of both characters. What are the possible outcomes of the way Sally is thinking? (Her ability to finish her work, her relationship with Joe.) What can Joe do to help Sally? (Ask her if she wants to stop feeling that way, suggest that she is overreacting to a very unpleasant event.)

Role-playing this activity on videotape can be useful for several reasons. The teacher and students can discuss the event twice, once without replaying the tape and again after viewing the tape. This will allow some students to alter their opinions after viewing what they had previously determined to be "facts." Also, the experience of seeing themselves on tape may be highly motivating.

The teacher may ask the students to script their own role-plays with one or more persons exhibiting rational (or sensible) thinking and the other verbalizing irrational or exaggerated thoughts (Zionts, 1992k).

The teacher gives the students the following irrational statements. Have them identify which statements are irrational (or exaggerated) and change the irrational statements to factual statements.

1. If I don't get my way, I'll die!
2. Boy, am I upset that it's raining. I can't go outside to play. I guess I'll just watch television.
3. I got a 50 on the quiz. This is the worst thing that could happen to me!
4. That teacher is so mean! He should be fair. All teachers should be fair!
5. I must do well so that others like me.
6. The consequence of failure is death!

**Answers**

1. Irrational: I will be very disappointed if I don't get my way. Chances are few that I would actually die!
2. Rational: It is upsetting when you can't do what you like. Watching television may be an appropriate alternative to sulking because you can't get your own way.
3. Irrational: Failing a quiz, while certainly unpleasant, is hardly the worst thing that could happen to anyone.
4. Irrational: This statement is not irrational because the teacher is described as mean (he may be), but because of the belief that all teachers must be fair. Teachers, like other people, are not going to be *all* anything. Some will be fair, others unfair. It's too bad that students sometimes end up with unfair ones.
5. Irrational: Again, it would certainly be preferable to do well. Yet, if you can't (because of lack of ability, lack of sleep, poor teacher, other conditions), you won't. If others don't like you because you don't do well, there is little you can do about it (tough, but true).
6. Irrational: The consequence may be unhappiness, disappointment, or a punishment, but rarely death!

For homework, the teacher can ask students to bring to class two statements (from anyone) that are irrational and to provide rational statements for each.

**Lesson 24. A Rational Belief a Day Will Keep the Crazy Thoughts Away**

This exercise by Grieger and Boyd (1980) can be used in teaching RET theory to explore the specific irrational beliefs as postulated by Ellis (see Chapter 8). The teacher can do the following:

1. Have the students list the pros and cons of a particular belief a day (or a week).
2. Divide the class into two groups to debate the rationality of the various beliefs.
3. Ask the students to create stories revolving around the irrational beliefs.
4. Have the students evangelize about RET.

### Lesson 25. I Am, I Do

This is one of many activities presented by Vernon (1989b, p. 173). This lesson focuses on the RET concept that one's behavior does not become one's essence. The objective is for the student to recognize the relationship between self-acceptance and behavior. It is important that students realize that how they feel about themselves is sometimes communicated through their behavior, and that this in turn influences others to treat them in a particular way. Alternatively, others may label them, and this in turn can influence how they feel about themselves.

The teacher does the following:

1. Write each of the following phrases on individual cards: bad kid, stupid, always in trouble, smart, never misses an answer, super friendly, "Mr. Popularity," "Miss Popularity," always chosen first, never does anything right. (More phrases and cards may be added if more than 20 students are participating.)
2. Divide the class into two teams and invite students to participate in an experiment about labels students assign based on the way students behave or the way students feel about themselves. Tape a card on the forehead of each Team 1 member. Team members should not see what is written on the card.
3. Assign each Team 1 member a Team 2 member. Each Team 2 member tries to communicate through words or actions what his or her partner's card says without stating exactly what is printed on it. (For example, the person communicating "bad kid" could say,"Can't you stay out of trouble?" or "Can't you ever be good?") Team 1 members try to guess what their teammates' labels say.
4. If desired, reverse team roles and repeat.

The teacher encourages discussion by asking the following questions:

1. Were you able to guess what your label said? If so, how were you able to do it?
2. In real life, how do you think people get labels?
3. Are you aware of having any labels that might determine how you feel about yourself or how you act? Share examples.

4. If you do have a label, how do you feel about having it? How do you think you got it?
5. Do you think that others tend to treat you in the way you're labeled?
6. If you could change your label, how would you like it to be changed?

### Lesson 26. My Personal Strengths

The aim of this lesson is to help students become aware of and focus on their personal strengths and positive traits. This lesson will demonstrate that people with poor self-concepts usually ignore positive attributes.

The teacher gives each student a copy of a blank "Strength Square" (a box with 36 squares, 6 by 6). The teacher completes his or her square in front of the group, writing in boxes personal strengths (e.g., I have good handwriting, I like to sew, I can run fast, I try to be friendly, I like to sing). The teacher places a star next to the strengths that he or she feels are very important. Next, the students complete their squares. When the squares are completed, the teacher asks the following questions:

1. On what squares did you attach stars?
2. What squares would you like to share that may have been a secret to the rest of the class. (It may be important to reinforce some of the group rules discussed in Chapter 1, specifically that reactions such as negative comments and laughter, as well as disputations about those strengths, are inappropriate.)

The teacher may want to have students attach or draw pictures next to the squares to illustrate the various strengths. Also, the Strength Squares can be enlarged on poster board.

For homework, the teacher asks students to complete a square, in small print, describing weaknesses. The teacher should tell them that the project is acceptable even if they cannot fill in all the squares.

### Lesson 27. RET Songs

An excellent activity to demonstrate that irrational beliefs constantly bombard students is to critically analyze the lyrics of popular music. This allows the opportunity for the students to examine their own beliefs about such topics as love, friendship, and sexual activity.

Because most students are interested to varying degrees in popular music, this means of expression can be used to illustrate several irrational beliefs concerning self-worth, being loved and wanted by others, rejection, and peers. Students, by examining the messages of certain popular records, can determine how irrational beliefs and feelings are influenced by outside factors. Once these beliefs are identified, the students can present and discuss alternatives.

The teacher begins the lesson by asking the students for various irrational beliefs people might have concerning their self-worth and acceptance by others. The group discusses whether they have heard any of these beliefs in any popular songs. The teacher passes out lyric sheets and plays several popular songs that contain irrational beliefs concerning self-worth, acceptance, and rejection. Then the class discusses these beliefs as to how they might affect people and how the students relate to these beliefs. The students should be asked to propose rational beliefs that encourage self-worth and self-acceptance. A homework assignment may be to have the students try to find a song that reflects rational beliefs.

Ellis (1977–1981) changed the lyrics to many popular songs and inserted rational statements. One of these songs is the following:

### Perfect Rationality (Tune: Luigi Denza, Funiculi Funicula)

> Some think the world must have a right direction
> And so do I, and so do I
> Some think that when there's the slightest imperfection
> They can't get by, and so do I
> For I, I have to prove I'm superhuman
> And better far than people are,
> To show, I have miraculous acumen
> And always great among the great
> > Perfect Perfect Rationality
> > Is of course the only thing for me
> > How can I even think of being if it must be fallibly?
> > Rationality must be the perfect thing for me. (Ellis, 1977–1981)

Songs also can be created by teachers and students, allowing them to use both their RET knowledge and creativity. It is recommended that one student's song be sung before each RET session. The following songs represent irrational beliefs. The teacher might present them to students and ask them to change the words to reflect rational beliefs.

### Shame (Tune: Frère Jacques)

> I am f-at, I am ug-ly.
> This is true, What'll I do?
> No-obody likes me. Ev-erybody hates me.
> Fat hog you. I'm so blue.
> Work all d-ay, never re-st
> 'Til I'm through, 'til I'm best.
> A messy paper's fine, as long as it's not mine.
> Clean work clean, never rest.
> Failed the t-est, tried my b-est
> I'm so dumb, really dumb.
> Teacher thinks I'm stupid, yes I'm really stupid.
> Shame, Shame, Shame, Shame, Shame, Shame. (Goebel, personal communication, 1981)

### RET (Tune: Camptown Races)

> I need an A or I'm a creep, Do Da, Do Da.
> Less than "great" and I won't sleep, Oh Do Da Day.

I love to worry all night, I need to worry all day.
This gives me an excuse to vegetate, and waste my life
    away.
Perfection is the thing for me, Do Da, Do Da.
The others will know "I'm okay," you see, Oh Do Da Day.
I love to worry all night, I need to worry all day.
This gives me an excuse to vegetate, and waste my life
    away.
RET and life, they both belong, Do Da, Do Da.
Being sad is often wrong, Oh Do Da Day.
Don't you worry all night, Don't you worry all day.
If you sit and reason things out, problems go away.
Don't let your problems get you down, Do Da, Do Da.
Think out answers that are really sound, Oh Do Da Day.
RET does work, but you've got to try
To live your life as you do please, or it will pass you by.
(P. Zionts & R. Bowles, 1984)

### Lesson 28. Bibliotherapy

The use of literature as examples of rational and irrational thinking is a very effective and interesting method of discussing RET. The books in the following annotated bibliography contain humorous and entertaining rational messages.

**Grades K–3:** *Sweet Pickles* by J. Reinach, 1977–1980, New York: Holt, Reinhart & Winston. In the world of *Sweet Pickles,* each animal gets into a pickle because of an all-too-human personality trait. For example, Very Worried Walrus has the irrational belief that something very terrible would happen if he falls off a bicycle, catastrophizing to the point that he imagines himself dangling out of a helicopter. Pig finally convinces him to try to ride the bike and, lo and behold, he crashes and falls, learning however, that nothing very terrible really happened.

**Grades K–3:** *Instant Replay* by S. Bedford, 1974, New York: Institute for Rational Living. Sandy hits her little brother because he teased her. Her father uses an "Instant Replay" to reach the ABCs of RET. Included in this short book is a brief manual explaining a method of counseling and talking to little (and other) people.

**Grades K–4:** *It Could Always Be Worse* by M. Zemach, 1976, New York: Scholastic Book Services. This Yiddish folktale teaches to accept situations that may be very uncomfortable, because catastrophizing about them will rarely make things better. The rabbi in this story listens to the story of a poor man who has many relatives living in a small hut. The rabbi advises the man to bring his animals into the hut until the man "can't take it anymore." Finally, the rabbi suggests that the animals be removed from the home, and everything seems "peaceful" in the hut.

**Grades K–4:** *Color Us Rational* by V. Waters, 1979, New York: Institute for Rational Living. Twelve short stories explore the principles of rational-emotive therapy. The consequences of thinking irrational, as it affects the characters' long-term goals, are presented. For example, Abigail Addington Brown ran away from home because of a new brother. She finally returns, thinking realistically that "I'm still not happy about Andrew Anthony Brown III. . . . But I'm going to do what I can to make the best of my rotten situation and maybe I can learn to make myself happy in the process. It would be nice to get lots of affection, admiration, and attention—but I don't need it to be happy" (p. 19).

**Grades K–6:** *Homer the Homely Hound Dog* by E.J. Garcia and N. Peggegrini, 1974, New York: Institute for Rational Living. Homer the hound dog learns to accept himself and his homely looks through rational-emotive therapy as applied by Henry the hound dog. In the end, Homer says, "I guess . . . people may like to dislike *things* about me, but since what they think really doesn't have anything to do with *me* then I'm neither good nor bad because they may think so" (p. 32).

**Grades K–8:** *The Ready Set Grow Series* (1978–1980). Waco, TX: Educational Products Division, Word, Inc. This is an excellent human development series of books dealing with such topics as fear, trauma, emotions, physical needs, human similarities, and human sequences. For example, *Tuff Stuff,* a book about trauma, discusses types of trauma and offers the following advice:

Step 1: Face it. Figure out what caused the trauma and face up to it. Don't try to pretend it didn't happen. (p. 110)

Step 2: Accept it. Try to get used to the way things are. (p. 112)

Step 3: Figure out if anything you did caused the traumatic experience. Sometimes you do things that bring on trauma; sometimes you do not. (p. 114)

Step 4: Decide what you are going to do about the traumatic experience, and if there is anything you can do, do it. Sometimes you can do something to change things, sometimes you can't. (p. 116)

Step 5: Do what you have decided to do. (p. 116)

Step 6: Talk about your thoughts and feelings. Don't keep them inside you. Share them with someone else. (p. 118)

**Grades 4–8:** *The Value of Believing in Yourself: The Story of Louis Pasteur* by S. Johnson, 1976, La Jolla, CA: Value Communications. This book is one of a series titled *Value Tales* that ties values to autobiographies. This book tells of the trials and tribulations of Pasteur, who reminds a group of children that "When I was working in my laboratory, I enjoyed the times when I believed in myself. In those days, I didn't always succeed. But even if I didn't, it always felt good to believe that I could" (p. 57).

**Grades 8–12:** *How to Make Yourself Miserable* by D. Greenburg with J. Jacobs, 1966, New York: Random House. This humorous book is dedicated to the true irrational believers. Chapter titles include: Basics of Self-Torture; Seven Classic Misery-Making Situations; Misery About the Past, the Present and the Future; How to Lose Friends and Alienate People; How to Lose Your Job; How to Avoid Deep Romantic Relationships; How to Destroy Deep Romantic Relationships; and How to Lose Any Remaining Friends. The "self-instructional" text has quizzes and tests to ensure irrationality.

**Grades 8–12:** Almost any book of short selections by Woody Allen are complete with irrational, self-defeating ideas.

**OTHER RET RESOURCES:**

The following resources provide many lessons that are developed to teach both the concepts of RET and RET readiness. The Institute of Rational Living (see address below) also provides a bulletin twice a year that includes the latest RET material for personal and professional use.

*Program for Affective Learning* (PAL) by Thomas R. Bingham, published by Metra, A Division of Utah Navajo Industries, P.O. Box 1000, Blanding, UT 84511. PAL is an extensive and comprehensive series of lessons and handouts that illustrate RET concepts. Designed for older students, this series will allow for a better understanding of RET. One criticism is that the packaging of this program is somewhat confusing.

*Rational-Emotive Education Manual for Elementary Teachers* by William J. Knaus, published by Institute for Rational Living, 45 East 65th Street, New York, NY 10021. This manual includes many excellent activities that students will enjoy and that will teach some valuable RET skills.

*Rational-Emotive Therapy as a Classroom Mental Health Curriculum* by Paul Zionts (in progress). Contact the author at Central Michigan University, Mt. Pleasant, MI 48859, or PRO-ED, 8700 Shoal Creek Boulevard, Austin, TX 78757.

*Think Aloud* by Bonnie W. Camp and Mary Ann S. Bash, published by Research Press, 2612 North Mattis Avenue, Champaign, IL 61821. This excellent series of books is for elementary school children and youth. It uses a cognitive behavioral approach to teach problem-solving skills and is complete with many lessons to illustrate concepts.

*Thinking, Changing, Rearranging* by Jill Anderson, published by Timberline Press, Box 70071, Eugene, OR 97401. In this RET curriculum book for adolescents, Anderson changed the terminology of many of the RET concepts to make them more attractive to these students. For example, irrational beliefs are called "junk thoughts."

*Thinking, Feeling, Behaving* by Ann Vernon, published by Research Press, 2612 North Mattis Avenue, Champaign, IL 61821. These well-organized and well-developed lessons are divided into two books: elementary and secondary.

*Thinking Straight and Talking Sense* by Mark Gerald and William Eyman, published by Institute for Rational Living, 45 East 65th Street, New York, NY 10021. This introduction to RET concepts seems to be most appropriate for early adolescents. The lessons are well designed, but there are too few to comprise a comprehensive mental health curriculum.

## Summary and Conclusions

Some educators who feel uncomfortable "therapizing" in a group setting may believe that the RET philosophy can be effective as a mental health curriculum. This chapter has presented examples of curricula that explore the principles of RET. They may be used either in conjunction with the intervention strategies in Chapter 10 or as a separate preventive mental health curriculum. Specific exercises that focus on certain RET concepts, as well as more general lessons, are included. The purpose of these exercises is to actively demonstrate the concepts of rational-emotive therapy, rather than to have the concepts "preached" to the students. If RET is taught solely as a mental health curriculum, students have the "choice" of adopting the principles that make the most sense to them. There are certainly other ways to teach RET concepts. For example, Edwards (1977) was a counselor who wrote a RET-like column for the school newspaper.

This chapter was organized in a developmental manner. Exercises were presented to give both teachers and students an active rather than a passive RET education. In Step 1 a story was used to invite the students into the RET process. Step 2 attempted to teach the students how to identify and understand the concept of feelings. The exercises were intended to encourage an interactive classroom discussion. The purpose of these examples was not to validate certain feelings as being particularly worthy, but to show that many feelings may accompany particular events. The third step indicated that, although a myriad of feelings may be the result of an event (depending upon the individual), it is one's unique interpretation that may determine the individual's reaction. Furthermore, this step suggested that disturbed students may be inaccurately perceiving these events from the beginning. Exercises were presented that provide a "scientific" method of examining the environment. The fourth step explored a variation of the ABC theory and showed how an individual could apply it for personal use. The theory of RET was explored through exercises, games, songs, and literature.

This unit has attempted to present a foundation of RET for classroom use. The reader is encouraged to utilize RET in any of the three ways suggested: (a) as a means to personal and professional growth, (b) as a classroom intervention for alleviating the emotional disturbance of students, or (c) as a preventive mental health curriculum. Furthermore, the interested educator may choose to participate in RET workshops as well as read the many RET resources available.

# Appendix 10.1: Outline of Concepts to Teach the Content of RET

## I. Lesson One

### A. *Objectives*

1. Student will state the words that describe common feelings.
2. Students will identify situations that occasion different feelings in themselves.
3. Students will state the rule that feelings can vary in intensity from strong to weak.
4. Students will demonstrate the rule by classifying their feelings on a continuum of intensity using the feeling thermometer. *Pleasant feelings:* Happiness, joy, love, enthusiasm, excitement, curiosity, relaxation, confidence. *Unpleasant feelings:* anger, hate, sadness, depression, fear, guilt, worthless, loneliness, frustration, disappointment, anxiety, annoyance.

### B. *New Ideas*

1. Different words describe different feelings.
2. Feelings can vary in intensity from strong to weak.

## II. Lesson Two

### A. *Objectives*

1. Students will state that thoughts cause feelings.
2. Students will state that pleasant thoughts cause pleasant feelings and that unpleasant thoughts cause unpleasant feelings.
3. Students will demonstrate by providing examples how their own pleasant thoughts cause them to feel pleasant and that their own unpleasant thoughts cause unpleasant feelings.

### B. *New Ideas*

1. Thoughts cause feelings.
2. Pleasant thoughts cause pleasant feelings. Unpleasant thoughts cause unpleasant feelings.

## III. Lesson Three

### A. Objectives

1. Student will identify which of his own thoughts lead to pleasant and unpleasant feelings.

2. Student will apply the happening–thought–feeling–reaction diagram [see Lesson 20 later in chapter] in analyzing himself.

3. Students will state in own words that it is often difficult to identify the thought that precedes a feeling because the thought may occur very quickly. The thought may be one word or a sentence fragment. Many times you do not hear yourself thinking the thought. Many times you may not realize that you have thought the thought.

4. Student will state that by changing your thoughts you change your feelings.

### B. New Ideas

1. Your feelings and behavior can be looked at in this way: HAPPENING + THOUGHT = FEELING—BEHAVIOR.

    a. Something happens to you.

    b. You think about what happened.

    c. The thought you have leads to a feeling.

    d. Your feeling will affect how you behave.

2. By changing your thoughts you can change your feelings.

## IV. Lesson Four

### A. Objectives

1. Student will state in his own words the definition of rational thought, irrational thought, and challenge.

2. Student will state in his own words that to know whether a thought is rational or irrational he must ask himself the question: "Is there enough evidence for me to say the thought is true?" If there is evidence, the thought is rational. If there is not enough evidence, the thought is irrational.

3. Student will identify examples and non-examples of rational and irrational thoughts.

### B. New Ideas

1. Definition of new words:

    a. Challenge: To question yourself to see if your thought is rational or irrational.

    b. Rational thought: A sensible and logical idea that seems to be true.

    c. Irrational thought: An unreasonable or absurd idea that is false.

    d. How to find out if a thought is rational or irrational. Ask yourself "Is there enough evidence for me to say the thought is true?" Yes or no. If YES, the thought is rational. If NO, the thought is irrational.

## V. Lesson Five

### A. Objectives

1. Student will state in his own words that when he thinks irrational thoughts he feels more unhappy, worthless, angry and frustrated than if he thinks rational thoughts.

2. Student will quantify the frequency of his rational and irrational thoughts.

### B. New Ideas

1. Thinking irrational thoughts makes you feel worse (unhappy, worthless, angry, and frustrated) than thinking rational thoughts.

## VI. Lesson Six

### A. Objectives

1. Student will demonstrate rule "thinking irrational thoughts makes you feel more upset than thinking rational thoughts" by analyzing his own behavior.

2. Student will state that when we get too upset we can do nothing to help improve the situation.

3. Student will state that we can control how upset we are by changing irrational thoughts to rational thoughts.

4. Student will demonstrate rule for identifying rational and irrational thoughts (Is the thought sensible and true, or absurd and false?) by analyzing his own thoughts.

5. Student will demonstrate rule for challenging and changing his irrational thoughts by restating them as rational thoughts.

B. *New Ideas*

1. When I get too upset, I can do nothing to improve the situation.
2. I can control how upset I am by changing my irrational thoughts to rational thoughts.

## VII. Lesson Seven

A. *Objectives*

1. Student will state that each of us is complex, not simple.
2. Student will state that he is made up of many positive and negative characteristics.
3. Student will identify some of his positive and negative characteristics.
4. Student will state that he is not all good or all bad because of some of his characteristics.
5. Student will state that when he focuses only on his negative characteristics, he feels worse about himself.
6. Student will demonstrate, by challenging the irrational thought that he is not what someone calls him, that he is made up of many characteristics.
7. Student will identify positive and negative characteristics of a teacher.
8. Student will state that a teacher is not all good or all bad because of some of the teacher's characteristics.
9. Student will state that when he focuses only on the negative characteristics of a teacher, he feels worse about the teacher.

B. *New Ideas*

1. Every person is complex, not simple. I am complex, not simple.
2. Every person is made up of many positive and negative characteristics. I am made up of many positive and negative characteristics.
3. A person is not all good or bad because of some of his or her characteristics. I am not all good or all bad.
4. When I focus only on the negative characteristics of a person, I feel worse about the person. When I focus on my negative characteristics, I feel worse about myself.

## VIII. Lesson Eight

### A. *Objectives*

1. Student will state that focusing only on the negative qualities of people (including himself) is irrational because people (including himself) have other positive qualities.

2. Student will state that people (including himself) are not good or bad.

3. Student will demonstrate rule for challenging and changing his negative irrational thoughts by restating them as negative rational thoughts.

4. Student will state that when he thinks irrational, negative thoughts about people (including himself), he gets more upset than if he thinks negative, rational thoughts.

### B. *New Ideas*

1. Focusing *only* on another person's negative qualities is irrational because people have other positive qualities. Focusing *only* on my negative qualities is irrational because I have other positive qualities.

2. When I think negative, irrational thoughts about someone else, I get more upset with that person than if I think negative, rational thoughts.

3. People are not good or bad. I am not good or bad.

4. When I think negative, irrational thoughts about myself, I get more upset with myself than if I think negative, rational thoughts.

## IX. Lesson Nine

### A. *Objectives*

1. Student will state the definition of "fact" and "opinion."

2. Student will state that people have different opinions.

3. Student will state that not everyone *should* have the same opinion.

4. Student will state that someone who disagrees with him is not bad or worthless.

5. Student will state that when he disagrees with someone else (has a difference of opinion with), it doesn't make any sense to get angry, upset, or behave stubbornly.

B. *New Ideas*

1. A fact is a statement that is true.
2. An opinion is someone's idea about something. It is neither true nor false.
3. People have different opinions.
4. Someone who disagrees with you is not bad or worthless.
5. People who disagree with you do not deserve to be punished.
6. When someone disagrees with you, it does not make sense to get overly upset, angry, or behave stubbornly.

X. **Lesson Ten**

A. *Objectives*

1. Student will state that just because he has an opinion about something doesn't make it true.
2. Student will state the definitions of "belief," "sound assumption," and "unsound assumption."
3. Student will state that some of the things he believes (his beliefs) are not true (are based on unsound assumptions).
4. Student will classify examples of his own beliefs as being based on sound and unsound assumptions.
5. Unsound assumptions lead to mistakes.

B. *New Ideas*

1. A belief: A conviction that something is true.
2. Sound assumption: A belief likely to be true.
3. Unsound assumption: Something that you believe to be true but which in reality is not.
4. Some of my assumptions are unsound (untrue).
5. When they are, I make mistakes.

## XI. Lesson Eleven

### A. Objectives

1. Student will state that everyone will always make mistakes.
2. Student will state that no one is perfect.
3. Student will state that mistakes do not change a person's good qualities.
4. Student will state that a person is not the same as his performance.
5. Student will state that people are not bad because they make mistakes.
6. Student will state that people who make mistakes do not deserve to be blamed or punished. They require help to change.
7. Student will state reasons why people make mistakes: (a) lack of skills, (b) carelessness or poor judgment, (c) not studying, poor student, (d) not having enough information, unsound assumption, (e) tired or ill, (f) different opinion.
8. Student will state that it is irrational to rate people as good or bad.

### B. New Ideas

1. No one is perfect; everyone will make mistakes.
2. Mistakes do not change a person's good qualities.
3. A person is not the same as his performance.
4. People who make mistakes do not deserve to be blamed and punished. They require help to change.

## XII. Lesson Twelve

### A. Objectives

1. Student will state the definitions of "want" and "need."
2. Student will identify examples of his own wants and needs.
3. Student will state the difference between a rational and irrational need.
4. Student will classify examples of his own rational and irrational needs.

5. Student will challenge irrational needs by restating them as rational wants.

6. Student will state that needs lead to making demands on another person.

7. Demands lead to anger and upset with another person.

B. *New Ideas*

1. A need is something one has to have to survive.

2. An irrational need is a demand for something that you don't really need to survive.

3. A want is a wish for something you would like.

4. When I demand something that I do not need, I am being silly (irrational).

## XIII. Lesson Thirteen

A. *Objectives*

1. Students will practice challenging "awfulizing" and "catastrophizing."

B. *New Ideas*

1. Situations and people are not as awful as I *think* they are.

2. Challenging awful thoughts improves the situation, and makes you feel less upset.

From *Rational-Emotive Therapy with Children and Adolescents: Theory, Treatment Strategies, Preventative Methods* (pp. 371–376) by M.E. Bernard and M.R. Joyce, 1984, New York: Wiley. Copyright 1984 by John Wiley & Sons.

# Unit 3 References

Algozzine, B. (1977). The emotionally disturbed child: Disturbed or disturbing? *Journal of Abnormal Child Psychology, 5,* 205–211.

Anderson, J. (1981). *Thinking, changing, rearranging.* Eugene, OR: Timberlane Press.

Apter, S. (1981). *Troubled children/troubled systems.* New York: Pergamon Press.

Beck, A. T. (1970). Cognitive therapy: Nature and relation to behavior therapy. *Behavior Therapy, 1,* 184–200.

Beck, A. T. (1976). *Cognitive therapy and emotional disorders.* New York: International Universities Press.

Bernard, M. E. (1980). Private thought in rational-emotive psychotherapy. *Rational Living, 15*(1), 3–8.

Bernard, M. E. (1990). Rational-emotive therapy with children and adolescents: Treatment strategies. *School Psychology Review, 19,* 294–303.

Bernard, M. E., & Joyce, M. R. (1984). *Rational-emotive therapy with children and adolescents: Theory, treatment strategies, preventative methods.* New York: Wiley.

Braswell, L., Kendall, P. C., & Urbain, E. S. (1982). A multistudy analysis of socioeconomic status (SES) and the measures and outcomes of cognitive-behavioral treatment with children. *Journal of Abnormal Child Psychology, 10,* 443–450.

Camp, B. W., & Bash, M. A. S. (1981). *Think aloud.* Champaign, IL: Research Press.

Cangelosi, A., Gressard, C. F., & Mines, R. A. (1980). The effects of a rational thinking group on self-concepts in adolescents. *The School Counselor, 27,* 357–361.

Castillo, G. A. (1978). *Left-handed teaching* (2nd ed.). New York: Holt, Rinehart & Winston.

Center, D. (1989). *Curriculum and teaching strategies for students with behavioral disorders.* Englewood Cliffs, NJ: Prentice-Hall.

Coleman, M. C. (1992). *Behavior disorders: Theory and practice (2nd ed.).* Needham Heights, MA: Allyn & Bacon.

Criddle, W. D. (1974). Guidelines for challenging irrational beliefs. *Rational Living, 9,* 8–13.

DeVoge, C. (1974). A behavioral approach to RET with children. *Rational Living, 9*(1), 23–26.

Dice, M. L. (1993). *Intervention strategies for children with emotional or behavioral disorders.* San Diego: Springer.

DiGiuseppe, R. (1975). The use of behavior modification to establish rational self-statements in children. *Rational Living, 10*(1), 18–19.

DiGiuseppe, R. (1986). The implication of the philosophy of science for rational-emotive theory and therapy. *Psychotherapy, 23,* 634–639.

DiGiuseppe, R. (1990). Rational-emotive assessment of school-aged children. *School Psychology Review, 19*, 287–293.
DiGiuseppe, R., & Bernard, M. E. (1990). The application of rational-emotive theory and therapy to school-aged children. *School Psychology Review, 19*, 268–286.
DiGiuseppe, R., & Kassinove, H. (1976). Effects of a rational-emotive school mental health program on children's emotional adjustment. *Journal of Community Psychology, 4*, 382–387.
Dryden, W., & DiGiuseppe, R. (1990). *A primer on rational-emotive therapy.* Chicago: Research Press.
Edwards, C. (1977). RET in high school. *Rational Living, 12*, 10–12.
Ellis, A. (1962). *Reason and emotion in psychotherapy.* New York: Lyle Stuart.
Ellis, A. (1972). Emotional education in the classroom: The living school. *Journal of Clinical Child Psychology, 1*, 19–22.
Ellis, A. (1973a). Are cognitive behavior therapy and rational therapy synonymous? *Rational Living, 8*(2), 8–11.
Ellis, A. (1973b). Psychotherapy and the value of a human being. In A. Ellis & R. Grieger (Eds.), *Handbook of rational-emotive therapy.* New York: Springer.
Ellis, A. (1973c). Rational-emotive therapy. In R. Corsini (Ed.), *Current psychotherapies.* Itasca, IL: F. E. Peacock.
Ellis, A. (1977a). *A garland of rational songs.* New York: Institute of Rational Living.
Ellis, A. (1977b). *How to live with—and without—anger.* New York: Thomas A. Crowell.
Ellis, A. (1977c). Psychotherapy and the value of a human being. In A. Ellis & R. Grieger (Eds.), *Handbook of rational-emotive therapy.* New York: Springer.
Ellis, A. (1977d). A rational approach to interpretation. In A. Ellis & R. Grieger (Eds.), *Handbook of rational-emotive therapy.* New York: Springer.
Ellis, A. (1977e). The rational-emotive facilitation of psychotherapeutic goals. In A. Ellis & R. Grieger (Eds.), *Handbook of rational-emotive therapy.* New York: Springer.
Ellis, A. (1977f). Rational-emotive therapy: Research data that supports the clinical and personality hypothesis of RET and other modes of cognitive-behavior therapy. *The Counseling Psychologist, 7*, 2–41.
Ellis, A. (1977g). Rejoinder: Elegant and inelegant RET. *The Counselor Psychologist, 7*, 73–82.
Ellis, A. (1979). Toward a new theory of personality. In A. Ellis & J. M. Whiteley (Eds.), *Theoretical and empirical foundations of rational-emotive therapy.* Monterey, CA: Brooks/Cole.
Ellis, A. (1980). An overview of the clinical theory of rational-emotive therapy. In R. Grieger & R. Boyd (Eds.), *Rational emotive therapy.* New York: Van Nostrand Reinhold.
Ellis, A. (1984). Is the unified-interaction approach to cognitive-behavior modification a reinvention of the wheel? *Clinical Psychology Review, 4*, 215–218.
Ellis, A. (1991). The ABCs of RET. *The Humanist, 3*, 11–12, 49.
Ellis, A. (1992). First-order and second-order change in rational-emotive therapy: A reply to Lyddon. *Journal of Counseling and Development, 70*, 449–451.
Ellis, A., & Abrams, E. (1978). *Brief psychotherapy in medical and health practice.* New York: Springer.
Ellis, A., & Dryden, W. (1987). *The practice of rational-emotive therapy.* New York: Springer.

Ellis, A., & Harper, R. A. (1975). *A new guide to rational living.* North Hollywood, CA: Wilshire.
Evart, C. K., & Thoreson, C. F. (1977). The rational-emotive manifesto. *The Counseling Psychologist, 7,* 52–56.
Forman, S. G. (1990). Rational-emotive therapy: Contributions to teacher stress management. *School Psychology Review, 19,* 315–321.
Forman, S. G., & Forman, B. D. (1980). Rational-emotive staff development. *Psychology in the Schools, 17,* 90–96.
Gerald, M., & Eyman, W. (1981). *Thinking straight and talking sense.* New York: Institute for Rational Living.
Ginter, E. J. (1988). Stagnation in eclecticism: The need to recommit to a journey. *Journal of Mental Health Counseling, 10,* 3–8.
Goodman, D. S., & Maultsby, M. C. (1978). *Emotional well-being through rational behavior training.* Springfield, IL: Charles C. Thomas.
Grieger, R. M. (1972). Teacher attitudes as a variable in behavior modification. *Rational Living, 7*(2), 14–19.
Grieger, R. M., & Boyd, J. (1977). Psychotherapeutic responses to some critical incidents in RET. In A. Ellis & R. M. Grieger (Eds.), *Handbook of rational-emotive therapy.* New York: Springer.
Grieger, R. M., & Boyd, J. (1980). *Rational-emotive therapy.* New York: Van Nostrand Reinhold.
Hajzler, D. J., & Bernard, M. E. (1991). A review of rational-emotive education outcome studies. *School Psychology Quarterly, 6,* 27–49.
Hall, R. J. (1980). Cognitive behavior modification and information-processing skills of exceptional children. *Exceptional Education Quarterly, 1,* 9–16.
Harris, R. (1977). Rational-emotive therapy: Simple but not easy. *Rational Living, 12,* 9–11.
Harris, S. R. (1976). Rational-emotive education and the human development program: A guidance study. *Elementary School Guidance and Counseling, 11,* 113–122.
Hobbs, S. A., Moguin, L. E., Tyroler, M., & Lahey, B. B. (1980). Cognitive behavior therapy with children: Has clinical utility been demonstrated? *Psychological Bulletin, 7,* 147–165.
Hooper, S. R., & Layne, C. C. (1985). Rational emotive education as a short-term primary prevention technique. *Techniques, 1,* 264–269.
Horney, K. (1950). *Nuerosisi and human growth.* New York: Norton.
Hughes, J. N. (1988). *Cognitive behavior therapy with children in schools.* New York: Pergamon.
Hurt, B. L. (1977). Psychological education for teacher education students: A cognitive-developmental curriculum. *Counseling Psychologist, 6*(4), 57–60.
Kassinove, H., Crisci, R., & Tiegerman, S. (1977). Development trends in rational thinking: Implications for rational-emotive school mental health programs. *Journal of Community Psychology, 5,* 266–274.
Kassinove, H., & DiGiuseppe, R. (1975). Rational role reversal. *Rational Living, 10*(1), 44–45.
Knaus, W. J. (1974). *Rational-emotive education.* New York: Institute for Rational Living.
Knaus, W. J. (1977). Rational-emotive education. In A. Ellis & R. Grieger (Eds.), *Handbook of rational-emotive therapy.* New York: Springer.

Knaus, W., & Bokor, S. (1975). The effect of rational-emotive education lessons on anxiety and self-concept in sixth grade students. *Rational Living, 10*(2), 7–10.

Knaus, W., & McKeever, C. (1977). Rational-emotive education with learning disabled children. *Journal of Learning Disabilities, 10,* 16–20.

Knaus, W., & Wessler, R. L. (1976). Rational-emotive problem simulation. *Rational Living, 11*(2), 8–11.

Kneedler, R. D. (1980). The use of cognitive training to change social behaviors. *Exceptional Education Quarterly, 1,* 65–74.

Kranzler, G. (1974). *You can change how you feel.* Eugene, OR: RETC Press.

Lazarus, A., & Fay, A. (1975). *I can if I want to.* New York: Morrow.

Livneh, H., & Sherwood, A. (1991). Application of personality theories and counseling strategies to clients with physical disabilities. *Journal of Counseling and Development, 69,* 525–538.

Mahoney, M. J. (1977). A critical analysis of rational-emotive theory and therapy. *The Counseling Psychologist, 7,* 44–46.

Malouff, J. M., & Schutte, N. S. (1986). Development and validation of a measure of irrational belief. *Journal of Consulting and Clinical Psychology, 54,* 860–862.

Malouff, J. M., Valdenegro, J., & Schutte, N. S. (1987). Further validation of a measure of irrational belief. *Journal of Rational-Emotive Therapy, 5,* 189–193.

Maultsby, M. (1970). Routine tape recorder use in RET. *Rational Living, 5*(1), 8–23.

Maultsby, M. (1971). Systematic written homework in psychotherapy. *Rational Living, 6*(1), 16–23.

Maultsby, M. C. (1975). Rational behavior therapy for acting-out adolescents. *Social Casework, 56,* 35–43.

Maultsby, M. C., Jr. (1977). Rational-emotive imagery. In A. Ellis & R. Grieger (Eds.), *Handbook of rational-emotive therapy.* New York: Springer.

Meichenbaum, D. (1977a). *Cognitive-behavior modification.* New York: Plenum Press.

Meichenbaum, D. (1977b). Dr. Ellis, please stand up. *The Counseling Psychologist, 7,* 43–44.

Meichenbaum, D., & Asarnow, J. (1979). Cognitive-behavioral modification and metacognitive development: Implications for the classroom. In P. C. Kendall & S. D. Hollon (Eds.), *Cognitive-behavioral intervention: Theory, research and practice.* New York: Academic Press.

Meichenbaum, D., & Cameron, R. (1974). The clinical potential of modifying what clients say to themselves. *Psychotherapy: Theory, Research and Practice, 11,* 103–117.

Meichenbaum, D., & Genest, M. (1980). Cognitive behavior modification: An integration of cognitive and behavioral methods. In D. H. Kanfer & A. P. Goldstein (Eds.), *Helping people change* (2nd ed.). New York: Pergamon Press.

Meichenbaum, D., & Goodman, J. (1969). Reflection-impulsivity and verbal control of motor behavior. *Child Development, 40,* 785–797.

Meichenbaum, D., & Goodman, J. (1971). Training impulsive children to talk to themselves: A means of developing self-control. *Journal of Abnormal Psychology, 77,* 115–126.

Mercer, J. R. (1975). Sociocultural factors in educational labeling. In M. Begab & S. Richardson (Eds.), *The mentally retarded and society: A social science perspective.* Austin, TX: PRO-ED.

Morris, K. T., & Kanitz, H. M. (1975). *Rational-emotive therapy.* Boston: Houghton Mifflin.

Muran, J. C. (1991). A reformulation of the ABC model in cognitive psychotherapies: Implications for assessment and treatment. *Clinical Psychology Review, 11*, 399–418.

Oliver, R. (1975). Overcoming test anxiety. *Rational Living, 10*(1), 6–12.

Paris, C., & Casey, B. (1979). *Project: You*. Vancouver, WA: Bridges Press.

Patton, P. L. (1985). A model for teaching rational behavior skills to emotionally disturbed youth in a public school setting. *School Counselor, 32*, 381–387.

Protinsky, H. (1976). Rational counseling with adolescents. *The School Counselor, 23*, 240–246.

Protinsky, H., & Popp, R. (1978). Irrational philosophies in populr music. *Cognitive Therapy and Research, 11*, 463–471.

Raynor, C. M. (1992). Managing angry feelings: Teaching troubled children to cope. *Perspectives in Psychiatric Care, 28*(2), 11–15.

Rhodes, W. C., & Paul, J. (1978). *Emotionally disturbed and deviant children: New views and approaches*. Englewood Cliffs, NJ: Prentice-Hall.

Robb, H. B., III, & Warren, R. (1990). Irrational Belief Tests: New insights, new directions. *Journal of Cognitive Psychotherapy, 4*, 303–311.

Rogers, C. (1969). *Freedom to learn*. Columbus, OH: Merrill.

Rossi, A. S. (1977). RET with children: More than child's play. *Rational Living, 12*(2), 21–24.

Saltzberg, L., & Elkins, G. R. (1980). An examination of common concerns about rational-emotive therapy. *Professional Psychology, 11*, 324–330.

Schwartz, R. M. (1982). Cognitive-behavior modification: A conceptual review. *Clinical Psychology Review, 2*, 267–293.

Shorkey, C. T., & Whiteman, V. L. (1977). Development of the Rational Behavior Inventory: Initial validity and reliability. *Educational and Psychological Measurement, 37*, 527–534.

Smith, M. L., & Glass, G. V. (1977). Meta-analysis of psychotherapy outcome studies. *American Psychologist, 32*, 752–760.

Smith, T. W. (1982). Irrational beliefs in the cause and treatment of emotional distress: A critical review of the rational-emotive model. *Clinical Psychology Review, 2*, 505–522.

Smith, T. W., & Zurawski, R. M. (1983). Assessment of irrational beliefs: The question of discriminant validity. *Journal of Clinical Psychology, 39*, 976–979.

Spirito, A., & Erickson, M. T. (1979). A developmental study of common concerns about rational-emotive therapy. *Professional Psychology, 11*, 324–330.

Vernon, A. (1989a). *Thinking, feeling, behaving: An emotional education curriculum for children (Grades 1–6)*. Champaign, IL: Research Press.

Vernon, A. (1989b). *Thinking, feeling, behaving: An emotional education curriculum for adolescents (Grades 7–12)*. Champaign, IL: Research Press.

Vernon, A. (1990). The school psychologist's role in preventative education: Applications of rational-emotive education. *School Psychology Review, 19*, 322–330.

Vertes, R. (1971). The should: A critical analysis. *Rational Living, 6*(2), 22–25.

Wagner, E. E., & Glicken, M. (1966). Counseling children: Two accounts. *Rational Living, 1*, 26, 28.

Walen, S. R., DiGiuseppe, R., & Wessler, R. L. (1980). *A practitioner's guide to rational-emotive therapy*. New York: Oxford University Press.

Warren, R., Smith, G., & Velten, E. (1984). Rational-emotive therapy and the reduction of interpersonal anxiety in junior high school students. *Adolescence, 19*, 893–902.
Wasserman, T. H., & Vogrin, D. J. (1979). Relationship of endorsement of rational beliefs, age, months in treatment, and intelligence to overt behavior of emotionally disturbed children. *Psychological Reports, 44*, 911–917.
Weinrach, S. G. (1991). Selecting a counseling theory while scratching your head: A rational-emotive therapist's personal journey. *Journal of Mental Health Counseling, 13*, 367–378.
Wilson, S. B., & London, T. (1977). Rational behavior education with young adults. *Rational Living, 12*, 16–19.
Woods, P. J. (1992). A study of "belief" and "non-belief" items from the Jones Irrational Beliefs Test with implications for the theory of RET. *Journal of Rational-Emotive and Cognitive-Behavioral Therapy, 10*, 41–52.
Young, H. S. (1979). Is it RET? *Rational Living, 14*, 9–17.
Zelie, K., Stone, C. I., & Lehr, E. (1980). Cognitive behavioral intervention in school discipline: A preliminary study. *The Personnel and Guidance Journal, 59*, 80–83.
Zionts, P. (1981). *Preventing teacher and student stress.* Paper presented at the Fifth Annual Conference on Severe Behavior Disorders of Children and Youth, Tempe, AZ.
Zionts, P. (1983). *Rational-emotive education worksheet.* Mt. Pleasant, MI: RETCO.
Zionts, P. (1992a). Catastrophizing. *Rational-emotive curriculum in the classroom.* Mt. Pleasant, MI: RETCO.
Zionts, P. (1992b). Exploring different feelings. *Rational-emotive curriculum in the classroom.* Mt. Pleasant, MI: RETCO.
Zionts, P. (1992c). Feelings are the results of our beliefs of events. *Rational-emotive curriculum in the classroom.* Mt. Pleasant, MI: RETCO.
Zionts, P. (1992d). InterpRETations. *Rational-emotive curriculum in the classroom.* Mt. Pleasant, MI: RETCO.
Zionts, P. (1992e). It's awful! It's terrible! How horrible! *Rational-emotive curriculum in the classroom.* Mt. Pleasant, MI: RETCO.
Zionts, P. (1992f). I yam what I yam and that's all that I yam, I'm Popeye the sailorman. *Rational-emotive curriculum in the classroom.* Mt. Pleasant, MI: RETCO.
Zionts, P. (1992g). Knowing your ABCs. *Rational-emotive curriculum in the classroom.* Mt. Pleasant, MI: RETCO.
Zionts, P. (1992h). My personal strengths. *Rational-emotive curriculum in the classroom.* Mt. Pleasant, MI: RETCO.
Zionts, P. (1992i). Shoulds of society. *Rational-emotive curriculum in the classroom.* Mt. Pleasant, MI: RETCO.
Zionts, P. (1992j). That's a fact! *Rational-emotive curriculum in the classroom.* Mt. Pleasant, MI: RETCO.
Zionts, P. (1992k). The consequence of failure is death! *Rational-emotive curriculum in the classroom.* Mt. Pleasant, MI: RETCO.
Zionts, P. (1992l). The difference between facts and opinions. *Rational-emotive curriculum in the classroom.* Mt. Pleasant, MI: RETCO.
Zionts, P. (1993). *Rational Emotive Education Worksheet–R.* Mt. Pleasant, MI: RETCO.

# Author Index

Abelson, A. G., 63
Abelson, M. A., 75
Abernathy, T. V., 62
Abrams, E., 320, 322, 325, 343
Adair, R., 11
Adams, D., 269, 273, 284
Adams, S., 129
Affleck, J. Q., 164, 167, 169
Alexander, R. N., 142
Algozzine, B., 19, 25, 33, 39, 48, 72, 80, 123, 318
Algozzine, K., 48
Allen, D., 68
Allen, W., 422
Allington, R. L., 62
Aloise, P. A., 254, 267
American Psychiatric Association, 98
Anderson, A., 246
Anderson, J., 391, 422
Anderson, K. E., 151
Anderson, T. H., 128
Annesley, F. R., 110
Apter, S., 318
Arbuthnot, J., 47, 252, 254, 261, 275
Archer, A., 164
Arkell, C., 104
Armbruster, B. B., 128
Arreaga-Mayer, C., 121
Asarnow, J., 311
Ashcroft, S. C., 104
Audette, B., 33
Ausubel, D. P., 17

Babigan, D., 46
Bailey, J. S., 47
Bakewell, D., 121
Bakken, J. P., 126
Baldwin, 234

Ballard, R. D., 105
Bandura, A., 235, 313
Barcikowski, R. S., 16
Barenboim, C., 216
Barker, R., 38
Barnett, R., 250
Barrett-Jones, K., 77
Bartlett, L., 30
Bash, M. A. S., 158, 311, 388, 422
Bauer, A. M., 12, 20, 177
Bauer, M. A., 11, 68
Baumrind, D., 257
Bear, G. G., 250
Beck, A. T., 309, 310, 311, 313, 333
Beck, M. A., 166
Becker, H. S., 44
Bedford, S., 420
Behar, L., 67
Beilke, R. L., 12
Bender, W. N., 137, 138
Bennett, M. A., 97
Bentley, J. L., 12
Berkowitz, M. W., 250
Berliner, D. C., 120
Berlinghoff, D. H., 62, 120
Bernard, M. E., 312, 315, 316, 324, 332, 335, 344, 352, 386, 387, 392, 431
Besharov, D. J., 63
Bettes, B. A., 44
Beyer, B. R., 269–270, 273, 275, 276
Bickel, D. D., 37, 129
Bickel, W. E., 36, 37, 129
Bierman, M. M., 131
Billingsley, B. S., 64
Bingham, T. R., 422
Biskin, D. S., 290
Black, F. L., 155

Blackney, C. D., 257
Blackney, R. A., 257
Blackorby, J., 11
Blalock, G., 137, 138
Blasi, A., 254
Blatt, M., 216, 248, 250, 254, 283, 287
Bokor, S., 344
Bond, L., 105
Boomer, L. W., 63, 137, 138
Bos, C. S., 105
Bower, E. M., 8, 9, 17, 18, 68
Bowers, K. S., 47
Bowles, R., 420
Boyd, J., 353, 355, 360, 365, 389, 416
Braaten, B., 26
Braaten, S., 26, 27, 173
Brading, P., 47
Brady, M. P., 125
Bramble, G. A., 266, 290, 292
Brandenburg, N. A., 19
Braswell, L., 309
Breton, W. A., 63
Breznitz, S., 226
Brion-Meisels, S., 252
Brophy, J. E., 120
Broughton, J. M., 250
Brown, G. B., 115
Brown, L. L., 101
Brown, V., 110
Buckley, N. K., 166
Bullis, M., 14, 25, 32
Bullock, L. M., 19, 110
Burke, J. C., 135, 178
Bursuck, B., 62
Bursuck, W., 120, 128
Butera, G., 62
Butler, L., 47
Byrne, D. G., 255

Cameron, R., 309, 346, 352
Camp, B. W., 158, 311, 388, 422
Campagna, A. F., 216
Cangelosi, A., 47, 344
Cantor, G. N., 251
Carlberg, C., 24
Carr, S. C., 178
Carrell, D. E., 166

Carri, L., 49
Carson, R., 68
Carta, J. J., 121, 134
Carter, J., 72, 76, 156
Carter, J. F., 25
Carter, W. J., Jr., 146, 149, 151
Casey, A., 85
Casey, B., 378
Castillo, G. A., 396, 403, 404
Cawley, J. F., 111, 117, 120, 121, 124, 127, 128, 129, 130, 132
Center, D., 19, 312, 9, 14, 231
Center for Quality Special Education, 49
Cessna, K. K., 120
Chadsey-Rusch, J., 68
Chaffin, J., 108
Chalfant, J. C., 75, 76, 77, 78
Chalmers, L., 127
Chandler, J. J., 216
Chandler, M. J., 254
Charles, C. M., 167
Cheng, Y., 12
Chesapeake Institute, 120
Chess, S., 46
Christenson, S. L., 16, 19, 38, 80, 85, 120–121, 127
Clarizio, H. F., 142
Clark, G. M., 129
Clifford, M. M., 219
Coder, R., 246
Coffey, O. D., 20
Cohen, A. K., 11, 213
Cohen, R., 123
Cohen, S. B., 135
Coie, J. D., 226
Colby, A., 235, 236, 241, 246, 257, 266, 283, 287
Cole, E., 47
Coleman, M. C., 8, 14, 16, 19, 31, 71, 95, 105, 108, 157, 231, 312
Coleman, T. W., 166
Conger, R. E., 47
Conley, M. W., 12
Cool, V., 68
Cooley, S. A., 77, 78
Coolman, M., 47
Cooney, E. W., 232

Cooper, D., 246
Cooper, L., 68
Costanzo, P. R., 226
Council for Children with Behavioral Disorders, 9, 14, 27
Council for Exceptional Children, 49
Cowan, W. A., 211
Cowen, E. L., 46
Crane, S. J., 65
Criddle, W. D., 373, 375
Crisci, R., 345
Cronin, M. E., 129
Cronis, T. G., 68
Cross, L. H., 64
Crowell, A. R., Jr., 105
Cullinan, D., 19, 44, 62, 147
Cumblad, C., 147
Curwin, R., 135, 171

Damon, W., 252
Darch, C., 25
Darwin, 411
Davis, J. U., 264
De Vries, B., 257
DeBettencourt, L. V., 135
Dedrick, C. V. L., 64–65, 65
Deffenbacher, J. L., 47
DeGiovanni, I., 47
Delquadri, J., 134
DeLuca, C. B., 128
Dembo, M. H., 32
DeMyer, M., 95
Denno, D., 216
Deshler, D. D., 125
Devlin, S. S., 12
DeVoge, C., 346
Dewey, J., 234
Diamond, S. C., 27
Dice, M. L., 312
Dickstein, E. B., 255
DiGangi, S. A., 135, 178
DiGiuseppe, R., 254, 312, 315, 320, 321, 345, 346, 363, 366, 367, 373–374, 375, 385, 391
Dodd, J. M., 179
Doerr, A. M., 252
Dollinger, S. J., 157

Donahue, C., 64
Donaldson, G. A., Jr., 63
Doris, D. A., 251
Dowis, C. L., 124
Downey, N., 215
Downing, J. A., 117, 176
Doyle, W., 127
Dryden, W., 312, 316, 322, 327, 333, 334, 363, 366, 367, 373–374, 375
Dudley-Marling, C., 110
Duke, D. L., 45
Dunn, L. M., 112
Durand, V. M., 26, 32
Duska, R., 219, 221
Dykes, M. K., 19

Edgar, E., 11, 67, 68
Edmonds, R. R., 36, 45
Edwards, C., 423
Eiserman, W. D., 134
Elfenbein, D., 247
Elias, M. J., 12
Elkins, G. R., 347
Elksnin, L. K., 25
Elliot, R. D., 12
Elliott, S. N., 155
Ellis, A., 310–323, 325, 327–334, 338, 343–344, 347, 353–355, 371, 377, 380–381, 385–389, 417, 419
Ellis, E. S., 25, 125
Enright, R. D., 235
Epanchin, B. C., 71, 164, 167
Epictetus, 314
Epstein, M. H., 19, 44, 62, 67, 147
Erickson, M. T., 345
Ericson, D. P., 257
Evans, D. W., 290
Evart, C. K., 347
Eyman, W., 391, 392, 401, 402, 403, 422
Eysenck, H. J., 313

Fad, K. S., 62
Fagan, J., 12
Failkov, M. J., 47
Fallen, N. H., 144
Fanning, P. N., 68
Fardig, D. B., 48

Farnell, D. A., 226
Farrell, D. T., 176
Faust, D., 261, 275
Fay, A., 359
Federal Register, 7
Federal Task Force on Homelessness and Severe Mental Illness, 11
Federation of Families for Children's Mental Health, 146
Feldman, D. H., 247
Fenton, E., 216, 239, 245
Fenton, F. S., 104
Fenton, K. S., 104
Fielder, J. F., 105
Fimian, M. J., 65
Fink, A. H., 49
Fischer, J., 24
Fleetwood, R. S., 252
Fleisch, B., 67, 71
Flowers, J., 166
Fodor, E. M., 216, 240
Foley, R. M., 62
Forman, B. D., 335, 337
Forman, S. G., 335, 337, 338
Forness, S., 9, 15, 19, 20, 67, 97, 172
Fowler, S. A., 134
Fox, J. J., 47
Fraenkel, J. R., 256, 287
Frame, C., 47
Frank, A. R., 63, 68
Freiberg, J., 125
Frick, P., 13
Friedman, R., 12, 19, 47
Friedrich, W. N., 12
Friesen, B. J., 146
Fry, R., 157
Fuhler, C. J., 136
Fulda, T. A., 232
Furth, H. G., 219

Gable, R. A., 25, 26, 49, 67
Gable, R. K., 108, 109, 110
Gajria, M., 124
Galbraith, R. E., 264, 266, 269, 273, 274, 278–279, 282, 287, 288, 290
Gallagher, P. A., 162, 174
Gallivan-Fenlon, A., 116
Gallup, G., 216, 232

Garcia, E. J., 421
Garcia, K., 47
Gargiulo, R. M., 12, 13
Garrod, A. C., 266, 290, 292
Gartner, A., 24, 27
Gast, D. L., 174
Genest, M., 311
George, M. P., 72
George, N. L., 72
George, P. S., 216, 240, 244, 245
George, S., 248
Gerald, M., 391, 392, 401, 402, 403, 422
Gerber, M. M., 110
Gersten, R., 25
Gest, T., 38
Gibbs, J., 235, 236, 241, 245
Gibbs, J. C., 244, 250, 256, 257
Gibson, E., 77
Gibson, S., 32
Gilliam, J. E., 31, 105, 108, 179, 181, 182
Gilligan, C., 257
Gillmore, J., 248
Gilmer, J. F., 75
Ginott, H., 167
Ginsburg, H., 219, 221
Ginter, E. J., 307
Glass, G. V., 343
Glavin, J., 19, 110
Glick, B., 231, 248, 252, 278
Glicken, M., 352
Goebel, 419
Goldbaum, J. L., 110
Goldhawk, S. L., 131
Goldman, R. L., 12
Goldstein, A. P., 231, 248, 252, 278
Goldstein, H., 104
Good, T. L., 120
Goodman, D. S., 322, 368
Goodman, G., 13
Goodman, J., 47, 310, 346
Goodman, J. F., 105
Goodman, L., 35, 66
Gordon, D. A., 47, 252, 254
Gordon, L., 68
Goulet, S., 261
Grabe, M., 38

Graden, J., 85
Graves, A., 61
Graziano, A., 47
Greenbaum, P. E., 12
Greenburg, D., 421–422
Greenspan, S., 216
Greenstone, J. L., 179, 180
Greenwood, C. R., 121, 126, 134
Greif, E. B., 246, 257
Gresham, F. M., 25, 46, 112, 155, 156, 238
Gressard, C. F., 47, 344
Grieger, R. M., 335, 353, 355, 360, 365, 389, 416
Griese, R., 270
Grosenick, J. K., 63, 72
Grumet, J. F., 226
Gunter, P. L., 166
Gust, A. M., 131
Guttman, M., 38

Haager, D., 128
Hains, A. A., 216, 254
Hajzler, D. J., 344
Halikas, J., 12
Hall, E., 38
Hall, R., 272, 273
Hall, R. J., 311
Hall, R. T., 264
Hall, R. V., 134
Hallahan, D. P., 44
Hammill, D. D., 81, 82, 101, 110
Harding, D. C., 131
Harmin, M., 214
Harper, G., 134
Harper, R. A., 320, 377, 380, 385, 387
Harrington, R. G., 77
Harris, K. R., 174
Harris, R., 322, 348
Harris, R. S., 345
Hartshorne, H., 254
Hasazi, S., 68
Hassibi, M., 46
Hendrickson, J. M., 26, 49
Hersh, R. H., 214, 217, 220, 225, 239, 240, 244, 256, 264, 267, 270–271, 274, 279
Hertzog, C., 46

Hetfield, P., 125
Hewett, F. M., 7, 171, 172, 209
Hickey, J., 222, 251, 260
Higgins, A., 251, 271
Hindman, S. E., 30
Hobbs, S. A., 343
Hogan, R., 12
Hogan, S., 134
Hooker, K. A., 46
Hooper, S. R., 344
Hophan, P., 269, 270
Horiuchi, C. N., 68
Horne, M. D., 25
Horney, K., 328
Horton, S. V., 125, 128
Horvath, M., 61
Hoskisson, K., 290
Howard-Rose, D., 121
Hudson, L. M., 257, 260
Hughes, J. N., 312
Hugo, K. E., 8
Hunter, S., 216
Huntze, S., 14
Hurley, O. L., 104
Hurt, B. L., 232, 308
Hutton, J. B., 67

Ianacone, R. N., 20
Inhelder, B., 226
Institute for Adolescents with Behavioral Disorders, 49, 61
Iwanicki, E. F., 65
Izzo, L. D., 46

Jack, S. L., 166
Jackson, D. A., 165
Jackson, N. E., 165, 166
Jackson, P., 233
Jacobs, J., 421–422
Janczak, T. M., 128
Janssen, K. N., 49
Jantz, R. K., 232, 248
Jenkins, V., 62
Jenne, T., 177
Jennings, W. S., 251
Jensen, W., 134
Johnson, A. B., 36
Johnson, D. W., 135

Johnson, L. J., 76
Johnson, R. T., 135
Johnson, S., 421
Jones, K. H., 137, 138
Jones, L. S., 122, 142, 183
Jones, R. R., 47
Jones, T., 264, 266, 269, 273, 274, 278–279, 282, 287, 288, 290
Jones, V. F., 62, 122, 142, 143, 150, 183
Joyce, M. R., 315, 316, 332, 335, 352, 386, 387, 392, 431
Justan, J. E., III, 68

Kanitz, H. M., 348, 349
Kansas State Department of Education, 76
Kantor, R. N., 128
Kashari, J., 12
Kassinove, H., 47, 345, 385
Katsiyannis, A., 174
Kauffman, J. M., 15, 19, 25, 26, 27, 44, 47, 62, 115, 119, 121, 154, 216, 231
Kauffman, K., 251, 260
Kaufman, M., 104, 105
Kavale, K., 9, 24, 157
Kazdin, A., 47, 71
Kearney, C. A., 26, 32
Keasey, C. B., 248, 254
Kelley, A. V., 215
Kelly, T. J., 19, 67
Kendall, P. C., 309
Keppler, R., 177
Kiehl, W. S., 155
Killen, M., 252
Kinder, D., 62, 120, 128
King, T. R., 63
Kinnison, L., 67
Klinger, J. K., 128
Knapcyzk, D. R., 156
Knaus, W., 325, 344, 388, 391, 406, 410, 411, 422
Kneedler, R. D., 311
Knight, R. R., 105
Knitzer, J., 9, 19, 62, 66, 67, 71, 72
Knoff, H. M., 111

Kohlberg, L., 214, 216–218, 233–243, 245–258, 260, 264, 265–266, 271, 274, 305
Konopasek, D. E., 25
Koorland, M. A., 178
Kortering, L. J., 11
Kranzler, G., 321
Krebs, D., 248
Kress, J. S., 12
Kroth, R. L., 142, 144
Kugelmass, S., 226
Kupersmid, J. H., 256
Kurtines, W., 246, 257

Lahey, B. B., 343
Lakin, K. C., 7
Lamphear, V. S., 12
Landers, M. F., 49, 129
Landman, S., 252
Landrum, T. J., 25
Langford, P. E., 248
Larivee, B., 125
Larrivee, B., 25
Larsen, S., 80, 81
Lawrenson, G. M., 63
Laycock, V. K., 25, 67
Layne, C. C., 344
Lazarus, A., 359
Ledingham, J. E., 13
Lehr, D. H., 111
Lehr, E., 309
Lelanc, M., 13
Leone, P. E., 30, 66
Lerner, J. V., 46
Lesar, S., 62
Leschied, A. W., 47
Levine, P., 68
Leviton, S. C., 179, 180
Lewin, P., 25, 32
Lewis, F. W., 218
Lewis, K. A., 20
Lickona, T., 216, 232, 237, 260, 266, 267, 269
Lieberman, M., 257
Lillie, D., 150, 151
Lilly, M. S., 104, 112
Lintz, F. E., 81
Lipsky, D. K., 24, 27

Livneh, H., 343
Locke, D., 254
Lockwood, A. L., 249
Lokerson, J., 49
London, T., 357, 358
Long, N., 180
Lopez, M., 9
Lovitt, T. C., 125, 128, 167
Lowenbraun, S., 164
Luchow, J., 61
Luria, 310

Maag, J. W., 135, 178, 257
Maccoby, E. E., 255
Mackenzie, D. E., 36
Mackey, J. A., 232
Maheady, L., 133, 134
Mahoney, M. J., 347
Malouff, J. M., 347
Mandlebaum, L. H., 126
Marion, R. L., 143
Marshall, K. J., 25
Marsing, L., 123
Masanz, J., 246
Mastropieri, M. A., 62, 121, 124, 126, 177
Matson, J. L., 47
Mattison, R. E., 11, 68
Maultsby, M., 322, 332, 361, 365, 368
Maxwell, J. P., 104, 105
May, M., 254
Mazak, S. G., 252
McAfee, J. K., 141, 142
McConnell, S. R., 156
McCoy, G. F., 142
McCoy, W., 273, 285
McDowell, R. L., 115
McGill-Franzen, A., 62
McGovern, J. E., 144
McGuire, M. D., 12
McIntyre, T., 117
McKenzie, R., 63, 134
McKinnon, A. F., 63
McManus, M. E., 62
McVey, D. L., 77
Mead, M., 234
Meadows, N., 68, 155, 156

Meichenbaum, D., 47, 309, 310, 311, 313, 346, 347, 352, 365, 388
Meller, J., 12
Melloy, K. J., 157
Mendelsohn, G. A., 254
Mendler, A. N., 171
Mercer, C. D., 143, 144
Mercer, J. R., 318
Meyen, E. L., 111
Michigan State Board of Education, 175
Miezitis, S., 47
Milin, R., 12
Miller, D. J., 216, 254
Miller, J. H., 120, 124
Miller, N., 47
Miller, P. H., 254, 267
Mines, R. A., 47, 344
Mirkin, P. K., 78
Mithaug, D. E., 68
Moguin, L. E., 343
Monda, L. E., 178
Monroe, C., 165
Morales, J., 11, 68
Moran, M. R., 176
Morgan, D., 12, 113, 120, 134
Morris, K. T., 348, 349
Morse, C., 12
Morse, W. C., 211
Morsink, C. V., 48
Mosher, D. L., 240, 248, 254
Mosher, R. A., 273
Moutrie, R., 76
Mueller, F., 66
Munk, D. D., 126
Muran, J. C., 308
Murray, H., 100
Muss, R. E., 232
Myles, B. S., 66, 72, 78, 117, 176

Napier, J., 264
National Education Assocation, 63
Neel, R. S., 68, 120, 155, 174
Nelson, C. M., 9, 20, 26, 29, 115, 174
Nelson, D. M., 174
Nelson, R. E., 25
Nelson, R. N., 179
Nelson, S. A., 226

Newcomer, P. L., 231
Nickles, J. L., 68
Nicolayev, J., 256
Niles, W., 252, 272
Nolet, V., 127
Novacek, J., 12
Novak, J. M., 39, 40, 41, 42, 42–43

Oates, 12
Obringer, J., 19
O'Connor, R. D., 47
O'Leary, K. D., 100
Oliver, R., 381, 383
Opler, M. K., 101
Opper, S., 219, 221
O'Reilly, M. F., 68
Ormsbee, 78, 80
Ormsbee, C. K., 117, 176
Osguthorpe, R. T., 134

Paolitto, D. P., 214, 220, 256, 264, 266, 274, 279
Pappanikou, A. J., 25, 113, 208, 232
Paris, C., 378
Parish, T. S., 252
Parker, G., 155
Parmar, R. S., 120, 121, 124, 128
Patterson, G. R., 47
Patton, J. R., 129
Patton, P. L., 344
Paul, J., 71, 208, 318
Paul, S., 157
Paulson, D., 68
Peacock Hill Working Group, 67
Pederson, A., 46
Peggegrini, N., 421
Pelavin Associates, 71
Perron, B. M., 13
Perry, C., 45
Perry, J. E., 248
Peters, R. S., 256
Phelps, L. A., 68
Phillips, D. C., 256
Phillips, E. L., 47
Piaget, J., 122, 167, 211, 217–227, 232, 234–235, 237, 245–246, 249, 255, 257–258, 262, 265, 266, 305, 318

Pillar, A. M., 290
Pittel, S. M., 254
Plato, 234
Poillion, M. J., 13
Poland, S. F., 78
Polloway, E. A., 129
Polsgrove, L., 26, 123
Poplin, M. C., 80
Popp, R., 319
Poppelreiter, T., 142
Prange, M. E., 12
Prater, M. A., 134
Prewitt, J., 67
Prillaman, D., 174
Protinsky, H., 319, 357
Pryzwansky, W., 75
Pugach, M. C., 76, 105
Pullis, M., 64
Punzo, R. P., 178
Purkey, S. C., 36
Purkey, W. W., 39, 40, 41, 42, 42–43
Putnam, M. L., 121, 128
Pysh, M. V., 76

Quay, H. C., 6, 9, 20, 110
Quinn, K. P., 147

Rankin, R., 39
Raschke, D. B., 64–65, 65
Raskin, J., 12
Raths, L. E., 214
Rauth, M., 62
Raynor, C. M., 346
Regan, M. R., 83, 85, 88
Reid, J. B., 47
Reiher, T. C., 116–117
Reilly, T., 64, 173
Reimer, J., 214, 251, 252, 264
Reinach, J., 420
Reith, H. J., 123
Repp, A. C., 126
Rest, J., 216, 246, 249, 250
Reynolds, M. C., 21, 24, 29
Rhodes, W. C., 318
Rich, H. L., 159, 166, 167
Richards, H. C., 250
Riggs, R. S., 290
Rist, M. C., 63

Rizzo, J. V., 117
Robb, H. B., III, 347
Robbins, L. N., 95
Roberts, C., 25
Roe, C., 68
Rogers, C., 320
Rorschach, H., 100
Rose, C., 121
Rose, T. L., 30
Rosell, J., 173
Rosenkoetter, L. I., 252
Ross, D., 273, 285
Ross, R. R., 47
Rossi, A. S., 343
Rothman, G. R., 249
Rucker, C. N., 104, 105, 108, 109, 110, 111
Ruhl, K. L., 62, 120
Ruma, E. H., 240, 248, 254
Rusch, F. R., 68
Rutherford, R. B., Jr., 9, 20, 26, 29, 174
Ryser, G. R., 62
Rzepski, B., 75

Sabatino, D. A., 68
Sacca, M., 134
Safran, J. S., 16, 24
Safran, S. P., 16, 24, 32
Saltzberg, L., 347
Salvia, J., 100, 124
Samuels, S., 144
Santilli, N. R., 257, 260
Santrock, J. W., 254
Sarbonie, E. J., 19, 25
Sasso, G. M., 157
Scharf, P., 212, 214, 215, 237, 238, 251, 260, 273, 283, 285, 288
Schloss, C. N., 155
Schloss, P. J., 124, 155, 182
Schmid, K. D., 66
Schonert, K. A., 251
Schumm, J. S., 126, 128
Schutte, N. S., 347
Schwartz, R. M., 311, 314
Schwartzman, A. E., 13
Scruggs, T. E., 62, 121, 123, 124, 126, 177

Sedlak, R., 68
Seixas, J. S., 12
Selman, R. L., 248, 249, 255, 257
Semmel, M., 62, 66, 123
Shapiro, E. S., 81
Shavers, D. M., 71
Shea, T. M., 177
Sherwood, A., 343
Shisler, L., 134
Shooki-Yetka, M., 49
Shores, 112
Shores, R. E., 166
Shorkey, C. T., 347
Shumaker, J. B., 125
Silver, S. E., 12, 19
Simon, S. B., 214
Simonds, J. F., 12
Simpson, 78
Simpson, R. L., 14, 66, 71, 72, 83, 85, 88, 105, 117, 142, 146, 149, 151, 173
Sitlington, P. L., 68
Skiba, R., 8
Skinner, B. F., 313, 318
Slenkovitch, J. E., 7, 8, 28
Smith, D. E. P., 174
Smith, D. J., 179
Smith, G., 345
Smith, G. J., 68
Smith, M. A., 182
Smith, M. L., 343
Smith, M. S., 36
Smith, S. W., 105, 176
Smith, T. W., 347
Sonis, W. A., 47
Speicher, B., 283, 287
Speicher-Dubin, B., 235, 236, 241
Spence, M., 67
Spirito, A., 345
Spivack, G., 67
Stainbeck, S., 24
Stainbeck, W., 24
Steele, B. F., 13
Steinberg, Z., 61, 67, 71
Stone, C. I., 309
Stone, F., 67
Strain, 112
Strain, P. S., 47, 155

Strayhorn, J. M., Jr., 155, 157
Sugai, G., 72, 76, 156
Sullivan, G. S., 124
Sullivan, P. R., 273
Swank, P. R., 125
Swarthout, D. W., 231
Swartz, G. M., 20
Sweeney, M. M., 226
Swift, M., 67

Takeuchi, D., 11
Talley, R., 75
Task Force on Children Out of School, 31
Task Force on Homelessness and Severe Mental Illness, 10
Taylor, F. D., 7, 171, 209
Taylor, J. H., 248
Taylor, R. D., 125
Teplin, L. A., 13
Thelen, M., 157
Thoma, S., 250
Thomas, A., 46
Thompson, R. H., 113, 120
Thoreson, C. F., 347
Thurlow, M. L., 38, 39, 72, 78, 120–121, 121
Tiegerman, S., 345
Timo, K., 155
Tindal, G., 127
Toch, T., 38
Tollefson, N., 25
Tomlinson-Keasey, C., 248
Tose, B. A., 97
Tremblay, R. E., 13
Trevethan, S. D., 257
Trost, M. A., 46
Tuma, J. M., 10
Turiel, E., 226, 237, 247–248, 249
Turnbull, A. P., 151
Turnbull, H. R., 151
Tyroler, M., 343

U.S. Department of Education, 19, 49, 71
Urbain, E. S., 309
Urquiza, A. J., 12

Vail, C. O., 178
Valdenegro, J., 347
Van Dusen Pysh, M. V., 75, 78
Van Ruesen, A. K., 105
Vaughn, S., 126, 128
Vautour, J. A. C., 104, 105
Velten, E., 345
Vergason, G. A., 141, 142
Vernon, A., 333, 391, 407, 412, 414, 417, 422
Vertes, R., 328
Vogrin, D. J., 344
Vygotsky, L., 310

Wagner, E. E., 352
Wagner, M., 71
Wahlers, D., 146
Walberg, H. J., 21
Walen, S. R., 254, 320, 353, 360, 388, 389
Walker, 5
Walker, B. L., 117
Walker, E., 44
Walker, H. M., 9, 14, 25, 29, 32, 39, 143, 155, 166, 167, 174
Walker, L. J., 248, 255, 257
Wallace, G., 81
Wang, M. C., 21
Warren, D. R., 255
Warren, R., 47, 345, 347
Wasserman, E. R., 251
Wasserman, T. H., 344
Waters, V., 420–421
Weaver, R., 129
Webber, J., 157
Wechsler, D., 97
Weddle, C., 10, 216, 240
Weinberg, L. A., 8
Weinrach, S. G., 308
Weis, J. G., 12
Werry, J. S., 110
Wessler, R. L., 254, 320, 370, 388
Wesson, C., 126
Wheeler, 68
Wheeler, L., 157
Wheeler, L. J., 64
Whelan, M., 219, 221

White, K. R., 113, 120
Whiteman, V. L., 347
Whittaker, M. E. S., 126
Whorton, D., 134
Wiederholt, J. L., 110
Will, M., 77
Williams, D., 11
Williams, S., 47
Wilson, B., 67
Wilson, R., 126
Wilson, S. B., 357, 358
Wolf, M., 47
Wolford, B., 20
Wonderly, D. M., 256
Wong, K. L. H., 121, 154
Wood, C. E., 155
Wood, F. H., 3, 5, 7, 19, 20, 103, 104, 153, 263
Wood, M., 180
Wood, P., 95, 97
Woodcock, R., 98
Woodman, R. W., 75
Woods, P. J., 347

Woodward, J., 124, 128
Wright, I., 252

Yell, M., 8
Yoshida, R. K., 104
Youcha, G., 12
Young, C. C., 49
Young, H. S., 348
Young, R. K., 179
Ysseldyke, J. E., 19, 25, 38, 39, 72, 78, 80, 81, 100, 104, 120–121, 123

Zabel, M. K., 64
Zabel, R. H., 19, 63, 64, 117
Zebarah, J., 10
Zelie, K., 309
Zemach, M., 420
Zionts, P., 10, 14, 68, 71, 95, 97, 145, 216, 226, 240, 335, 338, 387, 396, 397, 399, 407, 410, 415, 420, 422
Zubrick, S., 25
Zurawski, R. M., 347

# Subject Index

ABC(DE) model of rational-emotive therapy (RET), 322–332
Abused children, 12–13
Academic ability, assessment of, 97–98
Academic content, moral dilemmas on, 290–292
Academic needs of students, 122–123
Accidental injury, moral dilemma on, 283
Accommodation
   compared with remediation, 44–48
   Piaget on, 220
Achievement tests, 98
Activating events, in RET model, 323, 359–363
Adaptation process, 220
Addiction to drugs and alcohol, 12, 63
ADHD. *See* Attention-deficit/hyperactivity disorder (ADHD)
Administration
   administrators' reactions to students with EBD, 29–31
   definition of administrative, 2
   disinviting and ineffective schools, 38–39
   factors contributing to inviting and effective schools, 36–43
   institutional reactions to students with EBD, 29
   teacher competencies in, legal and administrative structure, 60–61
   and teachers having to deal with, 63–66

Adult retarded people, moral dilemma on, 286–287
Advocacy, 150
African American students, 11
Alcohol abusers, 12, 63
All or Nothing technique, 376
Allness or neverness, 328
All-or-none thinking, 327
Always-and-never thinking, 374
Anger, diagnosis of, 372
Anxiety, diagnosis of, 372
Argumentative students, 388
Assembly line activity, 229
Assessment. *See also* specific tests
   of academic and educational ability, 97–98
   achievement tests, 98
   of behavioral and emotional functioning, 99–101
   of cognitive ability, 95, 97
   direct observation, 83, 88–92
   formal assessment, 82
   group discussion of dilemmas, 262
   of health and physical abilities, 98–99
   of home and community, 101–103
   impersonal assessment, 262
   individual assessment, 261–262
   informal assessment, 82–96
   interviews, 82–88
   of moral development, 259–264
   parent interview, 82–83, 86–88
   product analysis, 92–93
   Pupil Assessment Summary, 96–97
   purposes of, 81, 93–96
   rating scales, 100–101, 102
   record review, 83
   referral for, 80–96

teacher competencies in, 57–58
teacher interview, 84–85
trial teaching, 93
Assimilation, 220
Association of Children with Learning Disabilities, 143
Association of Retarded Citizens, 143
Attention-deficit/hyperactivity disorder (ADHD), 13
Autism Society of America, 143
Awfulizing statements, 328, 374, 404–406

Bad Banana technique, 376
Behavior modification. *See* Cognitive behavior modification (CBM)
*Behavior Rating Profile–Second Edition* (BRP), 101, 102
Behavioral functioning, assessment of, 99–101
Behavioral management rules system
  administering negative consequences, 176
  administering positive consequences, 175–176
  chart of modifications for, 73, 74
  considering rules, 166–168
  crisis intervention, 179–183
  developing consequences, 171–175
  direct prompts, 166
  examples of consequences in, 170–171
  examples of well-written versus poorly written rules, 168
  generating rules, 167, 231, 233
  guidelines on administering consequences, 171
  identifying individual feelings about classroom rules, 231
  ignore–attend–praise technique, 166
  level systems and token economies, 176–179
  need for rule setting, 167
  negative consequences in, 173–176
  positive consequences in, 171–173, 175–176
  pre–rule setting, 165–166
  presenting rules, 168–171
  proximity control, 166
  rule reminders, 166
  sequence of warnings-consequences in, 169
  statement of rules in positive behavioral terms, 167–168
  suspension and expulsion in, 174–175
  teacher competencies in, 54–57
  timeout in, 173–174
Behaviorally disordered. *See* Emotionally/behaviorally disordered
Behaviors and feelings list, 364
Belief systems, in RET model, 324–330, 368–373. *See also* Irrational thinking
Bibliotherapy, 376–377, 420–422
Brainstorming, in moral discussions, 273–274
BRP. *See Behavior Rating Profile–Second Edition* (BRP)
Bulimia, moral dilemma on, 286
Burnout, 63–66

Camera Check technique, 360, 361
Car dealership, moral dilemma on, 282–283
Case studies, 22–24
Catastrophizing, 328, 404–406
Categorical need, 329
Cawley's process regulator, 130–132
CBM. *See* Cognitive behavior modification (CBM)
CBT. *See* Cognitive behavior therapy (CBT)
Change, nature of, 359
Change of placement, 176
Child abuse, 12–13
Clarification, in moral discussions, 273
Class discussions. *See* Moral discussions
Classroom interventions
  categories of, 73, 74
  curricular modifications, 73, 74

data summary form, 76
documentation of, 73, 75, 76
early interventions, 72–75
environmental modifications, 73, 74
management modifications, 73, 74
Classroom management
  behavioral management rules system, 165–183
  classroom characteristics, 158
  classroom structure, 158–165
  early interventions, 73–76
  instruction, 49, 51–53, 61–63, 116–117, 119–136
  philosophy of, as preventing maladaptive behavior, 154
  physical arrangement of classroom, 159–163, 269
  planning for, 153–154
  scheduling and routines, 162–165
  teacher competencies in, 53–54
  teaching social skills, 155–158
  working with paraprofessionals, 137–138
  working with parents of students with EBD, 138–152
Codification of rules, in moral judgment, 222
Cognitions concerning change, in cognitive behavior modification, 311
Cognitive ability, assessment of, 95, 97
Cognitive behavior modification (CBM), 308, 310–311
Cognitive behavior therapy (CBT), 308–311
Cognitive stages, Piagetian, 219–220, 227
Cognitive therapy, 308–310, 311, 332–333
Collaboration
  and identification of students with EBD, 73
  teacher competencies in, 58–59, 66–67
Collective normative values, 252, 253
*Color Us Rational* (Waters), 420–421

Communication
  with paraprofessionals, 137
  self-communication in RET, 322–323
  teacher competencies in, 58–59, 66–67
  teacher–parent communication, 151–152
Community, sense of, 252, 253
Community environment, assessment of, 101–103
Community resources
  advocacy and use of, 150
  for families, 149–150
  informational services, 150
  parent and family training programs, 150
  parent/family support, counseling, and consultation, 150–151
  teacher competencies in, 60
Competencies of EBD teachers, 50–61
Concrete operational stage, 219
Conduct disorders, 10–13
Confidentiality, 138
Conflict cycle, 180–181
Consciousness of rules, 225–226
Consequences
  activity on, 414–416
  development of, 171–175
  examples of, 170–171
  guidelines on administering, 171
  negative consequences, 173–176
  positive consequences, 171–173, 175–176
  in RET model, 323–324, 359–361, 363–366, 414–416
  sequence of, 169
  timeout, 173–174
Consultation, teacher competencies in, 58–59, 66–67
Content areas, teaching in, 126–128
Continuum of services, 66–67
Conventional reasoning, in moral development, 240, 241
Cooperation, incipient, in moral judgment, 221–222
Cooperative learning groups, 134–135

Copping out, 414
Crack babies, 63
Crisis intervention, 179–183
Culturally diverse, 11, 58
Curricular modifications, 73, 74

Damnation, 374
Decalage, 218–219, 235, 265
*Defining Issues Test* (DIT), 246
Demanding shoulds, 328–329, 404
Depression, diagnosis of, 372
*Diagnostic and Statistical Manual of Mental Disorders* (DSM-III-R), 98
"Difficult customers," and rational-emotive therapy (RET), 388–389
Dilemmas. *See* Moral dilemmas
Direct observation, 83, 88–92
Direct prompts, 166
Disciplinary problems, list of, 38
Discipline. *See* Behavioral management rules system
*Discipline with Dignity* (Curwin and Mendler), 171
Discussions. *See* Group sessions; Moral discussions
Disputation (D), in RET model, 330–331, 376–386
Disqualifying the positive, 328
Disturbance. *See* Emotionally/behaviorally disordered (EBD)
Disturbed–disturbing continuum, 16–19
Disturbed feelings and behaviors, definition of, 321
DIT. See *Defining Issues Test* (DIT)
"Doctor shopping," 143–144
Drug abusers, 12, 63
DSM-III-R, 98

Early classroom interventions, 72–75, 76
EBD. *See* Emotionally/behaviorally disordered (EBD)
Education for All Handicapped Children Act (P.L. 94-142), 7–8, 21, 27, 28, 48, 76, 101, 111, 114, 116, 139
Education of the Handicapped Act Amendments (P.L. 99-457), 147
Educational ability, assessment of, 97–98
Effect, in RET model, 332–333, 386
Egocentrism, in moral judgment, 221
EHA. *See* Education for All Handicapped Children Act (P.L. 94-142)
Elegant RET, 333–334, 367–368
Emotional functioning, assessment of, 99–101
Emotional reasoning, 328
Emotionally/behaviorally disordered
  administrators' reactions to, 29–31
  arguments against inclusion of, in regular classroom, 25–28
  assessment of, 95–103
  definitions of, 6–8, 14–15, 20–21, 33
  disturbed–disturbing continuum, 16–19
  early classroom interventions for, 72–75, 76
  exclusion clause and, 10
  federal definition of, 6–8
  identification of, 72–73
  incidence data on, 19–21, 71
  institutional reaction to, 29
  label for, 8–9, 13–15
  least restrictive environment for, 27–28
  legal interpretation of federal definition of, 7–8
  needs of, 5
  placement procedures for, 78–80, 103–116
  politics of, 6–21
  preassessment of, 72–80
  referral for assessment of, 80–96
  role of, in rational-emotive therapy (RET), 355–356
  societal factors influencing, 5
  stigma of label, 13–14
  teachers' reactions to, 31–32

teaching of, 35–69
Empathy, 352–353
Environmental modifications, 73, 74
Equilibrium, 220
Ethical practices, teacher
   competencies in, 61
Evaluation. *See* Assessment;
   Preassessment; and specific
   tests
Exclusion clause, 10
Exercises
   environmental expectations and
      reactions, 17
   inviting and disinviting teachers,
      42–43
   moral development, 224–225
   placement decisions, 105–110
   rational-emotive therapy (RET),
      332, 338
Expert model, 35
Expulsion, 30, 175

Fable of Ralph Ram, 392–394
Facts versus opinions, 397–401,
   428–429
Families
   assessment of, 101–103
   parent interview, 82–83, 86–88
   parent–teacher conferences,
      147–149
   support, counseling, and
      consultation with, 150–151
   support plan for, 148–152
   teacher competencies in working
      with, 59–60
   teachers' relationship with parents,
      138–152
   training programs for, 150
Family support plan, 148–152
Feelings. *See* Rational-emotive
   therapy (RET)
Feelings and behaviors list, 364
Feelings Charades, 396, 425–426
"Feelings" faces, 394
Feelings Thermometer technique,
   366, 401
Floor plans for classroom, 159–163
Focusing on the negative, 327

Follow-up
   after crisis intervention, 180
   for preassessment, 80
Formal assessment, 82
Formal operational stage, 219
Fortune-telling, 327
Friendship, moral dilemma on,
   291–292
Frustration tolerance, 329, 388,
   407–408

Gas station, moral dilemma on,
   279–282
*Getting Along with Others*, 166
Goals
   long-term goals set by
      multidisciplinary team,
      115–116
   in rational-emotive therapy (RET),
      366–367
Group sessions
   moral discussions, 268–278
   for rational-emotive therapy (RET),
      356–358
Guilt, diagnosis of, 372–373

Happening–Thought–Feeling
   Reaction (HTFR) diagrams,
   410–412
Health, assessment of, 98–99
Home environment. *See* Families;
   Parents
Homeless, 10–11
*Homer the Homely Hound Dog* (Garcia
   and Peggegrini), 421
Homework, in rational-emotive
   therapy (RET), 354, 386–388
*How to Make Yourself Miserable*
   (Greenburg), 421–422
HTFR diagrams, 410–412
Hyperactivity. *See* Attention-
   deficit/hyperactivity disorder
   (ADHD)

I Am, I Do activity, 417–418
I-can't-stand-it-itis, 374
I Yam What I Yam and That's All That
   I Yam! activity, 406

IDEA. *See* Individuals with Disabilities Education Act (IDEA)
IEPs, 94–95, 105, 115, 116–117, 122, 147, 154
Ignore–attend–praise technique, 166
Imagery, rational-emotive, 364–365
Impersonal assessment, 262
Incipient cooperation, in moral judgment, 221–222
Inclusion
   arguments against, for students with EBD, 25–27
   arguments for, 21, 24
   consultation services and, 66
   continuum of services and, 66–67
Incompatible thoughts and behaviors, in cognitive behavior modification, 311
Individual assessment, 261–262
Individualized Education Programs (IEPs), 94–95, 105, 115, 116–117, 122, 147, 154
Individualized versus generalized treatment, 113–115
Individuals with Disabilities Education Act (IDEA), 93, 101, 139
Indoctrinative education, 212–213, 238
Inelegant RET, 333, 334, 346, 367–368
Informal assessment
   direct observation, 83, 88–92
   interviews, 82–88
   parent interview, 82–83, 86–88
   product analysis, 92–93
   Pupil Assessment Summary, 96–97
   purposes of, 93–96
   record review, 83
   teacher interview, 84–85
   trial teaching, 93
*Instant Replay* (Bedford), 420
Institutional reactions to students with EBD, 29
Instruction. *See also* Teaching and teachers
   and academic needs of students, 122–123
   behaviors enabling, 125–126
   Cawley's process regulator, 130–132
   competencies in, 49, 51–53, 61–63
   in content areas, 126–128
   instructional design for teaching students with different abilities, 133
   learning strategies, 125
   motivation in, 135–136
   paraprofessionals and, 137–138
   peer tutoring, 133–135
   recall and reasoning, 124
   self-monitoring, 135
   significant considerations in, 119–123
   in social skills, 155–158
   specially designed instruction in special education, 116–117
   teaching skills and content, 123–124
   textbooks and, 128
   thematic units, 129–130
Integration model, 35
Intellectual ability. *See* Cognitive ability
Intellectualizing students, 389
Intellectually limited students, 389
Intent, perceptions of, 226
InterpRETations of Events, 412, 428–429
*Intervention in the School and Clinic*, 125
Interventions. *See* Classroom interventions
Interviews
   moral interview, 245–246
   parent interview, 82–83, 86–88
   purposes of, 82
   teacher interview, 84–85
Irrational thinking
   belief systems in RET model, 324–330, 368–373
   combated by rational-emotive therapy (RET), 314–319
   definition of, 322
   disputation of, 330–331, 376–386
   facts versus opinions, 397–401, 428–429

lesson on, 412–414
  perceived reality versus objective
    reality, 360–361, 399, 427
  of teachers, 334–338
  types of, in RET model, 324–330,
    368–369
Issue-related probes, 274
*It Could Always Be Worse* (Zemach), 420
It's Awful! It's Terrible! How Horrible!
  activity, 406–407
"It's-not-working" syndrome, 388

Job description of teachers of students
  with EBD, 48–68
Journal keeping, 361
Jump rope game, 222–223
Jumping to conclusions, 327
*Junior Eysenic Personality Inventory*,
  345
Just communities, 251–253
Juvenile delinquents, 13

Killer statements, 403, 430–431
Kohlberg's theory of moral
  development, 234–236, 237,
  239–257, 264, 265

Label
  choice of, 13–14
  of emotionally/behaviorally
    disordered, 8–9, 14–15
  stigma of, 13–14
Labeling and overgeneralization, 328
Laetrile, moral dilemma on, 285
Laws. *See* headings beginning with
  Public Law
Learner characteristics. *See also*
  Emotionally/behaviorally
  disordered
  teacher competencies in, 50–51
Learning disabled, 9, 10, 143
Learning environment. *See* Classroom
  management; Instruction;
  Teaching and teachers
Learning strategies, 125
Least restrictive environment (LRE),
  27–28, 103, 111–113
Lecturing, 389

Level systems, 176–178
*Life Space Intervention* (Wood and
  Long), 180
Linguistically diverse, 58
Listening checks
  in moral discussions, 273
  in rational-emotive therapy (RET),
    353
Literature, moral dilemma in, 291–292
Loaf of Bread technique, 382–383
Low frustration tolerance, 329, 388,
  407–408
LRE. *See* Least restrictive environment
  (LRE)

Mainstreaming, 21–25
Make Me activity, 403–404
Management of behavior. *See*
  Behavioral management rules
  system
Marbles, 221
Marijuana abusers, 12
MDTs. *See* Multidisciplinary teams
  (MDTs)
Mental retardation, 143, 286–287
Mercy death, moral dilemma on,
  288–290
Minimization, 328
Monitoring, teacher competencies in,
  57–58
Moral action, 254
Moral autonomy, 226
Moral development
  activities for elementary students,
    226-228
  activities for middle and high
    school students, 228–231
  assessment of, 259–264
  cautions pertaining to programs in,
    267
  classroom applications of, 259–296
  cognitive stages and, 219–220, 227
  consciousness of rules in, 225–226
  content and structure in, 234–235
  conventional reasoning in, 240, 241
  criticisms of Kohlberg's theory of,
    256–257
  description of, 215–217, 238

difficulties in implementing
    program in, 266–267
exercise on, 224–225
five-phase process of progression
    through stages of, 247
higher versus lower stages of, 250
implications of, to special
    educators, 231–234
importance of, 211
important concepts in, 235,
    237–239
indoctrinative education compared
    with, 212–213, 238
"justice" versus "care" orientation
    in, 257
Kohlberg's levels and stages of,
    239–245
Kohlberg's theory of, 234–236,
    237, 239–257
moral action and, 254
moral dilemmas in, 265–267,
    278–292
moral discussions for, 268–278
perceptions of intent in, 226
Piagetian stages of, 221–222,
    225–226, 227, 237
Piagetian theory of moral
    judgment, 217–231, 237, 265
postconventional reasoning in,
    240, 241
practice of rules in, 221–225
preconventional reasoning in,
    239–240, 241
role-playing, 227–228
role-taking and, 254–256
sequences of stages of, 248–249
sex-related patterns in, 221–223,
    257
stage changes in, 251–253
stage determination through moral
    interview, 245–246
stages of, as natural steps in ethical
    development, 247–248
stages of, as organized system of
    thought, 246–247
teaching of, 266–278
understanding of moral arguments
    based on stages, 249–250

values clarification compared with,
    213–215, 238
Moral dilemmas
    academic content dilemmas,
        290–292
    choice of, 278–279
    elements of, 278–279
    examples of, 279–292
    group discussion of, 262
    hypothetical classroom dilemmas,
        283–288
    hypothetical dilemmas, 279–283
    presenting, 272–274
    questioning techniques with,
        274–275
    real-life dilemmas, 287–290
    types of, 278–292
Moral discussions
    assessment using, 262
    bored group members and
        stagnated groups in, 277
    brainstorming in, 273–274
    clarification in, 273
    guidelines for, 275, 276
    ineffective education groups in,
        277–278
    initiating group discussions,
        271–272
    insensitive participation in, 275
    listening checks in, 273
    negative attitudes in, 277
    organization of, 268–269
    overactive participant in, 275, 277
    physical classroom arrangement
        for, 269
    preparing for, 268
    presenting moral dilemmas in,
        272–274
    preventing problems in, 275,
        277–278
    problematic leadership styles in,
        277
    questioning techniques in, 274–275
    rules of, 268
    size of group for, 269
    teacher's role in, 269–271
    time devoted to, 269
    underactive participant in, 277

Moral heteronomy, in moral
    judgment, 225–226
Moral interview, 245–246
Motivation, 135–136
Multidisciplinary teams (MDTs)
    administrative factors of, 111
    differing educational practices
        established by, at each level of
        education, 115
    implementing, 103–117
    individualized versus generalized
        treatment decided by, 113–115
    least restrictive environment
        defined by, 111–113
    long-term goals in education set by,
        115–116
    meetings of, 78–80, 104–117
    and placement decisions, 78–80,
        104–117
    for preassessment, 75–80
    roles of, 75
    selection of members of
        preassessment team, 77–78
    and specially designed instruction,
        116–117
    teacher assistance teams (TATs), 75
Musical Chairs, 227
Must statements, 374
My Personal Strengths activity, 418

Negative consequences, 173–176
Negative non sequiturs, 327
Nelson Modified Deviant Classroom
    Observation Scale, 89–92
Neverness or allness, 328
*New Guide to Rational Living, A* (Ellis
    and Harper), 376–377

Objective reality versus perceived
    reality, 360–361, 399, 427
Observation. *See* Direct observation
Opinions versus facts, 397–401,
    428–429
Organization process, 220
Overgeneralization, 328

P.L. *See* headings beginning with
    Public Law

PAL. *See* Program for Affective
    Learning (PAL)
Paraprofessionals, 137–138
Parent–teacher conferences, 147–149
Parents
    advocacy and resource use by, 150
    communication with teachers,
        151–152
    community programs and services
        for, 149
    current conceptualization of
        teacher–parent relationship,
        146
    family support plan and, 148–152
    informational services for, 150
    interview of, 82–83, 86–88
    involvement of, 101
    obstacles to inviting participation
        of, 141–143
    parent–teacher conferences,
        147–149
    reactions of, to learning that child
        is emotionally disturbed,
        143–144
    reasons for teachers' working with,
        138–140
    reporting pupil progress to,
        147–152
    stereotypes of, 144
    support, counseling, and
        consultation with, 150–151
    teachers' relationship with,
        138–152
    training programs for, 150
    typical parent–teacher contact
        opportunities, 143–146
Parties, moral dilemma on, 284
Peer tutoring, 133–135
Perceived reality versus objective
    reality, 360–361, 399, 427
Perceptions of intent, 226
Perfectionism, 328
Personalizing, 328
Philosophizing, 389
Phonyism, 328
Physical abilities, assessment of, 98–99
Physical arrangement of classroom,
    159–162, 269

Physical management, 182–183
Piagetian cognitive stages, 219–220
Piagetian theory of moral judgment
  activities for elementary students, 226–228
  activities for middle and high school students, 228–231
  cognitive stages and, 219–220, 227
  consciousness of rules, 225–226
  decalage and, 218–219, 235, 265
  exercise on, 224–225
  introduction to, 217–219
  perceptions of intent, 226
  practice and consciousness in, 217–218, 237
  practice of rules in, 221–225
  stages of, 221–222, 225–226, 227, 237
Placement decisions
  exercise on, 105–110
  made by multidisciplinary teams, 78–80, 104–105
Politics
  of emotionally/behaviorally disordered, 6–21
  of special education and general education, 21–28
  of teaching, 28–32
Poor, 11–12
Positive consequences, 171–173, 175–176
Postconventional reasoning, in moral development, 240, 241
Practice of rules, in Piagetian moral judgment, 221–225
Preassessment
  follow-up for, 80
  multidisciplinary teams (MDTs) for, 75–80
  purposes of, 75–76
  referral form for, 78, 79
  suggestions for preassessment procedures, 77–80
Preconventional reasoning, in moral development, 239–240, 241
Premoral state, in moral judgment, 225
Preoperational stage, 219

Problem-solving training, 157–158
Product analysis, 92–93
*Program for Affective Learning* (PAL), 422
Prompts, direct, 166
Proximity control, 166
Public Law (P.L.) 94-142 (Education for All Handicapped Children Act), 7–8, 21, 27, 28, 48, 76, 101, 111, 114, 116, 139
Public Law (P.L.) 99-457 (Education of the Handicapped Act Amendments), 147
Punishment, 173
Puzzle dot game, 228

Questioning techniques, in moral discussions, 274–275

Rating of self or others, 329–330, 406
Rating scales, 100–101, 102
*Rational-Emotive Education Manual for Elementary Teachers* (Knaus), 422
*Rational-Emotive Education Worksheet-R*, 387
Rational-emotive imagery, 364–365
*Rational-Emotive Therapy as a Classroom Mental Health Curriculum* (Zionts), 422
Rational-emotive therapy (RET)
  ABC(DE) model of, 322–332
  ability to identify and understand feelings in, 394–396
  activating events (A) in model of, 323, 359–363
  active-directive approach in, 353–354
  All or Nothing technique in, 376
  application of, 338–342
  Bad Banana technique in, 376
  belief systems (B) in model of, 324–330, 368–373
  bibliotherapy in, 376–377, 420–422
  Camera Check technique in, 360, 361
  change and, 359

and choice of intervention,
    307–308
cognitive behavior therapy and,
    308–311
compared with cognitive therapy,
    332–333
consequences (C) in model of,
    323–324, 359–361,
    363–366, 414–416
criticisms of, 346–348
disputation (D) in model of,
    330–331, 373–386
educational foundations of,
    317–318
effect (E) in model of, 332–333,
    386
efficacy of, with children, 342–346
eight basic concepts of, 318–321
elegant RET, 333–334, 367–368
empathy and, 352–353
exercises on, 332, 338
feelings and behaviors list, 364
feelings as result of beliefs about
    events in, 397–408, 425–431
Feelings Thermometer technique
    in, 366, 401
goal setting in, 366–367
ground rules in, 356–358
Happening–Thought–Feeling
    Reaction (HTFR) diagram of,
    410–412
"here-and-now" focus in, 355
homework in, 354, 386–388
implementation of, 356–391
inelegant RET, 333, 334, 346,
    367–368
as intervention, 351–392
introduction to, 392–394
irrational beliefs of teachers,
    334–338
irrational thinking combated by,
    314–319, 412–414
journal keeping as technique of,
    361
Loaf of Bread technique in,
    382–383
as mental health curriculum,
    395–431

outline of concepts to teach
    content of, 424–431
overview of, 312–313
philosophical foundations of,
    314–317
principles of, 348–349
problems in use of, 388–389
psychological foundations of,
    313–314
purpose of, 312
Rational Role Reversal in, 385
rational-emotive imagery as
    technique of, 364–365
recognizing total RET process
    including both theory and
    technique, 408–422
role-play as technique of, 363
self-communication in, 322–323
self-talk and, 322–323, 369–373
seriousness of problem determined
    in, 361–362
Shame Attacks in, 377–378
songs on, 418–420
steps in implementing, 356–391
students' role in, 355–356
teacher's role in, 351–355
teaching errors with, 389–390
techniques in, 361, 364–365, 366,
    375–378, 382–385
terms and definitions concerning,
    321–322
theory of, 307–349
Time Projection technique in, 376
Trust Me technique in, 384
uses of, 312
What Is the Worst that Can
    Happen? technique in,
    375–376
working with "difficult customers,"
    388–389
Rational-emotive therapy (RET)
    lessons
    Lesson One on Fable of Ralph Ram,
        392–394, 424
    Lesson Two on developing a RET
        vocabulary, 394–395, 424
    Lesson Three on exploring different
        feelings, 395–396, 425

Lesson Four on Feelings Charades, 396, 425–426
Lesson Five on difference between facts and opinions, 397–398, 426
Lesson Six on That's a Fact!, 398–399, 426–427
Lesson Seven on perceived reality versus objective reality, 399, 427
Lesson Eight on sifting facts from opinions, 399–401, 428
Lesson Nine on InterpRETations of Events, 401, 428–429
Lesson Ten on Feelings Thermometer, 413, 429
Lesson Eleven on Who Causes Your Feelings?, 402–403, 430
Lesson Twelve on killer statements, 403, 430–431
Lesson Thirteen on Make Me, 403–404
Lesson Fourteen on Shoulds of Society, 404
Lesson Fifteen on catastrophizing or awfulizing, 404–406
Lesson Sixteen on I Yam What I Yam and That's All That I Yam!, 406
Lesson Seventeen on It's Awful! It's Terrible! How Horrible!, 406–407
Lesson Eighteen on tolerating frustration, 407–408
Lesson Nineteen on Knowing Your ABCs, 408–410
Lesson Twenty on Happening–Thought–Feeling Reaction (HTFR), 410–412
Lesson Twenty-one on rational versus irrational beliefs, 412–414
Lesson Twenty-two on copping out, 414
Lesson Twenty-three on consequences, 414–416
Lesson Twenty-four on rational beliefs, 416–417
Lesson Twenty-five on I Am, I Do, 417–418
Lesson Twenty-six on My Personal Strengths, 418
Lesson Twenty-seven on RET songs, 418–420
Lesson Twenty-eight on bibliotherapy, 420–422
Rational Role Reversal, 385
Rational thinking
　definition of, 321–322
　lessons on, 412–414, 416–417
*Ready Set Grow Series, The*, 421
Reasoning skills, 124
Recall skills, 124
Record review, 83
Referral
　for assessment, 80–96
　after crisis intervention, 180
　for preassessment, 78, 79
　preassessment referral form, 78, 79
　purposes of systematic referral process, 80–81
Regular Education Initiative (REI), 21–24, 66–67
REI. *See* Regular Education Initiative (REI)
*Remedial and Special Education*, 125
Remediation
　accommodation compared with, 44–48
　definition of, 44
Reminders, 166
Reporting, of pupil progress to parents, 147–152
Residential treatment programs, 140, 145, 146
Resource room, 209
RET. *See* Rational-emotive therapy (RET)
Rewards, 171–173, 175–176
Role-playing, 227–228, 363
Role reversal, 385
Role-switch probes, 274
Role-taking, and moral development, 254–256
Rorschach test, 100
Routines, 164–165

Rule reminders, 166
Rules. *See also* Behavioral management rules system
    activities on, in moral development, 230–231
    consciousness of rules in Piagetian theory of moral development, 225–226
    examples of well-written versus poorly written rules, 168
    generating rules for behavioral management, 167, 231, 233
    identifying individual feelings about classroom rules, 231
    need for, 167
    practice of rules in Piagetian theory of moral development, 221–225
    pre–rule setting in behavioral management, 165–166
    presenting rules for behavioral management, 168–171
    in rational-emotive therapy (RET), 356–358
    reminders of, 166
    statement of, in positive behavioral terms, 167–168

Sales, moral dilemma on, 282–283
Scheduling, 162–164
Schools. *See* Administration; Teaching
SED. *See* Seriously emotionally disturbed (SED)
Self-concept, 330
Self-monitoring, 135
Self-observation, in cognitive behavior modification, 310–311
Self-rating, 329–330, 406
Self-talk in RET, 322–323, 369–373
Sensorimotor stage, 219
Seriously emotionally disturbed (SED), 8–9, 14. *See also* Emotionally/behaviorally disordered
Sex-related patterns, in moral development, 221–223, 257

Shame, diagnosis of, 373
Shame Attacks, 377–378
Shoulds, 328–329, 404
Simon Says, 227
SM/CD. *See* Social maladjustment/conduct disorders (SM/CD)
Social maladjustment/conduct disorders (SM/CD), 10–13
Social skills
    definition of, 155
    list of, 155–156, 157
    teaching of, 155–158
Songs on RET, 418–420
Special education. *See also* Teaching and teachers
    arguments against, 21, 24
    arguments against inclusion of students with EBD, 25–27
    beginning of process of, 103
    differing educational practices at each level of, 115
    implications of moral development in, 231–234
    individualized versus generalized treatment in, 113–115
    integration model in, 35
    least restrictive environment in, 27–28, 103, 111–113
    long-term goals in, 115–116
    politics of, 21–28
    resource room, 209
    specially designed instruction in, 116–117
Sports rules, 230–231
*State-Trait Anxiety Scale for Children*, 345
Stress, of teachers, 63–66
*Structural Issue Scoring Test*, 246
Students. *See* Emotionally/behaviorally disordered
Study guide, 125
Substance abusers, 12, 63
Suspension, 30, 174–175
*Sweet Pickles* (Reinach), 420

TAT. See *Thematic Apperception Test* (TAT)

TATs. *See* Teacher assistance teams (TATs)
Teacher assistance teams (TATs), 75
Teacher competencies, 50–61
Teacher interview, 84–85
Teaching and teachers. *See also* Instruction
  communication and collaboration in, 58–59
  communication with parents, 151–152
  community resources and, 60
  consultation and collaboration in, 58–59, 66–67
  cultural and linguistic diversity and, 58
  and dealing with administration, 63–66
  delivering instruction, 49, 61–63
  delivering instruction in, 51–53, 61–63
  and disinviting and ineffective schools, 37–39
  EBD teacher competencies, 50–61
  empathy of teacher, 352–353
  exercise on four types of teachers, 42–43
  factors contributing to inviting and effective schools, 36–38
  families and, 59–60
  and identification of students with EBD, 72–73
  intentionally disinviting teachers, 39–40
  intentionally inviting teachers, 41–42
  interviews of teachers as assessment technique, 84–85
  inviting and disinviting teachers, 39–43
  irrational beliefs of teachers, 334–338
  job description of teachers of students with EBD, 48–68
  and legal and administrative structure, 60–61, 63–66
  managing student behavior, 54–57
  managing the learning environment, 53–54
  monitoring and evaluation in, 57–58
  in moral discussions, 269–271
  politics of, 28–32
  professional and ethical practice in, 61
  remediation versus accommodation in, 43–48
  role of special educator, 43–48
  stress of, 63–66
  teachers' reactions to students with EBD, 31–32
  teacher's role in rational-emotive therapy (RET), 351–355
  teaching errors with rational-emotive therapy (RET), 389–390
  transition programs and, 57, 67–68
  trial teaching, 93
  unintentionally disinviting teachers, 40–41
  unintentionally inviting teachers, 41
  working with paraprofessionals, 137–138
  working with parents of students with EBD, 138–152
*Teaching Exceptional Children*, 125
Teams. *See* Multidisciplinary teams (MDTs)
Tests. *See* specific tests
Textbooks, 128
*Thematic Apperception Test* (TAT), 100
Thematic units, 129–130
*Think Aloud* program, 158, 311, 422
*Thinking, Changing, Rearranging* (Anderson), 422
*Thinking, Feeling, Behaving* (Vernon), 422
*Thinking Straight and Talking Sense* (Gerald and Eyman), 422
Time Projection technique, 376
Timeout, 173–174
Token economies, 176–179
Transfer out of school district, 30

Transition programs, teacher
 competencies in, 57, 67–68
Trial teaching, 93
Trust Me technique, 384
*Tuff Stuff*, 421
Tutoring, 133–135
Typing directions, 228

Undisturbed negative feelings and
 behaviors, definition of, 321
Universal consequence probes, 274

*Value of Believing in Yourself, The*
 (Johnson), 421

Values clarification, 213–215, 238

*Wechsler Adult Intelligence
 Scale–Revised*, 97
*Wechsler Intelligence Scale for
 Children–Third Edition*, 97
*Wechsler Preschool and Primary Scale of
 Intelligence–Revised*, 97
What Is the Worst that Can Happen?
 technique, 375–376
*Woodcock-Johnson Psycho-Educational
 Battery–Revised*, 98

"Yes, but!" students, 388–389